1993

The Enduring Constitution
A Bicentennial Perspective

The Enduring Constitution

A Bicentennial Perspective

JETHRO K. LIEBERMAN

West Publishing Company
Saint Paul   New York   Los Angeles   San Francisco

Library of Congress Cataloging-in-Publication Data

Lieberman, Jethro Koller.
  The enduring Constitution.

  Bibliography: p.
  Includes index.
    1. United States—Constitutional law. 2. United
States—Constitutional history. I. Title.
KF4550.L49 1987   342.73   86-32458
ISBN 0-314-32026-1   347.302

Photo Credits

Cover, The Granger Collection; **6,** Dennis Brack, Black Star; **8,** Courtesy, The Henry Francis du Pont Winterthur Museum; **11,** Richard Frear, National Park Service; **12,** The Granger Collection; **13,** From the Collection of Independence National Historical Park; **14,** The Bettman Archive; **15,** The Granger Collection; **16,** The Bettmann Archive; **17, (left)** The Granger Collection; **(right)** The Granger Collection; **18,** The Granger Collection; **20,** The Granger Collection; **22,** The Bettmann Archive; **23,** Connecticut State Library; **24,** The Granger Collection; **25, (left)** The Granger Collection; **(right)** The Granger Collection; **26, (top)** The Granger Collection; **(bottom)** The Bettmann Archive; **27,** From the Studio of A. Ramsay, c. 1767, Courtesy of The National Portrait Gallery, London; **29,** From the Collection of Independence National Historical Park; **31,** Library of Congress; **33,** From the Collection of Independence National Historical Park; **34,** The Granger Collection; **35,** The Granger Collection; **36,** The Granger Collection; **39,** The Granger Collection; **41,** Library of Congress; **46,** From the Collection of Independence National Historical Park; **48,** The Granger Collection; **50,** The Granger Collection; **51,** The Granger Collection; **54,** From the Collection of Independence National Historical Park; **55,** The Granger Collection; **56,** Stock Index International, Inc.; **58,** The Granger Collection; **60,** The Granger Collection; **61,** The Granger Collection; **62,** From the Collection of Independence National Historical Park; **64,** National Archives; **65,** From the Collection of Independence National Historical Park; **67,** Shelly Katz, Black Star; **69,** The Bettmann Archive; **71,** Miami Herald, C.W. Griffin, Black Star; **73,** The Bettmann Archive; **75,** John Chiasson, Gamma-Liaison; **79,** The Granger Collection; **80,** The Granger Collection; **83,** Dennis Brack, Black Star; **85,** The Granger Collection; **86,** The Bettmann Archive; **87,** Library of Congress; **89,** Library of Congress; **90,** The Granger Collection; **91,** Consolidated News Pictures by ISP; **93,** The Granger Collection; **94,** UPI/Bettmann Newsphotos; **96,** From the Collection of Independence National Historical Park; **97,** UPI/Bettmann Newsphotos; **98,** The Granger Collection; **99,** Library of Congress; **101,** The Granger Collection; **102,** The Granger Collection; **105 (left)** UPI/Bettmann Newsphotos; **(right)** UPI/Bettmann Newsphotos; **106,** UPI/Bettmann Newsphotos; **108,** Cynthia Johnson, Gamma-Liaison; **111,** From the Collection of Independence National Historical Park; **113,** UPI/Bettmann Newsphotos; **114,** Library of Congress; **115,** UPI/Bettmann Newsphotos; **118,** Library of Congress; **120,** The Granger Collection; **122,** Library of Congress; **127,** Library of Congress; **129,** Library of Congress; **135,** From the Collection of Independence National Historical Park; **138,** AP/Wide World Photos; **139,** UPI/Bettmann Newsphotos; **140,** R. Gyerman, Black Star; **143,** From the Collection of Independence National

(Photo credits continued following index)

For my brothers on Elm Street, 1963–1964

Don, Jon, Toby, Bob, Joe, Angus, John,
Richard, Thomas, Ron, David, and Phil

and to the memory of

Louis Tunick II
(1942–1963)

Some Thoughts on the Constitution

Though written constitutions may be violated in moments of passion or delusion, yet they furnish a text to which those who are watchful may again rally and recall the people; they fix too for the people the principles of their political creed.

—Thomas Jefferson, letter to Joseph Priestly, July 19, 1802

The subject is the execution of those great powers on which the welfare of a nation essentially depends. . . . This provision is made in a Constitution intended to endure for ages to come and, consequently, to be adapted to the various crisis of human affairs.

—John Marshall, *McCulloch v. Maryland*, 1819

A Constitution is framed for ages to come, and is designed to approach immortality as nearly as human institutions can approach it.

—John Marshall, *Cohens v. Virginia*, 1821

One country, one constitution, one destiny.

—Daniel Webster, Senate speech, March 15, 1837

The Constitution of the United States is a law for rulers and people, equally in war and peace, and covers with the shield of its protection all classes of men, at all times, and under all circumstances. No doctrine, involving more pernicious consequences, was ever invented by the wit of men than that any of its provisions can be suspended during any of the great exigencies of government.

—Justice David Davis, *Ex parte Milligan*, 1866

When the Constitution was first framed I predicted that it would last fifty years. I was mistaken. It will evidently last longer than that. But I was mistaken only in point of time. The crash will come, but not so quick as I thought.

—Aaron Burr, 1835

We are under a Constitution, but the Constitution is what the judges say it is.

—Charles Evans Hughes, Speech, May 3, 1907

Contents

Publisher's Foreword

In a world where it seems increasingly true that "Things fall apart: The centre cannot hold," the Constitution of the United States endures. No other written constitution has worked as well or as long to guide and protect a government and its citizens. Because, as Thomas Paine wrote in 1791, "The constitution of a country is not the act of its government, but of the people constituting a government," it is fitting that the people of the United States celebrate the two hundredth anniversary of the document they created.

As Jethro Lieberman states, "The Constitution is what lawyers and judges worry about—until something happens to bring it home." We hope, though, that this becentennial will bring home more than a sense of celebration. We hope it will bring home to more Americans the sober reflection and awed respect the Constitution never fails to elicit from those who work daily in service to the law.

It is a special kind of reverence. Not the distant respect accorded to a long-dead master, but the vital kind that leads each generation of Americans to wrestle anew with the spirit and the letter of the law. Over the years, this struggle for understanding has led to the publication of thousands of books on the Consti-

tution. An even greater number of articles have been circulated, and countless suggestions have been made concerning what the document means, or how it might be improved.

Still the arguments go on. Is the Constitution a "living document" to be interpreted in light of present day considerations; or do the "original intentions" of the framers still hold? Mr. Lieberman maintains that the Constitution remains vital not *in spite* of but *because* of the continuing debate: "Let the bicentennial nurture a sophisticated reverence for the most successful charter of freedom the world has ever known—and let the commemoration also fan the flames of disputation that have kept it that way," he writes.

As a publisher of legal materials, West Publishing Company has, since the Constitution was a mere eighty-nine years old, monitored the debate, recorded the arguments, and facilitated the dialogue. In 1976, to celebrate the nation's bicentennial and its own centennial, West published *Milestones!*, also written by Mr. Lieberman. In that volume, the author wove a legal history of the United States from eighteen events, as selected from a poll of American lawyers.

Not surprisingly, those events pivoted around the

U.S. Supreme Court. From Marbury v. Madison to U.S. v. Richard Nixon, the legal history of the United States centers on the Constitution and its interpretation.

The Enduring Constitution is an expansion of and further testament to that fact. It is meant to honor the document and those who so honorably and nobly uphold it. It is also meant to increase understanding, evoke thought, and illuminate disputes of the future with knowledge of our shared past.

Meanwhile, the debate goes on, as it must if the Constitution is to remain healthy. "Without a vital constitution," says Mr. Lieberman, "we could not hope to balance order and freedom, progress and conservation, stability and momentum."

DWIGHT D. OPPERMAN
President and Chief Executive Officer

Acknowledgments

I gratefully acknowledge the research assistance of Ellen M. Berrigan in the preparation of this book. Beyond living in libraries, answering scores of queries, and making dozens of telephone calls to ferret out additional facts, she was largely responsible for the preparation of the minibiographies scattered throughout the text.

Thanks also to Eric T. Freyfogle at the University of Illinois/Urbana-Champaign, William Nelson at New York University, and Stephen B. Presser at Northwestern University for their thoughtful comments on reading the manuscript; to my mother Elizabeth K. Lieberman, for proofreading the galleys and other editorial and cuisinary services; to Clark G. Baxter for all his editorial assistance since the inception of this project in early 1985; and to Bill Stryker and Kristen Weber and the other editors at West, and to Elaine Linden for her sensitive copyediting.

Although they may not realize how much it helped, I record special thanks to Ruth and Sandy Frankel for cajoling me to drop over for many bountiful meals, to Martha and Neal Cooper for all the tea, to Susan and Gerry Uram (he for his unflappable special courier service, she for her patience with my slamming car doors at 3 A.M.); for their forbearance, to students whose exams and papers last spring were graded late; to the friends who finally got the idea and stopped calling to ask when the manuscript would be finished; and because it will probably be the only opportunity, I record my gratitude to the person or persons who created WordPerfect, thus permitting me to rewrite and edit with remarkable ease many passages in this book twenty times or more (my writing students, please take note, though whether it was useful remains of course for the reader to judge).

For the record, Jessica is off to college and Seth is about to become taller than I am.

As usual, errors that remain are solely my responsibility, and for them I beg the reader's pardon. But after all, not even the Supreme Court always gets it right.

J.K.L.
Hastings-on-Hudson, N.Y.
September 17, 1986

Jethro K. Lieberman

Photograph © 1976 Jill Krementz

Lawyer, journalist, professor of law, and author of numerous articles and 20 books including *Milestones! 200 Years of American Law* (West Publishing, 1976), Jethro K. Lieberman brings to *The Enduring Constitution* impressive credentials in interpreting and popularizing the law.

As Director of the First-Year Writing Program at New York Law School, Jethro Lieberman opens up aspiring minds to the nuances and intricacies of the law by teaching Constitutional Law, Administrative Law, Advanced Writing Skills for Lawyers, and Dispute Resolution. Before joining the New York Law School faculty, he was Visiting Associate Professor at Fordham Law School.

Mr. Lieberman was founding editor of Business Week's Legal Affairs Department and served as that magazine's Legal Affairs Editor from 1973–82. His day-to-day responsibilities included relating and analyzing the changing law for millions of readers. In this responsibility, he followed legislation, court decisions, administrative regulations, and other aspects of law and legal institutions affecting our commercial and personal lives.

He received a B.A. from Yale, and J.D. degree from Harvard, graduating from both with honors. He has taught at Yale and was awarded a Phi Beta Kappa Bicentennial fellowship for a work still in progress.

Previous books include *The Litigious Society* (winner of the 1982 American Bar Association Silver Gavel award), *How the Government Breaks the Law, The Tyranny of the Experts, and Understanding Our Constitution*.

Prior to becoming a journalist, he spent several years in law practice in a variety of capacities: serving on active duty as a Navy lawyer, practicing antitrust law with a large Washington firm, and working as vice-president and general counsel of a New York publishing house.

He is the father of two children and lives in Hastings-on-Hudson, New York.

Prologue **To Celebrate a Constitution**

The Constitution of the United States looms overhead, a giant geodesic dome of practical political philosophy that for two centuries has shielded Americans from the twin disorders of anarchy and tyranny. Like most popular writing on the Constitution, the preceding sentence is both true and florid, and it suggests the dangers that lurk for authors who tackle so noble and overworked a subject as the hallowed charter of our liberties—especially at times of national observance.

On September 17, 1987, the nation celebrates the two-hundredth anniversary of the world's oldest continuing written constitution. That it should have lived so long is testament to both a small band of men who sweated for four months in a hot room in Philadelphia and to the character of Americans at large. But it is also testament to a relationship about which psychologists, sociologists, and anthropologists have, so far as I know, made nothing: The Constitution has shaped us all, as individuals, just as we, collectively, have shaped the Constitution.

The story of the Constitution is the story of a civilization, a culture, a society. It is also the entire history of a nation. And that is what makes writing about it so difficult. The author must take pains to see that he does not merely repeat what so many others for so long have already written, while yet telling the familiar story. He must see to it that he is accurate when nuance is sometimes all. He must shed personal opinions (or most of them, anyway) to make the account credible.

Above all, he must condense an abundant chronicle, recorded not merely on paper but also in much of what we see around us. The hurly-burly of the streets and the marketplace, the quotidian headlines of presidents and police chiefs, the currency that too rapidly departs our purses, the machines that surround us and elevate us and change us, the magazines we read and the movies we watch—all have a place in the Constitution that shapes us. The serenity that most of us feel at night (never for an instant supposing that a soldier will come bursting in to drag us off); the unconscious assurance with which we voice our opinions, snarling or smiling as is our style, defending or denouncing our politicians; the unembarrassed trip to church or synagogue (or unembarrassed stay at home)—all, and so much more, have a place in the Constitution that guards us.

Lest we turn the countryside into a semiotician's guide to the Constitution, the author's burden (and the reader's dilemma) can best be felt in examining the sheer paper commentary. The catalog of the New York Public Library lists 753 books directly under the heading "Constitution, U.S.," and thousands of other volumes touching on it this way or that are doubtless to be found there as well, for the Constitution embraces hundreds of topics on any one of which a lifetime can be spent in study. The public library has no special collection: Butler Library at Columbia University (the King's College that two delegates to the Constitutional Convention, Alexander Hamilton and Gouverneur Morris, attended) shows a similar dedication of shelf space: 564 volumes. And books are by no means the largest measure. Better to see the literary homage we pay in the learned commentary of legal scholars: Every year, the *Index to Legal Periodicals* shows more than 150 articles devoted to general constitutional studies (and again, specific constitutional topics consume much more index space). Better also to see the fealty we owe in the

opinions of courts: Every year federal courts alone devote thousands of pages to constitutional issues. In two hundred years, the glossators have rivaled the work of biblical scholars in all the past two thousand.

Of the writer's many problems, this torrent of commentary is one extreme—sifting through some of it and knowing when not to cull at all is a daunting prospect. No less treacherous a problem is the temptation to wax eloquent in vapid generalities about what is, after all, a subject that was formed in compromise and therefore demands balance.

Which brings us to Sol Bloom.

In 1939, New York Congressman Sol Bloom served as the "director general" of the United States Constitution Sesquicentennial Commission. The commission had a chairman: Franklin D. Roosevelt. It had other distinguished members. But in the volume that commemorates the festivities of the day, a recurring name is Sol Bloom. It appears on the title page, twice on the page that shows commission members, and on the page facing the introduction (a letter from FDR to the director general). Congressman Bloom writes the Introduction and is listed as the author of a 140-page excursus, "The Story of the Constitution." A section titled "Liberty Documents" contains the Magna Carta, the 1628 Petition of Right, the English Habeas Corpus Act of 1679, the English Bill of Rights of 1689, the Declaration of Independence, the Articles of Confederation, the Constitution, Washington's Farewell Address, the Monroe Doctrine—and concludes with, yes, "The Heart and Soul of the Constitution," an address by Sol Bloom. Photographs scattered through the volume depict Sol Bloom: with King George VI, at Washington's Tomb, at various other ceremonies, and even reading, with pince-nez in a stagey pose, the original document, then at the Library of Congress. Several other addresses by the Hon. Sol Bloom punctuate the proceedings, along with a photograph of Mrs. Bloom and daughter in the garden "studying historical material to be used in the Celebration." One almost expects to see Sol Bloom painted into Howard Chandler Christy's canvas of the signing of the Constitution, right behind Ben Franklin.

Sol Bloom resides now in a musty volume. The year of the sesquicentennial, 1939, was also the year of the New York World's Fair. But celebrations were tempered by heavy clouds of war. Seventeen days before the main ceremony, Germany invaded Poland. Though we face a corrosive terrorism (itself destructive of constitutional rights), thankfully we face no general war. Also, we have learned a great deal about how to throw a party for the nation. We stand in more danger that far greater impresarios than Sol Bloom will transform what ought to be a solemn occasion dedicated to real understanding of a constitutional culture into one of the largest pseudoevents in our history, even bigger than Bobby Riggs and Billie Jean King's tennis match, say, or the New York City Marathon. (But even these we can attribute to the Constitution: It permits—I did not say requires—an infectious enthusiasm for public events almost wholly devoid of meaning.)

As this is written, a year ahead of ceremonial events, one can begin to feel only a slight rise in temperature, a pale heat of the fever that will sweep the nation through our genius for public relations. Blessed by the Commission on the Bicentennial of the Constitution (headed by retired Chief Justice Warren E. Burger), one group plans to raise $6 million to sponsor a constitutional "trivial pursuits" among high school students, the winner to receive a four-year college scholarship. The group's advance scouts, promoting a story in the *New York Times*, contend that half the high school students in the country will participate. But if a board game can make even 10 percent of our youth constitutionally literate, we will all have something to celebrate.

Against a $6-million budget to promote a board game with prizes, what can a single volume on the Constitution (especially among all the dozens that are sure to be published) hope to accomplish? A book can do only one thing: Lend coherence and integrity to a subject that is merely mysterious if seen as the several answers to random questions. A book can provide perspective that is missing when one looks only to a single word or phrase or clause or looks at text without history or history without philosophy.

A book on the Constitution should, in a word, talk about *constitutionalism,* the spirit of law, rights, and orderly procedures that animate a free society and keep it free. It should help the reader see how unhelpful in the realm of society and politics is the old saw "If we can send a man to the moon, then why can't we . . . ?" for the task of keeping order and preserving freedom is far more complex than the engineer's application of physics to rockets. The engineer knows the goal—to go to the moon—whereas we here on earth must search for the goal each day in a never-ending debate with our fellow citizens. Without a vital constitution, we could not hope to balance order and freedom, progress and conservation, stability and momentum. Without a constitution, we could live a life—billions of people have—but it would not be a life of the fullest human potential. That much we owe the Constitution.

There are many ways to approach the constitutional order in America. A treatise would spell out the intricacies. A history would show how we have coped. But this book is not a legal treatise, nor is it (nor could it hope to be) anything approaching a constitutional history. Neither is it a commentary on the government nor a general history of the United States. But it inevitably partakes of all those things: constitutional analysis, institutional history, and narrative of events, political and social. The Constitution is not simply a collection of words on a fading parchment—even those words and that parchment—but a cause and a reflection of real events.

George M. Dallas, who served as James K. Polk's vice president (and as the eponymous inspiration for Dallas, Texas), once observed that "the Constitution in its words is plain and intelligible, and it is meant for the homebred, unsophisticated understandings of our fellow citizens." His bold proclamation is untrue. The Constitution is not intelligible without history, people, stories, litigants, cases, rulings, passion, enemies, philosophy, sociology, and economics. That is not because it is a lawyer's document, though a lawyer, Gouverneur Morris of Pennsylvania, formulated its final, often elegant, phrasing. Its intellectual father, James Madison, was not a lawyer; the political force for its ultimate ratification—Washington and Franklin, the two most respected men in America—were not lawyers.

No, the need for amplification, for interpretation, stems rather from its very nature. As the great Chief Justice John Marshall put it in 1819: "We must never forget that it is a *constitution* we are expounding."

A constitution cannot be a rule book, cluttered with definitions and cross-references. If, as Marshall said, it is "to be adapted to the various crises of human affairs," it must speak in majestic generalities—"due process of law," "equal protection of the law"—and it must use phrases whose meaning is not necessarily self-evident or self-limiting: "bill of attainder," "ex post facto," "judicial power." For that reason, the Constitution needs interpreters.

It has official ones, of course: the Supreme Court when it sits to construe a provision in the course of hearing an appeal; the president when he considers whether to veto a bill that trenches on constitutional rights or powers; Congress when it considers whether to pass a bill with constitutional implications. It also has as many unofficial interpreters as there are people with passion to think for themselves and debate with their neighbors.

En masse, the public is usually constitutionally inert: The Constitution is what lawyers and judges worry about—until something happens to bring it home. The last time that the great mass of unofficial interpreters talked long and loud about the Constitution was in 1974 when Richard Nixon, the greatest constitutional teacher of his generation, put the instrument to the test and the streets were abuzz with talk of impeachment.

In the end, it is usually the public interpretation that wins out. "The Supreme Court follows the election returns," says Mr. Dooley, and though few elections are more than Delphic on most issues, sooner or later the Court hears the rumble of the people, especially if a new president gets the chance to appoint his own justices.

Still, it is the fact of interpreting that matters. And because the Constitution will be interpreted—must be interpreted—it is a charter that ultimately has no absolutely fixed meaning. If porous open-endedness is vexatious, that is also the Constitution's strength and utility.

As we approach the bicentennial, it is fashionable opinion in the highest political circles of Washington that any understanding of the Constitution is wrong if it deviates from that which the framers held. For reasons of logic, philosophy, and probably law, that opinion won't wash. But it wouldn't matter if that opinion were right, for the entire course of American history shows that regardless of how passionately the "original intention" view is held, the Constitution is a living document. We adapt it even as we adapt to it, and it will ever be interpreted to fit the times, regardless of what anybody thinks.

That does not mean we can willy-nilly discard its language, flying off on a fancy to fit a sudden fashion. The words of the Constitution are not exactly anybody's whim. But the reality that it will be interpreted means it is *our* Constitution just as much as it was the framers' and our forebears'. The Preamble says that "We the People *do* ordain," not *once did ordain*. Each generation must rally to the Constitution and understand it anew.

This book tries to provide a basis for such an understanding. Because it is not a treatise, it does not pretend to deal with every word and phrase, nor to take the reader by the hand clause by clause. Other books do that. Because it is not a history, it does not attempt to deal with the impact of the Constitution on various institutions decade by decade (it presumes at least a nodding acquaintance with the great events of days past).

Rather, this book sketches a reciprocal transformation: how the Constitution has influenced important relationships in American history and how these evolving relationships have influenced our understanding of the Constitution. Here we explore government, the economy, liberty, equality, crime and punishment—not in detail, for the bindery will not permit the volume to grow so large, but with enough examples, I hope, that the reader will take away an appreciation for the complexity, importance, and ultimate genius of the document that two centuries later we rightly cherish.

For that reason, I ask the more cynical reader to excuse the occasional panegyric tone. I forthrightly concede that the words of the Constitution have not always been sufficient to preserve and protect us (or some of us) at any one moment, that human frailties, individual and institutional, have led often to moral obtuseness and political failure. But those who reflect on the reasons that America is a nation of immigrants, those who have heard the stories of oppression abroad in countries from which their ancestors fled (and from which people are still fleeing) cannot fail to marvel at the constitutional spirit in America, whatever the fashionable rhetoric of the moment and despite the immense political problems that bedevil policy-making in this country.

Let the bicentennial nurture a sophisticated reverence for the most successful charter of freedom the world has ever known—and let the commemoration also fan the flames of disputation that have kept it that way. The Constitution is no show dog to be held aloft at a lawn party; it is a battle plan at the center of the battle. What else ought a Constitution to be? Always open, oracular, waiting for a good argument to press constitutional imprimatur on a new cause, but always, at the same time, standing guard against old enemies in new robes. How else ought a Constitution to act?

The parchment is old, but we give the Constitution birth every day we invoke it.

Part 1

The Spirit of Constitutionalism

Chapter 1 The Search for Constitutionalism

One thing alone is common to all Americans. Not our language, though across the great land mass one language predominates and unites. Not our religion; America was founded on religious diversity. Not our ethnic roots or national origin, for peoples from every niche in the remotest archipelago have migrated to this land. Not our material possessions or the quest for riches. Not our ambition, drives, energy, commitment. Not our outlook or beliefs. Certainly not our fidelity to basic principles of justice and equity. Not our entertainments or our passions. Not even our hopes.

The Constitution alone is our common heritage.

Drafted over the summer of 1787 and ratified in 1788, the United States Constitution from its earliest days was said to have been divinely inspired, and on state occasions it inspires after-dinner speakers to wretched excesses:

> Our great and sacred Constitution, serene and inviolable, stretches its beneficent powers over our land . . . like the outstretched arm of God himself. . . . [T]he people of the United States . . . ordained and established one Supreme Court—the most rational, considerate, discerning, veracious, impersonal power—the most candid, unaffected, conscientious, incorruptible power. . . . O Marvellous Constitution! Magic Parchment! Transforming Word! Maker, Monitor, Guardian of Mankind!"

Even when its provenance has not been claimed quite so elevated, its admirers have spoken in terms only a little less exalted. "The most wonderful work ever struck off at a given time by the brain and purpose of man," gushed Britain's Prime Minister William Ewart Gladstone in the centennial year of its ratification.

The Constitution endures. In two hundred years, it has been amended but twenty-six times (most recently in 1971). Ten of those amendments came just three years after ratification and because of it; the Bill of Rights can justly be considered part of the original Constitution. Of the sixteen remaining amendments, two canceled each other out—Prohibition. Most of the rest were technical, affecting the method of elections—surely not unimportant, but not significantly changing the original charter.

Only four brought on fundamental changes. One ended slavery. Two others guaranteed to all the basic right to vote. A fourth—the Fourteenth Amendment—fundamentally altered the balance between federal and state power.

How could a shifting mixture of fifty-odd men sitting in a sweltering room in Philadelphia for four months lay down a charter under which we still live two hundred years later, in a world that would be unrecognizable to any of them? The short answer is that they gave their countrymen and their descendants a philosophy—constitutionalism—not a black-letter code. Philosophies, unlike codes, can outlast the conditions that give them birth. Far longer than codes, philosophies can shape the future. But the Founding Fathers did not need to anticipate the future; in prescribing a philosophy of politics by which they hoped to solve their own problems, they were progenitors of our own age—the age of freedom.

By freedom, they assuredly did not mean license. They meant, rather, the power of the people to share in the government. Liberty is "the happiness of living under laws of our own making"; hence, liberty is self-government. But freedom also came to be understood as something more: freedom *from* government as much as liberty to share *in* government.

We who are their beneficiaries often lose sight of what these framers wrought. Throughout human history, political freedom has been a chimera. Rulers, subjects, and philosophers, those theoreticians of the good life and proper government, have variously denounced freedom as unholy or impractical or have despaired of it as impossible. Here and there, briefly, some societies managed to survive in freedom (at least for many). But these were all small, homogeneous societies, and none lasted long free and unfettered.

In 1776, the sun shone on something new. A revolutionary generation proclaimed its independence in the name of the people, and five years later succeeded in wresting political power from an ancient monarchy. Unlike the Cromwellian uprising in the mother country more than a century earlier, the American Revolution depended on no single figure and easily outlasted George Washington, its most charismatic leader, a reluctant president eager to relinquish power. Throughout Washington's tenure and since, the system that the founders established preserved for an expanding nation a wide realm of freedom, so that today, scarcely two centuries later, we are the oldest republic in the world.

Just how unique was the spirit of constitutionalism that fell to the revolutionists to articulate? Constitutions had existed before, but none written in comprehensive form (only parts of the British Constitution had been reduced to writing). The American Constitution is the oldest, continuing written constitution in the world. It was for its time, and is still, a daring achievement: a public statement to Americans and to the world of the standards on which their government could be judged (a spirit perhaps manifested still in our live telecasts of rocket launches, come what may).

The idea of constitutionalism is very old, far older than the institutions that ultimately came to embody it. It means, in a single phrase immortalized in 1656 by James Harrington in his *Commonwealth of Oceana,*

Independence Hall, Philadelphia

"a government of laws and not of men." Or, as a leading scholar of constitutionalism has defined the term: "It is a legal limitation on government; it is the antithesis of arbitrary rule; its opposite is despotic government, the government of will instead of law."

The term itself has undergone a sea change in the two and a half millennia it has exercised philosophers of law, state, and society. To the Greeks, a constitution was simply the existing order of things. An unconstitutional law, if such a concept could even have been grasped, was not to be overturned unless a revolution not merely ousted the government but also changed the fundamental customs of the people.

Not until Roman republican times did constitutionalism acquire something of its modern meaning. To the republican writers, the state was bound by a higher law. In a famous passage in *De Republica*, Cicero says:

> True law is right reason, harmonious with nature, diffused among all, constant, eternal; a law which calls to duty by its commands and restrains from evil by its prohibitions. . . . It is a sacred obligation not to attempt to legislate in contradiction to this law; nor may it be derogated from nor abrogated. Indeed by neither the Senate nor the people can we be released from this law; nor does it require any but ourself to be its expositor or interpreter. Nor is it one law at Rome and another at Athens; one now and another at a late time; but one eternal and unchangeable law binding all nations through all times.

The idea of an eternal law of "right reason" has wandered in and out of political thought for two thousand years, slowly gathering force for those who would ultimately harness a cognate idea—that governments ought not be things unto themselves; only when they conform to natural rules of justice may they exercise their power.

Is the king under the law? If so, how can he be made to answer to it? These were the fundamental political questions of earlier centuries, and the tortured attempts to reconcile a sovereign power with a higher law show how difficult was the struggle to conceive a constitutionalism in the modern sense.

Some mileposts were there: Magna Carta, for one. In 1215, the abusive King John met the rebellious nobility at Runnymede and to save his throne yielded to a series of demands that would, in the language of generality in which his pledges were expressed, reverberate in a much later revolution. Most important was Chapter 29:

> No free man shall be taken or imprisoned or deprived of his freehold or of his liberties or free customs, or outlawed, or exiled, or in any manner destroyed, nor shall we go upon him, nor shall we send upon him, except by a legal judgment of his peers or by the law of the land.

Over the centuries, Magna Carta was absorbed into the political memory of England and assimilated into the laws of England and ultimately into the American Constitution itself.

By the seventeenth century, Lord Coke, for a time chief justice of the King's Bench, was asserting that law, a preexisting law, controlled the acts of Parliament; as he said in 1610 in the famous *Dr. Bonham's Case:*

> And it appears in our books, that in many cases, the common law will controul acts of parliament, and sometimes adjudge them to be utterly void: for when an act of parliament is against common right and reason, or repugnant, or impossible to be performed, the common law will controul it and adjudge such act to be void.

Here is a precursor of that judicial review that looms so large in the American system. But is is more generally a statement of constitutionalism: that government may not act however it wills.

This was the credulous age of the divine right of kings, when it was believed that God in his wisdom chose the Tudors or Stuarts for the throne of England—a notion approximately equivalent to

King John signing the Magna Carta at Runnymede.

supposing in our time that God selected George Steinbrenner to rule the Yankees or made J. Edgar Hoover director of the FBI for life.

The English struggles of the seventeenth century, which led to the execution of Charles I and the Glorious Revolution of 1688, revolved around the conflict between the king's power to govern and the people's (imagined) ancient rights—to security of person and property and to freedom from taxation to which Parliament had not assented.

By the end of the century, Parliament had subdued the crown, but that was merely to substitute one arbitrary power for another; as one observer noted: "Parliament can do anything except make a man a woman or a woman a man." The more general problem remained: how to subordinate governmental power to the rule of evenhanded law.

Political philosophers from earliest times have quarreled about the nature of the just society and of the proper type of government: rule by the one, the few, or the many. The ancient Greeks started it all by postulating an endless cycle of change—a law-abiding monarchy transformed into lawless tyranny, to be overthrown by an aristocracy that in turn degenerates into lawless oligarchy, replaced by lawful democracy that decays into mob rule, order finally being restored and the cycle renewed when a solitary leader assumes command to subdue the mob. Plato's horror at this disheartening cycle led him to postulate an even more depressing static society in *The Republic*, a utopia in which a special class of guardians would maintain order and others would lead rigidly prescribed lives. Aristotle sought a golden mean between tyranny and anarchy, proposing a "mixed constitution" that would moderate the worst features of each.

The philosophers were prompted by a keen sense of the dismaying realities that afflicted the societies in which they lived. As Alexander Hamilton noted in *Federalist* No. 9: "It is impossible to read the history of the petty republics of Greece and Italy without

Alexander Hamilton

feeling sensations of horror and disgust at the distractions with which they were continually agitated, and at the rapid succession of revolutions by which they were kept in a state of perpetual vibration between the extremes of tyranny and anarchy."

For two thousand years, the philosophers argued variations on these themes. In the medieval worldview, down to our own revolutionary era, rights were thought to inhere in three coexisting "estates"—crown, nobility, and the mass of commoners—and the dilemma was how each estate would best be represented in a government. The theorists sought to describe those arrangements that would yield order in a fractious world. They did not yet have a concept of government as a means, an instrument, for all the people. Group rights had not yet given way to individual rights. The monarch's claim to the right to govern

Founding Father

George Washington
Virginia

George Washington was born in Bridges Creek, Westmoreland County, Virginia, February 22, 1732, and died at Mount Vernon, Virginia, December 14, 1799. He was educated by his father and his older half-brother, from whom he inherited Mount Vernon, where he lived from 1752. Washington early assumed public responsibility. In 1749, he was appointed surveyor for Culpeper County. In 1752, he was commissioned a major in the Virginia militia. Seven years later, he was elected to the Virginia House of Burgesses, where he opposed the oppressive colonial rule. Between 1774 and 1775, he served as a delegate to the First and Second Continental Congresses. With war imminent, Congress chose him commander in chief of the Continental Army. Defeating Cornwallis at Yorktown in 1781, the final Revolutionary War victory, Washington was hailed a hero. Along with many, Washington believed that the government under the Articles of Confederation was too limited to be effective, and so attended the Annapolis Convention in 1786 and the Pennsylvania Convention the following year. Chosen president, he remained neutral during the debates and spoke only once. With the adoption of the Constitution, he was unanimously elected the first president of the United States in 1789. Although Federalist by tendency, he opposed factions, or parties. Most notably, while president, he supported Hamilton's fiscal policies, issued the Neutrality Proclamation in 1793, sent the governmental militia to suppress the Whiskey Rebellion in 1794, and used his influence to secure the unpopular Jay's Treaty in 1795. Weary of politics, he refused to serve a third term. After his Farewell Address in 1796, he returned to his beloved Mount Vernon, where he remained until his death nearly three years later.

Washington was dignified, tall, and good-looking. He was not a commanding speaker, though he commanded respect and admiration. He was a rather simple man, who preferred his life as a Virginia planter to the rigors of politics, but he was also a natural leader who took pains not to abuse the authority the people vested in him and whose simplicity and unregal bearing set an important precedent in American politics.

was not so much an instrumental power as a personal right of the king as the "owner" of the realm. Henry VIII could as rightfully issue decrees to his subjects as Henry Ford II could fire Lee Iacocca. Unlike automobile companies, however, the existence and relationship of the three estates was not something that men had brought on themselves: God placed the people in these estates and he divinely established their relationship one to the other.

With the social contractarians in the seventeenth century, political theory took a new turn. It was an age of science. Just as Newton demonstrated that universal forces controlled the movements of local objects and distant stars, so Thomas Hobbes built a science of politics on human motion. The more optimistic John Locke systematized the philosophy that found a home in the American constitutional tradition.

Locke supposed a time before government when people in a "state of nature" were free to act as they wished. As the world became more populous, inevitable conflicts led them to recognize the difficulties that stemmed from an intuited "natural law" that permitted anyone to punish another for violating it. So people came together and through a "social contract" created the state as an instrument to preserve their lives, liberties, and estates. The state was not an end in itself but a means to the fulfillment of individuals as they defined their own ends. A government that fails to perform its function forfeits the people's support:

John Locke

> Whenever the *Legislators endeavour to take away, and destroy the Property of the People,* or to reduce them to Slavery under Arbitrary Power, they put themselves into a state of War with the People, who are thereupon absolved from any farther Obedience, and are left to the common Refuge, which God hath provided for all Men, against Force and Violence. Whensoever therefore the *Legislative* shall transgress this fundamental Rule of Society; and either by Ambition, Fear, Folly or Corruption, *endeavor to grasp* themselves, *or put into the hands of any*

other an Absolute Power over the Lives, Liberties, and Estates of the People; By this breach of Trust they *forfeit the Power,* the People had put into their hands, for quite contrary ends, and it devolves to the People, who have a Right to resume their original Liberty, and, by the Establishment of a new Legislative (such as they shall think fit) provide for their own Safety and Security, which is the end for which they are in Society.

By the time the American colonies declared their independence, Locke's had become the modern conception. Individuals, not distinct classes or estates, are the center of the political universe. To secure their ends, the government must abide by the law, for sovereignty resides in the people, not in kings or states.

From the individualist perspective, the ideal embodiment of a constitutional government must be the republic. In technical terms, it could not be a democracy (though today we commonly suppose ourselves to be) because there always were too many people to fit into the legislative hall (not every New England town can have a town meeting) and because, as Rousseau noted, "it is impossible to imagine that the people should remain in perpetual assembly to attend to public affairs." This was the consensus of the revolutionary generation: The people would rule through representative agencies.

But the American Constitution makers did not hold with the republican theories of the British constitutional apologists, who claimed without warrant that great masses of people were represented in Parliament. This they knew firsthand. To the colonists' cry of "no taxation without representation," loyalists had remonstrated that of course Americans were represented in Parliament: They were "virtually" represented. Many parts of England had no legislative voice: Manchester and Birmingham sent no members to the House of Commons. Nevertheless, their citizens were said to be virtually represented because, as Edmund Burke explained in 1774, "Parliament is a *deliberative* assembly of *one* nation, with *one* interest, that of the

Colonists tearing down a statue of King George III while celebrating the first public reading in New York City of the Declaration of Independence on July 9, 1776. The lead in the statue was subsequently converted into Revolutionary ammunition.

whole, where, not local purposes, not local prejudices ought to guide, but the general good, resulting from the general reason of the whole." This gross confusion of "ought" with "is" rankled and festered in the colonial mind.

The republic Americans wanted was one in which they genuinely participated through true representation. The difficulty was that the philosophers had all claimed what they had in mind was impossible. Montesquieu and Rousseau, among others, had shown that for a true republic to work, certain conditions had to be fulfilled. In particular, republics had to be territorially limited with small, homogeneous populations; they had to be agricultural, or at least not industrial, and their citizens had to be virtuous, not greedy and devoted to material self-interest.

These conditions surely did not obtain in the states, for as Hamilton noted:

> When Montesquieu recommends a small extent for republics, the standards he had in view were of dimensions far short of the limits of almost every one of these States. Neither Virginia, Massachusetts, Pennsylvania, New York, North Carolina, nor Georgia can by any means be compared with the models from which he reasoned and to which the terms of his description apply. If we therefore take his ideas on this point as the criterion of truth, we shall be driven to the alternative either of taking refuge at once in the arms of monarchy, or of splitting ourselves into an infinity of little, jealous, clashing, tumultuous commonwealths, the wretched nurseries of unceasing discord and the miserable objects of universal pity or contempt.

Others concurred. Patrick Henry looked out on the continent and shuddered that transforming it into a republic was "a work too great for human wisdom." James Winthrop of Massachusetts said that "the idea of an uncompounded republick, on an average one thousand miles in length, and eight hundred in breadth, and containing six millions of white inhabitants all reduced to the same standards of morals, of habits, and of laws, is in itself an absurdity, and contrary to the whole experience of mankind." Could so many wise men be wrong?

The answer the Founding Fathers gave was twofold: institutional and political. Institutionally, they

James Madison

designed a complex mechanism of government, which the chapters that follow explore in some depth. The government was federal, not unitary; republican, not democratic; and its powers were separated among the three great branches. The framers thus found a practical way to ensure the constitutionalism that was so evidently lacking in all previous governments of Europe. Power splintered is power that cannot easily be turned against the people. As Madison put it in a famous passage in *Federalist* No. 51:

> Ambition must be made to counteract ambition. . . . It may be a reflection on human nature that such devices should be necessary to control the abuses of government. But what is government itself but the greatest of all reflections on human nature? If men were angels, no government would be necessary. If angels were to govern men, neither external nor internal controls on government would be necessary. In framing a government which is to be administered by men over men, the great difficulty lies in this: you must first enable the government to control the governed; and in the next place oblige it to control itself. A dependence on the people is, no doubt, the primary control on the government; but experience has taught mankind the necessity of auxiliary precautions.

Politically, the founders saw that the philosophers had the argument about republics backward; or else the revolutionists stood the argument on its head. Again, James Madison was the most cogent expositor of the new theory, one that would be tested, and is still being tested, in the America that they created.

In *Federalist* No. 10, he argued that a "well-constructed Union" must "break and control the violence of faction." By faction, he meant "a number of citizens, whether amounting to a majority or minority of the whole, who are united and actuated by some common impulse of passion, or of interest, adverse to the rights of other citizens, or to the permanent and aggregate interests of the community."

The greatest source of faction is the unequal distribution of property. "A landed interest, a manu-

The Thirty-Dollar Job: Who Penned the Constitution?

Who wrote the Constitution?—that is, who penned it by hand to create the solitary engrossed signed original that resides today at the National Archives?

The penman's identity was unknown for about 150 years, until a researcher for the Sesquicentennial Commission, after painstaking analysis of handwriting samples, discovered his man: Jacob Shallus, the assistant clerk of the Pennsylvania Assembly.

The assembly met in the same building as the delegates. It was then called the Pennsylvania State House (now known as Independence Hall). The call went out for an "engrossing clerk" to hurry down to the convention to engross the Constitution. For his extraordinary calligraphy, Shallus was paid thirty dollars.

Shallus had been quartermaster of the First Pennsylvania Battalion early in the war. He resigned in 1778 to become a privateer, capturing British ships, and after the war served as assistant clerk of the Pennsylvania Assembly and secretary of the state constitutional convention in 1790. He died at forty-six in 1796.

facturing interest, a mercantile interest, a moneyed interest, with many lesser interests, grow up of necessity in civilized nations, and divide them into different classes, actuated by different sentiments and views. The regulation of these various and interfering interests forms the principal task of modern legislation and involves the spirit of party and faction in the necessary and ordinary operations of government."

The violence of faction will not be muted in a pure democracy, that is, in "a society consisting of a small number of citizens." For in a small society, "there is nothing to check the inducements to sacrifice the weaker party or an obnoxious individual." But in the larger society, made possible by a representative government, "a greater variety of parties and interests" will flourish, and "you make it less probable that a majority of the whole will have a common motive to invade the rights of other citizens; or if such a common motive exists, it will be more difficult for all who feel it to discover their own strength and to act in unison with each other." In short, the greater the sweep of territory, the more people, the more numerous and diverse the factions, the less likely any one will control; divide them, and they shall not conquer.

So here, in the Constitution the founders wrote in 1787, was a reciprocity that would establish the conditions of constitutionalism: An institutional mechanism would prevent and restrain arbitrary power, and a political structure would support the mechanism of government it created. For it is not enough to deck out in Sunday best a noble government if no one bothers to attend to it. By its very nature, constitutionalism cannot be a mere abstraction. Like love, it has meaning only when it moves us. A constitution is useful only to the extent that it is used. The fit between the words on the parchment and the character of the people ensured that the constitutionalism devised in 1787 would be the terms on which Americans would earnestly debate ever after.

Chapter 2 Constitutionalism before the Constitution

Early Compacts

Nationhood was a long time coming. The founding of Jamestown in 1607 was separated from the writing of the Constitution by 180 years, almost as much time as has elapsed from the adoption of the Constitution to our own age. Though governed from abroad by king and Parliament, the colonists nevertheless gained some experience in constitution-making during those two centuries of maturation.

The earliest charter was the Mayflower Compact of 1620, in which the Pilgrims, clutching a somewhat dubious land grant from the Council for New England (a private land company), ordained a civil government of patent illegality:

> In the name of God, Amen. We whose names are under-written, the loyall subjects of our dread soveraigne Lord, King James . . . having faith, and honour of our king and countrie, a voyage to plant the first colonie in the Northerne parts of Virginia, doe by these presents solemnly and mutaly in the presence of God, and one of another, covenant and combine our selves togeather into a civill body politick, for our better ordering and preservation and furtherance of the ends aforesaid; and by vertue hereof to enacte, constitute, and frame such just and equall lawes, ordinances, acts, constitutions, and offices, from time to time, as shall be thought most meete

and convenient for the generall good of the Colonie, unto which we promise all due submission and obedience. In witness whereof we have hereunder subscribed our names at Cap-Codd the ll. of November . . . Ano: Dom. 1620.

King James had given the Pilgrims no authority to govern themselves, but the Puritans, landing ten years later, arrived with a royal charter for a trading company, "The Governor and Company of Massachusetts Bay." Nothing daunted, the Puritans converted the corporate charter into a civil state; they became the stockholders and ran the corporation as if it were a municipal government, confident of their ability to do so. From the very outset, the colonists displayed an appetite for self–governance and never doubted their aptitude.

The Massachusetts Bay charter gave its ruling body the power to make "Lawes and Ordinances for the Good and Welfare of the saide Companye, and for the Government and orderings of the saide Landes and Plantation, and the People inhabiting and to inhabite the same." But no Massachusetts law could be "contrarie or repugnant to the Lawes and Statutes of this our Realme of England." Exactly what "repugnant" or "contrary" meant was never entirely clarified, but the British Privy Council occasionally did veto colonial laws (perhaps 6 percent of the 8,500 laws submitted to it).

Other charters sprang up as new colonists arrived: the Fundamental Orders of Connecticut (1639) and the Articles of Confederation of the United Colonies

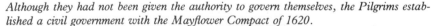

Although they had not been given the authority to govern themselves, the Pilgrims established a civil government with the Mayflower Compact of 1620.

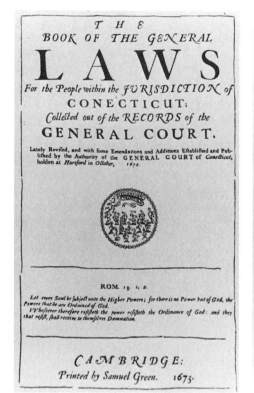

The title page (left) and page 9 from the first printed edition of the laws of Connecticut list such capital offenses as idolatry, blasphemy, and witchcraft. References to Biblical proof text follow each law.

of New England (then consisting of Massachusetts, New Plymouth, Connecticut, and New Haven, which were formed in 1643 and lasted until 1684). The Articles were a "consocation amongst ourselves, for mutual help and strength in future concernments," aimed "to advance the Kingdom of Our Lord Jesus Christ and to enjoy the liberties of Gospel in purity with peace." This association was tied to religious doctrine, and the Articles prohibited Quakers, Ranters, and other notorious heretics from entering or remaining in the United Colonies.

For roughly a century, between 1684 when the commissioners of the United Colonies of New England met for the last time, and 1765, the first meeting of the Stamp Act Congress, many suggestions would be seconded by respected colonists to form a defensive union against the aggressions of other nations: William Penn's Plan of 1696–1697, Robert Livingston's Plan of 1701, Coxe's Plan of 1722, Reverend Mr. Peter's Plan of 1754, Ben Franklin's Short Hints of 1754, the Albany Plan of 1754, also written by Franklin, and the Lord of Trade's Plan of 1754. These plans were as individual as their creators, but each expounded permanent union of the colonies.

The British Constitution in America

In the meantime, various leaders began to speak out on the meaning of the (unwritten) British Constitution and its applicability in the colonies. The clergy especially preached a Locke-like constitutionalism. Here is Charles Chauncey in 1747:

> Whatever power any are invested with, 'tis delegated to them according to some civil constitution. And this, so long as it remains the constitution, they are bound in justice to conform themselves to . . . Especially is this an important point of justice where the conclusion is branched into several parts, and the power originally lodged in it is divided in certain measures to each part, in order to preserve a balance in the whole. Rulers, in this case, in either branch of the government, are bound by the constitution and obliged to keep within the proper limits assigned them.

By the 1750s, it was generally (though mistakenly) agreed that "parliaments are not the constitution . . . but that they take their form, powers, and existence from it. That they cannot alter that form or alienate those powers . . . without breaking through that agreement of the society . . . which constituted them." And not just parliaments: "The throne as well as the cottage, the king as well as the subject, is bound by these laws." The government thus subordinated, this belief gave birth to the idea, though quite nascent before the revolution, that a law contrary to the constitution was "unconstitutional" and void.

What then of the constitutions of the colonies themselves? Royal governors and colonial legislatures engaged in a running debate throughout the eighteenth century: Were the colonies subject to the whim of the governors, appointed by the crown, or did the people in America "have the same fundamental rights, privileges, and liberties as [the people of England] have [and] hence . . . have a right to choose the laws by which [they] shall be governed," as one New York lawyer argued in 1734? The situation differed from colony to colony; some, like Maryland and Pennsylvania, had been granted explicit contractual rights to some form of self-government, but still just how much and on what terms was much disputed. Colonial legislatures were constantly being condemned by governor and royal councils for usurping authority ostensibly left in the executive's hands, authority, for instance, over the spending of public funds, a power many legislatures thought reserved to them.

Beginning in the 1760s, Parliament asserted itself with a much heavier hand than it ever had. Writs of assistance letting British agents invade colonial homes searching for rum smugglers aroused local wrath. These writs prompted James Otis's celebrated remarks, said to have been the spark that lit the long fuse of the revolution: "An act against the constitution is void. An act against natural equity is void."

The beginning of overt opposition was the Stamp Act of 1765, a tax on newspapers and legal papers. It was this act that gave rise to the cry "No taxation without representation." The colonists responded by calling the Stamp Act Congress, an extralegal convention to protest the tax. (Many, including some Englishmen, considered the congress a lawful assembly under the right to meet to petition the government, a right that would be made explicit in the First

Embossed tax stamp issued by the British government in 1765.

Amendment in 1791.) The outcry was so great that Parliament was forced to repeal the law the following year because royal stamp collectors resigned in droves when the colonists refused to cooperate.

When Parliament passed the British Tea Act of 1774, the colonies exploded and quickly acceded to Massachusetts's suggestion to convene the First Continental Congress in Philadelphia. This was clearly an extralegal body, represented by twelve of the thirteen colonies (many delegates were also part of the "Committees of Correspondence"). The Continental Congress acted by common consent, not by any inherent governing authority vested in it by a constitution.

Once the shot was fired in Lexington on April 19, 1775, that was heard round the world, the momentum was irresistible. In July, Ben Franklin called for "Articles of Confederation and Perpetual Union." In 1776, when the Continental Congress appointed a committee to draft the Declaration of Independence, it also appointed a committee to prepare a "form of confederation." The committee's work would eventually become the Articles of Confederation, which were in force from 1781 until the new Constitution was ratified in 1788. Eleven states had ratified by 1779, a year after they were proposed, but by their terms the

Two cartoons from the Revolutionary period: (above) Bostonian colonists tar and feather John Malcolm, an unpopular customs commissioner. (left) A satirical funeral procession following the repeal of the Stamp Act.

1775 engraving of the Battle of Lexington.

Articles could not become effective unless unanimously approved. Even before the Articles took effect, some prescient observers noted the inefficiency of the government the Articles would establish and called for a convention to create something else.

The Rise of American Power: Constitutions in the States

In the meantime, from 1776 until 1780, the rebellious states, independent as much from one another as from King George III, debated and adopted written constitutions. Constitution writing was not lightly undertaken; it answered a deeply felt need throughout

Congress voting independence.

America. In most states (but not in Massachusetts), it was the first order of business. As Lawrence Friedman has written:

> Constitutionalism answered to a deep-seated need, among members of the articulate public, for formal, outward signs of political legitimacy. This urge had driven tiny, isolated colonies in what is now Rhode Island or Massachusetts to express the structure and principles of government in the form of an agreement—a visible, legible bulwark against the lonely disorder of life outside the reach of the mother country. Much later, but by something of the same instinct, the remote Oregon pioneers, in a no-man's land disputed among nations, drew up a frame of government and called it a constitution. So did the residents of the "lost state of Franklin" in the 1780's, in what is now part of eastern Tennessee. So did the handful of citizens of the "Indian Stream Republic," in disputed territory near the border of New Hampshire and Canada. And so did the Mormons of the "State of Deseret." These "constitutions" . . . were short-lived and of dubious legality. But they illustrate how strong the *idea* of a constitution had become in American life.

None of the states deliberated in a vacuum. This was a fertile political age, and various figures proposed structures and codification of rights.

Virginia was the first state to act. The Convention of 1776, the successor to the royal government, adopted a constitution containing a bill of rights and a structure of government. It provided for a bicameral legislature; differences between members of the upper and lower house turned on minimum age and length of terms (four years in the upper house, one year in the lower). The legislature would elect a governor and an eight-man privy council with staggered terms. Voting eligibility was qualified by property ownership (one hundred acres of vacant land, twenty-five acres of land with a twelve-by-twelve-foot building, a net worth of twenty-five pounds, or completion of an apprenticeship in either Williamsburg or Norfolk). Counties and districts were equally represented, and "the failure of the convention to reapportion the leg-

King George III

islature in accordance with population left effective political power in the hands of its traditional possessors—the Tidewater aristocracy."

In securing rights to the people against invasion by the government, the Virginia Bill of Rights had a wide influence both in America and abroad. It contained some provisions later incorporated in the federal Bill of Rights. But many of its provisions seem peculiar by twentieth-century standards—for example, it listed as a fundamental right "the enjoyment of life and liberty, with the means . . . of pursuing and *obtaining* happiness and safety." The Virginia government was told that it "ought" not impose excessive bail and fines or cruel and unusual punishments and "ought" not to grant general search warrants—but not that it could not do these things. The free speech provision said that "the freedom of the Press is one of the greatest bulwarks of liberty, and can never be restrained but by despotic Government." Was this an invitation? James Madison, new to politics, persuaded the convention to substitute "free exercise of religion" in a provision that would merely have provided "toleration" for religious differences. But the peroration declared that "it is the mutual duty of all to practice Christian forbearance, love, and charity, towards each other."

One explanation for this form of wording is the different understanding of constitutionalism that Virginians possessed in those days. A constitution was taken to be a statement not just of legal rights but also of fundamental moral principles; it was a constitution in the Greek sense: a way of life. The statements of "ought" were not intended to weaken legal controls but to inform both government and people of what is right and wrong to do. That may be why Section 15 of the Bill of Rights proclaimed: "That no free government, or the blessings of liberty, can be preserved to any people, but by firm adherence to justice, moderation, temperance, frugality, and virtue, and by frequent recurrence to fundamental principles"—principles written out for all to read.

The most radical constitution was Pennsylvania's. It substituted payment of taxes for property ownership as the qualification for voting and established a unicameral legislature. To ensure that the people would control their legislature, its sessions were open to the public, bills had to be published in advance, and a bill introduced in one session could not be voted on until the next session. Legislators had one-year terms and could sit in only four of every seven years. The Virginia constitution had imposed no religious test, but members of the Pennsylvania legislature had to swear their belief that the Bible was divinely inspired. The executive authority was a rotating twelve-man council elected every three years. The constitution established a supreme court, the judges to have seven-year terms and be eligible for reappointment. It also created a "council of censors" elected by district every seven years who oversaw the legislature and executive and could "pass public censures" (these were not vetoes), order impeachments, and call for a convention to revise the constitution.

Pennsylvania copied many of the rights in Virginia's Bill of Rights, but added some of its own. It prohibited bribes offered and taken by candidates and voters. It told the legislature to enact certain types of laws: "Laws for the encouragement of virtue, and prevention of vice and immorality, shall be made and constantly kept in force, and provision shall be made for their due execution." Here was the notion, widespread at the time of the revolution, that "civic virtue" of the citizenry was essential to the maintenance of a republic. "Every state in which the people participated needed a degree of virtue; but a republic which rested solely on the people absolutely required it."

Massachusetts waited until 1780 to adopt its constitution, in part because many of the leaders thought a constitution was no ordinary business of the legislature. John Adams was the principal author of a constitution proposed by a special convention, and it was ratified by votes taken in each town. Feeling

John Langdon
New Hampshire

John Langdon was born in Portsmouth, New Hampshire, June 26, 1741, and died on September 18, 1819. After a time at local grammar schools, he became a clerk apprentice, went to sea, and eventually started a commercial business of his own. Early in life, he had acquired substantial property. Langdon supported the revolutionary cause from the beginning. In 1774, he engaged in one of the first overt attacks against the British, seizing supplies from a British fort in Portsmouth. In 1775, he was speaker in his state legislature and attended the Continental Congress, where he had considerable duties and many committee seats. The following year, he was named New Hampshire agent for Continental Army supplies and spent the war years amassing materiel. He also served as naval agent for the colonies, helping to build ships for attack against the British. Between 1777 and 1781, he was once again speaker in the New Hampshire legislature. Steadily active in the militia, he commanded several New Hampshire troops in support of Rhode Island. In 1783, he was a delegate in Congress; in 1784, a state senator. In 1785, he was elected president of New Hampshire. In 1786, he returned to his post as speaker. To aid the economically failing New Hampshire government, he absorbed the cost of sending the New Hampshire delegates to Philadelphia. Though he arrived near the close of the Convention, he accepted the document, advocated strong governmental power in areas of defense, taxation, and commerce, and followed through in his support in the New Hampshire ratifying effort. He was a member of the last Congress under the Articles of Confederation. In 1788, he was reelected president of New Hampshire. Early the next year, he resigned to become a U.S. senator. While senator, he was the first president pro tempore. He retired from the Senate and national politics in 1801, turning down Jefferson's offer to make him secretary of the navy. Instead, he returned to New Hampshire, where he was speaker from 1801 to 1805 and governor from 1805 to 1811 (except 1809). In 1812, he retired from politics at the state level, declining a Republican party nomination for the vice presidency.

Langdon was good-natured, sincere, and patriotic, if not remarkably brilliant. He was thrifty with his acquired wealth, though inclined to entertain with flourish. One acquaintance, the Marquis de Chastellux, described him as "a handsome man and of a noble carriage" with a home "elegant and well furnished."

strongly that their labors would forge a social contract, the organizers suspended property qualifications in the voting for delegates to the convention and for ratification by the towns. But the "frame of government that it established was among the most aristocratic or oligarchic of any."

The Massachusetts constitution established a bicameral legislature, with property qualifications for voting and for serving in the government. A candidate for governor had to own real estate valued at one thousand pounds, a large sum in those days. An executive council consisting of the lieutenant governor and nine other members, selected by the legislature, could impeach the governor, who was limited to a one-year term. The governor could veto legislation, but his veto could be overridden by a two-thirds vote, a provision that would find its way into the federal Constitution seven years later. Most of the judges served "during good behavior" unless the legislature recommended and the governor and executive council concurred in removal.

Reacting strongly to British institutions (and despite the governor's limited veto authority), the constitution echoed Cicero in declaring the ultimate notion of separation of powers: "In the government of this Commonwealth, the legislative department shall never exercise the executive and judicial powers, or either of them: The executive shall never exercise the legislative and judicial powers, or either of them: The judicial shall never exercise the legislative and executive powers of either of them: to the end it may be a government of laws and not of men."

The Massachusetts Bill of Rights copied Virginia's in several respects, but not its provision governing religious rights. To serve in government, one needed to be a Christian (some thought the provision did not go far enough and should have specified Protestant Christians). The legislature was empowered to support public worship and to pay for religious teachers out of public funds.

In these and many other ways, the former colonists, now citizens of independent states, set about to define the social compact under which they would live. They were conscious that they were *founding*—not just a form of government but an entire society as well. Some even said they were living once again in a "state of nature" and their constitution would indeed *constitute* a new people; they prayed that a new constitution would institute "such a broad basis of civil and religious liberty as no length of time will corrupt and which will endure as long as the Sun and Moon shall endure."

A Democratic Despotism

Alas for those who had thought it all possible, that a people of virtue could moderately govern themselves, subordinating private interests to a general good. What John Adams in 1776 had said was theoretically impossible—"a democratic despotism"—now seemed to rise like some monster from the legislatures. They were variously confiscating property, issuing paper money, demanding its acceptance as payment of debt, and throwing up obstacles to the recovery of debts. They passed laws permitting contracts to be torn up. Many felt the sting of ex post facto legislation. Madison complained in 1787 that the states were wantonly multiplying the laws, smothering the people.

The state legislatures had become omnipotent. Whatever theoretical force existed to the idea of separated powers dissipated in practice. The legislatures were not merely the first branch but largely the second and third branches too. They were little troubled at staying the execution of court judgments or even reversing the judgments of courts outright. They reduced governors to impotence.

This was unexpected. In the 1770s, republican theorists had thought it possible that if virtue failed, the people might become like a mob, licentious and lawless. But they did not suppose that the people's assemblies would become tyrants. In the 1780s, many feared that both lawlessness and tyranny were dooming their hope that a new human had evolved on the American shore.

For some, these were prosperous times, and everywhere could be seen the evidence of what much later Thorstein Veblen was to call "conspicuous consumption." The wealthy displayed their wealth extravagantly; the poor borrowed to do likewise. Many put on airs; others fumed about it. The newspapers decried the "visible declension of religion . . . the rapid progress of licentious manners, and open profanity." The clergy warned that the people were retreating into a private selfishness that left the commonwealth without support. Lawsuits increased like rabbits; in a county court in New England, eight hundred suits were being filed in a single year, most to collect on debts of five or six pounds. What a century later would be celebrated (by some) as the spirit of private gain that animates capitalism was taken as mere love of luxury and vice. Correspondents wrote Jefferson, in Paris in 1787, that his countrymen were "a Luxurious Voluptuous indolent expensive people without Economy or Industry." And many took especial umbrage at the "uppity" airs of those new men whom the revolution had thrust into positions of prominence. As James Otis had warned: "When the pot boils, the scum will rise."

Vacuum at the Center: The Articles of Confederation

The republican character was vanishing and virtue dissipated. The states, which were to be the political repositories for the new nation on which all the eyes of the world would be turned, were failing. If not quite so decadent, Americans were scarcely superior to their European counterparts. The experiment in

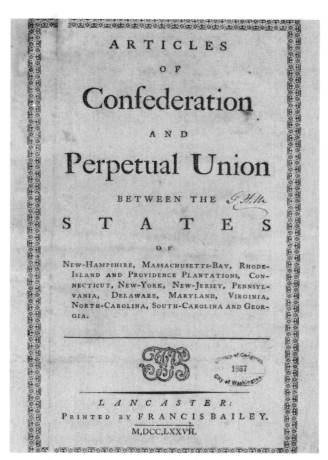

The Articles of Confederation failed to create a government with enough power to maintain national unity.

self-government seemed in serious jeopardy. The disappointments, threats, and dangers that led to the Constitutional Convention in 1787 were not due solely, as is often reported, to the failure of the Articles of Confederation, that compact among the states that had established a rudimentary central government. The movement toward a national government would not likely have progressed as fast as it did, nor have succeeded, had the states shown themselves capable of self-government. Nevertheless, it was the perceived failure of the Articles of Confederation that brought the delegates to Philadelphia.

The debate over the powers of a central government turned on sharply different economic interests that long antedated the revolution. A merchant and planter class dominated the legislatures of many states out of all proportion to their numbers. Many of these men were land speculators who gobbled up large tracts in the western wilderness and sold them back to farmers and artisans searching for subsistence and work. The speculators, operating often on the margin of legality and frequently on the other side of fraud, insisted that the renters and buyers punctiliously observe the letter of the law. For decades, fights between the speculators and farmers had flared up. Moreover, those who controlled the legislatures rarely voted taxes for better roads to bring goods to market or for protection against Indians on the frontier. "No taxation without representation" was not just an intermural cry against the mother parliament; the oppression of taxes imposed at home by those over whom one had no control was resented just as fiercely.

Aside from individual economic interests, the states themselves had territorial differences. Virginia had long claimed huge tracts of western land; landlocked states like Pennsylvania and Maryland were jealous of Virginia's expansion.

These and other differences led in turn to incompatible philosophies about the desirability of a central government. Some states could see the advantage of a central government to restrain land grabs by other states. Merchants could see the advantage of a central government to regulate commerce among states likely to impose all sorts of tariffs and regulations to further their citizens' interests. Farmers and others believed just as passionately that the states must retain ultimate political power, not merely for profound theoretical reasons but also because it was the only way their interests could best be represented.

Against this background of competing interests, members of the Continental Congress had met in 1776 to debate a form of union. The proposed Articles of Confederation left sovereignty with the states and gave the new Congress only those few powers specifically delegated to it. By 1779, Maryland was the lone holdout, refusing to ratify because it hoped to force western lands to be ceded to Congress. When this happened, after protracted maneuvering over the rights of those who claimed land from Indian sales, Maryland ratified on March 1, 1781.

The Articles proclaimed a league of friendship, but not a union. Each state had one vote in the unicameral Congress. This body had no authority to lay taxes. Although Congress conducted foreign relations, the states were largely responsible for troops, and Congress could not by treaty interfere with the right of each state to impose import and export duties as it saw fit. It took nine states to enact important legislation, so that most important legislation could not be passed. Congress was powerless to deal with issues, like the $42 million war debt, that aggravated a host of interests, including those of businessmen, creditors, soldiers, and which the states were only making worse.

Because the power granted was so limited and because the states did not in the Articles create a central, sovereign nation, no provision existed for separated powers; there was only Congress. The president was a member of Congress, with limited powers to exercise during his one-year term. Neither did the Articles create a judicial department, though Congress did have some judicial powers (boundary and other disputes between states, admiralty and prize cases, trials of piracy and felonies on the high seas).

Though it was the only one mentioned in the Articles, Congress was not the only organ of government. Congress created a small federal bureaucracy, which was destined to outlast the Articles of Confederation. As Merrill Jensen noted:

> The creation of a responsible staff of civil servants by the Confederation government is an almost unknown story. These men carried on the work of the departments of war, foreign affairs, finance, and the post office in season and out. The best example of this was Joseph Nourse of Virginia who became register of the treasury in 1779, a post which he held until 1829 when he retired because of old age. He kept books and prepared innumerable reports for Robert Morris, the board of treasury, Alexander Hamilton, and the secretaries of the treasuries who followed him. If it had not been for Nourse and men like him, with years of practical experience in the day-to-day affairs of government behind them, the Washington administration would have been badly hampered.

But the bureaucracy under the Confederation was small and had no general powers of government. Congress was the only significant national actor, and it was feeble. By the mid-1780s, talk of crisis could everywhere be heard.

As early as 1780, Alexander Hamilton, then only twenty-three, wrote a long letter to a member of Congress "At the Liberty Pole," calling for a constitutional convention. He further urged the idea the next year, publishing a series of papers in the *New York Packet* entitled "The Constitutionalist." In 1782, he and his father-in-law, George Schuyler, proposed constitutional reform to the New York legislature.

Others, including Washington, Henry Knox, and Gouverneur Morris, exchanged letters about the inadequacies of the existing government. James Wilson, desperate for corrections, wrote:

> When we had baffled all the menaces of foreign power, we neglected to establish among ourselves a government

that would insure domestic vigor and stability. What was the consequence? The commencement of peace was the commencement of every disgrace and distress that could befall a people in a peaceful state. Devoid of national power, we could not prohibit the extravagance of our importations, nor could we derive a revenue from their excess. Devoid of national importance, we could not procure, for our exports, a tolerable sale at foreign markets. Devoid of national credit, we saw our public securities melt in the hands of the holders, like snow before the sun. Devoid of national dignity, we could not, in some instances, perform our treaties, on our part; and, in other instances, we could neither obtain nor compel the performance of them on the part of others. Devoid of national energy, we would not carry into execution our own resolutions, decisions, or laws.

These and many other entreaties for stronger central authority were written in fear of the profound disturbances that rattled across the states throughout the 1780s. The army at Newburgh, payless, was on the verge of mutiny because it feared that the preliminary peace treaty of March 1783 would cancel their salaries.

The growing delinquency of the several states in paying war debts was undermining hopes of economic stability, but the fledgling central government was powerless to act. The debt was high; payment on the interest alone was estimated to be between 50 and 90 percent of some states' budgets. Regressive land taxes caused considerable discontent—for instance, the number of acres, rather than the value of land, was taxed, and the size of the assessment varied from state to state; also, rich holders often managed to shift the incidence of taxation from land to poll taxes. Slowness in paying the debt led many creditors, like soldiers with state certificates, to sell them to speculators at greatly deflated values, and resulting mob violence was feared in many states.

One way of paying off the war debt was to give market value (the market value of the paper certificates then circulating was far lower than the face of

the debt contracted). Creditors in those days were not simply large military contractors but small suppliers and thousands of soldiers, who had taken paper certificates in lieu of payment during the war. Virginia redeemed a sizable portion of its war debt by paying off certificates at a thousand to one: The paper was worth only one-tenth of 1 percent of the original debt contracted. The method arrived at in Massachusetts resulted in a windfall to speculators, who had gobbled up many of the notes, but left the taxpayers with a much heavier burden to carry (which they had to pay in specie, not in paper). State after state began to issue its own paper money, and Congress had no authority to regulate.

Throughout the 1780s, the Massachusetts legisla-

Daniel Shays's rebels confronting government troops at the Springfield arsenal on January 26, 1787.

ture was controlled by the merchant-creditor class, which resisted as long as possible reforms that would ease the plight of farmers and other debtors. Farmers were hard pressed in the wake of depression, the collapse of hard currency, and the crushing demands of taxation to meet payments on land they had bought from speculators at high prices. Consequently, farms were foreclosed, and numerous debtors were herded into jails. The state legislature, sitting in Boston, would not heed their demands for relief.

Farmers threatened with foreclosure began to take matters into their own hands, massing at the courts to prevent cases from being heard. Daniel Shays, a decorated captain of the Fifth Massachusetts Regiment during the war who had become a farmer, took up the cause. In 1786, he and his followers prevented the courts from hearing debt cases. In early 1787, Shays led a band of desperate fellow farmers in an armed attack on the federal arsenal in Springfield. Although the attack went awry, the local militia were at first powerless to disperse Shays's men, and not until the governor sent out state militia under the command of General Benjamin Lincoln were they routed (Shays fled to Vermont and was pardoned the following year).

The attack frightened people, not only in Massachusetts, but also through the states, for Shays's Rebellion demonstrated a state's difficulty in preventing armed uprisings. Some greater force was necessary, as was some stronger rule against the possibility that a state legislature might forgive debts legitimately incurred.

No wonder that John Quincy Adams worried aloud about this "critical period." Addressing the graduating class of 1787 at Harvard in July, he declared that America was "groaning under the intolerable burden of . . . accumulated evils." This was no usual graduation oratory. Thirteen sovereign states could not coexist without some central authority. That was the task of the Constitutional Convention, meeting in Philadelphia as Adams spoke.

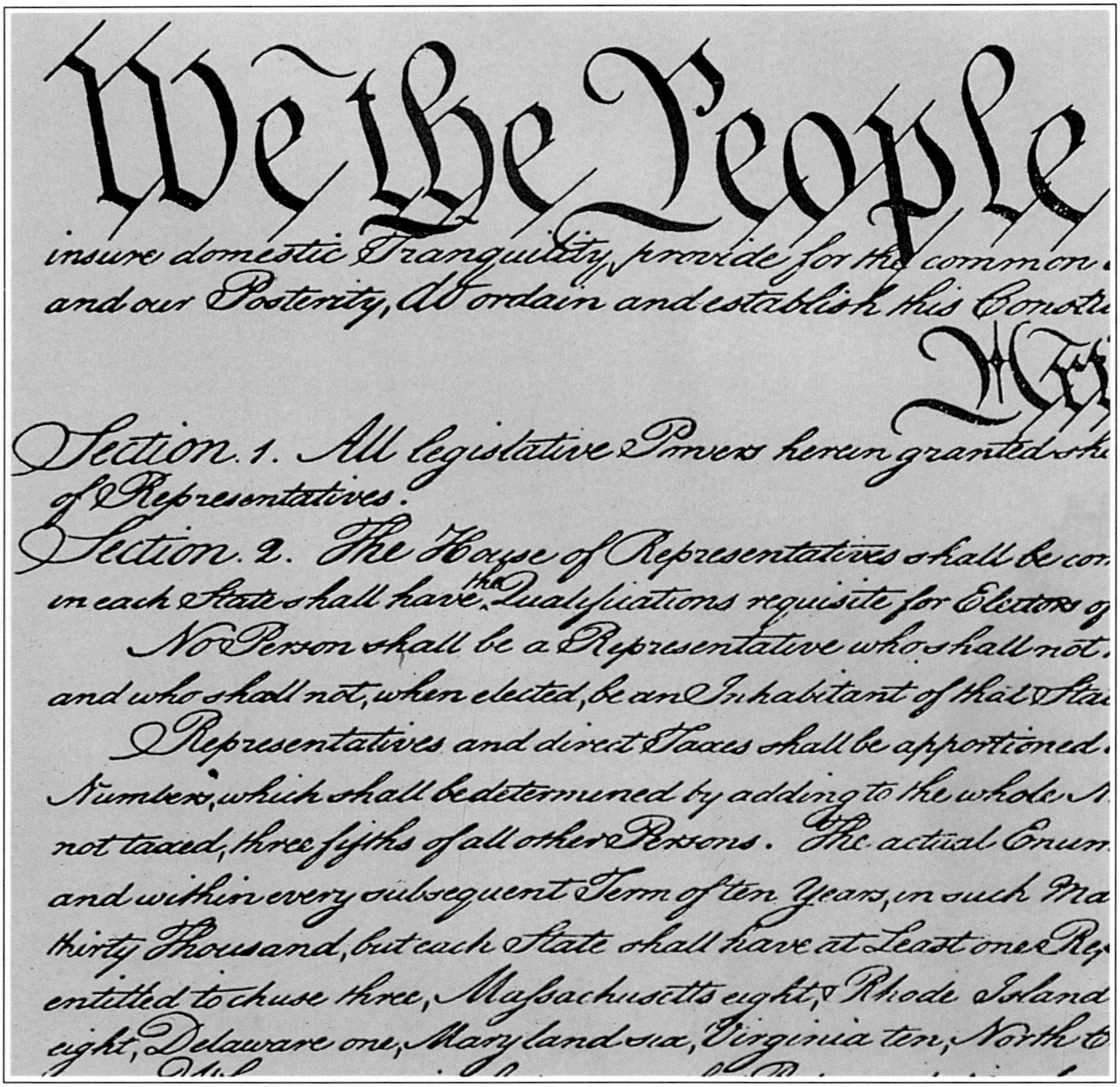
We the People
insure domestic Tranquility, provide for the common
and our Posterity, do ordain and establish this Constitu

Section. 1. All legislative Powers herein granted sha
of Representatives.
Section. 2. The House of Representatives shall be com
in each State shall have the Qualifications requisite for Electors of
No Person shall be a Representative who shall not
and who shall not, when elected, be an Inhabitant of that Sta
Representatives and direct Taxes shall be apportioned
Numbers, which shall be determined by adding to the whole N
not taxed, three fifths of all other Persons. The actual Enum
and within every subsequent Term of ten Years, in such Ma
thirty Thousand, but each State shall have at Least one Rep
entitled to chuse three, Massachusetts eight, Rhode Island
eight, Delaware one, Maryland six, Virginia ten, North C

Chapter 3 The Framing of the Constitution

By the People: Creating the Constitution

Having ousted the monarch from their house, the former colonists faced the more formidable problem of dealing equitably among themselves. Like squabbling siblings, the states saw largely to their own advantage—and in ways that could prove fatal to the well-being of all.

At the head of the list of questions to be resolved lay commerce and the navigation over the waterways that was its lifeblood. Bad as the Navigation Acts were when applied against the states as colonies, the British policies stung even worse now that they had gained their freedom and were treated by Westminster as foreigners. Congress sought power to act against Britain, but the states could not agree on a uniform approach to the naval menace across the sea.

Much less could they negotiate among themselves about the use of their own waterways. States with advantages took them. As James Madison put it, some states "having no convenient ports for foreign commerce, were subject to be taxed by their neighbors, through whose ports their commerce was carried on. New Jersey, placed between Philadelphia and New York, was likened to a cask tapped at both ends; and North Carolina, between Virginia and South Carolina, to a patient bleeding at both arms." But Congress was powerless to act.

A trade convention seemed a promising solution. Virginia and Maryland had agreed on joint navigation of the Chesapeake Bay and its tributaries, and they had invited Delaware and Pennsylvania to cooperate. In 1786, Virginia called on other states to send commissioners "at a time and place to be agreed on, to take into consideration the trade of the United States."

The time was the second Monday in September 1786. The place was Annapolis. Ten states appointed delegates, and five actually sent them: New York, New Jersey, Pennsylvania, Delaware, and Virginia. Connecticut refused to cooperate; nothing is known of Georgia's intentions; and Maryland, the host state, refused to send delegates because her leaders supposed the purpose of the convention was to reduce the powers of Congress, and they would have no part in such an endeavor. Three states were fully represented: Delaware, New Jersey, and Virginia—not so much from conviction, perhaps, but from proximity. Two delegates arrived from New York, Alexander Hamilton and Egbert Benson. One came from Pennsylvania.

The delegates convened on September 11, 1786. They waited fruitlessly on a quorum. On departing, they recommended to their legislatures that a new convention be called to meet in Philadelphia beginning the second Monday of May the following year to investigate "important defects in the System of the Foederal Government . . . of a nature so serious as, . . . to render the situation of the United States delicate and critical, calling for an exertion of the united Virtues and Wisdom of all the Members of the Confederacy . . . to·take into Consideration the situation of the United States to devise such further Provisions as shall appear to them necessary to render the Constitution of the Foederal Government adequate to the exigencies of the Union."

It remained to select the delegates. As in so many things, Virginia was first, and in being first established an important precedent. It appointed delegates to the convention in much the same way it sent representatives to Congress, a policy most other states followed. More important, Virginia set the high standard for delegates. By sending as the head of the delegation George Washington, Virginia's leading citizen and the leading citizen of the United States, Virginia ensured both that the position of delegate would be viewed as one of high honor and that those worthy of holding such positions would be appointed. As Thomas Jefferson wrote John Adams from Paris when he heard who had been named, "It is really an assembly of demi-gods."

New Jersey named delegates almost as quickly as Virginia. Pennsylvania, North Carolina, Delaware, and Georgia named delegates within weeks and instructed them to appear in Philadelphia as the Annapolis delegates had recommended. On February 21, 1787, Congress endorsed the proposal for a new convention, ensuring that it would meet. The long delay was attributable to conditions of the day: Transportation over such distances called for extensive preparation and collection of funds.

New Hampshire favored the second convention but lacked the money to send delegates until well into the deliberations that summer, when John Langdon, a wealthy businessman, offered to pay all the expenses from his private purse. Only Rhode Island refused to heed the congressional resolution, although several merchants and tradesmen sent the convention their regrets that Rhode Island would be unrepresented; they pledged to use their influence to help adopt any proposals that the delegates drew up.

And so the stage was set for a second convention. That it was necessary, most who deliberated on such things agreed. What it would accomplish was anyone's guess. As Henry Lee of Virginia wrote to a friend:

With difficulty the friends to the system adopted by the convention induced Congress to commit your report, altho' all were truly sensible of the respect manifested by the convention to this body, and all zealous to accomplish the objects proposed by the authors of the commercial convention. Indeed their conviction of the inadequacy of the present federal government renders them particularly zealous to amend and strengthen it. But different opinions prevail as to the mode; some think with the Annapolis meeting, others consider Congress not only the constitutional but the most eligible (efficient) body to originate and propose necessary amendments to the confederation, and others prefer State conventions for the express purpose, and a congress of deputies, appointed by these conventions with plenipotentiary powers.

On May 14, the second Monday of the month, far fewer than a quorum's worth of delegates gathered in the Long Room of the Pennsylvania State House. Muddy spring roads and high rivers contributed to the inauspicious start, but the delay in waiting once again for a quorum stemmed more importantly from the culture of the day: Forty-one of the delegates had served in Congress, and they knew from experience they would waste their time being prompt. By May 25, a quorum had arrived. The delegates were ready to begin. Outside, the city had covered the pavement with earth so that passing traffic would not disturb their deliberations.

Gouverneur Morris, James Wilson, and Robert Morris were present from the host state. Benjamin Franklin, then home ill, arrived later. George Washington, George Mason, George Wythe, James Madison, and Governor Edmund Randolph forcefully represented Virginia, as did Charles Pinckney, Charles Cotesworth Pinckney, John Rutledge, and Pierce Butler for South Carolina. Rufus King arrived from Massachusetts, Robert Yates and Alexander Hamilton from New York. From North Carolina and Georgia came one delegate each. Delaware, New Hampshire, Connecticut, and Maryland were not initially represented, and Rhode Island never was. Conspicuously absent were Thomas Jefferson and John Adams, both congressional representatives abroad—Jefferson in France and Adams in England.

The first order of business was to elect the convention president. Robert Morris nominated George Washington. Ben Franklin was to have had the honor

The Pennsylvania State House (Independence Hall), Philadelphia, at the time of the 1787 convention.

of placing Washington's name before the convention, but infirmities and heavy storms kept him from the opening proceedings. Though no one else was nominated, the delegates voted by formal ballot. Washington was unanimously chosen president and conducted to his chair, a raised platform at the head of the hall, by Robert Morris and John Rutledge. Aware of his moral authority, Washington was to act more as arbitrator than participant in the debates that followed; nevertheless, his opinions were evidently well known and he usually voted with Madison. He was to speak only once during the ensuing four months, although the story was told that he would frown or smile as the speakers pleased or disenchanted him.

The deliberations of the delegates were kept secret. At the outset, the delegates decided that "no copy be taken of any entry on the journal . . . without leave of the House," "members only be permitted to inspect the journal," and "nothing spoken in the House be printed or otherwise published or communicated without leave." This policy was adopted for the sound reason that the delegates wished to speak freely without fear of political pressure while the convention was in session. On Washington's suggestion, a secretary was selected; shrewd campaigning beforehand by William Jackson, a close friend of Washington's, handed him the victory over Franklin's nephew Temple Franklin. As it turned out, Jackson was a better politician than journal keeper. Most of what we know about the debates was recorded daily by James Madison, a task he later declared almost killed him.

The secretary appointed, the delegates chose a committee of three to prepare orders and rules of the debates and appointed a messenger and doorkeeper. Then they adjourned for the weekend.

From that late May day until September 17, they labored continually (with two days off for July fourth celebrations and another ten days off in late July and early August). Those who were assiduous in attending (and by no means all were—historians think that on average only thirty of the fifty-five delegates attended regularly) met every day from ten in the morning until three in the afternoon.

The delegates felt the historical moment. Madison told the delegates they "were now to decide forever the fate of Republican Government." Gouverneur Morris said that "the whole human race will be affected by the proceedings of this Convention." When it concluded, James Wilson opined: "After the lapse of six thousand years since the creation of the world, America now presents the first instance of a people assembled to weigh deliberately and calmly, and to decide leisurely and peaceably, upon the form of government by which they will bind themselves and their posterity."

Edmund Randolph of Virginia opened the deliberations on May 29 by offering fifteen resolutions. He called for a national government to consist of three branches—legislative, executive, and judicial. The principle of separating the powers of government was not seriously questioned; the difficulty was in finding the proper mechanism for doing so and the proper balance among them. The major conflicts among the delegates were over representation in Congress, the manner of electing the president, the nature of the presidency, and the powers and functions of the federal courts.

One burning issue would be compromised, but not resolved: slavery. That the question was vexed can be seen from the odd position of some, like Washington and Mason, who kept slaves on their estates, yet disdained the institution. Mason would not in the end even sign the Constitution because, among other things, it compromised on the slavery question (Chapter 15).

Representation was the key. Unless they could settle the question of how citizens would be represented in the national legislature, the delegates might just as well have packed up and ridden home. Two plans consumed most of the delegates' attention: Randolph's Virginia Plan and the New Jersey Plan, first offered by William Patterson on June 15.

How the Convention Notes Became Public

William Jackson, secretary of the Constitutional Convention, gave his official journal records to George Washington when the convention ended. When he left office in 1796, Washington turned the records over to the Department of State. There they remained until 1818, when Congress declared by a joint resolution that they should be printed. Interested readers then discovered that Jackson's records were sketchy, at most containing a list of formal motions and the voting by states.

Seeking to present a more accurate record, John Quincy Adams, then secretary of state, took these notes and others he collected from delegates and published them in a five-hundred page volume. Records maintained by certain delegates, notably Robert Yates of New York, Rufus King of Massachusetts, and James McHenry of Maryland, also came into the hands of historians.

Not until 1840, however, did historians find a treasure trove, the notes of James Madison. Published in 1840, these notes reflected Madison's unstinting labors day by day during the convention. As he himself wrote:

> I chose a seat in front of the presiding member, with the other members on my right and left hand. In this favorable position for hearing all that passed, I noted in terms legible and in abbreviations and marks intelligible to myself, what was read from the Chair or spoken by the members; and losing not a moment unnecessarily between the adjournment and reassembling of the Convention, I was enabled to write out my daily notes during the session, or within a few finishing days after its close.

In 1911, Max Farrand, a history professor at Yale University, compiled in three volumes the records that had come to light; the revised 1937 edition of this work, now in four volumes, remains the authoritative work.

Nevertheless, the various notes suffer from political bias and inaccuracies; future revisions of Farrand's work may establish a more secure basis from which to judge the Convention's labors.

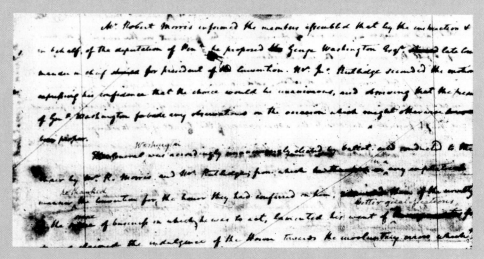

An excerpt from Madison's convention notes describing the unanimous election of George Washington as convention president.

The nub of the debate was the provision in the Virginia Plan that called for a national legislature to consist of two houses, whose members would represent the states in proportion to their free populations. The lower house would be elected directly by the people, the upper house would be chosen by the lower house from lists of candidates compiled by the state legislatures.

The Virginia Plan immediately created tension between large and small states. Three states alone—Virginia, Pennsylvania, and Massachusetts—held nearly half the population of the country. With proportional representation in each house, these three states could virtually command the nation.

Thus the New Jersey Plan—a counterreaction by the smaller states. Patterson proposed that each state be equally represented in a one-house Congress. So bitter was the battle between proponents of each plan that the convention was nearly undone.

Patterson's proposal brought to the fore the revolutionary nature of the proceedings: Let the Virginia proponents have their way and a new form of government would be imposed on the states—a national government, what Randolph called a "consolidated Union." This was no mere patching up of the Articles of Confederation to make them workable. This was nation building, the creation of a new nation-state.

Denouncing the Virginia Plan, Patterson said, "We shall be charged by our constituents with usurpation. We are met here as the deputies of thirteen independent, sovereign states, for federal purposes [in those days "federal" connoted simply an association, not a national government]. Can we consolidate their sovereignty and form one nation, and annihilate the sovereignties of our states who have sent us here for other purposes? . . . The people of America are sharp-sighted and not to be deceived. The idea of a national government as contradistinguished from a federal one never entered into the mind of any of them. . . . We have no power to go beyond the federal scheme, and if we had, the people are not ripe for it."

Founding Father

Nathaniel Gorham
Massachusetts

Nathaniel Gorham was born in Charlestown, Massachusetts, May 27, 1738, and died there, June 11, 1796. He was an apprentice to a Connecticut merchant at the age of fifteen for six years, when he went into business on his own in Charlestown. A member of the legislature from 1771 to 1775, he was also, during 1774–1775, a delegate to the Provincial Congress. Between 1778 and 1781, he had a seat on the Board of War. Gorham was a member of the state constitutional convention, 1779–1780, was elected to the state senate in 1780, then the state house in 1781. He remained at the house for six years, serving as speaker for three of those years. In 1782, 1783, and 1785–1787, he was a delegate to the Continental Congress, the last year as president. At the Constitutional Convention, he advocated strong central government, was active in the debates, and chaired the Committee of the Whole. Afterward, he was a member of the Massachusetts ratifying convention. In 1785, he was named a judge of the Middlesex Court of Common Pleas. He was a member of the Governing Council from 1788 to 1789. Land speculation in the six million acres that New York ceded to Massachusetts after the Revolution left him bankrupt in 1790.

James Wilson, the Pennsylvanian, responded: "Shall New Jersey have the same right or council in the nation with Pennsylvania? I say no! It is unjust. . . . If no state will part with any of its sovereignty it is in vain to talk of a national government."

On June 19, the assembly voted. The Virginia Plan drew seven votes, the New Jersey Plan three (New York, New Jersey, and Delaware). For a month, delegates debated and voted on issues such as the method of apportioning representation (should slaves count?), the length of representatives' terms, and the number of representatives in the lower branch. But on July 2, a vote was taken on a proposal to give each state an equal vote in the upper house. The delegates divided five states to five, with one state split.

As the delegates cast about for a way out of their quandary, they began to heed the possibilities of a proposal that Roger Sherman of Connecticut had been pressing as far back as 1776. The Connecticut Plan was simple: Let the states have it both ways. Give the states an equal voice in the upper house and proportional representation in the lower.

This compromise was put forth by a committee consisting of one delegate from each state. For two weeks, the committee proposed, and the delegates wrestled with, the details of such a compromise. How would representatives be apportioned? How would population growth be reflected in a future Congress?

By July 16, the details had been worked out. The first House of Representatives would consist of sixty-five members (actually, only fifty-nine showed up in the first Congress), and every ten years thereafter Congress itself would determine the number, following a census in which slaves would be counted as three-fifths of a person. Direct taxation by Congress was to be in proportion to representation in the House; a state with twice as much representation could be taxed twice as much. Money bills would originate in the House, not the Senate. The delegates defeated a proposal to count property or wealth of the citizens in each state as a factor in apportioning representa-

tives, a proposition championed by Gouverneur Morris because he wished to "secure to the Atlantic States," over new states that would be formed in the West, "a prevalence in the National Councils." Finally, senators would not be popularly elected but elected by the state legislatures.

This was the Great Compromise that saved the convention—and the Constitution. On July 16, the delegates adopted it five states to four. New Jersey, Delaware, Maryland, and North Carolina sided with Connecticut. Pennsylvania, Virginia, South Carolina, and Georgia opposed it. Massachusetts was divided. Yates and Lansing, the New York delegates, had walked out a few days earlier in disgust (Hamilton, the third delegate, had left after the vote on the New Jersey Plan and attended irregularly thereafter). By such a thin margin, the United States, as a political society, was given fundamental shape.

The essence of the compromise lay in the different modes of representation in a bicameral legislature. That was truly new. All else had been discussed before and incited far less passion. The three-fifths ratio for slaves, the money bill and taxation provisions, and even the election of senators by state legislatures were details—important details, to be sure—that made possible the new theory of representation.

For the next ten days, the delegates hashed out the dozens of other provisions that constitute the finished Constitution. Among the issues with which they had to grapple were these: the powers of the legislature, the nature and powers of the chief executive, the length of his term or terms, the method of electing him, the powers of the judiciary, how judges should be appointed, the relationship between national and state laws, and much more.

Some of the issues decided late in July proved decisive in shaping the nation's destiny; for example, the provision that laws enacted by Congress would be supreme over state laws and that the state courts were bound to uphold the federal laws. But many of the answers given even then were not the final an-

The Delegates: Some Vital Statistics

Fifty-five delegates attended the Constitutional Convention. Seventy-four had been appointed (there is some controversy over this number), but nineteen declined or could not attend. George Wythe, for example, was called home to care for his ailing wife immediately after the delegates convened, and Patrick Henry of Virginia and Charles Carroll of Maryland refused to appear.

Their average age was forty-two. Ben Franklin was the oldest, then eighty-one. The youngest was Jonathan Dayton, twenty-six, but the youngest active participant was Charles Pinckney, thirty. George Washington was fifty-five. Twenty-one delegates were under forty; fourteen were fifty or over. Eight were foreign-born.

Only forty-one of the fifty-five men who arrived in Philadelphia stayed to the end; most of the fourteen others attended but briefly. Of course, not every regular remained for every session: The average number of delegates present at each of the sessions through that hot summer was thirty. (Today, we call them "delegates," but some referred to themselves as "commis-sioners" or "deputies," as George Washington signed himself on the finished document.)

Some never spoke at the convention: Robert Morris, for one. Franklin was too feeble to speak out himself; James Wilson read his remarks. Some spoke more than one hundred times: Alexander Hamilton, George Mason, and James Madison. Mason spoke more often than any. Alexander Hamilton spoke the longest: A speech once lasted five hours. Luther Martin had to carry over to the next day his address on equal representation because he had become much too exhausted to continue.

Many who steadily took part in the deliberations refused to sign. In particular, Edmund Randolph, Elbridge Gerry, and George Mason, though present on the last day, refused—Randolph because he believed the Constitution did not sufficiently protect civil liberties. (He eventually spoke out at the Virginia ratifying convention urging its adoption, accepting the pledge of Virginians to seek a bill of rights as the first order of business of the new government.) Luther Martin, Robert Yates, and John Lansing would not sanction the finished document. Indeed, Martin and James Mercer of Maryland left the convention in disgust before the delegates had finished their work. Save for Alexander

swers. For instance, the convention decided that the president should be elected by Congress for a seven-year term and should be ineligible for reelection.

These were not final answers also because the numerous provisions had been adopted piecemeal and without form. They needed to be meshed, in content and style. That could not be done by a committee of the whole. Thus the convention delegated this work to a Committee of Detail and required that it report its results by August 6. Rutledge of South Carolina, Randolph of Virginia, Gorham of Massachusetts, Ellsworth of Connecticut, and Wilson of Pennsylvania were elected.

Theirs would be a difficult undertaking. As Page Smith has written: "This was the most trying and tiresome period of the convention. To descend from the plateau of lofty political principles to the precise wording of sentences and clauses, aware always of the vast implications in many words and combinations of words, is a singularly taxing enterprise."

The printed report, with wide left margins for the delegates to mark up as it was discussed, contained a preamble and twenty-three articles. These were subdivided into forty-three sections, themselves containing numerous paragraphs. Sixty percent of the document treated the composition and powers of

Hamilton, the New York delegates also departed. John Dickinson of Delaware departed before September 17, but had his colleague George Read sign for him.

Many of the delegates were among the most eminent men of the era (and some were among the most eminent in American history). Still others were relatively obscure then and are today even more obscure, as the short biographies throughout this book suggest. What follow are brief statistics that sum up the experience of those whose negotiating skill brought forth a nation.

Personal experience

College educated: 25
Military experience: 18 officers in the Continental Army; one a British army officer before the Revolution
Lawyers: 34 (the word had a different meaning in those days and the category includes those who had studied law for a time, even if they did not practice)
Planters: 6 (some of the others were part-time planters)
Merchants or financiers: 8
Ministers: 2
Physicians: 2

Political experience

Members of colonial or state legislatures: 46
Attended state constitutional conventions: 10
Delegates to the Continental Congress: 42
Signers of the Declaration: 8
Signers of the Articles of Confederation: 6
Attended the Annapolis Convention: 7
Governors or presidents of states: 16 (including those who had served or would serve after the signing)

Those who became

Presidents: 2 (Washington and Madison)
Candidates for president (other than above): 2
Vice presidents: 1 (Gerry)
Candidates for vice president (other than above): 3
Chief justice of the United States: 1 (Ellsworth)
Associate justices of the Supreme Court: 5
Senators: 19
Congressmen: 13
Speakers of the House: 1 (Dayton)
Territorial governors: 1
Cabinet members: 4
Ambassadors: 7

Congress. Given the number of sections and complexity of the task, it is not surprising that the committee drew heavily on language in the Articles of Confederation and the various plans and resolutions put forward during the previous three months.

For the next month, the convention as a whole debated the report that lay before the delegates. How the committee's proposals were refashioned into the present language of the Constitution is grist for later chapters. It was exacting work, especially in the grueling heat of a Philadelphia August. William Samuel Johnson recorded only five cool days, two of them Sundays. Despite the temperature, the delegates met during the next five weeks every day for five hours a day (and in one of those weeks for six hours a day). The most difficult problem that remained was how to elect the president, and that matter was not settled until September 8.

Now it was time to put the Constitution in finished form. The convention appointed a five-man committee on style and revision to devise the language that would be submitted to the people for ratification. The committee consisted of Johnson, Alexander Hamilton, Gouverneur Morris, James Madison, and Rufus King. The final draft, the language and style of the Constitution, is attributable to Morris. Years later,

Madison wrote to a friend that "the *finish* . . . fairly belongs to the pen of Mr. Morris. . . . A better choice could not have been made, as the performance of the task proved. It is true that the state of the materials . . . was a good preparation . . . but there was sufficient room for the talents and taste stamped by the author on the face of it."

On September 13, the committee submitted the printed report to the convention, which for three days thereafter compared the finished work with the provisions that the convention had agreed to throughout the summer. Some changes that had been inserted in the committee's draft were accepted—the provision that states may not impair the obligation of contracts. Other changes were made from the floor—the provision that no state, without its consent, would lose its equal suffrage in the Senate.

The final version grouped the dozens of scattered provisions into six basic articles. The first established the legislative power—Congress. The second created the office of president—the executive power. The third established the judicial power in the Supreme Court. The fourth governs relations between the states. The fifth prescribes the methods of amending the Constitution. And the sixth sets out the supremacy of federal law and the Constitution itself.

While they debated the substance of the Constitution for the last time, the delegates also adopted a preamble. As originally conceived, in language taken over from the Articles of Confederation, the preamble declared the Constitution to have been established by the states. The committee of detail suggested "We the People of *and* the States of New Hampshire, Massachusetts," and so forth. Subsequently, the "and" was dropped. But since the Constitution would be established if only nine states ratified it, how could the particular states be named in the document? It was by no means certain that this new Constitution would be unanimously accepted. So the committee of style put the Preamble in its final, telling form: "We, the People of the United States . . . " It is a measure of how far the convention had come that the delegates recognized by the end that with this Constitution they had created not only a new government but also a new nation.

On Saturday, September 15, Franklin eloquently urged the convention to respect the spirit of compromise that animated the undertaking. "I confess," he said, "that there are several parts of this Constitution which I do not at present approve. But I am not sure I shall never approve them. For having lived long, I have experienced many instances of being obliged by better information or fuller consideration, to change opinions even on important subjects, which I once thought right, but found to be otherwise. . . . I consent, Sir, to this Constitution because I expect no better and because I am not sure that it is not the best."

At six o'clock that evening, the delegates, in Madison's words, voted "on the question to agree to the Constitution, as amended. All the states—ay."

The next Monday, September 17, the Constitution was ready to be signed. Randolph, Mason, and Gerry balked. They pressed for a second convention to consider amendments that the states might wish to attach to the document about to be signed. Weary, and disbelieving that a second convention could do better than they had already achieved, the delegates unanimously rejected Randolph's proposal for a second convention.

Of the forty-two who were left at the convention, three—Gerry, Mason, and Randolph—refused to put their names to the parchment that today resides in the National Archives. Desiring unanimity, Morris suggested these words be tacked onto the end: "Done in Convention, by the unanimous consent of the States present the 17th of September . . . In witness whereof we have hereunto subscribed our names." At Morris's behest, Franklin himself proposed these words, which were promptly adopted.

As the delegates rose to sign, Franklin chanced to be looking at the president's chair, on which a picture of the sun had been painted. As Madison recalled, Franklin "observed to a few members near him, that Painters had found it difficult to distinguish in their art a rising from a setting sun. I have, said he, often and often in the course of the Session, and the vicissitudes of my hopes and fears as to its issue, looked at that behind the president without being able to tell whether it was rising or setting: But now at length I have the happiness to know that it is a rising and not a setting Sun."

To the People: Ratifying the Constitution

The one clear omission from the Constitution signed that day was a bill of rights, specific guarantees of personal freedom, like the freedom to worship. This was no oversight. The delegates certainly understood the nature of constitutional provisions for individual rights; eight states' constitutions had bills of rights. The convention had discussed the prospect, but opponents prevailed in the end by arguing that the Constitution they had just created granted no power to the government to violate the rights of citizens. On

The signing of the Constitution, September 17, 1787.

September 12, Gerry's motion to include a bill of rights was defeated ten to none.

This omission proved to be the major miscalculation of the convention. In state after state, reasonable men voiced their fear about a national government unburdened by restraints against interfering with personal liberties. Those who had defeated the motion in convention had clever rejoinders. Roger Sherman said that "no bill of rights ever yet bound the supreme power longer than the honeymoon of a new married couple, unless the rulers were interested in preserving the rights; and in that case they have always been ready enough to declare the rights, and to preserve them when they were declared." Noah Webster, not a delegate, sarcastically observed that a bill of rights might state "that everybody shall, in good weather, hunt on his own land, and catch fish in rivers that are public property . . . and that Congress shall never restrain any inhabitant of America from eating and drinking, at seasonable times, or prevent his lying on his left side, in a long winter's night, or even on his back, when he is fatigued by lying on his right."

These remarks did not meet people's real concerns. Why shouldn't the people worry about a government with the powers granted Congress, especially the power to do whatever is "necessary and proper" to carry out its other powers. What government in the history of humankind had ever resisted encroaching on the rights of those it governed? Had they not just fought the British to rid themselves of tyranny?

On this question, the framers were parochial and obtuse. That they, many of whom were destined for leadership in the government soon to be formed, would not interfere with the "rights of man" did not mean that all governments forever would stay their hands. As president, George Washington would not attempt to impose a national religion or shackle the press or abolish the jury system. But someone else might.

This was the issue on which much of the ratification debate turned. Article VII said that for the Constitution to take effect, conventions in nine states had to approve. The Continental Congress could not muster the votes to go on record as endorsing the Constitution. But on September 28, its supporters managed to pass a bill by which they could claim that Congress had voted "unanimously to transmit" it to the states, where the people would elect special conventions that would in turn decide whether to ratify the Constitution.

Pennsylvania convened the first such convention, but Delaware was the first to ratify—unanimously—on December 7. The Pennsylvania convention by a two-to-one majority ratified on December 12. Six days later, New Jersey unanimously ratified. But the critical conventions were yet to be held.

Massachusetts was the first hurdle. The Bay State's convention had more delegates than any other, and its records almost equal the records of all the conventions. Three issues predominated: biennial congressional elections, slavery, and the failure to require every public officer to be Christian. John Hancock presided over the debates, and Nathaniel Gorham and Rufus King traveled up from Pennsylvania to defend the Constitution. Though anti-Constitution at first, Samuel Adams came around.

But the opposition was hardy. General William Thompson argued against biennial elections: "O my country, never give up your annual elections! young men, never give up your jewel!" Amos Singletary spoke for the wariness of common people when he said:

These lawyers, and men of learning, and moneyed men, that talk so finely, and gloss over matters so smoothly, to make us poor illiterate people swallow down the pill, expect to get into Congress themselves; they expect to be the managers of this Constitution, and get all the power and all the money into their own hands, and then they will swallow up all us little folks, like the great *Leviathan*, . . . yes, just as the whale swallowed up Jonah.

And Thompson emphasized the mood of many Massachusetts men when he suggested that the "Old Confederation" would be better served amended than discarded:

There are some parts of this Constitution which I cannot digest; and, sir, shall we swallow a large bone for the sake of a little meat? Some say, Swallow the whole now and pick out the bone afterwards. But I say, Let us pick off the meat, and throw the bone away.

In the end, by a narrow nineteen-vote margin, the Massachusetts state delegates voted to ratify—but only after urging the immediate adoption of a bill of rights once the national government was formed under the new Constitution.

Georgia ratified on January 2, 1788, Maryland on April 2, and South Carolina on May 23. The next big convention was Virginia's, which began June 2. The atmosphere was heated. The delegates did not take lightly that Edmund Randolph and George Mason, delegates to the Philadelphia Convention, now opposed ratification, as did Richard Henry Lee and Patrick Henry. An able apostle of revolution and liberty ("give me liberty or give me death"), Henry had been a vociferous opponent of the Constitution from the start, refusing to attend the Philadelphia Convention. Now he excoriated the document for establishing

a great consolidated government, instead of a confederation. That this is a consolidated government is demonstrably clear; and the danger of such a government is . . . very striking. I have the highest veneration for those gentlemen; but, sir, give me leave to demand, What right had they to say, *We, the people?* My political curiosity, exclusive of my anxious solicitude for the public welfare, leads me to ask, Who authorized them to speak the language of, *We, the people,* instead of *We, the states?* . . . The people gave them no power to use their name. That they exceeded their power is perfectly clear.

But "Light Horse" Harry Lee made light of Henry's oratory, telling the assemblage:

The éclat and brilliance which had distinguished that gentleman, the honors with which he has been dignified, and the brilliant talents which he has so often displayed, have attracted my attention and respect. On so important an occasion, and before so respectable a body, I had expected a new display of his powers of oratory; but instead of proceeding to investigate the merits of the new plan of government, the worthy character informed us of the horrors he felt, of apprehensions to his mind, which made him tremblingly fearful of the fate of the commonwealth. Mr. Chairman, was it proper to appeal to the fears of this house? The question before us belongs to the judgment of this house. I trust he has come to judge, and not to alarm.

At Mason's suggestion, the Virginia debates tracked the Constitution clause by clause. The issues of slavery, taxation, and standing armies were disputed with vigor. At the end, Randolph dramatically changed sides to support the Constitution on condition that Virginia second Massachusetts's call for immediate adoption of a bill of rights. By eight votes, the Virginia convention narrowly defeated a proposal to defer ratification until a bill of rights was first drawn up. Like the Massachusetts convention, the second vote, to accept the Constitution as it stood, was approved by a margin of ten votes, on June 21, four days after New Hampshire became the ninth state to ratify (thus making the Constitution the law of the land).

The New York convention assembled in Poughkeepsie on June 17, one week before the Virginians voted. New Hampshire had just ratified by a narrow margin. As with the other two large conventions, New York was prepared for strong opposition. For six months, Alexander Hamilton, aided by Madison and John Jay, had been anonymously expounding the merits of the Constitution in what has since been admired as *the* classic American treatise on political theory, *The Federalist Papers*. Though some contend that *The Federalist Papers* were not effective in persuading those already opposed to accept the Constitution, they undoubtedly had a significant intellectual impact throughout the states, both in the ratification effort and in later efforts to understand its meaning and its framers' intent.

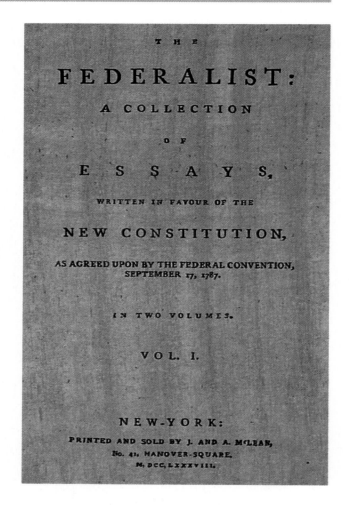

THE

FEDERALIST:

A COLLECTION

OF

ESSAYS,

WRITTEN IN FAVOUR OF THE

NEW CONSTITUTION,

AS AGREED UPON BY THE FEDERAL CONVENTION,
SEPTEMBER 17, 1787.

IN TWO VOLUMES.

VOL. I.

NEW-YORK:

PRINTED AND SOLD BY J. AND A. M°LEAN,
No. 41, HANOVER-SQUARE.
M, DCC, LXXXVIII.

Opposing the Constitution in New York were Robert Yates and John Lansing, both members of the Philadelphia Convention. Former Governor George Clinton, now president of the New York Convention, also opposed it. As in Virginia, the New Yorkers debated the Constitution clause by clause. When they voted, on July 26, they declared their "full confidence" that amendments would soon follow. Two votes decided the issue. It was a measure of the desire

to secure individual rights that in New York, Massachusetts, and Virginia, the Constitution was won by a margin of but eighteen votes altogether, "the greatest act of political prestidigitation in all recorded history."

Meantime, joyous celebrations had already begun. Cyrus Griffin, president of Congress, formally announced on July 2 that the Constitution was in effect. On July 4, 1788, ten ships, each bearing a white flag with the name of the ratified state embroidered in gold letters, moored in the Delaware River. Other river boats were decorated with flags and streamers. A procession of five thousand paraded the streets of Philadelphia, ending up at Union Square to join twelve thousand others to hear an address by James Wilson. Part of the procession included a car in the form of an eagle, occupied by the chief justice and two other supreme court justices, carrying a framed copy of the new Constitution.

On September 13, 1788, the Confederation Congress, acceding to the Philadelphia Convention's desire, named New York the seat of the new federal government. It also set out the timetable for starting up the government. The states would choose electors for president on the first Wednesday of the following January, and these electors would choose the first president on the first Wednesday of February, 1788. (George Washington's election was a foregone conclusion. Indeed, it was the knowledge that he would become president that calmed the fears of many about whether the presidency would turn into a monarchy.) Congress would meet the first Wednesday of March, about eight weeks before the first presidential inauguration on April 30.

For the People: The Constitutional Achievement

Few could have foreseen the shape of things to come on June 21, 1788, when New Hampshire became the ninth state to ratify and the Constitution became the organic law of the new United States of America. So embedded in our political consciousness is this Constitution (and the amendments that shortly followed) that we would blink in amazement were the habits of government that the Constitution fixed on this land suddenly to change.

In time, even before the paint yellowed on the canvases of the signing, the influential delegates became revered and then hallowed men—Founding Fathers. What they founded was a superstructure: a national government built on a strong predisposition to freedom and civil liberties within a political system that already existed. That is why, unlike the common law, the Constitution rules government, not people. Nothing in the original six articles lays duties on the people themselves. Rather, they and the amendments that followed imposed restraints on government. Only the Thirteenth Amendment speaks directly to the citizenry in outlawing forever the institution of slavery.

Impressive as it was, the founders' achievement should not be overstated. They did not create the United States out of whole cloth; they did not create the Constitution out of whole cloth. They did not divine the events that would constitute our nation's history.

For all its genius, the Constitution resulted from mature compromise and the keenly felt desire to be practical in solving pressing problems of the day. As important as the political theory was for those who read it—and Madison, for one, surely did—the Constitution itself was a response to specific defects in the Articles of Confederation. "Every provision of the federal constitution can be accounted for in American experience between 1776 and 1787," says Max Farrand, echoing Madison, who had written shortly after the Convention concluded:

> The truth is, that the great principles of the Constitution proposed by the convention may be considered less as absolutely new, than as the expansion of principles which are found in the Articles of Confederation. . . . If the new Constitution be examined with accuracy and candor, it will be found that the change which it proposes consists much less in the addition of *New Powers* to the *Union*, than in the invigoration of its *Original Powers*.

Historical Mystery: How Many Delegates Were There?

The Constitutional Convention met in secret, but thanks to Madison we know what happened in Independence Hall. Surprisingly, something of a historical mystery exists over what would seem a far simpler matter: How many delegates attended?

Most writers are agreed that fifty-five men were present at the convention at one time or another. But the reference guide *Notable Names in American History—A Tabulated Register* (third edition of White's *Conspectus of American Biography*, 1973), says fifty-eight delegates attended the convention.

Broadus and Louise Mitchell, in their *Biography of the Constitution of the United States*, note that beyond the fifty-five, ten more were appointed but never arrived and that two prominent figures, Patrick Henry and Charles Carroll, were named as delegates but declined the appointments, meaning that sixty-seven in all could have attended.

A study reprinted in the September 11, 1959, *Congressional Record*, entitled "Who Made the Constitution?" lists the fifty-five, plus an additional ten whose claim to fame was to have "muffed a great opportunity" (or sixty-five in all).

The sesquicentennial history (published by the Government Printing Office in 1943) says that seventy-four were named.

Max Farrand says, "Nearly seventy-five names have been mentioned."

What accounts for these discrepancies? Knowledgeable readers are encouraged to shed light on this mystery, in time to be included in the tricentennial edition of this book.

The most important correction was the legal basis of the Constitution itself. The Articles of Confederation were unenforceable. Not so the Constitution. "This Constitution," says Article VI, "shall be the supreme Law of the Land," in language refined by the committee of style and suggested by Luther Martin. As Farrand noted, this significant provision means that the Constitution is no mere treaty among sovereign states, but law, the one law that applies everywhere and uniformly throughout the United States.

That said, it remains inescapable that the Founding Fathers did possess a keen sense of theory—and faith. For as much as the Constitution was a compromise based on the practical realities of the day, it also was a vision of what would happen in a bountiful nation when people are free to pursue their ends. The twists and dodges of purely pragmatic compromise could never have evoked the language and purpose of the Constitution as it was written.

The theory was that of John Locke, that governments derive "their just powers from the consent of the governed," in the words of the Declaration of Independence. The supreme law that is the Constitution makes clear that the powers of government are *delegated* powers, not a gift of rulers, but a concession by the *people* to further their lives, liberties, and happiness.

The theory was also that of Baron Montesquieu. A government of delegated powers must be one of elected representatives, for how else can the people control their governors? But the powers delegated by the people must be divided up, else the governors would have too much authority and no one to check their abuse of it.

Still, we should be on guard against the tyranny of a label, especially one as hoary as separation of powers. Here was no rigid separation such as the Massachusetts constitution prescribed for the government of the Commonwealth. Assuming it is even possible to mark clearly the borders between government powers, a rigid exclusion of one from the other would preclude a system of checks and balances, not enhance it, for there could be no point of contact. Instead of a politics of compromise (as occurs now when, for example, Congress and the president must give and take to secure legislation acceptable to both), we would likely have inherited a system of bitter antagonism, if such a system could have lasted into our time.

So the theory of the founders was republican government, delegation and partial separation of powers, checks and balances, and human dignity. Their faith was that this compact document of some 4,300 words would be respected. If a constitution is to be worth more than the paper it is printed on, the people must believe it is worth adhering to even when it conflicts with their immediate parochial interests. The people must be prepared to take elections seriously, to abide by the laws their representatives write or the decisions of the courts construing those laws, to respect the limits placed on government power, to leave in peace those whose opinions are obnoxious to them, and to balk at all this only through the established procedure of amending the Constitution itself. Many nations have had constitutions; many have imitated the American one. But relatively few governments have enforced them—or abided by them. For all the staggering difficulties with which we have been confronted, a vicious cynicism that so often attends constitutionalism abroad is not one of them. Though our politics is greatly altered, the relationship between the branches surely different than the framers envisioned, and the Constitution's language often stretched, *constitutionalism* in America remains a central and potent force, not merely a symbolic good but a reality with which government and citizen alike must contend.

That the Constitution lives two centuries later, with most of its language intact—some delegates supposed it would not last out seventy-five—is testament both

William Samuel Johnson
Connecticut

William Samuel Johnson was born in Stratford, Connecticut, October 7, 1727, and died there, November 14, 1819. He was the son of an Anglican clergyman who was the first president of King's College. Johnson was directed toward education, graduating from Yale in 1744 and from Harvard with an M.A. in 1747. He soon became a leading member of the Connecticut bar. He was elected to the lower house of the Connecticut Colonial Assembly in 1761 and 1765. In 1766, he moved to the upper house, where he remained until the Revolution. He attended the Stamp Act Congress in 1765. Two years later, he traveled to London to act as colonial agent for Connecticut. He stayed until 1771, and developed strong ties to England. In 1771, he returned to the Connecticut Assembly. He was then named judge of the Superior Court. In 1774, he was elected to the Continental Congress, but he refused this post. For a time, he left the public eye, suspected of being a Loyalist. In fact, in 1779, he was held on suspicion of corresponding with the British. However, his known integrity won him release, and the event did not harm his political career. In 1784, he was elected to the government under the Articles of Confederation, where he stayed until 1787. That year, he was elected the first president of Columbia College, formerly King's College, reaffirming a tie to the school that his father had established. Also that year, he was elected a Connecticut delegate to the Constitutional Convention in Philadelphia. During the debates, he took an active role in the controversy over large and small state representation, and he proved to be especially helpful in resolving the issue. He served in the Connecticut ratifying convention, and in 1789 was elected one of the first Connecticut senators. When the federal government moved from New York, however, he resigned as senator to remain as president of Columbia College. Ill health in 1800 forced his retirement to his hometown, Stratford.

to theory and to faith. But it is also, finally, a testament to historical circumstances that are perhaps unique. The Founding Fathers were keen observers of human conduct; they understood what motivated their fellow citizens. Alone among the nations, America had had no experience with feudalism, as Louis Hartz has shown. With two searing exceptions, this was a nation of yeoman farmers, of merchants and traders, of small manufacturers—free men. (One exception was that of black slaves, and it was an exception that would prove the rule, for it almost wrecked the Constitution and the Union. The other exception was that of Native Americans—Indians—whom the founders treated as independent nations and whom their descendants did their best to kill.)

These citizens who now would rule had thwarted the "conspiracy against the rights of humanity" and had the confidence to think they could sit, collectively, as trustees for the governmental power that the Constitution unleashed. These also were citizens blessed beyond all others with the bounty of nature and the historical moment that saw the emergence of an industrial civilization that would create a material prosperity undreamed of by any philosopher or seer in ages past. Much can be forgiven when times are good.

In the end, the people were as much for the Constitution as the Constitution was for the people. It endures because it created a political system that allowed succeeding generations to adapt it to the perils they confronted. No one could reasonably hope for more.

Part 2

The Structure and Control of Government

Chapter 4 The Legislative Power

Basic Structure

"It could probably be shown by facts and figures that there is no distinctly native American criminal class except Congress," said Mark Twain, in one of his more mordant moments. The disenchantment that Twain felt a century after the framers brought forth the national assembly is scarcely a rebuke to the Constitution and only remotely to the framers themselves. Nothing in the Constitution compels members of Congress to be rapscallions; nothing in an imaginable constitution could prevent legislative venality. The cure, if there is a problem, lies in Congress itself. The Constitution gave power, for good or ill. The only other solution, the lack of power, was even worse.

Congress holds the central power in the federal government, even if it does not always successfully exercise it. The legislative power is the power to create law. In legislating, Congress gives voice to the people, who elect its members. Hence the Constitution reverses the age-old order of political responsibility: Unlike ancient monarchical systems in which parliaments consented to decrees of the sovereign, here the legislature may initiate and, formally at least, the executive consents (or vetoes). To indicate the central place of this legislative power, the founders put it first, in Article I. Nearly half the original text of the Constitution is contained there, and several other provisions scattered throughout the rest of the text and in several amendments add to the congressional strength.

The bicameral structure of the legislative branch—the essence of the Great Compromise at the Philadelphia Convention—endures unchanged from its conception to the present day. Congress consists of two chambers, the House of Representatives and the Senate. The original House consisted of fifty-nine members (sixty-five were authorized by the Constitution, but congressmen from North Carolina and Rhode Island were not seated until 1790 when those states had ratified the Constitution). The House now comprises 435 members. States are represented in proportion to their population. The Senate is composed of two members from each state; twenty-two Senators made up the original Senate (twenty-six when North Carolina and Rhode Island ratified), and it now seats one hundred.

Article I explicitly sets out the structure of Congress, the qualifications for its members, the method of their election, the process of legislation, and the powers Congress may exercise. Especially in conjunction with Articles II and III, Article I states two fundamental aspects of American government: checks and balances and the separation of powers. Before examining these systems in operation, a brief overview of Congressional history will provide a useful perspective.

The inauguration of George Washington at Federal Hall in Manhattan, the first seat of the U.S. Government under the Constitution.

A Brief History of the Early Congress

On March 3, 1789, the government under the Articles of Confederation faded away. A gun salute at Battery Park in Manhattan welcomed the nascent government under the new U.S. Constitution—on that day, the U.S. Congress was to convene officially for the first time. Its first home was Federal Hall in lower Manhattan. The House would meet downstairs, the Senate upstairs. In 1800 (after a ten-year residence in Philadelphia), the national government settled in a permanent capital in the District of Columbia, a ten-mile-square area on the Potomac, from land ceded by Virginia and Maryland.

The first Congress was an educated, experienced, and motivated group. Eleven of the twenty-two senators and nine of the fifty-nine representatives had been members of the Constitutional Convention. Eighteen senators and thirty-six representatives had served in the Continental Congress or the Congress of the Confederation. Four had signed the Declaration of Independence. One, Roger Sherman, prided himself on having signed every major document of the emerging nation since 1774 (the Articles of Association, the Declaration, the Articles of Confederation, and the Constitution).

On that first day, only thirteen representatives and eight senators arrived in New York. They were forced to put up in private homes and boarding houses to await a quorum. The chronic problem of lateness continued. A peeved representative, Fisher Ames of Massachusetts, wrote to a friend: "This is a very mortifying situation. . . . We lose credit, spirit, everything. The public will forget the government before it is born. The resurrection of the infant will come before its birth."

On April 1, the arrival of the thirtieth member of the House at last constituted a quorum. Frederick A. Muhlenberg of Pennsylvania was elected speaker; John Beckley of Virginia was named clerk. Also appointed were a doorkeep, assistant doorkeep, and later a sergeant at arms and an assistant to the sergeant at arms.

The next day, Muhlenberg named a committee of eleven members to establish rules and procedures for the House. Under Article I, each house may write its own rules, and this the House proceeded to do on April 7, adopting rules governing committees of the whole, decorum and debate, voting while in session, and duties of the speaker. A week later, the House created a Committee of Elections and set out rules for leaves of absence of House members.

Frederick A. Muhlenberg, first speaker of the House.

This relatively swift action attests to the members' seriousness of purpose—and the need for action. Compare it with the ninety-first Congress (1969–1970), which began a limited revision of House rules and took five years to complete the task.

Early on, it became necessary to adopt rules governing limitations on debate; a five-minute rule and a one-hour rule became standard. Permanent committees were also necessary, and by 1795 four were established. By 1809, six more were added. (Today, the House has twenty-two, the Senate sixteen.)

On April 6, 1789, the twelfth member of the Senate arrived, establishing its quorum. Members elected John Langdon of New Hampshire temporary president of the Senate, as required by Article I, until the

Founding Father

Roger Sherman
Connecticut

Roger Sherman was born in Newton, Massachusetts, April 19, 1721, and died in New Haven, Connecticut, July 23, 1793. He was self-educated and began his career as a cobbler, like his father. In 1743, he moved to New Milford and opened a cobbler shop, and was soon named county surveyor, a post he retained until 1758. In 1754, he was admitted to the Connecticut bar. The following year, he was elected to the Connecticut General Assembly. In 1761, Sherman moved to New Haven, where he worked as a retail merchant. From 1764 to 1766, he was again a representative in the assembly. He became an advocate of revolution while a Continental Congress member, serving for ten years from 1774. He helped draft the Declaration of Independence and proposed a plan of government during the time the Articles of Confederation was being created. In 1783, with others, he codified the laws of Connecticut, and, with Oliver Ellsworth, he drafted the Judiciary Act in 1789. At the Constitutional Convention, he first advocated indirect election for both houses, then presented the "Connecticut Compromise." He led the ratification fight for the Constitution in Connecticut. He was elected a Federalist representative in the First Congress, and in 1791 moved to the Senate. Sherman was the only signer of all four of the most important documents of the Revolution: the Articles of Association, the Declaration of Independence, the Articles of Confederation, and the U.S. Constitution.

---

vice president of the United States was elected. (The vice president is the permanent president of the Senate, but his powers are limited; he can vote only in the event of a tie.) Oliver Ellsworth was selected to go downstairs to inform the House that the Senate was in session and ready to count the electoral votes for president and vice president (in accordance with the procedure set forth in Article II). The entire House climbed to the Senate chamber for the first joint session. The ballots of the electoral college were unanimous: George Washington and John Adams were officially declared president and vice president of the United States.

After this urgent task, the Senate speedily organized itself, creating offices and rules. It elected James Mathers of New York the first doorkeep, an important role in those days because the Senate opted to conduct its business in secret, a rule it did not relax until 1795.

Senate absenteeism was a serious problem in the early years, an oddity since Congress met but three days a week for only three or four hours. One early explanation, which resulted in an enforcement clause to the Senate rule on absenteeism, had to do with the working style of each house. The House, open to the public, was large, noisy, and spirited, inducing the more subdued senators to leave their seats before recess to observe as spectators the antics in the chamber below.

For most of its history, congressional attendance has been a part-time affair, Congress meeting for only a few months (and rarely in the muggy Washington summer). Members all had other jobs or were wealthy enough not to have to work. Not until the past half-century or so, and especially the past quarter-century, has Congress sat in continuous session throughout the year and constituted, for most members, full-time (and more than full-time) work.

Salaries were set for both houses at $6.00 per day while in session, and up to $6.00 per twenty miles for travel expenses. This salary was low, even for the times, and the expense account was miserly, omitting many expenses today considered legitimate requirements of the job. Throughout our history, low pay has deterred many from entering politics (and skewed congressional membership toward the wealthy). One reason for the low pay may have been the Article I provision that members determine their own salaries, and fearing political repercussions members kept them low. As late as 1947, salaries for congressmen were still minimal at $10,000. In 1986, House and Senate salaries had increased to $75,100 (the speaker's salary is $97,900), with restrictions on outside income voted in the last few years.

Once the structure of the House and Senate had been determined, legislation began to emerge. The process is laborious, and the speed with which the first Congress acted is attributable mainly to its small size.

To enact a law, each house must pass a bill (by majority vote), and it must then either be signed by the president or, if he vetoes it, be passed anew by a two-thirds vote in each house. Except for revenue bills, which Article I declares must originate in the House, either chamber may introduce legislation. When one house passes a bill, it is sent to the other for consideration. During the committee process of drafting and revising, different versions are often adopted. To reconcile the versions so that each house can vote on the same language, Congress created an extraconstitutional device known as the conference committee. After a particular bill is passed in each house, a joint committee of congressmen and senators, appointed by each house, negotiates a compromise bill. When the conferees agree on the wording, they resubmit the new bill to the House and Senate for passage. Only at that point will the finished work be presented to the president for approval. This apparently cumbersome procedure is the direct consequence of a bicameral legislature and ensures a powerful set of checks and balances.

During the first three sessions of Congress (a total of 519 days), Congress received 268 bills and enacted 118 of them; 60 were major statutes. For the first twenty years, the House originated 78 percent of the bills introduced. In the first Congress, the Senate introduced only 5 bills, of which 4 were passed (including the significant Judiciary Act of 1789); the House introduced 26 bills. Within a half-century, the number would multiply dramatically: in 1837, the House introduced 1,000 bills; in 1869, 2,000; today, 10,000 bills are on average introduced yearly.

What follows is a brief chronology of significant actions of the early Congress.

May 19: The first debate on creating executive offices takes place.

June 1: George Washington signs the first legislation passed by both houses, a bill to carry out the oath provision of Article VI of the Constitution.

July 4: The first tariff bill, setting rates up to 15 percent, is passed. James Madison first raises the issue of setting duties on imports.

July 27: Congress creates the Department of Foreign Affairs and names John Jay head. It shortly becomes the Department of State.

August 7: The War Department is created. Henry Knox is soon named secretary of war.

September 2: Congress creates the Treasury Department and names Alexander Hamilton secretary.

September 22: The Post Office Department is created.

September 24: Congress enacts the first Federal Judiciary Act, creating the Office of Attorney General (to become the Justice Department) and fleshing out the structure and jurisdiction of the Supreme Court. John Jay is subsequently chosen as first chief justice of the United States, after resigning his post as head of Foreign Affairs.

September 25: Congress submits to the states what will become the Bill of Rights. The first 10 amendments become part of the Constitution on December 15, 1791 (New Jersey is the first state to ratify, on November 20, 1789). State conventions ratifying the U.S. Constitution had offered Congress 210. In June, Congressman James Madison pares these to 19, and presents them to the House. By August, after committee work, these are reduced to 17 and sent on to the Senate. By September 25, both House and Senate agree on 12. These are sent to the states for ratification. Ten are finally ratified.

January 14, 1790: Alexander Hamilton presents to the House his first report on public credit, part of his plan to have the federal government assume state debts left over from the government under the Articles of Confederation. As Treasury secretary, Hamilton regularly attends congressional sessions, seeing a legislative function in his executive position. Although for many years, Congress saw the Treasury Department as almost an arm of the legislature, this notion did not harden into precedent, and the practice did not continue.

March 1: Congress enacts the Census Act. The United States is the first country to carry out such a counting. The first census on August 1 finds a total population of 3,929,625 (including 59,557 free Negroes and 697,624 slaves).

March 26: The first naturalization act is passed.

John Jay, first chief justice of the United States.

April 10: Congress enacts the first patent act, and the Patent Office opens for business on July 31.

May 31: President Washington signs the first Copyright Act.

December 6: Congress meets in Philadelphia for the first time.

December 14: Hamilton reports to the House on the benefits of creating a national bank, kicking off a constitutional issue that would stir the government for more than half a century.

January 28, 1791: Hamilton reports to Congress on establishing a mint.

Founding Father

Alexander Hamilton
New York

Alexander Hamilton was born in Nevis, British West Indies, January 11, 1755, a bastard child. He died in New York City on July 12, 1804. Hamilton came to America in 1773 to study at King's College and wrote considerably on the patriot cause. With the outbreak of the Revolution, he enlisted in the Continental Army and served as an aide-de-camp to Washington. In 1782–1783, he served in the Continental Congress. Returning to New York to practice law, he remained politically active. He was a delegate to the Annapolis Convention and was fervent in advocating the Philadelphia Convention. With John Jay and James Madison, he wrote *The Federalist Papers*, an enduring work of political philosophy. He actively promoted ratification in New York. Washington named him first secretary of the treasury in 1789. He advocated such measures as the creation of a national bank, assumption of state war debts, creation of a flexible monetary system, and the funding of the national debt. He helped precipitate the split in the Federalist party through his intraparty struggle with Adams.

Hamilton was a colorful man, astute and dominating, who had many friends and as many enemies, among them Jefferson, Madison, Burr, Clinton, and Randolph. He had a pessimistic view of humanity, arguing at the Convention, "Give all power to the many, they will oppress the few. Give all power to the few, they will oppress the many." He was outspoken, arrogant, and motivated by a desire for fame, though not dishonest. He opposed slavery. Aaron Burr mortally wounded him in a duel in Weehawken, N.J., in 1804.

February 25: Washington signs the bill establishing a charter for the First Bank of the United States.

March 3: The first Internal Revenue Act becomes law (this is not the predecessor of the Internal Revenue Service, which did not come into existence until after Reconstruction).

February 21: Congress passes the Presidential Succession Act, which attempted, without great success, to clear up ambiguities in the Constitution arising from disability or death of the president.

April 2: Congress establishes the U.S. Mint and a decimal system of coinage, setting the silver-to-gold ratio at fifteen to one.

This brief listing suggests the range of congressional concerns existing from the start. In its seriousness of purpose and in the high level of debate, the first Congress and those immediately succeeding set precedents for two centuries of congressional activity to come.

The political structure of the modern Congress would be familiar to the first members, if not its splendid architecture atop Capitol Hill in Washington. But the demographics of its membership and the scope of its powers have changed in some ways beyond any expectation of the framers—largely because the United States has fulfilled Hamilton's vision and become a national economy with worldwide interests.

Membership

Members of the House of Representatives are elected every two years. They are chosen by popular election from districts in each state. The Constitution does not spell out how representatives are to be elected. Unless Congress chooses to intervene, the manner of election is left to the states. In 1842, Congress first required voters to choose from within districts, rather than statewide.

Article I imposes minimal requirements for election: A member must be at least twenty-five years old when taking his seat, a citizen of the United States (for at least seven years), and a resident of the state from which elected (but not of the district; it is a political custom, not a constitutional requirement, that a representative live in the district from which he is elected).

Senators serve six-year terms; originally chosen by the state legislatures, they have been popularly elected since the adoption of the Seventeenth Amendment in 1913. A senator must be at least thirty years old when seated and have been a citizen of the United States for nine years, and, like representatives, a resident of the state from which elected. This last qualification means less than it appears to say. Technically, the candidate need not be a resident until election day. When Robert Kennedy ran for the Senate in New York in 1964, some people protested that he was a citizen of Massachusetts (where he had previously voted while serving as U.S. attorney general). Even though he was ineligible to vote for himself in the election—because he had not lived in New York long enough before the election to satisfy the state requirements—he nevertheless was constitutionally entitled to run, since he was a resident of New York on election day.

Unlike the House, which is elected in its entirety every other year, the Senate is a "continuing" body. Only one-third of its seats are up for election in any election year. Article I specified that the original Senate was to be divided into three classes. The seats of senators in the first class expired in two years; those in the second class in four years, and those in the third class in six years.

The practical difference between being a continuing and noncontinuing body is that the House must reaffirm its rules before the start of each new Congress, whereas the Senate rules remain constantly in effect. Because some Senate rules require more than a majority vote (for example, to kill a filibuster), it is more difficult to change them than it is to change House rules, for the incoming House can adopt whatever rules it wants by a majority vote.

Article I says that each house is the sole judge of the elections, returns, and qualifications of its members. But its power to determine who can sit is limited by the qualifications for office stated previously. In 1967, the House of Representatives voted to exclude Congressman Adam Clayton Powell of New York on the grounds that he had misappropriated $40,000 in House funds and had been held in criminal contempt of court in New York for failure to pay a judgment in a lawsuit he had lost. He challenged the exclusion as unconstitutional, and the Supreme Court agreed. As long as a person, when elected, meets the age, citizenship, and residency requirements, neither house may exclude him.

But each house may judge whether the candidate in fact meets the constitutional requirements. In 1794, Congress denied a seat to Albert Gallatin because he did not meet the nine-year citizenship requirement.

The constitutional power to exclude has not often been exercised: As of 1984, only three senators-elect and ten representatives-elect were denied seats on these constitutional grounds.

Congress may also determine whether the candidate was properly elected, and its decision is final. In a contested election, a state may require a recount or even a new election, but the house may nevertheless hold its own recount and declare the winner as it determines. In 1985, the House of Representatives, controlled by the Democrats, gave a seat to the Democratic candidate from Indiana in a bitterly contested election, though the Republican candidate was the apparent winner. The election turned on the legitimacy of a number of ballots and the counting of absentee ballots, and the House's decision on the legitimacy of the ballots is final and cannot be reviewed in the courts.

Members of Congress enjoy certain immunities from the normal processes of law. Article I says they are privileged from arrest in attending sessions of Congress and in going to and coming from those sessions—but this privilege is relatively restricted, for it excepts cases of treason, felony, and breach of peace,

cases that constitute most of the grounds for arrest today. Its original intention was to exempt members from arrest for indebtedness.

More significant is congressional immunity from suit for libel and slander while participating in official proceedings. This provision the founders included to prevent the government from hauling away members who spoke out against the current administration. During the eighteenth century in England, members of Parliament could be snatched up who were heard to say things displeasing to the crown (such speech was labeled "seditious libel"). The present immunity is restricted to speech relating to deliberations in Congress. Thus Senator William Proxmire of Wisconsin was held to be immune from suit for a disparaging comment in a letter to another senator about an official Senate inquiry, but not immune for making defamatory comments in a newsletter mailed to constituents.

Though the formal qualifications for members of Congress have remained the same over two centuries, the election process has changed dramatically (Chapter 8). For as astute as they were, the Founding Fathers did not anticipate the rise of the political party—

The dominance of the two-party political system was unforeseen by the framers of the Constitution.

and consequently the Constitution gives it no formal sanction at all. Madison saw the virtue of faction against faction, but he did not see that factions would crystallize politically into self-perpetuating parties. This central feature of American political life lives in the interstices of the Constitution. Extraconstitutional, the two-party system survives by custom and necessity.

The Legislative Powers of Congress

Congress's substantive powers are the heart of Article I. Congress is said to be a body of limited powers; it is not empowered to legislate on anything that strikes its fancy. Two general sorts of restrictions limit its power to act. One is the constitutional prohibitions contained in the Bill of Rights and certain other provisions. (For example, Congress may not abridge the freedom of speech, nor may it enact a law "ex post facto.") These prohibitions might be called external limitations.

But an internal limitation also applies: Unlike state legislatures, Congress's legislative powers are limited to those "herein granted"; that is, to those powers specifically set forth in the Constitution—mostly in Section 8 of Article I and in several amendments (chief of which are the Fourteenth and Fifteenth). Following is a description of Congress's specific powers.

Taxing and Spending. Congress has the power to collect taxes at rates it sets. Congress may levy taxes on imports (but not exports), manufacture, sales, property, and income. The federal income tax is, of course, the major source of federal revenue today. It is a common myth that the federal income tax constitutionally came into existence only in 1913 when the Sixteenth Amendment was ratified. In fact, the original Constitution permitted Congress to tax income, but required, insofar as it was a "direct tax," that it

be laid in proportion to the population of each state, rather than uniformly on each individual. This was a cumbersome procedure, and the Sixteenth Amendment made the income tax practicable (page 73).

The taxes collected are to pay the debts of the government and "provide for the Common Defence and general Welfare of the United States." These are broad purposes that justify Congress in virtually any undertaking so labeled, as long as it does not violate specific prohibitions on congressional action (such as those in the Bill of Rights—for example, Congress could not decide to raise taxes to fund a movie censorship board, since censorship of movies is barred by the First Amendment).

Borrow Money. Congress can authorize the sale of savings bonds and other instruments on the credit of the United States.

Regulate Commerce. The commerce clause is an extensive power that has grown with the economy, permitting Congress to regulate commerce among the states, internationally, and with Indian tribes. More than any other, this clause gives Congress considerable autonomy in the regulation of economic matters. As the economy has grown and its many activities have become more interdependent, the scope of congressional action has widened, fully justifying the framers' desire to create a government that would not be impotent, like the government under the Articles of Confederation, to stave off economic chaos. More than any other, this clause bound the states into a single nation.

Naturalization. Congress has plenary authority to determine who shall be admitted to the United States, who shall become a citizen, and who, not being a citizen, may be deported.

Bankruptcy. Congress has exclusive power to enact a uniform bankruptcy law, covering both individuals and businesses. Only if it has failed to act may the states pass their own bankruptcy laws. Today, Congress has preempted most aspects of bankruptcy, leaving the states little ground on which to legislate (though the states do have a say in what possessions individuals may keep from their creditors when seeking to discharge their debts through bankruptcy).

Coin and Regulate Money. Congress has absolute power to fix a single value of money throughout the country, to issue coin or paper money, and to determine what kind of money may legally be used to pay debts. Congress may also fix the value of foreign money in relation to American currency.

Weights and Measures. To avoid the confusion that would stem from different units of weights and measures being used among the states, Congress has exclusive power to fix the system throughout the United States. Thus, if the metric system were ever to be adopted here, Congress would have to do the legislating.

Counterfeiting. Congress may provide for the punishment of counterfeiting of money and federal securities.

Post Offices. Congress may establish post offices, build the highways over which the mails travel, and to some degree (consistent with the First Amendment) regulate materials sent through the postal system.

Patents and Copyrights. Congress has enacted laws providing legal monopolies to inventors, writers, and others who transform ideas into tangible form. Thus copyright may be extended, not only to authors, but also to painters, sculptors, photographers, movie makers, designers, and others. Ideas themselves may not be legally protected, but their material expression can be.

Founding Father

William Livingston
New Jersey

William Livingston was born in Albany, New York, November 30, 1723, and died in Elizabethtown, New Jersey, July 25, 1790. He grew up in Albany, graduated from Yale in 1741, and was admitted to the bar in 1748. (An association with James Alexander, original counsel in the John Peter Zenger case, directed him to law.) In 1751, he was involved in a controversy against establishing King's College in an association with the Anglican Church. He also took part in New York provincial politics, a liberal opposed to the interferences of Parliament. Additionally, he established himself as an intelligent satirist. He served in the New York legislature from 1759 to 1760 and then left politics for a time, moving to New Jersey to live the life of a gentleman farmer. The slow pace was not agreeable, however; he became a representative for New Jersey in the First and Second Continental Congresses. By June 1776, he was commanding New Jersey troops. After the Declaration of Independence, he became the first governor of the state of New Jersey. At the Constitutional Convention, he supported the New Jersey Plan. He played a major role in the state ratifying convention, which approved the Constitution unanimously.

Lower Federal Courts. Congress may establish courts inferior to the Supreme Court.

Punish Infractions of International Law. Congress may establish criminal penalties for piracies, felonies on the high seas, and violations of international law (the "law of nations").

War Powers. Four clauses give Congress the power to declare war; raise, fund, and regulate armies and navy; and provide for the capture of enemy property. These clauses empower Congress to draft men (and women, if it chooses) into the armed forces. Because the president is, by virtue of Article II, the commander in chief of the armed forces, extensive conflict between the executive and legislative branches has arisen. With these clauses, Congress has considerable constitutional power (though not necessarily the political power) to check and balance actions of the president. In particular, because appropriations for the army cannot be made for more than a two-year period, Congress can control (or at least assert control over) the president's use of the armed forces.

Militia. The militia are citizen-soldiers not part of the regular armed forces (the National Guard and National Guard Reserve are parts of the militia). Under the militia power, Congress has authorized the president to call up the National Guard under specified emergencies and even to draft members of the Guard into the army.

Create and Govern the National Capital. Congress acquired land ceded by Maryland and Virginia to establish the District of Columbia as the national capital. Congress has the authority to legislate all law for the District (acting, for this purpose, like a state legislature); it has a like authority to govern all federal buildings and other federal facilities like dockyards and arsenals in the states.

Determine Succession to the Presidency. Under various provisions and amendments, Congress has power to determine the line of succession to the presidency and vice presidency and even, under certain circumstances, to choose the president and vice president.

Vest Appointment of Officers. Congress may determine who shall appoint certain inferior officers of the federal government.

Control the Jurisdiction of the Supreme Court. This power is discussed on page 119.

Admit States and Govern Territory of the United States. Congress has plenary authority to determine whether to admit a territory into the Union as a state (subject to the consent of a state from whose territory the new state is carved out). Congress also has sweeping power to govern the territories that it alone has the power to incorporate into the United States. (The courts have distinguished between "incorporated" and "unincorporated" territory. People born in incorporated territory are citizens and have all the constitutional rights of Americans born in the United States, whereas those born in unincorporated territory have only a few "fundamental rights" unless Congress chooses to extend other rights to them under this constitutional provision. The last incorporated territories were Alaska and Hawaii; the other U.S. possessions today are unincorporated territories—for example, Guam.) Finally, Congress may dispose of federal property, giving it away or selling it, as it sees fit.

Propose Amendments. Under Article V, Congress may propose amendments to the Constitution by a two-thirds vote and send them to the states for ratification.

Enforce Civil and Voting Rights. The Thirteenth, Fourteenth, Fifteenth, Nineteenth, Twenty-third, Twenty-fourth, and Twenty-sixth Amendments em-

In accordance with the War Powers Act, President Reagan would have been forced to withdraw the troops he sent to Grenada in October 1983 if Congress had not approved this action.

power Congress to enforce their provisions. In all, the power to enforce the provisions of the Fourteenth Amendment, ratified in 1868, was the most sweeping (see Chapters 10 and 15), though the power to enforce the voting rights provision of the Constitution has permitted Congress to give the federal government, in the Voting Rights Acts of 1965 and 1970, a sweeping authority to monitor and regulate state election procedures.

These are the enumerated powers, noted in necessarily abbreviated form here, that the Constitution entrusts to Congress. Had the Constitution stopped with this list, the course of constitutional history might have been quite different. For Article I adds one hugely significant power, quoted here in full:

> [The Congress shall have power . . .] to make all laws which shall be necessary and proper for carrying into Execution the foregoing Powers, and all other Powers vested by this Constitution in the Government of the United States, or in any Department or Office thereof.

This necessary and proper clause—sometimes called the elastic or coefficient clause—seems in one sense to be unnecessary and in another sense to undercut the concept of Congress as a body of limited powers. Why unnecessary? As James Madison argued in *Federalist* No. 44:

> Had the Constitution been silent on this head, there can be no doubt that all the particular powers requisite as means of executing the general powers would have resulted to the government by unavoidable implication. No axiom is more clearly established in law, or in reason, than that wherever the end is required, the means are authorized; wherever a general power to do a thing is given, every particular power necessary for doing it is included.

Even in the absence of this clause, no one doubted that Congress had the power to "punish any violation of its laws," in Chief Justice Marshall's words, even though "this is not among the enumerated powers of Congress," or that Congress could acquire territory for the United States simply because the Constitution does not explicitly set forth such a power. In other words, inherent in the term *legislative power* are certain modes of proceeding and certain powers that necessarily flow from the other grants. Thus, subject to some constitutional restrictions, Congress has the inherent power to investigate on any subject that falls within its purview, to subpoena witnesses, and even to punish reluctant ones for contempt. Also, Congress has an apparently limitless power to exclude aliens, not because the power is given in the Constitution, but because such a power necessarily follows as an attribute of sovereignty in the federal government. (However, the power to deport aliens is constitutionally circumscribed.)

Even so, powers inhering in the general concept of legislation and sovereignty would probably not have been sufficient to permit Congress to act as broadly as it has. The necessary and proper clause supplied the balance of power, opening up to Congress a vast range of activity—giving it, indeed, virtually limitless power to legislate, subject only to specific prohibitions in other parts of the Constitution.

In 1790, a debate on the breadth of the necessary and proper clause flared up between Secretary of State Thomas Jefferson and Treasury Secretary Alexander Hamilton over the constitutionality of a bill to create a bank of the United States. Jefferson argued that the only implied powers under the clause were those absolutely necessary to effectuate the specific powers granted. Hamilton responded, in effect, that the clause permits Congress to do whatever is convenient, useful, or conducive to ends that the Constitution explicitly says Congress can undertake.

This view was surely that of the first Congress in 1789 in proposing the Tenth Amendment, which says that "the powers not delegated to the United States by the Constitution, nor prohibited by it to the States, are reserved to the States respectively, or to the people." Some congressmen advocated language that said "powers not *expressly* granted." Madison objected.

There must, he said, "necessarily be admitted powers by implication, unless the Constitution descended to recount every minutiae."

The Supreme Court ultimately sided with Hamilton. In the famous case of *McCulloch v. Maryland*, Chief Justice Marshall upheld congressional power to create a national bank: "Let the end be legitimate, let it be within the scope of the constitution, and all means which are appropriate, which are plainly adapted to that end, which are not prohibited, but consistent with the letter and spirit of the constitution, are constitutional."

As broad as this reading suggests the clause is, the astute reader will have noticed that it permits Congress to legislate in areas far beyond those granted in Article I. For the clause says that Congress shall have the power to make all laws necessary and proper to execute "all other Powers vested by this Constitution in the Government of the United States, or in any Department or Officer thereof." A common example of the breadth of this provision is the power to legislate over maritime and admiralty matters, mentioned explicitly only in Article III, which extends federal judicial power to admiralty and maritime cases. The Supreme Court has ruled that Congress has "coextensive" power to shape that branch of law.

The Taxing and Spending Power

Along with its power to regulate the national economy, Congress makes itself most directly felt through its power to tax and spend. Two of its most important functions—measured by the time devoted to them and the significance of their ramifications—are to establish and monitor operations of the federal government and to raise, authorize, and appropriate federal funds for the myriad programs that it has established.

Congress has broad power to "lay and collect taxes." The original Constitution empowered Congress to raise two types of taxes—indirect and direct. Indirect taxes

Chief Justice John Marshall's opinions helped to define and strengthen the power of Congress and the Federal Government.

include duties and excises. A duty is a tax on imports. An excise is a tax on the doing of something, like the production, use, or sale of commodities or products and on the privilege of doing business. (The Social Security tax is an excise on corporate payrolls.) These indirect taxes must be imposed uniformly; that is, a federal excise tax cannot exact a higher percentage from a business in California than from one in Maine.

By contrast, a direct tax can be exacted only according to population; in effect, it is a tax on the people of a state, rather than on individuals. For a century, direct taxes were held to be confined to those imposed on property. Because apportioning taxes by population is impractical, direct taxation has not been an important part of congressional revenue raising.

But in 1895, the obscure distinction between direct and indirect taxes threatened the national solvency when the Supreme Court ruled that a tax on income derived from property is unconstitutional unless apportioned as required in Article I. Only fourteen years earlier, the Court had held a Civil War income tax law constitutional, but now five of its stalwart justices feared an encroaching socialism. The decision crippled federal power to raise taxes, and Congress was forced to overcome it with the Sixteenth Amendment, ratified in 1913. The Sixteenth Amendment permits Congress to "lay and collect taxes on incomes, from whatever source derived, without apportionment." Since then, with one exception, no federal tax has been adjudged direct.

With the Sixteenth Amendment in place, Congress has been free to tax as it has chosen, restrained only by political realities, not the Constitution. The authority to define income is broad and deep—Congress has said that even an embezzler must pay income taxes on the money he has embezzled. Those with larger incomes may be taxed proportionately more than those with smaller incomes. So complete is the congressional power to tax under the Sixteenth Amendment that a "retroactive operation of income tax legislation" has been held to be constitutional.

Moreover, it is no response to a federal tax measure that its effect is to severely regulate a company or industry or even put one out of business.

The taxes it raises Congress may spend "to pay the debts and provide for the common defense and general welfare of the United States." The "general welfare" clause is susceptible of different meanings. At its farthest extreme, it might be taken as a wholly independent power: Under it, Congress may spend whatever it likes on any program it likes as long as it is for the general welfare. This view has never been accepted, because it would render superfluous all the enumerated powers in Section 8.

At its narrowest, the power might mean that Congress could spend only to achieve goals permitted it under its other legislative powers. This was Madison's view, but it has not survived, because the listing of the spending power would be superfluous—under the necessary and proper clause, Congress may always spend whatever monies it deems necessary to carry out its programs.

Rather, Hamilton's view has prevailed. In his celebrated *Report on Manufactures to the House of Representatives,* he said that "the power of Congress to authorize expenditure of public moneys for public purposes is not limited by the direct grants of legislative power found in the Constitution," but is *in addition* to those powers. As a practical matter, this interpretation of the spending power means that Congress may establish broad programs such as unemployment insurance, Social Security pensions, and grants-in-aid to states for many types of welfare programs.

During the 1930s, when the Supreme Court was frowned on national regulation, it seemed for a time that such measures would be doomed. In cases testing the constitutionality of the Social Security Act, the argument was pressed that Congress could not create a fund to which employers and employees must contribute a percentage of their payroll and earnings. A shareholder of the Edison Electric Illuminating Com-

pany in Boston sued on behalf of the corporation, charging that Congress had invaded the powers of the states.

In 1937, the Supreme Court upheld the act. "Unless the choice is clearly wrong, a display of arbitrary power, not an exercise of judgment," said Justice Cardozo, any spending plan would be upheld as an exercise of the power to spend for the general welfare. "The concept of the general welfare [is not] static. Needs that were narrow or parochial a century ago may be interwoven in our day with the well-being of the Nation. What is critical or urgent changes with the times."

Thus the Social Security system was justified, not by recourse to congressional power over commerce or some other specific power that permits Congress to worry about pensions, but as an inherent aspect of the power to spend for the general welfare. This power Congress has construed very broadly. Today, the government spends billions of dollars, not only on federal operations and not only through revenue sharing with the states, but often directly on private individuals and groups to further some national purpose. Universities have received billions of dollars since World War II to undertake basic research, and lately even poets (through the National Endowment for the Arts) have been the object of the government's largess.

Indeed, so much money is recycled through the federal tax machine and back to various people that one conservative critic (Howard Phillips, chairman of the Conservative Caucus) has detected an attempt by the government to establish a religion: "Billions of taxpayer dollars are being dispatched annually to organizations which seek to influence our cultural, economic, political, and religious life, and this practice is an offense against the principle of the First Amendment to the Constitution forbidding federal support of a religious establishment." Of course, to his list of 175 "left-leaning groups" (he included the American Bar Association along with the Martin L.

Lincoln Center is among the beneficiaries of Congressional spending through the National Endowment for the Arts.

King, Jr. Center for Social Change, the Environmental Defense Fund, and the National Council of Churches), one should, in a spirit of fairness, add conservative groups like the American Bar Association and the National Rifle Association. Also, one should inquire about the propensity of the federal tax code to discriminate among various classes of people in their capacity to take deductions and other write-offs (a form of spending), the tendency here being to favor groups, like corporations, that have conservative inclinations.

The First Amendment argument, incidentally, is an example of the American habit of intellectual nimbleness in the cause of disputatious self-righteousness. Whatever else it is, the American Bar Association is not a religion (Chapter 12). Neither, more broadly, is mere advocacy of change. Corporations, for example, which benefit hugely from the federal spending power, are almost always engaged in influencing our economic life (one of Phillips's criteria for establishment of religion), and the Environmental Defense Fund seeks to preserve the environment against such

change. So although his categories are illogical and his constitutional argument a mere curiosity, his wrath is understandable, for Congress's ability to spend money does seem relentless and limitless, and the effects of federal spending are indeed pervasive.

The only limitation on Congress's general power to tax and spend is that it must not be "laid upon the condition that a state may escape its operation through the operation of a statute unrelated in subject matter to activities fairly within the scope of national power and policy." Congress could legitimately worry about the specter of unemployment and old-age helplessness in a country driven desperate by depression, but it could not, for example, tax corporations and then rebate or cancel the tax in states that lowered the voting age to sixteen.

Though the spending power belongs to Congress, it is one of authorization and appropriation; only the executive can actually disburse the funds. Suppose Congress authorizes the expenditure of public revenues for a particular program, like highway construction, and appropriates the money so that the Treasury can write out the check. Must the Treasury do so? For at least a century and a half, presidents have regularly asserted the authority to "impound" appropriated funds, and just as regularly the courts have denied them the power to do so. Thus in the 1830s, President Jackson's postmaster general refused to pay out a sum that Congress had determined (through an arbitrator) was appropriate for the carrying of the mails; Jackson thought a lesser amount was proper. The Supreme Court directed him to pay the congressionally approved sum.

But it is not always possible for the executive to do so. Congress appropriated funds to purchase gunboats in the event of war with France, but President Jefferson's purchase of the Louisiana Territory averted the crisis, and he told Congress he would not buy the boats. That was understandable. So, perhaps, were impoundments of funds that Presidents Truman, Eisenhower, and Kennedy thought necessary to keep the defense budget from being unmanageably swollen.

But the budgetary seesaw between Congress and the executive threatened to tilt dangerously when President Nixon declared, in effect, that he and he alone could determine whether to spend money Congress had appropriated. He denied Congress the power to add funds to his proposed budgets. On several occasions, he sought to terminate congressionally established programs by refusing to spend any money at all.

In fact, Nixon had the matter backward (as he had so much else backward: He once declared that the Senate was *required* to consent to his nominees for federal office, a constitutional theory wholly without merit). The president's budget is merely a proposal, and has no constitutional or legal standing. Only a congressionally approved budget, signed by the president, is legally binding, and the president may not withhold funds merely because he does not like the program.

In the wake of Nixon's numerous impoundments,

Congress passed (and Nixon himself felt obliged to sign, in the midst of his impeachment hearings) the Impoundment Control Act of 1974. This act requires the president to notify Congress of his intention either to terminate programs or delay expenditures. Congress had hoped to regulate impoundment through the "legislative veto," but since the Supreme Court has invalidated this device, Congress may be forced to take more draconian steps to exact compliance with its spending decisions.

Delegation of Power and the Creation of a Permanent Bureaucracy

Acting under its general commerce power and the necessary and proper clause, Congress has created, mostly in the twentieth century, a huge federal bureaucracy. As with the party system, the framers did not anticipate the creation of the administrative agencies of the modern state, and the bureaucracy sits uneasily in the constitutional scheme of separated powers. Indeed, it shows that the textbook model of separated powers misses a significant reality of government that must somehow be accounted for in the Constitution.

To be sure, Articles I and II are replete with references to departments of the government, and it is clear that the framers intended that the executive branch consist of more than the president and his personal assistants. As we have seen, the very first Congress created four major departments: Foreign Affairs, Treasury, War, and Post Office. But these (and the other departments) are for the most part subject to direct presidential supervision. Today, however, much of the federal administrative structure is not directly under the president's control—especially in the case of the independent agencies. A fair part of what Congress does is to create governmental structures for the carrying out of broadly worded policies.

So we return full circle to where we began: Article I says that all legislative powers are vested in Congress—not in administrative agencies. Yet it is the most common function of such agencies—the Securities and Exchange Commission, the Federal Trade Commission, the Federal Communications Commission, and all the others—to "make law," expressly under powers delegated to them by Congress. That is what they are there for.

On two occasions, the Supreme Court has held that Congress went too far in delegating its legislative power. In the most significant case, the Court in 1935 struck down President Roosevelt's National Recovery Administration. The National Industrial Recovery Act, which established it, permitted private groups to draft codes of fair competition, which on presidential approval became law. The Court held that Congress could not give away its power to the president without any standard to guide him in deciding what constitutes "fair competition." Said Justice Cardozo:

> The delegated power of legislation which has found expression in this code [dealing with live kosher poultry in New York] is not canalized within banks that keep it from overflowing. It is unconfined and vagrant. . . .
> Here in effect is a roving commission to inquire into evils and upon discovery correct them. . . . [If this delegation should stand] anything that Congress may do within the limits of the commerce clause for the betterment of business may be done by the President upon the recommendation of a trade association calling it a code. This is delegation running riot.

Yet it seems fair to conclude that the Court was particularly irked not so much at the formal delegation to the president but to that of private parties. For since that decision half a century ago, the Supreme Court has never struck down any congressional delegation of power to an executive agency, even though the agencies have been told to regulate in accordance with such loose standards as "public interest," "public convenience," and "public necessity."

Founding Father

David Brearly
New Jersey

David Brearly was born in Spring Grove, New Jersey, June 11, 1745, and died in New Jersey on August 16, 1790. His earliest American ancestor had arrived from England in 1680. Brearly was an attorney in his home state. At the outset of the Revolutionary War, he was arrested for high treason, suspected of Whig sentiment. During the war, he was released and was appointed lieutenant colonel of New Jersey. After the war, he took part in the New Jersey state constitutional convention and was elected chief justice of the state supreme court. He was an early upholder of judicial authority to strike down unconstitutional legislation. At the Philadelphia Convention in 1787, Brearly argued against proportional representation, against having joint ballots in presidential elections, and for the rights of small states. He was a member of the "grand committee" and regular in attendance—no ordinary feat! Later, he presided at the New Jersey state ratifying convention. From 1789 until his death, he was a U.S. district judge.

In addition to his political life, Brearly was active in religious pursuits. He was vice president of the New Jersey Society of the Cincinnati, a delegate to the Episcopal General Convention in 1786, a compiler of the Episcopal prayer book, and a member of the Masonic elite.

Separation of Powers

If Congress can delegate its power to executive agencies, how then are the branches of government separated? What kind of government has the Constitution given us? Indubitably, it is one far more complex than a simple model of divided powers.

In an 1881 case, the Supreme Court said that each branch must "be limited to the exercise of the powers appropriate to its own department and no other." Yet such a thing cannot be—and was explicitly rejected in both 1787 and 1789. The first Congress rejected what the Constitutional Convention had already rejected: a proffered amendment that would have added a "separation clause" to the Bill of Rights (modeled on that in the Massachusetts constitution): "The powers delegated by this constitution [it would have said] are appropriated to the departments to which they are respectively distributed: so that the legislative department shall never exercise the powers vested in the executive or judicial, nor the executive exercise the powers vested in the legislative or judicial, nor the judicial exercise the powers vested in the legislative or executive departments."

As usual, it was Madison who explained (in *Federalist* No. 48) the need for overlapping powers: "Unless these departments be so far connected and blended as to give each a constitutional control over the others, the degree of separation which the maxim requires, as essential to a free government, can never in practice be duly maintained." In other words, unless each branch of the government shares some powers with the others, none will have the capacity to check and balance the other. Or, as the Supreme Court has recently recognized: "[A] hermetic sealing off the three branches of Government from one another would preclude the establishment of a Nation capable of governing itself effectively."

This the framers themselves understood, for they were working their way out of the morass of a government with but one branch—the Confederation

Congress—which had so broken down that it had taken to delegating many of what tasks it had to agencies it created. The system created was a system of shared and overlapping powers, so that ambition could truly be made to counteract ambition (as Madison asserted in *Federalist* No. 51).

Of course, some ambitions are richer than others. Lobbyists, protected as they must be under the First Amendment, often seem to have the run of the legislative corridors. In many years past (and who can say what scandal will erupt tomorrow?), congressmen have shown the truth of Twain's dictum by taking bribes. Sometimes those bribes are packets of cash intended as direct payoffs. These days, the bribes more likely consist of campaign funds. Could James Madison ever have supposed that a single Senate race in North Carolina would cost $20 million?

More frequently (far more frequently than outright bribery, one likes to suppose), the lobbyists show Congress to consist of merely fearful creatures, who will against every grain of logical and moral sense put special breaks in the tax code or block or water down gun control legislation. This is American pluralism at work.

Congressmen as a rule do not like to be voted out of office—even jellyfish need to eat—and so in the end convince themselves they are doing what after all they really are doing: bowing to the will, however inchoately expressed, of the electorate.

If along the way Congress stumbles, unwisely legislating or foolishly failing to legislate at all, that is the price to be paid, not for having the Constitution, but for being human. A body of fallible men and women is not going to solve all the crises that erupt. Neither is it going to put things in such a tangle that the mess cannot ultimately be straightened out. A constitution, and the institutions it creates, can be judged only over the long haul.

The Constitution gives Congress the powers it needs to mirror more truly the American public. If the committee structure, the arcane rules, and the campaign

Office-seekers in the White House lobby (from which the word "lobbyist" derives) awaiting an interview with the newly-inaugurated President Rutherford B. Hayes.

financing system under which Congress usually operates have permitted special interests to "capture" congressional power and if this same structure and these same rules prevent Congress from acting in a truly democratic fashion, the remedy lies in the people, not in the Constitution. The Constitution does not compel the Senate to bend its knee to the filibuster, and it is unlikely that a constitutional amendment against such parliamentary devices would prevent a determined minority from bottling up bills that a less determined majority desires.

Many of the internal problems that beset Congress are beyond anything the framers imagined; certainly they did not suppose, for example, the existence, size, or power of professional staffs that operate like bureaucracies attached to congressional committees. But social reality is far more complex today than in the framers' time: The simple model of representative democracy they were constructing is too frail to do

justice to the vast and densely interdependent society that the Constitution helped create and protect.

Institutional reform is always slow but always possible. It remains within the means of Congress to accomplish. Indeed, many of the present difficulties are the results of reforms of a generation or more ago. For Congress does not exist in a political vacuum; it is but one branch of three in the federal system created two hundred years ago. Committee structure, for instance, is a response to the size and shape of the federal executive.

To appreciate fully the legislative power vested in Congress, therefore, we must see how that power intersects with the executive power vested in the president—a unique creation of the constitutional framers. To the powers of the president and the two-hundred-year struggle between legislature and executive that has shaped our daily political life we now turn.

Chapter 5 The Executive Power

Creating the President

"The President is at liberty," said Woodrow Wilson, "both in law and conscience, to be as big a man as he can. His capacity will set the limit; and if Congress be overborne by him, it will be no fault of the Constitution."

Nor of the framers. To head the national government, they determined on a single official, in whom they vested the entire executive power of the United States. Two hundred years later, the office seems perfectly obvious. But it was a new concept in the late 1780s, and the delegates may be forgiven if they did not fully appreciate what they had created.

The Founding Fathers could not imagine the pressures and perquisites of the modern presidency, but they were not naive and did not believe that human nature would fundamentally change in a republic. Even the revolutionaries in the 1770s who thought that Americans exhibited a new character thoroughly fit for republican principles had by 1787 seen the necessity for dividing power, putting "into the very form of government," in James Wilson's words, "such particular checks and controls, as to make it advantageous even for bad men to act for the public good." So although the office of president was a response, like so much else, to the weakness of the Articles of

Confederation (here the lack of any effective executive leadership), it was not set atop the Constitution but meshed with other powers. The powers of the president were, after all, set out second, following those of Congress, and if the president pushes Congress around, that is not, as President Wilson noted, the fault of the Constitution.

Under the Articles of Confederation, Congress was headed by a president, but no person could hold that office for more than one year in every three, and that president's powers were severely circumscribed. He was more like the head of a committee than an executive officer.

Early in the convention's proceedings, Edmund Randolph proposed in his Virginia Plan a national executive to be chosen by the legislature for a single term. This executive and the national judiciary would compose a Council of Revision with authority "to examine every act of the National Legislature before it shall operate." The council could veto any bill, and the bill could become law only if Congress then passed it by a much larger majority.

Off and on, the composition of the executive, powers, tenure of office, and method of election were debated until nearly the end. James Wilson of Pennsylvania suggested on June 1 that the executive be headed by a single individual. Though others believed Congress ought to choose the number, Wilson eventually prevailed, pointing to the existence of single executives in each state (some of them were then called "president" because they presided over the government).

Wilson advocated a three-year term and the possibility of reelection. George Mason of Virginia wanted a seven-year, nonrenewable term. Worried that a promising man might prove not to be fit for the job, Gunning Bedford of Delaware proposed a triennial election and a bar to a term longer than nine years.

Should the president have an absolute veto over legislation? Franklin argued against it: "[I have] . . . had some experience of this check in the Executive on the Legislature, under the proprietary Government of Pennsylvania. The negative of the Governor was constantly made use of to extort money. No good law whatever could be passed without a private bargain with him. . . . [I am] afraid, if a negative should be given as proposed, that more power and money would be demanded, till at last eno' would be gotten to influence & bribe the Legislature into a compleat subjection to the will of the Executive."

Tentatively, the delegates agreed to a seven-year term and postponed further debate on the executive to move on to other issues. They resumed the discussion in late July, considering a variety of schemes for electing the president and for determining the length of his term. Hugh William of North Carolina argued for one six-year term, noting that "the expence will be considerable and ought not to be unnecessarily repeated. If the Elections are too frequent, the best men will not undertake the service and those of an inferior character will be liable to be corrupted."

The delegates soon agreed to the proposition that the president (and other officers) should be impeachable. Impeachment was no new principle; it originated in fourteenth-century England and became a practical instrument of government in the seventeenth century. But the delegates were wary of a power that would permit the president to serve at Congress's whim, and so they eventually settled on restricted power to oust federal officials.

Other debate centered on appointments: Who should have the power to name government officials, including judges? The delegates wavered and tentatively decided to give the Senate the sole power to appoint them.

On July 26, a committee of detail was named to set forth the office of the executive so that the delegates could debate. The committee brought forward its proposal on August 6. It recommended that Congress have the appointment power, that the executive have a seven-year term and be ineligible for reelection, that the executive have a veto power over leg-

As Commander in Chief, President Reagan addresses U.S. troops in South Korea.

islation, that he command the armed forces, and that he be susceptible to impeachment and removal. For the first time, the executive was referred to as "president."

Pinckney of South Carolina suggested the president be required to have a net worth of $100,000; this precept that wealth would ensure high standards of eligibility brought a stinging rebuke from Franklin:

> Doctor Franklin expressed his dislike of every thing that tended to debase the spirit of the common people. . . . Some of the greatest rogues he was ever acquainted with, were the richest rogues. . . . This Constitution will be much read and attended to in Europe, and if it should betray a great partiality to the rich—will not only hurt us in the esteem of the most liberal and enlightened men there, but discourage the common people from removing to this Country.

Pinckney also suggested the Senate be given war authority, arguing that the House procedures would be too cumbersome and slow. Pierce Butler objected and proposed that the president should have the war power.

Madison and Gerry favored giving the executive power to defend against attacks, while placing the power to "declare" war in Congress.

Ellsworth proposed an executive cabinet, to be known as a council, composed of the president of the Senate, the chief justice, and the "Ministers as they might be established for the departments of foreign and domestic affairs, war finance, and marine who should advise but not conclude the President." Gerry spoke out strongly against department heads acting legislatively. (In the 1790s, Alexander Hamilton as treasury secretary would later come close to aping the parliamentary practice; he often attended congressional sessions and reported directly to the House, thinking himself almost an agent of Congress. Others did not follow his lead and no precedent was created.)

On the issue of succession, Morris opposed the Senate president's succeeding to the top job should the president fail to complete his term. He preferred the chief justice to step in. Madison thought the Council of Revision could serve in the president's stead. As late as August 31, this and other issues continued to roil the delegates, unable to settle on the powers and the nature of the office. Indeed, rumors circulated that the convention was even considering a limited monarchy, and there seems to be some evidence that several delegates had it in mind. Finally, however, they convened a committee consisting of one delegate from each state to rework the proposals yet again; the committee reported to the full convention on September 4. This version (or most of it) was ultimately embodied in the Constitution and gave us the office we know today.

The president must be at least thirty-five years old, a "natural-born citizen," and a resident of the United States for at least fourteen years. He serves a term of four years and is eligible for reelection. He is impeachable and removable by Congress under certain circumstances. He has full executive power, including the power to nominate officers of the federal government. Of this great power, and the way it can conflict with powers of Congress, we take note shortly.

Early Precedents

From long usage, the presidency seems commonplace now, but it was novel when introduced. The leader of the nation is elected (though not by popular vote) for a term of four years, though he is answerable to a popular assembly if he shows criminal or despotic tendencies. He cannot be an aristocrat, at least in the European sense, for the Constitution prohibits any federal officer from holding any title of nobility and denies to both federal and state governments the power to designate official marks of class.

Unlike the British parliamentary system, in which the prime minister is the leader of the majority party in the House of Commons and must first be elected to the Commons, the president is elected separately and has a different base of political power. He is answerable to the people but not directly to Congress. Indeed, the Constitution explicitly bars any member of Congress from holding an executive office. The framers thus created "presidential government."

Whether a national government headed by a president would work depended largely on the character of the incumbent, and it is no small matter that everyone knew—they even discussed his election openly at the convention—that George Washington was destined to be the first president. Washington himself was reluctant, tired, and desirous only of retirement. Writing in April, 1788, to his friend Lafayette, he said:

> In answer to the observations you make on the probability of my election to the Presidency (knowing me as you do) I need only say, that it has no enticing charms, and no fascinating allurements for me. However, it might not be decent for me to say I would refuse to accept or even to speak much about an appointment, which may never take place; for in so doing, one might possibly incur the application of the moral resulting from that Fable, in which the Fox is represented as inveighing against the sourness of the grapes, because he could not reach them. All that it will be necessary to add, my dear Marquis, in order to show my decided predilection, is, that, (at my time of life and under my circumstances) the encreasing infirmities of nature and the growing love of retirement do not permit me to entertain a wish beyond that of living and dying an honest man on my own farm. Let those who follow the pursuits of ambition and fame, who have a keener relish for them, or who may have more years, in store, for the enjoyment.

But once it became clear that the office would be pressed on him, Washington affirmed his dedication and his understanding of the care with which he would have to discharge his duties; he knew he was being watched, not simply by his generation, but by all to follow: "As the first of everything, in our situation, will serve to establish a Precedent, it is devoutly wished on my part, that these precedents may be fixed on true principles."

Washington served eight years, and those years were crowded with events, many of which indeed

The first cabinet (left to right): Henry Knox, Thomas Jefferson, Edmund Randolph, Alexander Hamilton, President George Washington.

hardened into precedents important to the conduct of the office and the image of the president of the United States. One was the dispensing with elevated titles. The Constitution itself had declared a policy against titles of nobility, and the question arose at one remove what to call the various officers to whom the Constitution gave political birth.

In the first months of the new government, a considerable storm was raised over the question. After lengthy debate, both House and Senate firmly rejected any title or manner of address for president or vice president other than those very words, the words that appear in the Constitution. Many believed that Vice President John Adams was agitating for titles in the hopes of getting one himself—strange business for so stalwart a republican. At any rate, it seems clear that he did suggest such titles for the president as "His Elective Majesty," "His Excellency," and "His Highness the President of the United States and Protector of the Rights of the Same." These were laughed away, and Senator Izard said that if titles were used, Adams's should be "His Rotundity."

Madison, in the House, declared himself "not afraid of titles, because I fear the danger of any power they could confer, but I am against them because they are not very reconcilable with the nature of our Government or the genius of the people. Even if they were proper in themselves, they are not so at this juncture of time. But my strongest objection is founded in principle; instead of increasing, they diminish the true dignity and importance of a republic, and would in particular, on this occasion, diminish the true dignity of the first magistrate himself."

Precisely what Washington felt about all of this is unclear, though it has been said that he preferred the title "His High Mightiness, the President of the United States and Protector of Their Liberties." But he saw how the winds blew; in a letter to a friend he wrote that "the question was moved before I arrived, without any privity or knowledge of it on my part, and urged after I was apprized of it contrary to my opin-

ion; for I foresaw and predicted the reception it has met with, and the use that would be made of it by the adversaries of the government. Happily the matter is now done with, I hope never to be revived." And it never was (though an echo of the debate sounded over the centuries when President Nixon unveiled new Gilbert-and-Sullivanish uniforms for Secret Service guards at the White House in 1970, amid guffaws at the apparent attempt to introduce some note of royalty into the White House; they were quickly withdrawn).

A more important matter arose even before Washington was inaugurated. While in Mount Vernon to hear whether the electors in New York had chosen him president, he was inundated with requests for jobs. In a letter to Benjamin Harrison, who had signed the Declaration and had been governor of Virginia, he explained his philosophy:

> In touching upon the more delicate part of your letter (the communication of which fills me with real concern) I will deal by you, with all that frankness, which is due to friendship and which I wish should be a characteristic feature in my conduct through life. I will therefore declare to you, that, if it should be my inevitable fate to administer the government (for Heaven knows, that no event can be less desired by me; and that no earthly

consideration short of so general a call, together with a desire to reconcile contending parties as far as in me lays, could again bring me into public life) I will go to the chair under no pre-engagement of any kind or nature whatsoever. But, when in it, I will, to the best of my Judgment, discharge the duties of the office with that impartiality and zeal for the public good, which ought never to suffer connections of blood or friendship to intermingle, so as to have the least sway on decisions of a public nature.

Though his policy of refusing to hire friends and relatives is no longer honored (at least often not, and with effects that Washington feared, as the headlines during the 1980s have made clear), his underlying philosophy has never been denied: The office is public, not private, and when private considerations move the incumbent, they lack legitimacy.

A third precedent of immense importance was Washington's decision after two terms to retire finally from public life. Many had expected him to remain president for life. But he chose to depart, stating that he thought two terms were sufficient for any man and establishing a precedent that lasted 150 years. (Franklin Roosevelt's breaking the tradition by running for four terms led to the Twenty-second amendment, ratified in 1951, constitutionally limiting the president to two terms). Washington's decision was crucial to the development of American political institutions, for it meant that the office was more important than the occupant and helped pave the way for the two-party system.

Electing the President

How the president would be selected was one of the most difficult issues facing the Constitutional Convention. If the chief executive were to be chosen by

Franklin Roosevelt, accompanied by Harry Truman, returns to Washington, D.C., in 1944 after his fourth election to the presidency.

the legislature, then he would be its captive, especially if he were eligible for reelection; the delegates assumed he would curry favor with the legislators to the country's detriment. Since the possibility of reelection was thought to be the best incentive to proper performance, some other way of selecting the president was necessary. The best would have been popular election, but the delegates could find no practical way to provide for it, given the technology and institutions of the times.

So the committee of eleven turned instead to what has come to be called the electoral college (this is not a constitutional term). In devising this unique institution, the framers were partially successful, for the electoral college persists formally despite the vast transformation in the American electorate and despite the persistent trend, evident for two centuries, toward popular election. But presidential election and succession has been the subject of four constitutional amendments.

Electors are chosen in each state according to methods adopted by the state legislatures. Although today presidential electors are selected by statewide popular vote, that is by virtue of political considerations, not constitutional command. State legislatures themselves could choose the electors, and other methods are not only possible but have been used (for instance, election within districts). Each state is entitled to as many presidential electors as the sum of its congressional representation (members of the House plus two). Today, with 538 electors (100 senators, 435 representatives, and 3 from the District of Columbia), a presidential candidate must secure 270 votes to win the office.

A candidate need not win a majority of popular votes to secure a majority of electoral votes. Presidents Truman (1948), Kennedy (1960), and Nixon (1968) were elected by significant majorities in the college despite carrying less than half the popular vote (because of minor party candidates). The states adhere to a winner-take-all rule, which is permitted but not required under the Constitution: Winning the popular vote by a fraction over 50 percent yields 100 percent of the electoral vote for that state. Thus a candidate with a number of close victories in states with large populations can take a majority of votes in the electoral college while losing the popular vote (because the losing candidate might have received overwhelming majorities in smaller states with fewer electoral votes). This happened in 1888 when Benjamin Harrison was elected with fewer popular votes than his opponent, President Cleveland.

By 1800, the electors ceased to perform any independent function. They had become stand-ins for the emerging political parties, the one major political oversight of the convention. Today, the November election is the news, not the results of the college's decision, which are reported on the inside pages of newspapers every fourth year on January 6 when they are officially counted by the House.

A nagging issue—unresolved for two centuries—is whether electors may vote independently for any candidate of their choice, even though they are pledged to vote for a particular candidate when selected as an elector from their state. In 1960, one Oklahoma elector, pledged to Vice President Nixon, voted for Virginia Senator Harry F. Byrd, but his defection had no bearing on the outcome.

The framers supposed the electors would be men of the highest moral character and educational attainments and that such a group would keep its task free from partisan politics. The mechanism they settled on was simple: A person winning the highest number of votes would be president and the next highest, vice president. A tie would throw the election into the House of Representatives, where each state would have one vote.

The emerging party system guaranteed a tie in the 1800 election, between Thomas Jefferson and Aaron Burr. The Democrats (the distant ancestor of the present party) had decided on Jefferson for president and Burr for vice president. Their electors were hand-

Aaron Burr

And if the House were controlled by the opposite party, as in 1800, then the wishes of the majority might well be thwarted. Or what would perhaps have been worse, the Federalists in 1800, knowing they would lose, might have cast half their votes for Burr, whom the Democrats had wanted to be vice president. With both Federalist and Democratic votes, Burr, rather than Jefferson, would have been president.

The party system made the difference and necessitated an amendment, the Twelfth, which was ratified in time for the 1804 election. Now electors must specify which vote is for president and which for vice president. If no one has a majority of votes, then the House, voting by states, chooses the president from the three highest vote getters; twenty-six votes are necessary for election. (This procedure has been invoked only once, in 1824, when the two-party system broke down and four candidates were nominated. John Quincy Adams, son of the first Federalist president, was elected, even though he had received fewer electoral votes than Andrew Jackson.)

Two hundred years after the convention, despite numerous attempts to abolish the electoral college, the formal system envisioned by the framers still stands, though its method of operation is far different. To critics who argue that a president should be popularly elected in the world's leading democracy, defenders of the system have pointed out that the electoral college requires that candidates be mindful of statewide issues as well as national ones and that a successful candidate will be one who appeals to many regions of the country and not simply to certain interests scattered throughout.

Succession

"Not worth a pitcher full of warm spit," said Vice President John Nance Garner about his job, the most "insignificant job" in the Constitution. The vice pres-

picked and were pledged to these candidates. The Democrats had the majority of votes, but under Article II they could not specify their votes for president and vice president, and so their candidates necessarily had an equal number of votes. The election was thrown to the House, still in Federalist hands, which took thirty-seven ballots before picking Jefferson as president.

The election alarmed the politicians. If each elector had to cast a ballot for two different people but could not specify which was for president, and if the party had only one set of candidates, then there would always be a tie and the House would always take over.

ident has two functions: to preside over the Senate and vote in the case of a tie and to wait for the president to die or become disabled. The Constitution was explicit in the case of the tie vote, somewhat less so in the case of succession.

Article II declares that the "powers and duties" of the office "shall devolve" on the vice president in case of the president's removal, death, resignation, or inability to carry out the office. Whether the vice president would become president or merely acting president was unclear and was settled definitively only when President William Henry Harrison died in 1841, a month into his term, and Vice President John Tyler took the oath of office and assumed the full powers of the office. The precedent he struck has been constitutionally accepted ever since.

But gaps in succession remained. What would happen if a president-elect were to die before inauguration? Or if a president has not been chosen by the time required for the start of his term? Or if there were no vice president and the president died? Or if the president were not dead but disabled?

Article II says that Congress may provide for a succession law in the event both president and vice president have died. The present law stems from 1947, and declares the line of succession to extend from the speaker of the house and the president pro tem of the Senate through the cabinet.

The Twentieth Amendment, the so-called Lame Duck Amendment, ratified in 1933, plugs other gaps. It lets the vice president-elect take over if the president-elect dies or fails to qualify before inauguration, and lets Congress decide who should serve as acting president if neither a president-elect nor a vice president-elect has qualified.

But the Twentieth Amendment still did not speak to the issue of presidential disability, an issue finally addressed in the Twenty-fifth Amendment, ratified in 1967. This amendment arose in the wake of President Kennedy's assassination. Suppose he had not been killed, but severely wounded. Who would de-

John Tyler set the precedent of presidential succession in 1841 when he assumed the office after William Henry Harrison died one month into his term.

Lyndon B. Johnson takes the oath of office aboard Air Force One following the assassination of John F. Kennedy in November 1963. Claudia Taylor "Lady Bird" Johnson is at the left; Jacqueline Bouvier Kennedy appears on the right.

clare whether Vice President Johnson would then have been entitled to exercise the powers of the president? In an age when nuclear war can be started, fought, and concluded in less than half an hour, it is vital to have a president who can act. Under the Twenty-fifth Amendment, the vice president becomes "acting president," a new constitutional term, in one of two ways: (1) whenever a president declares in writing to the speaker of the House and the president pro tem of the Senate that he is unable to discharge the powers and duties of his office, or (2) whenever the vice president and a majority of the cabinet likewise declare in writing the disability of the president.

The vice president immediately becomes acting president, with full presidential authority. The president may regain his office by writing the Speaker and president pro tem that "no inability exists." Suppose a vice president is installed as acting president

because the president is crazy, and in that state, the president declares his sanity. The Twenty-fifth Amendment provides that the vice president and a majority of the cabinet may within four days declare that the president still has a disability, and the issue is then left to Congress to decide, assembling within forty-eight hours. The president will regain his office unless by a two-thirds vote in each house, Congress declares within twenty-one days that the president is unable to carry on.

This mechanism is far from perfect. What happens if the crazy president immediately responds with yet another letter to Congress? And what happens if a physically disabled person takes too long to declare himself so? Nevertheless, it provides at least some method of legitimating a transfer of power under ordinary circumstances. In 1985, Vice President George Bush became acting president for about eight hours when President Reagan was under anesthesia during cancer surgery.

The Twenty-fifth Amendment also provided for the first time a method of filling the vice presidential slot when he resigns (as John Calhoun did in 1832), when he succeeds to the office of president (as happened in 1841, 1850, 1865, 1881, 1901, 1923, 1945, 1963, and 1974), or when he dies in office (as happened in 1812, 1814, 1853, 1875, 1885, 1899, and 1912). Altogether, during some thirty-eight years over the past two centuries, we have had no vice president. During all this time, no president has died or resigned, but the situation has always been uneasy (and but for the Twenty-fifth Amendment there would have been no vice president to succeed when President Nixon resigned in 1974).

The Twenty-fifth Amendment permits the president to name a vice president, subject to confirmation by a majority vote of both houses of Congress. This section has been invoked twice, shortly after its ratification: in 1973, when Spiro Agnew resigned in scandal, and in 1974, when President Nixon did likewise. Thus we have had one unelected president (Gerald Ford) and two unelected vice presidents (Gerald Ford and Nelson Rockefeller).

Impeachment and Removal

As important as is the line of succession, the framers were no less concerned about removal of an overweening chief executive. Just as limits had been placed on the powers of Congress (see Chapters 11–14, so some method of ensuring that the president would not overstep his powers would have to be found as well. That method was impeachment and removal. According to Max Farrand, impeachment was "the only new element in the constitution, that is, the only thing not originating in the correction of the defects noted" in the Articles of Confederation. Under the Articles, the executive was too weak for the people to have recourse to impeachment. Under the Constitution, the chief executive would be strong and the power of impeachment was felt to be a necessity.

The framers gave this power to the House of Representatives. Impeachment is nothing more than a formal accusation, like an indictment in a criminal case. The House can impeach by majority vote any civil officer of the United States, including the president and vice president (but not including members of Congress). Once impeached, the official must be tried by the Senate, where a two-thirds' vote is required to convict. If the Senate tries an impeached president, the chief justice must preside (to obviate the vice president's conflict of interest).

Under Article II, the president "shall be removed from office on impeachment for and conviction of treason, bribery, or other high crimes and misdemeanors." In once attempting to impeach Supreme Court Justice William O. Douglas, Congressman Gerald Ford said that "an impeachable offence is whatever a majority of the House of Representatives considers it to be." As a practical matter, that may be, since impeachment is not reviewable in any court, the power having been assigned exclusively to the House. But the framers did not suppose they were handing out so open-ended a power. The phrase "other high crimes and misdemeanors" connoted a certain category of offenses impeachable under English law. These included misuse of funds, abuse of power, neglect of duty, corruption, and encroachment on legislative prerogatives. Disapproval of presidential policies was not made a ground for impeachment, and it is generally agreed that the House abused its power in impeaching President Andrew Johnson in 1867 because it disliked his policies. By one vote, the Senate failed to convict him, a failure that preserved the narrower scope of impeachment and thus the powers of the presidency.

Impeachment and conviction have rarely been resorted to and even more rarely succeeded. As long ago as 1819, Jefferson said that "experience has al-

Contemporary engraving of the Senate impeachment trial of President Andrew Johnson in 1868.

ready shown that the impeachment the Constitution has provided is not even a scarecrow. It is a cumbersome, archaic process." In two centuries, the House impeached only a dozen officials (including President Johnson in 1867 and Supreme Court Justice Samuel Chase in 1804), and the Senate has convicted only four, all of them federal judges below the Supreme Court. Nevertheless, several others have resigned from office under threat of impeachment proceedings, and the House impeachment proceedings against President Nixon in 1974 show that the power is there and that it can have weighty consequences. Why else did Richard Nixon resign?

The President Is Not Above the Law

The president of the United States is the most powerful leader in the free world, not merely because he commands the technology of the mightiest nation, but also because, and more to the point, the Constitution confers on him as both head of state and government a wide range of powers. So nebulous are they that, from the very first, fears were expressed that the Americans had begot themselves what they had thought to rid themselves of. "The Constitution squints toward monarchy," said Patrick Henry, arguing against ratification in Virginia. From time to time, as the power of particular presidents waxes, commentators have found in the modern presidency imperial tendencies that not even Henry could have imagined. When dozens of ordinary rules and conventions are suspended for the convenience of the president, like the necessity of stopping at red lights, it is all too easy for him to consider the power from which the presidency stems to be his due rather than a trust to be discharged.

Yet the president is no monarch, neither in constitutional theory nor in political fact. The most imperial of modern presidents, Richard Nixon, was assuredly wrong, though he never seemed, even later, to grasp the depths of his constitutional ignorance, in professing the belief that "when the president does it, that means it is not illegal."

Richard Nixon leaving Washington, D.C., following his resignation from the presidency in August 1974.

Nixon made many sweeping claims to unbridled prerogative, resting in the main on the separation of powers. His most arrogant extrapolation from the separation of powers was his theory of executive privilege, which, put to the test in 1973 and 1974, demonstrated the limits beyond which no president can go.

A doctrine with ancient roots and resting on the separation of powers, executive privilege holds that communications between a president and his top advisers are confidential and may not be disclosed to the other branches of government against the president's will. It has long been accepted that under the right circumstances, a president may refuse to testify before Congress or deny a congressional committee access to papers from his advisers that go to the heart of the policy-making process. As the House Judiciary Committee expressed it in 1879: "The Executive is as independent of either house of Congress as either house of Congress is independent of him, and they cannot call for the records of his actions, or the action

of his officers against his consent, any more than he can call for any of the journals or records of the House or Senate."

Nixon took this doctrine to its illogical limits. To Senator Muskie's question whether executive privilege applies "to every one of the employees of the executive branch of the federal government of the United States," Attorney General Richard G. Kleindienst said: "Boy, if a president directed him not to, I think logically I'd have to say that's correct." Kleindienst soon backed off this preposterous claim that amounted to saying Congress could not call even a mail carrier to inquire into conditions at the local post office.

What remained, as Nixon was sucked into the vortex of Watergate, was the claim that no "private papers of [the president's] office, prepared by his personal staff," could be subpoenaed or handed over to either congressional investigators or to prosecutors or grand jury in a criminal case. To hand over the famous tapes would mean that "no president could function," Nixon wrote. His lawyers warned darkly that "a holding that the president is personally subject to the orders of a court would effectively destroy the status of the executive branch as an equal and coordinate element of government." In short, said presidential counsel Charles Alan Wright to Judge John Sirica, a court may not "compel the president to produce the evidence so long as he remains President. I cannot concede that a court has power to issue compulsory process to an incumbent president of the United States."

This was the claim of James I, that the king is above the law. Nixon was willing to distinguish the constitutional position of presidents from that of King James in only two respects: They can be denied reelection, and they can be impeached.

The Supreme Court rejected the imperial claim. In *United States v. Nixon,* it held unanimously that the doctrine of executive privilege does not encompass so absolute a bar to discovery of presidential documents. "The President's broad interest in confidentiality of communications will not be vitiated by disclosure of a limited number of conversations preliminarily shown to have some bearing on the pending criminal cases." The president, like anyone else, must yield to the courts when he is reasonably believed to have participated in a crime.

The Powers of the President

That presidents are not imperial, in the Nixonian sense, says little about the limitations of their more legitimate claims to power. Here, we encounter a vast realm. The scope of presidential duties, the conduct of the office, and the powers invested in the executive branch have grown immensely since the modest beginnings of President Washington's term on April 30, 1789. Congress voted him a salary of $25,000, though he had offered to serve for free if only his expenses were covered (recollecting his somewhat extravagant ways—his 1789 liquor bill alone came to $2,000—

Congress demurred). Today, the salary is $200,000, plus a personal expense allowance of $50,000. But official figures dramatically understate what is actually spent to support the president. Most of the budget for White House operations is hidden; estimates put it at more than $100 million. President Washington had at most a handful of personal assistants; the White House staff today numbers more than five hundred.

These numbers suggest the centripetal forces that have gathered into the executive office powers and duties that would have staggered the Founding Fathers. President Washington had so little to do at the outset of his administration that he took to advertising in the newspapers "visits of compliment" between two o'clock and three o'clock on Tuesday and Thursday afternoons. He also held dinners on Thursdays at four for government officials and their families on rotation, "levees" for men of the general public on Tuesdays at three, and tea parties on Friday evenings for anyone "properly attired." The executive branch remained modest for several years; when the executive was moved to the newly designated White House in 1800, President Adams's papers were packed in only seven boxes.

Today, the president's schedule is controlled minute by minute, it is nearly impossible for ordinary citizens to visit the president, and entire libraries have to be built to house just the presidential records of single administrations. The president has a fleet of airplanes and helicopters, limousines, and now and then a yacht or two (depending on whether it is fashionable to sail them or sell them); he has a communications network nonpareil, through which he can talk to anyone, anywhere, at a moment's notice; he has a military force at his command of several million men and women that at times is more than the entire population of the United States in Washington's day; he superintends a civilian work force of several more millions; and he has the keys to a device with which he can annihilate life on the planet.

Jonathan Dayton

New Jersey

Jonathan Dayton was born in Elizabeth-Town, New Jersey, October 16, 1760, and died on October 9, 1824. In 1776, he graduated from the College of New Jersey. During the Revolution, he served in the army, then studied law, and was admitted to the New Jersey bar. From 1786 to 1787, he served in the New Jersey Assembly. In 1787, he was chosen a New Jersey delegate to the Philadelphia Convention (after his father turned down the original nomination). At twenty-seven, he was the youngest delegate. He arrived June 21, remained until the end, and spoke frequently. William Pierce, an army comrade who was also at the Convention, described him as "of Talents, with ambition to exert them . . . There is an impetuosity in his temper that is injurious to him, but there is an honest rectitude about him that makes him a valuable Member of Society." In 1788, he was elected to the First Congress, but he declined the office. In 1789, he was on the New Jersey Council, and the following year, he was speaker in the assembly. Reelected to the Second, Third, Fourth, and Fifth Congresses, he was speaker during the Fifth. He served as senator for one term, from 1799 to 1805. In 1807, he was involved in scandal. A participant in the Burr action, though not an actual member of Burr's expedition, he was indicted for high treason. Although the indictment was eventually dismissed, his career in politics was substantially curtailed. He held some local offices and served two terms in the New Jersey Assembly, 1814–1815. He owned approximately 250,000 acres of land around Ohio Falls, and the town of Dayton, Ohio, was named for him.

All this immense power stems from a few sentences in Article II of the Constitution. The president is the commander in chief of the armed forces. He may demand a written accounting of departmental affairs from the heads of executive departments. He may pardon those involved in crimes against the United States.

He may make treaties with other nations, subject to ratification by the Senate. He nominates ambassadors, other ministers and consuls, justices of the Supreme Court and lower federal courts, and all other civil officers, again subject to confirmation by the Senate (though Congress is empowered to vest the appointment of those whose offices it creates in the president alone, in the courts, or in the heads of departments).

Cast in the form of duties, but stated so broadly that presidents have found in the language equally great powers, Article II commands presidents to give Congress information "from time to time" of the state of the Union, recommend measures to Congress "as he shall judge necessary and expedient," receive ambassadors, "take care that the laws be faithfully executed," and commission officers of the United States.

Informing Congress of the state of the Union is one of the presidential duties set out in Article II of the Constitution.

These specific provisions of Article II have been given expansive readings—by custom, by presidential claims, by congressional acquiescence, and in court. From these simple expressions, presidents have gained immense powers to govern. For example, the conduct of foreign affairs lies almost exclusively in the president's hands. He alone may decide whether to recognize a foreign government (a power said to stem from his authority to "receive ambassadors"), and he can commit troops abroad without waiting for a congressional declaration of war.

More important still is the argument for *inherent* presidential power stemming from the general grant in Section I of Article II, namely, that the "executive power" is vested in the president. Unlike the powers of Congress, which by the language of the Constitution are confined to those specifically granted (even though they are broad), the president's powers are more numerous. Most presidents have asserted inherent power to act far beyond the boundaries of the specific provisions just listed.

Thus as early as 1793, President Washington claimed inherent executive authority to proclaim American neutrality abroad; no statute or constitutional provision conferred this power. During the Civil War, President Lincoln emancipated the slaves by proclamation. He also seized a railroad, spent funds that Congress had failed to appropriate, impressed men into the army and navy, called up state militia, suspended the writ of habeas corpus, and blockaded the Confederate states. Inherent executive authority has even been relied on to immunize a federal marshal from charges of murder when sent to protect a federal judge, in the absence of a federal law permitting the attorney general to send him to do so.

Presidents have issued innumerable "executive orders," more than twelve thousand numbered executive orders by 1986 (and estimates of unnumbered orders range as high as fifty thousand). For example, President Kennedy created the Peace Corps by executive order.

Sometimes the authority claimed is so broad that

Abraham Lincoln reads a draft of the Emancipation Proclamation to his cabinet in 1862. Despite the executive proclamation's immediate effects, it did not alter the legal basis of slavery, which could be abolished only by individual state action or Constitutional amendment.

it seems to contradict other express language in the Constitution. For example, Article II plainly gives the Senate an important role in ratifying treaties. Yet presidents have historically exercised a power to enter into "executive agreements" that require no Senate approval at all. President Roosevelt entered into the "lend-lease" deal with England in 1938, exchanging ships for leases on Caribbean naval bases, as an executive agreement (though the deal violated federal law). And President Carter's extraordinary suspension of claims pending in United States courts against Iran as part of the deal to extricate the hostages in Teheran in 1980 was upheld despite the absence of any federal law permitting him to do so or any Senate approval of the agreement made with the Iranians.

This is not to say that presidents may do whatever they wish, whenever they want. The framers did not establish a monarchy, and presidents are not kings. Their powers may not infinitely be summoned from some constitutional vasty deep, as President Truman discovered in the celebrated *Steel Seizure* case. In December 1951, talks between the United Steel-

workers of America and the major steel-producing companies broke down, threatening a strike in an industry vital to American efforts in the Korean war. President Truman tried to head off the strike, but compromises failed. Two hours before the strike was to begin, the president ordered the secretary of commerce to "seize" the steel mills and operate them as government property. The president justified his seizure on national security grounds and his inherent executive authority to protect national security. The Supreme Court, for once, drew the line. It held that although Congress could have constitutionally seized the mills, the president had no independent authority to do so.

Indeed, throughout our history, it is the interaction of Congress and the president that ultimately has defined the scope of the powers of both. For the greatest extension of presidential power has not been unbounded interpretation of the president's inherent authority, but *power that Congress has given to the president*. Thus most of Lincoln's actions early in the Civil War were ultimately ratified by Congress. And

President Roosevelt's seizure in June 1941 of an aircraft plant, shipbuilding companies, a shell factory, a cable factory, and four thousand coal companies—the same thing President Truman was later told he could not do—was approved by Congress when it enacted the War Labor Disputes Act in 1943.

In a concurring opinion in the *Steel Seizure* case, Justice Robert H. Jackson laid out the relationship between the power of president and of Congress:

1. When the President acts pursuant to an express or implied authorization of Congress, his authority is at its maximum, for it includes all that he possesses in his own right plus all that Congress can delegate. In these circumstances, and in these only, may he be said (for what it may be worth), to personify the federal sovereignty. If his act

is held unconstitutional under these circumstances, it usually means that the Federal Government as an undivided whole lacks power. A seizure executed by the President pursuant to an Act of Congress would be supported by the strongest of presumptions and the widest latitude of judicial interpretation, and the burden of persuasion would rest heavily upon any who might attack it.

2. When the President acts in absence of either a congressional grant or denial of authority, he can rely upon his own independent powers, but there is a zone of twilight in which he and Congress may have concurrent authority, or in which its distribution is uncertain. Therefore, congressional inertia, indifference or quiescence may sometimes, at least as a practical matter, enable, if not invite, measures on independent presidential responsibility. In this area, any actual test of power is likely to depend on the imperatives of events and contemporary imponderables rather than on abstract choices of law.

3. When the President takes measures incompatible with the expressed or implied will of Congress, his power is at its lowest ebb, for then he can rely only upon his own constitutional powers minus any constitutional powers of Congress over the matter. Courts can sustain exclusive Presidential control in such a case only by disabling the Congress from acting upon the subject. Presidential claim to a power at once so conclusive and preclusive must be scrutinized with caution, for what is at stake is the equilibrium established by our constitutional system.

Though the Constitution by its terms confines legislative power to Congress and executive power to the president, the Constitution does not sharply define the break between them. To the contrary, the Constitution builds in numerous points of contact and overlap. Thus the president may conduct war by commanding the troops, but only Congress has the power to declare it. The president nominates government officers, but the Senate must create the offices and ratify his nominations. The president may oversee the great departments of the government, but Congress delegates rules of operation and often assigns them tasks. The president may create a sweeping program, but Congress may oversee its budget or

Justice Robert H. Jackson

deny it funds altogether. It is this overlapping power that comprises the system of checks and balances that has fueled most of the constitutional conflicts between Congress and president during the past two centuries—and that will go right on doing so as long as the Constitution endures.

The System of Checks and Balances

The powers of Congress and president are locked in an eternal tug of war, sometimes the one ascendant, sometimes the other. In our time, the era of the "imperial presidency," the president is thought to have the upper hand, but the story is more complex than simple catch phrases would lead us to believe. With limited space, we can examine only a few areas of controversy, but in all cases, the few words of the Constitution permit, indeed provoke, an extended debate.

The Removal Power

Article II says that the president shall nominate all officers of the United States, whose appointments are established by law, and shall appoint them by and with the advice and consent of the Senate. Congress is empowered to vest the appointment of such officers in the president alone, in the courts, or in the heads of departments. In plainer language, this clause says that when Congress establishes an office, the president names the officer to fill it, but the person he names cannot have the job unless the Senate by majority vote concurs. However, Congress may remove the Senate from this process by giving the president, courts, or department heads the power to appoint officers not otherwise mentioned in the Constitution.

What of removal? Since the Senate must concur in the appointment, must it concur in the dismissal? May Congress, which has the power to create offices, reserve to itself the power to participate in the decision to remove? Or may the president alone remove any officer (other than those constitutionally established, like justices of the Supreme Court), on the grounds that removal is an incident of the executive power? Or may officers be removed only through impeachment, as spelled out in Article I (impeachment by the House, conviction and removal by the Senate)? The Constitution does not answer these questions.

The removal issue stirred Congress from its earliest days. In 1789, the debate centered on whether the laws creating the Departments of Foreign Affairs, War, and Treasury should include language specifically permitting removal of the secretaries by the president. The debate turned on whether removal was an aspect of executive power, in which case the Constitution already vested that authority in the president, or was an aspect of legislative power to create offices. After three months of wrangling, Congress eventually voted in favor of an implied power, rejecting pleas that the secretaries be removable only with its concurrence.

Though Congress yielded on that occasion, the issue has never been free of contention. In firing his secretary of the treasury in 1833 over the issue of the national bank, Andrew Jackson incurred the wrath of the Senate, which actually censured him (though it ultimately conceded the legitimacy of his action and rescinded the censure). Congress later attempted to control dismissals in the Tenure of Office Act of 1867, and President Andrew Johnson's disregarding of that act in dismissing Secretary of War Edwin M. Stanton led to Johnson's impeachment. The Tenure of Office Act said that all officials of the federal government held their office until a successor was appointed by the president with the consent of the Senate, thus giving the Senate a veto over any appointment whatsoever.

After several confrontations, Congress finally repealed the act of 1887, but not before enacting several other laws restricting dismissal of federal officials,

BORN TO COMMAND.

OF VETO MEMORY.

HAD I BEEN CONSULTED.

KING ANDREW THE FIRST.

1832 cartoon satirizing Andrew Jackson's auto-cratic presidential behavior.

including certain categories of postmasters. In some of these laws, Congress specifically made its own (or the Senate's) consent a condition for removal (for example, the postmaster law in 1876); other laws limited the president to dismissing for cause (for example, "inefficiency, neglect of duty, or malfeasance in office").

For more than a century, the courts dodged the issue, though often called to rule on the constitutionality of removal when a dismissed official sued for back pay. The issue finally came squarely before the Supreme Court in 1926. Woodrow Wilson had concurred in the postmaster general's removal of the postmaster in Portland, Oregon, without the Senate's consent as required by the 1876 law. Was the president constitutionally entitled to remove a postmaster—or, by enacting the 1876 law had Congress overstepped its authority?

Chief Justice (formerly President) William Howard Taft declared for a six-to-three majority that the executive power of the president included the power to remove:

Made responsible under the Constitution for the effective enforcement of the law, the President needs as an indispensable aid to meet it the disciplinary influence upon those who act under him of a reserve power of removal. . . . The highest and most important duties which his subordinates perform are those in which they act for him. In such cases they are exercising not their own but his discretion. . . . [But even when they are performing duties prescribed by statute, those duties] come under the general administrative control of the President by virtue of the general grant to him of the executive power, and he may properly supervise and guide their construction of the statutes under which they act in order to secure that unitary and uniform execution of the laws which Article II of the Constitution evidently contemplated in vesting general executive power in the President alone.

Hence the 1876 law was unconstitutional, and the president could dismiss postmasters at will.

Founding Father

Benjamin Franklin
Pennsylvania

Ben Franklin was born in Boston, Massachusetts, January 17, 1706, and died in Philadelphia, Pennsylvania, April 17, 1790. A man of many talents, he was admired worldwide and justifiably so. Franklin was first an apprentice printer, later the publisher of the *Pennsylvania Gazette* and *Poor Richard's Almanack*. He joined the Pennsylvania Assembly as a clerk from 1736 to 1751, then as a member from 1751 to 1764. He was postmaster in Pennsylvania from 1737 to 1753 and for the colonies from 1753 to 1754. He was the Pennsylvania representative in the Albany Congress in 1754. Franklin served in England as agent for the colonies on issues of defense and taxation in 1757–1762, also acting as agent for Pennsylvania, Georgia, New Jersey, and Massachusetts. He formed Junto, a debating club in 1727, which became the American Philosophical Society in 1743.

He initiated many educational and social reforms, among them laying the base for the University of Pennsylvania. He was an inventor, and remains well known today for his electrical experiments during 1746–1752 and invention of the lightning rod. He spoke out for conciliation with the British until the Coercive Acts were passed in 1774. Then his energy was directed toward independence. He was a delegate to the Second Continental Congress in 1775, and was on the committee that drafted the Declaration of Independence. Congress sent him to France to gather support for the War of Independence. With John Jay and John Adams, he helped negotiate the peace treaty of 1783. He was later elected president of the Executive Council of Pennsylvania, and in 1787, he was a Pennsylvania delegate to the Constitutional Convention, the oldest member. There he helped draft the large and small state compromise. He signed the Constitution and retired from politics to write his autobiography.

Franklin was adept in many areas. His early career as a printer and businessman gave him enough financial stability to retire from business at forty-two. His philosophy of life fused wit to morality. He embraced the enlightened view that one could and should always continue to learn, as his words at the Convention attest: "Having lived long, I have experienced many instances of being obliged, by better Information, or fuller Considerations, to change Opinions even on Important Subjects, which I once thought right; but found to be otherwise."

But this absolute view was too confining, and it would not last. In a powerful dissent, Justice Brandeis addressed the issue of separation of powers:

> The separation of powers did not make each branch completely autonomous. It left each, in some measure, dependent upon the others, as it left to each power to exercise, in some respects, functions in their nature executive, legislative and judicial. Obviously the President cannot secure full execution of the laws, if Congress denies to him adequate means of doing so. Full execution may be defeated because Congress declines to create offices indispensable for that purpose. Or, because Congress, having created the office, declines to make the indispensable appropriation. Or, because Congress, having both created the office and made the appropriation, prevents, by restrictions which it imposes, the appointment of officials who in quality and character are indispensable to the efficient execution of the law. If, in any such way, adequate means are denied to the President, the fault will lie with Congress. The President performs his full constitutional duty, if, with the means and instruments provided by Congress and within the limitations prescribed by it, he uses his best endeavors to secure the faithful execution of the laws enacted.

Despite the seeming breadth of the opinion, the Court allowed for a federal civil service, employees of which could be protected against arbitrary dismissals by the president or his subordinate. Oddly enough, the Court found constitutional support for a protected civil service in the clause that permits Congress to vest appointment "in the president alone." It is odd, because the net effect of the case is that when a federal appointment is one that the Senate must approve, Congress can have no say in the removal, but when the appointment is one over which Congress has no say (because it has vested that authority in the president), then it may limit the president's power to remove. Such are the vagaries of constitutional interpretation—such, one might say, are the ambiguities of Delphic clauses in a constitution intended to endure.

The issue did not go away. Nine years later, in 1935, the removal power again came before the Supreme Court. President Roosevelt had removed William E. Humphrey, a member of the Federal Trade Commission, one of the so-called independent federal regulatory agencies, established in 1914. The FTC Act permitted removal only for "inefficiency, neglect of duty, or malfeasance in office." Roosevelt dismissed Humphrey, a mossback who took a dim view of the New Deal, for policy reasons: Roosevelt sought to put his own stamp on the agency. Now, however, the Court held against the president's removal power.

The distinction lay in the nature of the office. The FTC is a regulatory body, combining legislative, executive, and judicial powers. Speaking for a unanimous Court, Justice Sutherland said:

> The Federal Trade Commission is an administrative body created by Congress to carry into effect legislative policies embodied in the statute in accordance with the legislative standard therein prescribed, and to perform other specified duties as a legislative or as a judicial aid. Such a body cannot in any proper sense be characterized as an arm or an eye of the executive. Its duties are performed without executive leave and, in the contemplation of the statute, must be free from executive control.
> . . . The commission acts in part quasi-legislatively and in part quasi-judicially.

In other words, when Congress gives a job to do, sets a standard to be followed, commits the job to an agency, and gives that agency legislative, executive, and judicial power to do it, the president must keep hands off. The postmaster's case was limited to its facts: The president has exclusive authority to remove only "purely executive officers," not independent officers such as Humphrey. A quarter-century later, the Court affirmed this policy, again unanimously, in a case denying President Eisenhower the power to dismiss a member of the War Claims Commission.

Through these cases and others, the Supreme Court ratified the creation and operation of a powerful "fourth branch" of government, mentioned nowhere in the Constitution: the numerous federal administrative agencies. The administrative apparatus of the modern state is immense, and insofar as agencies are not directly under the command of the president (as the cabinet departments for the most part continue to be), they tend to be, as the President's Committee on Administrative Management declared in 1937, "in reality miniature independent governments, . . . a headless 'fourth branch' of the Government."

Although their independence is constitutionally anomalous, the independent federal agencies are not entirely autonomous. Presidents nominate their heads (and sometimes second-echelon employees); the Senate must confirm them. Congress can at any time rewrite the laws under which they operate. The president, through the Office of Management and Budget, can control their budget requests in Congress, and Congress may always appropriate larger or smaller sums or deny funds altogether for certain activities. Nevertheless, where their power counts—in the myriad regulations that affect numerous aspects of American life—recent developments suggest the independent agencies may be less vulnerable to direct control by either Congress or the president. Or, these developments may presage once again a seismic shift in the nature of the executive power vested in the president under Article II.

The Legislative Veto

The recent developments stem from the so-called legislative veto. In hundreds of statutes, Congress has granted administrative agencies power to issue rules and regulations to further some congressional purpose. Thus the Federal Trade Commission regulates unfair competition, the Federal Communications Commission oversees the airwaves, the Securities and Exchange Commission supervises the stock exchanges, and the Treasury Department, through the Internal Revenue Service, promulgates thousands of tax regulations. Because Congress has delegated its own legislative power, it has sought in many of these

instances to retain some control over the final regulatory product.

For half a century or so, Congress has done so by reserving to one house or the other the power to *veto* administrative regulations. Commonly, the law said a regulation would take effect only if one house, or even a congressional committee, failed to veto it within a specified period. In other words, a single house could, by majority vote, overturn an administrative regulation or other administrative action. In 1983, the Supreme Court declared all legislative vetoes unconstitutional.

The problem with the one-house veto, the Court said, was twofold. Article I specifies that for Congress to make a law, both houses must pass a bill. Also, the bill must be presented to the president for signature. Both bicameralism and presentment were avoided in the one-house veto. If Congress wants to amend or repeal an administrative regulation, it can do so by passing a bill and having the president sign it.

The result may seem queer. Congress can give the executive authority to issue regulations that have the force and effect of law. The exercise of that authority is said to be "executive." Congress can delegate lawmaking authority to the executive branch, but in the name of separation of powers cannot "invade" that power by reserving to itself the ability to control the regulation. In other words, Congress can give away its own lawmaking power to an executive agency, but not to one of its own committees or houses. This seems to stand separation of powers on its head: The executive may exercise a legislative function, but the legislature may not. The Court's response was simple (and not at all supple, as it might have been): The Constitution spells out how Congress is to exercise its function and any deviation from that procedure is invalid.

The decision voiding legislative vetoes has been severely criticized. Aside from weaknesses in the Court's reasoning, the decision threatens to upset a delicate balance between the legislative and executive branches: Congress has been willing to delegate some of its power only because it retained some control, through the legislative veto, over how that power was used.

How Congress will respond remains to be seen. But the issue has a significance that transcends the precise means by which Congress can assert control over executive rule-making. For it intersects with the hottest domestic political topic in Washington on the eve of the constitutional bicentennial: deficit reduction.

In 1985, Congress passed the so-called Gramm-Rudman Act (the Balanced Budget and Emergency Deficit Control Act of 1985), which requires the budget to be balanced by 1991. The act provides for "automatic" budget cuts if Congress and the president are unable to reduce the federal deficit by a specified amount each year through the normal process (the very process that the Court in the legislative veto case said must be done through formal enactment and presidential signature). The catch is that the "automatic" cuts are not automatic. In the peculiar semantics of Washington, an automatic cut is one for which neither Congress nor the president bears responsibility. In fact, the act directs the comptroller general of the United States to predict the size of the deficit and then to apply a formula to cut various programs to reach the year's target for reducing the deficit. The president must then "sequester" that much money from the budget. Both Congress and the president can duck and point a finger at someone else when losing constituents abuse them.

Unfortunately for Gramm-Rudman, the comptroller general, as head of the General Accounting Agency (the auditing arm of Congress), is not a member of the executive branch. Although nominated by the president, he is ultimately removable by a two-thirds vote of Congress. Therefore, said the United States District Court for the District of Columbia, in an unsigned opinion thought to have been authored by

Phil Gramm (left) and Warren Rudman (right).

then Judge Antonin Scalia, the budget-cutting procedure is unconstitutional because it delegates executive power to someone not within the executive branch.

The court's decision was potentially revolutionary; it suggested that a significant part of the administrative state, as it has developed for the past century, is unconstitutional because Congress has given executive powers to agencies whose heads are not removable by the president. This would have been the death knell of the fourth branch. Given the unconstitutionality of the legislative veto, the president might thus have discovered immense power flowing to the White House—control over the entire federal bureaucracy, with the power to write (or not write) all the regulations.

That transformation does not seem likely. In his last decision before retiring, Chief Justice Burger, for a seven-to-two majority, affirmed the nub of the District Court's opinion and struck down the core provision of Gramm-Rudman: The comptroller general, as a legislative branch official, may not be entrusted with the executive function of determining which budget cuts to make. But the decision apparently goes no further. Burger suggested that as long as Congress does not reserve to itself the power to remove heads of independent executive agencies, their constitutional status need not be disturbed and they need not be folded into the White House as policy-making bodies subject to the president's direct control.

The War Power

On April 14, 1986, President Reagan, the constitutional commander in chief of U.S. military forces, sent the United States Navy and Air Force into combat against Libya in the continuing war on international terrorism. For more than a week, following the bombing of a TWA airplane in flight over Greece and of a discotheque in West Germany popular with American troops, talk of retaliation had been in the air. Word leaked out that diplomats were briefing the heads of European governments. But our diplomats apparently were not visiting members of Congress, which under the Constitution has the sole power to declare war. Congress did not declare war. The planes dropped the bombs.

In all our history, Congress has declared war only five times, and yet American troops have been involved in scores of military actions, including ground war in both Korea and Vietnam (neither officially declared). Although Congress's power to declare war is virtually moribund, here again, the fault, if it is a fault, lies as much in the transformation of warfare as in the constitutional separation of powers.

The framers had little choice: The "war-making" power could never have been left to Congress, because a legislature moves too slowly to fight a war. That function, accordingly, had to be placed within the executive; Gerry and Madison suggested that the

Libyan officers guard a naval secondary school dormitory that was hit during the 1986 U.S. air strike on Tripoli. This action tested the 1973 War Powers Resolution because members of Congress were not consulted by the president until after the mission had begun.

word *declare* be substituted for *make* in the powers granted to Congress over war.

For two hundred years, Congress and presidents have argued over the extent to which the president has plenary power to order troops into action (and regardless of whether they have the constitutional or even statutory power, presidents have, of course, done so). And the powers presidents have asserted under their authority to make war as commander in chief have been broad: On these grounds President Roosevelt justified (and the Supreme Court of the United States, to its everlasting shame, supported) the roundup and detention of Japanese Americans on the West Coast during World War II (see page 280).

The Constitution deserted the Japanese Americans because all three branches of government failed, in the fear of the moment. Not one branch could muster the courage to call halt to a power that cannot be found in the Constitution. But that is scarcely attributable to a defect in the document. To the contrary, the Constitution does divide the power to regulate war, and in that division lies the only possibility of controlling national belligerency in a nuclear age.

In 1973, Congress overrode President Nixon's veto to enact the War Powers Resolution. The resolution recognizes that the president has the upper hand militarily, and so seeks to curb what he does by requiring him, first, to consult with Congress "in every possible instance"; second, to report to Congress within forty-eight hours after sending troops into action; and third, to terminate military action within sixty days (the president can extend it another thirty) unless Congress specifically authorizes continued fighting.

The intricacies of the law are beyond the scope of this book. But the difficulties with which it bristles can be seen at a glance: In sending the marines into Lebanon in 1982 and 1983, President Reagan ignored the resolution altogether, citing his authority as commander in chief and his power to conduct foreign relations. Congress responded with a law permitting the president to station troops in Lebanon for eighteen months (thus bypassing the 1984 elections). Also, not until the planes were airborne, three hours before they were due to drop their payload on Libya, did the president consult with certain members of Congress. The administration claimed there was still time to call off the raids had these congressional leaders objected, but the suggestion was so feeble that it might have made even John Wayne blush.

The clash between Congress and president, in matters of war, budget, spending, access to information, appointments, and governmental oversight, among many other matters, are woven into the fabric of American politics. Power to act and power to control are available to both. And when they fail, or conspire together, the Constitution provides a third and separate power to which the people may turn.

Chapter 6 The Judicial Power

The Passive Branch

"By ninth grade [reports a Washington journalist] . . . I heard about the Constitution of the United States. . . . I thought of the Supreme Court as something like a group of Super Bad guidance counselors who were always there to give an opinion on teen problems. I used to send the Court letters posing 'constitutional questions' that bugged me: 'Should wrestling coaches really be teaching psychology?' "

It took a "kindly librarian" to explain that the Supreme Court does not answer questions willy-nilly. But the student's endearing confusion is representative; many Americans know of the Supreme Court only from headlines announcing decisions. Unseen is the rich jurisprudential lode that must be mined to reach those results.

The federal judiciary is the least popularly understood major institution of American government. In the federal courts is vested "the judicial power," and together they constitute the third branch of government. Like the legislative power of Article I and the executive power of Article II, the judicial power of Article III is undefined. It takes substance from custom, usage, and history.

The judicial power is the power to *decide cases* under the law through legal procedures. It comprises several distinct powers. Thus courts can do the following:

- Determine rules of construction for interpreting statutes and the Constitution. For example, one court-made rule tells the judge faced with a statute whose meaning or reach is in doubt to construe it to make it consistent with the Constitution, if at all possible, rather than to give it a perhaps equally plausible reading that conflicts with the Constitution. The former course permits the court to uphold the law; the latter course would oblige the court to nullify the statute.
- Hold persons in "contempt of court," committing them to jail until they promise to obey a court order.
- Issue subpoenas directing witnesses to appear to testify or to bring documents.
- Appoint a special assistant known as a "master" to aid in a particular case and a special prosecutor (when called on to do so by the Justice Department) in matters involving conflict of interest by a high government official.
- Fashion remedies called for by the cases before them, unless Congress specifically prohibits them from using a particular remedy. In 1932, in the Norris-LaGuardia Act, Congress barred the federal courts from issuing injunctions in labor disputes.
- Make their own rules of procedure, as authorized by Congress.
- Admit to practice or disbar attorneys from practicing before them.

Judicial power differs significantly from executive and legislative power in one important respect: Unlike the other two branches, *the courts may not initiate action.* Congress may hold investigative hearings and pass legislation as it sees fit, without waiting for someone to call on it. The president and executive officers, acting under both inherent and delegated powers, may carry out a myriad of programs and policies without first being asked to do so. But the courts must wait for litigants to come before them. A judge may not look out on a controversy of the day and beckon the aggrieved into his courtroom to have their quarrel resolved. Several important principles promote this fundamental character of the judiciary.

Settle Cases or Controversies. The federal courts will not answer just any question propounded, like whether wrestling coaches should teach psychology. The courts answer *legal* questions. Moreover, you can't walk into court and ask the judge to answer even important legal questions, unless the answer is necessary to settle a case. Under Article III, the courts sit to hear "cases and controversies." Important legal issues that are not raised by adversaries in an actual legal dispute are not within the judicial purview.

This principle was laid down from the very start. In July 1793, at President Washington's behest, Secretary of State Jefferson wrote Chief Justice John Jay, asking the Court to respond to twenty-nine inquiries dealing with American neutrality growing out of the war between France and England. "These questions," Jefferson explained

depend for their solution on the construction of our treaties, on the laws of nature and nations, and on the laws of the land, and are often presented under circumstances *which do not give a cognizance of them to the tribunals of the country.* Yet, their decision is so little analogous to the ordinary functions of the executive, as to occasion much embarrassment and difficulty to them. The President therefore would be much relieved if he found himself free to refer questions of this description to the opinions of the judges of the Supreme Court of the United States, whose knowledge of the subject would secure us against errors dangerous to the peace of the United States, and their authority insure the respect of all parties.

Three weeks later, the justices wrote back declining to answer on the grounds that the Court constitutionally could hear only "cases or controversies" under Section 2 of Article III:

We have considered the previous question stated in a letter written by your direction to us by the Secretary of

John Dickinson
Delaware

John Dickinson was born in Talbot County, Maryland, November 8, 1732. He died in Wilmington, Delaware, February 14, 1808. He studied law in Pennsylvania and in London; once admitted to the bar, he had a law practice in Pennsylvania. In 1760, he was elected to the Delaware Assembly, in which he served from 1762 to 1765 and from 1770 to 1776. There he defended the notion of "proprietary government," believing that change would be for the worse. In his early political career, Dickinson wrote treatises on working with the British to prompt gradual change in the American condition. His *Farmer's Letters* gave him prominence as an American desiring change within (not apart from) the British Empire. He was a delegate to the Stamp Act Congress in 1765. In 1776, he voted nay to the Declaration of Independence. Also in that year, he penned the first draft of the Articles of Confederation. He was the president of the Delaware Supreme Executive Council in 1781, and of the same for Pennsylvania in 1782–1785. He attended the Philadelphia Convention and ultimately assented to the Constitution. He was not actually present on September 17, 1787, when the Constitution was signed, but asked his colleague George Read to sign his name on the document. Thereafter, he held no other political office.

Dickinson opposed rationalism and thus the politics of such figures as Ben Franklin and Thomas Paine. A conservative, he believed that Americans were asking only for ancient, fundamental rights that the British Parliament was trying to usurp. This gave him credence before the Revolution, but his opinions were discounted after. Respected for his writings, he personally did not command attention. In fact, he proposed the essence of the Connecticut Compromise early during the Convention debates, but was overlooked.

State, . . . regarding the lines of separation drawn by the Constitution between the three departments of the government. These being in certain respects checks upon each other, and our being judges of a court in the last resort, are considerations which afford strong arguments against the propriety of our extrajudicially deciding the questions alluded to, especially as the power given by the Constitution to the President, of calling on the heads of departments for opinions, seems to have been *purposely* as well as expressly united to the *Executive* departments. We exceedingly regret every event that may cause embarrassment to your administration, but we derive consolation from the reflection that your judgment will discern what is right, and that your usual prudence, decision and firmness will surmount every obstacle to the preservation of the rights, peace, and dignity of the United States.

Power to make final judgments. Not only must the courts act only on cases or controversies but also, under the requirement of separation of powers, they may not act even in "cases" if their decisions are subject to review by nonjudicial bodies. In the 1860s, Congress created the Court of Claims with jurisdiction to determine amounts due veterans. But the law permitted the secretary of the treasury to disallow the court's findings. The Supreme Court refused to hear an appeal of one such action, holding that the Court of Claims was therefore not a judicial court under Article III.

Many supplementary doctrines underscore the requirement that judges hear only cases. In most instances, the Supreme Court will not hear a case if its outcome would be "moot" by the time the Court has a chance to rule on the matter or if the matter is not "ripe" for review.

Standing. Even if a case exists—that is, if the issue is one in which those with adverse interests are contesting a claim of legal entitlement—the courts will still refuse to hear it if the plaintiff seeking judgment lacks "standing." In other words, not only must the *issues* be properly focused but also the *parties* must have some demonstrable legal interest in the proceeding.

In the simple nonfederal case, this rule is easy to understand. If I claim that you breached our contract, I have standing to sue because I am arguing that I was injured and have a legal right to redress. But my neighbor, with no personal stake in the outcome, has no standing to sue you on my behalf if I decide not to bring you to court.

On the federal level, the standing requirement has become quite complex. Back in the 1920s, Mrs. Harriett Frothingham found she had no standing when she sued the secretary of the treasury to contest a federal program giving aid to the states under the federal Maternity Act. She claimed that Congress could not through the states constitutionally give pregnant women federal funds; the Court held that her "injury" was no more or less than that of the millions of other federal taxpayers and hence was too slight to serve as the basis for a suit.

More recently, however, the Court has discerned standing for federal taxpayers when they are con-

testing congressional exercise of its taxing and spending power in the face of a constitutional provision that prohibits the particular expenditure. In the case, the plaintiff objected on First Amendment grounds to federal grants for instruction and teaching materials in religious schools.

Moreover, an "abstract" interest as a citizen in seeing that constitutional mandates are upheld is not sufficient to confer standing. For example, a provision in Article I prohibits members of Congress from holding "any office under the United States." A number of congressmen held reserve commissions in the armed forces, arguably an "office." An association of reservists opposed to the Vietnam war sued to enjoin the Defense Department from continuing their commissions. The Supreme Court dismissed the suit for lack of standing—as a result, citizens cannot test the constitutional question in court.

For all these reasons, the federal courts are "passive" institutions, waiting for cases to be brought. As Hamilton put it in *Federalist* No. 78:

Whoever attentively considers the different departments of power must perceive that, in a government in which they are separated from each other, the judiciary, from the nature of its functions, will always be the least dangerous to the political rights of the Constitution; because it will be least in a capacity to annoy or injure them. The executive not only dispenses the honors but holds the sword of the community. The legislature not only commands the purse but prescribes the rules by which the duties and rights of every citizen are to be regulated. The judiciary, on the contrary, has no influence over either the sword or the purse; no direction either of the strength or of the wealth of the society, and can take no active resolution whatever. It may truly be said to have neither FORCE nor WILL but merely judgment; and must ultimately depend upon the aid of the executive arm even for the efficacy of its judgments.

However, given the breadth of the federal courts' involvement today in policy at every level, we might well wonder at Hamilton's political acumen. Is a judiciary that instructs the executive (both federal and state) how it must operate its jails, police, schools, and hospitals truly a branch without Force or Will? Many have argued that the federal courts have greatly overreached themselves—one leading critic has branded them the "imperial judiciary"—but as usual, the answer is more complex than a surface look would indicate.

For one thing, Hamilton wrote before either the Bill of Rights or the Fourteenth Amendment, potent constitutional provisions authorizing the federal courts to review executive and legislative action. For another, no matter what their decisions, the courts remain dependent on the other branches to enforce their judgments. The judicial power is the power of *judgment:* to declare the law in a case, not to enforce it. The success of the courts is attributable to the esteem in which the people hold them. When the Supreme Court ruled in 1974 that President Nixon must turn over his tapes to the Watergate special prosecutor, the justices had none but moral authority to exact compliance. The president commanded the troops, not they. That he obeyed is testament to the enduring respect of the people for the Court's exercise of its judicial power.

The Structure of the Federal Courts

The Constitution created only the Supreme Court but does not describe its structure, leaving it to Congress to determine how many justices shall comprise it and leaving also to Congress discretion to establish lower federal courts. (The Constitution names the chief justice, though not in Article III; he is referred to only in Article I, Section 3, requiring that he preside over trials of the president in the Senate.)

For more than a century, the Supreme Court has consisted of the chief justice of the United States and eight associate justices. In the early days, the Court consisted of the chief and five associate justices. Congress gradually increased the Court's membership un-

Richard Nixon displays his office tape transcripts during a televised presidential address in April 1974.

til ten justices were sitting in 1863 (to correspond to the number of federal circuits). In 1866, to prevent President Johnson from putting his appointees on the Court, Congress passed a law reducing membership to seven through attrition. In fact, the number never dropped below eight, and in 1869 Congress set the number at nine, where it has stood ever since.

So seemingly insignificant was the Court in its early years that when the federal government moved to Washington in 1800, the capital architects forgot to design or build a place for it to sit. Two weeks before the start of its term that year, someone remembered the Court needed a place and the justices were assigned "a small and undignified chamber" on the main floor of the Capitol. Not until 1935 did the Supreme Court get its own building just east of the Capitol.

In the Judiciary Act of 1789, the first Congress created a system of federal trial courts called district courts, with limited jurisdiction. A district court was established in each state (plus an extra court in both Massachusetts and Virginia for the territory that would become Maine and Kentucky). Appeal from these courts was to a system of "circuit courts." These were not distinct courts with different judges but were made up of district judges and justices of the Supreme Court assigned to "ride circuit." These courts had important original jurisdiction, but they also had a drawback: In letting district judges hear appeals in their own cases, it permitted them to violate one of the oldest canons of judicial propriety, and it took Supreme Court justices away from more pressing work.

In fact, it was this onerous duty that led John Jay, the first chief justice, who had resigned in June 1795,

Chief Justice John Marshall (left) talks with local leaders at a tavern during his days as a circuit-riding judge.

to decline President Adams's nomination in 1801 to return to the high bench again as chief justice. (Jay had left the Court in April 1794, to become Washington's special envoy to London. Thereafter, he served two terms as governor of New York.) Jay's refusal cleared the way for Adams's portentous nomination of John Marshall on January 20, 1801.

For most of the nineteenth century, this cumbersome system (with some minor tinkering) was the mainstay of the federal judiciary. As new states entered the Union, Congress gradually increased the number of circuits, but Supreme Court justices were still required to ride circuit. In 1869, Congress legislated specific circuit judges and reduced the frequency with which Supreme Court justices would have to attend their circuits. Finally, in 1891, Congress created the modern federal court system. Federal district courts are the trial courts. Federal circuit courts, with their own judges, hear appeals from the district courts. The Supreme Court hears appeals from the circuit courts (since 1925, the Court has had discretion to determine which appeals it will hear).

On the eve of the Constitution's bicentennial, Congress has provided for 97 federal district courts, with 516 district judges. Each state has at least 1 federal district court and some states have as many as 4.

The United States has been divided into twelve federal circuits, and the appellate courts in each oversee the district courts in several states. For example, the U.S. Court of Appeals for the Second Circuit hears appeals from the federal district courts in New York, Connecticut, and Vermont. The U.S. Court of Appeals for the District of Columbia Circuit hears appeals not only from the federal district courts in Washington but also from numerous federal administrative agencies. A thirteenth federal circuit court, the recently created U.S. Court of Appeals for the Federal Circuit, hears patent and customs appeals from across the country. Congress has authorized 136 circuit court judges.

Federal judges, including Supreme Court justices, are appointed by the president, confirmed by the Senate, and serve during "good behavior"—for life, if they are inclined. They are to be paid regular sal-

William Rehnquist (right) is greeted by Senators (from left) Edward Kennedy, Howard Metzenbaum, and Strom Thurmond upon his arrival for confirmation hearings as chief justice nominee.

aries, which may not be reduced while they are in office. Federal judges are thus insulated from political pressure (both legislative and executive) and are free to discharge their judicial responsibilities independently of the administration that put them in office or of succeeding administrations (though pique at their decisions may lead Congress to refrain from increasing salaries to appropriate levels).

The Jurisdiction of the Lower Federal Courts

By assigning the judicial power to the Supreme Court and the lower federal courts that Congress establishes, the Constitution means to exclude the exercise of that power by the other branches. Although judicial power belongs to the courts, they do not have *carte blanche* to hear all the types of cases that may arise. The authority of a court to decide particular cases is de-

termined by its *jurisdiction*, and jurisdiction is not self-executing.

Article III sets forth the types of jurisdiction that Congress may confer on the federal courts. Congress has discretion to determine which categories should be conferred. The constitutionally permissible jurisdiction of the federal courts extends to cases (1) arising under the Constitution, the laws of the United States, and U.S. treaties, (2) affecting ambassadors, public ministers, and consuls, (3) involving admiralty and maritime matters, (4) in which the United States is a party, (5) between two or more states, and (6) between citizens of different states. (Certain other categories are also included in this jurisdictional grant.)

In the 1789 Judiciary Act, Congress granted only limited jurisdiction to the district courts. Congress gave them exclusive jurisdiction over admiralty and maritime matters, suits against consuls and vice consuls, and crimes under federal law (state courts could not hear these cases). The federal courts had "concurrent" jurisdiction in suits involving aliens and in which the United States was a plaintiff (meaning these cases could also be brought in state courts). The federal courts also had concurrent jurisdiction in all cases where "diversity of citizenship existed"—in which a citizen of one state wished to sue a citizen of another.

Not until 1875 did Congress extend to the lower federal courts jurisdiction to hear cases "arising under" the Constitution, federal law, or treaties—what today is by far the most important part of federal jurisdiction. If an inventor wished to sue for infringement of his patent, he had to take his case to state court—his rights would be determined by federal law under state procedures in a state court, subject to review in the Supreme Court.

The Law That Applies

Once it is clear that a federal court has jurisdiction properly conferred on it of the type permitted under the Constitution, the question remains what law the judge may apply to the case at hand. To say that a court may hear "patent cases" or "maritime cases" does not by itself establish the rules that govern the case.

When the federal courts finally got jurisdiction to hear cases arising under federal law, the source of the law they applied was the federal law itself: the provisions of the Constitution, congressional enactments, or treaties. But could they create law themselves?

Here it is necessary to consider the enduring myth that "courts don't make laws"—or stated in the imperative—"courts shall not make laws." At first blush, that proposition might seem self-evident, or what is "separation of powers" all about? Congress makes law, after all; aren't the courts merely to declare how they apply in the cases at hand?

But matters have never been so simple. Historically, at common law, courts had the power to make law. For centuries, British common law judges supposed they were merely "finding" the law, not making it; no longer bemused by medieval notions, we today know better. Tort (accident) law is largely judge-made, as is a significant portion of contract law. The common law is subject to legislative oversight, at least these days: The legislatures are free to alter or reverse the future effect of a judge-made rule (although they don't often do so because it is so difficult to tell, from any single case, what the rule actually is).

Under the Constitution, the state courts remain common law courts, subject only to limitations in state constitutions. But the federal courts, like the rest of the federal government, are bodies of delegated powers, and they are not given general authority to make up law. So the Constitution did not create a *federal* common law, at least not a general federal common law. That means the federal courts must look to a congressional enactment, a treaty, or the Constitution to resolve the disputes that are brought before them. (This last statement should be qualified a bit. In laying out the jurisdiction that federal courts

may exercise, Article III did permit the courts to create certain limited, but important, types of federal common law. A major example is the admiralty and maritime jurisdiction, which gives federal courts considerable authority to develop rules of the sea and of the navigable inland waterways.)

So the state courts were free to develop the common law; the federal courts were not. That sounds simple. But it led to a perplexing problem—the kind of problem, one supposes, that only lawyers could dream up.

During most of the nineteenth century (from 1789 to 1875), the "diversity jurisdiction" was the most significant part of federal courts' power to hear cases. This was authority to hear cases between citizens of different states. This jurisdiction encompasses all the ordinary cases that make up the lifeblood of the state courts, like contract and accident cases. At a time when states were jealous of their sovereignty and might desire to discriminate on behalf of their citizens, the diversity provision was designed to protect a "foreign" litigant from local bias.

The question remained what law should the federal courts apply. Must they apply the law of the state in which they were sitting? You might suppose they would have to do just that, for what else is there that governs a case based on state law? Clearly, if the same case had been tried in the state court, which the litigants could agree to do, the state court would have to refer to state law.

At any rate, a federal statute seemed to suggest that state law must govern. The framers wished to ensure that state law was fairly applied to noncitizens as well as citizens. That purpose might be defeated if the federal courts applied some other law. So in the 1789 Judiciary Act, the first Congress specified that "the laws of the several states . . . shall be regarded as rules of decisions in trials at common law in the courts of the United States in cases where they apply." This provision was known as the "Rules of Decision Act."

For fifty-three years, this somewhat obscure language was taken to mean that federal courts had to apply state law in diversity cases. In more than one case, the Supreme Court insisted that the Rules of Decision Act was to be taken seriously; the federal courts could not go about inventing rules on their own. "The injustice," said Justice Bushrod Washington in 1814, "as well as the absurdity of the [federal courts] deciding by one rule, and the [state courts] deciding by another, would be too monstrous to find a place in any system of government."

But Justice Washington had not reckoned with the genius of Justice Joseph Story, the great legal scholar whom President Madison appointed to the Supreme Court in 1811 at the age of thirty-two. In 1842, Justice Story talked the Court into turning the Rules of Decision Act upside down.

The issue in the case before the Court was whether the payment of a negotiable bill in return for a promise to cancel a preexisting debt constituted a valid contract. In New York, where the case arose, the law was unclear. The legislature had never enacted a statute on the point and the state courts had given no guidance. Justice Story assumed the rule in New York was that no valid contract existed. Nevertheless, he said, the federal courts were not bound by the state rule.

He reasoned that the Rules of Decision Act bound the federal courts only to state *statutes*. Decisions of the courts, he said, are not "laws." In the absence of a "law" so defined, the Rules of Decision Act did not apply. That left the federal courts free to develop a "general commercial law." Story thus transformed the jurisdictional grant in diversity cases into a powerful source of federal lawmaking.

Not surprisingly, the new federal law often conflicted with state rules. It led to a complex patchwork of law whose benefits could be enjoyed only if you could get into the right courts. Story wanted the law to be the same in Boston as in Des Moines. What resulted was a law that could differ in Iowa for citizens and noncitizens.

Justice Joseph Story

Just such an anomaly occurred in the famous municipal bond cases in the 1860s. The Iowa Supreme Court declared that private bondholders could not collect principal or interest from Iowa municipalities because the bonds were invalid under the state constitution. Out-of-state bondholders had better luck: They could go to federal court, which ruled that as a matter of "federal common law" they could collect. The Supreme Court upheld this decision. The diversity jurisdiction was supposed to provide equal treatment for citizens and noncitizens alike. But here noncitizens fared better than Iowa citizens, who could not avail themselves of the diversity jurisdiction in federal court.

Why did Justice Story create a federal common law? Justice Robert H. Jackson gave the most compelling explanation a century later. He pointed out that the bulk of cases coming to federal courts invoked the diversity jurisdiction. If the judges were bound by state rules, "there was obviously little opportunity for a Federal judge to exercise the legal talents which he might possess unless he was free to do more than echo the 'last breath' of a state judge." It also seems likely that Story and others were mesmerized by the old medieval notion that judges "found" law. They believed a common law court's ruling was not the law itself, but merely the "evidence," of the law. If a state court decision was only "evidence," the federal court could look for better evidence by searching its own mind.

In 1938, the Supreme Court finally reversed Justice Story's conclusion, holding that as a matter of constitutional law, "there is no federal general common law." State court decisions, no less than state statutes, are the source of law in diversity cases.

Of course, in the commercial arena, Congress has independent constitutional authority to legislate, so that today much commercial law once left to the states has now been absorbed in federal law.

Moreover, federal statutory law having grown to monumental proportions, the federal courts now exercise something very much like common law jurisdiction when they are called on to construe and apply federal statutes. And in many noncommercial cases, the federal courts have created something like a federal "common law," resolving important questions about the relationship between the branches and between the government and citizens.

For example, the federal courts have on their own determined the law of judicial and executive "immunity" from suit. In many cases over the years, the Supreme Court has ruled that judges and prosecutors may not be sued for damages arising out of official acts. These decisions do not rest on the Constitution; Congress could enact laws permitting federal officials to be sued. (In 1982, in a non-Watergate-related suit against President Nixon, a sharply divided Supreme

Court declared that presidents are absolutely immune from private damage suits for official activities carried on while they were president.)

The Supreme Court's Jurisdiction

Article III gives the Supreme Court "original jurisdiction" of cases involving ambassadors, public ministers, and consuls and in which a state is a party. "Original jurisdiction" means the power to try a case in the first instance. Only in these types of cases is jurisdiction constitutionally vested in the Supreme Court: Congress may not remove it. The Supreme Court only rarely uses its power to try cases involving ambassadors, and generally avoids trying cases in which states are parties.

In all the other categories of cases, the Supreme Court's jurisdiction is "appellate," meaning it may

---

Founding Father

Gunning Bedford

Delaware

Gunning Bedford was born in Philadelphia in 1747, and died in Delaware, March 30, 1812. He graduated from Princeton in 1771, a classmate of James Madison's. He studied law in Pennsylvania, and was admitted to the bar there. He moved to Delaware where he was a member of the legislature, the state council, and a delegate to the 1785–1786 Continental Congress. He represented Delaware at the Annapolis Convention. At the Philadelphia Convention, he was known as "the fat delegate." From 1784 to 1789, he was attorney general of Delaware. Washington named him a judge for the Delaware district, a post he held until his death.

The old Supreme Court chamber in the basement of the Capitol.

hear appeals from lower courts, whether state or federal. This jurisdiction is not automatically vested, for Article III explicitly declares that the Court's appellate jurisdiction is subject to "such exceptions and under such regulations as the Congress shall make." In other words, Congress has the power to limit the categories of appeals that the Supreme Court may hear.

In the 1789 Judiciary Act, Congress extended to the Supreme Court some but not all of the constitutional grant of appellate jurisdiction. It could review decisions of the lower federal courts in civil cases when the matter in dispute exceeded $2,000 (the bulk of these were diversity cases). It could not review federal criminal cases.

Its most significant appellate jurisdiction, however, was that over state court decisions. The Supreme Court could review decisions of state courts whenever they held (1) against the validity of a federal statute or treaty, (2) in favor of a state statute against the claim that it was contrary to federal law, or (3) against a claim based on a right enjoyed under the Consti-

tution or federal law. This power, never repealed, has enabled the Supreme Court to preserve the supremacy of federal law.

Since 1789, Congress has on several occasions markedly extended the appellate jurisdiction of the Supreme Court, commensurate with the extension of lower court jurisdiction. Under the Judges' Bill of 1925, Congress gave the Court virtually complete authority to determine which cases it would hear on appeal. (A complete description of federal jurisdiction is too complex to present here.)

If Congress giveth, may it taketh away? Congressional control of the Supreme Court's jurisdiction is not an issue for antiquarians. It is an important question in the current debate over the Court's role in American society.

Article III, Section 2, says that Congress may make exceptions to and regulate the Court's appellate jurisdiction as it chooses. If that provision means what it says, Congress has a potent check and balance against judicial action. To avoid a judicial declaration in a particular area, simply revoke the Court's jurisdiction to hear that type of case. For example, if Congress does not like the Court's abortion rulings, why not withdraw from the Court all power to hear abortion cases?

The only direct precedent for such an action goes back to Reconstruction. In the Habeas Corpus Act of 1863, Congress approved Lincoln's suspension of the great writ and provided legal shelter against state attempts to discharge civilian prisoners in military custody. The following year, an army court in Indiana sentenced a civilian antiwar activist, Lambden P. Milligan, to death for disloyalty. In 1866, the Supreme Court ruled that the trial was unconstitutional. Congress may not subject civilians to military tribunals and suspend habeas corpus in areas, like Indiana, where the civilian courts remained open. In ringing words, Justice Davis declared for the five-to-four majority: "The Constitution . . . is a law for rulers and people, equally in war and peace, and covers with the shield of its protection all classes of men at all times, and under all circumstances."

In 1868, another habeas corpus case came to the Supreme Court, this time from Mississippi, where William McCardle, an antiblack Vicksburg publisher, preached violent opposition to Reconstruction. The army arrested him for violating the Reconstruction law requiring all to keep the peace. McCardle's lawyers sought his release on a writ of habeas corpus. Angered at the Court's *Milligan* decision and desiring to keep the Court from pronouncing any further against Reconstruction, Congress passed a law withdrawing jurisdiction from the Supreme Court in any habeas corpus case, even those pending in the Court.

Even though McCardle's case had already been argued, the Court dismissed the appeal: "Without jurisdiction the court cannot proceed at all in any case. Jurisdiction is power to declare the law, and when it ceases to exist, the only function remaining to the court is that of announcing the fact and dismissing the cause."

Arguing from this case, modern congressional opponents of the Supreme Court have in recent years proposed a number of bills that would in effect withdraw the Court's jurisdiction to hear cases involving reapportionment, school prayer, confessions in criminal prosecutions, busing, abortion, and gender discrimination in military service. Whether the *McCardle* case controls these modern attempts to curb jurisdiction is open to doubt—or at least to serious argument.

The gist of at least one argument is that congressional powers under the Constitution are "*always* subject to the limitation that they may not be exercised in a way that violates other specific provisions of the Constitution." If Congress under the exceptions and regulations clause could limit the Court's jurisdiction however it chose, it could effectively block *any* provision of the Constitution from being enforced, including the provisions of the Bill of Rights that impose specific limitations on congressional power to act. "Federal damage actions could be made available to whites only; injunctions against censorship could be limited to those who publish from a federally approved list." Other, more subtle points and counterpoints have been advanced, and all we can say here is that the issue is unsettled—and may remain forever unsettled as long as Congress leaves well enough alone.

Judicial Review: The Court's Position as Constitutional Arbiter

The discussion so far has been like a game of baseball without the umpire. It could be played, but would the catcher count his pitcher's strikes? We would hear little controversy over the Supreme Court if it did not exercise the one power that sets it apart from courts around the world: the power to declare laws unconstitutional. A court to review the fairness of trials and the adequacy of lower courts' construction of statutes would continue to be essential, but it would excite little comment, for the reach of all decisions would be subject to legislative reversal. Congress, like Parliament, would be supreme, and that would be the end of that.

But under the Constitution as it has been interpreted for nearly two centuries, all the courts in America, state as well as federal, have the power in appropriate cases to declare legislative enactments unconstitutional. The most scorching criticism is aimed at the Supreme Court because that is where the final decision rests, not because it alone has the authority to void statutes.

The Supreme Court squarely claimed this awesome power in the most celebrated case in American history, *Marbury v. Madison*, the only case that continually makes its way into high school history textbooks.

Five days before President Adams's term expired and Jefferson was inaugurated, Congress passed a bill giving Adams a chance to appoint forty-two justices of the peace in the District of Columbia. Adams rushed the names of his nominees to the Senate, which confirmed them on his last day in office. The new judges' commissions were hurriedly prepared by Adams's secretary of state, who happened to be John Marshall, although he had been sworn in as chief justice of the United States a month earlier. But time was short, and at midnight on March 3, the last moment of Adams's term, four commissions had not been delivered. One was to go to William Marbury.

The next day, Thomas Jefferson, in one of his first acts as president, forbade their delivery. Although Marbury had been confirmed, it was thought he could not serve without the judicial commission. So Marbury and three others sought a writ of mandamus—a court order—requiring the new secretary of state, James Madison, to hand over the papers.

Marbury filed his suit in the Supreme Court of the United States, under a provision in the Judiciary Act of 1789 that gave the Court jurisdiction to issue writs of mandamus to other courts or to government officials. So alarmed was Jefferson at the possibility that the Court would grant the "midnight judges" relief

Five days before his term expired, President John Adams (above) nominated William Marbury as a justice of the peace.

that he persuaded Congress to abolish the Court's term; Marbury's cause was put off a year.

On February 9, 1803, the case at last came before the justices, who took testimony and evidence on the existence of the commissions and heard arguments on the legal issues. Less than three weeks later, on February 24, Chief Justice Marshall announced the decision on behalf of the entire Court.

"The Court seemed to face Hobson's choice," Archibald Cox has written. "To dismiss the case would apparently acquiesce in the Jeffersonian position [that elected representatives were supreme]. To issue the writ would invite President Jefferson and Secretary Madison to ignore it—a step they surely could and would have taken—while the country laughed at the Court's pretensions. Either result would confirm the independence of the Executive and Legislative from

Judicial control." But Marshall neatly sidestepped the dilemma.

Three issues had to be decided, Marshall said. First was whether Marbury was entitled to the commission. Did the Senate's confirmation and the president's signature on the commission suffice to vest the office or did Marbury need the piece of paper? Marshall held that the office had vested and Marbury was entitled to have Madison seal the commissions and hand them over.

The second question was whether the laws of the United States afforded Marbury a remedy, given that his rights had been violated. Again Marshall said yes. "Where a specific duty is assigned by law, and individual rights depend upon the performance of that duty, . . . the individual has a right to resort to the laws of his country for a remedy."

Then came the problem. Marbury was entitled to the commission, and a writ of mandamus was a legal remedy to compel Madison to perform his duty. But was the Supreme Court the proper court to issue it? Now the chief justice said no.

Marshall's reason was simple. The Judiciary Act of 1789 empowered the Court to issue writs of mandamus "in cases warranted by the principals and usages of law." But the Constitution says that the Court's *original* jurisdiction (that is, the jurisdiction to try cases) extends only to those involving ambassadors and states. Marbury's was assuredly not such a case. For the Court otherwise to involve itself with a writ of mandamus, it would have to do so by reviewing a lower court's issuance (or denial) of the writ, because Article III limits the Court's judicial power in all other cases to appeals. But this was not a case on appeal. The Judiciary Act thus gave the Court more power than the Constitution allowed. The act was therefore unconstitutional. Being unconstitutional, it could not be enforced. Marbury's case was dismissed; he would have to seek relief in a lower court.

Now, the Constitution does not say that the Court may rule on the constitutionality of federal laws or, for that matter, of any law. True, the supremacy clause in Article VI says that the Constitution and federal law are the supreme law of the land, but at most that supports the Court's power to void state laws as unconstitutional.

Marshall had no doubts. "Happily," he said, the question "is not of an intricacy proportional to its interest." The Constitution created a government of limited powers. For the Court to close its eyes to the Constitution in the face of a conflicting law would "subvert the very foundation of all written constitutions." To what end are judges required to take an oath to support the Constitution if they are not to read it or heed it when sitting in court? The Constitution would be a "solemn" mockery if judges had to abide by laws that violated its terms.

Jefferson was the winner, but it was not a victory he relished. His wily opponent had won a prize far greater than a seat for Mr. Marbury. The chief justice secured for the Court the power to pronounce the final word on the Constitution, as we can see by the numerous topics in this book. When we talk about the Constitution, we talk mainly about the Supreme Court's Constitution.

From our vantage point, the Court's role in passing on the constitutionality of legislation seems so obvious as to make its legitimacy unremarkable. Isn't that what the Court is supposed to do? In fact, the matter did not seem free of doubt, and during the year that political leaders in Washington waited for the Court to resume, the propriety of a court's striking down legislation was constant table talk.

Although the Constitution itself does not say that it is superior to a federal statute (the supremacy clause is no help here), Marshall was undoubtedly right in holding that a law that conflicts with the Constitution is void, or else what purpose does the Constitution serve? What was the problem, then?

Just this: The Constitution is by no means as clear that the *judiciary* has the power to make such rulings. For all the Constitution says, Congress has as strong a claim to determine the constitutionality of its laws. Should not the elected representatives of the people be presumed to have a dignity equal to that of the unelected justices in pronouncing our fundamental law? Although the issue is not free from historical doubt, it has been historically settled.

During the Philadelphia Convention, Edmund Randolph of Virginia had proposed that the president and federal judges make up a Council of Revision with power to review all congressional enactments. The idea was rejected. Opposing it, Elbridge Gerry said (as Madison recorded it) that the judiciary "will have a sufficient check against encroachments on their own department by their exposition of the laws, which involved a power of deciding on their Constitutionality. In some States the Judges had actually set aside laws as being against the Constitution. This was done too with general approbation." Gerry's proposition does not support a wholesale power, however, for his comment seems to suggest that the Court could void laws only when they were aimed at the judiciary itself (as in Marbury's case). This reading implies that at most the Convention thought the Court would necessarily rule on and refuse to follow laws that unconstitutionally interfere with the judicial power—not laws that violate other constitutional provisions. This was a point Madison had explicitly made at the convention. The Court should have jurisdiction over constitutional cases only when "limited to cases of a Judiciary Nature. The right of expounding the Constitution in cases not of this nature ought not to be given to that Department."

Alexander Hamilton was less modest in his appreciation of judicial review. In *The Federalist* No. 78, he spelled out essentially what Marshall would conclude fifteen years later:

> The complete independence of the courts of justice is peculiarly essential in a limited Constitution. By a limited Constitution, I understand one which contains certain specified exceptions to the legislation authority; such, for instance, as that it shall pass no bills of attainder, no

ex post facto laws, and the like. Limitations of this kind can be preserved in practice in no other way than through the medium of courts of justice, whose duty it must be to declare all acts contrary to the manifest tenor of the Constitution void. Without this, all the reservations of particular rights or privileges would amount to nothing.

> There is no position which depends on clearer principles than that every act of a delegated authority, contrary to the tenor of the commission under which it is exercised, is void. No legislative act, therefore, contrary to the Constitution, can be valid. . . .

> If it be said that the legislative body are themselves the constitutional judges of their own powers and that the construction they put upon them is conclusive upon the other departments it may be answered that this cannot be the natural presumption where it is not to be collected from any particular provisions in the Constitution. It is not otherwise to be supposed that the Constitution could intend to enable the representatives of the people to substitute their *will* to that of their constituents. It is far more rational to suppose that the courts were designed to be an intermediate body between the people and the legislature in order, among other things, to keep the latter within the limits assigned to their authority. The interpretation of the laws is the proper and peculiar province of the courts. A constitution is, in fact, and must be regarded by the judges as, a fundamental law. It therefore belongs to them to ascertain its meaning as well as the meaning of any particular act proceeding from the legislative body. If there should happen to be an irreconcilable variance between the two, that which has the superior obligation and validity ought, of course, to be preferred; or, in other words, the Constitution ought to be preferred to the statute, the intention of the people to the intention of their agents.

However, as Leonard W. Levy demonstrates, Hamilton's great pronouncement is less persuasive than it seems as historical evidence that the framers generally agreed with the power he was advancing. In discussing the powers of Congress in *Federalist* No. 33, he noted that the only judge of its powers under the necessary and proper clause would be Congress itself or the electorate. *Federalist* No. 78, says Levy, was

Where the Court Sits

The United States Supreme Court now occupies a huge marble building at One First Street, Northeast, in Washington. Its elaborate façades and monumental interior spaces have led critics to label it a "marble palace" and a "marble mausoleum." Chief Justice Harlan Fiske Stone called it "almost bombastically pretentious." It was, he said, "wholly inappropriate for a quiet group of old boys such as the Supreme Court." The justices would be, said one of them, "nine black beetles in the Temple of Karnak."

Opened in 1935, it was the Court's first permanent home. Until then, the justices had made do with a host of quarters not entirely their own. The Court first met, in 1790, in New York's Royal Exchange Building, at Broad and Water streets, now in the heart of the financial district. In 1791, the federal government having moved to Philadelphia, the Court met in City Hall on the first floor of the east wing. In 1796, however, a municipal court was scheduled to hold cases in the space, and so the federal jurists were bumped upstairs.

In 1800, the government moved again, this time to Washington, D.C. But no provision was made for the Supreme Court. Its first term in the new capital was held in an east basement room of the Capitol. During the next decade, because of renovations and other exigencies, the Court found itself in the library once occupied by the House of Representatives and then, to avoid the library's draft on winter days, in Long's Tavern. Finally, in 1810, the Court convened in a basement room under the Senate chamber. The room was designed especially for the Supreme Court. The War of 1812 interrupted proceedings, and the Court again moved, this time with Congress, and even settled into a house rented from Daniel Carroll, until it finally returned to the restored basement chamber in 1819. Chief Justice Marshall announced the opinion in the *Dartmouth College* case on the day he and his brethren returned to the Capitol. There the Court stayed until 1860.

During the Civil War, the Court moved to the old Senate chamber on the Capitol's first floor. In these quarters it remained for seventy-five years. The courtroom itself was capacious, but the justices' adjacent space was miserably cramped, and none had individual office space.

The Supreme Court building now provides each justice with a three-room office suite, and it also contains many ornate rooms for library, conference, staff offices, and other private and public functions. The courthouse was built at a cost of less than $10 million, probably fifteen times less than what it would cost to build today. Indeed, so efficient were its contractors that they actually returned to the treasury $94,000 of the funds appropriated for its construction and furnishings—an astonishing feat, at least to a modern era accustomed to the inexorable law of "cost overruns."

Hamilton's shrewd response to an anti-Constitution series of articles arousing fears that the Court would tyrannize the states; Hamilton showed that the Court could be a bulwark against *congressional* attempts to dominate the states. Still, if the Court on Hamilton's thesis had power to act in the states' interests, it had power to pass on the constitutional validity of any federal law, whatever its aim.

The records of debate being inconclusive, we could look to the practices of the day, if there had been any. If the courts were regularly in the habit of invalidating laws on constitutional grounds, that would strongly presume the founders' intentions. In one or two instances, judges did so, but it was no habit, indicating at most that these decisions were not made with any settled expectation of power.

Other shreds of evidence suggest, however, that Marshall's conclusion was no "usurpation," as has sometimes been charged since then. The First Congress—a particularly important one from this perspective, since in it sat many, including Madison, who had written the Constitution—stipulated in the Judiciary Act of 1789 that the Court had jurisdiction to hear cases in which state statutes were questioned as violating the Constitution. If that power was easily conceded, it is not a great leap—though a leap, to be sure—to the power to consider the constitutionality of federal law. Moreover, during the years between the Judiciary Act and *Marbury v. Madison*, the issue was frequently raised, and many on both sides of the aisle in Congress, Federalist and Republican, expressed the belief that the Court would settle the constitutionality of legislation.

In any event, as Levy says, "long acquiescence by the people and their representatives has legitimated judicial review. It was not 'imposed by self-anointed fiat on an unwilling people.' . . . [It] exists by the tacit consent of the governed."

Far less troubling was the Court's conclusion in 1816 that it has the power to pass on the validity of state laws under the federal Constitution. The supremacy clause declares unmistakably that the Constitution is superior to all state law if the two conflict, and state judges are bound by oath to support the federal Constitution. From the very beginning, Congress gave the Supreme Court jurisdiction to hear on appeal cases calling into question the validity of a state law under the Constitution. No respectable challenge has ever been made to this power. As Justice Holmes put it in a speech much later:

> I do not think the United States would come to an end if we lost our power to declare an Act of Congress void. I do think the Union would be imperiled if we could not make that declaration as to the laws of the several States. For one in my place sees how often a local policy prevails with those who are not trained to national views and how often action is taken that embodies what the Commerce Clause was meant to end.

Judicial Rulings and the Separation of Powers

The question remains whether and to what degree the other branches are bound by judicial rulings (constitutional or otherwise). If separation of powers means anything, it might be supposed to mean that one branch may not instruct another how not to act. Moreover, though *separation* connotes sharing, even sharing has its limits. Thus the president may veto a congressional enactment, but Congress is empowered to override the veto. May Congress override a judicial declaration?

On a nonconstitutional plane, Congress is free to disagree with the courts' interpretation of federal law, but only for the future, not to defeat a right recognized in a particular case, since to do so would be to invade the judicial power of the courts to decide cases.

Suppose a federal law entitles Vietnam veterans to certain benefits. The law requires, say, the veteran to have "served" thirteen months in Vietnam. Now assume the Veterans Administration, which administers the benefits program, denies a veteran the benefit because his thirteen months of combat was interrupted by a one-week emergency leave back home to attend his mother's funeral. The veteran sues the VA, and the court rules in his favor. Congress may not reverse the judgment. But Congress may certainly amend the law for future cases, making clear it did not intend to include service interrupted by home leaves in the benefit program. (However, if the law had been enacted before the veteran's service it would be treated as having "vested" the right to the benefit to all veterans in the plaintiff's shoes, and Congress would not be permitted to deny the benefit in like cases thereafter.) Now suppose instead the court ruled that the veteran was not entitled to the benefit. Nothing in the Constitution bars Congress from subsequently enacting a "private" bill telling the Treasury to give the veteran the benefit, nor from amending the law to give all veterans similarly situated the same benefit.

But once the Supreme Court has authoritatively construed a constitutional provision, Congress and the executive branch are bound by that interpretation in future like cases. If the Supreme Court rules that the Fourth Amendment requires a search warrant before federal agents can tap a citizen's phone, the attorney general is not free to decide that the ruling does not apply the next time he wishes to tap a phone. Since *Marbury v. Madison*, that has been the constitutional understanding.

As fundamental as this principle is, it should not be bent to service beyond its contours. A judicial decision is not a legal pronouncement on the wisdom of the challenged law or execution action. When the Court *upholds* the constitutionality of a federal policy, the ruling neither prevents Congress from repealing the policy nor requires Congress to undertake it in the future. And that means presidents and Congress may independently construe the Constitution themselves, within the limits of their powers.

A commonly cited example is President Jackson's message in 1832 vetoing an act extending the life of the Bank of the United States. In the seminal 1819 case of *McCulloch v. Maryland*, Chief Justice Marshall had upheld the constitutionality of the act creating the bank. Jackson disagreed, strongly voicing his opinion that the bank was unconstitutional. Because presidents have constitutional power to veto legislation, he was not bound by the Court's interpretation in vetoing the bill to extend the bank's life. *McCulloch* stands for the proposition that Congress acted within the scope of its powers in passing a bill establishing the bank. But nothing in such a ruling compels the president to sign a bill creating one. No court may tell the president that he has exercised his veto (or has failed to exercise it) unconstitutionally. Likewise,

1833 cartoon depicts President Jackson's battle over extending the life of the Bank of the United States. Jackson, as a cat, is seen "clearing Uncle Sam's Barn of Bank and Clay rats" to protect his "capital Corn Crib."

Congress may constitutionally enact antitrust laws, but its determination to repeal the Sherman Act would not be constitutionally faulty, even if the sponsors of the repealing legislation all stood up and professed their belief that antitrust laws are unconstitutional.

These situations aside, when the Court talks, Congress and the president (and the states) must listen. Though the principle is well established, it is not always heeded, even on the eve of the bicentennial.

Suppose Congress enacts, and the president signs, a Competition in Contracting Act (CICA), which permits the comptroller general to investigate claims, at a contractor's request, that the Pentagon has illegitimately awarded a contract without competitive bidding. The act tells the Pentagon not to pay the contractor who got the sweetheart deal while the comptroller general is investigating. This law does not please the Pentagon. The president signed the bill only because canny representatives attached it as part of another bill that the president could not afford to veto. What recourse does the president or secretary of defense have?

The Reagan administration, faced with just that situation, decided that CICA was unconstitutional. So far, so good, for the president is sworn to "preserve, protect, and defend" the Constitution. Because he was tactically forced to sign a bill does not mean that he must defend its constitutionality. If the sweetheart contractor sues for his pay, government lawyers are free to argue that the law is unconstitutional. (The constitutional problem the administration perceived was the same that sent Gramm-Rudman, the budget-balancing bill, to the Supreme Court.)

The Justice Department, however, did not wait for a case. It "declared" the law unconstitutional, and the budget director ordered government agencies to ignore the act. That is skirting close to the edge of a constitutional canyon—some might argue that the department's declaration hurls the administration into the abyss, for the president is sworn to "take care that the laws be faithfully executed." Still, a clearly unconstitutional law is not something the president would want to insist on enforcing.

But now a court passes judgment on the law. In a case brought by a disappointed contractor, the court says that the law is indeed constitutional. May the government continue to refuse to enforce the law?

Attorney General Edwin Meese thought so. In testimony before Congress, the attorney general denied the authority of a federal district court to pass on the constitutionality of the law and insisted on the administration's right to ignore it. This bizarre view was too extreme for Congress and courts. The district court ordered Meese to comply, and the U.S. Court of Appeals ultimately affirmed it. More persuasive authority for the attorney general, apparently, was a threat by the House Judiciary Committee to cut off funding for Meese's office, including money for his own and his assistants' salaries. Meese backed down and ordered the law enforced.

Political Questions

Even when constitutional rights are asserted, some questions are too political for the courts to give legal answers. This "political question" doctrine is another way of saying that over certain issues the Constitution commits complete discretion to the other branches. No matter how justiciable the claim seems—the parties have been injured, they have standing, the cause is ripe for appeal, it will not be moot before the decision is rendered, the claim is clearly based on a constitutional provision—the courts will dismiss it because they are the wrong place to take the grievance.

The earliest enunciation of the political question doctrine arose from Dorr's Rebellion in Rhode Island in 1842. When independence was declared, all the states except Rhode Island set about writing constitutions. Rhode Island retained its original charter, granted by King Charles II in 1663. The charter severely restricted suffrage and seriously malapportioned the legislature. In 1841, after thirty years of refusal by the legislature to reform the constitution, a militant group called the Rhode Island Suffrage Association held a convention and submitted a "People's Constitution" to an electorate broader than that permitted under the charter. At the same time, the legislature, now alarmed, put to the enfranchised voters a more restrictive constitution. The People's Constitution was ratified. The question then was which group of people represented the "people."

The existing government outlawed any government under the new constitution. But the Suffrage Association elected its president, Thomas Wilson Dorr, head of the new government. The two groups squared off, ready to fight. Ultimately, Dorr's government collapsed, and Dorr was convicted of treason, though his cause prevailed when within months a third reformist constitution was adopted.

During the rebellion early in 1842, each side sought the military assistance of President Tyler under the guaranty clause of Article IV. That clause says that the United States "shall guarantee" a "republican form of government" to every state. Tyler equivocated. Had events turned bloody, he probably would have dispatched federal troops to the fray. But as it happened, the appearance of a threat was enough to prevent a conflagration.

The following year, a test case wended its way to the Supreme Court. A shoemaker named Martin Luther had served as a "moderator" at the People's Convention in violation of martial law proclaimed by the charter government. He fled to Massachusetts. Luther Borden, the head of a government-inspired posse, raided his home and terrorized his female relatives. Luther sued Borden for trespass. Borden claimed his actions were authorized by the government. Luther claimed that Dorr's government was the only valid one, hence Borden's actions were unauthorized.

Thomas Wilson Dorr

In the Supreme Court, Chief Justice Taney declared that the Constitution put the issue beyond the Court's competence: Under Article IV, "it rests with Congress to decide what government is the established one in a State. . . . And its decision is binding on every other department of the government, and could not be questioned in a judicial tribunal."

The political question doctrine was the source of the Court's long reluctance to intervene in cases of malapportioned legislatures, a reluctance finally overcome in 1962. The Court has suggested that questions concerning the ratification of amendments to the Constitution are political and are to be answered solely by Congress. In a case distantly analogous to *Luther v. Borden*, the Supreme Court refused to intervene in a dispute over the credentials of delegates to the 1972 Democratic National Convention, reversing a lower court that had seated one faction and suggesting that the proper forum for resolving the dispute was the convention itself. And the Court steadfastly refused to become embroiled in considering the constitutionality of the arguably undeclared war in Vietnam, again on the ground that this was a political question for Congress and the president to resolve between them.

Judicial Policy Making and American Democracy

The issue Marshall settled in *Marbury* was the simple one. The much harder question is what limits are to be imposed on the Court's power to review. What logic divines the scope and meaning of contested provisions in the Constitution? In 1936, Justice Owen J. Roberts said it was all very simple, really:

> When an act of Congress is appropriately challenged in the courts as not conforming to the constitutional mandate the judicial branch of the Government has only one duty—to lay the article of the Constitution which is invoked beside the statute which is challenged and to decide whether the latter squares with the former.

Today, Roberts's remarks should be remembered as a mere *jeu d'esprit*, for no one doubts that any case that could be decided by laying the text of a statute next to the Constitution would have been settled in some place other than the Supreme Court. The difficult questions that reach the Court turn on vague phrases or constitutional silences. And when the justices are not simply engaged in close textual analysis, they become policy makers, no matter how they describe what they are doing.

The objection to this role is that it is not democratic. Our institutions are majoritarian, according to the standard critique. Unelected officials who serve for life should not substitute their values for those of the people's elected representatives, especially when the judicial decision cannot easily be reversed, for in constitutional matters, the Court's opinion is ex cathedra, and may be reversed only by constitutional amendment (or when a later Court changes its mind, as occasionally happens). "For myself," said Learned Hand, one of our greatest jurists, "it would be most irksome to be ruled by a bevy of Platonic Guardians, even if I knew how to choose them, which I assuredly do not. If they were in charge, I should miss the stimulus of living in a society where I have, at least theoretically, some part in the direction of public affairs."

The danger is not merely that the judges will thwart majority will. A far more insidious peril is that we will forget as a people the calling of politics and the necessity of political action. Judicial review may sap the moral sense that we the people are responsible for the conduct of public affairs and that what we and our representatives do matters. It might even tempt—it certainly has tempted—legislators into enacting laws they know are unconstitutional in order to feed the fears and paranoia of their constituents, confident that the laws will be overturned later on by the vigilant courts.

Judicial review might thus pervert self-government into buck passing. Said James Bradley Thayer, professor at Harvard Law School, in 1901: "The tendency of a common and easy resort to this great function [of judicial review], now lamentably too common, is to dwarf the political capacity of the people, and to deaden its sense of moral responsibility." To delegate responsibility for constitutional judgment to the courts is thus to seem to remove it from ourselves.

The "countermajoritarian force" of judicial review has long been pressed, and not simply by know-nothings eager to dispense with judicial restraints on legislative overreaction to disturbances in the body politic. Nor is the antidemocratic argument confined to one political persuasion; it has been as forcefully made by liberals as conservatives, because in different eras the Supreme Court has been infected by different social policy bugs. Once it found economic regulations to be gross violations of a Constitution designed to protect property, and the liberals winced. Today, or at least recently, it has found social regulations no less violative, and conservatives whine.

Let us admit, as anyone must, that judicial review is not majoritarian, if by that term we mean decisions made by those responsible to an electorate. The Court's constitutional policy-making changes, not immediately with elections, but more slowly with the random departures of aging justices and the accident of who happens to be president at those moments to name successors. But it is question-begging to assume that judicial review is illegitimate simply because the Court is not a majoritarian institution. The American system is not dedicated, nor has it ever been dedicated, to a strict and thoroughgoing rule by majority. The American political system is a complex mechanism that for two hundred years has operated through a host of governmental institutions that check and temper the power of temporary majorities to rule at the moment of their dominance.

The most obvious kind of majoritarianism is direct democracy, and for the most part we have rejected it in its town meeting form. Even our representative institutions are not entirely majoritarian; often they are not so at all. The rules of parliamentary procedure employed in both houses of Congress often thwart the majority will. Determined minorities can and do prevent even large majorities from passing legislation. For decades, the threat of a southern filibuster in the Senate kept from the floor civil rights legislation that would clearly have become law. That is not majoritarianism.

For many decades, besides, large numbers of Americans were barred from voting. Was that majoritarian? Large numbers of Americans do not vote now (in part, though not solely, because registration procedures remain something of a scandal), so that many national leaders take office with something less than a majority of the vote. Is that majoritarian?

Legislating is not an easy business; we are safer with representatives who must listen to the arguments of competing interests and attempt the compromises that keep us all alive than with ourselves at the levers of an electronic whim-registering machine. A mob inflamed by momentary passion never thinks straight; a legislature may not either, but it has a greater chance of coming to its senses.

Even so, legislators by and large register voter interests, and to the extent they do only that, we are all impoverished. Representatives should not be simple tuning forks. We need legislative leaders, not legislative followers. Occasionally, a president may advise the public of dangers and problems, but you can consult most State of the Union addresses and rarely find mention of anything wrong (unless the president has just begun his term and can blame it on his predecessor). Occasionally, an outgoing president will warn against some particularly potent threat, as Washington did about foreign entanglements and Eisenhower about the military-industrial complex. But generally, presidents and others who spoil the secret that the fault lies in us sooner or later fall out of grace, as Jimmy Carter did when he spoke of national malaise or Richard Nixon when he chided the American public for being like children. We are no better off for that. Our representatives too infrequently give us moral leadership. They generally refrain from arguing with their constituency, trying to persuade us of what must be done, although such persuasion can sensibly come from those uniquely situated to see all the forces that must be balanced and the nuances of the problems that must be resolved.

Without the threat of a Court looking over the legislative shoulder, the situation might be even worse. It can remind the legislator that some things are best resisted in the legislative chambers. For all the irresponsible legislators who might be tempted to vote for an unconstitutional measure to placate constituents, morally untroubled because they know the Court will rescue the nation, there may be an equal number of responsible legislators who simply need the shadow of judicial review to stiffen their backbones and to prompt them to tell their constituents why this will never do. The reality of judicial review can keep the legislators' eyes focused on policy making within constitutional bounds, for why waste time, and chance results, on a law that might well be overturned?

These are empirical questions, which cannot be answered by speculation. But it is far from clear that the countermajoritarian tendency of judicial review is, from that fact alone, detrimental to the commonweal.

Ought the Court, then, be free to act however it wishes? No one supposes that. The Court's role is not to decide what is wisest, not to cut a new Constitution from new cloth, ignoring the one we have, but to render decisions that are fashioned in some

way from the Constitution we have inherited and amended.

In what way? The central debate has always been loudest over the method by which the Court has carried out its function of judicial review. Various schools of jurisprudence have mapped out what to them has seemed the best approach: strict construction versus loose construction, intent of the framers versus the living Constitution, and today's constitutional buzz words, "interpretivism" versus "noninterpretivism."

Nuances aside, these pairs revolve around a basic concern: that the Court should (or should not) stick closely to the constitutional text. Those who favor strict construction, the necessity for interpreting only the words of the text, say that the Constitution is what the framers wrote. The Court should not look for values or ideas somehow encapsulated in the framers' phrases. It should stick to the plain meaning.

Many difficulties attend this jurisprudence of strict construction. Many phrases have no "plain meaning." Had the framers wished to express a meaning plainly, they could have done so. They chose, instead, sweeping, open-ended phrases. What did they mean when they said: "Congress shall make no law respecting an establishment of religion?" That is not plain. Little in the Constitution is plain, and that which is plain has rarely been the subject of controversy. Apparently, the government in two hundred years has never violated the Third Amendment; it says (figuratively) that a man's home is his castle and therefore soldiers can't be quartered there during peacetime unless the owner consents (or during wartime unless Congress does). That's clear enough, but little in the Constitution is that clear.

If the Court cannot always refer to plain meaning, then perhaps the justices should let the framers' *intentions* govern. Again, though, recovering their intentions is not easy (Chapter 15). A more insidious problem lurks in the jurisprudence of original intentions. If we are true to the point, we should insist on the governance of intentions, not what the framers said their intentions were. Many people will say many things to accomplish their ends; the scholastics, we are told, would cross their fingers so that the lie they were telling would not really count. Perhaps to win approval, the framers, or some of them, disguised their true intentions that the Constitution be an open-ended document. The words do not foreclose that possibility. Perhaps they intended that we not be bound by their intentions:

> One perpetrates no violence upon logic or known historical facts by assuming that the Founding Fathers *intended . . .* to empower the Court to serve as the Founders' surrogate for the indefinite future—interpreting the Constitution not as they themselves would have directed if they had been consulted in 1787, but as is thought right *by men who accepted the Founders' political philosophy— their commitment to self-government and the open society— and consider themselves obligated to effectuate that philosophy in the America of their own day.*

Anyway, *whose* intention is to govern? The Constitutional Convention, like the First Congress that drafted the Bill of Rights and the Thirty-ninth Congress that drafted the Fourteenth Amendment, did not have a solitary "intention." Different members had different intentions, and some, no doubt, had no intentions at all. And is it the *framers'* intentions that count, or those who ratified? That is why looking to history, the remedy for the vagueness of phrases, is so rarely helpful. History is not a dictionary; it is as much a repository of ambiguity as the phrases that are its external deposit.

No less significant, most of the problems that engage our attention today are not those to which the framers had given any thought. They could not have contemplated the impact of prayers in public schools because they did not have public schools. They could not have understood the potential reach of the search warrant provision because they did not know about electronic surveillance devices.

That we cannot know the framers' intentions—that they may not have had an intention to govern a par-

The Supreme Court's Caseload

Here is a brief accounting of the Supreme Court's modern caseload (the statistics are from its 1984–1985 term).

Total number of cases disposed of: 4,269.
Number of cases remaining on docket at term's end: 737.
Cases disposed of on original docket (cases between states): 8.
Cases disposed of on the merits on appellate docket: 226.
Appeals and petitions for review denied, dismissed, or withdrawn from appellate docket: 1,953.
Review granted as a percentage of appellate docket: 11.1.
Cases disposed of on the merits on miscellaneous docket (cases filed in forma pauperis; that is, unpaid cases): 32.
Appeals and petitions for review denied, dismissed, or withdrawn from miscellaneous docket: 2050.
Review granted as a percentage of miscellaneous docket: 1.1.
Number of opinions of Court: 151.
Number of cases decided by opinion whose principal issue was constitutional: 64.
Number of concurring opinions in all cases disposed of by opinion on the merits: 62.
Number of dissents in cases disposed of on the merits: 117.
Number of 5–4 decisions: 19.
Percentage of unanimous opinions or those with concurring opinions but with no dissents: 40.4.
Percentage of cases reviewed on writ of certiorari reversed by Court: 45.4.

ticular case—is not an argument for scrapping the language of the Constitution. To say that we cannot rely on founding intentions is not to say that the Supreme Court is free to disregard text. Judicial review is review of the Constitution. But the problem recurs: What do the words mean?

The debate over the canons of constitutional construction has not been nor ever will be settled. A sophisticated version of that debate today pits "interpretivists" against "noninterpretivists." The interpretivist believes that "judges deciding constitutional issues should confine themselves to enforcing norms that are stated or clearly implicit in the written Constitution." As Judge Robert H. Bork has put it: "Where constitutional materials do not clearly specify the value to be preferred, there is no principled way to prefer any claimed human value to any other. . . . There is no way of deciding [human rights questions] other than by reference to some system of moral or ethical values that has no objective or intrinsic validity of its own and about which men can and do differ."

Interpretivists differ among themselves in how far the text can be stretched. Some give a more expansive reading to, say, the First Amendment than others, but both would deny the validity of a ruling that finds, for example, a "right of privacy" lurking in the "penumbras" of various constitutional provisions (Chapter 13).

Interpretivism describes a judicial philosophy, not a particular political philosophy. Interpretivists may hold generally conservative political views, like Judge Bork, or liberal ones, like Justice Hugo Black. Their judicial philosophy tells them only that they must limit constitutional pronouncements to those that can be justified by looking at constitutional text; it does not dictate how broadly or narrowly the text itself is to be interpreted.

In contrast, the noninterpretivist is willing to search outside the language of the Constitution for constitutional values. But this is not a wholesale abandonment of the Constitution. The noninterpretivist looks for constitutional value in the structure of the document and in the consensus about rights that is said to be fairly implied from the text. Obviously, portions of the Constitution (and amendments) advance values that, while they are not made explicit with the labels that would comfort us, seem like values congenial to us: privacy, equality, liberty, democracy, republicanism. The noninterpretivist justifies the courts in their constitutional policy making, especially when the legislature enacts policies that tend to damage democratic process itself: laws that clog the channels of political expression or those that severely abridge the rights of "discrete and insular minorities" who cannot avail themselves of the democratic process. The critique of noninterpretivism is that no such consensus about fundamental values really exists: "What kind of 'fundamental presuppositions of our society' is it that cannot command a legislative majority?"

Where difficult questions abound, no "right" answers are definitively to be found. But our inability to "know" some ultimate does not invalidate the fact of judicial review or the process by which the Court, over time, has sought answers. Life is not a series of mathematical questions; it is, as Justice Holmes reminded us, "an experiment." Perhaps the most definitive response one can make to those who abhor judicial policy making is that it is the price we pay for a necessary judicial review. There may be no consensus of values to which the Court may legitimately refer, but there is a consensus that the Court try to articulate it. The full answer to those who decry the undemocratic character of judicial review is that the American people have acquiesced in this institutional role for their courts—indeed, have often gloried in it (unless their particular oxen were gored). The Constitution endures because the Court has the power to make it *our* Constitution in every generation. As Justice Holmes said:

When we are dealing with words that also are a constituent act, like the Constitution of the United States, we

James McHenry
Maryland

James McHenry was born in County Antrim, Ireland, November 16, 1723, and died near Baltimore, May 3, 1816. Formally educated in Dublin, he came alone to America in 1771, persuading his family to join him the following year. He studied poetry at Newark Academy, Delaware, and then medicine in Philadelphia. Early an active patriot, he traveled to Cambridge in 1775 to volunteer his services to the military. He was chosen for hospital work, and was commended by the Continental Congress. As a surgeon, he was captured and released by the British and promoted to senior surgeon of the Flying Hospital, Valley Forge. In 1778, he was made secretary to George Washington. Two years later, he was named to Lafayette's staff, an accomplishment of which he was particularly proud. In 1781, he left active military service to join the Maryland Senate. In 1783, he was named to Congress, an office he retained until 1786. While a congressman, he wrote considerably and adeptly. He was a Maryland delegate to the Constitutional Convention, arriving May 28, only to be called away by his brother's illness a few days later. He returned to the sessions in early August, and remained for the duration. Elected to the Maryland Assembly, he remained until 1791, when he was elected to the state Senate. In 1796, he succeeded Timothy Pickering as secretary of war. As secretary, he supported the ideas of Alexander Hamilton. Politically opposed to Adams, he retired from politics completely in 1800, to his home in Fayetteville, Maryland, where he became president of the first Bible Society in Baltimore, founded in 1813, and published several works. A conservative man who had influential associates, McHenry was a modest politician, surgeon, and soldier.

must realize that they have called into life a being the development of which could not have been foreseen completely by the most gifted of its begetters. It was enough for them to realize or to hope that they had created an organism; it has taken a century and has cost their successors much sweat and blood to prove that they created a nation. The case before us must be considered in the light of our whole experience and not merely in that of what was said a hundred years ago.

The Court sitting "almost as a continuing constitutional convention" has endured through numerous struggles. As Robert Jackson has noted:

As created, the Supreme Court seemed too anemic to endure a long contest for power. . . . Yet in spite of its apparently vulnerable position, this Court has repeatedly overruled and thwarted both the Congress and the Executive. It has been in angry collision with the most dynamic and popular Presidents in our history. Jefferson retaliated with impeachment; Jackson denied its authority; Lincoln disobeyed a writ of the Chief Justice; Theodore Roosevelt, after his Presidency, proposed recall of judicial decisions; Wilson tried to liberalize its membership; and Franklin D. Roosevelt proposed to "reorganize" it. It is surprising that it should not only survive but, with no might except the moral force of its judgments, should attain actual supremacy as a source of constitutional dogma.

Had the people not repeatedly supported, though tacitly, the Court's central function as it has evolved, one or the other of these presidents would surely have brought it to heel. True, Franklin Roosevelt scared the Court into changing its mind, and his longevity in the White House allowed him to reform it through appointment, but that is a part of the normal checks and balances that have functioned throughout our history.

A Brief Note on Remedial Decrees

No matter how passive the judiciary is in theory, a Court with the power to construe the Constitution will rarely be left alone. As Alexis de Tocqueville noted, in his most well-worn line, quoted now for 150 years, "There is hardly a political question in the United States which does not sooner or later turn into a judicial one." Unless constitutional restrictions (like "standing" problems) themselves stand in the way, any significant problem can be put before the Court.

If the resulting decision invalidates a law, the legal consequence, while it may be unpalatable to a vocal minority (or even majority), is sharply confined. A discriminatory law simply disappears and the people must go on their way as if it never existed.

Many modern decisions, however, have not confined themselves to erecting a barrier to governmental action. Courts in recent years have increasingly come to find in the Constitution *affirmative duties:* Not, the states may not segregate; rather, the states must integrate.

To impose duties on the government is far more difficult than merely to prohibit its actions. The remedy for a discriminatory law is to nullify it. But the remedy for an ongoing course of unconstitutional conduct (like cruel and unusual conditions in a prison) is not self-evident. Courts may know how to construe constitutions, but they are not adepts at social policy. Judges may have the legal power to direct hospitals, police stations, prisons, or schools deemed to have renounced the Constitution, but they do not thereby have the knowledge, resources, or time to do so intelligently.

Moreover, in opening the gate that separates legislative, executive, and judicial powers, the courts may squander their priceless political asset, the trust of the people, in attempting to fashion an affirmative decree. If a mental hospital to which people are committed against their will fails to treat its patients, it is no breathtaking conclusion to find that they have been unconstitutionally confined. What to do about their confinement is far more troublesome. May a federal court direct a state legislature to appropriate more money and tell the state mental health department how to spend it? (Some courts, in some cases, have come close to just such orders.) If the legislature balked, the court would be powerless to do more than sputter. Unheeded judicial decrees are worse than useless, for they teach contempt for all judgments.

Much of the contemporary criticism of courts, and the Supreme Court in particular, is directed toward their attempts to run things. The topic is beyond the limits of this book, but we can say that in all their dealings with these institutions, the courts rarely act unilaterally or impetuously. The process of framing decrees to nudge loath legislatures or balky bureaucracies into constitutional compliance is a dialogue— a discussion between the court and parties. Those who complain that courts do not understand should reflect that the "misunderstanding" is frequently that of the government, which resists the implication that it has erred and must develop manners. A government that demonstrates its willingness to right perceived wrongs is rarely likely to find a court rejecting good-faith proposals for doing so.

Assessing the Supreme Court's Performance

How well has the Court done? The question is loaded, of course. How well has Congress done? Or presidents? We're still around, might be one answer, perhaps adding, and we're doing fine. Whether we are doing fine depends on one's perspective; as in all questions of value, no definitive answer is possible. Or, if it is, the answer wouldn't satisfy everyone.

Evidence that the Court has behaved badly is not difficult to marshal. "Time has proved that its judgment was wrong on most of the outstanding issues upon which it has chosen to challenge the popular branches," said Justice Jackson, writing nearly half a century ago. "Its judgment in the *Dred Scott* case was overruled by war. Its judgment that the currency that preserved the Union could not be made legal tender was overruled by Grant's selection of an additional Justice. Its judgment invalidating the income tax was overruled by the Sixteenth Amendment. Its judgments repressing labor and social legislation are now abandoned. Many of the judgments against New Deal legislation are rectified by confession of error."

And Leonard Levy states: "One cannot doubt the pernicious, highly undemocratic influence of the series of decisions in which the Court crippled and voided most of the comprehensive program for protecting the civil rights of Negroes after the Civil War. These decisions paralyzed or supplanted legislative and community action, created bigotry, and played a crucial role in destroying public opinion that favored meeting the challenge of the Negro problem as a constitutional—that is, as a moral—obligation."

Henry Steele Commager (speaking of the Court before 1937) notes: "[The record] discloses not a single case, in a century and a half, where the Supreme Court has protected freedom of speech, press . . . against Congressional attack. It reveals no instance . . . where the Court has intervened on behalf of the underprivileged—the Negro, the alien, women, children, workers, tenant farmers. It reveals, on the contrary, that the Court has effectively intervened, again and again, to defeat Congressional attempts to free the slave, to guarantee civil rights to Negroes, to protect workingmen, to outlaw child labor, to assist hard-pressed farmers, and to democratize the tax system."

"So wretched a performance," Raoul Berger suggests, "inspires little confidence in the Court as the 'national conscience.' " To the contrary, history demonstrates only that the Court is not always dependable. The facts suggest that the Court fails when it *does not* act as the nation's conscience, not that it succeeds when it does so act. As Levy has also argued:

> Taking the long view . . . an historian may confidently assert that there has never been a single case of judicial review in favor of the Bill of Rights hurtful in any way to the democratic process, popular responsibility, or the moral sense of the community. The cases proving that judicial review has stunted the growth of the people or had undemocratic effects are those in which the Court checked statutory efforts, federal and state, to defend minorities or the underprivileged, but never those in which the Court has defended against legislatures, minorities, or the underprivileged or the unpopular.

Moreover, it is essential to take the long view. No Court opinion can be judged simply on its own terms (what did the Court say *today?*). To assess the Court's performance, we must inquire what the Court did (or failed to do) yesterday and the day before that. From the perspective of history, it is telling that the Court has rarely acted on the spur of the moment in exercising its awesome power to make constitutional policy. It almost always lags behind the social recognition of grievous wrong.

Its most significant decisions have been made against a long period of political abuse and the clear thwarting of minority rights.

Brown v. Board of Education, the seminal 1954 case holding school desegregation unconstitutional, was

NAACP attorneys George E. C. Hayes, Thurgood Marshall, and James M. Nabrit celebrating the Brown v. Board of Education *decision in 1954.*

no sudden fancy. Earlier decisions foreshadowed it, and for half a century the state legislatures had failed to give blacks even the minimal respect the Court's earlier decisions said were due ("separate but *equal*" school facilities). The legislative reapportionment cases came against a backdrop of decades of state legislatures' wanton violation of their own constitutions. The criminal law decisions applying the Bill of Rights to the states came only after decades had shown the police incapable of or unwilling to eliminate blatant brutalities in the station house and to extend even elementary rights to criminal suspects.

It is when the Court acts precipitately that it is likely to err. The most stunning modern example was its approval early in World War II of the incarceration of Japanese Americans on the West Coast. The Court did not have the benefit of the moral and intellectual sifting that usually precedes its forays into major constitutional policy making, and when it finally woke up, it began to retrench. Today, the Japanese exclusion cases have been thoroughly repudiated, and it is Congress that is considering some sort of reparations.

Those who find usurpation in the Court's historic role as constitutional policy maker have blinded themselves to real conditions. To suppose political life without a Supreme Court, capable of erring but also capable of restraining powerful majorities and minorities, is to suppose something we have never been and that is, ultimately, simply unthinkable. Would we be better off without a Court to tell the president he cannot simply seize private property, as President Truman tried to seize the nation's steel mills during the Korean war? Would we be better off without a Court to tell the president he cannot commit crimes and hide behind a cloak of executive privilege, as President Nixon tried when he hoped to escape the judgment of the people? Would we be better off without a Court to condemn racial discrimination, even if it took too long to say so? Are we worse off today as a nation than we were before *Brown v. Board?* Try to find anyone except the lunatic fringe to say

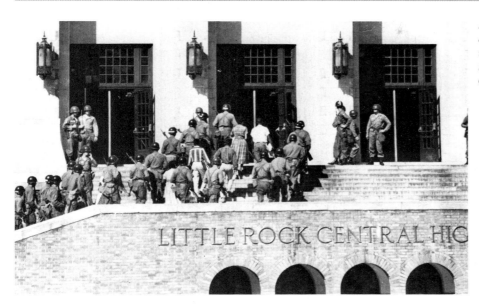

Federal troops escorting black children into Little Rock High School in 1957. President Eisenhower sent the troops to enforce the Supreme Court's school desegregation orders.

so. Probably no social transformation in history has been as complete in so short a time as that wrought by the *Brown* decision: certainly none before had ever been at the prompting of a court.

The response to these various decisions underscores the nation's acceptance of the Court's central role in constitutional interpretation, according to whatever rules it bends to the task. President Jackson is apocryphally reported to have said, "John Marshall has made his decision, now let him enforce it," when the Court in 1832 construed a federal treaty in favor of the Cherokees. The Court has no troops; they are under the president's wing in the constitutional scheme. Yet President Truman did not hesitate to return the steel mills, President Nixon barely wavered in releasing the tapes that he knew sealed his fate, and despite his apparent personal disinclination President

Eisenhower sent troops to Little Rock to enforce school desegregation orders. State legislators were appalled, but they reapportioned themselves. None of these things could be if the American people did not support the historical role of the Supreme Court. Despite repeated attempts by those unhappy at particular results, Congress after one try during Reconstruction wisely has refused to tamper with the Court's jurisdiction to serve as the nation's constitutional arbiter.

Sloppy in fact, inconsistent in theory, judicial review nevertheless works. This "undemocratic" institution operates daily in a nation made no less democratic, and arguably much more democratic, for it. The Constitution endures because the courts are an independent refuge, not always right but not always wrong, the one place where you can go to argue with the government face to face.

Chapter 7 Federalism: The Nation and the States

The Structure of Federalism

Jealous of the freedom they had wrested from the British, Americans in the crucial year between September 1787 and August 1788 understandably worried whether they would be surrendering it by ratifying the handiwork of the Philadelphia Convention. To a sizable segment of the populace, Antifederalists as they came to be known, the most serious defect in the Constitution was that it gathered up sovereignty, that mystical medieval notion, from the states and relocated it in a national government.

National was a dirty word. "I confess, as I enter the Building," said Samuel Adams during the ratification debates in Massachusetts, "I stumble at the threshold. I meet with a National Government, instead of a Federal Union of Sovereign States." In 1790, a correspondent wrote the president of New Hampshire: "To pray for the *national Government* is even deemed offensive in the Clergy. . . . I only mean that the word *national* is offensive—if we say the *federal*, or the *general* Government, it is tolerable."

The question was not the separation of powers, a different issue, and one for which the Federalists had ready answers. The question was whether, however its powers were lodged, the new government would keep from absorbing the state governments. It was obvious to all who thought about it that the Constitution would create a paradox: two separate legislatures—Congress and the state assemblies—operating over the same territory. Here on this soil, two governments would compete for control. Everyone knew—all the philosophers had always said so—that sovereignty had to reside ultimately in one place. How could it reside in two places at once? Such a thing could not be; "not knowing whether to obey the Congress or the State" made no sense, said James Winthrop. Amen, said George Mason: "These two concurrent powers cannot exist long together; the one will destroy the other."

One common answer was that the "two governments act in different manners and for different purposes, the general government in great national concerns, in which we are interested in common with other members of the Union; the state legislature in our mere local concerns. . . . They can no more clash than two parallel lines can meet." Madison noted, in debate and in *Federalist* No. 39, that the Constitution provided for neither an all-national nor an all-federal system "but rather a composition of both."

Still, the dilemma of sovereignty persisted. Suppose a conflict did arise? Where did the ultimate power lie? James Wilson provided the answer in the Pennsylvania ratifying convention: The power lies with the people. The people are sovereign, and "they can delegate [sovereignty] in such proportions, to such bodies, on such terms, and under such limitations, as they think proper. . . . The people of the United States are now in the possession and exercise of their original rights, and while this doctrine is known and operates, we shall have a cure for every disease."

The sovereignty of the people, reflected in the Constitution's Preamble ("We the People . . . ") and in the method of ratifying (specially chosen conventions, rather than existing political bodies), settled the argument. The liberal philosophy of John Locke had finally found its home. The people hold the power, not some hereditary monarch; governmental power is only on loan and may be called back at any time.

This proposition, while still formally the bedrock of American constitutionalism, poses an obvious problem, unresolved by Locke, who spoke airily of the people's right to challenge the government through revolution without distinguishing between legitimate rebellion and unlawful and self-serving insurrection. How many people does it take for their uprising to constitute a people's revolution; how few does it take to constitute them mere brigands? These are ultimate political questions; as we have seen, the Supreme Court in the aftermath of Dorr's Rebellion in Rhode Island refused to take sides.

The sovereignty of a people, surely a noble notion in the abstract, is a troublesome one when expressed concretely, for it inevitably ends in vigilantism. The San Francisco Vigilantes of 1856 proclaimed:

Embodied in the principles of republican governments are the truths that the majority should rule, and that when corrupt officials, who have fraudulently seized the reigns [sic] of authority, designedly thwart the execution of the laws and avert punishment from the notoriously guilty, the power they usurp reverts back to the people from whom it was wrested. . . . All law emanates from the people, so that, when the laws thus enacted are not executed, the power returns to the people, and is theirs whenever they may choose to exercise it.

Vigilantes since then have, if not so clearly, expressed much the same notion—to the great devastation of public law and order. The Constitution sought to answer such claims by providing, in Article V, a method for amending the fundamental law, so that it could never be said that any law or any policy was final. In that sense, and only in that sense, under a mature constitutionalism, are the whole people sovereign. The other way lies chaos.

Once the grand philosophical question had been answered, the practical relationship between the states and new federal government remained. In *Federalist* No. 51, Madison had made clear that the separation of powers, on which the system of checks and bal-

Founding Father

Robert Morris

Pennsylvania

Robert Morris was born around Liverpool, England, January 31, 1734, and died in Philadelphia, on May 8, 1806. He emigrated to America in 1747, first settling in Oxford, Maryland, later in Pennsylvania. He joined a shipping firm in Philadelphia, and through diligent work and financial genius was made partner in 1754. Without much formal education, Morris prospered in business. Growing revolutionary fervor prompted him in 1775 to join the Pennsylvania Council of Safety and Committee of Correspondence. The next year, he was a delegate to the Second Continental Congress, where he remained for two years. He wrote prodigiously and sat on the more prestigious committees, obtaining national acclaim. Before the Revolution, Morris favored conciliation, but he later signed the Declaration of Independence, in August 1776. He was not reelected to the Continental Congress in 1779, it having been alleged, without proof, that he was using his position for personal financial gain. By 1781, however, he was unanimously appointed superintendent of finance by the Continental Congress, and he remained at this post until 1784. While superintendent, he proved his prowess as financier, initiating the first national bank in U.S. history, the Bank of North America, and a new currency, called "Morris notes." In 1786, he was a delegate to the Annapolis Convention. The following year, he attended the Constitutional Convention as a Pennsylvania delegate. He served as senator from 1789 to 1795, and strongly supported Alexander Hamilton's policies at Treasury.

Morris was intelligent and creative. His business sense was remarkable. Ironically, however, he lost his fortune in land speculation, was sent to a debtor's prison (1799–1801), and died penniless. Had his schemes worked out, he would have been the wealthiest man in the nation.

ances depended, was not confined to the federal branches alone:

> In the compound republic of America, the power surrendered by the people is first divided between two distinct governments, and then the portion allotted to each subdivided among distinct and separate departments. Hence a double security arises to the rights of the people. The different governments will control each other, at the same time that each will be controlled by itself.

Also, just as the possibility of checks and balances within the federal government depends not on the absolute separation of powers but on powers that overlap and mesh, so too the relationship between the states and the federal government depends on overlaps within the Constitution. The relative position of the national and state governments and the scope of their powers—the question of federalism—has dominated constitutional theorizing for the past two centuries. History, economic development, a civil war, and evolving concepts of civil rights (under significant amendments) have altered the face of federalism more than any other single aspect of the Constitution.

Powers of the Federal Government over the States

The Constitution allocated some governmental powers exclusively to the federal government—for example, the power to declare and wage war, to control money, and to regulate immigration and naturalization. The states have no constitutional power in these spheres. Their powers lie over all areas not delegated to Congress.

Unlike planetary motions, however, the laws of human relationships are not subject to neat formulation. The rules designed to keep the bodies in separate orbits are unclear; the spheres of action cannot be sharply delineated. Sooner or later, conflicts will arise. For example, the states are free to regulate commercial matters within their borders, but their regulations may impinge on interstate commerce, which Congress is empowered to regulate.

In the event of a conflict between state and federal power, therefore, the supremacy clause (Article VI) of the Constitution makes clear that the federal power is paramount. The preemption of state laws by federal legislation has most often been brought into play when Congress exercises its commerce power. For the first century, this power was sparingly used, in part because economic conditions did not seem to call for national regulation. The past one hundred years, however, have seen an immense outpouring of federal legislation under the commerce power, so that the federal-state landscape today bears little resemblance to that which the framers knew. The story is more than a procedural one, and we defer to Chapter 18 a look at this major change in the locus of federalism.

Because federal power is divided, both Congress and the federal courts may exercise power over the states, and the effect of their actions is often different. At least in the early years, congressional enactments were not so much exercises of power over the states as of power over the people. When Congress taxes, it taxes people. When Congress provides for paper

> ## Ratification, State by State
>
> Here is the chronology of ratification. Delaware was the first to ratify, Rhode Island (which had not participated in the convention), the last.
>
> **Delaware**, December 7, 1787 (unanimous)
> **Pennsylvania**, December 12, 1787 (vote of 46 to 23)
> **New Jersey**, December 19, 1787 (unanimous)
> **Georgia**, January 2, 1788 (unanimous)
> **Connecticut**, January 9, 1788 (128–40)
> **Massachusetts**, February 6, 1788 (187–168)
> **Maryland**, April 26, 1788 (63–11)
> **South Carolina**, May 23, 1788 (149–73)
> **New Hampshire**, June 21, 1788 (57–46)
> **Virginia**, June 25, 1788 (89–79)
> **New York**, July 26, 1788 (30–27)
> **North Carolina**, November 21, 1789 (this was eight months after the new government had started)
> **Rhode Island**, May 29, 1790

money, it is not telling the states what to do so much as it is defining the rights and obligations of the people.

By contrast, the federal judicial power often oversees the actual powers and acts of the states. That is because, as we saw in Chapter 6, federal courts have jurisdiction over state cases when a federal question is raised. Then, the courts will be inquiring whether a state law or a state judicial decision conflicts with a federal statute or the Constitution itself. The effect of its ruling may well be to strike down some state policy or law.

These distinctions are by no means airtight. A congressional enactment under the commerce power may overrule a state law as surely as a court decision.

But in practice, the judicial power was far more likely, in the early years, to be seen as encroaching on state powers and prerogatives because the Constitution, by explicitly prohibiting certain state acts, gives the courts a basis for acting when someone complains. Thus the states may not "impair the obligation of contracts," and when a state law does so, the federal courts in the proper case may overturn the state act.

In two other particulars, the Constitution gave the federal government power to invade state interests. Article IV declares that "the Citizens of each State shall be entitled to all Privileges and Immunities of Citizens in the several States." Because these privileges and immunities are guaranteed by the Constitution, the federal courts may enforce them when state laws interfere, though as it developed, the courts drained most of the juice from this clause.

Article IV also sets out the guaranty clause: "The United States shall guarantee to every State in this Union a Republican Form of Government." Although this clause seems to invest the courts with a like power to determine when a state government is improper, as we have seen, the Supreme Court has declared that the question of whether and how to make such a guarantee is for Congress and the president.

Power of the States over the Federal Government

The supremacy clause might be supposed to give an advantage to the federal government. The election procedures furnished the states with a check and balance. For as ratified, the Constitution gave the states significant control over how the federal government would be constituted. Eligibility for voting depends on state law, and unless Congress acts, each state may determine the manner of electing members of the House. State legislatures chose their U.S. senators. And each state may establish procedures for selecting presidential electors. These rules gave the states considerable weight in determining the composition of Congress and in selecting the president. Congress might act contrary to state interests, but the states had the power to constitute (and reconstitute) Congress. A president who ignored a state or regional

Although their direct power over federal government has been weakened, state legislatures still retain a central lawmaking role.

interests would find his reelection jeopardized in the electoral college.

Interestingly, the Constitution does not prohibit state officials from holding federal office. Roger Sherman, who served as congressman and then senator from Connecticut, also was mayor of New Haven until he died in 1793. Washington appointed the president of New Hampshire, John Sullivan, to the federal district bench, and his refusal to resign from the state office provoked a storm. Maryland Senator Charles Carroll also sat as a state senator; when Maryland in 1792 enshrined in its constitution a ban on members of the federal government serving in the state's, he resigned his seat in the U.S. Senate, thinking the state office more significant. The political possibilities in state and national offices combined in a single person never had a chance to mature, however, because most states soon saw the potential conflicts and outlawed, either by legislative enactment or in their constitutions, the doubling up. (In some cases, the ban was a while in coming: New York and Massachusetts did not constitutionally prohibit the practice until 1821, North Carolina until 1835.)

Today, that direct power over the federal government is considerably weakened, in constitutional fact and political reality. For one thing, the Seventeenth Amendment removed from the state legislatures the power to elect senators. Judicial interpretation of Article I and the Fourteenth Amendment has remade the landscape of voting districts, so that the states have much less power to determine what interests shall be sufficient to elect representatives. Nevertheless, through the electoral college, the states as such continue to influence the outcome of presidential elections. And in long-established political custom, the states retain leverage over important federal powers. For example, the Constitution gives the power of nominating federal judges to the president and of consent to the Senate, but by custom (known as "senatorial courtesy"), the process is actually reversed. A state's senators usually tell the president whom he may nominate to the federal bench in their state, and the president ordinarily consents. (The constitutional forms remain intact: A majority of the Senate must agree to the president's nominee.)

No less important from the standpoint of federal-state power, at the outset the states had the central lawmaking role. The states predate the Constitution; they are not its creatures and do not need to be invested with power to act. If this were not clear, the Tenth Amendment, the last of the Bill of Rights, secured their position:

> The powers not delegated to the United States by the Constitution, nor prohibited by it to the States, are reserved to the States respectively, or to the people.

Most of what would affect the people would be the states' doing, and the people would naturally look to the states first. The states had wide powers—the common law and most criminal law derived from the states, not from the federal government. Congress could not define murder, for example, nor tell the states what procedures to use in prosecuting those accused of it. Nor could the federal courts oversee the state courts in their interpretation of state law; federal review was limited to federal questions. Also, the Constitution laid far fewer restrictions on the states than on the federal government. With the possible exception of the Ninth Amendment, the Bill of Rights secured the people against the federal government, not against the states.

The common understanding that the Constitution did not negate state sovereignty was reaffirmed by the ratification of the Eleventh Amendment in 1796. Alarmed by the Supreme Court's willingness to hear a suit against Georgia by a citizen of South Carolina, Congress quickly proposed an amendment to repeal that part of the Supreme Court's jurisdiction. States, as such, may not be sued in federal court (except by another state). The major purpose of the amendment was to underscore the states' sovereignty: A state may be sued only if it consents to be sued, and then only in its own courts.

Eleventh Amendment jurisprudence, it should be noted, is not as straightforward as the language of the amendment suggests. On the one hand, the Supreme Court has held that the Eleventh Amendment bars suits brought by a state's own citizens or by a foreign state, even though the language of the amendment certainly does not preclude them. On the other hand, the Supreme Court may hear an appeal of a suit brought by a state against an individual, and a plaintiff may seek a federal injunction against a state officer who is enforcing state laws alleged to be unconstitutional. With few exceptions, the Eleventh Amendment has proven to be a dead letter.

Equality of the States

Each state stands on an equal legal footing before the Constitution. There are no superior or inferior states, and Congress may not condition the admission of a state into the Union on matters left to the jurisdiction of the states. In 1911, for example, Congress barred Oklahoma, as a condition to its admission, from moving its state capital. But the power over locating a state capital is exclusively a matter for the states. The Supreme Court struck down the restriction, saying, "The power is to admit 'new States into *this* Union.' 'This Union' was and is a union of States, equal in power, dignity and authority, each competent to exert that residuum of sovereignty not delegated to the United States by the Constitution itself."

State Obligations toward Other States

The Constitution obligates each state to respect certain actions of sister states. The "full faith and credit" clause of Article IV says:

> Full faith and credit shall be given in each State to the public acts, records, and judicial proceedings of every other State.

Founding Father

Thomas Fitzsimmons (Fitzsimins)
Pennsylvania

Thomas Fitzsimmons was born in Ireland in 1741 and died in Philadelphia on August 26, 1811. He emigrated to America early in life, and spent his youth in Philadelphia, entering a mercantile career. He married well, which enabled him to form a mercantile and commercial partnership. With the outbreak of the Revolution, he quickly lent support to the American cause. He was on the Council of Safety and the Navy Board, and helped to build ships and other necessary military equipment. In 1782, he was elected to the Continental Congress. He served several terms in the state legislature. At the Philadelphia Convention in 1787, he advocated strong national government, governmental power to tax imports and exports, and equal treaty-making authority in both houses. In 1789, he was one of the first representatives from Pennsylvania. He remained in the House until 1795 as a Federalist sympathizer, and supported the retirement of the U.S. debt. Defeated by a Democrat, he retired from politics. Fitzsimmons was the founder and president of the Insurance Company of North America and president of the Philadelphia Chamber of Commerce for several years. He was a trustee of the University of Pennsylvania and a sometime philanthropist. In 1805, he was forced to declare bankruptcy because of obligations incurred by business associates, including Robert Morris. Unlike Morris, he recouped much of his wealth, escaping a pauper's death.

States are considered legal equals under the Constitution and are obligated to respect certain actions of sister states.

This reciprocity is an aspect of federalism, for if each state were free to disregard the juridical acts of other states, rights determined in one place could be undone in another.

The major utility of the full faith and credit clause is for the person with a court judgment. Suppose you win a money judgment in Arizona against the driver who smashed your car there. He moves to South Dakota. To collect your judgment, you need not sue him again in South Dakota. You need simply show the courts there that you already have an Arizona judgment establishing liability. Similarly, a divorce decree in one state may be used as a shield against a former spouse who attempts to get better terms by moving to another state and suing for a new decree.

Unhappily, the modern full-faith-and-credit jurisprudence is a complex affair, because judgments must have been validly obtained for the clause to operate. These days, state laws reach extraordinarily far; so-called long arm statutes confer jurisdiction over people outside the state if they have had certain kinds of "contact" with the state (perhaps they have done business in the state or caused an accident there). But not all contacts are sufficient, and the courts in sister states must first determine whether the original state court legally had jurisdiction over the defendant.

If they conclude that jurisdiction was lacking, the resulting judgment cannot be enforced in the other state. Vexing problems arise, especially in divorce cases, but their intricacies are beyond our scope.

The Tenth Amendment as a Source of State Sovereignty

The Tenth Amendment reserves to the states or the people all powers not otherwise delegated to the federal government. This might be taken as mere tautology, a statement of the obvious, as true without the Tenth Amendment as with it. If the Constitution gives Congress power to act, then it may do so; if the Constitution does not give a particular power, the states need no extra declaration to proclaim the unconstitutionality of its doing so.

For about fifty years, this was the received wisdom. In upholding the power of Congress to create a national bank, Chief Justice Marshall in *McCulloch v. Maryland* noted the irrelevancy of the Tenth Amendment: "Whether the particular power which may become the subject of contest has been delegated to the one government, or prohibited to the other, . . . [depends] upon a fair construction of the whole instrument," he said, upholding the power.

But for roughly a century, from Marshall's death to the New Deal, the Supreme Court saw the Tenth Amendment as a limitation on congressional power to regulate commerce. (We review that line of decisions in Chapter 18.) Finally, in 1941, the Court returned to Marshall's understanding, expressly overruling cases to the contrary.

In recent years, however, the Court has found some renewed vitality in the Tenth Amendment, at least insofar as Congress's attempts to regulate employment conditions of state officials are concerned. In 1974, Congress amended the Fair Labor Standards Act, previously applicable to corporate employees working in interstate commerce, and extended its provisions to state and local employees. The act sets minimum wage and maximum hour standards. The Court struck down this extension, saying: "This Court has never doubted that there are limits upon the power of Congress to override state sovereignty, even when exercising its otherwise plenary powers to tax or to regulate commerce. . . . One undoubted attribute of state sovereignty is the States' power to determine the wages which shall be paid to those whom they employ in order to carry out their governmental functions, what hours those persons will work, and what compensation will be provided where these employees may be called upon to work overtime." In other words, Congress may not do to the states what it has undoubted power to do to private individuals and corporations. But the reign of this new doctrine was not long; the Court specifically overruled it nine years later, after a series of perplexing cases that failed to shape the doctrine into usable precedent. So the Tenth Amendment once again is the confirmation of a truism, but no rule for sustaining state rights at the expense of federal powers lawfully exercised.

The "New Federalism"

In 1859, Chief Justice Taney declared that "the powers of the General Government, and of the State, although both exist and are exercised within the same territorial limits, are yet separate and distinct sovereignties, acting separately and independently of each other, within their respective spheres." This was the orthodox view of federal-state relations.

Even then, though, it was a shibboleth. The states and federal government had long cooperated in constructing railroads and overseeing banks, canal building, and the like. But the myth has persisted for nearly our entire history. In 1953, General Eisenhower ran for the White House on a ticket that promised, among other things, to restore to the states their proper powers and where possible to pluck the states from the labyrinth of federal law into which for decades Congress had drawn them. At the 1957 Governors' Conference, President Eisenhower said:

> I believe deeply in States' rights. . . . The States can regain and preserve their traditional responsibilities and rights. . . . Not one of us questions the governmental concepts so wisely applied by the framers of our Constitution. . . . We can revitalize the principle of sharing of responsibility, of separation of authority, of diffusion of power, in our free government. . . . I have a competent man and his assistants trying to identify those things where we believe the Federal government has improperly invaded the rights and responsibilities of States. . . . We must see that . . . each level of Government performs its proper function—no more, no less. . . . And so, America will continue to be a symbol of courage and hope for the oppressed millions over the world who, victimized by powerful centralized government, aspire to join us in freedom.

After a diligent search, a joint federal-state committee found little to back up Eisenhower's stirring words: "It proposed that the federal government eliminate grants-in-aid for vocational education and for sewage treatment plants, and that a portion of the tax on local telephone service be made available to the states." Congress rejected those modest proposals—and went on to transform the federal system.

In Eisenhower's time and before, federal appropriations to the states had been intended to enable the states to accomplish local goals—highway construction, hospital renovations, sewage treatment plants, airport expansion. This was no overbearing federal presence; to the contrary, the funds were ardently sought by the states and local government. Even when Congress required that the states obtain federal approval for state plans, the federal agencies acted more as technical advisers than political commissars.

By the time Eisenhower sought a way out, it was clear that the original concept of federalism had expired and could not be resuscitated. Beginning in the 1960s, joint state-federal programs increasingly were designed to achieve national objectives. Programs embodied in such 1960s laws as the Area Redevelopment Act, the Manpower Development and Training Act, the Economic Opportunity Act, the Demonstration Cities, Metropolitan Development Act, and the Law Enforcement Assistance Act (among hundreds to follow) brought policy-making functions of the federal government into areas that had once been thought to be purely local—education, crime control, public health and welfare, other social services, housing, urban renewal, environment, and transportation. These and other programs led to new concepts of federal grants-in-aid and revenue sharing, as Congress sought the appropriate balance between federal and state concerns.

Though some states' rights rhetoric remains and political leaders continue to speak boldly of a "new federalism," not even the Reagan administration, pledged to many of the old verities, has found it possible to create a political system that embodies the old philosophy. In a ruling fraught with some irony, the Supreme Court in 1986 struck down the administration's "Baby Doe" regulations, which required hospitals "to seek life-prolonging medical treatment for handicapped newborns and to give Federal investigators round-the-clock access to hospital records

Local state projects such as highway construction were the primary recipients of federal funding before the 1960s.

and facilities." The administration acted, the Court said, without legal authority. President Reagan condemned the Court for suggesting that the federal government had acted in a province properly reserved to the states: "If our Constitution means anything, it means that we, the Federal Government, are entrusted with preserving life, liberty and the pursuit of happiness." The president's misquotation of the Constitution was surely not deliberate, but it was telling, for his reading would obliterate any residue of federalism.

If the federal-state partnership is a problem, it is not ordinarily a constitutional one. Politicians may cry out melodramatically for more or less control over federal dollars and regulatory standards, but they do not seriously suppose that constitutional dramas are staged whenever a new program is enacted. That was reserved for the preservation and enlargement of civil rights.

State Sovereignty and the Theory of Nullification

Early on, the Supreme Court made clear its jurisdiction to hear cases challenging state laws and judicial decisions as contrary to the Constitution. Did the states have a like power to declare federal acts contrary to the Constitution (a power that the Supreme Court declared for itself in *Marbury v. Madison*)? In our time, this theory of "interposition" or "nullification" lacks constitutional logic, but for decades, mainly in response to the slavery question, the central political issue in American politics (Chapter 9), several theorists (and some states) asserted the proposition.

Interestingly, the earliest assertion of this doctrine came from Jefferson and Madison in response to the Federalist-inspired Sedition Act, pushed through Congress in 1798 at President John Adams's behest. Aimed at enemies of his administration, the act saw several editors into jail. Enraged by this apparent affront to the First Amendment, the Kentucky legislature, in November 1798, declared in a resolution drafted by Jefferson that the act was unconstitutional and void. Jefferson's theory was that the Union was a compact of sovereign states and the federal government was but the agent of the states, which retained the power to determine when the central government exceeded the scope of its delegated powers.

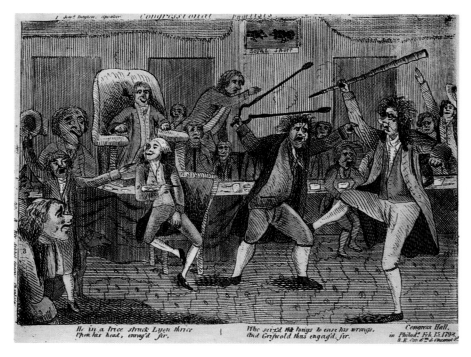

Congressional Pugilists, *1798 cartoon depicting the intense debate over the Sedition Act in which Roger Griswold, a Connecticut Federalist, attacked Matthew Lyon, a Vermont Republican, with a cane.*

Virginia's resolution, passed the following month, was even stronger. Drafted by Madison, it said

> that, in case of a deliberate, palpable, and dangerous exercise . . . of powers not granted by the [Constitution], the States who are parties thereto, have the right and are in duty bound to interpose for arresting the progress of the evil, and for maintaining within their respective limits the authorities, rights, and liberties appertaining to them.

The Sedition Act expired by its own terms in 1801, and the question of its constitutionality was never tested. The watershed *Marbury* case was still five years away when Jefferson and Madison wrote; the knowledge of a firm doctrine of judicial review to test the constitutionality of federal law might have kept Jefferson and Madison from penning such obviously unconstitutional sentiments.

The theory of interposition did not die. In 1828, John C. Calhoun, in *South Carolina Exposition and Protest*, advanced the thesis of a "concurrent majority": A majority within a state could veto federal actions and thereby avoid tyranny by the national majority. Calhoun argued that state interposition could legitimately block enforcement of a federal law. The interposed federal law could take effect only through a constitutional amendment.

Calhoun's theory of the concurrent majority was put to the test in 1832 when the South Carolina legislature called for a special convention, which adopted the Ordinance of Nullification to protest the federal tariffs of 1828 and 1832. The ordinance declared the tariffs "null, void, and no law, nor binding upon this State, its officers or citizens." It forbade anyone from appealing to the federal courts (threatening contempt if they did) and demanded that all state officials except members of the legislature swear on oath to support the ordinance. If the federal government tried to enforce collection of the tariffs, the ordinance declared the state's right to secede from the Union.

John C. Calhoun

President Andrew Jackson met the nullification crisis head on when, on December 10, 1832, he issued a "Proclamation to the People of South Carolina." "Be not deceived by names; disunion by armed force is treason," he declared, denouncing Calhoun's theory: "The Constitution of the United States, then, forms a *government*, not a league . . . in which all the people are represented, which operates directly on the people individually." For this proclamation, Jackson was canonized by nationalists, and South Carolina backed down in the face of the Force Act, enacted in March 1833, authorizing the president to use force if necessary to collect the tariffs.

Four years later, Calhoun pressed his interpositionist views in the Senate, urging a bill that would prohibit postmasters from carrying any publication dealing with slavery if addressed to anyone in a state that banned such literature. If Congress refused to act, Calhoun said, the states would, claiming they had an inherent power as sovereign entities to quarantine their inhabitants from antislavery propaganda. The bill failed, but the states did, for some time, interfere with the delivery of the mails.

Though southern states were the more persistent proponents of nullification and put the theory to its ultimate test during their attempted secession, which was resolved only by war, northern states too presumed to override federal law. The most notable example was sparked by an abolitionist editor, Sherman M. Booth, who helped rescue a fugitive slave in Wisconsin and was promptly arrested for violating the Fugitive Slave Act. In a welter of legal actions, the Wisconsin courts took the position that the Fugitive Slave Act was unconstitutional. Twice they released Booth in habeas corpus proceedings, the second time even though Booth had been convicted in federal court of violating the act. In *Ableman v. Booth*, the Supreme Court, speaking through Chief Justice Taney, reaffirmed the supremacy of federal law, and the Wisconsin Supreme Court ultimately backed down.

The Civil War settled the supremacy issue both politically and constitutionally, though for decades the issue of federal intrusion on the state's "police powers" would be heard in attempts, sometimes successful, to circumvent congressional exercise of the power to regulate interstate commerce (Chapter 18). Still, echoes of the mid-nineteenth-century interposition debates were occasionally heard much later. In the 1950s, after the Supreme Court ruled against racial segregation in schools, southern states heatedly denounced the justices and in the Southern Manifesto resurrected the old theories of state sovereignty. Segregationist politicians fell over each other in the stampede to reassert that the racist traditions were lawful. Senator James O. Eastland, for one, stated: "On May 17, 1954, the Constitution of the United States was destroyed because the Supreme Court dis-

Constitutional Peregrinations

After considerable traveling, the original signed Constitution is now at the National Archives. How did it get there?

William Jackson took the Constitution to New York and presented it to the president of the Confederation Congress on September 20, 1787, where it was placed in congressional archives and then delivered to President Washington. By the act of September 15, 1789, Congress directed him to turn it over to the State Department.

When the government moved to Philadelphia, the Constitution returned to Philadelphia; in 1800 it again moved with the government, to Washington, D.C.

In 1814, when Washington was under siege, Secretary of State Monroe took the Constitution and Declaration and stored them temporarily in Leesburg, Virginia, returning them after the war to the State Department, where they remained for 132 years. On September 29, 1921, they were transferred to the Library of Congress.

The Constitution and Declaration were exhibited at the library until December 23, 1941, when they were sent to Fort Knox for safekeeping. There they were stored until October 1, 1944, when authorities considered Washington secure against attack. They remained at the library until December 15, 1952, when they were transferred to their current display at the National Archives.

regarded the law and decided integration was right. . . . You are not required to obey any court which passes out such a ruling. In fact, you are obligated to defy it." Senator Harry F. Byrd of Virginia added: "[The decision is] the most serious blow that has yet been struck against the rights of the states in a matter vitally affecting their authority and welfare."

In 1958, the studied violence in Little Rock, fomented by local bigots, led the school board to ask the courts to give the city schools some breathing room in the plan to desegregate. It had tried to do its constitutional duty, it said, but massive resistance by Governor Orval Faubus, abetted by the state legislature and courts, would lead to more violence. In an unusual opinion, individually signed by all nine justices, the Supreme Court rejected the argument that the board could be excused from complying because some state officials made it difficult to do so. The Court reminded the board that the Supreme Court, not the states, is the final interpreter of the Constitution and that state officials who refuse to carry out federal court orders are warring against the Constitution by violating their Article VI oath to support it.

The Constitutional Revolution of the Fourteenth Amendment

The Civil War was the constitutional watershed, not simply because it overthrew the old order of slavery (Chapter 9) but because it also led directly to the most important constitutional revolution in America since the Philadelphia Convention itself. Three amendments—the Thirteenth, Fourteenth, and Fifteenth—radically extended federal power over the states. All three expressly granted Congress power to enforce their provisions—the first grants of legislative power to Congress outside the original Constitution—and as constitutional provisions, they necessarily likewise gave new power to federal courts. The Thirteenth

abolished slavery (Chapter 9). The Fifteenth extended the right to vote (Chapter 8).

The Fourteenth was less specific, and consequently far more potent. It set forth three principles in language of sweeping and majestic generality:

1. *The privileges or immunities clause.* No state shall make or enforce any law which shall abridge the privileges or immunities of citizens of the United States.
2. *The due process clause.* Nor shall any state deprive any person of life, liberty, or property without due process of law.
3. *The equal protection clause.* Nor [shall any state] deny to any person within its jurisdiction the equal protection of the laws.

The substance of these clauses must await later chapters. Here we are concerned with the application of the Fourteenth Amendment to the states, for in time it came to be understood as a sweeping revision of the original understanding of federalism.

The problem, with which we deal throughout most of the remainder of this book, lies in the way the Constitution guarantees basic rights. So far, we have examined the *powers* that the Constitution gave to the new federal government. But the Constitution also prohibited government from invading fundamental *rights* of the people. Some of these guarantees are expressed in the original text ratified by the states in 1788. Some are not.

For example, the states may not punish a person by enacting a law ex post facto—that is, they may not retroactively declare unlawful conduct that was legal when undertaken. Should a state do so, the Supreme Court on appeal will reverse a conviction obtained under the law on the grounds that it violates Article I of the Constitution. This is no interference with state jurisdiction, since the explicit prohibition in the Constitution binds the states.

However, most of our basic constitutional rights that justly distinguish America from much of the world are not contained in the original Constitution but in the Bill of Rights, ratified in 1791. And these rights, it became clear, do not bind the states.

The Bill of Rights was proposed by the first Congress, under Madison's leadership, because of genuine fears expressed at several of the state ratifying conventions in 1787–1788. Many state constitutions guaranteed fundamental rights to their citizens, but no comparable guarantees had been written into the Constitution. According to James Wilson, the idea of a bill of rights "had never struck the mind of any member" until George Mason casually suggested the possibility in the closing days of the convention. The suggestion was promptly voted down. Federalist apologists defended this omission in general on the ground that no power had been given the federal government to invade the rights of the citizenry. Hamilton, in *Federalist* No. 84, gave the orthodox argument:

> Bills of rights, in the sense and to the extent in which they are contended for, are not only unnecessary in the proposed Constitution but would even be dangerous. They would contain various exceptions to powers which are not granted; and, on this very account, would afford a colorable pretext to claim more than were granted. For why declare that things shall not be done which there is no power to do? Why, for instance, should it be said that the liberty of the press shall not be restrained, when no power is given by which restrictions may be imposed?

But this was legalistic mumbo jumbo. Jefferson, from France, wrote that "[a] bill of rights is what the people are entitled to against every government on earth, general or particular, and what no just government should refuse, or rest on inference." Madison, who had initially been in the Federalist camp and opposed to a bill of rights, soon came around, realizing that a bill of rights would serve a "double purpose of satisfying the minds of well meaning opponents, and of providing additional guards in favor of liberty."

In view of this debate, the ten amendments that comprise the Bill of Rights guarantee citizens fun-

The Bill of Rights, ratified in 1791.

damental freedoms against the federal government only, as the language of the First Amendment makes clear. It says that *"Congress* shall make no law" establishing religion or abridging freedom of speech and press; it does not say that the states may not. (The House had originally approved an amendment that said: "The equal rights of conscience, the freedom of speech or of the press, and the right of trial by jury in criminal cases, shall not be infringed by any State." Madison considered it the most valuable amendment on the list, but the Senate rejected it.)

It fell to Chief Justice Marshall to rule definitively on the point. In the 1830s, the city of Baltimore diverted several streams in the course of paving its streets.

The engineering project dried up the wharf belonging to John Barron, who sued the city under the Fifth Amendment for lost profits. The Fifth Amendment provides that no one's property may be taken for public use without just compensation. On appeal, Marshall dismissed the case, holding that the first ten amendments apply only to the federal government, not to the states. Unless restrained by the Maryland constitution, Baltimore could take anyone's property as it saw fit.

So matters stood until 1868, when the Fourteenth Amendment was ratified. The three clauses of Section 1—the privileges or immunities clause, the due process clause, and the equal protection clause—all impose constitutional restrictions on the states. They thus give the people a new forum—the federal courts—for redress of these fundamental rights. For the first time, the federal courts had a significant role to play in shaping the rights and freedom of persons under state law. So significant, indeed, that no other provision of the Constitution has been more litigated than the Fourteenth Amendment.

The Fourteenth Amendment had a Januslike impact on federalism. Paradoxically, the federal courts almost immediately fashioned the due process clause into a federal shield against state business regulation, a role that few had any inkling the Fourteenth Amendment was capable of filling. Simultaneously, the courts emasculated the privileges or immunities clause as a weapon in the struggle to overcome the handicaps under which were laboring the freed slaves, for whom the amendment was surely intended. And the equal protection clause, occasionally serviceable,

for the most part fell into a deep hibernation when blacks sought their rights. The story is complex, and awaits telling in Chapters 9, 10, 15, and 16.

But in time the Fourteenth Amendment would awaken, and its impact on the nature of government in the United States would be profound. It permitted the federal courts to pass judgment on the reasonableness of certain types of state legislation, enabling them to function as a council of revision over the states, the same kind of council that the framers had specifically rejected at the federal level. It also permitted the federal courts to apply the Bill of Rights, once a bulwark against the federal government alone, to the states as well. In thus committing to federal hands the protection of civil rights, liberties, and equality before the law for all persons in the United States, the Fourteenth Amendment was truly a second American revolution.

Chapter 8 Voting Rights: Citizen Control of the Government

"Suffrage," said Susan B. Anthony, "is the pivotal right." The right to cast a ballot is—along with the First Amendment's guarantee of a right to discuss the issues—the centerpiece of American democracy.

The vote is the means by which the people retain the power they have delegated to their government and by which strong popular sentiment is translated into law—subject to important constitutional restrictions against abridging fundamental rights. Without the vote, representative democracy collapses.

Despite popular cynicism, the clearest proof of the power of the vote is the dramatic change in the past quarter century in election districts with sizable black populations who finally gained the right to register and vote after a century of discrimination. What else prompted George Corley Wallace, four-time governor of Alabama, to reverse his segregationist stance of the early sixties to appeal to black voters (and to staff an administration with a number of black officials) in the early eighties? Voting works, when elections are free.

The Constitutional Extension of the Franchise

The history of voting in America is the story of a continually enlarging electoral franchise—coming in the main not by statutory enactment but by constitutional amendment. Eligibility for voting is set in the states. Whoever is entitled to vote for the "most numerous branch of the state legislature" (the state house of representatives or assembly) is constitutionally entitled to vote in national congressional elections. In the late eighteenth century, the vote was restricted to white males over twenty-one, and many states imposed property qualifications (or a poll tax) as well. So it is not surprising that as notions of democracy spread, so too would the right to vote. Seven of the sixteen amendments ratified after the Bill of Rights concern voting.

The change took place in four stages and in different ways—by amendment, by judicial decision, by statutory enforcement of the constitutional changes, and by a reworking of legislative districts. Four amendments to the Constitution formally established new classes of voters:

1. The Fifteenth Amendment in 1870 gave the vote to blacks in all state and federal elections. No one may be denied the right to vote on account of race.
2. The Nineteenth Amendment in 1920 gave the vote to women. Wyoming was the first state to grant women the right to vote, in 1890 when it was admitted to the Union. Twenty-eight states extended the vote to women during the next thirty years, until the Nineteenth Amendment capped the long push for women's suffrage.
3. The Twenty-sixth Amendment, ratified in 1971, extended the franchise to all citizens at least eighteen years old. In the Voting Rights Act of 1970, Congress had lowered the age for both federal and state elections—a response in part to drafting eighteen-year-old men to fight in Vietnam. But the Supreme Court

The women's suffrage movement achieved its goal with ratification of the Nineteenth Amendment in 1920.

held that Congress could not constitutionally legislate a voting age for the states, so the amendment was quickly passed and ratified.
4. The Twenty-fourth Amendment in 1964 abolished the poll tax in all federal elections. It does not cover state elections. Although the Fifteenth Amendment, some supposed, had already done that, the language of the amendment does not expressly say so and the Supreme Court never expressly ruled that it did. Two years later, the Supreme Court ruled that under the equal protection clause of the Fourteenth Amend-

ment, poll taxes in state elections are unconstitutional because they discriminate against the poor.

Local reaction to the Nineteenth, Twenty-fourth, and Twenty-sixth Amendments was relatively restrained, and voting officials generally observed them without fuss. Not so, the Fifteenth Amendment. A century of judicial construction and political activism was necessary to secure for black citizens the reality of participating in elections. A variety of devices adopted in the 1890s and early 1900s effectively choked off black voting. From 1896 to 1904, when Louisiana adopted literacy, property, and poll tax qualifications for voting, black registration fell from 130,334 to 1,342. Similar results occurred in other states.

The "grandfather clause" was one of the earliest devices to which southern states repaired to avoid the impact of the amendment. The states required a literacy test of all voters but exempted those eligible to vote on January 1, 1867, and their descendants. This exemption excluded the emancipated blacks, most of whom were not legally entitled to vote until ratifi-

cation of the Fifteenth Amendment in 1870. Hence illiterate whites could vote, illiterate blacks could not.

Another device was to require blacks to register during a short period (usually ten days) about six months before the election; if they did not, they lost forever their right to vote. Whites, on the other hand, did not have to register at all. The Supreme Court struck down these ploys, though the last not until 1939.

Redrawing district lines could also serve to disenfranchise voters. Tuskegee, Alabama, once carved itself into a twenty-eight-sided figure to dry up the black vote by placing the black residential sections outside its limits, but the Supreme Court held that this kind of gerrymandering violated the equal protection clause of the Fourteenth Amendment.

Meanwhile, a fundamental change in voting practice had taken hold throughout the United States: the primary election. Candidates within the same party run against each other in a primary and the winner (usually) gets his or her party's nomination to run in the election. Because the entire party system, includ-

New Hampshire residents participate in their primary election.

Thomas Mifflin

Pennsylvania

Thomas Mifflin was born in Philadelphia, January 10, 1744, and died in Lancaster, January 20, 1800. He attended Quaker schools in Philadelphia and graduated from the College of Philadelphia at sixteen. He went into business with his brother and prospered. In 1765, he opposed the Stamp Act. As a member of the Pennsylvania Assembly (1772–1775), he argued the need for a colonial congress and served in the First and Second Continental Congresses. In 1775, he was commissioned a major in the Continental Army. Later, he became quartermaster general, a brigadier general, and finally a major general. In 1777, he resigned as quartermaster, and the next year resigned from the army because of unsubstantiated allegations of involvement in a financial fraud against George Washington and the army. In 1783 and 1784, he served as president under the Articles of Confederation. Mifflin was the speaker of the Pennsylvania General Assembly from 1785 to 1788. From 1788 to 1790, he was president of the state supreme executive council. Under Pennsylvania's revised constitution in 1790, he became the first governor and served until 1799. Mifflin's unchecked extravagance forced him to flee Philadelphia from his creditors. He died penniless the following year.

ing primaries, is regulated by state law and because the Constitution on its face is quite oblivious to the existence of parties or primaries, segregationists found what they thought was a foolproof way to eliminate black voting.

For example, Texas's white primary law permitted only whites to vote in the primary. This law effectively nullified the black vote, because whoever won the Texas Democratic primary, as in other southern Democratic primaries at the time, won the election. Texas defended its law on the ground that a primary is not an election and the Fifteenth Amendment protects the right to vote in elections only.

In 1927, the Supreme Court held that this artifice violates the equal protection clause. So Texas repealed the white primary law, enacting in its place a law giving executive committees of the political parties the authority to determine who should vote in the election. Texas reasoned that the Fourteenth Amendment protected only states, not private political parties, from discriminating. But again the Supreme Court struck down the law: The executive committee had become an agent of the state and it was barred, just as the state is barred, from exercising its power in a discriminatory manner.

Not deterred, Texas turned over to all party members the decision whom to enroll in the party. At first, the Court upheld this subterfuge, holding that when all party members act, they do not constitute an agency of the state. But in 1941, the Court finally recognized that a party primary is a true election, whether or not the word is used in the Fifteenth Amendment, and three years later struck down discrimination in any primary organized under state law.

Congressional Enforcement of the Fifteenth Amendment

The Fifteenth Amendment did more than formally declare the rights of all to vote, regardless of race. It also gave Congress power to enforce its provisions. This enforcement clause for the first time gave Congress power over state elections. Immediately after the amendment was ratified, Congress sought through two statutes to enforce the rights of the emancipated slaves to vote, the Enforcement Act of 1870 and the Force Act of 1871. But the Supreme Court, reversing most of the political gains of the Civil War as expressed by Congress, struck down these laws, or most of the vital sections of them. For nearly a century thereafter, as political forces changed and the rise of a one-party system below the Mason-Dixon line gave southern Democrats a stranglehold on civil rights legislation, Congress left the power dormant.

Not until 1957 did Congress act again to enforce the Fifteenth Amendment, by creating the Civil Rights Commission with power to investigate deprivations of voting rights and by conferring on the attorney general the power to sue voting officials implicated in those violations. That was a start, but the law was not efficient enough to deter continuing widespread state disobedience of the Fifteenth Amendment (largely

because it required case-by-case adjudication), nor did the Civil Rights Acts of 1960 and 1964 adequately address the problem. Finally, in the wake of Barry Goldwater's defeat in the 1964 elections, an unusually large Democratic majority in Congress was positioned to respond to President Johnson's call for action. This occurred ten days after Governor Wallace's state-sponsored violence on the march from Selma to Montgomery, a spectacle of unmatched brutality televised for a world to watch and culminating in the shooting of a white civil rights worker from Detroit, Mrs. Viola Liuzzo. "The time for waiting is gone," Johnson said, pointing to "the outraged conscience of a nation—the grave concern of many nations—and the harsh judgment of history on our acts." By wide margins (71–18 in the Senate, 328–74 in the House), Congress enacted the Voting Rights Act of 1965, according to Laurence Tribe "probably the most radical piece of civil rights legislation since Reconstruction."

In that act (extended in 1970, 1975, and 1982), Congress gave sweeping power to the U.S. Justice

The march from Selma to Montgomery led to swift passage of the Voting Rights Act of 1965.

Blacks waiting to vote in Peachtree, Alabama, following enactment of the Voting Rights Act of 1965.

Department to oversee elections in states that had once discriminated. It is this act, more than anything else, that has brought blacks to the registration rolls in record numbers, enough to significantly change voting patterns, rhetoric, and laws in those states.

Although applicable on its face to all states, the law actually subjects to its terms only those states (or counties) with a long history of discrimination. It applies to any state that (in the attorney general's determination) on November 1, 1964, conditioned the right to vote on a "test or device" (such as a literacy test) and that, by the reckoning of the director of the census, had less than 50 percent of eligible voters actually registered or voting in the November 1964 elections. In operation, the act governed all of Alabama, Alaska, Georgia, Mississippi, Louisiana, South Carolina, and Virginia, thirty-four counties in North Carolina, and single counties in Arizona, Idaho, and Maine. The Supreme Court quickly upheld the act against a constitutional challenge that Congress had no power to fashion specific remedies.

The act is tough. It permits the attorney general to suspend the various tests or devices that kept minority registration sluggish and to send federal voting examiners to supersede local officials in registering blacks. It also requires states to submit for approval, of either the attorney general or the federal district court in Washington, D.C., any proposed change in voting laws that would add a "test or device." To forestall any lengthy court battles over the attorney general's findings, Congress explicitly precluded judicial review, and the Supreme Court upheld this foreclosure of the usual right to challenge administrative action as a valid exercise of Congressional power under the Fifteenth Amendment. Within months, the black voter rolls swelled appreciably; a year later, total southern black registration nearly doubled, and within the next two decades, more than ten million blacks became a substantial electoral force.

Twice in the next ten years, Congress significantly strengthened the act, and so strong has been its appeal (and so demonstrably effective) that not even the opposition of President Reagan to a further extension could dissuade Congress in 1982 from reenacting it. In addition to prohibitions against literacy tests, the various amendments greatly expanded the number of citizens covered: Alaskan natives, American Indians, Chinese, Filipino, Japanese, Korean, and Spanish minorities are now included. More than thirty additional states were made subject to the attorney general's preclearance procedures, and individual citizens can file suit to bring their cities or counties within the act's coverage.

Literacy Tests

In 1898, the Supreme Court declared that a literacy test applicable on its face to all potential voters did not violate the equal protection clause of the Fourteenth Amendment, unless someone could show that a test was being discriminatorily administered. That situation finally was squarely put a half century later, in a case arising from the Alabama state constitution's requirement that only such persons could vote who understood and could explain the United States Constitution to the "satisfaction" of the local registrars. Because registrars were given no standard for judging the answer (hence they had wholly arbitrary power to discriminate—whites, in any event, were rarely asked to expound on the Constitution), the Supreme Court struck it down.

On its face, a literacy test poses no constitutional difficulty. The Supreme Court has never struck down literacy tests fairly applied, according to measurable standards; its last pronouncement found no constitutional fault with the concept of requiring all voters to be literate.

However, in the Voting Rights Act of 1965, Congress declared that a person illiterate in English but literate to the sixth-grade level in Spanish may not be denied the right to vote, and the Supreme Court has upheld that provision. Moreover, in the Voting

Thomas Nast's cartoon illustrating the use of literacy tests and strict educational qualifications to disfranchise many black voters in some Southern states appeared in the January 18, 1879, issue of Harper's Weekly *with the caption "The color line still exists—in this case."*

Rights Act amendments of 1970, Congress extended to all fifty states a ban on using literacy tests to enroll voters. In 1975, Congress took the final step and permanently banned all literacy tests for all elections.

Residency Requirements

Voters must vote from a specific place. A New Hampshire resident is not entitled to vote in the election for mayor from the next town, representative from Vermont, and senator from Massachusetts, just because she would rather cast her ballot for those candidates. To prevent the casual tourist from spending election day in out-of-state voting booths, every state (and municipality) maintains a territorial rule: Voters must be residents.

But like every other law that restricts voting, the residency requirement can be used to eliminate certain classes of people from the polls. In recent years, courts have scrutinized residency rules especially carefully, striking down laws that incorporate overly lengthy waiting periods. In a Tennessee case, the Supreme Court held that a one-year wait for eligibility to vote in the state (and three months in the county) was unconstitutionally long when it was conceded that the voter in question had indeed moved to the county and was a bona fide resident. The Court rejected Tennessee's claim that it had the power to restrict voting to "knowledgeable voters" or that the one-year rule was tailored to accomplishing that end. On the other hand, a fifty-day residency requirement was upheld as serving the state's "important interest in accurate voter lists."

Apportionment and Districting

Votes alone are not enough. Going behind the curtain and pulling the lever is useless if the vote doesn't count. Outright theft of ballots is unlawful under state and federal laws. But a vote can also be lost if it counts for less than other votes. For decades, votes were diluted by skewed districts in both federal and state elections. Voters in an urban congressional district, for example, might be four or five times as numerous as those in a rural district, and yet each district would send one representative to Washington. In effect, the vote in the less populous district would count for four or five times as much as that in the urban district.

The problem of malapportionment has two dimensions: equality of representation among the states and equality within the states. The only congressional inequality permitted in the Constitution is that for states with small populations: Every state is entitled to at least one representative (and, of course, every state gets two senators). Article I directs Congress to apportion seats state by state according to a decennial census. The original apportionment was not to exceed one representative for every thirty thousand people. As the population grew, that ratio would have created a House more than politically unwieldy. (The original ratio today would yield a House of eight thousand members.) So Congress has consistently reduced the ratio; by the turn of the twentieth century, it was roughly 1 per 200,000.

However, Congress has not always reapportioned itself according to the census: in 1920, for instance. The temptation is always strong to avoid this duty, since shifts in population among the states give more seats to some states, fewer to others, and incumbents find themselves without a seat at all or running in a drastically altered district to account for the change in the number of seats allocated to each state. So in 1929, Congress changed the method of determining the number of seats, setting 435 as the total number of House seats and requiring an apportionment among the states that would yield this number (meaning that the ratio is today approximately 1:545,000).

If this formula yields a representation roughly equal among the states, it does nothing for equality of districting within the states. Malapportioned districts

were the norm until very recent times. In 1946, the Supreme Court expressly declined to hear a case involving malapportionment, refraining, in Justice Frankfurter's words, from entering the "political thicket." Not until 1962 did the Supreme Court overcome its reluctance to let voters sue over such questions. In 1964, the Court ruled for the first time that Congressional districts with skewed populations within a single state are unconstitutional; the case arose in Georgia, where residents of Atlanta with 20 percent of the population elected only 10 percent of the state's representatives. The Court based its ruling on Article I, which states that representatives are to be "chosen . . . by the people," language that the Court majority took to mean: "One man's vote . . . is to be worth as much as another's."

This decision, and others that followed, did not control malapportioned state legislatures, where population disparities were far worse than in Congress. Some states for decades had ignored their own constitutional requirements to redistrict after the federal census. In time, Alabama, for one, had developed disparities as great as 46:1 in her senate and 16:1 in the lower house. It took only one-quarter of the population to elect a majority in both houses. The Supreme Court, also in 1964, voided state legislative malapportionment, on the ground that it violated the equal protection clause. Said Chief Justice Warren:

> Legislators represent people, not trees or acres. Legislators are elected by voters, not farms or cities or economic interests. As long as ours is a representative form of government, and our legislatures are those instruments of government elected directly by and directly representative of the people, the right to elect legislators in a free and unimpaired fashion is a bedrock of our political system. . . . The Equal Protection Clause demands no less than substantially equal state legislative representation for all citizens, of all places as well as of all races.

These decisions sparked a decade of lawsuits that remade the legislative map of the United States. Among its many decisions, the Court held that elections to each house in a state bicameral legislature must be from districts with equal population and that it does not matter that the people of a state in a general referendum approve some other arrangement, since citizens in one state cannot vote to rescind the U.S. Constitution. The United States Senate is the only legislative body exempted from this constitutional rule because its two-senators-per-state basis of apportionment is expressly set forth in the Constitution (as part of the Great Compromise). States may not model elections to their own senates on the federal system.

The reapportionment cases sparked an outcry in some quarters during the 1960s. One political wag impishly declared that after these cases the only people interested in state lines would be Rand McNally (the publisher of maps), and several political scientists decried the Court's simplemindedness in the face of important historic and political reasons for constructing election districts on geographic lines rather than on population. Several constitutional amendments were proposed to overturn the Court's ruling, but all such attempts failed.

The equal vote rule did not by itself answer all questions, and for a quarter-century the courts have found themselves saddled with a new class of litigation and a host of perplexing questions: Does the rule apply to every election (local as well as state)? How equal must election districts be to satisfy the rule? May elections be restricted to people who are "primarily interested" in the results?

In general, the courts have held that the rule applies to any local governmental body with "general governmental powers over an entire geographic area" and, even more strongly, that whenever persons are elected "to perform governmental functions," voters must "be given an equal opportunity to participate in that election." Moreover, "a state [must] make an honest and good faith effort to construct districts . . . as nearly of equal population as is practicable." Under some circumstances, however, an election may be restricted to those who are "primarily interested"; for example, voters in an election for directors of a water storage district may be limited to landowners in the district.

Regulating Campaigns

Even if voters can vote, and votes are counted equally, they would not count for much if the government could restrict in any significant way *who* can run for office or the ability of candidates to campaign. Legislatures are often tempted to bar candidates or restrict campaigns, because doing so eliminates the competition. One party is always struggling to make it more difficult for other parties to win; an officeholder always finds some threat in the noises that a potential or actual opponent makes. Among the many constitutional difficulties that inhere in campaigns, these stand out: (1) keeping candidates or parties off the ballot and (2) regulating campaign financing.

Ballots

A myriad of state laws govern listings on the ballot. The major parties are always listed; they control the process. Because Republicans and Democrats are wary of third-party movements, legislatures usually make it difficult for minority parties to put their candidates before the voters, as Adlai Stevenson III discovered in attempting to place his name on the Illinois ballot in 1986 after quitting the Democratic ticket as gubernatorial candidate; he refused to run with two adherents of the right-wing maverick Lyndon LaRouche, who had captured other spots on the ticket in a primary that spring. The more hampered minority candidates are in getting on the ballot, the more likely the courts will view their plight with sympathy.

One extreme was George Wallace's travail in Ohio in 1968. The Ohio rules required a minor-party candidate (Wallace was running as the American Independent party candidate for president) to round up signatures of registered voters equal to 15 percent of the votes cast in the previous gubernatorial election if his party had not garnered at least 10 percent of the vote in that election. Moreover, the nominating petition had to have been filed nine months before the presidential election. Even those requirements, onerous as they were, did not suffice; the party would be kept off the ballot unless it conducted primary elections and held a national nominating convention, neither of which the American Independent party had done. The Supreme Court held that the Ohio rules violated the equal protection clause and interfered with the "right of individuals to associate for the advancement of political beliefs, and the right of qualified voters, regardless of their political persuasion, to cast their votes effectively."

The Ohio rules were so draconian, the Court noted, that they "made it virtually impossible for a new political party . . . to be placed on the state ballot." By contrast, the Court upheld a Georgia law that simply required signatures of 5 percent of voters registered in the previous election. Reasonable petition requirements have been upheld to protect the election process; if the states did not require a "significant, measurable quantum of community support," a suf-

George Wallace

ficient number of cranks, branding themselves a "party," could make the general ballot meaningless and even impossible to contain within a voting booth.

Campaign Financing

The campaign financing problem is more intractable. Campaigns cost money, and the temptation to outspend one's rival is as old as democratic politics. Many gladiatorial contests in ancient Rome were early forms of public relations, sponsored by candidates for public office to draw comment on their candidacies. The first election law in history is said to be a 432 B.C. regulation barring Roman candidates from whitening their togas with chalk to attract attention. George Washington was spared having to campaign in 1788 because he had no opponent, but he was no stranger to the political arts. In running for the Virginia House of Burgesses in 1757, he followed the custom of the day, dispensing twenty-eight gallons of rum, fifty gallons of rum punch, thirty-four gallons of wine, forty-six gallons of beer, and two gallons of cider royal, all to seal the affections of 391 voters. By 1796, campaign funds had become an issue, and they have never since ceased being one.

The money has been used to buy votes, to buy election officials to withhold ballots, and even to buy seats outright. In the late nineteenth century, before the Seventeenth Amendment, when U.S. senators were still elected by state legislatures, the ticket to selection was usually cash. Mark Hanna, William McKinley's campaign manager, elevated the shakedown into a high art, probably not rivaled in elegance until Maurice Stans took on the job for Richard Nixon in the 1972 election, though no presidential campaign since John Adams's time has been untainted.

To be sure, much of what the moneymen did was illegal, violating all sorts of laws against bribery and extortion. But prosecutors are reluctant to prosecute those who, when they win office, hold the keys to appropriations. Moreover, many direct laws regulat-

ing campaign financing have been riddled with loopholes. The Federal Corrupt Practices Act, which governed federal campaign financing from 1925 until 1972, was practically worthless in deterring the bagmen and candidates from flouting its spirit.

In 1971, Congress enacted the Federal Election Campaign Act, which President Nixon signed and promptly tried to sidestep. To avoid the reporting requirements (public disclosure of all contributions and expenditures in excess of $100), Stans raised millions of dollars before the date (April 7, 1972) on which the act took effect, largely by promising anonymity (he suggested as contributions one-half of 1 percent of the net worth of various corporations, which were barred by law from contributing). By the fall of that election year, the General Accounting Office reported more than seven hundred violations of the law by all individuals, corporations, candidates, and officials.

As an outgrowth of Watergate, Congress amended the Election Campaign Act in 1974, imposing spending and contribution limits. The law limited the amount that could be contributed to candidates or their committees and the amounts that candidates could spend on themselves and that others could spend on their behalf. Individuals, groups, and campaign committees are limited to contributing $1,000 to any single candidate; political committees, to $5,000. No individual can contribute more than $25,000 to candidates altogether. The Supreme Court upheld the contribution limitations against a challenge that they violated contributors' rights of free speech and association.

However, it struck down the spending limitations. The law set a ceiling of $1,000 that anyone could independently spend to promote a specific candidate and a ceiling of $25,000 that a candidate or his family could spend on his own behalf. These limitations, the Court ruled, violated the First Amendment. The intent of the law was to equalize the relative ability of individuals and groups to influence the outcome of elections. But "the concept that the government may restrict the speech of some elements of our society in order to enhance the relative voice of others is wholly foreign to the First Amendment."

The net result of this ruling is that candidates and others may spend as much as they want to promote a particular candidacy as long as they do so independently of the campaign committee. Countering claims of independence is difficult. "A group like ours could lie through its teeth and the candidate stays clean," said the founder of one influential national political action committee, convicted in 1986 of violating the law four years earlier by spending ten times the limit on a rival of Senator Daniel Patrick Moynihan's, though not independent of his rival's campaign. The loophole remains large, and the problem of corruption bred by the need for campaign financing remains unsolved.

To some degree, therefore, Ambrose Bierce's cynical definition of an elector as "one who enjoys the sacred privilege of voting for the man of another man's choice" rings true. We are increasingly free as a population to vote, but increasingly we do not, and those for whom we vote are increasingly determined by those with money to spend. Under the Constitution, money will always talk.

But it does not dictate. As long as debate remains robust and the channels of debate remain open, voters at least have a choice. The alternative is to give over the source of funding to a single party and let the philosophers (usually known as party secretaries) decide. Then only one candidate will run, and the possibility that government will be controlled by the people will vanish even from historical memory.

Part 3

The Quest for Liberty

Chapter 9 Realizing Freedom: The Abolition of Slavery

In the long sorry history of man's inhumanity to man, slavery as an institution loomed large enough to have found a place in the original Constitution. Despite the generosity of their philosophical beliefs, the Founding Fathers could not dislodge ancient habits of mind, at least not sufficiently to risk the failure of their enterprise by forcing the moral issue.

Slavery's roots in America are nearly as old as British colonization. Even before the founding of the New World colonies, English slavers introduced kidnaped Africans into many lands over which His Britannic Majesty held dominion, and the slave trade followed the colonists across the Atlantic as a matter of course.

By the late seventeenth century, slavery had been incorporated in the legal systems of many of the colonies. The law did not formally establish slavery as an institution; that was accepted as a matter of custom, justified, when justifications were needed, with the kind of polite fictions that John Locke resorted to—that slaves were captives in just wars, who, having lost their right to life, could not be heard to complain if their lives were spared for the service of others. Thus in 1698, Locke drafted the Instructions to Governor Nicholson of Virginia, in which Negro slaves were regarded as justifiably subservient because they had committed "some Act that deserves Death" in a "just war" against them. (How he could have supposed that the Royal Africa Company's sweep into the Dark Continent qualified as a "just war" can only be explained as an early example of "public relations": Locke was an administrator of the slave-owning Carolinas, whose *Fundamental Constitutions of Carolina* proclaimed that every freeman "shall have absolute power and authority over his negro slaves.")

When the colonies became states, they did not formally establish slavery as an institution but continued to regulate slavery by statute and common law. All assumed, that is, that slavery as a custom and social arrangement was beyond question; even those who abhorred it supposed slave owners had a legal right to their property. The law was needed, not to originate, but to regulate.

This notion was so widely held that it became known as the "federal consensus": Slavery was legitimate within states that sanctioned it and the federal government was powerless to abolish it within those states. The states alone were competent to regulate or abolish slavery as they saw fit. Though some disputed it (Samuel Hopkins proposed in 1776 that the Continental Congress abolish slavery), the federal consensus was remarkably powerful in keeping minds closed to the underlying moral issue. The Articles of Confederation did not tamper with slavery, leaving the legal issues squarely up to each state.

It was this consensus that led to the famous "federal number": A slave counts for three-fifths of a man. The issue first arose just after the Declaration of Independence. How should the populations of each state be enumerated for purposes of a per capita tax to pay for federal expenses? Southern representatives vociferously objected to counting slaves as any part of the population. Not doing so would, of course, keep their tax burden smaller, but it would also avoid any suggestion that a slave was human. In a debate on July 30, 1776, Thomas Lynch of South Carolina declared: "If it is debated, whether their slaves are their property, there is an end of the confederation. Our slaves being our property, why should they be taxed more than the land, sheep, cattle, horses, &c?" Benjamin Franklin's telling retort: "Sheep will never make any insurrections." In 1783, a committee of the Continental Congress proposed in an enumeration of populations state by state that all free persons (excluding untaxed Indians) be counted "and three-fifths of all other persons not comprehended in the foregoing description." This three-fifths ratio would work its way into the Constitution four years later.

Although slavery itself did not occupy any considerable amount of the framers' attention, it was the central division within the convention. As Madison noted: "The real difference of interest lay, not between the large & small but between the N & Southn. States. The institution of slavery & its consequences formed the line of discrimination."

The delegates did not propose a federal power to abolish or even immediately to regulate slavery, but several subsidiary issues assumed major importance. Once it was settled that representation in the lower house would be based on population within each state, the question arose how to decide who should be counted. Ultimately, the delegates settled on the federal number: The entire white population would be added to three-fifths of the slave population. The three-fifths ratio would also serve to define the limits of federal power to enact a direct tax on each state.

These provisions were not met with unanimity. Gouverneur Morris, for one, denounced the Connecticut Compromise and unsuccessfully sought to undo it, declaiming that "when fairly explained, [the Compromise] comes to this: that the inhabitant of Georgia and S.C. who goes to the Coast of Africa, and in defiance of the most sacred laws of humanity tears away his fellow creatures from their dearest connections & damns them to the most cruel bondages, shall have more votes in a Govt. instituted for protection of the rights of mankind, then the Citizen of Pa. or N. Jersey who views with a laudable horror, so nefarious a practice." To add to the insult, northern states would be obligated to send troops to southern

states to put down slave rebellions, while all the time the southern states, safe from taxation and induced to increase their representation in Congress, would continue to import slaves.

The slave trade was even more hotly contested. Northerners who opposed slavery on moral grounds wished Congress to have the power to end trafficking in human beings; southerners, in particular the delegates from the Carolinas and Georgia, who saw slavery as an economic necessity, argued against any prohibition. In the end, the delegates compromised, reaching what Farrand has called "one of the conspicuous and important compromises of the convention."

The compromise provided that Congress would have no power to end the slave trade until 1808; from then on, if Congress wished, it could prohibit the importation of slaves into America. Any slaves who were imported could be taxed, but not more than $10.00 a head. Congress could impose direct taxes only in proportion to the ratio between each state's population and the total population, counting the slave population in each state as three-fifths of the whole. The provisions governing importation of slaves and direct taxes could not be amended out of the Constitution. Although not directly part of this compromise, a provision earlier accepted against taxing exports was important in creating an atmosphere that permitted the slave-trade compromise to be made: By prohibiting export taxes, the delegates had ensured that Congress could not indirectly impair the institution of slavery by taxing the product of slave labor.

The final aspect of the compromise was the provision governing navigation acts—laws requiring that goods in commerce be carried only in vessels made in America and manned by American crews (the same

kind of law to which the colonists had so vocally objected before the Revolution when imposed on them in reverse by Parliament). The delegates had earlier debated a requirement that navigation acts would require a two-thirds vote in Congress. The two-thirds requirement pleased the southern states, because navigation acts increased the cost of shipping goods, and displeased northern states whose economies would have benefited by the spur to their shipping industries that the acts would have induced. But now, in return for the absolute ban against congressional interference with the slave trade for twenty years, the southern states yielded to a congressional power to pass navigation acts by majority vote.

Two other slavery-related provisions passed the convention with less debate. One was the fugitive slave clause in Article IV. It prohibited one state from enacting laws that would emancipate a fugitive slave escaping into that state. Instead, the master could demand the slave's return. The other was a twin provision that empowers Congress to quell domestic strife. By Article I, Section 8, Congress is authorized to call up state militias to "suppress Insurrections," and under Article IV, Section 4, the federal government must protect the states against "domestic Violence."

Altogether, the document that emerged from the convention dealt with slavery in ten separate provisions:

1. Article I, Section 2: the "federal number" clause apportioning House seats on the basis of population, counting slaves as three-fifths of a person.
2. Article I, Section 2: apportioning direct taxes the same as representatives.
3. Article I, Section 8: establishing congressional power to call up the militia to suppress insurrections, including slave rebellions.
4. Article I, Section 9: prohibiting a congressional ban on the slave trade before 1808 and permitting a head tax on slaves of up to $10.00.
5. Article I, Section 9: prohibiting a direct tax not based on the federal census as provided for in Article I, Section 2 (this clause is redundant, being the same as the first provision).
6. Article I, Section 9: prohibiting Congress from taxing exports from any state.
7. Article I, Section 10: prohibiting the states from taxing exports (and thus from taxing the products of slave labor).
8. Article IV, Section 2: prohibiting states from emancipating fugitive slaves.
9. Article IV, Section 4: requiring the federal government to protect the states against domestic violence (including slave insurrections).
10. Article V: making the slave trade and direct tax provisions unamendable.

Although these provisions were undeniably inserted to protect southern interests in slavery, the delegates nowhere used the words *slave* or *slavery*. Sensitive to the anomaly of these provisions in the Constitution, the committee on style found circumlocutions that avoided saying what they meant. Thus in the apportionment clause, slaves were referred to as "other Persons." In the fugitive slave clause, they were called "Person[s] held to Service or Labour." And in the slave-trade clause, Congress was told that it could not prohibit the "Migration or Importation of such Persons as any of the states now existing shall think proper to admit." Why these euphemisms? Luther Martin explained that the framers wished to bypass "expressions which might be odious in the ears of Americans, although they were willing to admit into their system those things which the expressions signified."

But they were not so much admitting slavery into the new constitutional system as they were sticking to the consensus that slavery was for each state to deal with, not for the federal government. If slavery was to be abolished, it would have to be done by the states. Six of the original thirteen states—Massachusetts, Rhode Island, Connecticut, New York, New Jersey, and Pennsylvania—were taking initial steps in this direction in 1787, although in some cases it would take decades for complete abolition to become a legal reality. Not until 1843, for instance, did the Rhode Island constitution finally declare that "slavery will not be permitted in this state." In two other states, slavery was abandoned sooner. Vermont was the first to abolish slavery constitutionally (in 1787, three years before it became the fourteenth state). In New Hampshire, slavery simply faded away. On its face, the federal Constitution seemed almost neutral, neither advancing nor limiting these state-by-state developments.

Yet the Constitution remained somewhat ambiguous. The slave-trade clause, for instance, prohibited Congress from interfering with the trade only in those states "now existing." It was apparently free to restrict slavery in any new state or in territories of the United States. Almost at the time the delegates were in convention, the Continental Congress was enacting the Northwest Ordinance of 1787, which declared that in the Northwest Territories (from which Ohio, Indiana, Illinois, Michigan, and Wisconsin ultimately emerged as states, "there shall be neither slavery nor involuntary servitude . . . otherwise than in the punishment of crimes, where of the party shall have been duly convicted." Had Congress been able to restrict the spread of slavery, it is conceivable that the "peculiar institution" would in due course have withered

Civil war era photograph of slave quarters.

in the original southern slave states without a war. Whether Congress could do so was the battleground during the next three-quarters of a century, leading to constitutional crises in 1819–21, 1832 (the "nullification crisis,") 1846–50, 1854, and in 1861 when the nation finally exploded in civil war. Unlike any other issue in American history, the slavery question dominated political and constitutional thinking for decades; never since has any single constitutional issue so exercised the population at large or for so long a time—not segregation, not abortion, not Watergate. Constitutional disputation was the stuff of pamphleteering, street argument, vigilantism, and occasional rioting—day after day, year after year.

Whether or not the Constitution was neutral on its face, congressional enactments that followed ratification were not. In the first Fugitive Slave Act, in 1793, Congress acceded to southern claims and enacted a draconian law that made it difficult and sometimes impossible for free blacks who had been kidnaped to prove they had been born free or had been manumitted. Despite continual criticism, the act was repeatedly held to be constitutional.

Congress also protected slavery in all territories outside the free states and the Northwest Territories. In particular, it adopted the Maryland and Virginia slave codes for the nation's capital in the new District of Columbia in 1801. These laws, sometimes conflicting, were particularly severe. Slaves could have their ears cropped for striking a white; Maryland repealed this law in 1821, but it remained on the district's books. District slaves, seized as runaways, could be held in jail and sold if not claimed. This law led to the sale of numerous free blacks, who were left unprotected by the statute. The problem was that jailers were responsible for the costs of keeping their captives, and to recoup these costs they were permitted to sell unclaimed "slaves." Since no one could claim a free black, only the most scrupulous and moral jailer would refrain from selling free men and women into slavery to recover his costs. The Maryland statute that permitted this outrage had been enacted in 1719 and was repealed in the early 1800s, but it lingered on in the District, and it and other provisions of the District code permitted a flourishing slave trade within sight of the White House.

In 1803, South Carolina, after a state-imposed ban in 1787 to reduce indebtedness, reopened the high seas trade in slaves, to near universal denunciation. Within four years (at the first opportunity, constitutionally speaking, in 1807), Congress would ban for good the international trading in slaves, defining it as piracy for which the penalty was hanging (although it has been estimated that during the next half-century, thousands of slaves were imported despite the ban). Once the twenty-year ban expired on congressional interference with slave trading, the constitutional anomalies began to surface. A person could be hanged for shipping another person from Africa to Georgia. But if the shipment originated in one of the southern states, the American navy itself would protect the seller and the shipper. Also, blacks who were unlawfully imported from abroad were not returned home through federal authority; rather, under state laws, they were sold into slavery to profit the state. Against this backdrop, and with developing agitation against slavery in the north, came the Missouri crisis of 1819.

At the time of ratification, the populations of the free and slave states were roughly in balance. By tacit understanding, not law, the Mason-Dixon line and the Ohio River divided north and south, separating Pennsylvania from Maryland and Virginia; Ohio, Indiana, and Illinois from Virginia and Kentucky. By common consensus, slave states and free states were admitted to the Union in tandem to preserve the balance: Ohio (free) in 1803, Louisiana (slave) in 1812, Indiana (free) in 1816, and Mississippi (slave) in 1817. Illinois became a state in 1818; though nominally free, its constitution contained protoslavery provisions, and Alabama was to follow as a slave state. At the same time, the question of admitting Arkansas and Missouri arose, and the ensuing debate suggested that

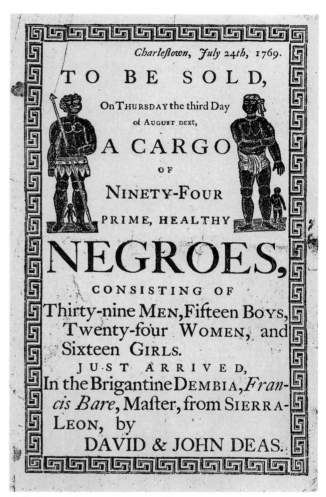

1769 slave sale announcement published in Charleston, South Carolina. Congress banned the international trading of slaves in 1807, but the practice continued illegally for the next half-century.

the Constitution might not be as neutral as it had once been supposed.

Missouri lay above the line dividing slave states from free. Northerners were perturbed at the continuing admission of slave states, not just on moral grounds, but also on highly political ones: The three-fifths clause was producing a skewed representation in Congress for slave states. Between 1792 and 1802, the clause gave southern states twelve representatives they would not otherwise have had; between 1802 and 1811, fifteen; and between 1811 and 1822, eighteen. Admitting Missouri to the Union as a slave state would considerably upset the balance.

So in February 1819, New York Congressman James Tallmadge introduced a bill in the House making Missouri's admission as a state conditional on a prohibition against any further slavery and the gradual emancipation of slaves in the territory. For constitutional justification, Senator Rufus King of Massachusetts argued that Article IV—permitting Congress to admit new states and to make "all needful Rules and Regulations respecting the Territory or other Property belonging to the United States"—empowered Congress to lay down whatever rules it wished as a condition for admission, including a ban on slavery. King's speech caused a sensation, for it struck hard at the notion that the Constitution was neutral on the question of the spread of slavery. Beyond the legalistic response that the Constitution conveyed no such power on Congress, southerners conjured up all manner of nightmares that such a power would bring. These included perhaps the earliest claim in American history that communism would surely follow, as an interference with the property rights of Americans, which the due process clause of the Fifth Amendment guaranteed against government expropriation, at least without just compensation. Other arguments pro and con sprung from the ambiguous, euphemistic language that the framers chose in 1786 to avoid putting the word *slave* into the Constitution. Thus restrictionists pointed to Article I, Section 9 (prohibiting Congress from banning the slave trade until 1808), as implicitly showing that Congress had the power to regulate *migration* of slaves after 1808; antirestrictionists argued that "migration" did not refer to slaves but to the movement of free white aliens.

In the end, Congress accepted the so-called Missouri Compromise: Missouri would come into the Union as a slave state, Maine as a free state, and no slavery would be permitted in any territory north of Missouri's southern border (excepting Missouri itself). The compromise, said historian Samuel Eliot Morison, "put the question of slavery extension at rest for almost a generation. It was a fair solution. The South obtained her immediate object, with the prospect of Arkansas and Florida entering as slave states in the near future; the North secured the greater expanse of settled territory, and maintained the principle of 1787, that Congress could keep slavery out of the Territories if it chose."

Political quietude at the federal level was not mirrored by any cooling of moral fervor or legal change within the states. Northerners organized the underground railway, spiriting thousands of slaves to freedom. Slave revolts in the south, including the Nat Turner Rebellion in 1831, left southerners terrorized and led them to enact repressive slave codes and laws governing relations between whites and free blacks.

Gradualism was dying. The hope that in time slavery would simply fade away seemed increasingly unlikely to a host of northern abolitionists. Extremists on both sides of the issue became more militant. The New England Anti-Slavery Society was formed in 1831; two years later, the American Anti-Slavery Society included in its founding constitution the doctrine of "immediatism": The government should, the society held, abolish slavery everywhere at once. Local societies spun off from the American Anti-Slavery Society, and they sought reform by helping runaways, organizing state conventions, and publishing an increasing stream of papers against slavery. One important work that acted as a spur was William Lloyd

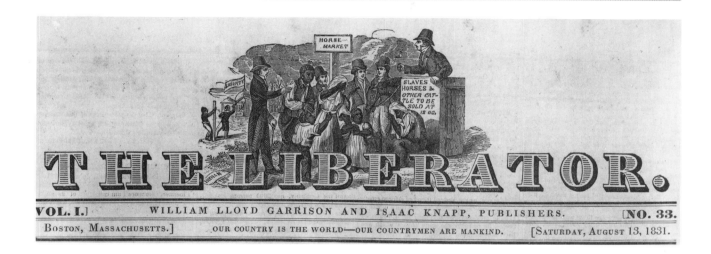

THE LIBERATOR.

VOL. I.]   WILLIAM LLOYD GARRISON AND ISAAC KNAPP, PUBLISHERS.   [NO. 33.

BOSTON, MASSACHUSETTS.]   OUR COUNTRY IS THE WORLD—OUR COUNTRYMEN ARE MANKIND.   [SATURDAY, AUGUST 13, 1831.

Garrison's newspaper *Liberator* in 1831. The Garrisonians saw the Constitution as inherently proslavery and urged northern states to secede from the Union.

At first, abolitionists distributed their publications through the mail. But in 1835, an ad hoc group, the "Committee of 21," took over the municipal government of Charleston, South Carolina, and prevented the delivery of such mail. In blatant violation of the spirit of the First Amendment guaranteeing free speech and press against federal encroachment (and, many thought, against encroachment by the states as well), the legislatures in Maryland, Mississippi, Missouri, and Tennessee followed suit, banning publications "calculated to excite discontent . . . amongst the slaves or free persons of color." Other states actually demanded that northern states enact laws censoring all antislavery activity; North Carolina had the effrontery to denounce northern states for countenancing freedoms of speech and association in their constitutions. It was left to South Carolina Governor George McDuffie to express southern extraconstitutional policy in its most naked form: He argued that under principles of international law, northern states were bound to make antislavery activity a capital offense.

By such measures, southerners were transforming the constitutional question into the rights not solely of slave owners but also of all Americans. Political activity intensified, as abolitionists discovered the efficacy of petition drives. More than a million signatories demanded that Congress abolish slavery in the District of Columbia and elsewhere.

From the 1830s on, cases concerning slaves and free blacks were tried at all judicial levels in the United States. Abolitionists in northern states hoped to secure judicial rulings that invalidated slavery and some of the worst aspects of race prejudice, but they were generally unsuccessful, frequently because of judicial racism. Thus, with no precedent to guide him save his own personal prejudice, the chief justice of the Pennsylvania Supreme Court, John Bannister Gibson, one of the most eminent nineteenth-century jurists, ruled that blacks could not vote because they were not "freemen" under the meaning of the term in the 1790 state constitution.

In Connecticut, the Prudence Crandall case drew considerable national attention. Crandall ran a school for girls in the town of Canterbury, and in 1832 started to admit blacks. Whites objected, so she converted

Schoolteacher Prudence Crandall's conviction for teaching nonresident black students at her Connecticut girls' school was overturned, but the court's decision sidestepped the issue of full state citizen rights for free blacks.

the school to an all-black institution. The legislature enacted the Connecticut Black Law, barring her from teaching nonresident blacks unless the town first approved. She was convicted of violating the statute. Her conviction was overturned on a technicality in the state supreme court, but she failed to persuade the judges on the major issue being pressed by abolitionists from Massachusetts, Rhode Island, Connecticut, and New York—that the "privileges and immunities" clause (Article IV, Section 2) guaranteed free blacks full rights as citizens of the state. Citizenship was not well defined in the Constitution. Proslavery advocates denied that blacks could be citizens of any state; abolitionists argued that free blacks as citizens of one state automatically had national citizenship. The court ducked the issue.

Over one question—the rights of slaves traveling with their master in a free state—legal doctrine held some promise for the abolitionists. The law governing so-called sojourners stemmed from a 1772 decision of Baron Mansfield, chief justice of the King's Bench, in the celebrated *Somerset* case. An American slave, James Somerset, was brought to England by his master; Somerset escaped, was recaptured, and was put on the block for sale to Jamaica. Emancipationists in England secured a writ of habeas corpus, hoping to have the court declare slavery unlawful throughout England. Mansfield did not quite go that far, but he did hand down a far-reaching opinion. He held, first, that the law governing what coercion a master could exercise over runaway slaves was that of the country in which the slaves were found, not the country in which they were held as slaves. In other words, Virginia colonial law (where Somerset was originally bought by his master) could not dictate what would happen to him in England. English law applied, and English law would not permit him to be enslaved under these circumstances. That was because, Mansfield said, second, only "positive law" could establish slavery; some official legal pronouncement of the sovereign was required. There being none in England,

Gouverneur Morris

Pennsylvania

Gouverneur Morris was born in Morrisania, N.Y., January 31, 1752. He died there November 6, 1816. He graduated from Kings College in 1768 and was admitted to the bar in 1771. Morris favored conciliation early on, but by 1775 was for the patriot cause. He helped draft the New York state constitution with John Jay and Robert Livingston. In 1778, he was in the Continental Congress, but lost his seat in 1779 through the machinations of his adversary George Clinton. He lived in Pennsylvania for a few years, where he became assistant to the superintendent of finance (1781–1785). At the Philadelphia Convention, he advocated a strong central government and life terms for the president and senators, and opposed equal representation in the Senate and the three-fifths compromise. As chairman of the committee on style, he was responsible for the language of the Constitution. In 1789, he traveled to Europe on private business and stayed until 1798, sometimes as a U.S. official, and observed the French Revolution at first hand. From 1800 to 1803, he was a U.S. senator. He was the canal commissioner of New York from 1810 to 1813 and voted for the Erie Canal. He opposed the War of 1812, and two years later supported the antiwar states' rights convention in Hartford.

Morris was a tall and attractive ladies' man. One-legged, he is said to have lost his limb fleeing from an angry husband. He had a long affair with Talleyrand's mistress. At fifty-seven, he married.

Somerset had to be freed. (Some limited forms of slavery continued in England until final emancipation in 1833.)

The case reverberated throughout the colonies and for decades afterward in the states, for it seemed to suggest that a slave who stepped onto free soil was thereby emancipated. Not only that, but, as abolitionists recognized when in the mid-1800s the issue was the spread of slavery into new territories, *Somerset* was a powerful argument for restriction: If Congress refused to permit the territories to adopt slavery, there would be no positive law establishing it and slave owners taking their slaves into the territory (or later the state) would find them immediately emancipated.

Such was the result in the "Med Maria" case in 1836 in Boston. Med, a six-year-old slave, traveled with her mistress, vacationing in Massachusetts. Abolitionists obtained a writ of habeas corpus, and when the case came up to the state supreme court, Chief Justice Lemuel Shaw held, on the principles of *Somerset*, for Med, whose champions renamed her "Med Maria Somerset." Shaw's opinion held that the "free and equal" clause of the state constitution showed there was no positive law creating the right of slavery, rather the opposite. And since no state law permitted a sojourner to keep her slave, Med had to be freed.

Despite such occasional antislavery victories, the politicians tried to avoid coming to terms with the constitutional arguments pro and con. In 1836, Congress adopted so-called gag rules, designed to table all petitions and censor floor debates about slavery. The gags lasted for eight years, and during this time, the constitutionality of the gag became a prominent issue. John Quincy Adams, former president and then a congressman, earned the nickname "Old Man Eloquent" for his creative attempts to bypass the rules; he once spoke for ten days on an issue related to slavery, unimpeded by his angered southern colleagues, leaving one "sprawling in his own compost."

By 1844, the gags were a dead letter and Congress repealed them. By this time too, fierce questions arose about the extension of slavery into vast tracts of land that were about to be acquired. Between 1845 and 1853, the land mass of the United States increased by 73 percent, as follows: Texas annexation, 1845 (Texas and parts of New Mexico, Oklahoma, Nebraska, and Colorado); Oregon Territory, 1846 (Washington, Oregon, Idaho, and parts of Montana and Wyoming); the Mexican cession following the Mexican War, 1848 (California, Nevada, Utah, and parts of Colorado, Wyoming, New Mexico, and Arizona): and the Gadsden Purchase, 1853 (the southern tips of Arizona and New Mexico). What had once been a stable balance between slave state and free in the provisions of the Northwest Ordinance and the Missouri Compromise was now seriously threatened. Would this immense territory to the west be slave or free?

In 1846, Pennsylvania Congressman David Wilmot proposed the language of the Northwest Ordinance to bar all slavery in any lands acquired as a result of the Mexican War. He reasoned that since that territory had had no tradition of slavery, any states carved out of it should be free. This Wilmot Proviso sparked a furious, lengthy debate in a Congress no longer disposed to gentlemanly behavior over the issue. Massachusetts Senator Charles Sumner was so severely beaten at his seat on the floor of the Senate after a speech denouncing South Carolina Senator

David Wilmot

Andrew Butler, while his colleagues stood by watching, that it took him three years to recuperate before he could return to the Senate.

The issue turned on whether Congress had the constitutional power to prevent slavery in new territories. Against the northern position that through its power to govern the territories and to regulate the flow of interstate commerce, Congress could halt slavery at the borders of the new territories, southerners argued their right to take their property with them anywhere in the United States they wished. For many southerners, this was the last chance to maintain their way of life; they saw the rapidly increasing population of the northern states threatening their hold on political power in Congress. In 1850, only seven of the twenty-three million Americans lived in the eleven

1856 cartoon depicting the assault on Senator Charles Sumner by Congressman Preston S. Brooks following Sumner's speech attacking the pro-slavery stance of Senator Andrew Butler, who was a relative of Brooks.

states that would become the Confederacy a decade later.

Congress overcame the crisis provoked by the Wilmot Proviso by accepting Henry Clay's Compromise of 1850. Northerners won the admission of California as a free state. Southerners saw to it that the states that would emerge from the Mexican cession would be organized without regard to slavery; Congress would neither introduce nor exclude slavery in these territories. Instead, the question of whether slavery would ultimately be permitted was left to the courts.

The second sop to the South provoked a firestorm of opposition: the Fugitive Slave Act of 1850, updating the badly weakened fugitive slave law originally enacted in 1793. The new law explicitly required the federal government to capture and return fugitive slaves. This was a response to the Supreme Court's 1842 decision that all state personal liberty laws themselves were unconstitutional because they conflicted with the federal law. The 1850 act empowered a new set of federal agents to assist in recapturing runaway slaves. The act's provisions were severe: A bystander who refused to aid a federal marshal could be tried for treason. A federal marshal who lost his prisoner would be personally liable to pay a large fine. The standard of evidence for seizing a fugitive was, by the standards of our age, highly suspect: Only the claimant need demand the capture; the alleged runaway was prohibited from disputing the claim and could not sue to protect her freedom. Those who hid runaway slaves were liable to a $2,000 fine and six months in prison. No wonder the national temper rose: As free blacks were kidnaped, riots and murder attended attempts to recapture them, and the states passed personal liberty laws that sharply conflicted with the federal act. The federal consensus was unraveling.

Four years after the Clay Compromise, the slave-state, free-state balance was wrecked with the passage of the Kansas-Nebraska Act. Senator Stephen A. Douglas, who would shortly debate Abraham Lincoln, saw a way to ensure that the transcontinental railroad would be kept from the south: Organize the Nebraska Territory. To counter southern opposition, he proposed that the Missouri Compromise of 1820

Henry Clay's Compromise of 1850 proved to be only a short-term solution to the slavery issue.

be abrogated and the people of the territory be permitted to determine for themselves whether to allow slavery (he called this "popular" or "squatter's sovereignty"). Congress concurred, after a fierce debate that split the territory into two. The act explicitly repealed the Missouri Compromise to allow slavery into "free soil" territory above the time-honored line. As before, Congress ducked the issue of how far slavery could extend by leaving it to the courts. And when the issue finally came to a head in the case of the Missouri slave Dred Scott, the Supreme Court administered its "self-inflicted wound," from which it—and the nation—would take long to recover and which would fundamentally alter the course of American constitutionalism.

The case was wending its way through the courts during the struggles of 1854, which narrowed constitutional options drastically. Of the five constitutional alternatives open to the nation in 1848—Wilmot Proviso (Free Soil), territorial sovereignty, extension of the Missouri Compromise line, Calhounite slavery-ubiquity, and the Clayton Compromise [essentially embodied in Clay's Compromise of 1850]—two lay dead or dying in 1854. The Missouri Compromise was politically defunct, and the view that it had always been unconstitutional was gaining support. Territorial sovereignty was perverted in northern eyes, stripped of its pseudo-democratic implications and revealed for what it was: a proslavery disguise, concealing the flanking movements of slavery in the western empire. This left only the Free-Soil and Calhounite polar opposites as constitutionally viable, together with the unpredictable Clayton possibility of abandoning the constitutional issue to federal judges. In this sense, Abraham Lincoln's "House Divided" speech of 1858 expressed an important constitutional truth. The constitutional house had become divided; the scope available for evasion and ambiguity had constricted; the time left for temporizing was running out.

Could slavery be extended westward? That question lay at the heart of the case that would rend the nation, shattering its fragile unity beyond the power of any person to restore. Scott was born in the late eighteenth century, the property of Peter Blow of Virginia. In 1827, when Scott was thirty, the family moved to St. Louis. When Blow died, Scott was sold to Dr. John Emerson, an assistant army surgeon. In 1834, Dr. Emerson began a series of fateful travels: first to Illinois (a free state), then to Fort Snelling in the Wisconsin Territory (in what was to become Minnesota, by virtue of the Missouri Compromise, also free). In 1837, Scott and his family were sent back to St. Louis to be hired out, while Dr. Emerson attempted to recover his health elsewhere. In 1843, Emerson died, and his widow, Irene Sanford Emerson, inherited his property, including the slaves.

In 1846, Dred Scott sued for his freedom in a Missouri state court. Following the *Somerset* reasoning, he argued that he had become irrevocably free when he entered Illinois and Minnesota with Emerson. In 1850, a jury held in his favor, but the Missouri Supreme Court reversed its decision two years later, overruling a precedent squarely to the contrary. The state supreme court held that under Missouri law, Scott had become a slave again when he reentered the state.

That should have ended the case, for the question was not appealable to the U.S. Supreme Court, slavery being an issue for each state to settle. But fate intervened. Mrs. Emerson had remarried and moved to Massachusetts. A Missouri law made married women ineligible to administer a trust, so administration of her father's estate passed to her brother, John F. A. Sanford of New York. Because Sanford was not a citizen of Missouri, he could be sued in federal court under the "diversity of citizenship jurisdiction"; and a federal case would be appealable to the Supreme Court.

This new suit—a test case fabricated for the purpose of putting the slavery issue squarely before the Supreme Court—alleged that Sanford had assaulted Dred Scott and his family. Scott sought $9,000 in

Dred Scott's suit for freedom in 1846 was eventually lost eleven years later when the U.S. Supreme Court found the Missouri Compromise of 1820 to be unconstitutional.

damages. The U.S. Circuit Court in St. Louis ruled that Scott was a citizen for jurisdictional purposes, thus permitting the suit to be heard. Sanford (whose name would be misspelled "Sandford" in the Supreme Court Reports) defended on the grounds that he was entitled to lay his hands "gently" on his slaves. In 1854, the circuit court upheld that defense, and the case was ready for its rendezvous with Chief Justice Roger Brooke Taney, from slaveholding Maryland.

The appeal reached the Supreme Court in February 1856, but the Court was evenly divided on the question whether the case was properly before it; a ninth justice, Samuel Nelson of New York, concluded that the threshold question, whether Scott was a citizen, should be reargued, and that was put off until December 1856, after the national elections that brought James M. Buchanan to the White House. The reargument lasted four days and excited speculation throughout the country. Obscure when it first was docketed, by now the appeal and its significance were known to anyone who read the newspapers.

Four years earlier, in *Strader v. Graham*, the Supreme Court had ruled unanimously that slaves' status must be determined by referring to the law of the state to which they returned, not to the state in which they sojourned. By this rule, Scott would clearly remain a slave, because the Missouri Supreme Court had already ruled that he was when he returned. And if he was a slave, then he could not bring his suit, and that would be the end of the matter.

But the Supreme Court decided not to adhere to so narrow a chain of reasoning. For a variety of political reasons, the justices determined to reach the larger issue—whether the Missouri Compromise of 1820 was constitutional. If it was not, then Congress could do nothing to prevent the westward expansion of slavery.

On March 6, 1857, two days after James Buchanan took the oath of office as the nation's fifteenth president, the Supreme Court handed down its decision— in the form of nine separate opinions, totaling more than 250 pages in the official reports. Although the opinions muddy the reasons, the Court's holding was clear: The Missouri Compromise was declared to be unconstitutional, and Dred Scott was held to have remained a slave.

Taney's opinion was remarkable for the sweep of its conclusions. First, he declared that "a negro, whose ancestors were imported into this country, and sold as slaves," was not a citizen of the United States and no state could make him a citizen. Taney rested this conclusion on the assumption that blacks were not "people of the United States," not members of the political community, at the time the Constitution was written. Here was "strict construction" with a vengeance: The Constitution meant in 1857 what it meant when it was adopted. How Taney "knew" that the Constitution meant this in 1786, when written, or

Justice Roger B. Taney

1787, when ratified, is mysterious, since free blacks did exist in many states at the time. In fact, Taney was simply wrong. As Justice Curtis noted in his dissent: in 1781, "all free native-born inhabitants of the States of New Hampshire, Massachusetts, New York, New Jersey, and North Carolina, though descended from African slaves, were not only citizens of those States, but such of them as had the other necessary qualifications [such as sufficient property] possessed the franchise of electors, on equal terms with other citizens."

Perhaps because only two other justices followed Taney to this conclusion, he demonstrated an alternative reason for concluding that the courts lacked jurisdiction to hear Scott's case: the unconstitutionality of the Missouri Compromise. In governing territory belonging to the United States, the federal government is bound by the Fifth Amendment to the Constitution, which provides that no person may be deprived of life, liberty, or property, without due process of law. "And," said Taney, "an act of Congress which deprives a citizen of the United States of his liberty or property, merely because he came himself or brought his property into a particular Territory of the United States, and who had committed no offence against the laws, could hardly be dignified with the name of due process of law." Since Congress did not have the power to extinguish an owner's property right in slaves, neither did the territorial governments, which derive their powers from Congress.

Thus the principle of the Missouri Compromise was smashed, and there could be no preventing the march of slavery. Not even a majority of the territorial inhabitants could abolish it. With those words, Taney smote popular sovereignty, and in this aspect of his opinion, six other justices joined.

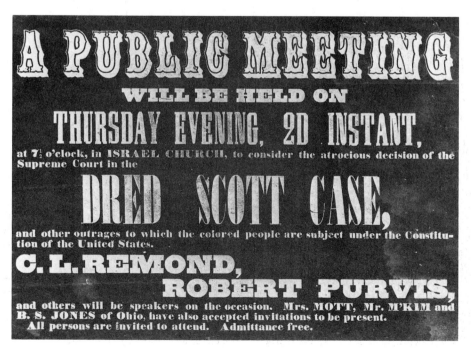

Notice denouncing the Dred Scott *decision and inviting the public to attend an abolitionist-sponsored meeting to consider the effects of the court's actions.*

Among the many peculiar aspects of Taney's reasoning, perhaps the strangest was the mechanism by which slavery was "created" in the territories. Slavery was a legal nullity without positive law—that is, without a legal pronouncement of a competent political authority. But Congress had declared certain territories forever free. What then created the right of slavery there? The laws of a slave state. But how could the laws of Missouri extend to Minnesota, there being no declaration of the right to slavery in that territory? Taney did not address himself to this paradox.

The Court declared Dred Scott a slave. Those who had used him, unsuccessfully, to secure a ruling against slavery, now took steps to emancipate him. In May 1856, he became a free man, but he died of tuberculosis only fifteen months later.

For four bitter years, to be followed by another four even more bitter, the *Dred Scott* case tore the nation apart. The Democratic party was hopelessly split between northern and southern factions, allowing the Republican Abraham Lincoln his plurality victory in a four-way race in 1860.

"Both parties deprecated war," Lincoln was to say in his second inaugural, "but one of them would *make* war rather than let the nation survive, and the other would *accept* war rather than let it perish. . . . and the war came." South Carolina in convention voted to secede on December 20, 1860, and twelve other states joined within nine months. Only through war could slavery finally be destroyed.

The end came finally, officially, on December 18, 1865, when the Thirteenth Amendment was declared ratified. "Neither slavery nor involuntary servitude," it declares "shall exist within the United States, or any place subject to their jurisdiction." This is the only provision in the Constitution that applies directly to all people in the United States. That is, it reaches private conduct as well as public law, outlawing slavery in any form by whoever attempts to hold another in bondage. And it protects everyone. The Thirteenth Amendment is not "a declaration in favor of a particular people. It reaches every race and every individual, and if in any respect it commits one race to the Nation, it commits every race and every individual thereof. Slavery or involuntary servitude of the Chinese, of the Italian, of the Anglo-Saxon are as much within its compass as slavery or involuntary servitude of the African."

Moreover, the Thirteenth Amendment bans more than slavery. In outlawing "involuntary servitude," it strikes at peonage, compulsory service to pay a debt. Thus the Supreme Court in 1905 voided an Alabama statute that subjected farm laborers to imprisonment for quitting their jobs to take up employment with someone else. By the same reasoning, the Thirteenth Amendment precludes state courts from ordering an employee to abide by an employment contract and continue working, even in the absence of criminal sanctions. You can always quit your job; you cannot be forced to work for someone against your will. However, a contract that forbids the employee from quitting to work for a competitor, but leaves him free to do other work, is not unconstitutional, as baseball players alleged in trying to break out of the "reserve" system, a contractual system that bound them to play for their own ball club only (though the reserve system fell apart on other grounds).

As significant as it is, the courts have limited the Thirteenth Amendment to its primary objective. Certain time-honored forms of compulsory service—like the military draft and being held as a material witness in court at one dollar per day—do not violate the amendment.

For blacks, emancipated by President Lincoln's proclamation, an exercise of executive power ratified and secured by the Thirteenth Amendment, the abolition of slavery was paramount, but by no means sufficient. Removed from a social system that at least had fed them, the question remained how they would survive in a hostile culture that had to regard them as constitutionally equal but saw them as inferior in every other way.

The Thirteenth Amendment gave Congress significant power to enforce its objective, and Congress acted. The Civil Rights Act of 1866, for example, gave blacks the right to contract, to sue and be sued, to marry, to travel—civil rights, in the nineteenth-century meaning of the term, that had been denied them, not only as slaves, but even as free persons before the Civil War. But following Reconstruction, the Supreme Court took a narrow view both of the meaning of the Civil War amendments and of the powers of Congress to enforce them. So harsh was the Court's blow in the 1870s and 1880s that it would be eighty-seven years before Congress chose once again to exercise its power and almost as long (Chapter 15) before the federal courts extricated themselves from the terrible racial morass into which they had sunk.

Three-quarters of a century late, formal freedom became the law of the land. But the Thirteenth Amendment was, then, less a law than a pledge. A century and more later, we are still redeeming it.

Chapter 10 **Latent Possibilities: the Promise of the Fourteenth Amendment**

"There's no better way of exercising the imagination than the study of law. No poet ever interpreted nature as freely as a lawyer interprets truth," said the French playwright and propaganda minister Jean Giraudoux. He could have been speaking about the fate of the Fourteenth Amendment in the late nineteenth century. Intended to change the face of justice, the Fourteenth Amendment sought nourishment from judges who strained at interpretation to avoid the larger effort of imagining a different world. Instead of bedrock, it became a sieve, through which rights of blacks could pour out and rights of commercial interests could pour in. Contradictions abounded, historical reality was lost, and the rights of Americans were for a long time forgotten.

The story is complex, and is told here in separate places because it is central to much of modern constitutionalism. In this chapter, we consider the roots of the transformation in the federal system of rights and how the Fourteenth Amendment came to protect the liberty of Americans, not just from acts of the central government, but from that of the states as well, a development of profound importance for the system of individual rights today (Chapters 11–13). Eventually, the Fourteenth Amendment was returned to its intended purpose of fighting racial and other inequalities (Chapters 15–16). It also became the device through which the Bill of Rights has come to apply to the criminal law of the states (Chapter 14). And for a long time the Fourteenth Amendment gave extensive protection to private property, broadly defined, and still functions as its protector today, although in altered fashion (Chapter 17).

The Thirteenth Amendment as Precursor

Although the opinion was not universally shared even among themselves, the radical Republicans who controlled Congress immediately after the Civil War believed the Thirteenth Amendment would do more than merely signal the formal abolition of slavery. That, as a practical matter, had already been accomplished. In empowering Congress to enforce its provisions, its framers thought the Thirteenth Amendment gave ample latitude to the earnest desire to abolish as well the badges of slavery.

Blacks and whites were not equal in legal theory after the Civil War, just as free blacks had not been the legal equals of whites in antebellum America. Throughout the South before the war, blacks were civilly disabled: They could not sue, they could not testify in court (in some states they could not testify at all, in others they were prohibited from testifying against whites), they could not enter into binding contracts, they could not hold property equally with whites. The Thirteenth Amendment was intended to do away with these disabilities that as surely rob a person of freedom as the status of slavery itself. In the Civil Rights Act of 1866, Congress prohibited the states from enforcing many of these laws (or extended these rights to blacks to overcome local custom).

But during the mid-1860s, beginning before the ratification of the Thirteenth Amendment and continuing afterward, the southern states adopted the so-called Black Codes. These "acknowledged the Negroes' free status but provided blacks only severely truncated forms of freedom": Given the political realities, the states permitted blacks to buy, sell, and own property, to make contracts, to marry (other blacks), to travel, to sue and be sued, and to testify in court whenever other blacks were parties to the case.

But in other respects, the Black Codes were harshly repressive, "recreating the race-control features of the slave codes":

> They defined racial status; forbade blacks from pursuing certain occupations or professions (e.g., skilled artisans, merchants, physicians, preaching without a license); forbade owning firearms or other weapons; controlled the movement of blacks by systems of passes; required proof of residence; prohibited the congregation of groups of blacks; restricted blacks from residing in certain areas; and specified an etiquette of deference to whites, as for example, by prohibiting blacks from directing insulting words at whites. The Codes forbade racial intermarriage and provided the death penalty for blacks raping white women, while omitting special provisions for whites raping black women. They excluded blacks from jury duty, public office, and voting. Some Codes required racial segregation in public transportation. Most Codes authorized whipping and the pillory as punishment for freedmen's offenses.

The practical effect of the codes was to severely degrade blacks and to make it virtually impossible to obtain even the most rudimentary form of justice. For example, by barring their testimony in trials involving whites, it was impossible for black workers to challenge unlawful acts of their white employer.

That the Thirteenth Amendment was equal to eradicating the worst excesses of the codes was an article of faith among most Republicans. Thus Michael Hahn, head of Lincoln's Reconstruction effort in Louisiana, in a speech in Washington in November 1865, proclaimed that the Thirteenth Amendment was open-ended in committing the federal government to protecting the equal rights of everyone.

No one doubted that the Thirteenth Amendment gave Congress the authority to legislate in ways that touched the private conduct of citizens ordinarily regulated under state law—a problem that would loom large in Fourteenth Amendment jurisprudence. Also, there could be few doubts that the enforcement clause was open-ended to some degree, or else why grant such a power at all? But some reservations were raised about the breadth of the terms *slavery* and *involuntary servitude*. Was the inability to testify a mark of servitude or something else? Was the disenfranchisement of blacks throughout the South an abridgment of civil rights or political rights? Were state indictments aimed at suppressing free speech by those who pressed for black suffrage a threat to civil rights that should be enjoyed by all Americans? Were social restrictions—lack of access to various institutions that by their nature are "public" accommodations (hospitals, restaurants, schools, inns)—abridgments of civil rights or social rights?

As two historians of the constitutional currents of the Civil War era note, our conception of civil rights does not mirror the meaning of the term twelve decades ago. Civil rights were those that were truly essential to freedom and which beyond question the Thirteenth Amendment covered, else how could a person be free? But these did not necessarily include the right to vote or to seek treatment in a hospital. The problem was that no one had any clear understanding of the terms that were bandied about so freely, nor was there consensus on which rights should be deemed fundamental. Some rights seemed more certain than others, even rights that seemed to have little direct connection with racial equality. Thus James Wilson, chairman of the House Judiciary Committee, declaimed in debates over the Thirteenth Amendment that the First Amendment surely belonged "to every American citizen, high or low, rich or poor,

Founding Father

Daniel Carroll
Maryland

Daniel Carroll was American born, July 22, 1730, and died in Rock Creek, Maryland, May 7, 1796. In 1742, his family sent him for six years to Flanders for his formal education. He inherited a large estate and considerable fortune. In 1781, he was elected a delegate to the Continental Congress from Maryland. He signed the Articles of Confederation. At the Philadelphia Convention, he advocated, as did most wealthy property holders of the era, a strong centralized government. He was elected to the First Congress, where he argued for assumption of state debts and supported a bill to locate the capital on the Potomac. George Washington appointed him in 1791 to survey and limit the ten-square-mile territory that would become the nation's capital. He remained commissioner of the District of Columbia until ill health forced him to resign in 1795.

where ever he may be within the jurisdiction of the United States. With these rights no State may interfere without breach of the bond which holds the Union together."

Many others echoed Wilson's view, though they differed on exactly which rights ought to be secured to all Americans regardless of state residence. They also disagreed on which rights had been made secure by virtue of the Thirteenth Amendment. But even those who spoke in favor of rights at all agreed that the "privileges and immunities" of citizens included an array of rights not exhausted by a narrow definition of freedom. Clarification was in order.

Beyond the Thirteenth Amendment

In the midst of these debates, on the first day of the Thirty-ninth Congress, December 6, 1865, Representative John Bingham of Ohio introduced the first resolution on what would become the Fourteenth Amendment. Early in 1866, Senator Lyman Trumbull of Illinois introduced a bill that would become the Civil Rights Act of 1866. Proponents of the civil rights bill argued that the Thirteenth Amendment was sufficient constitutional warrant for Congress to act. Bingham was not so sure. In any event, the debate over the Fourteenth Amendment—against the backdrop of perceived deficiencies in the language of the Thirteenth Amendment—seemed to show that the sponsors supposed the new amendment would reinforce the Thirteenth, not subvert it in any way.

That something more was needed to enforce rights became clear as 1866 wore on. Before the Civil Rights Act of 1866 was enacted, many courts concluded that by itself the Thirteenth Amendment did no more than abolish the status of slavery, defined narrowly. After the act was passed (over President Johnson's veto), several courts concluded that it was unconstitutional. Beyond the courts' definition of legalities, enforcement was scanty of whatever rights did exist. The states largely ignored the federal law, and President Johnson was not warmly disposed to any laws that seemed to interfere with state autonomy. He was anxious to end Reconstruction and restore to the states all powers that had been absorbed by the federal government in the wake of war. Enforcement of the law depended on unenthusiastic state officials and case-by-case adjudication in the state courts. Appeal to federal courts was difficult in the extreme.

This was the backdrop against which the Fourteenth (and Fifteenth) Amendment was debated. Unfortunately, in the mysterious way of history, those later charged with interpreting the laws focused on foreground and overlooked background. The Fourteenth Amendment came to be seen as implicitly nar-

President Andrew Johnson's moderate Reconstruction policies were too conservative for the more radical Republicans in Congress who overruled his veto of the Civil Rights Act of 1866.

rowing the meaning of the Thirteenth (even though the latter had been ratified before anyone had contemplated a Fourteenth Amendment), confining the Thirteenth to a restricted definition of slavery, rather than extending it. Any larger protection would thereafter be sought in the different terms of the Fourteenth.

One of the most portentous consequences of this interpretation was its effect on the federal Civil Rights Acts. The Civil Rights Act of 1866, in abolishing blacks' civil impediments, acted directly on the states and on private individuals (a still revolutionary intrusion on "states' rights"). Recall that although the Thirteenth Amendment was understood to permit this direct effect of federal legislation, many doubted whether it embraced the particular provisions of the act. However, if the greater constitutional backing those provisions required were to be found in the Fourteenth Amendment, then troubles could arise. The Fourteenth might not permit such direct legislation—indeed, it was ultimately held not to permit federal legislation that affected private conduct.

The Demise of Privileges and Immunities

The first clause of the second sentence of Section 1 of the Fourteenth Amendment is the privileges or immunities clause. Quoted earlier, it is worth repeating here: "No state shall make or enforce any law which shall abridge the privileges or immunities of citizens of the United States." It seemed to provide a broad mantle of protection, and not only for blacks. Sadly, that was not to be.

This clause echoes the provision in Article IV that "the citizens of each State shall be entitled to all privileges and immunities of citizens in the several States." This murky language can be taken one of four ways. It might mean that Congress must treat everyone equally. It might mean that every state must treat its own citizens equally. It might mean that citizens carry the citizenship rights of their state when they go to another state. Or it might simply mean that a state may not favor its own citizens by discriminating against other citizens who come within its borders. The last view is the one that has stuck. "The primary purpose of this clause," said the Supreme Court in 1948, "was to help fuse into one nation a collection of independent, sovereign states. It was designed to insure to a citizen of State A who ventures into State B the same privileges which the citizens of State B enjoy." (Notice that the clause speaks in terms of citizens; it does not encompass corporations or aliens.)

As understood today, the doctrine has no substantive content: It does not say what rights a state must guarantee to its own citizens; it simply says that a state may not deny *fundamental* rights to citizens from other states unless it also denies them to its own citizens. Moreover, a state may even discriminate between citizens of other states and its own citizens as long as the inequality is reasonable given legitimate state interests, though that test is difficult to pass. For instance, in 1973 the Supreme Court invalidated a law that banned non-Georgians from obtaining abortions in Georgia because the state could not prove that the law would conserve scarce public hospital resources, in itself a legitimate purpose.

But this line of cases was after the fact. When Bingham was proposing the present language of the Fourteenth Amendment, the leading decision was *Corfield v. Coryell,* a lower court case decided by Supreme Court Justice Bushrod Washington while riding circuit. The case concerned New Jersey's ban on out-of-state fishermen gathering oysters in state waters. Washington's famous conclusion was that the privileges and immunities clause in Article IV encompasses all rights "which are in their nature fundamental; which belong of right to the citizens of all free Governments; and which have at all times been enjoyed by the citizens of the several States which compose

Justice Bushrod Washington was responsible for the Corfield v. Coryell *decision in 1823.*

maintain actions of any kind in the courts of the state; to take, hold and dispose of property, either real or personal; and an exemption from higher taxes than are paid by the other citizens of the state.

Had the Supreme Court accepted Washington's approach, the federal courts would have had sweeping jurisdiction over state laws that discriminated against nonresidents, for *Corfield* did not talk in terms of equality between citizens and nonresidents; it said nonresidents were entitled to those fundamental rights, period. Although the Court ultimately would reject this view, in the mid-1860s, it had not yet done so. Nevertheless, *Corfield* left a gaping hole in the protection of individual rights: It did not say a state was obliged to extend these rights to its own citizens.

To make up for this deficiency, Bingham proposed the privileges or immunities clause of the Fourteenth Amendment. It seems to say, and Bingham and others almost certainly intended that it mean, that states must respect fundamental rights of American citizens.

What were these fundamental rights? On this question a vehement historical debate has centered for half a century. This much is clear. Bingham himself and Senator Jacob M. Howard of Michigan, the floor manager of the amendment in the Senate, both were aware of *Barron v. Baltimore*, the case of John Barron's wharf, in which Chief Justice Marshall had said that the Bill of Rights applies only to the federal government. Bingham and Howard believed the amendment they were proposing would overturn that decision and make the Bill of Rights apply to the states also. Said Howard: "To these [Article IV] privileges and immunities, whatever they may be[,] for they are not and cannot be fully defined . . . to these should be added the personal rights guaranteed and secured by the first eight amendments to the Constitution. . . . The great object of the first section of this amendment is, therefore, to restrain the power of the states and compel them at all times to respect these fundamental guarantees."

this Union, from the time of their becoming free, independent, and sovereign." Washington did not spell out all such rights: "What these fundamental principles are it would perhaps be more tedious than difficult to enumerate." But he did list these:

> Protection by the government; the enjoyment of life and liberty with the right to acquire and possess property of every kind, and to pursue and obtain happiness and safety; subject nevertheless to such restraints as the government may justly prescribe for the general good of the whole. The right of a citizen of one state to pass through, or to reside in any other state, for purposes of trade, agriculture, professional pursuits, or otherwise; to claim the benefit of the writ of *habeas corpus;* to institute and

But it was not to be. Five years after the Fourteenth Amendment was ratified, the Supreme Court betrayed its inability to imagine the import of the revolution that had swept America, and in deciding the infamous *Slaughterhouse Cases*, showed that it had the power to stay that revolution. The framers of the Fourteenth Amendment were after a change too great for the Supreme Court of the 1870s to stomach; they could not understand a federalism in which Congress and the federal courts could monitor state laws involving such intimate matters as the very rights of the people.

In 1869, a corrupted Louisiana legislature passed a bill establishing a monopoly over the landing and butchering of livestock in New Orleans. All livestock had to pass through the Crescent City Stock Landing and Slaughterhouse Company, chartered by the legislature. More than one thousand butchers and livestock dealers were excluded from the monopoly and several took their cases to court, protesting that the monopoly violated the Thirteenth and Fourteenth Amendments and the 1866 Civil Rights Act. The state said it was a routine health control measure, common to many states at the time. In 1873, the Supreme Court in a five-to-four decision sided with Louisiana and dismissed the appeal.

For the majority, Justice Samuel Miller held that the inability to pursue one's business (because of a legislatively created monopoly) was not the kind of servitude banned by the Thirteenth Amendment or legislated against under the Civil Rights Act. Regulation of property was permissible under the states' traditional "police powers." The Thirteenth Amendment, Miller said, was intended to protect former slaves, not to enlarge the rights of whites against the state.

Nor would the Fourteenth Amendment avail the butchers. The privileges or immunities clause encompassed only rights of *national* citizenship, not those of state citizenship, and commanded the states to refrain only from abridging national rights. What were

Justice Samuel Miller's decision in the Slaughterhouse Cases *declined to find federal power to intervene in state affairs.*

these national rights? Like Washington, Miller could not specify them in detail, but he suggested these:

> To come to the seat of government to assert any claim he may have upon that government, to transact any business he may have with it, to seek its protection, to share its offices, to engage in administering its functions . . . of free access to its seaports . . . to the subtreasuries, land offices, and courts of justice in the several states . . . to demand the care and protection of the Federal government over his life, liberty and property when on the high seas or within the jurisdiction of a foreign government . . . the writ of habeas corpus . . . to use the navigable waters of the United States, however they may penetrate the territory of the several states.

How the Supreme Court Decides Cases

Nothing in the Constitution or federal statutes dictates how the justices go about deciding the cases they have chosen to hear. The procedures they use are set by the Court itself and have evolved over many years.

The justices have almost complete control over which cases they will hear of the thousands of cases that pour in. All that is needed is four justices to vote to "grant cert"—that is, to grant a writ of certiorari to a lower court to bring a case up on appeal. (The justices are legally required to hear a few types of cases.)

The arguments in every case the justices hear are submitted by the opposing lawyers first in written briefs. Each case is then argued orally. Oral arguments are open to the public. In the early years of the Court, oral argument could sometimes last for days in important cases. No longer. Today, each side is allotted thirty minutes to present its case—and usually advocates barely begin to make their arguments when they are peppered with questions from the raised, irregularly shaped bench. (The Supreme Court does not sit in panels, as most other appellate courts do; all the justices sit for each case.) When the lawyer has five minutes left, an amber light at the podium winks on. When time has expired, amber turns to red, and the lawyer must stop.

The Court does not decide the case immediately. Each week, at a conference of the justices, every argued case is discussed and tentative votes are taken. Unlike oral arguments, the conference discussion is closed to everyone but the nine justices—indeed, the conference of the justices is one of the most secret meetings in a town full of secret meetings, but unlike most meetings in Washington, what occurs there is leakproof.

By long tradition, the senior justice in the majority assigns the task of writing the Court's opinion to one of the justices. If the chief justice is in the majority, he is the senior justice. If he is in the minority, then the senior justice in the majority is the one who has served longest on the bench.

The writer may take one week to several months to circulate the majority opinion, and during that time, or in reaction to the opinion itself, votes may change. The Court's decision is never certain until it is printed in the Court's basement printery and announced publicly.

Because the conference proceedings are confidential, the public rarely glimpses the inner workings of the Court. In 1986, Justice William J. Brennan, Jr., gave a rare newspaper interview in which he discussed how the justices go about deciding cases. What follows are excerpts from the interview he gave to *New York Times* reporter Stuart Taylor, Jr.:

One reason I do [that is, review] my own certs [petitions for certiorari], excepting summertime when I let my incoming clerks do them, is that I think the screening process to decide what we should take and decide is as important as the decisional process. I don't think it's fair to put on clerks who are here only for a single term the responsibility to recommend whether we should or shouldn't take them, except, as I said, the summer list.

And then, the cases that we do agree [to review] we will pick to pieces every single case, the record, the briefs, that we're going to hear argument in. And clerks get into the damnedest wrangles over some of these things, which is the way they most help me. And I get in the middle of a number of pitched battles, too.

The result is that when I go into oral argument, I think I am as aware of what the issues are, and the positions of everybody and the things I've got to worry about, as I possibly could be.

And then on the very day of argument, we meet that afternoon after the argument session and we go over every one of the cases and the arguments that we have heard, and it's at that juncture that I decide which way I want to vote tentatively. And I emphasize the tentatively, because the final outcome is more than just the tentative consideration we give at conference following argument.

But I go to conference on the argued cases with a two- or three-page—I always try to keep it within that size—statement of my views on the case and why I'm voting tentatively to reverse or affirm, as the case may be. That's the system I arrived at after experimenting with some others, and that has proved the most effective and satisfactory for me and the most helpful to me in arriving at decisions.

Now, when an opinion is assigned to us, I ask one of the clerks to make an initial draft, which I don't want to see until after his three colleagues have critiqued it and given me the benefit of their view. Then when I get it I finally complete it, and before I circulate it I have them examine it again in print. Quite often they come up with more suggestions.

Now that's the system that I follow. I don't know that it's the same system that all my colleagues follow. But it, as you can see, involves an intensity and concentration that repeated 160 times a year can leave you a little tired at the end of it.

The process [of seeking to get a majority of the Court to sign an opinion] is very simple, really. I get an opinion to write or a colleague gets an opinion to write. And when a colleague circulates an opinion, we don't have, as we did more often at least in my first years, as much one-on-one conversation, largely because there's so damn much to do, and so we exchange comments.

I get an opinion, say from Justice Stevens. I've voted with him, but I don't like the way he's addressed a particular problem. I write him a memo. Sometimes I circulate it to the conference, sometimes I send it to him directly, depending on what the nature of the issue is.

And as you'll see if you read this [holding up a copy of a recent book by Bernard Schwartz entitled *Swann's Way*, about the behind-the-scenes process by which the Court upheld desegregation through busing in 1971], the number of exchanges, particularly between me and my colleagues, it's startling to see how much I've had in the way of exchanges and how the exchanges have resulted in exchanges of view, both of my own and of colleagues. And all of a sudden at the end of the road, we come up with an agreement on an opinion of the court.

Collegiality is an overworked word. That's supposed to be a description of the process that we ought follow. But as Henry Hart [a prominent Harvard law professor, now dead] coined it, Henry Hart meant we ought to sit down and bat this out the way you and I are this afternoon.

That doesn't work for me, because among other things, I send not only comments but actually am bold enough to suggest, "write it this way rather than that way." and send him a proposed revision of something he's written or a proposed addition.

Now that's the way the system really works. That's why I said you have to remember that the original conference vote is always tentative. It's necessary so that you get a general understanding and when I'm writing an opinion I take very copious notes at conference of what my colleagues' positions are, and they have mine from this two- or three-page thing that I send.

And the result is when I'm writing I have notes about everybody and I know pretty much what pitfalls I have to avoid and how many agree on a given approach, at least as expressed at conference. But that's only tentative, because after you've had more time to think about a case, notwithstanding all the work you've done on it to get to this point, you may change and often do.

So after all the Sturm und Drang, it had come down to this: The constitutional revolution of the Civil War protected the rights of blacks and whites to ply the waterways and to travel to Washington, D.C.! The rights that really counted—all the civil and political and social rights for which the freedmen contended—all these were remitted to the tender mercies of the states that had for the most part been steadfastly denying them.

What of the Article IV privileges and immunities clause that at Justice Washington's hands promised so much? The Court noted that a decision a few years earlier had stricken Washington's laundry list of rights the states must honor: Article IV protects no fundamental rights but merely commands the states to treat citizens and nonresidents equally when they choose to grant any.

The *Slaughterhouse* decision made no sense, because it mooted the privileges or immunities clause. Even before the Fourteenth Amendment, the states never could constitutionally abridge the rights of national citizenship that Miller offered as solace to the losers.

What then was the purpose of the privileges or immunities clause in the Fourteenth Amendment? The majority had no answer. The dissenters saw that the decision emptied the amendment of any real promise for the very people that the majority said the provision was intended to protect. The result was this: The Article IV privileges and immunities clause granted equality only between citizens of a state and nonresident visitors; among its own citizens a state could discriminate. The Fourteenth Amendment privileges or immunities clause protects only national rights, excluding virtually all the civil rights that blacks were lacking. Only the equal protection clause might help, but even that was, with a few notable exceptions, rendered useless for three-quarters of a century (Chapter 15).

The Court need not have pronounced such tragic conclusions. It could have reached the same result simply by saying that even supposing the privileges and immunities clause requires that states guarantee fundamental rights to their citizens, the right to be free of a monopoly was not one of them. That was essentially its position against the argument that the "due process clause" required the monopoly to be upset—an argument that would shortly be stood on its head (Chapter 17).

The Court went as far as it did because it feared the consequences, the intended consequences, of the Fourteenth Amendment. "So serious, so far-reaching and pervading, so great a departure from the structure and spirit of our institutions" would a contrary decision be, Justice Miller declaimed, that the consequences of such a decision would "fetter and degrade the State governments by subjecting them to the control of Congress, in the exercise of powers heretofore universally conceded to them of the most ordinary and fundamental character." The dissenters' view, Justice Miller said, would "change the whole theory of the relations of the State and Federal governments" and "would constitute this court a perpetual censor upon all legislation of the States . . . with the authority to nullify such as it did not approve." The argument from such consequences "has a force that is irresistible in the absence of language [too clear] to admit of doubt." (Justice Miller meant, one supposes, that Bingham and Howard should have added to the privileges and immunities clause: "And we really mean it.")

The dissenters responded: "It is objected that the power conferred is novel and large. The answer is that the novelty was known and the measure deliberately adopted. . . . Where could it be more appropriately lodged than in the [federal] hands to which it is confided?"

In the end, the majority quailed before the prospects of the Fourteenth Amendment. That it would do precisely what they feared, that it *was* intended to work a revolution in the relationship between federal and state power in the matter of basic human rights, was what they could not face. So they sliced from the amendment the privileges and immunities clause, and it has never been stitched back in.

Extending the Bill of Rights to the States

Despite the majority's belief in *Slaughterhouse* that the Civil War amendments were intended to benefit the emancipated slaves, the Court would go on during the next quarter-century to give the lie to this prediction. That story, and the Court's ultimate reversal, is told in Chapter 15. Because much of the rest of this book deals with basic rights that the Court, after all, has ultimately applied as much against the states as against the federal government, it is worth considering here how the Court eventually upset Justice Miller's confident expectation that he had preserved the structure of the Union as it had been given by the framers nearly a century before.

The issue is whether and to what extent the Fourteenth Amendment extends the Bill of Rights to the states. If the whole Bill of Rights, on what theory? If not the whole Bill of Rights, which rights, and how and why?

It was the first Justice John Marshall Harlan (on the Court from 1877 to 1911) who declared that the due process clause of the Fourteenth Amendment *incorporates* the entire Bill of Rights. The Constitution says that no state shall deprive any person of life, liberty, or property without due process of law. Suppose a state fails to abide by the command of the Fifth Amendment that before individuals can be tried for a "capital or otherwise infamous crime" they must first be indicted by a grand jury. Is that failure a denial of due process of law? Such a case came to the Supreme Court in 1879, in an appeal from a death sentence after a California trial that lacked a preliminary grand jury indictment. The Supreme Court concluded that the grand jury process is not essential

For a quarter of a century, Justice John Marshall Harlan was alone in asserting that the Fourteenth Amendment incorporated the Bill of Rights.

because it is merely preliminary to the trial itself; because it is not a fundamental right, the due process clause does not oblige the states to adhere to it.

In a powerful dissent, Justice Harlan said the grand jury indictment procedure was binding on the states simply because it is found in the Fifth Amendment. To him, the issue was not whether a transient Supreme Court majority could be found to conclude that a particular procedure was part of the process that is constitutionally due under the Fourteenth Amendment but that the Fifth Amendment made it fundamental, and the Fourteenth Amendment made it applicable to the states through the due process clause.

In two later cases, Harlan was the lone dissenter, pressing the same view that the due process clause "incorporates" all provisions in the Bill of Rights. One case, in 1895, again concerned failure to indict through a grand jury; in this case, the defendant was tried by an eight-person Utah jury rather than the usual twelve jurors. The Court found nothing constitutionally amiss. The second case, in 1908, turned on the right against self-incrimination, also found in the Fifth Amendment. Again the Court saw no deprivation of due process. But this time the Court majority did declare a "possibility" that "some of the personal rights safeguarded by the first eight Amendments against national action may also be safeguarded against state action." Why the change? Eleven years earlier, the city of Chicago, exercising its power of eminent domain, took property belonging to the Chicago, Burlington & Quincy Railroad, which sued for compensation. The Fifth Amendment says that no property may be taken without "just compensation." This time the Court unanimously declared that the right to be compensated for taking of private property is so fundamental that it applies to the states through the due process clause in the Fourteenth Amendment. No amount of wriggling could let the Court slither out: If at least one principle enunciated in the Bill of Rights is included within the meaning of due process, then others might be as well.

How could such rights be determined? The Court's answer was the following test: "Is it a fundamental principle in liberty and justice which inheres in the very idea of a free government and is the inalienable right of a citizen of such a government?" Harlan had warned that this test permitted the courts to pick and choose, and he denied any such power: "No judicial tribunal has authority to say that some of [the Bill of Rights] may be abridged by the States while others may not be abridged." If a right was important enough to have been included in the Bill of Rights by the likes of James Madison and others of the First Congress, it was important enough, for Justice Harlan, to apply to the states.

For a quarter of a century, Justice Harlan was the lone proponent of this concept that the Fourteenth Amendment incorporates the Bill of Rights. So matters stood until 1925. In that year, almost as an afterthought in a case involving the conviction of Benjamin Gitlow for criminal anarchy in advocating revolution in certain pamphlets, Justice Edward T. Sanford said:

For present purposes we may and do assume that freedom of speech and of the press—which are protected by the First Amendment from abridgement by Congress— are among the fundamental personal rights and "liberties" protected by the due process clause of the Fourteenth Amendment from impairment by the States.

All nine justices agreed with this statement, though it did not help Gitlow, whose conviction was affirmed on the ground that his particular pamphlets were not protected by the First Amendment because they directly incited revolution.

Once having stated the proposition in concrete terms, it was not long before the Fourteenth Amendment due process clause actually became operative in holding a state to rights laid down in the Bill of Rights.

Seven of the Scottsboro case defendants meet with New York attorney Samuel Leibowitz at a Jefferson, Alabama, jail in 1932.

In a series of free speech and press cases from 1927 to 1931, the Supreme Court struck down state criminal convictions on the grounds that they violated the First Amendment, as made applicable to the states through the Fourteenth Amendment.

In 1932, the Court went further, invoking for the first time a specific provision in the Bill of Rights as essential to the process due criminal defendants in state cases. The Scottsboro boys, nine illiterate black teenagers traveling on a freight train in northeastern Alabama, got into a fight with white youths, including two girls. A white boy who was thrown from the train summoned the police. One of the girls falsely accused the blacks of having raped her companion, Victoria Price. The sheriff jailed them in the town of Scottsboro; they barely escaped lynching before the trial. At the trial two weeks later, eight of the nine were convicted in a single day. Mindful of the appearance of justice, the trial judge had agreed to let a Tennessee

lawyer, unfamiliar with Alabama procedure and ignorant of the facts, to "assist" the defendants. He was their only lawyer. The Supreme Court saw through the sham and declared in a seven-to-two opinion that in a capital case, the right to the assistance of counsel was an essential ingredient of due process.

From that time, the Court determined case by case whether a particular provision in the Bill of Rights would apply to the states. Freedom of religion was absorbed into the Fourteenth Amendment in 1934; freedom of assembly in 1937. In that same year, in *Palko v. Connecticut*—a case involving the double jeopardy clause of the Fifth Amendment—Justice Benjamin N. Cardozo discussed at length the concept of incorporation, holding that some rights are part of "those fundamental principles of liberty and justice which lie at the base of all our civil and political institutions," principles "so rooted in the traditions and conscience of our people as to be ranked as fundamental." Some of these rights are "of the very essence of a scheme of ordered liberty" and are therefore part of due process, applicable to the states. Other rights listed in the Bill of Rights are not so essential; without them, "justice would not perish." It is up to the judges to determine which rights fall into which category.

If the Bill of Rights was not yet in its entirety a bulwark against the states, it was becoming so. In 1947, the no establishment of religion clause in the First Amendment, requiring separation of church and state, was made applicable to the states, and in 1948 so was the Sixth Amendment's requirement of a public trial.

In that same year, a five-to-four Supreme Court majority had held in *Adamson v. California* against a defendant's claim that the self-incrimination clause of the Fifth Amendment had been violated. Angrily dissenting, Justice Hugo L. Black boldly stated his belief in total incorporation of the Bill of Rights:

> My study of the historical events that culminated in the Fourteenth Amendment, and the expressions of those who opposed its submission and passages, persuades me that one of the chief objects that the provisions of the amendment's first section, separately, and as a whole, were intended to accomplish was to make the Bill of Rights applicable to the states. With full knowledge of the *Barron* decision, the framers and backers of the Fourteenth Amendment proclaimed its purpose to be to overturn the constitutional rule that case had announced. . . . I cannot consider the Bill of Rights to be an outworn Eighteenth Century "straight jacket." . . . I believe [that] the original purpose of the Fourteenth Amendment [was] to extend to all the people of the nation the complete protection of the Bill of Rights. To hold that this Court can determine what, if any, provisions of the Bill of Rights will be enforced, and if so to what degree, is to frustrate the great design of a written Constitution.

Forty years after his last dissent on the subject, Justice Harlan (whose grandson and namesake was to sit with Black as a colleague through the late fifties and sixties

Founding Father

Daniel of St. Thomas Jenifer
Maryland

Daniel of St. Thomas Jenifer was born in Charles County, Maryland, 1723, and died in Annapolis, November 16, 1790. The origins of his rather elegant name are unknown. Quite wealthy, he lived at an impressive estate called Stepney, in Charles County. In his early adulthood, he was agent and receiver general for the last two proprietors of Maryland and justice of the peace. In 1766, he was a member of the Provincial Court. From 1773, until the outbreak of the Revolution, he served on the Governor's Council. Right up to the Revolution, he remained a supporter of conciliation. In 1775, he was president of the Maryland Council of Safety. Two years later, he was elected president of the state Senate, and in 1778, he was elected to the Continental Congress, where he remained until 1782. In 1782, he became a financial agent for the state. In 1785, he was a commissioner from Maryland to arbitrate the Virginia dispute over navigation in the Chesapeake Bay and on the Potomac. He was not active at the constitutional debates. Jenifer was a pleasant, good-natured, and well-liked individual, with such well-placed, genuine friends as George Washington. He never married.

and to retire on the same day in 1971) had won his first convert.

Black's great antagonist was Justice Felix Frankfurter. In *Adamson*, Frankfurter responded to Black's dissent that of the forty-three Supreme Court justices who had had the chance to side with the incorporation doctrine, "only one, who may respectfully be called an eccentric exception [that is, the first Harlan], ever indicated the belief that the Fourteenth Amendment was a shorthand summary of the first eight Amendments, theretofore limiting only the Federal government, and that due process incorporated those eight Amendments as restrictions upon the powers of the State." After all, Frankfurter pointed out, if Black's theory were true, then such provisions as the Seventh Amendment's requirement of a jury trial in civil cases involving more than $20.00 would force many states to change their laws, and who would suppose that such a particularistic requirement was what the framers of the Fourteenth Amendment had in mind? Who would suppose that justice required it?

In a 1952 case, Frankfurter set out his view. The police had unlawfully broken into the defendant's home and pumped his stomach against his will to recover narcotics he had swallowed. Justice Frankfurter wrote for a unanimous Court that what had happened violated due process. But Frankfurter's notion was not Black's: No particular provision in the Bill of Rights needed to be cited, for this was "conduct that shocks the conscience":

> Illegally breaking into the privacy of the petitioner, the struggle to open his mouth and remove what was there, the forcible extraction of his stomach's contents—this course of proceeding by agents of government to obtain evidence is bound to offend even hardened sensibilities. They are methods too close to the rack and the screw to permit of constitutional differentiation.

Frankfurter's approach to the problem was one he called "absorption": Over time, case by case, the Court would absorb certain fundamental rights into the Fourteenth's due process clause.

For nearly a quarter-century, Black and Frankfurter carried on the debate in opinions that pepper the pages of the *United States Reports*, the official reports of Supreme Court decisions. Justice William O. Douglas subscribed to Black's thesis; they held that the "shocks the conscience" test is too vague and gives neither the Court nor the states standards to

Justice Felix Frankfurter believed that the court would gradually absorb certain fundamental rights into the Fourteenth Amendment's due process clause on a case by case basis.

determine which rights are fundamental and which are not. Other justices sided with Frankfurter. Some justices thought the Bill of Rights could not be entirely incorporated because some of the provisions (like the Seventh Amendment) are too confining. Other justices have thought that the Fourteenth Amendment could not be limited to the Bill of Rights because some rights not specifically mentioned there are equally fundamental—for example, the right to privacy of the marital bedroom. Consistently, when the Supreme Court threw out a Connecticut law against the use of contraceptives on the grounds that it violated due process (page 265), Black dissented because he could find no provision governing privacy in the Bill of Rights.

Black's incorporation theory, first announced in 1948 in *Adamson*, stirred up a historical storm that has not abated. In an influential article, Charles Fairman concluded after a painstaking review of the debates that the historical record "overwhelmingly" refuted Black. But, says Leonard Levy,

> the difficulty with Charles Fairman's article, despite its superb scholarship and exacting standards of proof, is that its compass is limited to the immediate background of the Fourteenth Amendment. Fairman focused only on the period after December of 1865. Moreover, to the extent possible, he adhered rigorously to the literal meaning of the words used and understandably construed them in a lawyer's terms. He therefore missed the history that was behind those words and that suffused them with a content that can be appreciated only by understanding them and the language of the amendment as expressions of the constitutional ideology of the abolitionists. Because Frankfurter curtly dismissed the notion that the clauses of Section One were a "shorthand summary of the first eight Amendments" and because Fairman used an excessively narrow and legalistic lens, neither had the full story. . . . From press, pulpit, and platform, the phrases that found their way into the Fourteenth Amendment's trilogy were invoked [by abolitionists] to support not only the abolition of slavery and equal civil rights for

Negroes, but also freedom of speech, press, conscience, petition, and assembly, as well as the procedural rights of the criminally accused and such rights of property as making contracts and enjoying the fruits of one's labor. The clauses of Section One were at the least "a shorthand summary of the first eight Amendments" for the abolitionist generation whose constitutional climacteric found expression in the Reconstruction Amendments.

Other historians, after Fairman, have concluded with Levy that he ignored significant developments before the narrow period he examined and that on balance the record of debate shows that the framers did intend incorporation.

To conclude that the record does not clearly reveal intentions does not imply that the debate has been

---

Founding Father

John Blair
Virginia

John Blair was born in Williamsburg, Virginia, in 1732, and died there on August 31, 1800. He was educated at the College of William and Mary and at the Middle Temple in London. He was elected to the Virginia House of Burgesses in 1766. He remained at this post until 1770, then served for five years as clerk of the Governor's Council. In 1776, he was part of the Virginia state constitutional convention, and elected to the Privy Council. Two years later, he was elected judge of the General Court. From there, he became judge of the High Court of Chancery and judge of the Court of Appeals. In 1789, George Washington appointed him to the U.S. Supreme Court, on which he served until 1796.

miscast. If the framers of the Fourteenth Amendment did not intend for later courts to treat their language in an evolving fashion, from which to draw moral norms of the current generation, why did they express themselves so vaguely, instead of deliberately confining their intention in unmistakable language? The thirty-ninth Congress knew very well that the Court was capable of drawing meanings that were not obvious from vague phrases. If they knew of the power and tendency, perhaps they meant that process to continue.

Whatever the historical intent, beginning in the 1960s the Supreme Court increasingly sided with the implications of Black's view, if not his theory. In a string of cases (page 286), the Court "selectively" incorporated one provision after another of the Bill of Rights into the Fourteenth Amendment, and thus imposed significant constitutional restraints on the states. The Fourteenth Amendment had come full circle, and was at last a significant means by which national standards of both procedural and substantive rights could be, and would be, applied to all the states. Though purists on both sides might find their reasons suspect, no one could any longer fault the imagination of the justices nor their obvious and continuing attempt to do justice through a Fourteenth Amendment revivified and nourished and ready for long-term service.

Chapter 11 Freedom of Expression

The Blessings of Liberty

The Constitution, its Preamble reminds us, was ordained to "secure the blessings of liberty" for all time.
We have every reason to be grateful to the framers
that this was one of their principles. We should be
grateful also that they stated their objective in so general a fashion for few words have meant so much and
referred to so many different possibilities as the beguiling concept of liberty.

The Whigs of the Revolution took liberty to mean
the people's power over government against the selfish interests of a ruling coterie. "Who could be more
free than the People who representatively exercise
supreme Power over themselves?" asked a Charleston
paper in 1775. Because the people would never vote
to injure themselves, the revolutionaries did not suppose it necessary to protect *individual* liberty against
the state. A "democratical despotism is a contradic-
tion in terms," said John Adams.

We know better, and so did the people thirteen
years later. During the battle for ratification in 1787
and 1788, the Federalists defended the omission of a
bill of rights by demonstrating that the Constitution
gave the new federal government no powers to abridge
such rights as the freedom to speak, publish, and
worship. All rights and all powers not delegated were
reserved to the states and to the people. The argument
was unpersuasive. "A bill of rights," Jefferson wrote

to Madison, "is what the people are entitled to against every government on earth, general or particular, and what no just government should refuse, or rest on inference." Jefferson also observed that the courts "will consider themselves in a peculiar manner the guardians of those rights . . . [and] resist every encroachment upon rights expressly stipulated . . . by the declaration of rights."

Though he was at first skeptical, Madison warmed to the task as a member of the First Congress and was largely responsible for drafting the amendments that comprise the Bill of Rights. Of the hundreds of amendments proposed, Congress eventually sent twelve to the states. Three-fourths of the states ratified ten of these by 1791 (Virginia was the eleventh and last state to ratify, on December 15), and a gratified Jefferson, then secretary of state, proclaimed the first ten amendments part of the Constitution. Connecticut, Georgia, and Massachusetts were holdouts, finally ratifying as a symbolic gesture in 1941 on the sesquicentennial of the Bill of Rights.

The value of a bill of rights to an age psychologically disposed to exalting the freedom of the individual is too obvious to merit much comment. But it may be useful to consider a reason for a declaration of individual freedoms much less often mentioned—the safety and well-being of the whole society.

The usual excuse for denying individual freedom is that the people will abuse their liberties. The argument runs like this. Our limited powers of reason conflict with our unlimited capacity for what the framers called "self-love" and what we call self-interest. Encourage liberty, and you encourage people to neglect the larger society for their own selfish aims. Republican virtue is a chimera; remove restraints and the people tend toward anarchy. No government can preserve order that cannot act against all the causes of disorder. That is why the state must have the power to regulate what people write and say as much as what they do.

A government should have the power to regulate venom in a voice as much as pollution in the water, the authority to preserve society by punishing those who would disturb it as much by undermining respect for its leaders as by causing fear for safety in its streets. More, by controlling the press, the government can avoid those inefficiencies that arise when it must constantly justify its course to still the public doubts that open discussion breeds.

These are the arguments of dictators and totalitarians. Proponents of an open society respond that curtailing freedom alleviates none of the problems that dictators have identified. Self-interest and limited reason are fixtures of human nature, and they persist in any regime. In totalitarian societies, self-interest and the limitations of reason are concentrated in a smaller circle, causing greater damage. To the proposition that people will abuse their liberties through self-interest, we need but retort that unchecked, governments even more will abuse their power through the same self-love. Liberty is the cure for these limitations, not their cause.

Unfree societies have a propensity for gigantic mistakes. Mistakes are made when debate is abolished, when voices are stilled. The history of totalitarian societies is the history of "great leaps forward" that become opportunities foregone. Soviet agriculture suffered for a generation because no one was permitted to dispute Trofim Lysenko, a mad agronomist whose faulty scientific theories were thought to vindicate communist social ideology. Soviet planning abilities were retarded for nearly thirty years because Leonid Kantorovich, the inventor of linear programming, was regarded as a heretic from the communist faith. For a decade in China, political ideology triumphed over technological skills, shattering the already fragile economy. Argentinian generals plunged the nation into an unwinnable war against Great Britain because those who knew the facts could not afford to say the unthinkable out loud. The nuclear power station at Chernobyl blew up because nuclear safety is not openly debated in Russia. (And, yes, the space shuttle *Challenger* blew up because even in an open society, people may be silenced for reasons of greed, vanity, or prestige.)

Totalitarian societies have it backward. Liberty is no obstacle. It is a source of efficiency. It confines mistakes and permits self-correction far short of revolution. It exposes rulers and popes to the proofs of carpenters and patent clerks. In recognizing the limits of reason and the power of self-interest, it opens up society to the welter of opinion and facts that alone can conquer dogma.

We value liberty intrinsically, because freedom is essential to the human spirit. But we value it also as a hard-headed necessity. Liberty is not a luxury, not a rationalization for hedonism; it is an instrumental good, which protects each of us from the errors of those who would dominate us all.

In securing to the people their freedoms, the Bill of Rights ultimately did more than express in other words the proposition that the federal government was one of limited powers. That still would have allowed the "sovereign people" to interfere with the rights of individuals. Indeed, for more than a century, that was the theoretical effect, since the Bill of Rights applied only to the federal government, not the states. Nothing in the Bill of Rights prevented a state from restraining the press if it chose to ignore or abolish its own constitutional prescriptions (and some state constitutions provided no press freedoms). But in this century, the Bill of Rights, through the Fourteenth Amendment, has gradually been taken to proclaim a novel theory. In the sphere of essential human freedoms, *not even "the people" are sovereign*. The rights laid down in the Constitution withdraw even from the people—the people, that is, in the corporate sense— the power to impose on the freedom of each of us.

In important spheres—of thought, conscience, expression, worship, affiliation—we are each of us,

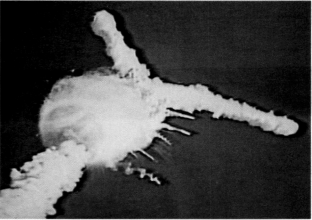

Governmental or social restraints on free speech can result in disasters such as the Chernobyl and Challenger *explosions.*

therefore, sovereign unto ourselves. *Sovereignty resides in every one of us individually.*

That is a remarkable philosophical doctrine. It is an even more remarkable political accomplishment. To those who believe that ultimate sovereignty must reside somewhere, it poses rather obvious political difficulties, for it means that sovereignty has been divided—some of it delegated to government and some of it to each person in the United States, leaving everyone free to speak his or her mind, though the heavens may fall. To the tension between individual freedom and state power, this chapter and the chapters that follow are devoted.

Preconstitutional Restraints on Expression

Throughout human history, governments have sought to silence disagreeable persons. Their pamphleteering might stir political disorder, their blasphemies religious revulsion, their pornographies sexual anarchy. The impulse to still these perils is worldwide; it has affected all governments at all times in all societies, including ours today.

Those who have the power to move against dissent are fearful creatures, invariably afraid that the heavens *will* fall at the merest murmuring of discontent from the crowd. In the sixteenth century, a subject of His Majesty King Henry VIII could be imprisoned for saying, "I like not the proceedings of this realm, I trust to see a change of the world." Earlier, such expressions were punishable by death as treason.

As troublesome as the drunken toast might be, kings found Johann Gutenberg's movable type far more disturbing. In the late fifteenth century, the art of printing spread like a flash fire across Europe. The printed word could ignite a population. For one thing, printing led to literacy, the most powerful weapon against political oppression ever devised. For an-

Johnann Gutenberg's invention of movable type was a threat to those holding religious or secular power, and restraints on publications were quick to follow.

other, the printed word lasts, unlike the rabble rouser's imprecations over a lifted tankard in the pub. Printing's earliest revolutionary beneficiary was Martin Luther; the Protestant Reformation would never have occurred if Luther's message could not have been spread in printed books. And so, with the invention of the press came censorship—by popes, by monarchs, and ultimately by Victorian citizen groups offended at naughty words in the Bible and Shakespeare and impure thoughts in dime novels.

Censorship of books and licensing of the press came early in England. By the 1520s, power to suppress heretical books was in the hands of ecclesiastical authorities, and in 1529 Henry issued the first index of prohibited books (the papal *Index librorum prohibitorum* was not promulgated until 1564). In the 1530s, until Henry renounced the church of Rome, sellers of Lutheran Bibles were burned at the stake. In his Proclamation of 1538, Henry created a licensing system for all books printed in England, and shifted administration from ecclesiastical to civil officials. The proclamation aimed, among other things, at "seditious opinions." In 1559, Queen Elizabeth required all new works to be submitted to censors for approval. Practical administration of the censorship laws ultimately fell to the Stationers Company, the guild of book publishers, binders, and sellers, which came to hold a monopoly over the printing of all books in the country. Members of the Stationers Company were granted wide powers to "search whenever it shall please them in any place, shop, house, chamber, or building of any printer, binder or bookseller whatever within our kingdom of England . . . for any books, or things printed, or to be printed, and to seize, take, hold, burn, or turn to the proper use of the . . . community, all and several of those books and things which are or shall be printed contrary to the forms of any statute, act, or proclamation made or to be made."

In 1644, John Milton in his often-quoted *Aeropagitica* condemned the licensing system: "[T]hough all

Queen Elizabeth I enforced a strict censorship policy on all new publications during her reign.

the winds of doctrine were let loose to play upon the earth, so Truth be in the field, we do injuriously by licensing and prohibiting to misdoubt her strength. Let her and Falsehood grapple; who ever knew Truth put to the worst, in a free and open encounter?" But not until 1694 did Parliament abolish the licensing system.

In the meantime, the common law courts had developed a law of "seditious libel"—"the intentional publication, without lawful excuse or justification, of written blame of any public man, or of the law, or of any institution established by law." It did not matter that the writer spoke the truth; indeed, that was worse, for "the greater the truth, the greater the libel." People were far more likely to be inflamed, the theory went, by learning facts that showed the government was indeed corrupt than by hearing that which could easily be shown false. Therefore, speak no ill of king or his ministers, parliament or its members, whatever the provocation.

The colonial press was licensed too. Although enforcement of the system was spotty, until the mid-eighteenth century, the royal courts did prosecute for seditious libel. But in 1735, with the crown's defeat in a New York seditious libel trial, the practice halted virtually overnight.

The trial was that of John Peter Zenger, printer of the *New-York Weekly Journal*, first published on November 5, 1733. A German immigrant with little command of English, Zenger acted as a front for a number of New York lawyers, avowed enemies of the colonial governor William Cosby. Chief among them was "editor" James Alexander, an ally of Chief Justice Lewis Morris, leader of the opposition to Cosby. To avoid prosecution, the writers kept their identities secret; only Zenger's name appeared on the masthead.

Cosby was an inept, greedy, and arrogant administrator, who richly deserved condemnation in the press. Week after week, the *Journal's* anonymous writers pilloried Cosby for his corruptions and abuse of office. Nettled after a year of ceaseless criticism,

Cosby ordered Zenger arrested on November 17, 1734, on four counts of seditious libel. A grand jury had earlier refused to indict him; Cosby had him charged by an "information."

Zenger was held at the jail on the third floor of the colonial city hall. It was there, for nine months, that he established a journalistic tradition for which he should be celebrated (especially in these days when the principle is in trouble): He kept his mouth shut. Against the possibility of a death sentence, if convicted, Zenger steadfastly refused to reveal who had actually written the articles for which he stood condemned. (Twice Cosby had tried to have Alexander indicted as editor and twice grand juries had refused, insisting they could not pierce the anonymity of the *Journal's* editorship.) No less remarkable were the actions of Zenger's wife, Anna Catherine Maulin, a native of Holland, who kept the paper going every Monday during his imprisonment, risking her own neck to publish the continuing attacks on Cosby.

Finally, on August 4, 1735, one floor below his jail cell, Zenger was brought to trial. Cosby had removed Morris as chief justice and appointed a thirty-two-year-old loyalist, James DeLancey, and DeLancey did not disappoint. He forbade Alexander to represent Zenger. So Alexander brought in the venerable Philadelphia lawyer, Andrew Hamilton.

In those days, the only function of the jury in a libel case was to determine whether the defendant had made the statements. Whether a particular statement was libelous was a question of law for the judge to decide. Hamilton surprised everyone by admitting that Zenger had printed the offending issues, but argued that truth was a defense. DeLancey thereupon agreed with the prosecution that the jury had nothing left to decide, because truth was not legally a defense. He directed the jurors to retire, deliberate, and return with a verdict of guilty.

But Hamilton appealed directly to the jurors to take the law into their own hands. His peroration still resounds:

Andrew Hamilton defends John Peter Zenger in his 1735 seditious libel trial. Zenger's acquittal became an important milestone in the struggle for American free press.

Men who injure and oppress the people under their administration provoke them to cry out and complain; and then make that very complaint the foundation for new oppressions and prosecutions. I wish I could say there were no instances of this kind. . . . [T]he question before the Court and you gentlemen of the jury is not of small nor private concern, it is not the cause of a poor printer, nor of New York alone, which you are now trying: No! It may in its consequences affect every freeman that lives under a British government on the main of America. It is the best cause. It is the cause of liberty; and I make no doubt but your upright conduct this day will not only entitle you to the love and esteem of your fellow citizens; but every man who prefers freedom to a life of slavery will bless and honor you as men who have baffled the attempt of tyranny; and by an impartial and uncorrupt verdict, have laid a noble foundation for securing to ourselves, our posterity, and our neighbors that to which nature and the laws of our country have given us a right—the liberty—both of exposing and opposing arbitrary power (in these parts of the world, at least) by speaking and writing truth.

The jury retired and obliged Hamilton within minutes, acquitting Zenger. News of the trial was jubilantly received throughout the colonies. Hamilton returned to Philadelphia with gun salutes from ships in the harbor. Cosby died shortly thereafter. Zenger returned to the *Journal* and was even appointed "printer to the King's most excellent Majesty, for the Province of New York," serving two years in the new administration. He died in 1746.

Though Zenger's case did not change the law, common law seditious libel in the colonies was dead. The case made sensational reading, and James Alexander's account was widely circulated in England and America. But colonial legislatures retained licensing power and continued to make trouble for printers until the Revolution.

The First Amendment: The Framers' Intentions

Freedom of speech and press became constitutional rights in 1791 with the ratification of the First Amendment. But in denying Congress the power to abridge "the freedom of speech or of the press," what exactly did Madison and the First Congress have in mind? What was "the freedom" that Congress may not abridge? Historians do not agree, and an old debate still rages.

William Blackstone, whose *Commentaries on the Laws of England* (published in 1765–1769) made an immense impression on the legal mind in America, declared that "the liberty of the press consists in laying no *previous* restraints upon publications, and not in freedom from censure for criminal matter after an offending article is published." As he went on to say:

> Every freeman has an undoubted right to lay what sentiments he pleases before the public; to forbid this is to destroy the freedom of the press; but if he publishes what is improper, mischievous, and illegal, he must take the consequences of his own temerity. . . . To punish (as the law does at present) any dangerous or offensive writings, which, when published, shall on a fair and impartial trial be adjudged of a pernicious tendency, is necessary for the preservation of peace and good order, of government and religion, the only solid foundations of civil liberty. Thus the will of individuals is still left free; the abuse only of that free-will is the object of legal punishment. Neither is any restraint hereby laid upon freedom of thought or enquiry: liberty of private sentiment is still left; the disseminating, or making public, of bad sentiments, destructive of the ends of society, is the crime which society corrects.

Did the framers mean to enshrine Blackstone's crabbed definition in the Constitution? So Justice Holmes felt

in 1907: "The main purpose of [free press clauses in constitutions] is to prevent all such previous restraints as had been practised by other governments, and they do not prevent the subsequent punishment of such as may be deemed contrary to the public welfare."

Holmes later changed his mind, but in a searching history of the eighteenth-century meaning of freedom of speech and press, Leonard W. Levy argues that the framers "were sharply divided and possessed no distinct understanding" of the phrases they used. On balance, Levy concludes, they meant to do nothing more (or not much more) than receive the Blackstonian definition. "If . . . a choice must be made between two propositions, first, that the clause substantially embodied the Blackstonian definition and left the law of seditious libel in force, or second, that it repudiated Blackstone and superseded the common law, the evidence points strongly in support of the former proposition." Since the common law of seditious libel did not permit truth as a defense nor the jury to pass on the libel, Levy acknowledges that the framers probably intended to incorporate these "Zengerian principles" in the First Amendment.

Another school, led by Zechariah Chafee, Jr., holds that the framers did mean to abolish the crime of seditious libel. "The First Amendment was written by men . . . who intended to wipe out the common law of sedition, and make further prosecutions for criticism of the government, without any incitement to law-breaking, forever impossible in the United States of America." As Chafee pointed out, licensing by royal authority had been abandoned in England nearly a century earlier and was moribund in America by 1725. "There was no need to go to all the trouble of pushing through a constitutional amendment just to settle an issue that had been dead for decades." Rather, the framers had in mind, Chafee argued, a "definite popular meaning" of liberty of the press: "the right of unrestricted discussion of public affairs."

Can these conflicting views be resolved? William W. Van Alstyne suggests that the framers had in mind

Printing the Constitution

According to Maryland delegate James McHenry, the first draft of the Constitution as devised by the Committee of Detail was ordered "in the hands of Dunlap the printer to strike off copies for the Members" on August 4, 1787. James Madison's notes confirm that the copies were distributed to the convention delegates on August 6, 1787. A seven-page broadside, this draft was referred to a revision committee on August 8, 1787.

On September 12, the Committee of Style and Arrangement reported its revisions to the convention, and a newly printed version was distributed to the delegates. This copy reduced the Constitution from a seven-page broadside to four large folios. The following day, according to McHenry, the convention "Recd. read and compared the new printed report with the first printed amended report."

On September 15, 1787, the third and final draft of the Constitution was approved for printing. McHenry wrote on this day that the delegates voted five hundred copies to be "struck." Two days later, McHenry added in his notes, "Members to be provided with printed copies." The Constitution was finally struck on September 17, 1787, as a six-page broadside bearing the imprint of Dunlap & Claypoole. On that same day, the delegates signed the engrossed (that is, handwritten) original.

On September 19, 1787, Dunlap & Claypoole published this final version of the Constitution, using the identical Caslon type of the September 17 printed copy, in their Philadelphia newspaper, *The Pennsylvania Packet and Daily Advertiser*.

The six-page broadside includes the text of the Constitution, the signatures of the convention members as "done in convention, by the unanimous consent of the States present," the resolutions of submittal adopted on September 17, 1787, and George Washington's letter of transmittal to the existing government under the Articles of Confederation.

On receipt and consideration of the broadside, Congress unanimously resolved on September 28, 1787, to submit the document to the states for ratification. The next day, as confirmed by its "Register of Accounts," Congress paid John Dunlap three pounds and ten shillings for "printing 100 copies of the new Constitution," and on October 3, 1787, one pound and four shillings plus paper expenses for an additional one hundred copies of the Constitution.

Today, the engrossed copy of the final Constitution is displayed at the National Archives.

Other copies of the Constitution in its three printed stages have been preserved. George Washington retained a copy of the seven-page broadside, as well as a copy of the four-page folio with handwritten notes (by Washington and William Jackson) on the changes that were made to the second draft between September 12 and September 15. Washington sent Congress this copy along with the official papers of the convention. These are now housed in the Library of Congress.

A copy of the final broadside with annotations by Edmund Pendleton, president of the Virginia ratifying convention, is also at the Library of Congress, as is a copy of the September 12 broadside signed and annotated by New Jersey delegate David Brearley and a copy on which James Madison penned changes that were made before the Constitution was finally adopted. Still other copies of the first printed draft are preserved at the Library of Congress with the Madison and Brearley papers.

James Madison

Virginia

James Madison was born in Port Conway, Virginia, March 16, 1751. He died in Orange County, Virginia, June 28, 1836. He graduated from the College of New Jersey in 1771. In 1776, he helped draft the Virginia Constitution. From 1780 to 1783, he was a member of the Continental Congress and from 1784 to 1786 a member of the Virginia House of Delegates. A diligent and scrupulous keeper of notes of the proceedings of the Constitutional Convention and coauthor of *The Federalist Papers*, Madison was the intellectual father of the Constitution. He was a member of the House from 1789 to 1797, where he questioned the constitutionality of a national bank. He later changed his mind, advocating a national bank as the means of preserving national currency. In fact, he signed a new twenty-year charter for the Bank of the United States as president in 1816.

Madison was of slight build, five feet six inches and 130 pounds. Though he had a weak voice, he was an excellent orator—and his thoughts carried. He was at ease in politics. He wrote the Virginia Resolutions in response to the Alien and Sedition Acts in 1798, arguing the right to nullify unconstitutional acts. He was Thomas Jefferson's secretary of state, from 1801 to 1809, and twice elected president, serving from 1809 to 1817. He was a member of the 1829 Virginia constitutional convention and rector of the University of Virginia from 1826 to 1834.

not a "what" but a "who." As he says, "What in fact the evidence suggests most strongly is that . . . [there was no direct connection between] seditious libel and the [framing of the] first amendment. At the time of the debate about the first amendment, the principal issue to be settled was quite different. It was the federalism issue: not *what* speech was worth protecting, but rather *who*, as between Congress and the state governments, would have definitive power over that subject." The evidence clearly suggests, Van Alstyne says, that the framers of the First Amendment had no substantive theory of free speech. Rather, they intended to deny Congress all power to legislate on the subject. Governmental power over speech and press was left to the states exclusively. Therefore, no *national* law of seditious libel was possible.

Since the First Amendment now applies to the states through the Fourteenth Amendment (page 206), the search for the meaning of freedom of speech and press cannot rest in the framers' intentions. They intended the states to have a continuing power to oversee the press and speech. But the Fourteenth Amendment subjects this power to the same limitations as the First Amendment sets for Congress—arguably giving Congress and the states no power at all to regulate speech or press.

However, a complete lack of power is intuitively implausible. Can the government really be impotent to prevent people from driving down the street in the middle of the night with loudspeakers blaring or from committing perjury or from publishing details of military codes that would be invaluable to the enemy? As Justice Holmes once said: "The most stringent protection of free speech would not protect a man in falsely shouting fire in a theater and causing a panic." To make sense of these freedoms, then, we need a theory.

Freedom of Expression: A Theory

In the spring of 1986, a real "Polish joke" making the rounds in Warsaw asks the difference between the Polish Constitution and the American one. The answer is: The Polish Constitution guarantees freedom of speech and the American one guarantees freedom after speech. For the First Amendment to have any utility, it must protect speakers from legal consequences of a majority's contempt for their utterances. If the state had power to punish any statement after it is made, freedom of speech would be a mere "privilege" revocable at the legislature's whim.

Yet so it has been argued. As a Connecticut judge once declared: "Freedom of speech and press does not include the abuse of the power of tongue or pen, any more than freedom of other action includes an injurious use of one's occupation, business, or property."

But if the press were free to publish only so long as it did not abuse that freedom—a conception central to the Soviet Constitution—then we would have no freedom of press (or speech), for the government (any government) holds a monopoly on the defining of injury. The press would always be subject to legislative limits—any limits. That is the view of most governments, which see the press as a propaganda arm of the state, not as a Fourth Estate that serves as private watchdog over abuse of government power.

The paramount importance of autonomous expression in a constitutional regime leads directly to a conclusion that makes some people highly uncomfortable. It means that even harmful statements and publications must be allowed. In other words, Congress (and the states) may not legislate against those who arguably abuse these freedoms. "To argue that the federal Constitution does not prevent punishment for criminal utterances begs the whole question, for utterances within its protection are not crimes. If it only safeguarded lawful speech, Congress could escape its operation at any time by making any class of speech unlawful." So the First Amendment must mean that people are free to speak and write as they see fit, not as the government sees fit. Constitutionalism means that rights cannot be accompanied by binding legal responsibilities.

An analogy underscores the point from a different angle. Citizens have the right to vote. That right is not conditional on a responsible exercise of the ballot. You are not obliged to vote for the responsible candidate; you may not be questioned or punished for your choice. Just so, our rights to expression are not conditional on any presumed responsible exercise of them.

The history of free speech in America is the gradual expansion of two notions: (1) that the responsibility for expressing matters of public concern "properly" is moral, not legal, and (2) that matters of public concern are not narrowly confined to expressly political issues such as elections. The expression of ideas, any and all ideas, is the province of the individual, not the government. Opinion must circulate freely; the Constitution does not distinguish. Under the First Amendment, as Justice Powell has said, "there is no such thing as a false idea." Sorting out true from false is for all of us to discuss, not for the government to impose.

Setting out in 1927 the justification for exempting political speech from the exactions of the law, Justice Brandeis explained "why a State is, ordinarily, denied the power to prohibit dissemination of social, economic and political doctrine which a vast majority of its citizens believes to be false and fraught with evil consequence":

> Those who won our independence believed that the final end of the State was to make men free to develop their faculties; and that in its government the deliberative forces should prevail over the arbitrary. They valued liberty both as an end and as a means. They believed that freedom to think as you will and to speak as you think are means indispensable to the discovery and spread of political truth; that without free speech and assembly discussion would be futile; that with them, discussion affords ordinarily adequate protection against the dissemination of noxious doctrine; that the greatest menace to freedom is an inert people; that public discussion is a political duty; and that this should be a fundamental principle of the American government. They recognized the risks to which all human institutions are subject. But they knew that order cannot be secured merely through fear of punishment for its infraction; that it is hazardous to discourage thought, hope and imagination; that fear breeds repression; that repression breeds hate; that hate menaces stable government; that the path of safety lies in the opportunity to discuss freely supposed grievances and proposed remedies; and that the fitting remedy for evil counsels is good ones. Believing in the power of reason as applied through public discussion, they eschewed silence coerced by law—the argument of force in its worst form. Recognizing the occasional tyrannies of governing majorities, they amended the Constitution so that free speech and assembly should be guaranteed.

> Fear of serious injury cannot alone justify suppression of free speech and assembly. Men feared witches and burned women. It is the function of speech to free men from the bondage of irrational fears. . . . Every denunciation of existing law tends in some measure to increase the probability that there will be violation of it. . . . But even advocacy of violation, however reprehensible morally, is not a justification for denying free speech where the advocacy falls short of incitement and there is nothing to indicate that the advocacy would be immediately acted on. . . . No danger flowing from speech can be deemed clear and present, unless the in-

cidence of the evil apprehended is so imminent that it may befall before there is opportunity for full discussion. If there be time to expose through discussion the falsehood and fallacies, to avert the evil by the process of education, the remedy to be applied is more speech, not enforced silence.

What then of limits—of sound trucks in the night or disclosing national secrets? The general answer, explored in the topics that follow, is that when the government acts to restrict speech simply for the sake of banning its *content,* the law violates the First Amendment. The government may not enjoin or punish messages (unless they are provably false and affect only private matters). Limits on speech and press can be upheld only when they are an incidental effect of the government's acknowledged powers to act against other substantive evils.

These general statements, it must be conceded, are insufficient to explain the multitude of cases that make up First Amendment doctrine. No general statements are sufficient, for the issues are as varied as life itself. Probably no other single substantive constitutional provision penetrates so far and wide, implicating so many interests, activities, and concerns of the people. It embraces their politics, social relations, scientific discovery and technological advance, religious concerns, emotional feelings, and commercial dealings. It covers every means they have of contacting one another: daily conversations and newspaper stories; magazines, books, and pamphlets; radio, television, and film; telephone and door-to-door surveys; mails and leaflets; theater and pulpit; homes, auditoriums, and streets on which to congregate. The human species is a communicating species, and the society we have constructed in America is a communicating society. The conflicts that arise are so numerous, the interests affected so diverse, that no account here could begin to exhaust the subject.

The topics that follow, therefore, are necessarily limited in number and scope. A leading constitutional law casebook lists eleven major topics and twenty-nine subtopics (and dozens of sub-subtopics) under the heading freedom of speech and press. The leading constitutional law treatise lists thirty-six topics under the same heading. Moreover, since First Amendment law has evolved almost entirely during the past seventy years, from the end of World War I, in cases of widely divergent issues, we don't explore this law chronologically.

No Prior Restraint

The First Amendment sweeps most broadly in preventing "prior restraints" on expression. In 1931, the Court pronounced the modern version of this doctrine in voiding a Minnesota statute that permitted a court to suppress any "malicious, scandalous and defamatory newspaper, or other periodical." On the prosecutor's application, a state court had ordered the *Saturday Press* to cease publishing because it had carried vicious articles charging that law enforcement officers were not energetically moving to stamp out gambling, bootlegging, and racketeering in Minneapolis. The power to abate "is of the essence of censorship," said Chief Justice Hughes. The law was aimed at shutting down newspapers voicing opinions about public officials. A proscription against such laws is the heart of the First Amendment—no matter how raw the sentiments expressed.

Hughes did note that under extremely limited circumstances, an injunction against the press might be appropriate: "No one would question but that a government [in wartime] might prevent actual obstruction to its recruiting service or the publication of the sailing dates of transports or the number and location of troops."

Forty years later, the United States Justice Department, referring to this limited exception, sought to enjoin the *New York Times* and the *Washington Post* from publishing a classified military study entitled "History of U.S. Decision-Making Process on

Founding Father

William Blount
North Carolina

William Blount was born in Bertie County, North Carolina, March 26, 1749, and died in Knoxville, Tennessee, March 21, 1800. During the Revolution, he served in the North Carolina state militia. Between 1780 and 1789, he served six terms in the North Carolina legislature: Three of these terms were as a delegate to the Congress under the Articles of Confederation, another was as a delegate to the Constitutional Convention in 1787, and another was as a member of the North Carolina convention to ratify the federal Constitution. In 1789, he ran unsuccessfully for a seat as senator. The following year, President Washington named him governor of the Southwest Territory. There he presided over the 1796 convention to organize the state of Tennessee. Once Tennessee became part of the nation, he was elected senator. Implicated in a land speculation conspiracy that may or may not have been related to the Aaron Burr conspiracy, he was expelled from the Senate in 1797 after President Adams obtained a damaging letter which he forwarded to the Senate. Blount left the capital and returned to Tennessee. In 1798, he was elected to the state legislature and became president of the state Senate.

Viet Nam Policy," more commonly known as "The Pentagon Papers." Although the government succeeded temporarily in stopping the papers from publishing further installments (lower courts issued temporary restraining orders until the legal issue could be resolved), the Supreme Court (by a six-to-three vote) vacated the restraining orders within less than two weeks. The justices wrote nine separate opinions; the short per curiam opinion simply stated that the government has a "heavy burden" to meet in trying to prevent a story from being aired and that the government had not met that burden. Among other things, the material in the Pentagon Papers was entirely historical, none dealing with issues more recent than 1968, three years before publication, and the government could say only that its revelation "might" prejudice the national interest. But as Justice Brennan said, "The First Amendment tolerates absolutely no prior judicial restraints of the press predicated upon surmise or conjecture that untoward consequences may result." Justice Stewart took the position that the problem was for the president to solve by preventing disclosure in the first place, not to enjoin newspapers once information is in their hands.

Other asserted interests against publication have failed to move the Court. In 1959, it struck down a movie licensing scheme (film and other media are forms of expression entitled to First Amendment protection) when New York refused a license to *Lady Chatterley's Lover* on the grounds that it unlawfully presented adultery as "desirable, acceptable, or proper." For the Court, Justice Stewart denied that a state could prevent a theater from exhibiting a film that

> advocates an idea—that adultery under certain circumstances may be proper behavior. . . . The First Amendment's basic guarantee is of freedom to advocate ideas. The State, quite simply, has thus struck at the very heart of constitutionally protected liberty. [The constitutional] guarantee is not confined to the expression of ideas that are conventional or shared by a majority.

It protects advocacy of the opinion that adultery may sometimes be proper, no less than advocacy of socialism or the single tax.

In 1976, the Court rejected a state trial court's "gag order," which barred publishing or broadcasting any information about an accused's confession before trial. And a Georgia statute that outlawed reporting the name of a victim in a rape case was overturned; the state may not prohibit accurate reporting of names that appear in public records of court cases.

Nevertheless, the problem of prior restraint is far from dead, as events stemming from espionage trials in 1986 have made clear. Fearing the effects of disclosures at trials of American intelligence agents for selling secrets to the Soviet Union, the director of the Central Intelligence Agency publicly warned newspapers not to publish certain information, and he seemed to have threatened prosecution if they did not comply. The government's position was apparently that the disclosures would alert foreign powers to further American intelligence secrets by disclosing the damage that the leaks had caused. Although the government did not seek an injunction, the warnings by various officials, including the president, had an effect in preventing some stories from being published.

Access to Writings

If the government may not restrain the press from publishing, may it prevent readers from reading? A law would clearly be unconstitutional that said people could not shop in "socialist" bookstores or that orders Mark Twain out of the library. What about a school board that removes books from school library shelves on the grounds that the books are unsuitable? A sharply divided Court has ruled that a school board may not in effect censor what students can read by removing from library shelves books that board members do

May 1985, FBI agents arresting Michael Lance Walker on charges he helped pass secrets to the Soviet Union.

not like. A New York school board had ordered removed such books as *Slaughterhouse Five* by Kurt Vonnegut, *The Naked Ape* by Desmond Morris, *Down These Mean Streets* by Piri Thomas, and *Best Short Stories by Negro Writers*, edited by Langston Hughes, because they were "anti-American, anti-Christian, anti-Semitic, and just plain filthy." Justice Brennan's plurality opinion declared that "local school boards may not remove books from school library shelves simply because they dislike the ideas contained in those books." This case came in the midst of a wave of school censorship in the 1970s. By 1981, according to the American Library Association's Office for Intellectual Freedom, more than nine hundred cases of attempted censorship in primary and secondary schools had been reported across the country. (For more on censorship, see section on obscenity, page 235.)

Punishing Subversive Ideas

The government may not enjoin speech or publication, unless it poses a highly particular, immediate, and grave danger to the national security and then probably only in wartime. But may the government punish those who advocate subversive acts or otherwise lawless activity, even though the advocacy itself may not be enjoined? The story is long and tangled and we cannot fully unravel it here.

In 1798, Congress enacted the infamous Sedition Act, which made it a crime to "write, print, utter or publish . . . any false, scandalous and malicious writings against the government of the United States, or either house of the Congress . . . or the President of the United States, with intent to defame . . . or to bring them . . . into contempt or disrepute; or to excite against them the hatred of the good people of the United States, or to stir up sedition within the United States." Several people were prosecuted and jailed under the act, which was heatedly denounced as unconstitutional by anti-Federalists like Jefferson.

The act lapsed by its own terms in 1801 and was never reviewed in the Supreme Court.

Not until World War I did Congress again enact legislation, like the Espionage Act of 1917, that could be used to stifle political speech. The act was aimed at antiwar efforts; it specifically outlawed attempts to cause insubordination in the military and to obstruct military recruitment. In a series of cases in 1919, the Court, speaking through Justice Holmes, developed a test for determining the limits of advocacy: "[The] question in every case is whether the words used are used in such circumstances and are of such a nature as to create a *clear and present danger* that they will bring about the substantive evils that Congress has a right to prevent."

But the clear-and-present-danger test is murky at best, and as a general formula must be applied to the facts of each case, about which judges could—and did—disagree until their ink ran out. In the very case, the defendant was convicted for mailing out fifteen thousand leaflets urging that the draft was unconstitutional; would anyone suppose today that such a mailing presents a "clear and present danger" to the ongoing recruitment of soldiers? By that test, our jails would have burst apart during the height of the Vietnam antiwar protests.

Indeed, that very same year, another subversion case provoked Holmes to pen one of the most famous declarations of free speech in history. Five Bolshevik sympathizers printed up leaflets attacking President Wilson's decision to send troops to Vladivostok and Murmansk in 1918; they suggested workers stop making bullets that "German militarism" and "American capitalism" would use to crush the Russian Revolution. Five thousand of these leaflets were thrown out of an office building window and otherwise distributed in New York City. The Supreme Court upheld convictions for unlawfully writing with intent to "incite, provoke and encourage resistance to the United States" and to incite curtailment of war production. "The government was confronted with demonstrat-

Vietnam anti-war demonstrators in New York City, October 1969.

ing that the action in some way interfered with the war with Germany. The charge was only provable through the claim that the leaflets had a tendency to cause armed revolts and strikes and thus diminish the supply of troops and munitions available against Germany on the regular battlefield."

Holmes dissented. Noting the lack of evidence that the defendants had the statutory intent or that the distribution could interfere in any way with the war effort, Holmes said:

> Persecution for the expression of opinions seems to me perfectly logical. If you have no doubt of your premises or your power and want a certain result with all your heart you naturally express your wishes in law and sweep away all opposition. To allow opposition by speech seems to me to indicate that you think the speech impotent, as when a man says that he has squared the circle, or that you do not care whole-heartedly for the result, or that you doubt either your power or your premises. But when men have realized that time has upset many fighting faiths, they may come to believe even more than they believe the very foundations of their own conduct that the ultimate good desired is better reached by free trade in ideas—that the best test of truth is the power of the thought to get itself accepted in the competition of the market, and that truth is the only ground upon which their wishes safely can be carried out. That at any rate is the theory of our Constitution. It is an experiment, as all life is an experiment. Every year if not every day we have to wager our salvation upon some prophecy based upon imperfect knowledge. While that experiment is part of our system I think that we should be eternally vigilant against attempts to check the expression of opinions that we loathe and believe to be fraught with death, unless they so imminently threaten immediate interference with the lawful and pressing purposes of the law that an immediate check is required to save the country.

The effect of these cases, and others that followed, "left a restrictive legal residue available for government use. . . . State legislatures rushed sedition, criminal syndicalism, and red flag laws onto their statute books." Antisubversive organizations were established. In the midst of the "red scare," Attorney General A. Mitchell Palmer sanctioned raids and arrests so lacking in constitutional regularity that the Court in reaction moved a long way toward the "exclusionary rule" (page 289) that so exercises contemporary critics.

In time, Holmes's dissent became constitutional understanding, as the Court narrowed the range of discussion that could be criminalized. A new type of organization, the American Civil Liberties Union began to have an impact on the Constitution. The ACLU is an advocacy group whose political strategy was to litigate and thus to influence the course of judicial review. For the first time, an organization with a commitment to constitutional rights became a long-term adversary of the government, building an expertise in litigation to match that of the Justice Department and often to surpass that of state agencies.

In 1937, the Court overturned a conviction under Oregon's criminal syndicalism law of the leader of a meeting held under Communist party auspices. The meeting was orderly and none of the speakers advocated any unlawful acts. Oregon claimed that because the party advocated violence, anyone conducting a meeting under its banner could be jailed. Other decisions denied similar claims. But the undoing of the harm done by the World War I sedition laws was a project of nearly half a century.

After World War II, the government prosecuted several Communist party members under the Smith Act (the Alien Registration Act of 1940), which forbade the knowing advocacy of the need to overthrow the government or the desirability of doing so. It also forbade membership in any organization with such beliefs. A similar state law had been upheld in 1925, in the same case in which the Supreme Court first held that the First Amendment applies to the states through the Fourteenth (page 206). For a time, the Court upheld convictions under the federal statute as well, substituting a "clear-and-*probable*-danger" test for the clear-and-present-danger test.

A period of frenzy and suspicion that turned to hysteria began in the late 1940s. The House Un-American Activities Committee (on which Congressman Richard Nixon first practiced his diplomatic skills) and the Senate Subcommittee on Internal Security assumed the task of uncovering communists in government. Senator Joseph McCarthy gave his name to an ideology and a technique, making reckless charges of subversion through the highest levels of government, but he was not alone in his eagerness to ferret out "traitors"; Senators Patrick McCarran and William Jenner distinguished themselves in the art of red-baiting. Loyalty-security programs swept the government and much of private industry. In the early 1950s, one critic acidly charged, "the McCarthy-McCarran era could scarcely roll the repression along fast enough to keep pace with the Vinson Court's approval of it."

But the Court did not uniformly defer to the rampant know-nothingism, and by the mid-1950s, it was shying away from a too-easy acceptance of probabilities in seditious speech cases. Mere advocacy of the use of force or unlawful actions is not sufficient to sustain a conviction. By 1969, the Court finally proclaimed that the First Amendment bars criminal penalties "except where such advocacy is directed to inciting or producing *imminent* lawless action and *is likely to* incite or produce such action." By then the political fury of the late forties and fifties had abated, supplanted by new furies. The sixties and seventies would bring new problems, new rebellions, and a new political vocabulary, made possible by the long move toward the abolition of sedition.

The net effect of sedition doctrine, then, is that we are free in the realm of public affairs and politics to argue, exhort, and persuade, no matter how outrageous our ideas, purpose, logic, manner, or style may appear to others. Opponents may denounce their leaders' approach to public life. The disgruntled may declare the foundations of the republic rotten. The disaffected may deride the very Constitution that permits them to speak. We do all this constitutionally

Senator Joseph McCarthy identifying the numbers and locations of alleged communists during a congressional hearing.

free from the hangman's noose. (For much milder sins, "democratic" Athens gave Socrates hemlock.)

We may not merely offer our ideas as theory but also we may exhort for fundamental change. It is no objection that the shouting, even the ranting, are incitements, for as Justice Holmes said:

> Every idea is an incitement. It offers itself for belief and if believed it is acted on unless some other belief outweighs it or some failure of energy stifles the movement at its birth. The only difference between the expression of an opinion and an incitement in the narrower sense is the speaker's enthusiasm for the result. Eloquence may set fire to reason.

We light the fire; the First Amendment fans the flames. So it must be in a republic, where one man's media is another's poison.

Defamation

After midcentury, the legal doctrine of sedition declined along with the social forces that prompted the postwar red-baiting. But new forces were ascending, as a revolution in "rights consciousness" led to what some would call a "litigious society." More and more, Americans brought their grievances to courts, and in the realm of speech and press the question was whether private lawsuits for libel and slander might accomplish what public prosecutions had not.

The law of defamation of character was established early in the common law of each state; barnacle encrusted, it boasted odd inconsistencies between the oral variety (slander) and the written version (libel). Rules for what constituted libel or slander, how it could be proved, who bore the burden of proof, and how to measure damages varied from state to state. Mostly, defamation suits were for private wrongs: the credit-rating service that falsely reported a debtor's bankruptcy; the newspaper caption that mistakenly referred to a couple in a picture as Mr. and Mrs.

when they were not married to each other (implying that one or another was a bigamist); the doctor called a quack in a waiting room full of patients. But the potential danger to those speaking out on public issues was always apparent: Suppose in the heat of the campaign a candidate intemperately characterized her opponent in a way she would not have wanted her grandmother to hear? Suppose a television broadcaster misstated a fact about the campaign? Suppose an editorialist asserted an unprovable proposition: The politician is a liar. What then?

Using private damage suits to harass or silence the press became a serious possibility in the early 1960s. If public figures could persuade juries that false statements injured their reputations, the laws in many states permitted juries to assess damages they thought "fair," without proof of the actual extent of the harm.

The test came in 1964. The *New York Times* had carried a fund-raising advertisement for civil rights groups in the South. One paragraph talked about "truckloads of police armed with shotguns and tear-gas [who] ringed the Alabama State College Campus." The ad was signed with sixty-four prominent names and was "warmly endorsed" by twenty southern clergymen. L. B. Sullivan, supervisor of the police department in Montgomery, sued the *Times* for libel. The ad had not named him, but he claimed that people would think the word *police* referred to him and that they would suppose him responsible for the various acts mentioned. In minor respects, the ad misstated events; for example, although the police were at the college in abundant numbers, they did not "ring" the campus. Although Sullivan's witnesses testified to the jury that they "would not want to be associated with anybody who would be a party to such things as are stated in the ad," they did not testify that they had shunned him on account of the ad.

Without any evidence of how the ad had hurt him, the jury awarded Sullivan $500,000. The Alabama Supreme Court upheld the award, saying that the jury could infer that the *Times* had acted with malice because it irresponsibly failed to screen the factual accuracy of the ad by checking its morgue for its own stories about the events in question. The ad was placed through an agency that forwarded a letter from its chairman, A. Philip Randolph, a nationally known civil rights activist. His letter vouched that the signatures were all valid; the *Times* had no other reason to check the details.

The result was astonishing, and like so much else in the realm of constitutional law, had one side not so overreached, the counterreaction might not have been so strong. A man whose name was never used and who was only inferentially involved in the matters mentioned, matters of highest public interest, won half a million dollars for an ad that appeared in a newspaper that circulates mainly one thousand miles away, without a shred of proof that he had been injured, by statements true in substance though not in every detail. The award was one thousand times greater than the maximum sum ($500) allowed by the Alabama code for the crime of maliciously and falsely calling someone a criminal.

In *New York Times v. Sullivan*, the Supreme Court unanimously reversed the state court and dismissed the suit. Because the ad discussed "one of the major public issues of our time," it qualified for First Amendment protection, unless falsity alone would support a verdict. But to require proof of every assertion would have a "chilling effect" on those who would speak out on public issues. Said Justice Brennan: "A rule compelling the critic of official conduct to guarantee the truth of all his factual assertions—and to do so on pain of libel judgments virtually unlimited in amount—leads to . . . self-censorship. . . . Under such a rule, would-be critics of official conduct may be deterred from voicing their criticism, even though it is believed to be true and even though it is in fact true, because of doubt whether it can be proved in court or fear of the expense of having to

do so. . . . The rule thus dampens the vigor and limits the variety of public debate."

The new constitutional rule of libel requires public officials, suing for defamation of their official conduct, to show that the statement was made with "actual malice": that it was uttered or published either "[1] with knowledge that it was false or [2] with reckless disregard of whether it was false or not."

Later cases spell out the contours of a doctrine that is still evolving. Thus the *Sullivan* rule applies not only to public *officials* but to "public *figures*" who are "involved in issues in which the public has a justified and important interest" (like allegations that the football coach at the University of Georgia had fixed a game or that a retired general had sparked a crowd to violently oppose the desegregation of the University of Mississippi). However, a private individual does not fall within the scope of the rule, as long as the court does not impose liability without fault and as long as all punitive awards are made only on proof of actual malice.

Fighting Words, Hostile Audiences

Sweeping political conspiracies, subversive underground organizations, and the exhortations of radical revolutionaries are not the only kinds of efforts that urge or lead to lawlessness. Much more mundane are intimidations of bullies on the corner, victims pushed beyond their limits, self-righteous hecklers, and minor urban agitators. People say things that lead others to react. Inciting a crowd to go over to the jailhouse, right now, and take the suspect out and lynch him is surely punishable. But suppose the speaker merely insults? Is the likely response of the audience justification for suppressing the speech?

The Court has enunciated the so-called fighting words doctrine: A state may outlaw the use of words communicated face to face that are "plainly likely" to provoke retaliation. But words are not automatically "fighting" whenever the audience is unsympathetic. Thus the Court has overturned convictions for breach of peace stemming from a peaceful march to protest segregation, when the crowd turned ugly but the marchers stayed calm. The heckler may not so easily veto the speaker.

In a significant case at the height of the Vietnam war, the Supreme Court reversed a conviction of a young man who appeared in the Los Angeles County Courthouse with a jacket on which were embroidered the words "Fuck the Draft." The conviction was based on a statute that prohibited disturbing the peace by offensive conduct. Though the words may be offensive, especially to the "women and children present in the corridor," the defendant himself engaged in no violent conduct, nor did anyone react violently. The Court held that the state sought to punish for the use of words, not conduct. The defendant was making a political statement, which the state may not prohibit.

The contours of the fighting words doctrine are difficult to discern, because unsurprisingly judges disagree over the import of foul language and spirited insults and the potential for violence. The most important recent national controversy over this issue came in the late 1970s when the American Nazi party decided to hold a march in Skokie, Illinois, the home of many Jews who had survived the Holocaust. In a series of rulings that went back and forth between the federal courts in Illinois and the Supreme Court, the right of the demonstrators to march was effectively upheld, although the Court avoided pronouncing directly on the question, refusing to review a Court of Appeals decision that various municipal

The rights of American Nazi party members to demonstrate in Skokie, Illinois, were upheld by the Supreme Court; however, the demonstrators subsequently canceled the march.

ordinances curbing the march were unconstitutional. In the end, the marchers themselves canceled the demonstration. The problem and the cases continue, doctrinally unresolved.

Symbolic Speech

The First Amendment, it is often said, protects expression, not conduct. But the line between the two is never easy to draw, for "a message may be delivered by conduct that is intended to be communicative and that, in context, would reasonably be understood by the viewer to be communicative." This "communicative conduct" has come to be called "symbolic speech." A California statute prohibited the display of a red flag "as a sign, symbol, or emblem of opposition to organized government"; in the 1931 *Red Flag* case, the Court held the law unconstitutional. In later flag cases, state attempts to prescribe how the American flag could be flown have been voided when the purpose of the laws was to prohibit the flag waver from communicating a message—for example, the Court upset a Washington State conviction for displaying the flag with a peace symbol affixed to it. On the other hand, a conviction was upheld for publicly burning a draft card, in violation of a statute against mutilating draft cards, even though the purpose of the act was to protest American involvement in Vietnam. Also, demonstrators could not seek to avoid a regulation prohibiting sleeping on a national park ground not specifically designated for camping by arguing that their actions were intended to call attention to the plight of the homeless.

Time, Place, and Manner Regulations

Speaking and writing are the characteristic means by which humans carry out all other activities to accomplish their ends. Laws that prohibit or regulate harmful activities therefore frequently trench on speaking and writing. But a law that incidentally inhibits expression is not unconstitutional if it is reasonably aimed at an evil that the legislature has authority to police. How is the balance to be drawn?

The problem crops up frequently in cases involving laws designed to keep the streets and other public spaces free from litter (for example, proscribing handbills and leaflets), from congestion (regulating marches and demonstrations in myriad ways and in many places—streets, parks, and near courts, prisons, municipal, and other public buildings), and from noise (banning loudspeakers). The variety of cases makes doctrinal summary hazardous, but in general it is probably safe to say that the courts will upset "time, manner, and place" regulations unless they are narrowly drawn to attack only the particular harm against which the legislature is empowered to act.

On numerous occasions, the Supreme Court has struck down laws and regulations because they were "overbroad"—lumping together conduct that could be prohibited and speech that could not. As Justice Blackmun has expressed it, "The use of the overbreadth analysis reflects the conclusion that the possible harm to society from allowing unprotected speech to go unpunished is outweighed by the possibility that protected speech will be muted."

For example, a Birmingham, Alabama, parade ordinance during the early 1960s said that the city commission must issue a parade permit on application "unless in its judgment the public welfare, peace, safety, health, decency, good order, morals, or convenience require that it be refused." The commission refused a permit to black ministers, including Martin Luther King, Jr., who wished to lead a civil rights march on Good Friday in 1963. The Court held that the parade ordinance was unconstitutional because it gave the commissioners, in Justice Stewart's words, "virtually unbridled and absolute power." In failing to set standards for the commissioners to follow, the law empowered them to disapprove any parade and thus gave them complete discretion to discriminate between demonstrations they approved and those they did not.

But regulations narrowly drawn that do not ban altogether the right to speak or publish have survived constitutional challenge. In these cases, the courts undertake some sort of balancing test to determine whether the state's interest in preventing the injury outweighs the effect of the regulation on the speech or publication sought to be made. What these regulations may not do is regulate by distinguishing among the types of messages that will be presented. Thus the Court felled an ordinance prohibiting picketing in front of schools, but exempting schools involved in labor disputes: "[Government] may not select which issues are worth discussing or debating in public facilities."

Obscenity

The First Amendment offers no protection to the obscene (whether in books, magazines, films, or on stage). Astonishingly, despite three-quarters of a century of literary censorship by federal postal and state officials, the constitutional status of obscenity did not reach the Supreme Court until 1948 and was not decided until 1957. Of course, ruling against obscenity merely panders to popular prejudice; the real question is how to define it.

Reflecting the full flowering of American Victorianism in the last quarter of the nineteenth century, various "vice societies," including most prominently the New York Society for the Suppression of Vice, led by Anthony Comstock, and the New England Watch and Ward Society (both founded in 1873),

An ordinance that allowed picketing in front of schools exclusively for labor disputes was felled by the Court.

lobbied for tighter censorship ("Comstock") laws. Through social and political pressure, blacklists, and boycotts, the vice societies became virtual censors from the 1890s into the 1920s. For a time, some even enjoyed what today we might suppose to be an unconstitutional delegation of power to work with public prosecutors and courts. Their targets were not merely the works of little redeeming value: They struck hard at noted novelists (for example, Stephen Crane, Walt Whitman, Theodore Dreiser, Erich Maria Remarque, John Dos Passos), at classics (works by Aristophanes, Rabelais, Boccaccio, Voltaire), at straightforward sex hygiene books, and at thinkers like Sigmund Freud. Hundreds of books, wholly unobjectionable by modern standards, succumbed to the censors' prudery.

In those days, it was not usually the words they found offensive but the thoughts. Sometimes, though, it was the words: "Anglo-Saxon" words—the kind Richard Nixon called "expletive deleted"—occasionally cropped up, as in D. H. Lawrence's *Lady Chatterley's Lover* (banned in Boston in 1930). Often their anxiety leaves us today simply scratching our heads: In 1929, for example, the American publisher of *All Quiet on the Western Front,* in a passage describing field hospital smells, used his blue pencil to change the word *pus* to *ether.* (Federal postal officials had barred imports of the unexpurgated European version.) To the pompous arbiters of moral taste and sensibility, it did not matter what the author intended or what the effect was of the work as a whole; a single suggestive passage was enough to condemn it. The vague British test, adopted by American courts in the late nineteenth century, was whether the work had a tendency "to deprave or corrupt those whose minds are open to such immoral influences." Beginning after World War I, the lower courts increasingly dismissed indictments and overturned convictions (although as late as 1947, the New York courts declared obscene Edmund Wilson's *Memoirs of Hecate County*). With the famous *Ulysses* decision by Judge John Munro

Woolsey in 1933, it became clear that isolated passages in a book of obvious literary merit could not be used to suppress it.

The trouble with all this, and one need scarcely be bold to say it, is that sex is an idea too, and like all ideas, one that government officials must leave alone. Moreover, assuming that some expressions of sex might be somehow sufficiently dangerous or offensive to suppress, the concept of "obscenity" is so malleable that almost anything can be suppressed in its name. The Police Board of Censorship in Chicago once held obscene a Walt Disney movie on the vanishing prairie because it showed a buffalo giving birth, and the censorship board of a southern town banned a movie as obscene because it depicted black and white schoolchildren playing together.

In the 1957 case, the Court upheld federal and state statutes prohibiting mailing and selling of material variously described as "obscene, lewd, lascivious, filthy, vile, or indecent." Whether a work should be so labeled depended on "whether to the average person, applying contemporary community standards, the dominant theme of the material, taken as a whole, appeals to prurient interests." This prurient interest test was better than what the courts had used before, but not much better. "Prurient" refers to lustful desire. But how does a work "appeal to" desire? What is a "contemporary community standard": Is it whatever a jury unanimously measures a charged work by or the standard of at least five of the nine justices? And if a "dominant theme" test is eminently sensible for a novel in which the sexual aspect is but one part, does it make sense for a monthly magazine that intersperses lascivious photographs with articles on how to make the most of your stereo?

In later cases through the 1960s, the Court expanded its early holding into a three-pronged test, narrowing the definition. To be legally obscene, the dominant theme of the work taken as a whole must (1) appeal to prurient interest in sex, (2) be "patently offensive because it affronts contemporary commu-

nity standards relating to the description or representation of sexual matters," and (3) be "utterly without redeeming social value." The enunciation of this test, in a case emancipating *Fanny Hill* in Massachusetts, arguably led to (it certainly coincided with) a great wave of sexually explicit books, movies, and magazines. Themes that were once raised in movies by the arching of an eyebrow and consummated discreetly off-camera now were depicted in color, if not always in the clearest focus. Four-letter words became obligatory. Pornography was no longer obscene: America was liberated.

Still, obscenity—the remnant of it—continued unlawful, and a powerful conservative tide, vocally expressed by the 1970s, inveighed against the hard core manifestation of our newly won permissiveness. In 1972, the emerging Burger Court announced a new and more restrictive test, broadening the types of material that can be condemned: (1) Instead of a national standard, the Court said that the "average person" must apply local (meaning state) standards. (2) State statutes must specifically spell out the types of sexual conduct, depiction of which is prohibited. In other words, the statute may not simply refer vaguely to "lewd or lascivious" conduct. Even so, the material is constitutionally protected unless it depicts the forbidden acts in a *patently offensive way*. (3) Taken as a whole, the work must lack "serious literary, artistic, political, or scientific value."

Do these new guidelines help? The best answer is that one year after announcing it, the Court unanimously reversed a Georgia ban on the movie *Carnal Knowledge;* the justices held that only material depicting "patently offensive hard core sexual conduct" remains outside the constitutional shield. And what does "hard core" mean? Who can improve on Justice Stewart's famous answer: "Perhaps I could never succeed in intelligibly [defining it]. But I know it when I see it."

The battle over pornography rages. A presidential commission on pornography in 1970 found no substantial link between pornographic materials and sexual violence; an attorney general's commission in 1986, without substantially new evidence, found the opposite. Feminist groups (allied, unlikely enough, with religious fundamentalists) have lobbied for laws that define pornography as discrimination against women; the mayor of Minneapolis vetoed the first such ordinance in 1983, but the Indianapolis pornography-as-discrimination ordinance took a trip to the Supreme Court to be nullified. A new manifestation of the old vice societies has sprung up in the 1980s, as organizations, some sponsored by fundamentalist religious groups, have begun to pressure merchants to remove "offensive" material like *Penthouse* and other widely circulating national magazines. In 1986, more than eight thousand convenience stores reportedly obliged, some when notified by the Attorney General's Commission on Pornography that they would be identified in the commission's report as purveyors of smut. Whether the government may constitutionally maintain such lists (calling to mind the attorney general's listing of subversive organizations during the political witch hunts of the 1950s) may yet be tested in court. (But in a statewide referendum in Maine in 1986, voters rejected by a two-to-one margin a proposal that would have provided jail sentences for those who sell, distribute, or promote obscene material.)

After a quarter-century of life in a sexually permissive society, about all we can conclude is that although obscenity is not constitutionally safe from the legislature's skewer, the courts will remind prosecutors how narrow is the category of material that can be roasted in the fire:

1. Minors have no constitutional right to pornography, even if it might not be obscene for adults.
2. Pornographers have no constitutional right to depict children in sexual poses, even if the conduct is not obscene.
3. Material may not be banned to all simply because it might not be suitable for children. The state may not quarantine "the general reading public against books not too rugged for grown men and women in order to shield juvenile innocence."
4. In the privacy of one's home, the possession of even obscene material, defined by any test, is constitutionally protected. "If the First Amendment means anything," Justice Marshall wrote, "it means that a State has no business telling a man, sitting alone in his home, what books he may read or what films he may watch."
5. But ogling pornographic stars on a VCR at home is not the equivalent of consenting to watch them at a local movie house. The states may prevent the showing of obscene films at adult theaters, even if all the patrons have knowingly entered.
6. The majority through the legislatures may not enforce norms ("community standards") against expression that gives it psychic offense. The problem of pornography is not simply that it might incite crime

(a link probably forever unprovable) but that it undermines the "tone" of society. "The real case against pornography is so unfashionable as to have little hope of a hearing," writes one correspondent. "It is that pornography distorts the personality of the addict, especially if he is a child, and that a society addicted to pornography is itself distorted. . . . A pornographic society . . . creates a frame of mind—the playboy philosophy—antithetical or even hostile to the institution of marriage, hence to the family." All that may be, but pornography is not our only addiction; much else also arguably threatens family and other social institutions: mindless television, home computers, glorification of material success, the "yuppie" ideals of the "me decade." Ideas incite. Incitements change things.

Still, the concept of the "sexually offensive" may be sui generis. In the absence of strong proof that the sexually explicit incites criminal behavior, may states insulate the passerby from the sights of sex—the garish movie marquees, the dirty bookstore window displays, the lurid magazine racks? The Supreme Court has held that a state may zone adult movie theaters into "red-light" districts, even though the movies shown, while sexually explicit, are concededly not obscene. But the Court has also invalidated a statute prohibiting drive-in movie theaters from exhibiting films with nudity if the screen can be seen from a public street. Because these are issues that will always exercise the public as social moods change, no confident answer can ever be given, though the very question shows how far we have come since the days when fiction editors would delete as too lurid a sentence such as this from the stories that America read: "A painted girl glanced at him as he moved away."

Commercial Speech

That the *motive* for speaking or publishing is economic does not remove the First Amendment shield from the message. Likewise, that the *message* of the speech is commercial no longer permits the government to condemn it. Without thinking much about the issue, the Supreme Court in 1942 upheld a ban on the distribution of leaflets promoting the tour of a submarine. The municipal ordinance prohibited circulation of any printed materials dealing with "commercial and business advertising matter." Purely commercial advertising, the Court said, was not constitutionally protected.

In 1975, the Supreme Court came around. It reversed a Virginia ruling that under state law an abortion clinic in New York could not advertise its services in Virginia. In that case, the ad carried a message of some public significance. In 1976, the Court went further to restore First Amendment rights to commercial advertising in striking down another Virginia law, this one prohibiting pharmacists from advertising drug prices.

Nothing in these decisions prevents regulation against advertising for unlawful activities or for false or misleading advertisements. Nor do they prevent regulation of commercial speech under narrow circumstances. The Court refused to uphold a state public service commission regulation that forbade promotional advertising by an electric utility to conserve energy. It would not sanction an ordinance prohibiting home owners from posting "for sale" signs to promote a racially integrated community and stem "white flight." But it did uphold a ruling that a newspaper could not publish separate "men" and "women" help-wanted listings in its classified ads in violation of an antidiscrimination ordinance.

In the commercial marketplace, no less than in the wider arena of public discussion, ideas are beyond the government censor. This too remains an unsettled area—especially after the Court ruled in June 1986 in a murky opinion that Puerto Rico may ban its casinos from advertising gambling domestically. By implication, states might conceivably be free to ban advertising of cigarette, liquor, and other legal products considered "harmful." Whether the Court will now backslide remains to be seen. But we ought to recognize the folly of those who would preserve a society against the encroachment of ideas, like the French, who impose criminal penalties on commercial advertisers who use foreign words, to guarantee the purity of the French language.

Problems of Access

A. J. Liebling, press critic and satirist, once quipped that there is freedom of the press for the man who owns one. In most other countries, the very jest would be incomprehensible; totalitarian states are wary even of Xerox machines, which threaten revolution in speed and ease of their copying. In America, anyone is free to own a printing press, and many private individuals do. Of course, the humor of Liebling's observation lies not in the ownership of technology but in the size of the audience. What counts, according to this view, is not the right to speak or publish, but the ability to get a message to listeners, readers, and viewers.

The First Amendment guarantees the right of everyone to speak out and to listen to those who do. But it does not follow that freedom of speech and press ought to guarantee a right to communicate in the broadest sense; that is, in the sense of being guaranteed access to an audience. An audience does not exist in the abstract; it must be assembled through patient work and great expense. Newspaper and magazine circulation wars, television lineups, talk show promotions, and bookstore window displays are designed to lure readers, watchers, and listeners. What works in one week does not necessarily succeed in another; audiences are always unstable and must always be won anew. The First Amendment says that government must not stand in the way of one who would try to build an audience, but it does not say that one who has an audience must yield it to another.

This proposition was tested in 1974, when a candidate for the Florida House of Representatives sued the Miami *Herald* under a 1913 state right-of-reply law. The Florida statute required a newspaper to publish on demand the reply of any candidate whose personal character or official record was attacked in its columns. The law said the reply had to be printed in the same place and in the same type size as the offending article. The Supreme Court unanimously held the law unconstitutional as an interference with editorial freedom to decide what to publish. To the candidate's argument that the right-of-reply law did not censor, the Court responded that it "exacts a penalty on the basis of the content of a newspaper," a penalty in time and money spent on the reply and loss of space for other matters. Even if the law were workable, it might lead papers to lose their enthusiasm for controversy, and "such self-censorship under legal threat is banned by the First Amendment." (This same absolute standard, it should be noted, is not applicable to radio and television. The Court has upheld the fairness doctrine, a rule imposed by the Federal Communications Commission, requiring a station to give free air time to a person other than a political candidate whose character or integrity has been attacked.)

If members of the public have no constitutional access to the press, neither does the press have constitutional access to members of the public—at least, not to events to which the public at large is uninvited. In cases in which the press sought special rights under the press clause of the First Amendment, the Court declined to grant them. Thus a newspaper is not constitutionally entitled to talk to specific inmates in prisons: The "Constitution does not . . . require government to accord the press special access to information not shared by members of the public generally."

In 1979, the Court rejected a newspaper's demand that its reporters be admitted to cover pretrial hearings in a murder case from which the public was barred. In that case, the prosecutor and defendant both wanted the proceedings closed. But the defendant has an independent Sixth Amendment right to have all criminal proceedings open, so if he refuses to let the judge close the doors, the press may not be kept out. Finally, in 1980, the Court declared for the first time, in a decision with seven separate opinions, that the press has a right under the First Amendment to attend criminal trials (in the absence of special circumstances that rarely will be present.) But this holding does not distinguish between the public generally and the press as representative of it—the right of access is a public right, which the press shares with anyone interested in seeing justice done.

Freedom of Association

Neither in the First Amendment nor elsewhere does the Constitution mention the right to associate. The First Amendment does guarantee the "right of the people peaceably to assemble, and to petition the government for a redress of grievances." From the assembly and petition rights, the Court has fended off six types of governmental interference with people's joining organizations "to pursue goals independently protected by the First Amendment."

1. *Prohibiting creation of or participation in an organization.* We have already seen that through criminal syndicalism acts the government sought to outlaw or cripple political organizations such as the Communist party. Both the organization itself and membership and participation in it are constitutionally protected unless the group is clearly engaging in lawless conduct, not merely speech advocating future lawless conduct.

2. *Conditioning association on taking loyalty oaths.* During the 1950s, Congress and many state legislatures conditioned public employment on the employees' swearing loyalty or taking an oath that they had not supported the Communist party (or a party advocating the overthrow of the government). During the 1960s, the Supreme Court struck down

Although the Constitution guarantees the right of peaceful assembly, laws may be invoked to control the time and place of the event.

most of these requirements, largely on the grounds that they were unconstitutionally broad or vague. Some laws required employees to swear they did not belong to organizations they were constitutionally entitled to join. Other laws used terms that were not defined or could not be defined. For example, a law forcing job applicants (and employees) to swear they did not belong to "subversive organizations" and that they would promote "respect for American institutions" gives no guidance on which organizations are included within the term or what institutions deserve respect and how that respect should be promoted.

3. *Meddling in an organization's internal affairs.* The government may not attempt to dictate how an organization operates if in doing so the government trenches on First Amendment values. For example, the state may not dictate how or whether a priest is defrocked by his church, nor may it control the seating procedure of delegates at political conventions.

4. *Prohibiting a group from engaging in otherwise protected activity.* We have already seen that governmental attempts to control marches and demonstrations must be narrowly drawn to further purposes wholly independent of the speech in which the group wishes to engage. Traffic regulations may be invoked to keep marchers from tying up Main Street during rush hour, but they may not be used to prevent the demonstration altogether. Those who assemble to air grievances are allowed especially wide latitude. As Justice Douglas put it:

The right to petition for the redress of grievances has an ancient history and is not limited to writing a letter or sending a telegram to a congressman; it is not confined to appearing before the local city council, or writing letters to the President or Government or Mayor. Conventional methods of petitioning may be, and often have been, shut off to large groups of our citizens. Legislators may turn deaf ears; formal complaints may be routed endlessly through a bureaucratic maze; courts may let the wheels of justice grind very slowly. Those who do not control television and radio, those who cannot afford to advertise in newspapers or circulate elaborate pamphlets may have only a more limited type of access to public officials. Their methods should not be condemned as tactics of obstruction and harassment as long as the assembly and petition are peaceable.

5. *Denying benefits to members of organizations.* A New Bedford, Massachusetts, ordinance once forbade city policemen from engaging in certain political activities. When a politically involved policeman was dismissed from the force and sued for reinstatement, Justice Holmes (then on the Massachusetts Supreme Court) sustained the dismissal with these words: "The petitioner may have a constitutional right to talk politics, but he has no constitutional right to be a policeman." The notion that a "privilege" can be conditioned on the surrender of a constitutional right has since been considerably weakened, if not abandoned. Thus the Court has held that mere membership in a "subversive" organization like the Communist party may not be a condition for denying a passport to travel abroad or a license to a person otherwise qualified to practice law. In other words, the government may not foreclose to a person who exercises his First Amendment rights the prospects of life that are open to others equally situated.

6. *Forcing disclosure of members' identities or affiliations.* Some organizations are too unpopular or fragile to withstand disclosure of their members' identities. When the NAACP sought to open an office in Alabama during the 1950s, the state tried to force it to turn over its membership lists to the state attorney general. The Supreme Court held that "compelled disclosure . . . may constitute a restraint on freedom of association." Likewise, an Arkansas statute was voided that required public school teachers to file lists of all organizations to which they belonged or contributed during the previous five years.

Preferred Freedoms

For about fifty years, the Supreme Court has suggested, with more or less force as the political complexion of its membership changed, that the rights guaranteed by the First Amendment, the freedoms of expression, of conscience and religion (Chapter 12), and of assembly are "preferred freedoms." Justice Cardozo said that "freedom of thought and speech . . . is the matrix, the indispensable condition, of nearly every other form of freedom." In the famous Footnote 4 of the *Carolene Products* case, Justice Stone suggested the possibility that "legislation which restricts those political processes which can ordinarily be expected to bring about repeal of undesirable legislation . . . [might] be subjected to more exacting judicial scrutiny . . . than are most other types of legislation." Justice Wiley Rutledge referred to "the preferred place given in our scheme to the great, the indispensable democratic freedoms secured by the First Amendment."

Even justices like Felix Frankfurter, who disavowed the term, have not retreated from a general notion that the First Amendment brings to the Court a "momentum of respect" for the freedom of expression above claims to liberty resting on less specific language. This is surely correct, a judicial recognition of the wisdom stated best of all by John Stuart Mill in his classic essay *On Liberty:*

> If all mankind minus one, were of one opinion, and only one person were of the contrary opinion, mankind would be no more justified in silencing that one person, than he, if he had the power, would be justified in silencing mankind. . . . The peculiar evil of silencing the expression of an opinion is, that it is robbing the human race; posterity as well as the existing generation; those who dissent from the opinion still more than those who hold it. If the opinion is right, they are deprived of the opportunity of exchanging error for truth: if wrong, they lose, what is almost as great a benefit, the clearer perception and livelier impression of truth, produced by its collision with error. . . . We can never be sure that the opinion we are endeavoring to stifle is a false opinion; and if we were sure, stifling it would be evil still.

Despite seventy years of contention, the First Amendment remains the stalwart repository of the liberty that keeps us rich, strong, and free.

Chapter 12   Freedom of Conscience: Separating Church and State

Origins of Religious Liberty

Religious oppression is older than the pyramids of Egypt and as current as dour autocrats in Moscow, Peking, Teheran, Baghdad, and divers other capitals of the world today. One of the dominant themes of human history, religious intolerance unhappily continues, its ferocious thirst unslaked by centuries of killing, torture, and repression. You might suppose after all this time, after the Pharoanic cruelties, the lion pits of Rome, the Crusades, the Inquisition, and the carnage of the twentieth century, that those who kill or maim in God's name might have become a trifle embarrassed, but that's not how they think.

You might especially suppose that those to whom it has been done would be sober enough not to do it unto others, but that's not how even most victims think—not our very own Puritans, for instance. Forced to support the Church of England, the Pilgrims fled, first to Holland and then to America. But travel did not make them more tolerant. They wished religious freedom for themselves, not for others.

Until 1692, the established church in Massachusetts was Congregational: residents of each town were

Religious toleration did not exist in many of the early colonies. In 1637 the Massachusetts Bay Colony banished Anne Hutchinson, believing that the unorthodox religious views she preached in her home would threaten the unity of the colony.

assessed for the payment of a minister. After 1692, the law dropped the requirement that the church be Congregational, though it remained so in most towns until 1727 simply because a majority of taxpayers were Congregational. In 1727, the law was changed to permit Episcopalians to pay taxes to their own church; they were no longer required to contribute to the Congregational church. In 1729, Quakers and Baptists were exempted from paying taxes for ministers' salaries, even of their own churches, although the law was not always fairly applied. For more than a century, until 1833, Massachusetts had two established churches.

Other colonies too had officially established churches. New York, Connecticut, and New Hampshire had multiple establishments. In New York, towns that were religiously heterogeneous taxed each congregation to build and support its own churches. In five southern states—Georgia, Maryland, North Carolina, South Carolina, and Virginia—the Episcopalian church (the transplanted Church of England) was the sole established state church. Every person was bound to go to that church on Sundays and to pay taxes to maintain the church, regardless of belief. Only Delaware, New Jersey, Pennsylvania, and Rhode Island were free of officially established churches.

Laws establishing churches, it should be understood, were not intended simply to raise revenue. They were, at least initially, punitive regulations designed to force conduct conforming to the majority's religious tenets. A 1614 Virginia law mandated whipping for those who refused to be tested by a minister for "examination in the faith." The third time a parishioner broke the Sabbath, he or she could be executed. The death penalty was also available for speaking "impiously of the Trinity or one of the Divine Persons, or against the known articles of Christian faith."

During the next century, the medieval belief that people must avow publicly, by word and conduct, their adherence to a particular creed gradually waned.

By the time of the Revolution, some states stood firmly against church establishment, although the practice was not wholly abolished. The constitutions of New Jersey and Pennsylvania were explicit that no person could be obligated to pay for any church building or minister's salary. The North Carolina constitution of 1776 and New York's constitution of 1777 eliminated establishment outright.

Other states ceased their preference for one particular religion. In its 1780 Constitution, Massachusetts empowered the legislature to make public worship compulsory and to collect taxes to support ministers, but the money was to go to those of the taxpayers' own denomination, if a minister of that persuasion preached in their town or nearby. The legislature was barred from subordinating "any one sect or denomination to the other." Connecticut, Georgia, Maryland, New Hampshire, and South Carolina followed this pattern to varying degrees (in 1778, South Carolina proclaimed the "Christian Protestant religion" to be the state religion, a provision that was dropped in 1790 when religion was disestablished).

But it was Virginia's abolition of the established Church of England in 1785 that was to have the most pregnant consequences for American constitutionalism. The fight was led by Jefferson, whose Statute of Religious Liberty, drafted in 1777, was adopted eight years later, and by Madison, whose "Memorial and Remonstrance Against Religious Assessments" had "staggering" political effects in electing a disestablishmentarian legislature that enacted Jefferson's bill. Jefferson regarded the statute and Declaration of Independence as the two most important products of his ever fertile mind.

Jefferson always held religion to be a private matter. Granting that the government could prohibit injurious acts, he declared: "But it does me no injury for my neighbor to say that there are twenty gods, or no god. It neither picks my pocket nor breaks my leg." Although by 1776, Virginia had considerably moderated its laws against dissenters, it remained a jailable offense to deny the trinity or the divinity of the Bible. Jefferson wished to free the human mind from every shackle, to sweep away the intellectual baggage of previous centuries that imprisoned free inquiry and the expression of opinion.

The Virginia Statute of Religious Freedom provided that

> no man shall be compelled to frequent or support any religious worship, place, or ministry whatsoever, nor shall be enforced, restrained, molested, or burthened in his body or goods, or shall otherwise suffer, on account of his religious opinions or belief; but that all men shall be free to profess, and by argument to maintain, their opinions in matters of religion, and that the same shall in no wise diminish, enlarge, or affect their civil capacities.

This provision applied to all; not merely dissenters from the established church but also non-Christians and even atheists were guaranteed absolute freedom of conscience. Madison saw the statute as forever extinguishing "the ambitious hope of making laws for the human mind." So strong were the sentiments of Jefferson and Madison that both, as president, would later refuse even to proclaim national holidays of thanksgiving because they believed that doing so unconstitutionally entangled state and church.

The framers, in Article VI, had laid down the principle that no religious test could ever be required as a qualification for federal public office. Taking up the broader cause in the First Congress, Madison penned the language of an amendment denying Congress power to legislate in religious matters. The constitutional phrases themselves were gradually extended during the course of debate, to ensure that Congress have *no* power to legislate in religious matters, rather than, as certain Senate versions implied, a power to aid religion generally as long as it did not prefer one religion over another. The House version was ratified in the First Amendment: "Congress shall make no law respecting an establishment of religion, or prohibiting the free exercise thereof."

The "Wall of Separation"

In 1802, President Jefferson wrote the Danbury (Connecticut) Baptist Association that the First Amendment built "a wall of separation between church and state." His famous statement remains the central metaphor for interpreting the freedom of religion clauses. But like all metaphor, it suggests more questions than answers.

The Founding Fathers meant to sever religion and government, the better that the people could achieve their secular purposes through the state and their religious purposes through independent churches. (The founders, of course, meant to deny all power over religion to Congress; today, by virtue of the Fourteenth Amendment, that power is denied the states as well.)

The First Amendment seeks to ensure these possibilities by simultaneously barring "an establishment of religion" and prohibiting state interference with the "exercise" of religion. These clauses can work in tandem: Imposing a tax on the citizenry to build and maintain a particular church both establishes that church and interferes with dissidents' freedom to worship as they will. But frequently there is tension between the establishment and free exercise clauses. For example, a provision in the Tennessee constitution prohibited priests "of any denomination" from sitting in the state legislature—a position Jefferson advocated. Yet by seeking to prevent any entanglement between state and church, Tennessee imposed a severe burden on a person's profession of religious belief. In 1978, the Supreme Court unanimously voided the ban. Likewise, to prevent entanglement, a city might argue that it could not provide police or fire protection to churches within its boundaries, but so rigid a policy would discriminate against churches and interfere with the right of their congregants to exercise their religion.

Beyond the potential conflict between the clauses lies the question of degree: How much state action toward religion constitutes an establishment or an

Thomas Nast cartoon from 1871 depicts Columbia rejecting the pleas of various religious denominations. The cartoon was titled Church and State—No Union upon Any Terms.

infringement? In other words, how high (or straight) can the wall be—or must it be?

Establishments of Religion—The Modern View

In 1947, in a case involving public funds for bus transportation to and from all elementary schools, both public and parochial, Justice Black wrote:

> The "establishment of religion" clause of the First Amendment means at least this: Neither a state nor the Federal Government can set up a church. Neither can pass laws which aid one religion, aid all religions, or prefer one religion over another. Neither can force nor influence a person to go to or to remain away from church against his will or force him to profess a belief or disbelief in any religion. No person can be punished for entertaining or professing religious beliefs or disbeliefs, for church attendance or non-attendance. No tax in any amount, large or small, can be levied to support any religious activities or institutions, whatever they may be called, or whatever form they may adopt to teach or practice religion. Neither a state nor the Federal Government can, openly or secretly, participate in the affairs of any religious organizations or groups and vice versa. In the words of Jefferson, the clause against establishment of religion by law was intended to erect "a wall of separation between church and State."

A powerful religious current in recent years has led some to suppose that Black was wrong in declaring that the First Amendment bars government from aiding religion (in the particular case, public funding for parochial school buses was upheld). According to proponents of this view, the First Amendment was intended only to prevent the state from preferring one religion over another, not to stop the state from aiding religion in general. As William F. Buckley has put it, the First Amendment "was not designed to secularize American life, [but was intended] merely to guard against an institutionalized preeminence of a single religion over others on a national scale."

Founding Father

Richard Dobbs Spaight
North Carolina

Richard Dobbs Spaight was born in Newbern, North Carolina, March 25, 1758, and died in his home state, September 6, 1802. Of a prominent family, he was orphaned at the age of eight and traveled to Ireland for his formal education, receiving a degree from the University of Glasgow. In 1778, he returned to America and quickly became involved in the revolutionary cause, volunteering for the militia. In 1789, he became a member of the General Assembly and continued to serve in this post until 1783 when he became a member of the Continental Congress. After the Convention in 1787, he persuaded George Washington to visit North Carolina in an attempt to push North Carolina's ratification; the tactic succeeded. In 1792, he was again a member of the General Assembly, which chose him governor. In 1797, he was elected to Congress to fill a vacant seat. Reelected, he remained until 1801, when he became a North Carolina senator. The fervor of early American politics and the sensitivities of eighteenth-century gentlemen led to Spaight's demise. A Jeffersonian, he was challenged to a duel on political grounds and was mortally wounded.

Buckley is twice wrong. This narrow interpretation of the establishment clause is not plausible. Nor does the broader interpretation of the First Amendment thereby "secularize American life."

Establishment did not mean to the framers an official status for a single, particular church; it meant an official position for any churches that citizens could be compelled to support through taxes and attendance. In barring an establishment, the framers intended not merely to prevent a particular church from receiving state endorsement over others but also to prevent any endorsement at all. Recall that those who opposed a bill of rights did so not because they wished their rights to be taken away but because they held that Congress had been given no power to do so. This was particularly true about power to enact legislation concerning religion. A bill of rights was therefore unnecessary; worse, some feared, it might even be dangerous because it would imply that whatever was not explicitly forbidden might somehow be implied as a power of the federal government (hence the Ninth Amendment, page 266.) The modern suggestions that Congress may aid religion show that those dangers were rightly apprehended.

The impotence of Congress to foster religion does not, however, "secularize American life." To the contrary, the First Amendment leaves Americans free, on their own, to live as religious a life as they desire, short only of government involvement. Because the government may not prevent Buckley's neighbor from profaning the Lord does not mean that Buckley must go about blaspheming. Because the government may not force me to attend church does not mean that you cannot go as often as you like. Because the government may not lead my children in prayer in public school does not mean that my children may not pray there on their own.

To determine the constitutionality of legislation or other government action that affects religion, the Supreme Court has followed a porous, three-pronged test: "a legislative enactment does not contravene the Establishment Clause if it has a secular legislative purpose, if its principal or primary effect neither advances nor inhibits religion, and if it does not foster an excessive government entanglement with religion." If a state practice fails any part of this test, it is unconstitutional.

The test is easy to state, but here especially, as Justice Holmes taught, "general propositions do not decide concrete cases. The decision will depend on a judgment or intuition more subtle than any articulate major premise." What follows is a summary of the intuition that has guided the Court during the past four decades, the period of active religion jurisprudence.

Financial Support for Religious Activities

A string of federal and state enactments have tested the limits of government financial aid to religious institutions, in particular to sectarian schools. The three-pronged test, largely developed through these cases, has proven notoriously difficult to apply, and throughout the 1970s and 1980s, shifting majorities of justices have led to results that have seemed contradictory, if not paradoxical. As Leonard F. Manning has summed them up:

Lawyer and layman alike must have been wondrously perplexed when the Court told us that the state would be compelled to police the teaching of the partially subsidized secular instructor in the church-affiliated elementary and secondary schools, although surveillance is not mandated to guard against indoctrination in the wholly funded public school; that the state may lend text books to parochial school students but that it may not lend those same students, or their parents, movie projectors, tape records, record players, maps and globes, science kits or weather forecasting charts; that a state may exempt church property from taxation but that it may not provide state income tax credits or income tax deductions for parents who pay tuition to church-related elementary and secondary schools; that the state may provide free bus transportation, to and from school, for children attending parochial schools but it may not provide the same transportation for the same students for trips to governmental, industrial, cultural and scientific centers designed to enrich their secular studies; that the state may provide direct, noncategorical funding of church-related colleges, but may not provide indirect, and restricted financial assistance for church-affiliated secondary schools; that the state may not provide for children with special needs, remedial and accelerated instruction, guidance counseling and testing, speech and hearing services, on nonpublic school premises, but that it may provide speech and hearing diagnostic services in the nonpublic school; and that the state may provide—in public schools, public centers or mobile units—therapeutic services for deaf, blind, emotionally disturbed, crippled and physically handicapped nonpublic school children but that it may not provide the same services for the same children on the nonpublic school premises.

Contradictory though the results may seem, they are perhaps best explained as the Court's groping attempt to construct a zigzagging wall of separation to accommodate some secular interests that somehow "feel"

as though they would neither advance nor hinder anyone's religious practice. To use another set of examples, the Court has rejected a "released-time" program in which public schools ended an hour early one day a week to permit students to attend voluntary religious instruction in the schoolrooms, whereas it has permitted a similar program in which students who volunteered could leave the school grounds to go to religious centers for religious instruction. In the latter case, the students were pursuing their religion elsewhere; in the former, the school was inextricably entangled in the religious activity. The distinction suggests the subtle feel by which the Court has been constructing the wall.

Government spends money on religious activities in ways other than schools. For example, it pays for chaplains in the armed forces and prisons. Though given the opportunity, the Court has never disapproved these activities because although the expenditures obviously tend toward a religious establishment, the failure to do so would amount to government interference with soldiers' and inmates' free exercise

The government's school lunch program includes assistance for church-affiliated schools without violating the constitutional requirement for separation of church and state.

of religion. In a contest between the two religion clauses, the free exercise clause will usually be paramount.

School Prayers

In cases that have infuriated more than arch-fundamentalists, the Court has struck down prayers and Bible reading in public schools. The first prayer case, in 1962, involved a "nondenominational" prayer actually written by the New York Board of Regents. Said Justice Black: "[It] is no part of the business of government to compose official prayers for any group of the American people to recite as part of a religious program carried on by the government." In 1963, the Court rejected a Pennsylvania law that required teachers to read aloud passages from the Bible and students to recite in unison the Lord's Prayer. Despite the outcry, the practice surely flunked all three prongs of the establishment test: There was no secular legislative purpose, the primary effect of the reading was to advance religion, and public readings fostered excessive government entanglement in religious activity. That the practice of government-sponsored prayer is an impermissible establishment seems especially clear in view of prayer advocates' failure to be satisfied by the obvious alternative. Nothing that the Court has ever said prohibits individual schoolchildren on their own to pray in the schoolyard before classes, in the opening minutes while the teacher is calling the class to order, or at any quiet moment during the day. The only purpose in school prayer is to place the government's imprimatur on the practice, and that is precisely what the establishment clause forbids.

To be sure, children who did not wish to participate in the prayer or Bible reading could sit silently or be excused. Erwin S. Griswold, then dean of Harvard

Before Engel v. Vitale *in 1962, many schools required the day to begin with a prayer.*

Law School, argued that the state does not do ill in thus setting these children apart:

> Is it not desirable, and educational, for [the child of a nonconforming or minority group] to learn and observe this [difference in beliefs], in the atmosphere of the school—not so much that he is different as that other children are different from him? And is it not desirable that, at the same time, he experiences and learns the fact that his difference is tolerated and accepted? No compulsion is put upon him. He need not participate. But he, too, has the opportunity to be tolerant. He allows the majority of the group to follow their own tradition, perhaps coming to understand and to respect what they feel is significant to them.

This is an odd way to put the matter: Ought we not prefer that the majority learn to tolerate the practices of the minority? Minorities have many (and a lifetime's) ways to learn what sets them apart. Something is inherently unequal in the equality of tolerance that Griswold so facilely proposes—rather like the nineteenth-century Supreme Court justices who said that laws requiring racial segregation did not stamp blacks as inferior; it was all in their minds (page 307).

Bans on Secular Doctrines: "Monkey Laws"

Evolutionists have been fighting fundamentalists (who today call themselves "creationists") ever since Darwin. Gaining national notoriety in the Scopes trial in 1925 in Tennessee, the issue is whether a state may bar teachers from talking about the theory that Homo sapiens has evolved from lower animal orders. In 1968, a case testing an Arkansas "monkey law" reached the Supreme Court, which unanimously struck it down on the finding that the state had selected "from the body of knowledge a particular segment which it proscribes for the sole reason that it is deemed to conflict with a particular religious doctrine."

Government-Sponsored Religious Symbols: The "Crèche" Case

It ought to follow that when the government affirmatively sponsors religious symbols, it is similarly violating the establishment clause. But symbols have proved more resilient, perhaps because they have become so cheapened that we scarcely notice them. Our

Clarence Darrow (center) beginning his defense at the start of the 1925 "Scopes Monkey Trial" in Dayton, Tennessee.

currency recites that "In God We Trust" (as do any number of public buildings). Is that motto an establishment of religion? The issue has never been tested.

But in 1984, the Supreme Court narrowly approved the public funding in Pawtucket, Rhode Island, of a crèche, a nativity scene displayed in a park in the heart of the downtown shopping center. The Court's stated rationale was that Christmas is a national holiday and the crèche fulfilled an essentially secular purpose; in any event, it was a "passive symbol" of a "celebration acknowledged in the Western World for 20 centuries."

Concurring, Justice O'Connor sought to square the result with the three-pronged test. Even if the crèche had a secular purpose, she noted, it would still fail the test if government intended nevertheless "to convey a message of endorsement or disapproval of religion." The crèche passed the test, she said, because Pawtucket did not intend to endorse Christianity: The crèche had become one of the symbols of a "holiday [that] itself has very strong secular components and traditions."

Dissenting, Justice Brennan condemned a "beguilingly simple, yet faulty syllogism": that to recognize Christmas as a public holiday permits the conclusion that the crèche is constitutionally permissible because the crèche is "nothing more than a traditional element of Christmas celebrations." Brennan would separate the secular from the sectarian elements and symbols of the holiday: Santa Claus is secular, Jesus is not.

Interpreting Religious Doctrine

The courts may construe symbols to determine secular meaning, but they may not sit to interpret religious doctrine to determine which faction in a fight over church property or church office is entitled to its use. A state court may not decide that a national religious organization has so departed from the ecclesiastical doctrines of the church that a local congregation is entitled to sever the parent body's control over the local church property. Ecclesiastical questions are for church authorities, not civil courts. Nor may a court set aside a church's defrocking of its bishop despite a claim that the church had violated its own rules: "A civil court must accept the ecclesiastical decisions of church tribunals as it finds them." (These cases demonstrate that the First Amendment prohibits any branch of government, not just legislatures, from actions that tend toward an establishment of religion.)

Free Exercise of Religion—The Modern View

The government may undertake neither to establish nor to prohibit individuals from freely exercising their religions. But the free exercise clause has its own difficulties: May the religious eccentric justify any action by pointing to its religious significance? In a nation devoted to hucksterism, that seems a tall proposition. Here, as in the case of the free speech clause, the courts have tended to distinguish between belief

The free exercise clause allows religious groups such as the Hare Krishnas to proselytize.

and conduct, though the words again mask how difficult it is to distinguish at the margin.

Right to Proselytize

Communicants' active proselytizing on behalf of their faith is largely protected against claims that in so doing they may offend others and thus disturb the peace. In an early case, a Jehovah's Witness played a phonograph on a public street; the record attacked all organized religious systems as instruments of Satan, in particular the Roman Catholic church. His intention was to persuade passersby to contribute money "in the interest of what [he], however misguided others may think him, conceived to be true religion." Passersby were in fact offended; the neighborhood in which he had set up his booth was 90 percent Catholic. He was convicted of violating both a breach-of-peace law and a licensing law requiring him to obtain the permission of the secretary of the public welfare council, who was empowered to determine whether solicitations were for religious or charitable causes. The Supreme Court reversed. A narrowly drawn statute that prohibited all noise from the public streets might have withstood challenge, but not a prosecution obviously aimed at clamping down on "obnoxious" religious discussion. The licensing scheme was struck down on the same grounds that the Court had voided similar ordinances involving nonreligious speech (page 234).

Enforced Speech Repugnant to One's Creed

The free exercise clause will not permit the state to dictate what a person must say or affirm. In the "flag salute cases," the Supreme Court in 1940 upheld a Minersville, Pennsylvania, public school rule requiring all students to salute the flag and recite the usual pledge of allegiance on pain of expulsion. The pledge offended the Jehovah's Witnesses' literal interpretation of the Bible. The Court's ruling upholding the flag salute ("the symbol of national unity") set in motion in many communities across the country a series of violent reactions to the Witnesses' very presence. (Pious and unyielding, considered beyond the pale of mere eccentricity by many mainstream Protestants, "a sect," in Zechariah Chafee's phrase, "distinguished by great religious zeal and astonishing powers of annoyance," Jehovah's Witnesses have figured in a substantial number of the significant free exercise cases, to the greater benefit of all religions in America.) Scores of school boards rushed to adopt flag salute rules, but as Judge J. Skelly Wright concluded, "the words of the Supreme Court, that the protection of freedom could best be left to the responsibility of local authorities, were perverted and used as an excuse for what was in effect religious persecution by the local school boards."

Three years later, the Supreme Court reversed itself in a case coming from West Virginia. In an often-quoted passage, Justice Jackson declared: "If there is any fixed star in our constitutional constellation, it is that no official, high or petty, can prescribe what shall be orthodox in politics, nationalism, religion, or other matters of opinion or force citizens to confess by word or act their faith therein."

Well into the nineteenth century, many states required just that: Public officeholders were required to swear a belief in Christianity or even Protestantism. Though this restriction disappeared by 1877 (New Hampshire was the last holdout), a similar oath of belief in God remained in the constitutions of eight states. The Supreme Court finally struck these down in 1961, in a case in which Maryland refused to commission a notary public because he refused to declare that he believed in God. And in 1977, the Court voided a New Hampshire law that car owners display the state motto "Live Free or Die" on their license plates, again in a case brought by Jehovah's Witnesses.

Forced Choices

A Seventh-Day Adventist in South Carolina was discharged from her job because she refused to work on Saturday, her Sabbath. She applied for but was denied state unemployment compensation because she had refused, "without good cause," to undertake suitable work offered her (namely, her job). Although the compensation law was "religion blind," it worked an obvious discrimination against the applicant, and in 1963 the Supreme Court struck down the state's work test. Her ineligibility stemmed entirely from her religion. The rule imposed on her "forces her to choose between following precepts of her religion and forfeiting benefits, on the one hand, and abandoning one of the precepts of her religion to accept work, on the other. Governmental imposition of such a choice puts the same kind of burden upon the free exercise of religion as would a fine imposed against appellant for her Saturday worship."

This case suggests the possibility that the Court's earlier decisions in the Sunday Closing Law Cases (page 322) might in time be reversed. In one of those cases, an Orthodox Jew had protested a law that compelled him to close his store on Sunday, even though his religion compelled him to close on Saturday, closings that together imperiled his economic survival. The Court upheld the Sunday ordinance.

Exemption from a Secular Duty: Conscientious Objection

The tangled history of the conscientious objector provisions in the federal draft laws is beyond our scope. The Supreme Court has never ruled definitively that Congress must exempt from the military draft those who object to "war in any form" on religious grounds. But Congress has long provided such an exemption. An important subsidiary question, however, is what exactly constitutes a religion for purposes of the exemption. Until 1967, the federal law defined *religion* as a "belief in a relation to a Supreme Being involving

Alvin York's application for exemption from the draft as a conscientious objector was denied in 1917 and he eventually became a popular army hero during World War I.

duties superior to those arising from any human relation but [not including] essentially political, sociological, or philosophical views or a merely personal moral code." In a 1965 case, the Court construed that provision to include a "sincere and meaningful" belief that "occupies a place in the life of its possessor parallel to that filled by the orthodox belief in God," and in 1970, the Court held that, as construed, the exemption applied to those whose sincere beliefs were based on a personal philosophical, moral, or ethical code. But the exemption does not apply to a "selective conscientious objector," one who opposes only certain wars, even if that opposition is grounded in a clear theological belief.

Sincerity of Belief

Constitutional protection for the exercise of religion cannot be a shield for every mountebank who claims a religious justification for his actions. Suppose a huckster solicits funds, asserting that he is a divine messenger of God. In fact, he believes no such thing; he is interested only in how much he can rake in. In a mail fraud case on these facts, the Court permitted the jury to consider the sincerity of the defendants' claim, but not the truth of it. If the jury concluded that the defendants honestly believed they were divine messengers, there could be no conviction: "If one could be sent to jail because a jury in a hostile environment found [religious] teachings false, little indeed would be left of religious freedom."

This problem remains a live and vexing one, as recent news stories attest. If a state exempts a minister's real estate from taxation, may others claim to be ministers of their own religion to obtain the exemption?

Unlawful Religious Conduct

Protected religious practice obviously must not be confined to belief or expressions of belief. Labeling a practice "conduct" to avoid the free exercise clause would put much religious ritual at risk: drinking wine, eating wafers, affixing symbols to buildings. But it is not less true that religiously justified conduct has its limits: Ritual murder will not be condoned because someone somewhere has called it religious.

The classic instance of state power over conduct claimed to be integral to the religion is the now-lapsed Mormon belief that polygamy was a religious duty for men. The Supreme Court in 1878 sustained a conviction of a Mormon who had taken a second wife in the then territory of Utah in violation of a federal law. The Court reasoned that American society was founded on the monogamous family and that Congress would clearly prohibit polygamy in the territories to all who did not profess a religious belief in the necessity of it. Did the First Amendment shield those who did affirm it as a religious duty? No, said the Court, for Congress "was left free to reach actions which were in violation of social duties or subversive of good order." It is doubtful that so broadly worded a justification would be entertained today, for religion often teaches a violation of some people's social duties and others' "good order." (For example, suppose a

1868 photograph of a Mormon polygamist and his family outside their Great Salt Lake Valley home.

religion taught the necessity of a man's living with several women at once, in a state akin to marriage, if not in the marriage relationship. Could the state today ban the arrangement? Indeed, on the principles explored in Chapter 13, it might not be able to ban multiple living arrangements even without religious justification.)

Nevertheless, the belief-action distinction retains some validity. Thus the Court has upheld a hospital's decision to override a parent's objection on religious grounds to a child's being given a lifesaving blood transfusion.

On the other hand, the California Supreme Court reversed the conviction of members of the Native American church for using peyote in religious ceremonies. Though the state may deny its use to others, the court held that for the Navaho priest, peyote was central to the religious practice of a genuine and ancient church, the drug amounting in effect to a deity.

Also, in 1972, the Supreme Court held that Wisconsin could not enforce its compulsory public education laws against the Amish, whose religious convictions preclude them from sending their children to school beyond the eighth grade. Finding that the entire Amish way of life was "not merely a matter of personal preference but one of deep religious conviction, shared by an organized group, and intimately related to daily living," the Court held that enforcing the state's education law "would gravely endanger if not destroy the free exercise" of the Amish religious beliefs.

To preserve a way of life against the admittedly secular purposes of the state suggests how high a deference the Court can pay to the free exercise clause. But that deference poses a difficulty in turn, for the free exercise of religion must be that of individuals, not a way of life. The Court expressly noted that nothing in the record suggested that the children wished to attend school despite their parents' desires. But suppose they did? Not even parents may maintain an indefinite power to shape the beliefs of their children.

A 1972 Supreme Court ruling permitted exemption for the Amish from a compulsory public education law in Wisconsin on the grounds that it would endanger the free exercise of that religion.

In the end, the liberty that the First Amendment protects is that of the individual—even if the child (at least above a certain age) deserts the faith of her fathers and joins the rankest of cults. Or at least so it must be if we are to remain true to the spirit of religious freedom in America.

Chapter 13   The Farther Reaches of Liberty: Privacy and Personal Autonomy

Substantive Due Process

A free life consists in more than thinking and talking and writing. If the freedoms of expression and conscience are the indispensable matrix of political liberty, if they are even worth dying for, still they do not define all that is worth living for.

A constitution that distinguishes between thought and action, expression and conduct, shielding the former from invasion and exposing the latter to encroachment, would not be a document worthy of our highest praise. A rational life plan encompasses *doing,* and that implies, in a constitutional order, some realm of personal autonomy. Yet that realm is difficult to locate in the constitutional text. The conduct that comprises symbolic speech is limited, and the sphere of religious practice shrinks when it begins to have social effects.

It is not plainly crazy to argue that we must look to legislatures, not constitutions and courts, to preserve the essential freedom of action. In a system that respects everyone's right to vote and everyone's right to speak out, a legislature will not curb our essential needs. Why constitutional protection for speech but not for action? We accept as a basic principle that even when speech might be deemed harmful, its social impact may not be regulated. In other words, freedom of speech must be enshrined in a constitution, for its very tendency will be to sting and to send its victims to seek legislative balm. But we can hardly accept as a basic proposition that all conduct likewise must be unregulated. That is not freedom but anarchy. Regulating harm is one of the principal activities of the state. A major part of legislation must necessarily be to curb the means, ends, and consequences of human activity.

Still, any governmental power can be abused. An impassioned majority will not delay in pouncing on conduct it finds offensive, no matter how essential that conduct may be to the person for whom it defines her very being—or for whom that conduct is merely pleasurable. A simple example is the right to imbibe. Those who pressed temperance on the nation, successfully when the Eighteenth Amendment was ratified in 1919, thought to liberate the American soul, to "promote the cause of human progress." The evils of alcohol were well documented, but prohibitionists went far beyond regulating or banning its use in saloons and public places. Prohibitionists told people that they could not have a glass of wine in their own home. They got away with it in legal theory, though scarcely in practical fact, by overriding whatever restraints against dry legislation might have been found in the Constitution. And if none, should there not have been? It was laudable to end the worst excesses of the prevalent public drunkenness of the nineteenth century, and contrary to legend Prohibition apparently accomplished just that, despite repeal. But the question remains whether a legislative majority may impose its morality on an unwilling segment of the public.

Not just instinctively, but because we have been tutored by him, John Stuart Mill's classic exposition of the liberty to act is often accepted as appropriate constitutional wisdom:

A *crowded speakeasy during Prohibition.*

The sole end for which mankind are warranted, individually or collectively, in interfering with the liberty of action of any of their number, is self-protection. . . . The only purpose for which power can be rightfully exercised over any member of a civilized community, against his will, is to prevent harm to others. His own good, either physical or moral, is not a sufficient warrant. He cannot rightfully be compelled to do or forbear because it will be better for him to do so, because it will make him happier, because, in the opinions of others, to do so would be wise, or even right. . . . The only part of the conduct of any one, for which he is amenable to society, is that which concerns others. In the part which merely concerns himself, his independence is, of right, absolute. Over himself, over his own body and mind, the individual is sovereign.

Unfortunately, perhaps, Mill was born too late for the framers to insinuate this passage in the Constitution. In any event, the Millian principle would pose severe difficulties of interpretation these days, even if it were embodied in a separate article of the Bill of Rights. We need not strain to show that almost everything we do in our complex, interdependent modern society affects others to some degree and in a way that could plausibly be said to be harmful. The current public debate on the right to smoke (cigarettes or dope), for example, turns on that point.

In the earliest days of the Constitution, some supposed a "natural right" of individual liberty for which no explicit guarantee was necessary—the "inalienable rights" of the Declaration of Independence. In 1798, Justice Samuel Chase opined:

> I cannot subscribe to the *omnipotence* of a *State Legislature*, or that it is *absolute* and *without controul;* although its authority should not be *expressly* restrained by the *Constitution*, or *fundamental law*, of the State . . . The *nature*, and *ends* of *legislative* power will limit the *exercise* of it. This *fundamental* principle flows from the very nature of our free *Republican* governments. . . . There are acts which the *Federal*, or *State*, Legislature cannot do, *without exceeding their authority*. There are certain *vital* principles in our *free Republican governments*, which will determine and over-rule an *apparent and flagrant* abuse of *legislative* power; . . . An ACT of the Legislature (for I cannot call it a *law*) contrary to the *great first principles* of the *social compact*, cannot be considered a *rightful exercise* of *legislative authority*.

But in the very case, Justice James Iredell answered Chase in terms that would carry the Court for nearly a century:

> If . . . the Legislature of the Union, or the Legislature of any member of the Union, shall pass a law, within

the general scope of their constitutional power, the Court cannot pronounce it to be void, merely because it is, in their judgment, contrary to the principles of natural justice. The ideas of natural justice are regulated by no fixed standard: the ablest and the purest men have differed upon the subject; and all that the Court could properly say, in such an event, would be, that the Legislature (possessed of an equal right of opinion) had passed an act which, in the opinion of the judges, was inconsistent with the abstract principles of natural justice.

Natural law and natural justice, by those names, were not to grace the canons of constitutional interpretation.

"Substantive due process" would, however, take its place. This imposing term draws its meaning from the due process clauses of the Fifth and Fourteenth Amendments: "No person shall . . . be deprived [nor shall any state deprive any person] of life, liberty or property, without due process of law." The clause seems to mean that a person may indeed be deprived of life, liberty, or property, as long as it is *lawfully* taken; that is, following whatever legal process is due him—for instance, a fair trial by an impartial jury. But in a development the main lines of which are traced in Chapter 17, the Supreme Court in the late nineteenth century concluded that some deprivations were illegitimate no matter the process.

In this view, the evil is not a procedural irregularity (or lack of procedure at all) in the taking of property or loss of liberty—to sentence individuals to jail without having first convicted them at trial is a denial of *procedural due process*. The evil is rather, the taking or deprivation itself. The adherent agrees that it is legitimate to jail persons who are properly convicted, but holds it impermissible to deny them their *substantive* right to work twelve hours a day, no matter how scrupulously the legislature enacted the law.

The Court's foray into substantive due process occurred mainly to vindicate property rights and economic "liberties"—hence the doctrine is often called "economic due process." It was this concept that the butchers of New Orleans pressed on the Court in the *Slaughterhouse Cases* (page 201)—unsuccessfully. Their argument was that the monopoly handed the Crescent City Livestock-Landing Co. deprived them of their freedom to earn a living. That was in 1873, and the Court was not yet ready for this expansive reading of the new Fourteenth Amendment. But in 1897, it was. In *Allgeyer v. Louisiana,* the Court struck down a state law that made it a criminal offense to take out an insurance policy on property in Louisiana unless the company had qualified to do business there. Said Justice Rufus W. Peckham:

> The liberty mentioned [in the Fourteenth Amendment] means not only the right of the citizen to be free from the mere physical restraint of his person, as by incarceration, but the term is deemed to embrace the right of the citizen to be free in the enjoyment of all his faculties; to be free to use them in all lawful ways; to live and work where he will; to earn his livelihood by any lawful calling; to pursue any livelihood or avocation, and for that purpose to enter into all contracts which may be proper, necessary and essential to his carrying out to a successful conclusion the purposes above mentioned.

Economic due process held sway for about forty years, until the Court rather abruptly reversed itself in the late 1930s. From that time, it has broadly deferred to the judgments of Congress and the state legislatures in matters involving economic regulation.

Despite retreat on the economic front, however, the Court in recent years has revivified the substantive due process doctrine, turning it to noneconomic concerns—in particular, issues of privacy and personal autonomy.

Early Noneconomic Liberty Cases

The stirrings were felt earlier in the century. Nebraska outlawed teaching any subject in the public schools in a language other than English. A teacher was convicted for teaching German. The Court reversed the conviction in 1923. Fourteenth Amendment liberty, said Justice James C. McReynolds,

> denotes not merely freedom from bodily restraint but also the right of the individual to contract, to engage in any of the common occupations of life, to acquire useful knowledge, to marry, establish a home and bring up children, to worship God according to the dictates of his own conscience, and generally to enjoy those privileges long recognized at common law as essential to the orderly pursuit of happiness by free men.

The Nebraska law interfered "with the calling of modern language teachers, with the opportunities of pupils to acquire knowledge, and with the power of parents to control the education of their own." Two years later, the Court overturned an Oregon law that required all children between the ages of eight and sixteen to attend public schools. In foreclosing parents' choice to send their children to parochial schools, the law again interfered "with the liberty of parents and guardians to direct the upbringing and education of children under their control."

These cases closely implicate the values of free speech and thought and might be explained as resting on the explicit text of the First Amendment—except that they came before the Court recognized that the Fourteenth Amendment specifically applies the freedoms of speech and religion to the states. (And in the Oregon school decision, a companion case raised the issue of a parent's right to send his son to a military school; no religious question led the Court to decide in the same way—that a constitutional right of liberty outweighs the state's interest in standardizing its children.)

For forty years, noneconomic substantive due process lay waiting—a doctrine in search of interests to protect. These came, with a vengeance, in 1965 and again in 1973, when the Court fashioned a new constitutional right of privacy in its birth control and abortion decisions.

Founding Father

Charles Pinckney
South Carolina

Charles Pinckney was born in Charleston, South Carolina, October 26, 1757, where he died on October 29, 1824. Educated in his home town, he was admitted to the bar in 1779. He enlisted in the militia during the Revolution, was captured in the British attack on Charleston, 1780, and remained a prisoner of war until 1781. From 1784 to 1787, he was a delegate to Congress under the Articles of Confederation. An active debater during the Constitutional Convention, he was on the Committee of Rules and Procedures, and submitted the "Pinckney Draught" at the opening of the debates; thirty-two of his provisions were incorporated in the final Constitution. Though an important contributor to the debates, he later boasted of single-handedly creating the "supreme law of the land," a remark that weakened his credibility. In 1789, he was elected governor of South Carolina and held this office until 1792. He presided over the South Carolina state constitutional convention of 1790. Initially a Federalist, by 1796 he supported Thomas Jefferson in the presidential election. In 1798, he was elected a U.S. senator. In 1801, Jefferson appointed him U.S. minister to Spain. As minister, he was frustrated by his inability to persuade Spain to cede or sell Florida in the aftermath of the Louisiana Purchase. In 1806, he returned to South Carolina and was elected governor as a Democrat. From 1810 to 1814, he was a member of the state legislature. In 1818, he was elected to Congress, where he opposed the Missouri Compromise of 1820.

The Right of Privacy

The word *privacy* does not appear in the Constitution or Bill of Rights. Yet the Constitution assuredly protects aspects of privacy: the Fourth Amendment says that the police may not search our homes, possessions, or bodies without a warrant obtained on reasonable cause; the Fifth Amendment prohibits self-incrimination; the First Amendment has been interpreted to preserve the privacy of individuals in their homes and of various associations; the Third Amendment prohibits soldiers from being quartered in our homes in time of peace without consent. What then of a state that outlaws the use of birth control devices and makes criminals of those who give advice about birth control to married couples?

The executive director of the Planned Parenthood League of Connecticut and the medical director of the league's New Haven center were arrested for giving such advice. In *Griswold v. Connecticut*, the Court reversed the convictions and struck down the law. Justice Douglas's majority opinion discerned a broad right of marital privacy in "penumbras formed by emanations from" guarantees in the Bill of Rights. The case "concerns a relationship lying within the zone of privacy created by several fundamental constitutional guarantees." But the right of privacy of the marital bedroom is not merely to be found there:

Justice William O. Douglas authored the majority opinion in Griswold v. Connecticut.

We deal with a right of privacy older than the Bill of Rights—older than our political parties, older than our school system. Marriage is a coming together for better or for worse, hopefully enduring, and intimate to the degree of being sacred. The association promotes a way of life, not causes; a harmony in living, not political faiths; a bilateral loyalty, not commercial or social projects. Yet it is an association for as noble a purpose as any involved in our prior decisions.

Justice Arthur J. Goldberg sought to ground the Court's holding in another part of the Constitution, the rarely noted Ninth Amendment. It reads: "The enumeration in the Constitution, of certain rights, shall not be construed to deny or disparage others retained by the people." These open-ended words suggest a different basis for protecting the people's liberties. As Justice Goldberg said: "To hold that a right so basic and fundamental and so deep-rooted in our society as the right of privacy in marriage may be infringed because that right is not guaranteed in so many words by the first eight amendments to the Constitution is to ignore the Ninth Amendment and to give it no effect whatsoever."

Yet until *Griswold*, the Court had never even suggested sustaining on the strength of the Ninth Amendment a right not otherwise found in the text of the Constitution. The Ninth Amendment, says one commentator, "was not intended to add anything to the meaning of the remaining articles in the Constitution. It was simply a technical proviso inserted to forestall the possibility of misinterpretation." Hamilton and James Wilson importuned Madison to avoid the implication that the federal government might possess all sorts of powers not specifically denied to it by the Bill of Rights, even if not mentioned in the text of the Constitution. For example, the First Amendment precludes Congress from abridging freedom of speech. It does not say that the president may not do so. Madison's answer was the Ninth Amendment, intended to ensure that such an argument would carry no weight.

But to say that the Ninth Amendment is a "technical amendment" is neither to confine it nor shrivel up the rights that it protects. Its text is plain, and as Charles L. Black sardonically urged in the Holmes Lectures in 1979, it is time that "having been proposed by the requisite majorities in Congress, and ratified by the requisite number of states, the Ninth Amendment to the Constitution of the United States at long last be adopted." Black's solution to its meaning is straightforward: "the unnamed right is *closely analogous or functionally similar to a named right.*" For example, the double jeopardy clause (page 291) does not say that it applies in the case of jail sentences; the Fifth Amendment speaks only of "life or limb" (that is, death sentences or mutilation). Yet the courts will certainly apply it when a convicted felon has been sentenced to jail, and, says Black, the Ninth Amendment makes it perfectly appropriate that they do so. That said, the Supreme Court has not yet seen fit to adopt the suggestion, and the right of privacy must seek its foundation in penumbras and radiations.

Since the *Griswold* case, the Court has effectively overturned most state laws against contraception. In 1977, it struck down a New York law that permitted only pharmacists to sell or distribute contraceptives to anyone over sixteen and that prohibited sale or distribution to anyone under sixteen, confirming the general proposition that matters of procreation are for individuals (even unmarried individuals) to decide, not the state.

The contraceptive cases provoked relatively mild response to this new recognition of a right of privacy. The storm came with the seven-to-two abortion decision in *Roe v. Wade* in 1973. That case tested the Texas abortion laws, typical of about three-quarters of the state abortion statutes. The Texas law made it a crime to "procure an abortion" unless on medical advice abortion was necessary to save the mother's life. In a discursive opinion on the history of abortion laws in the United States, Justice Blackmun held that the fetus is not a "person" within the meaning of the Fourteenth Amendment; that the right of privacy, founded in the Fourteenth Amendment concept of "personal liberty," encompasses the decision to terminate a pregnancy; and that the state has "compelling" interests in the mother's health and in safeguarding "potential life."

These factors led the Court to promulgate a three-tier constitutional rule. The state may not interfere with a woman's decision to have an abortion during the first three months of pregnancy—Justice Blackmun noted that mortality during first trimester abortion is less than that of mortality in normal childbirth. After the first trimester, however, the state's interest in the mother's health becomes compelling, and so it may determine the qualifications of those it will permit to perform abortions and the facilities in which abortions are done. Because the fetus "presumably

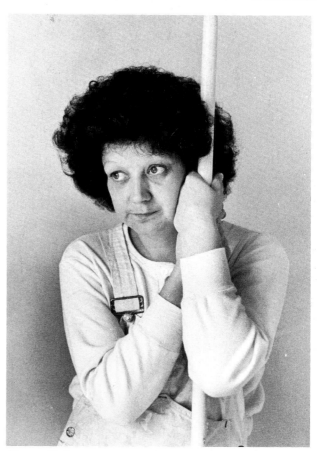

Norma McConey, ten years after her suit under the alias of "Jane Roe" resulted in the controversial Court ruling on abortion.

has the capability of meaningful life outside the mother's womb" around the third trimester, the state may invoke its compelling interest in preserving potential life by banning abortions at that stage, unless necessary to preserve the mother's health.

Rarely has such a storm burst over a decision by the Supreme Court—in both the academy and on the streets. There are in fact two debates. The scholars are arguing over the constitutional legitimacy of the Court's ruling. Within the scholarly community, as within the Court itself, the issue is unsettled—and unsettling. Just how far ought the Court go in ferreting out fundamental values that an electoral majority may not disturb?

On the streets, the questions are more direct, and more polarizing. Is abortion murder? Ought a woman have complete control over her body? Though the public reaction to *Roe v. Wade* has been less ferocious than it was to *Dred Scott* or *Brown v. Board* (Chapter 15), it has been national in scope and import. The case has become, in the eyes of those who detest it, part of the demonology of American conservatism (though decided by the Burger Court, in a decision to which the chief justice assented), and it was soon the centerpiece of a debate that went far beyond fraying tempers. "Prolife" and "prochoice" are more than slogans to wear on buttons in a parade. Protests against *Roe* have sparked violence in scores of cities, not merely in clashes on picket lines but also in bombings of abortion clinics. Some have labeled these incidents "domestic terrorism," though the FBI so far seems disinclined to investigate clues that a conspiracy, not random violence, is to blame.

Abortion quickly became a litmus test of ideological purity in politics at the local, state, and national levels, as candidates even for the presidency were queried on their views. Priests and ministers spoke out for and against candidates in ways not seen since at least the 1960 election (provoking a subsidiary debate about the role of the clergy in electoral politics). Rarely has the venom been more poisonous, nor single-issue

politics more single-minded. Vicious political attacks on legislators and other political officials became de rigueur.

The issue crops up everywhere. Tax reform was almost scuttled in the spring of 1986 when a senator threatened to attach an abortion-related provision to the tax reform bill then being debated.

The Reagan administration made it clear in deed, if not in word, that those who favor abortion will not be favored with judicial appointment. When the Senate rejected a Reagan judicial nominee clearly unqualified for the federal bench, the attorney general's Orwellian complaint was uncommonly naked: It was, he said, "an appalling surrender to the politics of ideology." (An opponent of abortion, the nominee, Jefferson B. Sessions, 3d, had made astoundingly insensitive racial remarks while serving as U.S. Attorney in Mobile, Alabama.)

Various constitutional amendments to prohibit abortion have been proposed in Congress, although so far they have all foundered. All this is the legacy of *Roe v. Wade*.

So too are the many subsidiary cases that followed. For the states were not shy about seeking ways around the decision, and since 1973 abortion cases have become a staple of the judicial dockets. Thus the Court voided a Missouri statute that required women under eighteen to obtain their parents' consent before having an abortion—parents may not veto the decisions of a "mature minor." The decision also struck down a provision requiring a wife to obtain her husband's written consent before a doctor can perform an abortion. It is the *woman's* choice. The Court invalidated as too vague a Pennsylvania statute that required physicians, on pain of criminal penalties, to follow a prescribed procedure if they had "sufficient reason to believe that the fetus may" survive outside the womb. But the Court has also ruled that the Constitution does not require state or federal authorities to fund abortions for indigent women, not even when those abortions are medically necessary.

In 1986, another Pennsylvania statute, this one requiring physicians to present the woman with detailed information about the risks of and alternatives to abortion and to file reports open for public inspection with state authorities, met the Court's scalpel—but in this latest decision, the vote was five to four, and Chief Justice Burger has called for a fundamental reexamination of *Roe*. The administration had vigorously pressed the Court in this case to overrule *Roe*, and eighty-two members of Congress had filed antiabortion briefs in the case. That overruling now seems unlikely to come at the hands of the present Court, and the immediate constitutional future of abortion rights will hinge on whether President Reagan or a like-minded successor has a chance to appoint someone to a seat on the Court vacated by a justice who adheres to the principles announced in *Roe*.

Should the Court ever reverse itself, the outcome even then would be uncertain. Abortion opponents are louder than they are numerous; a majority of Americans appears to favor access to at least many kinds of abortions. How and whether that majority would organize to defeat its well-organized opponents would then become the focus of attention. A reversal of *Roe* would not prohibit abortion; it would return the question to the states.

Nonpolitical Associational Rights

May people freely choose to live together, lunch together, and socialize together when no political or religious interests are at stake? Clearly, no general absolute nonpolitical or nonreligious right exists to associate with whomever one chooses and exclude all others. Federal and state law may clearly control the workplace; an employer may not refuse to take on black or female employees by pointing to some constitutional freedom to associate only with whites or

males. Does state power follow into the home or social club?

No one can yet confidently state a general answer, although doctrine is beginning to emerge. Families may not be lightly barred from living together. The city of East Cleveland, Ohio, adopted a zoning ordinance that barred nonnuclear families from sharing a home. The ordinance resulted in the criminal conviction of a grandmother who lived with her son and two grandsons who happened to be cousins. Had they been brothers, the ordinance would not have applied. The Supreme Court reversed, though by the thinnest margin. Said Justice Powell: "Our decisions establish that the Constitution protects the sanctity of the fam-

ily precisely because the institution of the family is deeply rooted in this Nation's history and tradition [a tradition not limited to] respect for the bonds uniting the members of the nuclear family. . . . The tradition of uncles, aunts, cousins, and especially grandparents sharing a household along with parents and children has roots equally venerable and equally deserving of constitutional recognition."

The Court has limited this rule to families. The village of Belle Terre, a square mile on Long Island consisting of two hundred families, zoned out groups of more than two unrelated persons living together. In a case brought by six unrelated college students sharing a house, the Court upheld the restriction, in part because the ordinance did not preclude anyone's right to associate as long as they did not do so on a permanent basis. As Laurence Tribe explains it: "The argument appears to be: hippies can always visit." But may they stay overnight?

Between the large business enterprise and the family lie a host of associations that have varying reasons for wanting to discriminate in membership. Those engaged in specific activities protected by the First Amendment—like a church or a political party—may exclude those who are of different religious or political persuasions. But the position of civic organizations is more ambiguous.

In the *Jaycees* case in 1984, the Court sustained a Minnesota statute that prohibits sex discrimination in "places of public accommodation." The Jaycees restrict voting members to men between the ages of eighteen and thirty-five. The Court found that although the Constitution protects "certain intimate human relationships . . . against undue intrusion by the state," the Jaycees did not qualify. It did not have that "relative smallness, a high degree of selectivity in decisions to begin and maintain the affiliation, and seclusion from others" that distinguishes the constitutionally protected association. Whether a men's luncheon club would be secure from the intrusion of a state order to desegregate remains an open question. (Note that the question is not whether in the absence of a state law forbidding discrimination the Court could order a *private* club to desegregate. The Constitution does not restrict private groups, and the Court has held that even some degree of public involvement, like the granting of a liquor license, is not sufficient to convert a private group into a public one for the purpose of applying the equal protection clause to group membership or activities.)

Sexual Preference and Activity

Though the logic of the privacy decisions arguably embraces sexual conduct by consenting adults in the privacy of their homes, the Court remains skittish in reaching that conclusion. A narrow view would hold that the privacy right the Court has discerned is one rooted in the historical American concern for the family and that laws prohibiting fornication, adultery, and homosexuality do not contravene but support that concern. A broader view would note that as enunciated, the right of privacy found in *Roe* is for personal autonomy over one's body and that if the state may not prohibit abortion, it should surely not stand in the way of those who wish to express their physical love for each other.

But in June 1986, in a five-to-four decision, the Supreme Court upheld a Georgia sodomy law, at least as applied to male homosexuals. In the majority opinion, Justice White characterized the Court's previous privacy decisions as family oriented and denied any "connection between family, marriage, or procreation on the one hand and homosexual activity on the other." The Court is "quite unwilling" to announce "a fundamental right to engage in homosexual sodomy." Earlier privacy decisions, Justice White said, were rooted in fundamental liberties "implicit in the concept of ordered liberty" such that "neither liberty nor justice would exist if [they] were sacrificed." The earlier decisions could also be seen as embracing liberties that are "deeply rooted in the nation's history and tradition." But homosexual sodomy has no such roots. Until 1961, all fifty states criminalized it, and in 1986 twenty-four states and the District of Columbia continued to proscribe it. Justice White said the Court could not agree to see the case as calling for a right limited "to the voluntary sexual conduct between consenting adults." For how could it then distinguish, "except by fiat," between consenting homosexual rights on the one hand and adultery, incest, and other sexual crimes committed in the home on the other? Finally, the Court said that even if the only basis for state sodomy laws is "the presumed belief of a majority of the electorate that sodomy is immoral," that is not sufficiently irrational to upset it. "The law . . . is

Protest following the 1986 Court decision upholding a Georgia sodomy law.

constantly based on notions of morality, and if all laws representing essentially moral choices are to be invalidated under the Due Process Clause, the courts will be very busy indeed."

A bitter dissent from Justice Blackmun, the author of the Court's original abortion decision, criticized the Court's "obsessive focus on homosexual activity," since the Georgia statute outlaws heterosexual sodomy as well. "The Court claims that it today merely refuses to recognize a fundamental right to engage in homosexual sodomy; what the Court really has refused to recognize is the fundamental interest all individuals have in controlling the nature of their intimate associations with others." Noting that the conduct for which the defendant had been arrested occurred in the privacy of his home, Justice Blackmun denied that a majority's morality could determine the limits of personal conduct: "This case involves no real interference with the rights of others, for the mere knowledge that other individuals do not adhere to one's value system cannot be a legally cognizable interest, let alone an interest that can justify invading the houses, hearts, and minds of citizens who choose to live their lives differently."

Both fundamentalist and "gay rights" spokespersons thought the decision would "slow the advancement of homosexual rights." But the decision seems unlikely to have any impact on the enforcement of sodomy laws, since in their nature they are virtually unenforceable. Moreover, the Court explicitly left open whether the decision is strictly homophobic or more broadly strikes at heterosexual conduct as well. But it seems reasonable to suppose that the Constitution will not likely be construed as hospitable to the broadest sexual liberty for at least another generation.

Personal Appearance

Throughout history, rulers have promulgated sumptuary laws dictating the colors, clothes, jewels, and other personal items that the various classes could wear within the realm. Solon, the great Greek lawgiver, declared that no bride could take to her marriage home more than three robes. During the Middle Ages, European city states prescribed the manner of dress with great particularity: the height of bonnets, the width of shoes, the amount of silks and satins, the width of lace. England, which abolished its sumptuary laws in 1604, required the populace to wear English woolen caps and to refrain from using imported cloths. The custom crossed the Atlantic; Massachusetts, for example, had sumptuary legislation from 1634 to 1676. Wearing lace was an indictable offense.

In our day (or at least through the 1970s), the authorities have worried themselves into a frenzy over long hair. Dour bureaucrats, who need not try to keep a straight face because they can discern no humor in their demands, have decreed the length of hair of all sorts of subversive characters: students, teachers, police officers and firefighters, soldiers and sailors, and many others. In the only major case the Supreme Court has heard (it has declined many other opportunities), the majority declined to upset a police department hair regulation. It found a "rational connection between the regulation" and "the promotion of safety of persons and property." A uniformed police force might need to impose on its members similarity in appearance "to make police officers readily recognizable to the members of the public, or [to foster] the esprit de corps which such similarity is felt to inculcate within the police force itself."

Significantly, the Court noted that the police officer challenging the regulation was not "a member of the citizenry at large," suggesting that should a city council actually try to impose a general sumptuary law, the Court would void it. That is of small comfort to public employees or wards of public bureaucracies who wish to express their individuality. On occasion, though, a bold lower court has liberated students (and, why not say so, school officials as well) by invalidating local hair length ordinances. The judge's job was made easier by listening to the purported justifications for the regulations: long-haired males might not be able to write on the blackboard because the hair would fall in their eyes; long-haired males might prompt confusion about which rest room they should use. The issue, it should be borne in mind, is not some general public interest in short hair or

Prior to a 1968 court hearing, this billboard appeared in Norwalk, Connecticut, after four students were suspended for having excessively long hair.

Pierce Butler
South Carolina

Pierce Butler was born in County Carlow, Ireland, July 11, 1744. He died in Philadelphia, February 15, 1822. A major in His Majesty's Twenty-ninth Regiment, he married in 1771 and soon traveled to South Carolina to establish a new home. In 1773, he resigned his commission for the quiet life of a South Carolina planter. In 1779, he was named state adjutant general. From 1778 to 1782 and 1784 to 1789, he served in the state legislature. In 1786, he was named to a commission that would set the state boundaries. Wealthy and aristocratic, he was elected within two days in 1787 as a delegate to both the Congress of Confederation and the Constitutional Convention. At the Convention, he authored the fugitive slave clause. In 1789, he was elected to the U.S. Senate as a Federalist, and in 1792 was reelected, but was reluctant to observe Federalist party politics. In 1796, he resigned and returned to South Carolina. Six years later, he was reelected to fill an unexpired seat in the Senate. He resigned from political office for good in 1806.

wearing ties in public places or long pants instead of skirts, but how each of us chooses to appear. A constitution that cannot honor that aspect of personhood is timid indeed.

The Right to Dare Death

The thoroughgoing libertarian has no trouble concluding that we each must have the liberty to take risks that may injure or kill us. Favorite examples are taking of drugs, refusing to "buckle up," and riding helmetless on motorcycles. These may provoke endless Millian debate: Does cocaine hurt only the user or the larger society? If cocaine were legally available, so that it did not create a lucrative black market, with all the subsidiary crime that breeds, would its use in the privacy of a home be any different from the private consumption of the most depraved pornography, a right the Court has determined is ours? Whatever the philosophical answer, the constitutional position is clear: These are not fundamental liberties, and the state may criminalize these risk-taking activities. Is it rational to outlaw marijuana and not alcohol, the former arguably safer than the latter? Perhaps not, but here the rationality is for the legislature, and the change, if it is to come, must be sought in political action at the polls.

The Right to Die

If we do not have the right to dare death, do we have the right to choose it outright? Questions undreamt of only a few years ago now obtrude almost daily, courtesy of our powerful technologies. One that has come to the political, though not yet fully to the constitutional, consciousness is the right to die—may we refuse a machine that can artificially prolong life?

The issue probably was first nationally discussed in the case of Karen Ann Quinlan, who fell into a coma after swallowing a destructive mixture of alcohol and drugs and was connected to a life-support machine. Doctors held out no hope she would ever recover from her vegetative state. Her family saw no need to prolong their misery (it is not clear that it was *her* misery). The doctors refused to disconnect the machine without a court order. The New Jersey Supreme Court eventually gave it, and the plugs were pulled.

On close inspection, the state court's decision did not confirm Karen Ann's right to die; rather, it confirmed her family's right to determine whether to continue her life. Karen Ann did not request that the doctors cease their ministrations. She was wholly unconscious and could not speak for herself.

The issue has been posed far more poignantly during the 1980s in the case of Elizabeth Bouvia, a California woman who has been paralyzed from birth and who suffers intractable pain. For years she has been battling hospitals and courts to have her feeding apparatus disconnected because she no longer wishes to live. Does the Constitution guarantee her that right if the doctors refuse and the state courts decline to order them to do so? The answer may not come definitively in her unhappy case, but the growing sophistication of medical technology ensures that this will soon become an issue of highest constitutional concern.

The Right to Travel

The right to travel has been repeatedly reaffirmed as a basic liberty of Americans. This right implies that states may not put impediments in the way of those who would go about or of those who would assist them. Thus the Court had no difficulty striking down a California law that made it a criminal offense to bring an indigent person into the state and Pennsylvania and Connecticut laws that refused welfare payments to those who had lived in the state for less than a year. The Court likewise invalidated a federal law that prohibited members of the Communist party from obtaining passports.

The right to travel need be nothing so grand as the desire to see the world, journey across country, or relocate. The liberty encompasses the simple act of walking outdoors, "hanging out," and strolling at night. These common pleasures were always threatened by municipal "vagrancy" laws. Here is the vagrancy ordinance of Jacksonville, Florida:

> Rogues and vagabonds, or dissolute persons who go about begging, common gamblers, *persons who use juggling or unlawful games or plays*, common drunkards, *common night walkers*, thieves, pilferers or pickpockets, traders in stolen property, lewd, wanton and lascivious persons, keepers of gambling places, common railers and brawlers, *persons wandering or strolling around from place to place without any lawful purpose or object, habitual loafers*, disorderly persons, persons neglecting all lawful business and habitually spending their time by frequenting houses of ill fame, gaming houses, or places where alcoholic beverages are sold or served, persons able to work but habitually living upon the earnings of their wives or minor children shall be deemed vagrants and upon conviction in the Municipal Court shall be punished as provided for Class D offenses.

Said Justice Douglas for the Court in striking the ordinance: "A presumption that people who might walk or loaf or loiter or stroll or frequent houses where liquor is sold, or who are supported by their wives or who look suspicious to the police are to become future criminals is too precarious for a rule of law." More recently, the Court voided as too vague a California ordinance "that requires persons who loiter or wander on the streets to provide a 'credible and reliable' identification and to account for their presence when requested by a peace officer."

Registering with the police is not a pastime in which Americans care to indulge. Nor should we have to. It is fundamental that we are at liberty to seek our own ends, as long as they are lawful, no questions asked.

Chapter 14 The Procedural Guarantees of Criminal Justice: Making the Government Safe for the People

Procedural Safeguards Against Official Whim

To this point, we have looked at substantive constitutional safeguards of liberty: the abolition of slavery, the freedoms of speech, press, and religion, and substantive rights to personal privacy and conduct. In a constitutional system, government must have no legitimate power to suppress the range of activities that together constitute the meaning of a free society.

But total freedom of personal conduct can be no part of our constitutionalism. Ours is a system, as Justice Cardozo put it in his famous paradoxical phrase, of "ordered liberty." Government exists, according to the Lockean tradition, to deter and to provide redress for crimes and injuries to the people's liberties and estates. The government obviously must often abridge the liberty of criminals in the most elemental sense: by confining them or otherwise punishing them for criminal conduct.

Some things may not be made crimes. But that which can be made criminal must not be permitted to serve the regime as an excuse to rid itself of those whom it dislikes through capricious prosecutions. Criminal sanctions must be meted out in a regular way, according to known rules. Equal in importance to substantive guarantees, therefore, are procedural rights, for as Felix Frankfurter reminded us: "The history of liberty has largely been the history of observance of procedural safeguards."

These safeguards are found in certain provisions of the original Constitution, in the due process clauses, and in the Fourth, Fifth, Sixth, and Eighth Amendments. Because these provisions are often decried as mere "technicalities" (when they operate to free a felon or reverse his conviction), it is worth underscoring their vital importance in a constitutional system.

Ours is an "accusatorial" system of criminal justice. It is rooted both in the separation of powers and in the common law tradition. The legislature defines crimes, the executive prosecutes, and the judiciary sits in judgment. The prosecutor must prove the defendant guilty "beyond a reasonable doubt," and the accused is entitled to defend (through independent counsel) against the prosecutor's accusations. This "adversary system" contrasts with the European "inquisitorial" approach, in which the judge is largely responsible for conducting the inquiry.

The adversary system is highly contentious, and has produced an immense body of doctrines and rules. Many see them as nit-picking distinctions that frequently serve to minimize defendants' culpability, mitigate their punishment, or free them altogether. Because the conventional wisdom is that most defendants are guilty, the fundamental presumption of innocence and the rules that attend the quest for conviction are often pilloried. Why be so solicitous of the guilty? Thus the Warren Court's breathtaking extension of defendants' rights in the 1960s became the centerpiece of candidate Richard Nixon's successful presidential campaign in 1968.

But the Nixonian critique (and many others) that finds virtue in constitutional rights only for the in-

The Warren Court (1953–69) made substantial contributions to the criminal justice process with its extension of defendants' rights.

nocent misses the essential point. The whole purpose of a criminal trial is to determine guilt, so that extending constitutional rights to the innocent only is a self-defeating exercise in question begging. Moreover, that the overwhelming number of accused are guilty demonstrates the strength of the American system of criminal justice. Totalitarian regimes that dispense with adversary procedures prosecute significant numbers of people who are palpably innocent. The great virtue of the adversary system, therefore, with all its attendant rules and constitutional guarantees, "is not so much that it permits the innocent to defend themselves meaningfully, [as] that in the main it prevents them from having to do so" in the first place. Prisons are no happy place in the United States, but the innocent do not languish in them, as they do, for lack of basic constitutional restraints, in the Soviet gulag and in the prisons of tyrannies, right-wing and left-wing, around the world today.

The procedural safeguards provided in the Constitution were hard won. For centuries, the English suffered from notorious abuses like the Star Chamber, the feared court of the sixteenth century (finally abolished in 1641) that tried defendants for offenses the crown did not want to put before a jury. The Star Chamber interrogated by torture to elicit confessions, and the punishments it meted out were cruel in the extreme, including flogging, branding, and dismemberment.

Though Star Chamber procedures were no part of the colonial experience, they were part of historical memory. Other invasions of the colonists' rights, like the writs of assistance and general search warrants that led agents of the crown to ransack their homes, were a reality in the 1770s that still rankled when the Bill of Rights was drafted a decade and a half later. If we do not prize our rights to procedural justice, it is because we have forgotten what the revolutionaries knew—and what revolutionaries around the world continue to fight for today.

The Writ of Habeas Corpus

The writ of habeas corpus (literally, "you may have the body") is the most important guarantor of personal liberty in Anglo-American jurisprudence. Unless the jailer can show reason to hold a prisoner, either because the prisoner has been validly convicted or because he was validly arrested and is awaiting trial, a court on demand will issue the writ, freeing the prisoner. Habeas corpus thus prevents a person from being held without charges—a practice common in despotic regimes that imprison enemies without cause.

Charles II of England's ascent to the throne in 1679 led to Parliament's enactment of the Habeas Corpus Act.

The framers provided for the Great Writ, well known in England by the seventeenth century, in Article I. The writ may not be suspended except at times of "rebellion or invasion." Even then, courts may not be prohibited from granting the writ unless the state of hostilities makes it impossible to enforce civil law—so the Court held in voiding the military trial of a civilian when Lincoln suspended habeas corpus during the Civil War. The power to suspend is for Congress, not the president (Congress ultimately ratified Lincoln's suspension of the writ).

Habeas corpus is largely resorted to today in connection with federal review of state court proceedings. Under the federal habeas corpus statute, federal courts may hear the pleas of state prisoners that they are being unconstitutionally incarcerated. The prisoner must first exhaust the procedures afforded under state law; habeas corpus is not a means by which state defendants can interrupt a trial or appeal and remove the case to federal court. But a federal court hearing an application for the writ may try the facts anew; it is not bound by the state court's prior determination.

Though the writ sees service principally in state cases, it remains available for those times when the federal government, spooked by sizable dissent, fearfully or brazenly arrests demonstrators and others without legal cause, as happened, for example, during the red scare in 1920 and the antiwar demonstrations in the early 1970s. But the most notable instance of unlawful arrest occurred in 1942, when a presidential decree led to a massive roundup of American citizens of Japanese descent (and resident Japanese aliens ineligible for citizenship).

As a result of "race prejudice, war hysteria and a failure of political leadership," the U.S. Army obtained Executive Order 9066 from President Roosevelt (who history suggests was on more than this occasion insufficiently attentive to civil liberties). The order provided for the exclusion and removal of 110,000 Japanese Americans from the West Coast and detention in "relocation camps" scattered throughout the West (actually as far east as Arkansas). In retrospect, as a careful study by the congressionally established Commission on Wartime Relocation and Internment of Civilians showed in 1982, the military had not a shred of justification for Order 9066.

Nevertheless, the Supreme Court upheld it, in one of the worst civil liberties decisions it ever wrote. Citing "military necessity," Justice Black's majority opinion deferred to the army, overlooking the dearth of facts to support the military judgment. The army's demand for the exclusion order was nothing more than the statement of a desire to rid the West Coast (but not Hawaii, where the Japanese American population was far larger) of an indigenous population that local bigots had been seeking to eliminate for decades. The Court held that the exclusion was not a "group punishment based on antagonism to those of Japanese origin" but a "military imperative."

Because most Japanese Americans were not inclined to pursue test cases, they forsook the opportunity to avail themselves of the one remedy that would ultimately have worked—habeas corpus. The exclusion order was based on a military fear of possible espionage, and that possibility in turn was the basis for the Supreme Court's upholding of the plan in general terms. (Not a single case of espionage ever turned up.) But a concededly loyal American surely could not be excluded from her home and incarcerated, for she would not fit within the justification of the order even if, because of ancestry, she fit within its terms. And the legality of imprisoning a loyal citizen charged with no crime is precisely what the writ of habeas corpus is designed to deter.

When such a case was finally brought on a writ of habeas corpus, the Supreme Court unanimously ruled that the government could not hold Mitsuye Endo, an admittedly loyal American citizen, in a camp against her will. The dismantling of the camps proceeded apace. (The evacuees returned to find most of their

Although Americans of Japanese ancestry were legally U.S. citizens, President Roosevelt's executive order in 1942 allowed them to be confined in camps and treated as enemy aliens.

property stolen, and little restitution has ever been made—a frightening glimpse of what can happen when constitutionalism is abandoned.)

No Bills of Attainder or Ex Post Facto Laws

Two ancient and inherently arbitrary powers claimed by Parliament that the framers wished to ensure would never be exercised in the United States were the legislative attainder and the ex post facto law. Article I explicitly prohibits Congress and the states from exercising either of them.

The bill of attainder was originally a parliamentary act that charged a person with treason, sentenced him to death, and confiscated his property. Such an act is an obvious violation of the separation of powers, for the legislature would charge and convict without a trial. Following the Civil War, the Supreme Court broadened the definition of attainder to strike down state and congressional enactments requiring priests

and lawyers to take an oath that they had never supported the Confederacy. The Court held that to remove a person's means of earning a livelihood is a punishment and that any punishment legislatively prescribed without trial violates the bill of attainder clause. In more recent times, the Court has struck down federal laws that denied compensation to three named government employees whom the House Un-American Activities Committee had investigated for subversive activities and that made it a criminal offense for a member of the Communist party to serve as an officer or employee of a labor union. But the Court turned back President Nixon's challenge to a congressional enactment that put his presidential papers in the custody of the General Services Administration.

An ex post facto law has been succinctly defined as "one which renders an act punishable in a manner in which it was not punishable when it was committed." A law that provides for a penalty when none existed at the time the act was committed or that increases the penalty is ex post facto. Such laws ob-

William Few was born near Baltimore, Maryland, June 8, 1748, and died at Fishkill-on-the-Hudson, New York, July 16, 1828. He moved to North Carolina in 1758 and later to Georgia. Living the frontier life, he was a self-educated man. At the onset of the Revolution, he was made a lieutenant colonel. He was a member of the Georgia General Assembly twice, a member of the Executive Council of State, surveyor general of Georgia, commissioner to the Indians, and two times a delegate to the Continental Congress. In 1783, he returned to the General Assembly and the Continental Congress. In 1787, he was one of the two Georgia delegates (six were originally present) to remain to the close of the Constitutional Convention. He became one of the first U.S. senators from Georgia, leaving office in 1793 to return to the Georgia State Assembly for his fourth term. In 1796, he was named a judge of the Second Federal Judicial Circuit of Georgia and served until 1799, when he moved to New York City. There he met quick political success. He spent four years in the New York General Assembly and served as inspector of the state prisons and as an alderman. From 1804 to 1814, he was director of the Manhattan Bank and later became president of the City Bank. Few was dignified and somber, a religious man who gave his wealth to worthy causes.

viously offend the sense of regularity; they are clearly arbitrary. Indeed, even without the specific constitutional prohibition, a legislative enactment purporting to penalize particular conduct committed before the act is passed would undoubtedly run afoul of the due process clause. So much seems unexceptionable. But the actual operation of the clause has led to dubious results.

The ex post facto clause is limited to penal laws. A law that retroactively increases taxes or sets aside a court's construction of a will and grants a new hearing is not unconstitutional. Also, not every sanction has been labeled penal. Thus the Court has held that a state law prohibiting doctors convicted of crime from practicing medicine was not ex post facto when applied to a doctor convicted before the law took effect, because the act merely policed the fitness of all doctors to practice medicine. More dubiously, the Court has held that deportation is not a punishment. In the particular case, decided in 1952 during the postwar red mania, a resident alien was deported for being a member of the Communist party at a time during which such membership was not a deportable offense. In that case, the Court labeled deportation a civil rather than a criminal proceeding and rested its holding largely on Congress's plenary power over aliens.

Changes in the law that can be labeled "procedural" often escape the ex post facto ban, even though what differentiates a procedural from a substantive change is elusive. Changes in evidentiary rules disadvantaging a criminal defendant have been held not to be ex post facto. Likewise, the revocation of a law that precluded the death penalty when a jury recommended mercy was held not to offend the ex post facto clause.

Due Process Clause as a Curb on Arbitrary Procedures

The lineage of the due process clauses of the Fifth and Fourteenth Amendments has been traced to a charter of Henry I in 1100, but it is more commonly found in the Magna Carta of King John in 1215 (and repeated in the more enduring Magna Carta of 1225 issued by his son King Henry III). In Chapter 29, the kings declared the great rule of law, that

> no free man shall be seized or imprisoned, or stripped of his rights or possessions, or outlawed or exiled, or deprived of his standing in any other way, nor will we proceed with force against him, or send others to do so, except by the lawful judgment of his equals or by *the law of the land*. To no one will we sell, to no one deny or delay right or justice.

In the Statute of 1354, the phrase is first used in the form that we copy to this day: "That no man of what estate or condition that he be, shall be put out of land or tenement, nor taken nor imprisoned, nor disinherited, nor put to death, without being brought in answer by due process of law."

Due process connotes fair procedures. Specific procedures, like the right to jury trial, are guaranteed in the Fourth, Fifth, Sixth, and Eighth Amendments, and we examine these shortly. But the procedures specifically enumerated in these amendments do not exhaust the rules that apply in criminal prosecutions. As Justice Frankfurter once described the judge's task in delineating those rules: "Regard for the requirements of the Due Process Clause 'inescapably imposes upon this Court an exercise of judgment upon the whole course of proceedings in order to ascertain

The King John Magna Carta of 1215.

whether they offend those canons of decency and fairness which express the notions of justice of English-speaking peoples even to those charged with the most heinous offenses.' " To Justice Cardozo, due process connoted those basic rights that are "of the very essence of a scheme of ordered liberty," or as previous courts had expressed it, "those fundamental principles of liberty and justice which lie at the base of all our civil and political institutions," principles "so rooted in the traditions and conscience of our people as to be ranked as fundamental."

These generalizations express a depth of feeling, but are weak guides to fixing the rights and principles that should be considered fundamental. Determining what fundamental procedures are due has provoked one of the largest debates in our constitutional history, as we have already seen in Chapter 10 in the debate over applying the federal Bill of Rights to the states through the Fourteenth Amendment. But the question cannot be simply whether all or only some of the Bill of Rights applies to the states. The due process clause of the Fifth Amendment must be supposed to have a meaning independent of the substantive guarantees of the rest of the Bill of Rights. In other words, some procedures beyond those mentioned in the other amendments must necessarily be included in the term *due process of law*.

Over the years, the Supreme Court has held just that. Not for lack of importance but for lack of space, what follows is but a sketch of the procedures that due process requires in criminal cases (other than those set forth in the Bill of Rights).

The trial must be open and the hearing officer must be neutral—a judge may not preside over a hearing to try charges that arose out of a grand jury proceeding in which he was the sole grand juror. A judge cannot have a "direct, personal, substantial pecuniary interest in reaching a conclusion" against the defendant, as was once the rule in Ohio towns where the mayor, sitting as judge, received a percentage of the fine in cases involving violations of the liquor laws.

No one may be convicted of a statute "so vague,

The Sixth Amendment guarantees the right to a trial by an impartial jury.

Abraham Baldwin

Georgia

Abraham Baldwin was born in North Guilford, Connecticut, November 22, 1754, and died in New Bedford, Connecticut, March 4, 1807. Conscientious from an early age, he paid off the debts of his father's estate, gave up his inheritance claims, and educated his several brothers and sisters at considerable personal expense. In 1772, he graduated from Yale. Three years later, he was licensed as a minister. From 1775 to 1779, he tutored at Yale. He resigned to become a chaplain in the Continental Army. In 1781, to replace a vacancy, he was unanimously elected a professor of divinity at Yale. He declined, however, and on leaving the army, did not return to either the ministry or education. In 1783, he was admitted to the Connecticut bar. The following year, he relocated to Georgia and was admitted to the bar there. In 1785, he served in the Congress of the Confederation and was elected to the Georgia House of Assembly. At the Philadelphia Convention, he originally opposed equal representation in the Senate and supported representation based on property standards. However, he later changed his vote, perhaps motivated by his link to Connecticut, and served on the committee formed to work out the final Connecticut Compromise. He became a U.S. representative and then a senator in 1799. A moderate Democratic-Republican, he remained a U.S. senator until his death. In the first session of the Seventh Congress, he was president pro tempore. Baldwin was a skilled, modest, well-liked, and good-natured innovator, concerned his entire life with the human condition. Baldwin County, established in 1803, was named in tribute to him.

indefinite and uncertain" that its meaning cannot be reasonably determined—for example, a statute that subjected to penal sanctions a person who was a "gangster" or a "vagrant" or "annoying." Closely related to this rule is the Court's historic declaration that a person can be tried only for violations of a statute duly enacted by the legislature; there can be no prosecution for common law crimes. This ruling came in 1812 in a case growing out of the prosecution of two Hartford, Connecticut, newspaper editors for seditious libel of President Jefferson. The federal Sedition Act had lapsed in 1801; they were prosecuted on the theory that the common law independently prohibited seditious libels. Since a common law jurisdiction implies the power to create new crimes, individuals might be prosecuted for crimes of which they would have no notice, and notice is fundamental to due process.

A proceeding must be free from threats of mob violence. When a white state jury in 1923 was hounded into bringing back a death penalty for black defendants in five minutes after a forty-five minute trial under extremely hostile and ugly circumstances, the convictions would have to be reversed.

Knowing use by prosecutors of perjured testimony or false evidence to secure a conviction violates due process, and the conviction cannot stand.

Tricking a person into committing a crime will negate the conviction. What constitutes the requisite degree of trickery—*entrapment,* in the legal phrase—is a much-disputed question. The usual rule is that the defendant must not have been of a mind to commit the crime, and her will must have been overborne by the police. Merely supplying her with means to commit a crime, as by offering to sell her illegal drugs, is not sufficient to establish an entrapment defense.

Under the due process clause, the burden of proof in criminal cases rests with the prosecution, which must prove "beyond a reasonable doubt . . . every fact necessary to constitute the crime with which [the defendant] is charged."

Incorporating the Bill of Rights

Beyond the fundamental fairness required by the due process clause, exemplified in the foregoing list of prohibitions, the Bill of Rights specifies for federal criminal proceedings a number of rights of equally ancient lineage—among them rights against unreasonable searches and seizures, self-incrimination, double jeopardy, cruel and unusual punishment; rights to jury trial, confrontation of witnesses, and assistance of counsel. For the most part, during the 1960s, the Supreme Court "selectively incorporated" most of the Bill of Rights into the Fourteenth Amendment so that today those specific protections apply in state as well as federal proceedings—as illustrated in the brief historical table that follows. Bear in mind that the capsule description of each right masks nuances of great complexity, worked out in scores of cases for each provision during the past quarter-century, still being worked out today, and yet to be worked out in the foreseeable future.

Incorporation of the Bill of Rights in the Fourteenth Amendment

Amendment	Year of Incorporation	Right Incorporated
First	1927	Freedom of speech
	1931	Freedom of press
	1937	Freedom of assembly
	1940	Freedom to exercise religion
	1948	Ban on religious establishment
Fourth	1949	Ban on unreasonable search and seizure
	1961	Extension of exclusionary rule
Fifth	1897	Just compensation clause
	1964	Ban against compulsory self-incrimination
	1969	Ban on double jeopardy
Sixth	1932	Assistance of counsel, capital case
	1948	Right to public trial
	1963	Assistance of counsel, felony cases
	1965	Right to confront adverse witness
	1966	Right to impartial jury
	1967	Right to subpoena favorable witness
	1967	Right to speedy trial
	1968	Right to jury in nonpetty criminal cases
	1972	Counsel in imprisonable misdemeanor cases
	1979	Right to unanimous verdict of six jurors
Eighth	1962	Ban on cruel and unusual punishments

Although the Burger Court since 1970 has often restricted the potential reach of the Warren Court's dramatic expansion of these rights, it has not retreated altogether, and defendants' rights today remain far broader than they were a quarter of a century ago. But their delineation has become the vocation of specialists, for the simple characterization of rights masks the incredible complexity of their meaning worked out from case to case. The federal courts' due process rulings have created a thick procedural rulebook difficult for police, prosecutors, and defense lawyers to master. What follows are but highlights of some of the Bill of Rights doctrines as they apply today.

Search and Seizure Problems

The Fourth Amendment stemmed from search practices that had evolved for centuries in England. In cases involving seditious libel and the possession of other prohibited goods, the king's ministers issued "general warrants" that did not specify who or what was sought or which premises were to be searched. In the colonies, the crown used writs of assistance, a form of general warrant, to ransack homes and businesses. These writs were both universal and perpetual: They never expired and anyone was authorized to search. Writs issued in Massachusetts in the 1760s provoked riots and led to James Otis's impassioned pleas against the writs, which, according to John Adams, sparked the Revolution itself: "Then and there the Child Independence was born."

The Fourth Amendment seeks to avoid the evils of open, unending searches by requiring the police to swear before a neutral magistrate that they have "probable cause" to believe that the thing they are looking for is where they say it is. This general statement masks a host of problems: By what standards is an informant to be judged as trustworthy? What if the exact location of the thing is unknown? What kinds of things are properly the subject of a search? In one significant recent case, the Court upheld a warrant to search the offices of a student newspaper for negatives and film of student demonstrations, which would show who was involved in an illegal takeover of university buildings, even though no one suspected illegal activity by any of the editors or photographers.

The Fourth Amendment prohibits only *unreasonable* searches and seizures. In many cases, a search or seizure is defined as unreasonable unless the police have first gone to court to obtain a warrant. But the courts have decreed many exceptions to the warrant requirement, so that the inquiry then focuses on the reasonableness of the search itself. Among the cases held not to require warrants (though the police must still have probable cause to believe that the crime has been committed or that the goods sought are within the area of search) are arrests of a person in a public place or when the police are in "hot pursuit" of a suspect, "stop and frisk" searches, searches to which consent has been given voluntarily, searches incident to a valid arrest (but only of his person or the area within his immediate reach), and searches of motor vehicles.

Difficult questions have arisen over body searches. In one famous case, the police forcibly pumped the stomach of a person against his will to remove drugs he had swallowed: the Court held that the pumping violated due process because, in Justice Frankfurter's words, it was conduct that "shocks the conscience." But in later cases, the Court held that involuntary taking of blood samples in a drunk-driving case is permissible.

The question in most of the warrantless search cases is whether the suspect had a reasonable expectation of privacy. The variety of cases is endless: a jacket on a coat rack in a workplace? garbage pails placed by the curb? a package on the seat of a car parked in the suspect's own driveway? student lockers? Courts have given varying answers. Reasonable expectation

A warrant is not required for "stop and frisk" searches, although the police must have probable cause to conduct the search.

does not always dictate: Border searches of incoming automobiles are permissible, even without probable cause, but the border patrol may not stop automobiles twenty miles inside the border and search without probable cause, except for permanent checkpoints at which limited questioning is permitted without even any suspicion that something is amiss. The Supreme Court has not ruled on the constitutionality of airport screening, but all lower courts have concluded that, as routinely administered, the practice is necessary to ensure airport security, as long as actual searches of luggage or one's person proceed only on reasonable suspicion. What of police roadblocks to ferret out drunken drivers? Presumably, the mere stopping of cars at a fixed point and talking to drivers to check for sobriety would pass muster, but indiscriminate spot checks, without reasonable cause to believe that the driver is inebriated, would not.

Wiretapping and other forms of electronic eavesdropping have posed numerous difficulties. In 1928, the Court first considered wiretapping and concluded that the Fourth Amendment did not cover this kind of eavesdropping, provoking Justice Brandeis's dissent:

> The makers of our Constitution . . . conferred, as against the government, the right to be let alone—the most comprehensive of rights and the right most valued by civilized men. . . . Every unjustifiable intrusion upon the privacy of the individual, by whatever means employed, must be deemed a violation of the Fourth Amendment.

For the next forty years, the Court grappled with cases involving microphones placed against walls, undercover agents wired for sound, microphone spikes stuck into walls, listening devices stuck into a wall with a thumbtack, and listening in on an extension phone. Finally, in 1967, the Court overruled the 1928 case and held that wiretapping and other forms of electronic surveillance are subject to the Fourth Amendment and therefore may not be undertaken without warrants. In the Omnibus Crime Control and Safe Streets Act of 1968, Congress authorized the attorney general to seek warrants to wiretap. Attorney General John N. Mitchell claimed the power to wire-

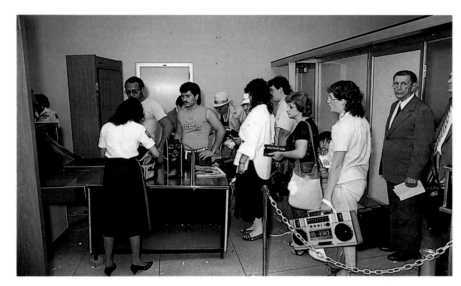

Lower courts have ruled that airport screening is necessary for security. The Supreme Court has not reviewed that constitutionality of this practice.

tap without warrants in cases involving "domestic subversion." The Court told him otherwise, although it has declined so far to hold that the Fourth Amendment applies to wiretaps of foreign groups arguably dangerous to national security.

When the police seize evidence in violation of the Fourth Amendment, the courts invoke the exclusionary rule, a remedy heatedly debated since it was first applied to the states in 1961. Evidence taken in an unlawful search may not be used in court. The exclusionary rule was first announced for federal cases in 1914; the Court said that if private papers unlawfully taken by a federal marshal could be used in court, "the protection of the Fourth Amendment declaring [a person's] right to be secure against such searches and seizures is of no value, and . . . might as well be stricken from the Constitution."

The rule is easily stated but applied often only with difficulty, for it also controls the use of involuntary confessions that violate the Fifth Amendment. The question is whether the police may use information based on an involuntary confession to seek other evi-

dence, and the answer is that unless the evidence is independently obtained, the "fruit of the poisonous tree"—the evidence resulting from an unlawful search or involuntary confession—may not be used at trial (though grand juries may use such evidence as the basis for questioning).

The exclusionary rule has been bitterly denounced by many critics of the Warren Court. In 1984, the Burger Court announced the "good-faith" exception to the rule: "Evidence obtained by officers acting in reasonable reliance on a search warrant issued by a detached and neutral magistrate but ultimately found to be unsupported by probable cause" may be introduced at trial. Because determining "probable cause" is often vexed with exceedingly fine judgments, the question remains what constitutes "reasonable reliance." In seeking alternatives to the exclusionary rule, the Burger Court has suggested the possibility of private damage suits against officers who violate the Fourth Amendment, and in 1986 it held that although a judge may not be sued for issuing an invalid warrant, police officers are not necessarily immune from suit simply because they actually believe the facts they allege in seeking the warrant. It will doubtless be the work of several years to reconcile the good-faith exception with the tort damage suit.

Right Against Self-Incrimination

From earliest colonial days, Americans enjoyed a privilege against self-incrimination, a right that Parliament recognized in the mid-seventeenth century after John Lilburne, a printer, heroically refused to take a general oath to answer questions that amounted to a "fishing expedition," despite excruciating torture by the Star Chamber. This right is embodied in the Fifth Amendment, which declares that "no person . . . shall be compelled in any criminal case to be a witness against himself." The right to "plead the Fifth" is available to witnesses as well as defendants, but only to natural persons, not corporations or other organizations. It is not restricted to trials but applies in any situation in which one might become the target of criminal prosecution; for example, a statute requiring members of the Communist party to register with the attorney general was held to violate the Fifth Amendment. Moreover, sanctions other than jail or fines are sufficient to establish a violation: The government may not fire a public employee or disbar an attorney who pleads the Fifth. In a criminal prosecution, the Fifth Amendment gives the defendant the absolute right to refuse to take the stand, "and forbids either comment by the prosecution on the accused's silence or instructions by the court that such silence is evidence of guilt." But if a defendant does take the stand, she is subject to cross-examination and may not then refuse to answer questions. Should the government determine that a witness's testimony is necessary, it may overcome the Fifth Amendment by granting the witness immunity from prosecution, in which event her testimony may be compelled.

During the 1950s, the major controversy over the Fifth Amendment stemmed from its invocation by reputed communists. Today the focus is quite different. The modern controversy surrounds the many cases that require involuntary confessions to be excluded from trial. The principle is simple: A confession obtained through beating or some other abusive means is inherently untrustworthy. Around the world, trumped-up confessions extracted through torture make it clear what would happen if the courts tolerated third-degree methods in the stationhouse. But the modern rules go far beyond outright physical or even mental abuse. Combining the Fifth Amendment right against self-incrimination and the Sixth Amendment right to counsel, the Court has fashioned a doctrine, epitomized in the *Miranda* case, but by no means resting there, that requires the police in a variety of circumstances to desist from even questioning suspects.

Miranda held that suspects in police custody must be told that they may (1) remain silent, (2) consult with a lawyer before answering questions, (3) have an attorney appointed free if they cannot afford one, and that (4) whatever they say may be used against them in court. Furthermore, even if questioned, they may stop answering at any time. If the police fail to advise suspects of their rights or question them after they say they do not wish to talk, any resulting confession is inadmissible.

Since 1966, the Court has retreated from the seemingly absolutist posture of *Miranda*, most notably in *Harris v. New York* in 1971, which held that even if a confession is involuntary, it may be introduced into evidence for the limited purpose of impeaching the defendant's credibility. In other words, if the police secure a confession in violation of *Miranda* and the defendant subsequently takes the stand to deny his complicity in the crime, the prosecutor may introduce the confession to demonstrate to the jury that the defendant is a liar—a rather large loophole in the right that *Miranda* was seeking to preserve.

Ernesto Miranda (right) with attorney John J. Flynn. Since overturning Miranda's conviction in 1966, the Court has reduced the scope of its ruling on the rights of a suspect.

Suppose a suspect remains silent while in police custody but at trial takes the stand with an alibi. The Court has held that the defendant's prior silence—his failure to tell the police the alibi—may also be used to impeach him before the jury.

Dozens of problems arise in this ticklish area: Was the suspect in custody? Was he given a complete warning? May the police resume questioning a few hours after a suspect refuses to discuss the case? Is a statement volunteered by a person not being interrogated, even if in custody, admissible without *Miranda* warnings? May the police plant an informer in his cell while he is awaiting trial to see what he will say? Since every case is different, and new cases present new situations each year, the constitutionality of confessions in criminal cases will remain an active part of the Court's docket.

Double Jeopardy

The Fifth Amendment also provides that no person shall "be subject for the same offense to be twice put in jeopardy of life or limb." The double jeopardy clause protects a defendant from being prosecuted again for the same offense after she is acquitted—if the jury says "not guilty," no further proceeding is possible, and the state may not appeal. Likewise, if a defendant is finally convicted, she may not be retried. Difficult questions remain: A hung jury does not preclude a retrial, nor does a defendant's successful motion for mistrial or her appeal of a conviction because of legal error. But if a trial is stopped at the prosecutor's or judge's instance after the jury is sworn (or her conviction is upset on appeal because there was insufficient evidence to convict), no further prosecution is allowed. This rule prevents a prosecutor from avoiding an acquittal by seeking a mistrial whenever he concludes he is likely to lose.

The double jeopardy clause protects the defendant against the burden and anxiety of repetitive prosecutions, but only when the offense is the same. In a country with multiple jurisdictions and complex criminal laws, the question of what constitutes the same offense is often difficult to answer. The general rule is that a court may not impose additional punishment for an offense proved by the same set of facts

William Jackson was born in Cumberland, England, March 9, 1759, and died in Philadelphia, Pennsylvania, December 18, 1828. Orphaned at a young age, he came to America under the guardianship of a South Carolina gentleman. During the Revolutionary War, as an aide to Major General Benjamin Lincoln, he became a major. In 1781, he traveled to France, Holland, and Spain to oversee the shipping of Continental Army supplies. In 1782, he returned to the United States, where Secretary of War Benjamin Lincoln saw to his appointment as assistant secretary of war. After two years, he resigned and returned to Europe to engage in mercantile business. At the Constitutional Convention, he became secretary, nominated by Alexander Hamilton. As secretary, Jackson's role was limited. His only official papers were the journal proceedings of the yea and nay votes, void of descriptive texture. In 1788, he was admitted to the Pennsylvania bar. Two years later, he was an unsuccessful candidate for the position of secretary of the U.S. Senate. That year, George Washington appointed him his personal secretary. At the end of 1791, Jackson resigned and went into a business partnership. Always loyal to Washington, he volunteered his services when Washington's secretary was called away. Washington reciprocated by appointing him U.S. surveyor of customs at Philadelphia, a post he lost when Jefferson swept many Federalist government agents from their positions in 1800.

that have already proved another offense for which the defendant has been sentenced—for example, a defendant was sentenced on a conviction for car theft; double jeopardy prevented him from later being prosecuted for joyriding, because joyriding was included in the definition of car theft under state law. But if a particular act is criminal under separate federal and state laws, then the double jeopardy clause does not bar two prosecutions.

Speedy Trial

The Sixth Amendment guarantees defendants the right to a "speedy and public trial." What constitutes constitutional promptness depends on a balance of four factors, weighed in each case: length of delay, reason for the delay, prejudice to the defendant because of the delay, and his assertion of the right to a speedy trial. In one case, the Court held that a delay of five years between the commission of the crime and the return of an indictment was speedy enough. If, however, the trial is not speedy, the "only possible remedy" is dismissal of the charges. In the Speedy Trial Act of 1974, Congress established fixed time limits within which the federal government must commence criminal prosecutions. At the outside, trials must begin within 130 days of the arrest. Many states have recently adopted similar statutes.

No Cruel and Unusual Punishments

The Eighth Amendment denies the power to inflict "cruel and unusual punishments." This provision is rooted in the Magna Carta, which set forth a rule of proportionality: Only grave crimes merit grave punishment. The Eighth Amendment (and comparable provisions in state constitutions) have eradicated the unspeakably inhuman physical tortures that had once been permitted in England—"dragging through the streets to the place of execution, embowelling alive, mutilation by cutting of the hands or ears, branding on the face or hand, slitting the nostrils, public dissection, beheading and quartering, burning alive, the pillory, stocks, and the ducking stool, the thumb screw, and the rack"—and that are still employed (and worse) by barbaric governments that pretend to be civilized.

Though the government is formally barred from administering these odious punishments, the effect of prison life on many inmates comes close. From the late 1960s, a spate of lawsuits in lower courts has successfully attacked prison systems in many states on Eighth Amendment grounds. Thus the Arkansas Penitentiary was held to be "a dark and evil world completely alien to the free world."

Occasionally, the Supreme Court has found certain punishments to be disproportionate. Thus it struck down statutes that stripped soldiers who deserted in wartime of their citizenship, sent drug addicts to jail simply for being addicted, and permitted capital punishment for a rape not ending in death. But in a bizarre 1980 case, the Court upheld as not disproportionate a life sentence for a man who obtained $120.75 by false pretenses under a habitual offender statute (in his previous two felony convictions, the defendant had netted a total of $108.36), and so it is unlikely that many defendants will succeed in challenging their sentences, despite the crazy-quilt pattern of sentencing in the United States today.

In 1972, the Supreme Court vacated death sentences of six hundred prisoners in the United States in ruling that the death penalty as then applied was cruel and unusual, because it was essentially arbitrary and often racist. But in 1976, the Court upheld the death penalty as such, under rewritten statutes that guard against arbitrary imposition. Death penalty jurisprudence is large and growing; the Court continues to scrutinize dozens of capital sentences each year. It has voided laws permitting death in nonhomicide cases and those making death the "mandatory" sentence in a particular case; the jury must be able to consider relevant aspects of the character of each defendant before sentencing him to die. Whether capital punishment serves a useful function is a large question, but so far not a constitutional one.

Twenty years after the "criminal law revolution," *Miranda* and related decisions continue to stoke the furnace of social controversy, though the temperature of the debate is markedly cooler. Numerous studies have shown that the constitutional decisions of the 1960s have not interfered with police work, and "most law-enforcement officials admit that, as a practical matter, Miranda has not hurt them very much." Despite the continued doubters, who argue more on the symbolic than the factual plane, that is an agreeable result, but perhaps a constitutionally irrelevant one. For constitutionalism demands that the government obey the law. As Justice Brandeis said, in the wiretap case, in words that stir sixty years later:

> Our government is the potent, the omnipresent teacher. For good or ill, it teaches the whole people by its example. Crime is contagious. If the government becomes a lawbreaker, it breeds contempt for law; it invites every man to become a law unto himself; it invites anarchy.

How much worse if, its history forgotten, the Constitution were precluded from standing guard against the relentless power of a government estranged from the people.

Part 4

The Quest for Equality

Chapter 15 · Ending America's Original Sin: The Abolition of Racial Discrimination

Voltaire somewhere wrote that history is the joke we play on our ancestors. If so, we are only getting even, for the present seems a larger trick they have played on us. In no part of our past is this truer than the legacy of race relations. Despite the promise of the Civil War amendments, the practical Constitution had to wait until our own time to redeem the pledge of the Thirteenth, Fourteenth, and Fifteenth Amendments that all shall be equal under the laws of the land.

Citizenship: The Promise of Equality

In the aftermath of the Civil War, America seemed bright promise for the freed slaves. The Fourteenth Amendment restored to them in practice what Taney in *Dred Scott v. Sandford* had so woefully denied in theory: citizenship. The first sentence of Section 1 of the Fourteenth Amendment reads: "All persons born or naturalized in the United States, and subject to the jurisdiction thereof, are citizens of the United States and of the State wherein they reside." This section effectively reversed the primacy of national and state citizenship. What was once murky is now clear. Citizenship in a state derives from national citizenship, and anyone born here (except children born to foreign diplomats in the United States) is a citizen.

This is a strong rule, never later denied in theory or practice, despite a century of lingering racism, and not just toward blacks. From 1875 until 1952, Congress precluded certain resident aliens, like Chinese and Japanese, from becoming citizens, no matter how many years they lived here, no matter their contribution. But their children were citizens the instant they were born.

Formal citizenship is only the beginning of equality, not its summation. In retrospect, a reading of the Constitution that took seriously the meaning of citizenship to treat all citizens equally would have simplified our life immensely, but the word was not freighted with such a meaning, nor would it have provided protection for those who live here but are not citizens. So some other ground was necessary on which to rest legal equality.

The Civil Rights Act of 1866 was one possibility, extending to blacks equal rights to contract, to sue

Until 1952, Congress precluded certain resident aliens, including Japanese, from citizenship, while their children became citizens at birth.

and be sued, to marry, and to testify. The Fourteenth Amendment, with its equal protection clause, was a far stronger possibility, enacted in part to shore up doubts about the constitutionality of the 1866 act. The Civil Rights Act of 1875 was even stronger: Among other things, it forbade discrimination against blacks in all public accommodations.

With or without these laws, until the 1890s it still seemed possible that blacks and whites might mingle freely throughout the South—much more freely than was apparently the norm in the North, which had never known the closeness of the races that the personal contact of slavery had fostered. Though it was by no means universal, racial integration in civil, social, political, and religious institutions was for a time widespread in many places. In 1868, the legislatures of Mississippi and South Carolina enacted comprehensive antidiscrimination laws. Even after Reconstruction, until the turn of the century, blacks voted without intimidation in many counties of the South and were regularly elected to office. As C. Vann Woodward reports:

Every session of the Virginia General Assembly from 1869 to 1891 contained Negro members. Between 1876 and 1894 North Carolinians elected fifty-two Negroes to the lower house of their state legislature, and between 1878 and 1902 forty-seven Negroes served in the South Carolina General Assembly. In 1890 there were sixteen Negro members of the session of the Louisiana General Assembly which passed the Jim Crow railway bill that led to the case of *Plessy v. Ferguson* [page 306]. Southern States elected ten Negroes to the U.S. House of Rep-

The first black senator and representatives were among the many blacks who were elected to office after Reconstruction and before the turn of the century.

resentatives after Reconstruction, the same number elected during Reconstruction. Every Congress but one between 1869 and 1901 had at least one Negro member from the South.

Popular attitudes seemed to permit this socialization as entirely normal. An editorial in the *Richmond* (Virginia) *Dispatch* in 1886 states:

> Our State Constitution requires all State officers in their oath of office to declare that they "recognize and accept the civil and political equality of all men." We repeat that nobody here objects to sitting in political conventions with negroes. Nobody here objects to serving on juries with negroes. No lawyer objects to practicing law in court where negro lawyers practice. . . . Colored men are allowed to introduce bills into the Virginia Legislature, and in both branches of this body negroes are allowed to sit, as they have a right to sit.

In many parts of the South in the 1870s and 1880s, in restaurants, parks, trains, public halls, picnic grounds, churches, and even cemeteries (though usually in separate parts), the races mixed. Charles Dudley Warner reported in 1885 that "white and colored people mingled freely, talking and looking at what was of common interest" at the International Exposition in New Orleans. "On 'Louisiana Day' the colored citizens took their full share of the parade and the honors. Their societies marched with the others, and the races mingled in the grounds in unconscious equality of privileges. . . . [A] colored clergyman [sat] in his surplice . . . in the chancel of the most important white Episcopal church in New Orleans, assisting the service."

By the 1890s, however, extensive political changes had unraveled the progressive political understanding and enthroned a greatly different legal understanding. The end of Reconstruction spelled the end of federal political control over secessionist states. Once slavery was formally abolished, moral fervor over the issue of black rights waned. A split in the political feelings of whites, causing white populists to seek political alliance with black voters, faded. Severe economic difficulties and the depression of the 1890s led demagogues to make blacks the scapegoats for the suffering of poor whites. Massive voting fraud stole most black ballots. National xenophobia stirred up by overseas wars led northerners to articulate their long-held feelings that non-Caucasians were clearly inferior to whites. In sum, "while northern and national restraints upon race extremists were relaxing, internal Southern resistance was also crumbling."

Invalidating Federal Protection

Had the Supreme Court acted early and steadfastly to prevent the erosion of legal support for blacks, the nation might have been spared a century of oppression. And the outcome might well have been different—for one thing, resistance to black equality might have come far more strongly from the North than the South, with unforeseeable results. But the Court did not wrap blacks in the blanket of the Fourteenth Amendment. To the contrary, the Court eroded their constitutional protection almost from the start.

The washing away began early, as we saw (page 201), when the Supreme Court in 1873 emasculated the privileges or immunities clause of the Fourteenth Amendment in the *Slaughterhouse Cases*, holding that the protection of the Bill of Rights did not apply to the states. A far more drastic curtailment of constitutional power to guarantee blacks equal rights was to come ten years later.

The Civil Rights Act of 1866 and cases under the Fourteenth Amendment established that the worst features of the Black Codes were unlawful. But the disabilities that officially lay on blacks were by no means the only obstacles to equality. Aside from poverty and ignorance—sufficient to subordinate most people for decades if not centuries—blacks suffered from social prejudice that prevented them from engaging in the myriad activities of daily life enjoyed

by whites. This ostracism stemmed not from the edicts of states but from the racism of people in their private dealings. As Senator Charles Sumner, chief proponent of the Civil Rights Act of 1875, stated to a convention of blacks in South Carolina in 1871:

> How much remains to be obtained you know too well in the experience of life. Can a respectable colored citizen travel on steamboats or railways, or public conveyances generally, without insult on account of color? Let Lieutenant-Governor Dunn, of Louisiana [a black], describe his journey from New Orleans to Washington. Shut out from proper accommodations in the cars, the doors of the Senate Chamber opened to him, and there he found the equality a railroad conductor had denied him. Let our excellent friend, Frederick Douglass, relate his melancholy experience, when, within sight of the executive mansion, he was thrust back from the dinner table where his brother commissioners were already seated [Douglass had been appointed secretary of the federal San Domingo Commission that year]. . . . I might ask the same questions with regard to hotels, and even common schools. An hotel is a legal institution, and so is a common school. As such each must be for the equal benefit of all. Now, can there be any exclusion from either on account of color? It is not enough to provide separate accommodations for colored citizens even if in all respects as good as those of other persons. . . . The discrimination is an insult and a hindrance, and a bar, which not only destroys Comfort and prevents equality, but weakens all other rights.

The national political consequence of these difficulties, and the last gasp of the radical Republicans in Congress, was the Civil Rights Act of 1875. It declared that "all persons within the jurisdiction of the

United States shall be entitled to the full and equal enjoyment of the accommodations, advantages, facilities, and privileges of inns, public conveyances on land or water, theatres, and other places of public amusement; subject only to the conditions and limitations established by law, and applicable alike to citizens of every race and color, regardless of any previous condition of servitude." This was legislation at its broadest. It did not merely strike down state laws that officially discriminated but also forbade people from discriminating in their private acts.

Amidst warnings of unconstitutionality, tests were not long in coming. Federal prosecutors brought scores of prosecutions, and six cases, collectively known as the *Civil Rights Cases,* wound their way to the Supreme Court. Ironically, the lead case came from New York City, where Samuel Singleton, doorkeeper of the Grand Opera House, refused to admit William R. Davis, Jr., and his date, both black. Other cases concerned refusals to serve food, to give lodging in a hotel, to provide a seat in the ladies' car of a railroad, and to let a black sit in the dress circle of a San Francisco theater. In 1883, by an eight-to-one decision, the Supreme Court held the Civil Rights Act unconstitutional and dismissed the prosecutions.

The Court rejected both Thirteenth and Fourteenth Amendment support for the act—the Thirteenth Amendment because, said Justice Joseph Bradley, "it would be running the slavery argument into the ground to make it apply to every act of discrimination which a person may see fit to make as to the guests he will entertain, or as to the people he will take into his coach or cab or car, or admit to his concert or theatre." A shut door does not a slave make.

The Court's slap at the Fourteenth Amendment was a more brutal blow. The Court ruled that the equal protection clause applies only to the states themselves, not to "private action": "The wrongful act of an individual, unsupported by any [state] authority, is simply a private wrong, or a crime of that individual." It did not matter that these establish-ments had been licensed by the state to serve the public. The Negro, declared Justice Bradley, must descend from his elevated status as "the special favorite of the laws" and assume "the rank of mere citizen."

The *Civil Rights Cases* continue to haunt constitutional law to this very day, for they established the dogma of "state action," according to which the Constitution applies only to those acts that states take and not to deeds of private citizens (and consequently Congress is powerless to legislate against private discriminations). The state action doctrine, as it has evolved, is mystifying, because it is anyone's guess what will or will not be construed as an "action" of the state. In 1961, for example, the Supreme Court ruled that when a state parking authority leases space to a private restaurant on a public highway, the decision of the restaurateur to exclude blacks is state action. But in 1972, the Court ruled that it is not state action for a state to limit the number of liquor licenses it issues and then to grant one to a private club that discriminates on racial grounds.

The decision in the *Civil Rights Cases* was not foreordained nor logically compelled. Indeed, Bradley's reasoning was deficient on its face. For after noting that the wrongful act of an individual is a private wrong, he went on to note that it is nonetheless "an invasion of the rights of the injured party, it is true, whether they *[sic]* affect his person, his property, or his reputation: but if not sanctioned in some way by the State, or not done under State authority, his rights remain in full force, and may presumably be vindicated by resort to the laws of the State for redress." In other words, a person excluded from public accommodations is no less wronged for the exclusion's being private, *even without a federal civil rights law.* It is just that the poor fellow who can't get into the restaurant or theater or train must seek his remedy in state court. A trifling thing, surely: the same right, just a different court. But if the state courts would not go along?

Seven years earlier, the Supreme Court had declared that "the equality of the rights of citizens is a principle of republicanism. Every republican government is in duty bound to protect all its citizens in the enjoyment of this principle, if within its power. That duty was originally assumed by the States; and it still remains there. The only obligation resting upon the United States is to see that the States do not deny the right. This the [Fourteenth] Amendment guarantees, but no more." The Court was plainly suggesting that if a state, including its judiciary, refuses to protect a citizen in the equality of rights, Congress could surely intervene. The point is that state inaction, no less than state action, denying equal rights violates the equal protection clause. The Fourteenth Amendment does not talk in terms of *making* discriminatory laws; it says that states shall not *deny* the equal protection of the laws.

The Court dismissed this argument in the *Civil Rights Cases* because the 1875 act did not distinguish between states that provided positive protection and those that did not: "It applies equally to cases arising in States which have the justest laws respecting the personal rights of citizens, and whose authorities are ever ready to enforce such laws, as to those which have arisen in States that may have violated the prohibitions of the amendment." But this is too facile. As Laurence Tribe points out, Bradley did not explain why the Court voided the act in its entirety, rather than limiting its application to states that did not provide equal protection. One of the states involved, Tennessee, had explicitly repealed its common law rule of equal access. As a practical matter, even on Bradley's crabbed reasoning, a litigant would "simply" (it wasn't simple but expensive and time consuming to) seek redress in state court first and appeal to the Supreme Court if the state court refused to provide access to public accommodations. Never mind that the trip to the state courts in most instances would be fruitless.

Only Justice John Marshall Harlan dissented. This powerful proponent of equal rights began his political career as a conservative Kentuckian. Loyal to the

Founding Father

George Mason
(did not sign the Constitution)

George Mason was born near Dogue's Neck on the Potomac below Alexandria in 1725, and died in Virginia, October 7, 1792. His early life was devoted to the study of law, plantation management, and land speculation. He was quite wealthy, owning a five-thousand-acre plantation on the Potomac. He was also a close neighbor to George Washington. He penned the Virginia Declaration of Rights, on which the Bill of Rights was modeled, and served in the Virginia House of Burgesses. Mason helped organize George Rogers Clark's expedition, which led to the acquisition of the Northwest Territory. He was named an Annapolis delegate, though he did not attend the convention. A delegate from Virginia at the Constitutional Convention, he was one of the most frequent speakers. To the very end, he supported revisions aimed at compromise, but refused to sign the finished document because it lacked civil rights provisions and contained a slavery clause. (Mason was the loudest against slavery during the debates, though he kept many of his own.) After the Constitution was signed, Mason fought diligently against approval at the Virginia state ratifying convention. He died before he could witness the success of the newly created government.

The first Justice John Marshall Harlan

Union, he nevertheless opposed abolition. Converting to Republicanism in 1868, he found that he was converting his basic convictions as well. From 1871 until 1877, when President Hayes named him to the Supreme Court, he spoke out fervently for Negro rights.

Confronting the rest of the bench on this most sensitive issue in the nation, Harlan succumbed to writer's block. The solution was Mrs. Harlan's. She unearthed one of his most prized possessions, which had been missing for a few years: the inkwell Taney had used to write the *Dred Scott* opinion. As Alan Westin tells the story: "After Harlan had spent a sleepless night working on his dissent, Mallie Harlan remembered the inkstand. While the Justice was at church, she retrieved it from its hiding place, filled it with a fresh supply of ink and pen points, and placed it on the blotter of his upstairs desk. When the Justice returned from church, she told him, with an air of mystery, that he would find something special in his study. Harlan was overjoyed to recover his symbolic antique. It broke his writer's block at once. . . . [In Mallie Harlan's words] 'his pen fairly flew on that day and, with the running start he then got, he soon finished his dissent.' "

Harlan grounded his forceful dissent on several points. The facilities were licensed to serve the public equally. Congress had power to govern railroads under its commerce power (a point that would ultimately be decisive in upholding the constitutionality of the substantially similar Civil Rights Act of 1964). Moreover, in 1850 Congress had enacted the draconian Fugitive Slave Law that jeopardized those who helped runaway slaves and the Supreme Court had upheld that law, certainly an act that forbade private discriminatory actions. "I insist that the National Legislature may . . . do for human liberty . . . what it did . . . for the protection of slavery and the rights of the masters of fugitive slaves." And responding to Bradley's complaint that it was time to stop singling out blacks for special protection, Harlan declared: "Today it is the colored race which is denied, by corporations and individuals wielding public authority, rights fundamental in their freedom and citizenship. At some future time, it may be that some other race will fall under the ban of race discrimination. If the constitutional amendments be enforced, according to the intent with which, as I conceive, they were adopted, there cannot be in this republic, any class of human beings in practical subjection to another class."

The *Civil Rights Cases* were a decisive force in the unfolding relations between the races. They signaled the end of federal attempts to police racially discriminatory acts, and they encouraged a rising generation of southern political leaders to climb to office on the backs of blacks. The decision, Alan Westin has written, "destroyed the delicate balance of federal guarantee, Negro protest, and private enlightenment which was producing a steadily widening area of peacefully integrated public facilities in the North and South during the 1870's and early 1880's."

The Rise and Decline of "Separate but Equal"

In short order, the Court's ruling led to federal judicial blessing of an early form of apartheid: the Jim Crow segregation laws that spread rapidly throughout the South, beginning with a Florida railroad law in 1887. Blacks were excluded, not only from transport, hotels, restaurants, theaters, parks, and other public places, but also from white neighborhoods, telephone booths, and elevators in public buildings. Florida and North Carolina even separated the public school textbooks used by blacks and whites, and Atlanta used different Bibles for black and white witnesses in court to swear on. New Orleans segregated white and black prostitutes. Was all this constitutional? Here, after all, were states legislatively requiring discriminating against blacks—state action, if ever there were such a thing.

In Louisiana, in 1891, a group of black citizens set about to test Jim Crow. They formed a "Citizens' Committee to Test the Constitutionality of the Separate Car Law." Officially labeled "An Act to Promote the Comfort of Passengers," and popularly known as the Jim Crow Car Act of 1890, the law directed railroads to "provide equal but separate accommodations for the white and colored races" and prohibited anyone, with significant exceptions, "to occupy seats in coaches other than the ones assigned to his race." The committee began soliciting funds to bring a lawsuit. To direct the suit, they hired Albion W. Tourgee of New York, a leading North Carolina Reconstructionist carpetbagger.

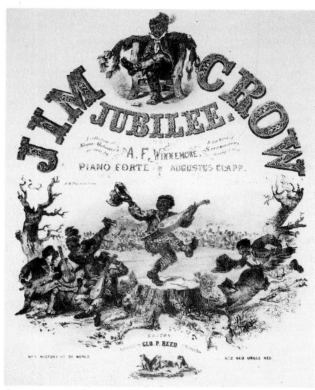

American song-sheet cover from 1847. The term Jim Crow *was derived from a song performed by minstrel Thomas Dartmouth Rice.*

In June 1892, they set in motion an elaborate plot to put the question before the Supreme Court. A man who could easily have passed for white, Homer Adolph Plessy, climbed aboard the East Louisiana Railroad in New Orleans and sat down in the white-only coach. By prior arrangement, a conductor requested that Plessy move back to the colored car. When he refused, a train detective arrested him. At his arraignment, he pleaded that the law was unconstitutional. Tourgee sought an order prohibiting the criminal court judge, John H. Ferguson, from holding the trial. By the end of the year, the Louisiana State Supreme Court had upheld the law, paving the way for an appeal, in *Plessy v. Ferguson,* to the Supreme Court.

Louisiana argued that it could separate the races in public accommodations as long as the accommodations assigned to persons of one race were equal to those assigned to the other. Tourgee saw the case in an entirely different way. "The question," he said in his brief, "is not as to the equality of the privileges enjoyed, but the right of the State to label one citizen as white and another as colored in the common enjoyment" of a host of daily activities.

Underscoring this point was Plessy himself, specially chosen for his appearance. Plessy was seven-eighths white (one of his eight great-grandparents had been black). If the justices could have been forced to concentrate on how the law classified people as black or white, Plessy might at least have prevailed on the singular facts in his case. (The South was scarcely worried about people who looked white and were known to be partly black only by their own affidavits.) Could a law be constitutionally valid if it defined a person of one-eighth African blood as "colored" but did not also define a person with one-eighth Caucasian blood as white? If the Court had concentrated on this point—the classification of a person as black or white for purposes of legal disabilities—it is at least possible that the issue of the dubious justification of segregation might have been kept alive for later cases, in

Signs of segregation at a Durham, North Carolina, bus station in 1940.

which the manifest absurdity of trying to define on the basis of their genes what people may or may not do would have been shown.

In an era that subscribed to the genetic superiority of whites, the justices were unwilling to grapple with Tourgee's point. The Court focused on what the law might legitimately do with the distinction between white and black, however the line was drawn; it was uninterested in what it was that made a person white or black.

Tourgee pointed out that "nurses attending the children of the other race" could sit in the forbidden cars (how many white nurses attended black children on railroad trips, or anywhere else?). "The exemption of nurses shows that the real evil lies not in the color of the skin but in the relation the colored person sustains to the white. If he is a dependent, it may be endured: if he is not, his presence is insufferable. Instead of being intended to promote the *general* comfort and moral well-being, this act is plainly and evidently intended to promote the happiness of one class by asserting its supremacy and the inferiority of another class. Justice is pictured blind and her daughter, the Law, ought at least to be color-blind."

The Court rejected every argument against state-enforced segregation. Justice Henry B. Brown said that the equal protection clause does not prevent a state legislature from drawing lines or making classifications. All laws do that to some degree. All that the equal protection clause prohibits are those that arbitrarily or unreasonably distinguish between the races. Reasonableness depends on the "established usages, customs, and traditions of the people, and with a view to the promotion of their comfort, and the preservation of the public peace and good order."

This analysis was tautological, for when will the people ever deviate from their own usages, customs, and traditions? When enacted into law, these will always turn out to be constitutionally permissible under the Fourteenth Amendment. In preserving the state's customs, Jim Crow could always be shown to promote the racial peace necessary to the good order of the state.

Nor did the discrimination unconstitutionally brand one race inferior to another, a Thirteenth Amendment argument: In an oft-quoted passage, Justice Brown said the Court considered

> the underlying fallacy of [Plessy's] argument to consist in the assumption that the enforced separation of the two races stamps the colored race with the badge of inferiority. If this be so, it is not by reason of anything found in the act, but solely because the colored race chooses to put that construction upon it.

To all this, Justice Harlan replied in one of the greatest dissents (and prognostications) in American history. The purpose of the law was not to provide equal facilities but to discriminate against blacks. The state's intention was to put flesh on the idea of supremacy that the white race feels. But, Harlan declared,

> in view of the constitution, in the eye of the law, there is in this country no superior, dominant, ruling class of citizens. There is no caste here. Our constitution is color-blind, and neither knows nor tolerates classes among citizens. In respect of civil rights, all citizens are equal before the law. The humblest is the peer of the most powerful. The law regards man as man, and takes no account of his surroundings, or of his color when his civil rights as guaranteed by the supreme law of the land are involved. . . . We boast of the freedom enjoyed by our people above all other peoples. But it is difficult to reconcile that boast with a state of law which, practically, puts the brand of servitude and degradation upon a large class of our fellow citizens—our equals before the law. The thin disguise of "equal accommodations" for passengers in railroad coaches will not mislead any one, nor atone for the wrong this day done. . . . In my opinion, the judgment this day rendered will, in time, prove to be quite as pernicious as the decision made by this tribunal in the Dred Scott case.

From 1896 until 1954, separate but equal was constitutional dogma. Segregation reigned in every area of social and political life: Jim Crow applied to housing, schools, employment, public accommodations, the military, and marriage. Segregation was widespread, not limited to the South; in its heyday, it governed school attendance in thirty states, including New York. It ruined more than race relations; like slavery the century before, the policy of political and social inequality that the Court permitted states to enforce tarnished the entire American promise, wasting lives, squandering talent, impoverishing the nation in countless ways.

That the separate-but-equal doctrine was fraudulent is no longer a surprise, though it took several decades for the courts to open their eyes to the deceit they had fostered. We deal with that fraud shortly. Here it should be noted that the doctrine was not coextensive with all racial discrimination. When a law discriminated in a way that left nothing even theoretically "equal," the Court struck it down.

As early as 1880, the Court voided a West Virginia law restricting jury service to white adult males (though it took the Court until 1986 to void the common practice of prosecutors in peremptorily challenging prospective black jurors to keep them from judging black defendants). Likewise, a state could not legitimately provide a dining car for whites but none for blacks (on the ground that the relatively few black riders made the operation of diners for them uneconomical). In 1917, the Court said a state could not preclude blacks and whites from moving onto a block the majority of whose residents were of the other race. As we saw in Chapter 8, the Court also began to enforce black voting rights, relying in part on the equal protection clause. In 1948, the Court invalidated the invidious system of racially restrictive land covenants, under which a seller could bind all future buyers of the land to sell only to whites. Although the covenant itself was a private agreement (hence no state action), the Court reasoned that its enforcement implicated an organ of government (the courts). Thereafter, you could enter into a racial covenant, you just could not enforce it.

Still, the colored curtain of segregation hung across America, and it was to destroy that barrier to equality that a new type of organization was formed: an issue-oriented, litigating arm of a national association—the Legal Defense and Education Fund of the National Association for the Advancement of Colored People (NAACP). Its creation was sparked by the NAACP's victory in 1938 in a crucial desegregation case. A black had been turned down for admission to the University of Missouri Law School, the only public law school in the state. Under Missouri law, he was entitled to scholarship funds to attend law outside the state, but he declined. Although the Supreme Court had upheld school segregation in 1927, the Court now agreed this case was different: Since no out-of-state law school taught Missouri law, the treatment accorded the would-be student was separate and *unequal*. Missouri responded by establishing a black law school at an existing black university.

The next year, the NAACP founded the Legal Defense and Education Fund, and appointed Thurgood Marshall its general counsel. In 1939, Marshall's determined mission was to eradicate segregation throughout the United States. (Ten years earlier, the University of Maryland Law School had refused to admit Marshall because he is black; his greater personal triumph over this adversity was to integrate the Supreme Court itself, in 1967, when President Johnson named him the one-hundredth justice to sit on the high court.)

The defense fund began to carry out its mission by jabbing at segregation's weakest points. The very weakest, on which the entire edifice would ultimately collapse, was the dubious equality of separateness. Was separate in fact equal? Could it even in theory be made equal?

Because a crack in the doctrine's facade had already been established in professional education, the defense fund found further targets there. In 1950, it scored a notable victory when the Supreme Court declared that a new law school established hurriedly

A sit-in by black students at a Charlotte, North Carolina, lunch counter in February 1960. Lunch counters and theaters in the town were reopened to all citizens five months after the demonstration.

to keep blacks out of the University of Texas wouldn't wash. The fund shrewdly chose a law school, because the justices would know firsthand the difference between a quality education and an inferior one. Chief Justice Fred M. Vinson noted that in excluding whites, the black law school would prevent the black law student from coming into contact with representatives of the racial group that includes "most of the lawyers, witnesses, jurors, judges, and other officials with whom [he] will inevitably be dealing when he becomes a member of the Texas Bar." The "reputation of the faculty, experience of the administration, position and influence of the alumni, standing in the community, and tradition and prestige" of the new black school could never hope to compare with that of the University of Texas. On that same day, the Court ruled that whenever a state chose to enroll black professional students in a white school (this time the School of Education of the University of Oklahoma), it could not rope them off from the white student body in class, library, dining room, and other places.

The Demise of Separate but Equal: Brown v. Board of Education

The fall of separate but equal at the hands of the newly installed Chief Justice Earl Warren in 1954 has been told so well and in such depth that it will be unnecessary to spin out the tale here at any length. *Brown v. Board of Education* was the consolidation of four cases originating in Delaware, Kansas, South Carolina, and Virginia challenging racial segregation of public elementary and secondary schoolchildren. The cases were originally argued in December 1952. During the Court's initial deliberations several days later, five justices were inclined to uphold segregation. But as the weeks wore on, one or two changed their minds, and so the Court set the cases down for reargument in the hopes of reaching a more nearly unanimous opinion.

Before the Court reconvened to hear the cases the following December, Fred Vinson died and President Eisenhower named California Governor Earl Warren

Linda Brown outside of a Topeka, Kansas, school.

chief justice. By all accounts, his presence made a crucial difference in fashioning a unanimous opinion overturning *Plessy*.

The Court directed the lawyers to focus on several issues, including the question whether the framers of the Fourteenth Amendment had intended to act against school legislation. Possessing both the opportunity and power to terminate segregation in the District of Columbia, the Thirty-Ninth Congress had taken no steps to do so. Indeed, by amending the bill that would become the Civil Rights Act of 1866 specifically to continue segregation in the district, the Congress that wrote the equal protection clause had declared itself undisposed to integration.

To this difficulty, Thurgood Marshall, chief counsel for the schoolchildren, responded that the historical record was unclear; at worst, it could not be shown that the framers conclusively meant to exclude the possibility that the Supreme Court would, at some later time, find school segregation a denial of equal protection of the laws.

The Court agreed. Warren dismissed the historical argument as "at best . . . inconclusive." Doubt about the framers' intentions was due not merely to the difficulty of probing the minds of people gone seventy-five years but also to "the status of public education at that time." Public schooling in the 1860s was neither universal nor so vital as it was in 1954:

In approaching this problem, we cannot turn the clock back to 1868 when the Amendment was adopted, or even to 1896 when Plessy v. Ferguson was written. We must consider public education in the light of its full development and its present place in American life throughout the Nation. . . . Today, education is perhaps the most important function of state and local governments. Compulsory school attendance laws and the great expenditures for education both demonstrate our recognition of the importance of education to our democratic society. It is required in the performance of our most basic public responsibilities, even service in the armed forces. It is the very foundation of good citizenship. Today it is a principal instrument in awakening the child to cultural values, in preparing him for later professional training, and in helping him to adjust normally to his environment. In these days, it is doubtful that any child may reasonably be expected to succeed in life if he is denied the opportunity of an education. Such an opportunity, where the state has undertaken to provide it, is a right which must be made available to all on equal terms.

And so, the chief justice concluded, "separate educational facilities are inherently unequal. . . . To separate [elementary and high school children] from others of similar age and qualifications solely because of their race generates a feeling of inferiority as to their status in the community that may affect their hearts and minds in a way unlikely ever to be undone. . . . Whatever may have been the extent of psychological knowledge at the time of *Plessy v. Ferguson,* this finding is amply supported by modern authority."

These words, lacking rhetorical elegance or warmth, were scathingly attacked—mostly by those who could not stomach the result. But they have also been assaulted by more analytical minds than those of southern politicians who profited from fanning racial flames. The gist of the criticism is that Warren rested on illegitimate (or at least unproven) sociological and psychological assertions about the effects of segregation and not on legal principles.

The seeming sociological cast of the decision has been linked to its rhetorical flatness: Through its blandness Warren secured unanimity, so critical to acceptance by a nation that would read it in either shock or amazement. As J. Harvie Wilkinson has pointed out, the justices then on the Court were unusually antipathetic toward each other; it required remarkable tact and skill for Warren to pull them together. "Unanimity here appeared to breach the Court's most hallowed tradition: that of open and spirited dissent. Yet it was precisely this break with tradition—the unusualness of unanimity—that made it so effective. To speak with one voice was to speak with force and finality; to speak otherwise was but to lend comfort to an enemy already in prey."

Moreover, the one voice had to be the voice of tact if the decision was to have any chance of winning over the South. So rather than rest on a ringing declaration that *any* law dividing on racial lines is unconstitutional (a holding that would have satisfied Herbert Wechsler's quest for "neutral principles" of decision), the Court pointed to empirical evidence that segregation in schools hurt children, evidence that was immediately attacked as insufficient, intellectually suspect, even communist inspired.

More than thirty years later, and a world removed from the "mind-set" that then characterized the nation, these difficulties seem, if not wholly beside the point, at least niggling. How could anyone suppose that in the nature of things enforced separation from white society was equal treatment?

But the intellectual problem has not worn away with age. It continues to haunt those who wish to know how to legitimize the Supreme Court's apparent imposition of a new policy on a nation, in the face of determined majorities who wished it another way and in the absence of explicit constitutional language to support the choice.

The problem inheres in the basic doubt about whether the framers of the Fourteenth Amendment intended that school segregation would yield its ghost to their handiwork. If they all assumed that whatever else it meant, the equal protection clause did not invalidate laws mandating school segregation, what did the 1954 Court do but write its own predilections into our fundamental law? And by what right?

In our own time, it is difficult to understand how a clause that speaks in terms of equality could at the same time exclude so basic an equality as attending schools established for the majority race. In the post-Civil War era, the term *civil rights* did not mean what it means to us. James F. Wilson of Iowa, Republican chairman of the House committee that drafted the Civil Rights Act of 1866, said that "civil rights and

immunities [do not mean] . . . that all citizens shall sit on juries or that their children shall attend the same schools." From these and like comments, Raoul Berger forcefully insists that school desegregation was not encompassed by the equal protection clause. Concurring with Justice Robert H. Jackson, Berger concludes that the justices were "declaring new law for a new day."

If you believe that the Constitution is open-ended, that conclusion will not be greatly troubling, at least not when the Court's decision is grounded in a moral principle fairly within the spirit of the constitutional phrase it is construing. Such a belief is respectable. If the framers did not intend that later courts treat their language in an evolving fashion, from which to draw moral norms of the current generation, why didn't they deliberately confine their ideas in unmis-

takable language? Members of the Thirty-ninth Congress knew very well that the courts were capable of drawing meanings from fuzzy words that were arguably not there. So if the framers knew of the power and tendency, perhaps by their nebulous phrases they meant for the courts to continue to engage in that process.

But if you believe instead that the Constitution must mean to us what it meant to those who wrote it (no matter how difficult it might be to uncover what they meant), then the decision in *Brown* might seem greatly troubling, for what is to stop some other Court from finding some other moral principle?

Let us be clear on the point at issue. It is not any longer that the Court *said* its decision rested on empirical evidence. The scores of decisions the Court has announced since then have made it clear that the real basis was indeed that constitutional harm lies in the very act of drawing legislative distinctions based on race. The intellectual problem is, rather, that the Court arguably reached this conclusion by resorting to a clause not broad enough to cover it.

Several responses are in order. First, if the equal protection clause was not intended to embrace school desegregation, then why in the first half of the twentieth century was the Court so beguiled by the slogan "separate but equal"? Take Bingham and Wilson and all the others at their word that they meant to leave segregation where it was, why then insist on any schooling at all for the disfavored race? If schooling was a social, not a civil, right, why bother even to debate? Surely the segregated schools in the District of Columbia and elsewhere were far from equal in the framers' time. If historical practice is the decisive factor, then the framers cannot be heard to have said even that separate black schools ought to be equal.

Consider the peculiar origin of the separate-but-equal doctrine. It was announced by Lemuel Shaw, chief justice of Massachusetts from 1830 to 1860, in a suit challenging the Boston school board's decision to segregate schoolchildren by race. The plaintiff's lawyer was Charles Sumner, who sponsored the Civil Rights Act of 1875 a quarter-century later in the Senate. The Massachusetts constitution said that "all men are born free and equal," and it prohibited the legislature from granting "particular and exclusive privileges." Sumner argued that the state constitution thus forbade "any institution founded on inequality or caste." Shaw agreed that "all persons without distinction of age or sex, birth or color, origin or condition, are equal before the law." However, when he applied this principle it somehow did not yield equal treatment but doubletalk. In Shaw's jejune formulation: "The rights of all, as they are settled and regulated by law, are equally entitled to the paternal consideration and protection of the law. . . . What those rights are, to which individuals, in the infinite variety of circumstances by which they are sur-rounded in society, are entitled, must depend on laws adapted to their respective relations and conditions." The law that assigned black children to one school and white to another did not offend the constitution, Shaw concluded, as long as the schools were equal. In other words, the separate-but-equal doctrine was created out of whole cloth to avoid the embarrassment of a state constitution that actually demanded equality of the races.

The doctrinal roots of separate but equal are thus wholly independent of the Fourteenth Amendment. In ordering segregated schools in the District of Columbia, Congress was not bound by the Massachusetts rule. To argue from the framers' supposed intention not to scuttle school segregation that the Fourteenth Amendment encompasses separation of the races, it is necessary to concede that the separate-but-equal formulation could not have been part of the equal protection clause. Whatever else they did, the framers of the Fourteenth Amendment surely did not propose to graft the jurisprudence of Lemuel Shaw onto the federal Constitution.

Plessy, to be sure, was not about school segregation. Yet something troubled even the *Plessy* Court, which itself bathed in the sociology of the times—a fact on which the detractors of Chief Justice Warren's use of social science findings somehow usually avoid comment. The *Plessy* Court held that transportation was a social, not a political or civil, right. But if the equal protection clause applies only to civil rights, and transportation is not one of them, again why try to pretend that a separate caboose is an equal one? Why not just tell blacks that they cannot ride the rails at all?

(Why wasn't *Plessy* really about the right to travel, a right that even then was more than arguably a privilege or immunity of national citizenship? Suppose Plessy had been traveling to Washington to speak to his representative in Congress. Even the *Slaughterhouse* Court (page 201) recognized that as a fundamental right protected by the Fourteenth Amendment.)

Second, in this light, the most that can be said against the Supreme Court in 1954 is that it reconstructed the meaning of "civil rights." It did not reinterpret the meaning of equality. The Court saw through the fatal flaw in the proposal of Bingham and Wilson and others that school and jury segregation could be separated from "the rights of personal security, the rights of personal liberty, and the right to acquire and enjoy property." In their concern over an electorate hardening their position on white rights, the framers might have found it politically wise to articulate this position to secure enactment of the 1866 Civil Rights Act and even the Fourteenth Amendment, but it made no underlying sense. It simply collapses of its own dead weight.

Third, the right to contract *was* a civil right, clearly intended to be secured by the equal protection clause. Even if school segregation somehow falls outside its shadow, most of the Jim Crow laws upheld by the courts directly impinged on this right. More astonishing, the Supreme Court in an entirely different realm—that of labor and property—concluded that the due process clause of the Fourteenth Amendment protected the "liberty of contract"—that is, the right of workers to contract with employers free of restrictive regulations (such as those limiting the number of hours that could be worked in a day; see Chapter 17). No less did the Jim Crow laws prevent blacks from "contracting" with whites to ride in white cars and attend white theaters. (That whites were equally forbidden from contracting to ride in black cars is beside the point, for the inequality lies in the proscription against blacks mingling with whites, when whites are permitted to do so, and not in the equal punishment that might be visited on either for violating the law.)

Fourth, the framers clearly intended equality to prevail in the basic political right of voting; that is why they proposed, and the states ratified, the Fifteenth Amendment. Had the courts vigorously enforced it, so that blacks could have become a significant

factor in elections from 1870 on, as they should have been, the electoral process would not likely have led to the legacy of Jim Crow racism with which the courts have had to do battle these past thirty years. It is stacking the deck to an intolerable degree to conclude that a person is not entitled to redress for woes caused by the unlawful deprivation of a right the exercise of which would have avoided them.

Finally, *Brown* and the revolution that followed cannot be understood except against the backdrop of the other massive constitutional deprivations visited on blacks by all southern states and probably most northern ones as well—and by Congress and the White House too. The states never disagreed that they were bound by the separate-but-equal criterion, but in education, health care, social services, public employment, and transportation, they defaulted on meeting even this minimal obligation. The default was no small or transitory thing; it lasted at least four generations and its last vestiges have by no means been eradicated. To dispute the Court's constitutional bona fides because certain representatives and senators in the late 1860s thought they could extend equality without affecting school enrollment is to enshrine political theories over political reality. The Supreme Court was the last possible institution in America to order the piper paid.

Moreover, no one should be heard to complain that the Supreme Court had acted precipitately or without warning: It took fifty-eight years to act decisively, and anyone with a finger to the wind should have known which way it was blowing. The course of race relations is the most telling example in American history of the precept that the Supreme Court reacts slowly to willful violations of the law by the other branches of government and decrees "policy" (if that is what *Brown* was) only when the breach is continuing, massive, and harmful in the extreme.

In any event, the moving finger writes, and having writ, moves on. Not even Raoul Berger, the scourge of the Court's equal protection interpretations, pretends his belief that the Court usurped the policy-making functions of Congress and the people logically compels us to return to the ill-famed theories of *Plessy:* "It would . . . be utterly unrealistic and probably impossible to undo the past in the face of the expectations that the segregation decisions . . . have aroused in our black citizenry—expectations confirmed by every decent instinct. That is more than the courts should undertake and more, I believe, than the American people would desire."

In this belief, Berger is more realistic than *Brown's* chief legal adversary, John W. Davis, the 1924 Democratic presidential candidate and solicitor general of the United States, who was regarded as the greatest appellate advocate of his time. In his last hurrah, Davis argued *Brown* for South Carolina. "Somewhere, sometime," he told the Court, "to every principle comes a moment of repose when it has been so often announced, so confidently relied upon, so long continued, that it passes the limits of judicial discretion and disturbance." He was speaking of *Plessy* and he was wrong, but the same words surely now apply to *Brown.*

Davis's position was scorned by the United States itself. Solicitor General J. Lee Rankin argued as amicus ("friend of the court"—the United States was not a party) that continued segregation was doing the United States incalculable harm in its foreign relations with newly emerging third world countries.

By its decision in *Brown,* the Supreme Court for the first time cleansed American constitutionalism of its racist stain. It would follow from then on that legislative line drawing could no longer turn on the distinctions of race. That was constitutional theory, of course. Constitutional fact has never been in harness with declarations, even authoritative ones, of constitutional values. Prejudices are not shaken in a day, nor did anyone suppose they would be (though Marshall wrongly predicted that school integration would be accomplished by 1960 and all forms of segregation would be eradicated by 1963).

The story of reaction to *Brown v. Board of Education* is largely the story of race relations in America during the past three decades, and race relations are a large part of the public affairs of our age. In school segregation itself, the Court in 1955 in the second *Brown* case declared its famous remedy: The lower federal courts should come up with plans to admit blacks to public schools "on a racially nondiscriminatory basis with all deliberate speed." The "all deliberate speed" requirement turned out to be no requirement at all, leaving the door open to massive resistance and hideous violence by whites determined to preserve a way of life they cherished without reason and without understanding how much it degraded them. It is no accident that the Sunbelt emerged as a potent economic competitor of the North only after the South had finally begun honestly to purge itself of its racist heritage.

During the generation that the new racial philosophy incubated, political processes, long frozen because the Constitution did not appear to require politicians to act, finally began to function. New hopes led to determined political action by blacks as well. At great cost in human life, bloodshed, and suffering, the sit-ins, demonstrations, and finally riots led to congressional action. Though President Eisenhower waffled, failing to exert the immense moral leadership that was his, when finally provoked he did federalize the Arkansas National Guard and ordered the soldiers to Little Rock. The Civil Rights Act he signed in 1957 was the first such law since the ill-fated Civil Rights Act of 1875. Stronger medicine came from Congress in the 1964 Civil Rights Act, for the first time enforcing legislatively the Court's decision ten years earlier. That act declares unlawful all employment discrimination based on race, religion, creed, national origin, and sex, and bars discrimination in public accommodations and in any enterprise receiving federal funds. This time, in the Second Reconstruction, the Supreme Court upheld the laws that its predecessor had so mercilessly struck down.

Across a broad front during the 1960s, voting rights and other laws were put on the books, presidents issued executive orders, and the courts built a broad mosaic of equal protection doctrine. The Supreme Court led the way, striking down racial discrimination in area after area, finally reaching the most intimate relationship of all, marriage. In 1967, the Court unanimously voided miscegenation laws that prohibited blacks and whites from marrying.

Though battles raged over this entire front, the strongest resistance and the most difficult policy choices continue to this day in school desegregation. For fifteen years, the lower federal courts bore the brunt of the struggle. Conspicuous by its absence, the southern bar in its pusillanimity showed itself morally bankrupt—a relative handful of northern lawyers, scorned, jailed, and harassed, supplied their courtroom services until the southern bar could be transformed. The major agent of change was the U.S. Court of Appeals for the Fifth Circuit, which took appeals from across the deep South. On that bench, probably fortuitously, but fortunately, sat four wise and courageous judges—Elbert P. Tuttle of Georgia, John Minor Wisdom of Louisiana, John R. Brown of Texas, and Richard Taylor Rives of Alabama—who along with Alabama Federal District Judge Frank M. Johnson, Jr. (now on the Fifth Circuit), unflinchingly moved to carry out the Supreme Court's constitutional understanding in the absence of any guidance from the Court itself, doing battle with governors, legislators, state courts, and even their own recalcitrant brethren on the lower federal courts of the south.

In 1969, the Supreme Court finally explicitly abandoned its *Brown II* stance of "all deliberate speed"; for a unanimous Court, Justice Black said: " 'All deliberate speed' is no longer constitutionally permissible. . . . The obligation of every school district is to terminate dual school systems at once and to operate now and hereafter only unitary school systems." Black's opinion was joined by the new Chief Justice, Warren E. Burger, signaling that even conservative judges (for so President Nixon, who had named him that year, surely saw him) would not retreat from the Warren Court's basic commitment to equal protection. And in 1971, the Court issued its toughest ruling, approving busing to achieve integration. Numerous lower court busing decisions now became the target of local wrath, and a more conservative Congress attempted to control federal court busing decrees; the issue continues to smolder to this day. Fully integrating the schools, it turns out, creates problems of a different order of magnitude than eradicating formal segregation; their explication would take us far afield.

But we cannot leave this discussion of constitutional equality among the races without noting that in 1968 the Court came full circle and revivified both the long-dormant Civil Rights Act of 1866 and the original hope of many sponsors of the Thirteenth Amendment. In a housing case, the Court declared that the second section of the Thirteenth Amendment, giving Congress the power to enforce the antislavery provision, permits Congress to legislate against racial discrimination in housing, whether sale or rental:

> Negro citizens, North and South, who saw in the Thirteenth Amendment a promise of freedom—freedom to "go and come at pleasure" and to "buy and sell when they please"—would be left with "a mere paper guarantee" if Congress were powerless to assure that a dollar in the hands of a Negro will purchase the same thing as a dollar in the hands of a white man. At the very least, the freedom that Congress is empowered to secure under the Thirteenth Amendment includes the freedom to buy whatever a white man can buy, the right to live wherever a white man can live. If Congress cannot say that being a free man means at least this much, then the Thirteenth Amendment made a promise the nation cannot keep.

In 1976, the 1866 act was taken one step farther, overcoming the state action problem that Justice Bradley found in the *Civil Rights Cases*. In 1883, the Court had instructed Congress that it could not interfere with private relations; those were for the states

to deal with. By that logic, private secondary schools that received absolutely no funds from the government should be immune from legislative or judicial requirements to integrate.

Now, in 1976, the Supreme Court found a way around that state action dilemma, at least in the case of private schools. Again it repaired to the Civil Rights Act of 1866, which gives blacks the same right "to make and enforce contracts . . . as is enjoyed by white citizens." The Court concluded that the Thirteenth Amendment gives Congress ample power to enact a right to contract, enforceable by all throughout the United States. "Private, commercially operated, non-sectarian schools" that refuse admission to blacks violate the federal right to contract.

Much too belatedly, but nevertheless finally, the nation was committed to a course of constitutionalism that banished invidious discrimination based on color—working a transformation in our culture greater and faster than any change that had ever before come from the declarations of courts. The "invisible man" was at last becoming seen and heard and accepted.

In *Plessy v. Ferguson*, Justice Brown had expressed his conviction that the Fourteenth Amendment was "undoubtedly designed to enforce the absolute equality of the two races before the law . . . [but] could not have been intended in the nature of things . . . [to] abolish distinctions based upon color or to enforce social, as distinct from political equality." In other words, "legislation can't enforce morality," as too many social Darwinists, north and south, never tired of maintaining to salve their consciences for failing to act. *Brown* and the laws that followed proved them wrong.

The constitutional consensus seems likely to hold. When the Reagan administration attempted in 1983 to sanction tax breaks for segregated academies, the courts firmly said no, and the Administration pulled back. The most relentlessly conservative administration in sixty years could not breach the fundamental principle that in a constitutional republic, no badge of inferiority can be stamped on a race by the hand of government.

Chapter 16 **Beyond Race: Equality for All?**

Suspect Classifications

Few political words arouse partisan passions or quicken the convictions as powerfully as *equality*. Mostly the debate is tedious, for it is futile to deny that people differ markedly in mental facility, physical. agility, emotional stability, and in every other possibility. Jefferson's self-evident truth, that all men are created equal, was never intended to imply that people are everywhere equal in every respect but, rather, that in the eyes of the state, all people deserve equal respect. A good society knows no political orders, no higher and lower estates, no nobles and commoners. All stand equal in the eyes of the law.

A constitutional regime of equality before the law is simpler to state than to achieve, however, for law frequently classifies. It includes and excludes, penalizes and profits, prohibits and permits. Legislating is line drawing, and the judge must decide, when the question arises, whether those who are put on one side are the equals of those left on the other.

If it is unfair, because unequal, to exclude a person from a classroom because of her skin color, is it wrong to exclude her because of disease? If an apple peddler is permitted to sell his fruit on the street corner, may the city bar a hot dog vendor from hawking his franks? Is equality offended if some people are too poor to pay the fee to obtain a divorce decree? Is it discriminatory to draft men and not women? May a state force police officers over fifty to retire (thus favoring younger people)? May a state restrict welfare benefits to citizens? If a child born in wedlock may sue for damages resulting from the death of her mother, is it unequal treatment to deny an illegitimate child the same right?

Moreover, if a law is neutral on its face, applicable by its terms to all, should the Constitution be offended if its impact is unequal? Anatole France's celebrated quip that the "law in its majestic equality forbids the rich as well as the poor to sleep under bridges, to beg in the streets, and to steal bread" poses the dilemma. But wit does not dictate the solution.

The equal protection clause stands guard over the illegitimate classification and evil execution of fair-faced laws, but it often takes a subtle nose to sniff the odor of impermissible inequality in a world as complex as ours. The child sent to bed an hour before her older sister may protest that "she's a child too" and smart at the unfairness of life; the appeal to equity may be for parents to enlarge their categories and relent or to remind younger daughter that mother and father know best. Circumstances tell; the term *equality* settles no issues by rigid formula.

Until recent years, the courts interpreted the equal protection clause as mandating equal treatment "except upon some reasonable differentiation fairly related to the object of regulation." Unlike due process, at least as it was long interpreted, equal protection is concerned with the means by which the legislature acts, not with the ends it seeks. If the legislature has a reasonable purpose—for example, guaranteeing safety in the skies—it can classify in ways reasonably expected to achieve that end (age limitations for pilots).

Not all legislative purposes are equally legitimate, however. Some classifications may amount to a regime of inequality: the desire simply to treat certain people differently. That was the vice of racial segregation. During the 1960s, the Warren Court developed a two-tier approach to equal protection. Some classifications need merely be "rationally" related to a legitimate legislative goal, and that rational relationship can be quite minimal. Other classifications are "suspect," and the courts will strictly scrutinize the legislature's purpose; unless the state's interest is "compelling" and the classification is tightly connected to the state's goal, the courts will invalidate the lines that the legislature draws.

The "suspect class" rule actually predates the Warren Court and has two dimensions. One, illustrated by a 1942 case, suggests that when a fundamental right is at stake, the Court will carefully scrutinize the distinction the law draws between groups. In that case, the Supreme Court declared that because the right of procreation is fundamental, the state may not compel people to be sterilized on an unequal basis. Oklahoma had a law requiring sterilization for two-time felons whose crimes involved "moral turpitude." The law exempted embezzlers but included those who committed grand larceny. The Court said the distinction was "a clear, pointed, unmistakable discrimination. . . . We have not the slightest basis for inferring that that [distinction] has any significance in eugenics, nor that the inheritability of criminal traits follows the neat legal distinctions which the law has marked between these two offenses."

The other dimension of suspect classes lies in their relative power and status in society. In 1938, in "the most celebrated footnote in constitutional law," Justice Harlan F. Stone suggested that the Court would not necessarily indulge a law in the usual presumption of constitutionality if the law is "directed at particular religious, or national, or racial minorities" or if "prejudice against discrete and insular minorities . . . tends seriously to curtail the operation of the political processes ordinarily to be relied upon to protect minorities."

For the past three decades or so, the judicial task has been to identify the "discrete and insular minorities," those suspect categories to which the "strict scrutiny" test applies. Business or economic groups are rarely considered discrete or insular, whereas ra-

Founding Father

William Richardson Davie

(did not sign the Constitution)

William Richardson Davie was born in Egremont, Cumberlandshire, England, on June 20, 1756, and died in North Carolina, November 29, 1820. He came to America in 1763, settling in South Carolina. Later, he was adopted by his maternal uncle, a clergyman. He studied at Queen's Museum College in Charlotte, North Carolina, and at Princeton, graduating in 1776 with first honors. Immediately after, he returned to North Carolina where he studied law. Admitted to the bar in 1780, he rode circuit in his state until 1787. Also during the 1780s, he enlisted in the military to participate in the revolutionary cause. An able soldier, he quickly rose from lieutenant to major. From 1786 to 1798, he represented the county of Halifax in the North Carolina legislature, and was largely responsible for the codification of North Carolina laws. The state named him commander of its troops and boundary commission chairman in 1797, as well as governor in 1798. As a

North Carolina delegate to the Constitutional Convention, he favored the Connecticut Compromise, election of senators and presidential electors by the legislature, and representation for slave property. After the Convention, he helped push for ratification. Under Adams's administration, Davie was named brigadier general, and in 1799 was named peace commissioner to France. In 1802, Jefferson appointed him to negotiate the Tuscarora Treaty. However, the following year, he was pushed from politics by the Jefferson-Mason machine for his aristocratic leanings. He retired to his home, Tivoli, in Lancaster County, South Carolina in 1805, devoting much of his time to farming, riding, and reading. In 1813, he declined an appointment by Madison to become a major general.

Tall and commanding, Davie was more comfortable as a military man than as a politician. He was largely responsible for the endowment of the University of North Carolina, and as grand master of the Masons, placed the cornerstones for its first building. He was also the first president of the South Carolina Agricultural Society.

cial groups are. (It was a sublimely ironic moment when the Court first specified race as a "suspect" category in the Japanese exclusion case, page 280, upholding the federal government's power to imprison Japanese Americans during World War II solely on the basis of their ancestry—the only time the Court has ever sustained an invidious discrimination since announcing the doctrine.) In between racial and commercial classifications lie distinctions based on parentage, alienage, gender, wealth, and tribal status—distinctions of groups whose members suffer from various disabilities that have long kept them from participating in the political process and hence rendered them relatively powerless to prevent the discriminations imposed on them by those in charge.

Commercial Classifications

Normally, economic legislation is permissible that draws lines between different types of businesses or even two different businesses in the same industry. For example, a New York City ordinance banned vehicles from displaying advertisements, except for vehicles advertising the business in which they are regularly employed. Railway Express operated 1,900 trucks carrying goods across the country. It rented the sides of its trucks to advertisers. Under the ordinance, Railway's rental was illegal, whereas a dairy company's delivery trucks could devote the outside of its vehicles to advertising the company's milk and cheese. The Supreme Court upheld the regulation against the argument that it unfairly discriminated against Railway.

The height—or depths—of the minimal rationality test applied to business was the Warren Court's approval in 1961 of Sunday closing laws against a strong challenge on religious as well as equal protection grounds. Spottily enforced (the randomness of enforcement itself raising equal protection problems),

An 1895 cartoon comment on blue laws in New York City.

the blue laws in three-quarters of the states prohibit merchants from selling a variety of goods, while permitting them to sell others. The logic of the distinctions is usually elusive. What can one make of a law that permits the sale on Sundays of "antiques" but not "reproductions," or hosiery in drugstores but not in hosiery stores? Can Sunday be a day of rest if the law exempts from a closed-store policy the sale of "milk, bread, fruits, gasoline, greases, drugs and medicines, and newspapers and periodicals"? Said Chief Justice Warren of the latter list: "It would seem that a legislature could reasonably find that the Sunday sale of the exempted commodities was necessary either for the health of the populace or for the enhancement of the recreational atmosphere of the day."

The Burger Court has followed in these footsteps. In 1976, the Court unanimously upheld a law that distinguished among pushcart vendors in the French Quarter of New Orleans. A grandfather clause exempted from a ban on selling in the quarter those who had been selling food continually "for eight years prior to January 1, 1972." Said the Court in an unsigned opinion: "The judiciary may not sit as a superlegislature to judge the wisdom or desirability of legislative policy determinations made in areas that neither affect fundamental rights nor proceed along suspect lines." Or, as Justice Rehnquist put it in a 1980 opinion dealing with a congressional enactment that restructured the federal railroad retirement system: "Because Congress could have eliminated windfall benefits for all classes of employees, it is not constitutionally impermissible for Congress to have drawn lines between groups of employees for the purpose of phasing out those benefits. . . . The only remaining question is whether Congress achieved its purpose in a patently arbitrary or irrational way." If it did, the law is unconstitutional; if Congress did not divide irrationally (that is, if plausible reasons can be found for its action), the law will be upheld. What constitutes plausibility remains controversial.

Gender Distinctions

The equal protection clause speaks of "persons." Until the 1970s, distinctions drawn on sex lines were not suspect enough to require strict scrutiny. This almost always meant that women suffered by comparison with men. The most dazzling example of the refusal to treat women equally was Justice Bradley's bold declaration in 1873 in the case of a woman who unsuccessfully sought admission to the Illinois bar to practice law:

Man is, or should be, woman's protector and defender. The natural and proper timidity and delicacy which belongs to the female sex evidently unfits it for many of the occupations of civil life. The constitution of the family organization, which is founded in the divine ordinance, as well as in the nature of things, indicates the domestic sphere as that which properly belongs to the domain and functions of womanhood. The harmony, not to say identity, of interests and views which belong, or should belong, to the family institution is repugnant to the idea of a woman adopting a distinct and independent career from that of her husband. [The] paramount destiny and mission of woman are to fulfil the noble and benign offices of wife and mother. This is the law of the Creator.

Thirty-five years later, the Court upheld a law thought to favor women by limiting the number of hours they could work: "That woman's physical structure and the performance of maternal functions place her at a disadvantage in the struggle for subsistence is obvious. . . . Differentiated by these matters from the other sex, she is properly placed in a class by herself, and legislation designed for her protection may be sustained, even when like legislation is not necessary for men and could not be sustained." In 1948, the Court upheld a Michigan law forbidding women from becoming bartenders unless they were wives or daughters of male owners of the bar in which they sought to work.

1869 Currier and Ives cartoon satirizing the women's rights movement.

Though this was the state of things until relatively recently, today no such sentiments survive; these justifications would be branded "romantic paternalism" that "put women not on a pedestal but in a cage." In 1971, for the first time, the Supreme Court announced that a rule favoring men in the administration of a decedent's estate is unconstitutional. An Idaho law said that in a case in which a man and woman were "equally entitled" to be the administrator, "males [shall] . . . be preferred to females." The Court voided the law.

The Court began its still unfolding analysis of sex discrimination the same year that the House passed the Equal Rights Amendment (ERA). Sent to the states by the Senate in 1972, the ERA declared: "Equality of rights under the law shall not be denied or abridged by the United States or by any State on account of sex." Given seven years to ratify and then three more, the states failed to do so: Proponents of the ERA were three states short of the necessary thirty-eight on June 30, 1982, when time ran out.

Passed by comfortable margins in the House and Senate, the ERA fell victim to a number of forces: opposition by President Reagan, strident opposition by antiabortion activists, and doubts shared by many of its likely effect on such institutions as the armed forces. In a 1972 minority report, Senator Sam J. Ervin Jr. of North Carolina lambasted the ERA on a number of grounds, among them that the Fourteenth Amendment already sufficiently protected women; that a variety of laws also protected them, including Title VII of the Civil Rights Act of 1964, which guarantees equality in hiring; that it "would have undesirable effects on the military, on criminal and domestic relations law, and on protective labor legislation; [and] that an ERA would violate the right to privacy in schools, restrooms, dormitories, and prisons."

In 1983, an effort to revive the ERA failed in the Senate when Senator Orrin Hatch of Utah showed that the amendment's chief sponsor, Senator Paul Tsongas of Massachusetts, was unable "to discuss the

ERA's effects on . . . abortion rights, fair housing, women in the military, homosexual marriages, veterans' preference, seniority practices, insurance rate distinctions, and noncoeducational colleges." Senator Tsongas's limp response was that the courts would decide. That was precisely what the ERA's opponents feared: that the open-ended language would permit the courts to integrate the army, to permit homosexual and lesbian marriages, to strike down veterans' preferences, and the like. In fact, just such a state of affairs has come to be, though not those particular rulings: In the absence of the ERA, the courts have rediscovered the possibilities of legal equality between the sexes implicit in the Fourteenth Amendment.

Legal equality almost became the rule in 1973, when four justices declared that sex-based distinctions were inherently suspect. Justice Powell refused to join this plurality opinion. He pointed to the ERA, then pending, as a "compelling reason for deferring a general categorizing of sex classifications as invoking the strictest test of judicial scrutiny." Despite the ERA (or perhaps because of it), the Court has shown a heightened awareness of gender discrimination since the early 1970s.

In the 1973 case, the Court struck down as unconstitutionally discriminatory a military rule governing allowances for dependents. The rule said that a serviceman could claim his wife as a dependent, and thus be entitled to increased housing allowances and medical and dental benefits, whether or not she was actually dependent on him financially. However, a female member of the armed forces could obtain a like benefit only if her husband depended on her for more than half his support.

Many of the cases that followed struck down in the name of equality laws that seemed to favor women: a law permitting women at eighteen to drink 3.2 percent beer but requiring men to be twenty-one, a law permitting only mothers of illegitimate children to block their adoption, and a rule barring men's admission to the Mississippi University for Women

Time ran out for ERA proponents in June 1982 with three more states needed for the amendment's ratification.

ERA *opponents feared the far-reaching effects of the amendment.*

School of Nursing. Some cases struck down rules favoring men—for example, a Louisiana law that permitted men but not women to dispose of property jointly owned without the spouse's consent. Still other decisions refused to void laws favoring women—significantly, the draft registration case, in which the president under the Military Selective Service Act may require men but not women to register for military service, and also a case upholding laws that make only men criminally liable for statutory rape.

Squaring these varied results (and results in many other cases dealing with insurance and survivors' benefits under Social Security and other laws) is difficult, perhaps impossible. No tidy rule can be confidently stated, because the outcome turns so heavily on the Court's perception of the legitimacy of the underlying goal and how necessary the discrimination is to carrying it out. In a recent statement of the rule the Court intends to follow, Justice Brennan said that gender classifications will not be upheld unless the government satisfies a burden of "(A) showing a legitimate and 'exceedingly persuasive justification' for

[a] gender-based classification" and "(B) demonstrating 'the requisite direct, substantial relationship' between the classification and the important governmental objectives it purports to serve."

Aliens

The equal protection clause is not limited to citizens; it speaks broadly of "persons." In 1915, the Court was content to uphold second-class treatment of aliens—for example, a New York law that prohibited employing aliens in public works projects. But by 1948, the Court began to take a narrow view of allowable discriminations toward resident aliens when it declared that California could not deny resident aliens commercial fishing licenses. In 1971, the Court held that states may not refuse to pay aliens welfare benefits, and it later ruled that states may not prevent aliens from practicing law, from serving as notaries public, or from holding permanent positions in the competitive civil service. (Most of these rulings turned

Founding Father

Oliver Ellsworth

(did not sign the Constitution)

Oliver Ellsworth was born in Windsor, Connecticut, on April 29, 1745, and died on November 26, 1807. His ancestors had come to Connecticut from England in 1650. Brought up on a farm in Connecticut, he entered Yale at the age of seventeen. Two years later, he transferred his studies to Princeton and received an M.A. in 1766. His father had intended him to go into the ministry, but Ellsworth took up the study of law. He was admitted to the bar in 1771 and made a successful practice in Hartford. Concurrently, he was named state attorney general. His workload was large; he had a docket of between 1,000 and 1,500 cases. In 1775, he became a member of the Connecticut General Assembly and served on the committee of military accounts. In 1777, he was elected to Congress. For the next six years, he was an intermittent member of Congress, acting on the committee to regulate army supplies and on a special committee to suppress mutiny by military troops in Pennsylvania. From 1780 to 1784, he was part of Connecticut's governor's council. Then, from 1784 to 1789, he was a state Supreme Court judge. As a member of the Constitutional Convention, he favored equal representation in the Senate, proposed the name of "the government of the United States," and advocated the Constitution as an amendment to the government under the Articles of Confederation. He was one of Connecticut's first two U.S. senators. As such, he chaired the committee that originated the first judiciary bill, supported Jay's Treaty, Hamilton's plan to assume state debts, and the creation of a national bank. John Adams described him as "the firmest pillar of Washington's whole administration in the senate." Well liked, he was reelected senator in the second elections. In 1796, he was named chief justice of the United States. A distinguished judge, he remained in this seat until 1800. Ellsworth's legal prowess was recognized with LL.D. degrees from Yale (1790), and Dartmouth and Princeton (1799). In 1799, along with fellow delegate William Davie, he was named envoy to France. Ill health forced him to leave France, and after a time in England, he returned to America. Back in Connecticut, he was renamed a member of the governor's council, and was also made a member of Yale's Board of Fellows. In 1807, he was offered the post of state chief justice. However, he declined for health reasons and died that same year.

on Congress's power to admit aliens to this country. State laws barring them from ordinary pursuits conflict with congressional intent that they be free to live in the United States and thus violate the supremacy clause.)

Unlike resident aliens, "undocumented" (illegal) aliens are not a suspect class "because their presence in this country in violation of federal law is not a 'constitutional irrelevancy.'" Still, even they are entitled to protection from some harsh commands of the state. The Court has ruled that illegal aliens of school age may not be denied enrollment in the public schools; a Texas law prohibiting their attendance and cutting off funds to school districts that admit them is irrational, the Court said, because it furthers no important state goal. The law "imposes a lifetime hardship on a discrete class of children not accountable for their disabling status. The stigma of illiteracy will mark them for the rest of their lives. By denying these children a basic education, we deny them the ability to live within the structure of our civic institutions, and foreclose any realistic possibility that they will contribute in even the smallest way to the progress of our Nation."

But citizenship has not become an empty category. The Court has found rational reasons for linking citizenship as a qualification to holding certain jobs. For example, the states may require American citizenship as a condition of employment as state troopers and as "deputy probation officers, Spanish speaking." It has also upheld as a condition of employment as a public school teacher that the applicant at least declare an intention of becoming a citizen.

Indians

Unlike every other group protected by the Constitution, American Indians occupy a special place in our legal relations, for they alone, in their corporate

Leaders of the American Indian Movement preparing for a purification ceremony at the site of the massacre at Wounded Knee, South Dakota.

capacity, are held to be sovereign nations. In 1832, Chief Justice Marshall said that the "Indian nations had always been considered as distinct, independent political communities, retaining their original natural rights, as the undisputed possessors of the soil. The very term, 'nation,' so generally applied to them, means 'a people distinct from others.' " The Court reaffirmed this principle as late as 1959. For all the good it has done them, the Indian nations have the legal capacity to enter into treaties with the federal government, though not the political or military power to enforce them. This unique status means that within the reservation, a state may not exercise legal jurisdiction; the tribes are self-governing, subject only to overriding power in Congress. Indians are U.S. citizens, and they can place themselves within the jurisdiction of the states simply by ceasing to live on the reservation. Despite tribal sovereignty, federal law can preempt even the treaties that have been made, subject to the Fifth Amendment's prohibition against taking property without paying just compensation. But the equal protection clause stands guard against statutes that "put [them] at a serious racially based disadvantage"; Indians may "not be treated worse than similarly situated non-Indians."

Illegitimate Children

The Supreme Court has never declared illegitimate children a suspect classification, but it has increasingly, if not always consistently, looked askance at laws that burden only those children whose parents' had been too hurried to marry. The first such case, in 1968, struck down a law that precluded unacknowledged illegitimate children from suing for the wrongful death of their mother. Three years later, however, the Court upheld a state law that gave priority to relatives other than acknowledged illegitimate children in inheriting from the parent, and a state law that required illegitimate children to establish paternity during the lifetime of the father in order to inherit was also approved as constitutionally inoffensive. But a law that absolutely forbade illegitimate children from inheriting from their fathers because their parents had not married went too far and could not stand, at least when the paternity had been decided in court. Also, a law that required an illegitimate child to bring a paternity suit within one year of birth to obtain child support was held to be constitutionally defective because legitimate children could sue for support at any time.

Indigence

Poverty as such is not generally a suspect classification for purposes of equal protection analysis. It is not unconstitutional to charge for the use of a public facility, like the toll on a bridge, merely because people who are too poor to pay it might be disadvantaged. But certain fees can work an unconstitutional harm. Access to courts cannot be burdened by onerous financial requirements impossible for some to meet. So an indigent defendant may not be denied the right to appeal his conviction because he is unable to afford trial transcripts. Nor can a person too poor to pay a fine after conviction be required to serve in jail in lieu of paying the fine for a period longer than the maximum jail term set forth in the statute.

Residency requirements that deny welfare or hospital benefits to indigents who have not lived in the state for more than a year have also been struck down on equal protection grounds. Such also was the fate of Alaska's statute distributing income from oil reserves to citizens in amounts that varied with the length of time they resided in the state.

But the apparent judicial move toward labeling indigents a suspect category requiring courts to strictly scrutinize legislative discriminations was slowed practically to a halt in the 1970s. In one case, the Court saw no constitutional harm in a state statute that limited payments to families under the Aid to Families with Dependent Children program to a maximum of $250 per month, regardless of family size or need.

Also during the 1970s, various litigants strongly challenged the system of financing public secondary education in the United States. Under many state laws, education is financed by taxes levied on property within each district. A richer district would have relatively more to spend per pupil than a poor district. Residents of poor districts attacked the general financing scheme on an equal protection premise: The state should provide equal sums to every pupil within the state, not merely within the district. Two school districts in the San Antonio, Texas, area, for instance, varied between expenditures per pupil of $356 and $594. The Supreme Court turned back this challenge, holding equal protection unavailable in part because it could not be assumed that the poorest people necessarily live within the poorest districts and in part because, unlike earlier cases in which the lack of wealth made some essential service or right unavailable, here there was no claim that schooling itself was beyond the means of any pupil. Said Justice Powell for the five-to-four majority: "At least where wealth is involved, the Equal Protection Clause does not require absolute equality or precisely equal advantages. Nor indeed, in view of the infinite variables affecting the educational process, can any system assure equal quality of education except in the most relative sense." (Although there is thus no federal constitutional restriction on unequal funding, many state courts, construing state constitutions, have disagreed with the Court's reasoning and have issued orders requiring school districts to be equalized throughout their states.)

If there is a connecting strand in these disparate opinions, it is that shifting majorities of justices have sought to walk an exceedingly fine line between manifest injustice and the disparities that will inevitably occur in a market economy. Although indigence is not a suspect category, the impact of some laws on this group of people will on occasion elicit special concerns from courts moved by the plight of those lacking resources to fight for themselves in the legislative arena.

Neutral Terms, Discriminatory Effects

A law neutral on its face may nevertheless have discriminatory effects. It might, for example, be administered in an unequal way. The equal protection spotlight shines as much on an executive's power to administer the laws as on the legislature's power to enact them. That was the vice of literacy tests for voter registrants (page 165)—they gave unbridled power to registrars to enforce in a wholly discriminatory manner.

In the case that established the principle that administrators do not enjoy complete discretion to enforce or fail to enforce the laws as they see fit, a San Francisco ordinance required all laundries to be operated in stone or brick buildings, unless the board of supervisors consented to laundries in some other type of building. Of the 320 laundries in the city, all but 10 were made of wood; 240 were operated by Chinese. Non-Chinese laundry operators in wooden buildings were granted permits to run their businesses; the Chinese laundry operators were not. In 1886, the question reached the Court, which reversed the conviction of a Chinese operator who had not obtained a permit:

The cases present the ordinances in actual operation, and the facts shown establish an administration directed so exclusively against a particular class of persons as to warrant and require the conclusion, that, whatever may have been the intent of the ordinances as adopted, they are applied by the public authorities charged with their administration, and thus representing the State itself, with a mind so unequal and oppressive as to amount to a practical denial by the State of that equal protection of the laws. . . . Though the law itself be fair on its face and impartial in appearance, yet, if it is applied and administered by public authority with an evil eye and an unequal hand, so as practically to make unjust and illegal discriminations between persons in similar circumstances, material to their rights, the denial of equal justice is still within the prohibition of the Constitution.

Aside from regulations administered with an evil eye and an unequal hand, laws neutral on their face can nevertheless have a disparate impact on different groups of people. Large numbers of minority applicants for public jobs might fail a legally required written test, not because the test is intended to discriminate, but because those who failed had not been adequately schooled (perhaps because of past racial bias). In some cases, Congress by statute has declared that discriminatory effect, quite aside from motive of the legislators or purpose of the statute, is enough to invalidate a result. The Supreme Court has read Title VII of the 1964 Civil Rights Act to bar employers from relying on general intelligence tests and high school diplomas unless those criteria were directly helpful in predicting job performance, if blacks were disadvantaged by the requirements.

But suppose the statute is silent about discriminatory effect. Will the Constitution block the enforcement of a law that discriminates only in effect? No, the Court has said; the constitutional standard is different: "Our cases," Justice White has said, "have not embraced the proposition that a law or other official act, without regard to whether it reflects a racially discriminatory purpose, is unconstitutional *solely* because it has a racially disproportionate impact."

How can an invidious purpose be discerned if the inequality is not manifest on a law's face (like a provision barring blacks from serving on a jury)? Not easily, is the answer; the less invidious the effect, the less likely a court will infer an invidious purpose. Thus the Court in 1979 ruled that a Massachusetts law passed constitutional muster in giving preference to veterans over nonveterans in hiring for public employment. A woman challenged the law on the grounds that it discriminated against women as a class. The

Supreme Court, noting that women veterans also got the preference and that the law discriminated against significant numbers of men as well, found that the state did not intend to discriminate against women but against nonveterans—that is, the state was motivated to favor veterans, not to disfavor women.

The problem of intention versus results loomed large when Congress debated reenactment of the Voting Rights Act in 1981 (page 163). In 1980, the Supreme Court had ruled that an at-large election system in the city of Mobile, Alabama, was constitutional, even though it might have had a discriminatory impact on the black community's ability to elect blacks to the city commission, the governing body of the city. Noting that thousands of municipalities employ an at-large (rather than district) system for voting, the Court held that no discriminatory purpose could be shown. In response, the Democratic House voted to adopt a "results" standard in judging the validity of a voting system; the Republican Senate voted to retain the Supreme Court's "purpose" standard. Senator Robert Dole of Kansas offered a compromise that was ultimately accepted: Courts may look to results as one factor in the "totality of circumstances" that establish a case of invidious discrimination, but they may not infer from the Voting Rights Act any right of a particular group to be elected to office in proportion to their numbers in the population.

Benign Use of Suspect Categories: Affirmative Action

In laws requiring "affirmative action" (the pejorative term for which is "reverse discrimination"), the equal protection clause may be asked to swallow its tail. Suppose that Congress, acting under its Fourteenth Amendment and commerce clause powers to enforce equal rights and to redress past wrongs, passes laws requiring race or gender to be taken into account (as Congress has done and as several presidents have done in executive orders). To achieve an integrated community in a black area, some blacks will have to be excluded; likewise, whites in a white area. Is this a "benign" use of otherwise suspect categories?

The intense debate over affirmative action garnered national headlines for months in 1978 before and after the Court's decision in the famous *Baake* case. The University of California at Davis Medical School, with a class size of one hundred, had a special admissions program designed to ensure enrollment in 1973 of sixteen minority applicants (to be selected from three thousand total applicants). Allan Baake, a white ap-

plicant, was refused admission in 1973 and 1974, even though his test scores were significantly higher than some of the minority applicants who were admitted. Baake sued, charging the school with violating the equal protection clause and Title VI of the Civil Rights Act of 1964. The California Supreme Court held that the special program violated the equal protection clause, since it disqualified Baake because of his race in favor of someone less qualified, measured solely by standards that would have applied in the absence of racial concerns.

On appeal, the U.S. Supreme Court, in a welter of opinions, split the baby: Baake was ordered admitted to the school, but the school was not foreclosed from ever using race as a criterion in its admission process. Justice Powell's "swing vote" led to this curious result. Four justices believed that the Fourteenth Amendment bars race from ever being a factor in the admissions process of a public school; hence they voted to admit Baake. Four justices believed that race can properly be considered, and hence voted to overturn the state court's injunction against the school's program. Justice Powell believed that as applied, the school's admission program was constitutionally flawed, and so his was the fifth vote to admit Baake. But he also believed that race could properly be a factor in a revamped admissions program, and so with the other four he made up a majority that permitted some forms of affirmative action.

The school asserted four reasons to support its special admissions program: (1) to reduce the "historic deficit" of groups traditionally disfavored in medical schools and the profession; (2) to counter the effects of past discrimination; (3) to increase the number of physicians who will serve minority communities currently underserved, and (4) to obtain the "educational benefits that flow from an ethnically diverse student body."

Justice Powell and four other justices concluded that the first reason is constitutionally impermissible: "Preferring members of any one group for no reason

Justice Lewis Powell's (left) "swing vote" allowed Alan Bakke (right) to enter medical school but also permitted some forms of affirmative action.

other than race or ethnic origin is discrimination for its own sake. This the Constitution forbids."

The second reason is not absolutely invalid, but a public school may not simply point to it to justify a discriminatory policy. Some legislative, administrative, or judicial findings must first be made that past discriminations existed. No such findings had been made for Davis or for the medical profession in California; moreover, the school was "in no position to make" such findings.

The equal protection clause does not prohibit attempts to increase service to a community that a profession has historically slighted. But again, Justice Powell noted, the school had not demonstrated that its special admissions program "is either needed or geared to promote that goal."

Finally, an institution of higher education may constitutionally seek to attain a diverse student body, even by considering race a relevant factor in that diversity, but not in the rigid way of the Davis Medical School. Its

explicit racial classification . . . tells applicants who are not Negro, Asian, or "Chicano" that they are totally excluded from a specific percentage of the seats in an entering class. No matter how strong their qualifications, quantitative and extracurricular, they are never afforded the chance to compete with applicants from the preferred groups for the special admission seats. At the same time, the preferred applicants have the opportunity to compete for every seat in the class. The fatal flaw in [the school's] preferential program is its disregard of individual rights as guaranteed by the 14th Amendment. Such rights are not absolute. But when a State's distribution of benefits or imposition of burdens hinges on the color of a person's skin or ancestry, that individual is entitled to a demonstration that the challenged classification is necessary to promote a substantial state interest. [Davis] has failed to carry this burden.

The school's failure lay in its determination to assign a fixed number of places to a minority group. However, when minority status is but one among many considerations, it will withstand constitutional attack:

> The file of a particular black applicant may be examined for his potential contribution to diversity without the factor of race being decisive when compared, for example, with that of an applicant identified as an Italian-American if the latter is thought to exhibit qualities more likely to promote beneficial educational pluralism. Such qualities could include exceptional personal talents, unique work or service experience, leadership potential, maturity, demonstrated compassion, a history of overcoming disadvantage, ability to communicate with the poor, or other qualifications deemed important. . . . This kind of program treats each applicant as an individual in the admissions process. The applicant who loses out on the last available seat to another candidate receiving a "plus" on the basis of ethnic background will not have been foreclosed from all consideration for that seat simply because he was not the right color or had the wrong surname. It would mean only that his combined qualifications, which may have included similar nonobjective factors, did not outweigh those of the other applicant. His qualifications would have been weighed fairly and competitively, and he would have no basis to complain of unequal treatment under the 14th Amendment.

In later cases, the Court has stepped gingerly through the minefield of affirmative action. It approved a voluntary affirmative action plan that was collectively bargained by a union and employer, setting aside half of all openings in a plant training program until the time when the proportion of the black workers in the plant equals the proportion of blacks in the local workforce. It also affirmed a congressionally imposed requirement that 10 percent of any federal grants for local public works projects be "set aside" for "minority business enterprises," defined as business at least 50 percent owned by minority group members. On the other hand, the Court condemned a lower court's decree, attempting to remedy the past effects of discrimination in the Memphis Fire Department,

that newly hired minority firefighters would take precedence in a seniority system over whites who would otherwise be retained during layoffs necessitated by a downturn in the economy. It also held unconstitutional a Michigan school board policy of laying off more senior white teachers before minority teachers.

Despite the Reagan Administration's extreme unhappiness with affirmative action, the Court has made it clear that certain programs, handled with finesse and intended to redress past wrongs, do not offend the Constitution. In July 1986, a six-to-three majority strongly rebuffed the administration's central argument that racial preferences may never be used except to redress actual victims of discrimination. The Court held that race-conscious remedies "may be appropriate where an employer or a labor union has engaged in persistent or egregious discrimination, or where necessary to dissipate the lingering effects of pervasive discrimination." Moreover, said the Court, affirmative action hiring plans are not necessarily illegitimate even when the benefits go to members of minority groups who were not personally discriminated against. At the same time, the Court unanimously held that a racial preference should not be an automatic remedy and that courts should be sparing in ordering or approving preferences for minority members who were not themselves victims of discrimination.

The core of affirmative action is unlikely to be eliminated, though its application in particular cases will doubtless continue to perplex and to be unpredictable. It is part of the larger debate over the meaning of equality, a debate that can never be wholly resolved in a society that constantly changes.

As I write, the day's paper brings the news that a rising number of Americans who work at home—spurred by advances in computer and telephone technology—is stirring a controversy over local zoning ordinances, which tend to prohibit businesses in residential neighborhoods. A Chicago ordinance bans "the installation of any mechanical or electrical equipment customarily incident to the practice" of a profession. Two computer programmers were told that in working at home they violate the ordinance. But many zoning regulations customarily permit doctors and lawyers to work at home. Are distinctions between old professions and new ones constitutionally sound? In the changing patterns of life are thus born disputations over equality, arguments that will flourish as long as Americans cherish the right to formal equality before the law.

Part 5

Business and the Economy

Chapter 17 Protecting Property and Economic Interests

The Importance of Property

No constitutional term has undergone a greater metamorphosis, nor been the subject of a vaster outpouring of commentary, than that of property. For more than two millennia, philosophers have argued over its meaning and justification, and for three centuries it has been central in a debate over the scope of political power. It is, moreover, a concept over which people retain a passionate concern, from their earliest days in the sandbox when the child first learns about "mine" and "yours" to the adult's lifetime occupation in using nature and machine to grow and build, distribute and sell, and store and consume.

Property rights are often contrasted with human rights, like the liberty interests discussed in Chapters 11–14, but the distinction is artificial. I am no more free if my home is gone when I return at night than if I were prevented from complaining about its disappearance. Neither social nor personal life is possible without stability and the fulfillment of a wide array of expectations. A state that winked at theft would be lawless twice over. As Justice Stewart once put it:

> The dichotomy between personal liberties and property rights is a false one. Property does not have rights. People have rights. The right to enjoy property without unlawful deprivation, no less than the right to speak or the right

to travel, is, in truth, a "personal" right, whether the "property" in question be a welfare check, a home or a savings account. In fact, a fundamental interdependence exists between the personal right to liberty and the personal right in property. Neither could have meaning without the other.

Just as the right to speak and publish must be guaranteed if we are to have any hope of tempering the power of government, so the right to own and use property privately must be guaranteed if we are to have a place, an Archimedean refuge, from which to exercise those freedoms. Societies in which all productive property is publicly owned afford their citizens no space from which they can resist the encroachment of government into their lives. Quite aside from its economic value, the private realm is an essential aspect of the general political system of checks and balances. Government may check the exercise of private economic power, as we will see, but if it does so by abolishing the private realm altogether, nothing is left to check the ultimate power of government itself.

From an economic perspective, of course, private property is what makes a capitalist market system possible—with all that implies for production and innovation. Capitalism could not have developed without the rule of law, which protected property from arbitrary seizure by the state and hence provided the incentive to invest. Only the fear of rebellion occasionally restrained absolutist monarchies from simply confiscating what they wanted. According to Friedrich A. Hayek, "There is probably no single factor which has contributed more to the prosperity of the West than the relative certainty of the law which has prevailed here."

Part of the difficulty of the subject, however, and with portents for constitutional law, is that the failure of the rule of law contributed mightily, in England and elsewhere, to the creation of private property— the centuries-long enclosure movement essentially deprived the peasant class of land that generations had worked in common and gave dominion of the commons to a landlord class. The effect of this movement surely was, as Paul Johnson has written, "the universal establishment of rights of freehold property which encouraged the cultivator to invest in agriculture, and so brought about the slow but cumulatively astonishing agricultural revolution which marked the seventeenth and eighteenth centuries." That revolution helped spark the industrial revolution itself, with the benefits and pains we have felt ever since, but it was largely accomplished by the radical redistribution of property rights and benefits that rule-of-law theorists deplore when carried on by activist welfare states today. As the old quatrain expressed it:

> They put in jail the man or woman
> Who steals the goose from off the common,
> Yet let the larger felon loose
> Who steals the common from the goose.

Redistribution was also a fact in early America; until roughly the middle of the nineteenth century, much private land was taken, without compensation, to aid entrepreneurs in building roads, bridges, canals, and railroads.

The rights of property were unquestionably a fundamental concern of the framers. They knew their English history; they had lived, after all, under an English king. Madison, showing why the causes of faction could not and ought not to be controlled, had said in the fateful *Federalist* No. 10 that "the first object of government" is to protect the diverse "faculties of men, from which the rights of property originate." Here was a more sophisticated version of Locke's fundamental dictum that "government has no other end but the preservation of property."

The framers had seen what could happen when, in times of recession, representative assemblies were pressed to defer payment of debts or abrogate indebtedness altogether, a situation no less important than the propensity of monarchs to tax or steal as they desired. The framers also understood the consequences of uncoordinated economic policy that left the states to squabble among themselves, acting like petty and jealous principalities, erecting trade barriers and seeking to protect their citizens at the expense of other Americans. Alexander Hamilton was a forceful proponent of creating a political system receptive to capital development. Given all this, an economic determinist might argue that property and financial well-being were the driving forces of the convention.

In 1913, Charles Beard published his famous *An Economic Interpretation of the Constitution*, contending just that. Beard argued that the Constitution was essentially the work (and a conspiratorial coup d' etat at that) of a conservative economic minority—capitalists, not farmers—who created a national government to protect their interests from the depredations of the states. Hence they gave sweeping and exclusive power to the new federal government to regulate commerce, conduct war and international affairs, and govern the vast tracts of land to the west. They diminished state power—one of the few instances in the original Constitution—in economic matters. States are forbidden from issuing bills of credit, substituting paper currency for gold and silver in payment of debt, and "impairing the obligation of contracts."

For more than forty years, the Beard thesis became the dominant explanation of the motivation that underlay the framing of the Constitution. But in 1956 and 1958, two works—Robert E. Brown's *Charles Beard and the Constitution* and Forrest McDonald's *We the People: The Economic Origins of the Constitution*—effectively demolished Beard's claim that the framers had undemocratically staged a coup d' etat to further their narrow economic interests. The rights of property and economic expectation are significant values, protected not only in the Constitution itself but also in the Fifth (and later in the Fourteenth) Amendment's due process clause and in the just compensation clause. But they do not explain and cannot be made to explain the entire structure of government or the spirit of constitutionalism in America.

Founding Father

William Churchill Houston

(did not sign the Constitution)

William Churchill Houston was born around 1746 and died in Frankford, Pennsylvania, on August 12, 1788, while en route to the South to recover from tuberculosis. He studied at Princeton, receiving an A.B. in 1768, after which he was made a master of the grammar school and a tutor. In 1771, he was promoted to professor of mathematics and natural philosophy. Five years later, he joined the revolutionary effort, first as captain of the foot militia of Somerset County and later on active duty at Princeton. He left the military in 1777. In 1775–1776, he was deputy secretary of the Continental Congress, and in 1777, a member of the New Jersey Assembly. The following year, he was named a member of the New Jersey Council of Safety, and the year after that elected to the Continental Congress. In 1781, he was admitted to the bar and also named clerk of the New Jersey Supreme Court. From 1782 to 1785, he was collector of Continental taxes in New Jersey, a member of several official state committees, and a prosperous attorney, as well as serving again in the old Congress from 1784 to 1785. He was a New Jersey delegate to both the Annapolis and Philadelphia conventions.

Defining Property

Property, like obscenity, is one of those concepts that seems intuitively easy to define until we try to do it. We do not always even know it when we see it, as the eighteenth-century French writer Jean Francois Marmontel bitterly recalled in his *Memoirs*. Marmontel

> tells us of an interview with Bassompierre, a bookseller, or, as we should now call him in this department of his business, a publisher of Liege. Bassompierre had made such a good thing out of the sale of Marmontel's famous *Belisaire* that he felt compelled to call upon the author, who was passing through his town, and thank him for the service he had rendered. Marmontel was furious. "What," says he, "you first rob me of the fruits of my labours, and then have the effrontery to come and brag about it under my nose!" Bassompierre was amazed. It had not struck him in that light. "Monsier," said he, "you forget Liege is a free country, and we have nothing to do with you and your *privileges*."

Walton Hamilton and Irene Till once wittily defined property as "a euphonious collocation of letters which serves as a general term for the miscellany of equities that persons hold in the commonwealth." Blackstone, whose opinion was taken as law in revolutionary America and for many years after, said: "The right of property is that sole and despotic dominion which one man claims and exercises over the external things of the world, in total exclusion of the right of any other individual in the universe. It consists in the free use, enjoyment, and disposal of all a person's acquisitions, without any control or diminution save only by the laws of the land." The modern legal definition is crisper: Property is the "legal relationship between persons with respect to a thing."

These definitions are purely formal. They do not tell us what equities may be held in the commonwealth or what the property relationship must or may be between persons. A commonsense view might hold that "things" means just that: objects, land, trees, houses. But from a constitutional perspective, what constitutes a "thing" is not so easily answered. Not merely corporeal things are of value: In a market society, people's right to sell their labor is no less valuable than their horses or cars. Moreover, as Blackstone noted, the essential value is not ownership, but "use, enjoyment, and disposal." What good is it to say that the law must afford me a remedy against trespassers if the state may prevent me from operating a mill or factory on my land?

Like other terms in the Constitution, the meaning of the property and liberty protected by the due process clauses is not confined to a dictionary definition—or even to what the framers intended. Indeed, it is no small irony that those who would press on the courts a jurisprudence of original intention find congenial a radically changed meaning of property. Originally, *property* meant a thing owned. As the legal historian Morton J. Horwitz notes: "The premise underlying the law [in the late eighteenth century] . . . was that land was not essentially an instrumental good or a productive asset but rather a private estate to be enjoyed for its own sake." In time, at least for a time, constitutionally protected property came to mean every use to which a thing could be put, including its "exchange value" (the value to be extracted from any thing, by selling, renting, or otherwise exchanging it). As we will see, the courts overlooked Blackstone's important caveat, that the despotic dominion an owner exercises over his property is always subject to control by the law of the land—in constitutional terms, by due process of law.

In the widest sense, protecting property means protecting economic transactions beyond mere title. It encompasses the contracts we make for the exchange of land, goods, and services, and the right to dedicate our personal energies toward productive goals. No more than personal liberty, however, the constitutional right to property in this widest sense cannot be absolute, for actions and use can hurt. A government that surrendered its power to prevent and redress harm in the name of constitutionalism would have exalted one aspect of life over many others. That much our Constitution does not do (though many, including a majority of the Supreme Court, once supposed it did). The Constitution shields economic interests from irrational and wholly arbitrary behavior, but it does not validate a particular economic theory.

The Contract Clause

The Constitution prohibits states (but not the federal government) from passing any "law impairing the obligation of contracts." The contract clause was aimed at legislation that would absolve debtors of their financial obligations. But it was first pressed into service in cases involving state efforts to rescind public grants, and it would later become the core of an argument that the states could do nothing that interfered with the benefits of the bargain that individuals had struck.

The first important contract clause case involved the fraudulent grant in 1795 of huge tracts of land along the Yazoo River, encompassing most of Ala-

bama and Mississippi, to several companies in Georgia. Many legislators were bribed to vote the land grants, and the stink prompted a new legislature the next year to vote to annul the grant. But the land was no longer in the grantees' possession, for they had in the meantime sold it to investors, who understandably resisted the state's attempt to regain it. In 1810, in the landmark case *Fletcher v. Peck,* Chief Justice Marshall declared that title had vested in the good faith purchasers from the original grantees and that the contract clause prohibited Georgia from reclaiming it. (The political fallout from the Yazoo scandal was long lasting. As its chronicler, C. Peter Magrath, observed: "For three decades the name 'Yazoo' stood for a series of events which scandalized the state of Georgia, troubled Congress and the administrations of Washington, Adams, Jefferson, and Madison, and divided Jefferson's Republican party.")

Marshall, who himself was a land speculator (at least once on the brink of ruin), followed *Fletcher* in *Dartmouth College v. Woodward* in 1819. Dartmouth's royal charter provided that its board of trustees would be self-perpetuating. The New Hampshire legislature passed a law to permit the state to appoint trustees,

Dartmouth College

thus changing it from a private to a public college. Marshall held that the charter was a contract and that the state was bound to respect it. (It was in this case that Dartmouth's counsel, Daniel Webster, concluded his plea to a mesmerized Court with the words, "It is, Sir, as I have said, a small college. And yet there are those who love it!")

A few weeks later, the Court turned the contract clause against a New York insolvency law that permitted debtors to discharge all financial obligations by surrendering their property. By allowing debtors to avoid their preexisting commitments, the state law was thus unconstitutional. This case went to the heart of the contract clause; it was the very reason the framers included it in the original Constitution. (The contract clause does not bar Congress from passing bankruptcy laws that have the same effect as the law voided in the New York case. Article I, Section 8, explicitly empowers Congress to enact bankruptcy laws.)

Eight years later, in 1827, the Court heavily dented the clause in holding in *Ogden v. Saunders* that debtors could be discharged by a state law enacted before they obligated themselves to their creditors—the earlier rule was limited to application of insolvency laws enacted after the debt was made. *Ogden* was the only constitutional case in which Marshall dissented in thirty-four years as chief justice, and it led to the unraveling of the contract clause as an important bulwark of private interests against the state, for it meant that those who make contracts must do so subject to existing laws of the state.

Nor was that the only limitation on the seemingly broad sweep of the contract clause. In the *Dartmouth* case, Justice Story had noted that in granting a corporate charter, a legislature may always reserve to itself the power to amend the charter (a power that New Hampshire had failed to reserve in Dartmouth's charter). Two years after Marshall's death, the new chief justice, Roger Brooke Taney, held in the famous *Charles River Bridge* case that a Massachusetts charter

Justice Joseph Story's opinion in the Dartmouth *case was a major early contribution to the law of corporations.*

to a private turnpike company to build a toll bridge did not bar the state from later granting a charter to another company to build a competing free bridge. In the absence of explicit language, the Court refused to read into the earlier charter an agreement to perpetuate the toll company's monopoly.

More sweepingly, the Court held in a series of cases that the states' "police power"—the common law power to protect the health, safety, good order, comfort, and general welfare of the community—may not be bargained away. A legislature may not bind its successors by promising, for example, not to exercise its power of eminent domain or to refrain from prohibiting lotteries.

The line is thin between impermissible retroactive aid for the insolvent and permissible retroactive prohibitions based on the police power. If I may be stopped from doing something that I had been given a charter to do, because a later legislature believes that what I am doing is noxious, may not the legislature interfere with the payment of debts, on the ground that the creditor should understand that money is lent subject to laws that the state might one day make? In 1934, the Supreme Court appeared to be but a step away from emasculating the contract clause when it approved Minnesota's "mortgage moratorium" law barring banks for two years in the midst of the Depression from foreclosing mortgages. But such a view was too severe. The Court noted that the Minnesota law was temporary and did not repudiate the debts, but was limited to changes in the remedy provided in the law for breach of the contract. Said Chief Justice Hughes: "If state power exists to give temporary relief from the enforcement of contracts in the presence of disasters due to physical causes such as fire, flood, or earthquake, that power cannot be said to be nonexistent when the urgent public need demanding such relief is produced [by] economic causes."

Nevertheless, until recently the Court did not struggle to uphold contract clause claims. In a 1965 case, the Court permitted Texas to extinguish a contractual right (not merely a remedy) it had granted to landowners to reclaim their interest in lands they had forfeited for failure to pay delinquent interest.

But in 1977, the Court held against New Jersey on a contract clause claim. In 1962, New Jersey and New York enacted a statutory covenant on behalf of the Port Authority of New York and New Jersey as security for its bondholders. The covenant made it difficult for the Port Authority to use bond revenues to subsidize rail operations. Twelve years later, New Jersey repealed the covenant, and a four-to-three Court majority held that although courts must generally defer to states when they interfere with private contracts, the courts must scrutinize any state attempts to impair their own contractual obligations, as in this case. The Court held that New Jersey had not acted reasonably and struck down the law repealing the covenant.

In 1978, the Court expanded the reach of the contract clause to protect private contracts against state claims of necessity when it struck down a Minnesota law requiring employers with established pension plans to modify retroactively the obligations they assumed toward their employees. But in later cases, the Court appears to have pulled away from the more exacting scrutiny it announced in the Minnesota case. Thus, in a 1983 case, the Court upheld a Kansas law that effectively blocked a private supplier of natural gas from taking advantage of a clause in a contract that required a private utility to pay more for gas whenever the federal government increased the price at which gas could be sold. The Court said that when a contract clause claim is asserted, courts must undertake a three-part inquiry: Was a contractual right substantially impaired? If so, did the state have any significant and legitimate public purpose in regulating? If it did, was the contractual modification reasonably related to the reasons justifying the legislation? Unless the complainant can show that the state had no legitimate purpose in imposing a substantial impairment or that it had failed to adjust the modification to the purpose, the courts must defer to the states. It seems unlikely that many challenges will withstand the rigors of this test, given a Court that in modern times is generally willing to defer to legislative judgments in the economic arena.

A "Strange Misconception": Economic Due Process

In a fit of moralism in the 1850s, the New York legislature enacted a broad prohibition statute, requiring the immediate destruction of all liquor except that used for medicinal purposes. A liquor seller challenged the law in court. The seller's theory was startling: Since the commercial value of its liquor stock, undoubtedly property before prohibition, was "annihilated" by the law, the ban amounted to a deprivation of property without due process of law. Without explaining why the statute, duly enacted, lacked due process, in 1856 the New York Court of Appeals (the state's highest court) struck down the law on due process grounds. This was perhaps the earliest application of a doctrine that would hold sway for more than forty years in the United States Supreme Court, the doctrine of substantive due process of law. Under this doctrine, courts felled laws that were substantively "unfair" or that "wrongly" interfered with a person's use of property or liberty to contract.

The Supreme Court first alluded to this conception of the federal due process clause in 1857 in the *Dred Scott* case. In striking down the Missouri Compromise, which forbade slaveholding in the territories, Chief Justice Taney said that "an Act of Congress which deprives a citizen of the United States of his liberty or property, merely because he came himself or brought his property into a particular Territory of the United States, and who had committed no offense against the laws, could hardly be dignified with the name of due process of law." Taney did not elaborate. He may have been supposing that individuals could be deprived of their property only after a trial, though as we have seen, the nature of this "property" was unlike any other kind for which Americans could claim constitutional protection.

These were precursors. The full-bodied doctrine awaited the Fourteenth Amendment's due process clause, giving the Supreme Court new language with which to scrutinize state regulations that seemed to impinge on economic activity during the burst of industrialization in the later nineteenth century. It was the age of laissez-faire: To the adherents of the new economic orthodoxy, prompted by the social Darwinism of the day (in particular by the writings of Herbert Spencer and William Graham Sumner), any governmental interference in business was a danger to the natural order. By the 1890s, a new Court, imbued with these notions, saw anything that upset the natural economic order as a violation also of the Fourteenth Amendment.

That was not the Court's initial instinct. In the 1873 *Slaughterhouse Cases,* the Court explicitly declined to read in the due process clause any absolute protection for the livelihood of butchers against a municipal ordinance creating a monopoly of the slaughtering business. Indeed, Justice Miller proclaimed (in one of the worst predictions the Court has ever made), that "we doubt very much whether any action of a State not directed by way of discrimination against the negroes as a class, or on account of their race, will ever be held to come within the purview" of the due process clause. Dissenting, Justice Bradley said that "a law which prohibits a large class of citizens from adopting a lawful employment, or from following a lawful employment previously adopted, does deprive them of liberty as well as of property, without due process of law. Their right of choice is a portion of their liberty; their occupation is their property." He overlooked the opportunity to quote an ancient authority, Sir Edward Coke, whose writings profoundly influenced

the growth of the common law. Railing against the 1624 Statute of Monopolies, Coke contended that "if a grant be made to any man, to have the sole making of cards, or the sole dealing with any other trade, that grant is against the liberty and freedom of the subject, that before did, or lawfully might have used that trade, and consequently against this great charter" Magna Carta itself (source of the due process clause).

For two decades or so, the *Slaughterhouse* majority view survived, but it grew increasingly infirm. In the 1877 *Granger Cases,* the Court upheld Illinois's regulation of the rates grain elevators charged their customers. Chief Justice Waite rebuffed the silo owners,

claiming violation of due process, by viewing the property as "clothed with a public interest" (because "used in a manner to make it of public consequence and [affecting] the community at large"). Jurisprudence reaching back to the seventeenth century permitted governments to regulate property "affected with a public interest." The Court refused even to look at the reasonableness of the rates set. "We know," Waite said, "that this is a power which may be abused; but that is no argument against its existence. For protection against abuses by legislatures the people must resort to the polls."

Later that year, Justice Miller noted that "the docket

of this court is crowded with cases in which we are asked to hold that state courts and state legislatures have deprived their own citizens of life, liberty, or property without due process of law. There is here abundant evidence that there exists some strange misconception of the scope of this provision as found in the 14th Amendment."

But this "strange misconception" would soon capture a judicial majority. Three strands of doctrine intertwined to make the due process rope that would strangle state regulations from the 1890s into the 1930s. First, regulations governing purely private businesses that did not affect a public interest would be more carefully scrutinized. What was or was not "clothed with a public interest" was ultimately a metaphysical question that had no firm answer in legal theory, permitting the judges a wide discretion to void laws of which they disapproved. Second, state laws could not limitlessly regulate; "this power to regulate is not a power to destroy." Third, the due process clauses protect "persons," but most of the business interests affected by rate and other regulations were business corporations. Is a corporation a person? Yes. In 1886, without discussion, Chief Justice Waite cut off debate on this point at the outset of oral argument in a case turning on the power of a state to discriminate in taxation between natural persons and corporations. "The Court does not wish to hear argument on the question [whether corporations are persons]. We are all of the opinion [that they are]."

In 1897, the Court took the fateful step. In *Allgeyer v. Louisiana*, the Court for the first time struck down a state law on the grounds that it violated substantive due process. The particular law prohibited anyone from insuring property in Louisiana through any marine insurance company that had not "complied in all respects" with Louisiana law. The next year, the Court invalidated a railroad rate regulation scheme, having earlier held that the reasonableness of rates was a matter for "judicial investigation." The Court

held that a railroad is constitutionally entitled to a "fair" rate of return on the value of its land. Dubbed the "fair value fallacy," because the value of the land depended on the rates railroads could charge, this circular doctrine meant that the states had to give back to the railroads the value of what the regulation took away because the rates were exorbitant. The Court finally rejected the doctrine in 1940.

Substantive due process came into its prime in 1905. From then until the mid-1930s, the doctrine of economic due process consisted of two broad strands mirroring the operative words in the constitutional clause: liberty to contract and the right to use property free from state regulation. (Contractual liberty is different from contractual impairment: The former deals with laws that prevent people from entering into contracts, the latter with laws that interfere with contracts already made.) The hallmark of this doctrine was inconsistency, since it depended so much on judicial intuition about what was reasonable or not. From 1899 to 1937, the Court voided state and federal laws under the due process clause in 197 cases; it upheld 369 state laws during the same period. But the numbers are perhaps less important than the perception, for the Court's willingness to scrutinize economic legislation—and to strike down many state laws—undoubtedly kept many more off the books.

Liberty of Contract

The case that launched the liberty of contract doctrine was *Lochner v. New York*. If *Dred Scott* is the Court's Benedict Arnold, *Lochner* remains its Aaron Burr—popular for a time, but remembered with more than a faint distaste. After an extensive investigation into conditions in the baking industry, the New York legislature passed a law limiting bakery employees to ten-hour days and sixty-hour weeks. Discounting the plentiful evidence that long hours in bakeshops were unhealthy, Justice Peckham for the five-to-four majority declared that the law was "an illegal interference with the rights of individuals, both employers and employees, to make contracts regarding labor upon such terms as they may think best, or which they may agree upon with the other parties to such contracts."

In earlier cases, the Court had upheld an eight-hour day for miners and a six-day week for barbers. Justice Peckham distinguished the miners' case, but ignored the barbers' case.

Perhaps too great embarrassments are better forgotten. Perhaps, too, the distinction between bakers and barbers inheres in the regularity with which judges frequent barbers and the infrequency with which they talk to bakers. The scientific difference between resting on Sundays and stopping after ten hours seems too shallow to support the difference. It may also be that state commmissions and public investigating bodies smacked a little too much of socialism. In the *Barbers' Case* and in at least one state case upholding the power of the state to regulate the practice of barbering, the political muscle of barbers— a free people asking the legislature for help to protect the public—outshone the efforts of public bodies making inquiries. Noble motives will go for naught when not disguised by public relations men.

It is one of the many curiosities of this case that the Court upheld the rights of bakers in a case brought by a bakery. No baker asked for this sweeping protection of his sacred right to contract. As the Court had pointed out in the earlier mining case, the defense of the employer was "not so much that his right to contract has been infringed upon, but that the act works a peculiar hardship to his employees, whose right to labor as long as they please is alleged to be thereby violated. The argument would certainly come with better grace and greater cogency from the latter class." Lochner, the owner of the bakery (whose con-

Justice Rufus Wheeler Peckham's decision in Lochner v. New York *overturned a law limiting the work hours for bakery employees.*

viction for letting an employee work more than sixty hours a week the Court set aside), was arguing less for his employee's right to agree to spend all his time baking than for his own right to contract with an employee who was legally free to work for as much time as Lochner cared to have him work (on pain of not hiring him at all).

This was laissez-faire rampant. Justice Holmes, dissenting, found the "case decided upon an economic theory which a large part of the country does not entertain. . . . The Fourteenth Amendment does not enact Mr. Herbert Spencer's Social Statics." Noting the many regulations the Court had sustained, though they interfered with a similar liberty, Holmes said that "a constitution is not intended to embody a particular economic theory, whether of paternalism and the organic relation of the citizen to the State or of laissez-faire."

Nevertheless, liberty of contract had become an established gloss on the due process clause, and the Court applied it in a wavering line of cases in two ways: striking down the law when the legislative goal was held to interfere with a fundamental liberty interest and, if the goal was permissible, when the means chosen were not reasonably related to it. The legislative goal would always be illegitimate if it took property from Peter and gave it to Paul solely for the purpose of redistributing wealth or if it sought solely to equalize bargaining power. Thus a state could not outlaw "yellow dog" contracts—a worker's agreement not to join a union as a condition of employment—for this would be to prevent workers from exercising their right to bargain away their union membership, an exchange that would perhaps land them a job. The only exceptions were hour limitations for women, who were held to be a disadvantaged class because of their physical characteristics and social role as childbearers, although the Court subsequently struck down a District of Columbia minimum wage law for women.

Oliver Wendell Holmes, Jr.

Economic Regulations

In many other cases that could not be squeezed into a liberty of contract frame, the Court struck down economic regulations because they interfered with the businessperson's property interest. State legislatures were barred from enacting price regulations, except for a few rare industries that the Court deemed "affected with a public interest" (like utilities). Nor could legislatures restrict companies from competing in a new line of business—for example, by requiring an ice company to demonstrate that existing plants were insufficient to meet public need or by prohibiting corporations from owning pharmacies unless all stockholders were pharmacists.

Not just ends but also means fell victim to the Court's due process axe. Thus it was permissible for a state to regulate the materials used in manufacturing mattresses to protect consumer health. But a law that prohibited use of "shoddy" (cut-up fabric) was unconstitutional because it was "purely arbitrary." The Court emphasized other, less intrusive measures the state might have taken, like requiring the shoddy to be sterilized and the mattresses to be inspected. Justice Holmes dissented, as he did in most of these cases, on the ground that the Court was substituting its judgment for the legislature's on the adequacy of remedy; he thought the degree of danger in unsanitary fill and the difficulty of inspection should permit the legislature to opt for the more drastic remedy.

The Fall of Economic Due Process: Toward Minimal Rationality

Economic due process unraveled in the 1930s in the midst of the Great Depression, when the general population would no longer countenance the results of laissez-faire theories. The Court disentangled itself in two decisions, one in 1934 and the other in 1937. In the earlier case, the Court upheld a New York law establishing an administrative scheme to stabilize the price of milk in the state. Said Justice Roberts:

> Neither property rights nor contract rights are absolute; for government cannot exist if the citizen may at will use his property to the detriment of his fellows, or exercise his freedom of contract to work them harm. Equally fundamental with the private right is that of the public to regulate it in the common interest. [The] guaranty of due process [demands] only that the law shall not be unreasonable, arbitrary or capricious, and that the means selected shall have a real and substantial relation to the object sought to be attained. . . . [But] the public control of rates or prices is [supposedly] per se unreasonable and unconstitutional save as applied to business affected with a public interest, . . . a business . . . such as is commonly called a public utility; or a business in its nature a monopoly.
>
> . . . The milk industry, it is said, possesses none of these [characteristics]. . . . But if, as must be conceded, the industry is subject to regulation in the public interest, what constitutional principle bars the state from correcting existing maladjustments by legislation touching prices? We think there is no such principle. The due process clause makes no mention of sales or of prices any more than it speaks of business or contracts or buildings or other incidents of property. . . . There is no closed class or category of businesses affected with a public interest. . . . So far as the requirement of due process is concerned, [a] state is free to adopt whatever economic policy may reasonably be deemed to promote public welfare, and to enforce that policy by legislation adapted to its purpose. The courts are without authority either to declare such policy, or, when it is declared by the legislator, to override it. If the laws passed are seen to have a reasonable relation to a proper legislative purpose, and are neither arbitrary nor discriminatory, the requirements of due process are [satisfied].

The Court thus returned to the logic of the *Granger Cases*, now seeing that modern conditions made it impossible to divine a line between businesses that do and do not affect a public interest.

In the later case, the Court overruled its earlier holding that a state minimum wage for women is unconstitutional. "The legislature was entitled to adopt measures to reduce the evils of the 'sweating system,' the exploiting of workers at wages so low as to be insufficient to meet the bare cost of living, thus making their very helplessness the occasion of a most injurious competition. The legislature had the right to consider that its minimum wage requirements would be an important aid in carrying out its policy of protection."

From the late thirties, the Court has demonstrated a determination to avoid the role of economic czar that it had played during the first decades of the twentieth century. In the *Carolene Products* case, in sustaining a federal ban on the interstate shipment of "filled milk," the Court held that economic regulations would be presumed constitutional and announced that the review of such laws henceforth would be minimal. If the legislature has a "rational basis" for enacting a law, the courts may not interfere.

For fifty years, the Court has adhered to the minimal rationality standard of review in economic cases. In 1963, in upholding a Kansas law limiting the business of "debt adjusting" to lawyers, Justice Black remarked that "unquestionably there are arguments showing that the business of adjusting debts has social utility, but such arguments are properly addressed to the legislature, not to us. We refuse to sit as a 'super legislature' to weigh the wisdom of legislation, and we emphatically refuse to go back to the time when courts used the Due Process Clause 'to strike down state laws, regulatory of business and industrial conditions, because they may be unwise, improvident, or out of harmony with a particular school of thought.' . . . Whether the legislature takes for its textbook Adam Smith, Herbert Spencer, Lord Keynes, or some other is no concern of ours."

Justice Stone's famous footnote four in *Carolene Products* sharply distinguished between the deference courts must pay to legislatures when enacting laws affecting business and the economy and laws that affect "discrete and insular minorities" and that are within the specific prohibitions of the Constitution. Economic due process has practically vanished, but substantive due process lives on, not always internally consistent, as we saw in Chapter 13.

"The Petty Larceny of the Police Power": Taking Versus Regulating

At common law, the sovereign could take private property for public use, as long as he compensated the owner for the loss. This power of "eminent domain" was recognized in the Fifth Amendment, which requires the federal government to pay "just compensation" for any property taken. Both a public purpose and a just compensation are constitutionally prerequisite to the taking. In the revolutionary days that saw the just compensation clause become part of our fundamental law, it was unlikely that the state would take someone's land for a private purpose— the usual reason for confiscation was to permit construction of a highway, canal, or bridge.

The Fifth Amendment applied, of course, only to the federal government. By 1800, only three state constitutions—those of Massachusetts, Pennsylvania, and Vermont—required compensation for takings, and despite the provision, the Pennsylvania Supreme Court hewed in 1802 to the medieval notion that landowners held their property at the sufferance of the state, which could take the land to build roads without compensation. Most state legislatures, including Pennsylvania's, began to provide for compensation in turnpike and canal statutes, while denying any necessity to do so. As late as the 1830s, South Carolina took and did not pay, with the approval of the state courts. But many states would furnish compensation only if the taking was for a public purpose, and until about 1850 railroad companies and others in many states, exercising what amounted to a power of eminent domain, took property without being held liable to compensate the owners.

By midcentury, those who had profited from the loose rules permitting transfer of property came to understand that their own holdings were under threat unless the constitutional standards were tightened, and so the rules began to change. With the ratification of the Fourteenth Amendment, landowners could look to the federal courts for protection. By the end of the century, the constitutional rule was fixed. In 1896, the Supreme Court held that a state may take property only for a public use, and in 1897 it held that just compensation is an essential element of any exercise of eminent domain.

What constitutes a public use is largely for the states themselves to say. Just as the courts defer to legislatures in passing on the validity of economic regulations, so they are ordinarily unwilling to contradict a state's declaration that the taking is for a public purpose. In a very recent case, the Supreme Court upheld the Hawaii legislature's decision to force the seventy-two private landowners who held nearly half the state's private property (nearly half the rest was held by the state and federal government) to sell to their tenants. As long as the landowners were compensated, the legislature's determination to correct "the land oligopoly problem" was held to be a rational exercise of eminent domain. Said Justice O'Connor: "The mere fact that property taken outright by eminent domain is transferred in the first instance to private beneficiaries does not condemn that taking as having only a private purpose. . . . It is only the taking's purpose, and not its mechanics, that must pass scrutiny under the Public Use Clause."

The framers did not envision a modern economy. Had *property* remained what it meant to them, few

Founding Father

John McClurg

(did not sign the Constitution)

James McClurg was born near Hampton in Elizabeth City, Virginia, around 1746, and died in Virginia on July 9, 1823. He attended the College of William and Mary, graduating with an outstanding record in 1762. He traveled to Scotland to study medicine at the University of Edinburgh, received his M.D. in 1770, and continued postgraduate studies in Paris and London. A capable individual, his medical writings were acclaimed. In 1773, he returned to his home state. He was not an early participant in the revolutionary cause, but during the war served as physician general and director of hospitals under Virginia's militia. In 1779, he was named professor of anatomy and medicine at his alma mater. However, the chair was discontinued in 1783 and he lost this post. Around this time, he moved to Richmond, where he stayed for the rest of his life. McClurg's interest in medicine always took first priority. In 1820 and 1821, he was president of Virginia's medical society. In 1787, he became a delegate to the Philadelphia Convention, but only after Patrick Henry and Richard Henry Lee both declined the post. At the debates, he favored life tenure for the executive, separation of all executive and legislative functions, and a federal negative on state laws. For a few years during Washington's administration, he was on the Virginia executive council. That was his last involvement in government.

constitutional difficulties would plague the exercise of eminent domain. Today, however, we value property for its productive capacity, not simply for the possession of it as evidenced by a title deed. Modern regulations constantly interfere with the ways we use that property; indeed, that is their very purpose. The problem of taking is thus transferred from the confiscation of title to the losses that flow from regulation.

When government regulates an activity that is clearly injurious to the public, the courts are unlikely to find compensable harm done to the owner. A manufacturer that pollutes the air or waterways will not find the courts receptive to its plea that it be compensated for loss of the opportunity to continue to pollute (measured by the costs of installing and operating pollution controls). But if the town council decides it wants to preserve old buildings, so that the current owner is hamstrung in how her house or office may be used, has her property value been destroyed, in Holmes's arresting phrase, through "the petty larceny of the police power?"

The premise, Holmes observed, was necessity. "Government could hardly go on if to some extent values incident to property could not be diminished without paying for every such change in the general law. As long recognized, some values are enjoyed under an implied limitation and must yield to the police power. But obviously the implied limitation must have its limits." When are the losses only incidental to regulation so that no compensation need be paid? When is the regulation so severe that it amounts to a taking for which just compensation becomes a constitutional requirement?

The general rule—that the government must compensate whenever the regulation amounts to a taking—is vacuous. Each case turns on its particular facts. The Court has upheld the general principle of zoning, for example, so that a municipality may determine that some property may be used as residences and others only for business, without having to compensate owners who would rather devote their prop-

Declaring Laws Unconstitutional

It is always news when the Supreme Court declares a law unconstitutional. The Court is less likely to excite attention when it upholds a congressional or state enactment. That is perhaps why some people suppose the Court has struck down more laws than it has—or has a proclivity for finding constitutional difficulties with legislative actions. In fact, the numbers suggest otherwise.

In 1936, or roughly a century and a half after the Court got into business, the Legislative Reference Service of the Library of Congress estimated that the Court had upset 70 federal laws. In its first 150 years, Congress had enacted about 24,000 laws.

In 1942, Professor Benjamin F. Wright, having sifted through the court reports, concluded that from February 1790 to June 1941 the Court had overturned 79 federal statutes and 658 state statutes out of 2,000 cases contesting the constitutionality of state and federal law.

Between 1943 and 1964, the Court struck down ten more federal statutes on constitutional grounds, according to Professor Arthur E. Sutherland. Through 1972, noted the Congressional Research Service of the Library of Congress, the Supreme Court had voided another 26, for a total of 106 federal statutes declared unconstitutional in more than 180 years. By then, the Court had struck down as unconstitutional a total of 803 state statutes as well.

erty to another use. Even when the zoning ordinance drastically limits the use of land, the Court ordinarily will uphold it if the land may be used at all. An ordinance that rezoned suburban land so that a developer could no longer build as many housing units as he had planned withstood a just compensation challenge. And landmark preservation laws that prohibit owners of buildings specially denominated as historic likewise do not require compensation if the building remains usable, even if in a restricted manner. In one recent case, the Court held that New York City had not taken the property of the owners of Grand Central Terminal when it enacted an ordinance requiring the facade to be maintained in good repair and the owners to seek permission of a landmarks commission before altering the exterior in any manner.

On the other hand, when the government declared an airplane flight path barely one hundred feet above a residence, the Court held that it had obtained an easement for which compensation was required. During the 1980s, the Court has discerned two types of compensable takings in modern government regulations. In one, a New York ordinance required owners of rental buildings to let cable television companies install cables on the buildings without charge; the Court said any "permanent physical occupation," even a minor one, is a taking for which compensation must be paid. In another, the federal Environmental Protection Agency refused to license the Monsanto Company to market certain pesticides unless it first disclosed its trade secrets for making them so that the general public could benefit from the knowledge. The Court held that since the trade secrets were property under state law, the government must compensate for the company's loss of its intangible property (that is, the benefit to be gained from keeping the knowledge confidential) during any time that the company had an "investment-backed expectation" that the EPA would keep the secrets.

Public Entitlements

Just as the modern industrial economy created property interests that the framers had not foreseen, so also the modern welfare state has created new types of expectations. Public assistance programs—payments for health care, unemployment, old age, phys-ical and mental disabilities, and the like—confer benefits on millions of people. Does one who qualifies for welfare benefits or a driver's license have a "vested" interest in the financial aid or license? Or is this assistance a mere "privilege" that the administrative apparatus of the modern state may decide as it wishes to revoke or terminate?

In an influential article in 1964, Charles Reich argued that citizens depend on public programs and that it is manifestly unfair to view the many benefits as privileges revocable at will. Benefits declared by statute should be recognized as a "new property" right that deserves constitutional protection. Since 1970, the Supreme Court, by expanding the concept of liberty and property under the due process clauses, has begun to develop a new procedural right for those who claim public benefits. This right is not limited to welfare-type financial assistance; it applies as well to certain types of government employment, licenses, and other public programs, including even the right to attend school.

The premise of this emerging doctrine is that statutory rights are a form of liberty or property and that the government may not revoke or terminate these rights except by due process of law. In *Goldberg v. Kelly,* the case that heralded the doctrine of public entitlements, the Court held that New York could not unilaterally terminate welfare assistance without first affording recipients an evidentiary hearing. Likewise, a state may not revoke a driver's license without first giving the driver an opportunity to show that she was not at fault. Nor may a public school suspend a student, even for a limited time, without giving the student some notice of the charges and an opportunity to rebut them.

Two perplexities arise in this line of cases. The first is how to define those entitlements that sufficiently implicate a property or liberty interest. An untenured teacher with a one-year contract at a public college protests the school's failure to rehire him. Must the college give him a hearing on the question whether

to grant him a new contract or may the hiring decision legitimately rest in the wholly unfettered discretion of the college? The Court held that due process does not protect all conceivable interests: "To have a property interest in a benefit, a person must have more than an abstract need or desire for it. He must have more than a unilateral expectation of it. He must, instead, have a legitimate claim of entitlement to it." That legitimate claim of entitlement could come, in the college case, only from the state law; since the law did not provide for tenure until the teacher had been at the school for four years, the teacher could not have had any expectation that he would be rehired. The state may decide to vest absolute discretion in the college whether to rehire its untenured faculty.

Whether a person has a legitimate claim of entitlement depends on the facts in each case. Although a purely subjective expectation does not amount to a constitutionally protected property right, the statute or regulation need not explicitly set out the entitlement. Thus the Court held that even though a college had no tenure system, its faculty handbook gave an instructor who had taught for ten years sufficient claim to continued employment so that the college could not dismiss him without a hearing. The faculty handbook specified that "the administration of the college wishes the faculty member to feel that he has permanent tenure as long as his teaching services are satisfactory and as long as he displays a cooperative attitude toward his co-workers and his superiors."

In later cases, the Court found against a police officer who claimed a property entitlement to permanent employment, against a citizen who claimed that his liberty interest had been invaded by a police department that defamed him in falsely naming him an "active shoplifter" in a flyer circulated to local merchants, and against a prisoner who claimed that his transfer from a medium-security to a maximum-security prison was unconstitutional because he was not allowed to cross-examine adverse witnesses at a hearing before the transfer.

Once a person is held to have a protectible due process liberty or property interest, the second perplexity is what process is due. Before denying or terminating a benefit, must the state grant in effect a trial—a hearing with full-scale rights to cross-examine all adverse witnesses? Or may the state limit the scope of the hearing? Must the hearing be held first or may the state provide for a hearing some time after the benefit has been denied?

Since 1970, the Court has been wrestling with these questions and no definitive answer is yet possible. Only in *Goldberg* did the Court hold that the beneficiary was entitled to a full-scale hearing before termination. In other cases, the Court has determined that a minimal hearing was all that due process required—in the school case, for instance, a suspension of less than ten days required the principal to notify the student informally of the charge and an explanation of the evidence and to allow the student a chance to give his side of the story, but it did not permit the student to confront witnesses or cross-examine them.

Whether the claimant to a statutory benefit is entitled to a pretermination hearing depends on a balancing of various factors: the private interest at stake, the risk that without a prior hearing the state will erroneously deprive the claimant of his entitlement, and the burden to the government of being forced to hold a hearing first. In the 1976 case that announced this balancing test, the Court found that the balance weighed against a hearing before the Social Security administrator terminated the recipient's disability benefits, as long as the claimant had the right to contest the termination before an administrative law judge thereafter. In a more astonishing case a year later, the Court held that public school students could be paddled in Dade County, Florida, without any prior hearing on the charges; the possibility of a damage suit for excessive punishment (but not necessarily for unwarranted punishment) was held to be sufficient protection against a severe beating. This is one of the rare cases in which the Court has said that punishment may be administered without a hearing. Even the Red Queen was prepared to grant a trial after the sentence.

How far the courts will go in protecting the populace against arbitrary denials or terminations of public benefits and other expectations aroused by law remains unclear. Here, as with much of the constitutional claim to protection against governmental interference with property, the courts are likely to defer broadly to the legislatures and executive agencies and to act cautiously, case by case. If this means the Supreme Court has erected a double standard, giving higher constitutional protection to noneconomic than to property interests, it is a distinction that is not likely to vanish—and that is based, for the most part, on the language of the Constitution itself.

Chapter 18 A Commercial Republic: The Commerce Power and the National Economy

Many of the most intense controversies of our day were, for the framers, constitutional afterthoughts. The issue that most aggravated them, prompting the Philadelphia Convention, was commerce. Jockeying for competitive advantage, the states, independent republics, regulated the waterways and inland transportation, interstate trading, and commerce with other nations and taxed imports and exports. In *Federalist* No. 22, Alexander Hamilton denounced the "interfering and unneighborly regulations of some states" that "not restrained by a national control" would become "sources of animosity and discord" and might eventually make the states into nothing more than selfish German principalities that through a multiplicity of duties had rendered the "fine streams and navigable rivers of Germany useless."

Prodded by the tireless, farsighted Hamilton, who as much as any man laid the seeds from which would grow the commercial republic of the United States, the framers gave Congress the power to regulate commerce among the states and with foreign nations. This single provision in Article I, coupled with congressional power to do that which is necessary and proper to carry out the commerce power, gave the national legislature the means by which to forge a national economy—and a nation.

What is the "commerce" committed to congressional care? How broad or narrow is the power that the Constitution grants? May Congress enact however and whatever it pleases by declaring an enactment to be a regulation of commerce? May the states regulate commerce if Congress is silent? These are the central questions, unanswered in the Constitution itself.

In the early years, Chief Justice Marshall gave life to a national economy in his celebrated decision in *Gibbons v. Ogden* extolling the federal power to regulate. This concept was vigorous and would lead to a web of federal law in scores of areas and to a vast federal administrative apparatus that reaches into the nooks and crannies of far more than our economic life. For a time, however, the Supreme Court would discern limits on Congress's power to act. Though never wholly constricting, the Court's restriction of the commerce clause seemed to threaten national attempts to recover from economic crisis and tempted President Franklin D. Roosevelt to attack the Court's very independence. The Court's "switch in time" averted FDR's Court-packing plan and restored the commerce power to its national role, as we shall see.

The Sweep of Federal Power: Rise, Decline, and Triumph

The Power to Regulate

The first test came in 1824. Years earlier, the New York legislature had granted a steamboat monopoly to Robert Livingston and Robert Fulton. Under the grant, only these two could legally operate steamboats in New York waters. Other states rushed to protect the interests of their citizens (or a favored few of them with money for steamboats). Occasionally, hotheads would shoot at each other, and facing states had

threatened war. The states might yet fulfill Hamilton's grim foreboding of a nation rent by the greed of petty sovereigns up and down the waterways with power to exclude those who carried the nation's commerce.

Through a series of deals, Aaron Ogden, leading Federalist lawyer and former governor of New Jersey, purchased from the Livingston-Fulton interests the right to run a steamboat ferry from Elizabethtown in New Jersey to the port at New York. His sometime partner, Thomas Gibbons, a Georgia loyalist during the Revolution, eventually began to cheat on their partnership by running an independent steamboat. A complex set of lawsuits ensued, and the New Jersey legislature was eventually persuaded to enact retaliatory legislation. But when New York Chancellor James Kent (affirmed by the state's highest court) enjoined Gibbons from operating his steamboat ferries in New York waters in violation of Ogden's rights, the stage was set for a crucial appeal to the Supreme Court.

The argument in February 1824 took place before a large audience—members of Congress, leading journalists, Harriet Martineau, the English novelist, and an "assemblage of ladies [so great] that many of them were obliged to find seats within the bar." They had come to hear Daniel Webster and William Wirt plead for the release of "every creek and river, every lake and harbor in our country from the interference of monopolies." Webster, who had stayed up all night preparing his argument, later wrote that "I think I never experienced more intellectual pleasure than in arguing that novel question to a great man who could appreciate it, and take it in; and he did take it in, as a baby takes in its mother's milk."

The novel question was to what the word "commerce" applied. Ogden's lawyers argued that it was limited to "traffic," buying and selling, and did not encompass navigation. Holding for Gibbons, Chief Justice Marshall did not agree: "Commerce, undoubtedly, is traffic, but it is something more—it is

Thomas Gibbons

Aaron Ogden

intercourse." As he noted, it is impossible to separate the two:

> The mind can scarcely conceive a system for regulating commerce between nations, which shall exclude all laws concerning navigation, which shall be silent on the admission of the vessels of the one nation into the ports of the other. . . . All America understands, and has uniformly understood, the word "commerce" to comprehend navigation. It was so understood, and must have been so understood, when the constitution was framed. The power over commerce, including navigation, was one of the primary objects for which the people of America adopted their government.

Marshall easily dismissed through reductio ad absurdum the argument that the congressional power to regulate foreign and interstate commerce operated on interstate waterways or the high seas but could not be exercised within a state. For if it could not, what power did Congress then have to regulate the commerce between adjoining states: "Can a trading expedition between two adjoining states, commence and terminate outside of each?"

What, then, is this power to regulate commerce? In sweeping words, Marshall enfused the commerce clause with a scope so broad that we are yet under the power of his language and interpretation:

> It is the power to regulate; that is, to prescribe the rule by which commerce is to be governed. This power, like all others vested in congress, is complete in itself, may be exercised to its utmost extent, and acknowledges no

limitations, other than are prescribed in the constitution.

. . . If, as has always been understood, the sovereignty of congress, though limited to specified objects, is plenary as to those objects, the power over commerce with foreign nations, and among the several states, is vested in congress as absolutely as it would be in a single government, having in its constitution the same restrictions on the exercise of the power as are found in the constitution of the United States. The wisdom and the discretion of congress, their identity with the people, and the influence which their constituents possess at elections, are, in this, as in many other instances, as that, for example, of declaring war, the sole restraints on which they have relied, to secure them from its abuse. They are the restraints on which the people must often rely solely, in all representative governments.

So Congress had the power—and Congress had in fact acted. Gibbons had licensed his boats under a federal law governing "vessels employed in the coasting trade." Chancellor Kent had held that this law merely immunized American ships from taxes and other burdens imposed on foreign shippers. The Court disagreed. The federal law permitted licensees to ply interstate waters. The injunction, based on a state law granting a monopoly in those waters, thus directly conflicted with the federal law, and under the supremacy clause must fall. Gibbons prevailed. So did nationalism, against a localism that would have suffocated the mighty commercial empire America was to become.

For more than half a century, the federal commerce power lay largely dormant. One form of federal economic involvement—the government's contentious entry into national finances with the First and Second Bank of the United States—came to an end with President Jackson's veto in 1836 (and would not be resuscitated until Congress created the Federal Reserve System in 1913). The later constitutional problems over commerce concerned the states' authority to reg-

1799 engraving of The First Bank of the United States in Philadelphia.

Founding Father

Luther Martin

(did not sign the Constitution)

Luther Martin was born near New Brunswick, New Jersey, around 1748, and died in New York on July 10, 1826. He attended the grammar school of the College of New Jersey, graduating from the college in 1766. His young adulthood was spent as an educator. He was a teacher at Queenstown, Queen Anne's County, until 1769, left for a year to study law, and returned to education in 1770 as superintendent of the grammar school at Onancock, Accomac County, Virginia. He continued to study law, though financial troubles had forced him back to work. In 1771, he was admitted to the Virginia bar, practiced for a while in Virginia, then moved to Somerset County, Maryland, where his practice prospered until the onset of the Revolution. In 1774, he was named to the patriot committee of Somerset County. That same year, he was made a delegate to

the convention of Maryland at Annapolis. In 1778, he was appointed state attorney general and he transferred to Baltimore. In 1785, Martin was a delegate to the Continental Congress. Two years later, he represented Maryland at the Constitutional Convention, but left with fellow delegate John Francis Mercer before the debates were concluded. An opponent of strong central government, he assailed the Constitution in a speech to the Maryland House of Delegates and fought to prevent ratification at the Maryland state convention. In 1804, he defended Justice Samuel Chase in his impeachment trial. The following year, he resigned as attorney general, but his interest in law did not diminish. In 1807, he defended Aaron Burr at his trial for treason. In 1813, he became chief judge of the Court of Oyer and Terminer for the city and county of Baltimore. This position lasted for three years. In 1818, he was reappointed attorney general and accepted. His last assignment of note was the famous case of *McCulloch v. Maryland*. In 1820, Martin suffered a stroke and he was forced to resign as attorney general.

Martin was a bright legal figure, although he had many personal misfortunes. He was constantly in debt, was prone to drink, and had tragic luck with women. He was once described as "the rollicking, witty, audacious Attorney-General of Maryland; . . . drunken, generous, slovenly, grand; bull-dog of federalism, . . . the notorious reprobate genius."

ulate in the absence of congressional action, and these problems we examine shortly. Here, we first consider the gradual expansion of federal commercial regulation, judicial resistance, and the eventual vindication of Marshall's sweeping vision.

Congress did not begin to regulate actively until the economy developed sufficient national characteristics after the Civil War to moot state efforts to control baneful effects. For a time, few supposed that Congress would be the centralizing force it has become. Just after the Civil War, a foreign diplomat told Senator Sumner that "from this time, your government and ours are the same" because of the large public debt and the bureaucratic machinery necessary to run the war. "These official establishments will govern your country, as such establishments govern our countries."

Sumner repeated this conversation to Edward Everett Hale, who responded that the fears were groundless. Americans would not countenance a large peacetime army and would closely cabin the bureaucracy. Hale said, "Given two courses of national conduct the nation must always select that which will employ the fewest people, that which will have least distinct corporate organization, and that which will finish its business the sooner. It was a pity, perhaps, to abolish the Freedmen's Bureau at the moment we did it; but the principle which abolished it was the true one; and the moment was only a question of weeks or months. To work by special [that is, temporary] machinery . . . even if then the machinery be given away . . . this is the true policy of the Republic."

Hale was a poor prognosticator. By the 1880s, Congress assumed, slowly at first, a new business: economic regulation. The novelty lay in the federalizing, not in the subject, for the states had been regulating furiously for decades. Much of it was masked, however, by disguising economic regulations in the dress of criminal statutes. The Indiana criminal code of 1881 contained dozens of prohibitions against economic crimes: shooting prairie hens out of season, falsely weighing and selling coal, using nets to prevent fish from swimming into or out of any creek emptying into the Ohio River, advertising or selling any drug that cautioned pregnant women against using it. Ten years later, Indiana made it a punishable offense for railroads to fail to employ flagmen at crossings. In New York, in 1898, the legislature prohibited labeling commodities as "sterling silver" unless they were 92.5 percent pure. Other states, egged on by an unlikely coalition of unions and ministers, enforced dormant Sunday closing laws, to give workers a day of rest.

"The multiplication of economic crimes," Lawrence Friedman has argued

> did not mean, necessarily, that people looked on sharp business behavior with more and more sense of moral outrage. It meant, rather, a decision, to socialize responsibility for enforcing certain parts of the law. Crimes are, among other things, wrongful acts punished wholly at the expense of the state, and largely on the state's initiative. The states, and the federal government, were invoking criminal law in one of its historic functions—a low-level, low-paid administrative aid. [The alternative, private lawsuits, were ordinarily not worth the cost.] In a criminal action, enforcement and punishment were entirely at public expense. The enforcing officials, of course, were only the usual array of policemen, district attorneys, and judges. They were not specialists in regulatory crimes, and rarely bothered with them. Criminality was often only a halfway stage on the road to administrative law—to professional, specialized policing of some area of economic life.

During the 1870s and 1880s, as we have seen, these state regulations escaped due process attack in the courts, which held them to be an acceptable exercise of the police power over commerce within the states. Just a century ago, in 1887 and 1890, Congress enacted two major laws that set the pattern for most of the regulation of national commerce that followed.

The first statute was the Interstate Commerce Act, which established the first federal regulatory agency, the Interstate Commerce Commission. Congress gave the ICC power to set interstate railroad rates to eliminate the gouging of farmers and other shippers. With state legislatures in their pockets, railroads had been effectively beyond control. The ICC was the first of dozens of federal administrative agencies, outside the regular departments of government, that Congress has established under its commerce power to regulate every aspect of the national economy. Others include the Federal Trade Commission (1914), the Federal Communications Commission (1934), the Securities and Exchange Commission (1934), the National Labor Relations Board (1935), and the Environmental Protection Agency (1970). Other important agencies, most of them independent when established, are now part of the executive departments. These include the Food and Drug Administration (part of the Department of Health and Human Services); Nuclear Regulatory Agency (formerly the Atomic Energy Commission) and the Federal Energy Regulation Agency (formerly the Federal Power Commission), both now parts of the Department of Energy; the Occupational Safety and Health Administration (part of the Labor Department); and various agencies within the Agriculture Department with broad supervisory powers over farm practices and pricing.

Administrative enactments delegate power to agencies to regulate in minute detail. In 1890, Congress took another route to economic regulation when it passed the Sherman Antitrust Act, the first of a series of antitrust laws, including the Clayton Act (1914) and the Robinson-Patman Act (1936). These create broad codes of civil wrongs—for example, Section 1 of the Sherman Act prohibits "every contract, combination . . . or conspiracy in restraint of trade or commerce among the several states"—and require judicial enforcement.

Almost immediately, these congressional forays into the general regulation of commerce came under attack as improper enactments under the commerce clause. In the Sugar Trust Case in 1895, the Court ruled that the Sherman Act could not be applied to the monopolization of the sugar refining industry. The American Sugar Refining Company acquired four other refi-

1889 cartoon depicts a Senate "of the monopolists, by the monopolists and for the monopolists."

neries, giving it control of 98 percent of national refining capacity. Section 2 of the Sherman Act outlaws monopolization of any part of interstate trade or commerce. But the Supreme Court distinguished between "commerce" and "manufacture," holding that the business of refining sugar was not part of commerce. It was therefore left to state regulation, if at all. Later cases permitted antitrust prosecutions to go forward on different grounds—for instance, an agreement to restrain prices of goods was held to be not merely a restraint on manufacturing but also on commerce, because price obviously affects the degree to which goods will be bought and sold in the market.

Another line of cases, developed early this century, gave Congress a federal commercial police power. Congress was not limited to regulating to improve the functioning of markets. Its commerce power allows it to *prohibit* goods from circulating or services from being offered that it deems noxious. In 1903, the Court upheld a ban on interstate sale of lottery tickets, against the argument that the commerce clause conferred a power to regulate but not to prohibit. Likewise, Congress may bar merchants from selling impure foods under laws regulating food and drugs; that adulterated foods are seized within a state and not while in transit is no objection to the validity of the laws or of the seizure. Congress may even ban the transportation of women across state lines for immoral purposes, said the Court in upholding the well-known Mann Act.

But in 1918, the Court signaled a major shift in its jurisprudence in rejecting a federal law prohibiting sales in interstate commerce of all goods produced by child labor. The Court looked at the character of the goods shipped and pronounced them harmless. Distinguishing between interstate transportation and the production of goods for sale, Justice Day denied Congress a power to "standardize the ages at which children may be employed in mining and manufacturing." Dissenting, Justice Holmes pointed to numerous other decisions approving commercial prohibitions, and said:

> It does not matter whether the supposed evil precedes or follows the transportation. It is enough that in the opinion of Congress the transportation encourages the evil. . . . If there is any matter upon which civilized countries have agreed—far more unanimously than they have with regard to intoxicants and some other matters over which this country is now emotionally aroused—it is the evil of premature and excessive child labor. . . .
>
> It is not for this Court to pronounce when prohibition is necessary to regulation if it ever may be necessary—to say that it is permissible as against strong drink but not as against the product of ruined lives. The act does not meddle with anything belonging to the States. They may regulate their internal affairs and their domestic commerce as they like. But when they seek to send products across the state line they are no longer within their rights.

The *Child Labor Case* prompted Congress to send a constitutional amendment to the states—one of the few still pending because Congress imposed no time limit on its ratification. Its desirability became moot a quarter-century later when the Court explicitly

The 1918 Child Labor Case *denied Congress the right to standardize employment ages for children, but the decision was reversed and protective legislation was passed during the New Deal.*

overruled the *Child Labor Case*. But it was a harbinger of difficulties to come.

The New Deal Crisis

National woe and constitutional curbs on federal power to act intersected in the mid-thirties at the flow tide of the Depression. The Court sustained some early state efforts to combat the Depression's effects despite due process arguments—the Minnesota mortgage moratorium law and the New York milk-pricing scheme. It sustained some federal efforts too—laws banning gold clauses in contracts and payments in gold were upheld in 1935.

But that same year, the Court began to strike down the New Deal. In the "hot oil" case, it rejected the petroleum code promulgated under the National Industrial Recovery Act (NIRA), not on commerce, but on delegation grounds (Congress had given the National Recovery Administration, an executive agency, too much legislative power). It reached the commerce clause when voiding the Railroad Retirement Act of 1934, declaring that a compulsory retirement and pension plan for employees of carriers subject to the Interstate Commerce Act was an unlawful social welfare scheme, not a regulation of interstate commerce.

On May 27, Black Monday, it tossed out wholesale the NIRA in the "Sick Chicken" case—the power to promulgate any of the industrial codes was "delegation running riot." Also on that day, the Court rebuked Roosevelt for attempting to fire Federal Trade Commissioner William E. Humphrey and invalidated the federal Frazier-Lemke Act for the relief of farm mortgagors.

At a press conference, Roosevelt said that the decision against the NIRA had turned the Constitution back to the "horse-and-buggy days," leaving the federal government without jurisdiction over construction, mining, manufacturing, and agriculture, which, with transportation, were the five basic American economic activities. The United States would have to

face up, the president said, to "whether we are going to relegate to the States all control over social and working conditions throughout the country regardless of whether those conditions have a very definite significance and effect in other States."

In October, the Court threw out a Vermont tax on the novel grounds that it violated the privileges and immunities clause of Article IV, the first time this had been done, leading Thomas Reed Powell of the Harvard Law School faculty to comment that "if the Court is going to pick new, strange clubs out of the air to swat anything that it doesn't like, the subject of constitutional law will be as stable as a kaleidoscope operated by an electric battery." (The Court overruled this case just five years later.)

The following spring, sitting for the first time in its new building (the first that it had ever had of its own), the Court upset the Bituminous Coal Conservation Act of 1935, again on the ground that the Constitution gave Congress no power to set maximum hours and minimum wages, this time of coal miners. In January, it had voided the first Agricultural Adjustment Act, one of the key measures of the New Deal, holding that Congress's spending power would not permit the federal government to alleviate the farm crisis by paying farmers to take acreage out of production. In late May, it struck down the Municipal Bankruptcy Act, passed to save thousands of small towns by letting them readjust their debts.

By this time it was clear, said Robert Jackson, that the Court was conducting a "dual campaign against the powers which the Congress thought had been granted it by the Constitution":

On the one hand, [the Court] *narrowed* the scope of the great clauses of the Constitution granting powers to Congress. It seriously contracted the interstate commerce power and it read startling exemptions into the taxing power. Simultaneously, it *expanded* the scope of clauses which limited the power of the Congress, such as the "due process clause" and the clauses withholding power

Members of the 1936 Supreme Court, whose invalidations of New Deal legislation led to President Roosevelt's court-packing proposal.

from the federation. At the same time it used the "due process" concept to cut down the effective powers of the states. Division of opinion on constitutional interpretation ceased to be along the classic lines of a liberal as against a strict construction. The same Justices used both in the interests of private economic power: they were strict and niggardly in construing *powers* of government and liberal to the point of extravagance in construing *limitations*—even inventing such limitations as "freedom of contract" where none existed in the Constitution.

At the end of the Court's term that June, Justice Harlan Fiske Stone judged his brethren:

> I suppose no intelligent person likes very well the way the New Deal does things, but that ought not to make us forget that ours is a nation which should have the powers ordinarily possessed by governments, and that the framers of the Constitution intended that it should have. . . . We finished the term of Court yesterday, I think in many ways one of the most disastrous in its history.

The monotonous regularity of the five-to-four votes (usually with Justice Owen J. Roberts in the "swing" position), the minority's relentless denunciation of justices given to reading their predilections into clauses intended for the "various crises of human affairs" (in Marshall's words a century earlier), the heavy thud of New Deal laws fallen as so much scrap on the Court's constitutional refuse pile—all led the administration to expect the worst for the two key laws yet to be tested: the Wagner Act (the National Labor Relations Act) and the Social Security Act.

Court opponents saw two alternatives. The Constitution could be amended to provide Congress with the explicit powers the Court professed not to see in the existing text. Or the Court could be pressed somehow to change its interpretation.

The amendment approach seemed untenable. First, no one could agree on the language. Second, as Roosevelt saw, it would be impossible to secure ratification soon, and perhaps at all. "If I were John W. Davis and had five hundred thousand dollars," Roosevelt said, "I could stop a constitutional amendment cold." That left the second approach—and the most promising avenue to changing the opinions of the Court seemed to be to add new justices, in other words, to pack it.

The Court-Packing Plan

Roosevelt waited until after his crushing defeat of Governor Alfred M. Landon in 1936. In early February 1937, he unveiled his plan. He asked Congress for authority to appoint a new judge to every federal court for each judge on that court who turned seventy years old and, having served at least ten years, failed to retire within the next six months. Judges who chose to retire would continue to draw full pay. Under the plan, the Supreme Court would be limited to a maximum of fifteen justices. At that time, six of the Court's nine members were over seventy. During his first term, Roosevelt had been unable to appoint anyone to the High Court.

Had the plan been forthrightly presented, Congress might have responded positively—his election sweep had given him the largest House majority since 1855 and largest Senate majority since 1869. But Roosevelt dissembled. Ignoring the patent reason for his plan, he spoke only of the aging justices' infirmities and the need for "constant infusion of new blood." Moreover, in speaking generally of all courts, he diffused a message that should have been pointed at the Supreme Court.

By avoiding the central issue, he lost valuable support across the political spectrum. In particular, Roosevelt alienated Justices Brandeis, Stone, and Cardozo, "in effect [charging] the Justices collectively with inefficiency and inadequate discharge of duty," certainly not the case with any of these three who might have spoken up in favor of a plan more obviously directed at the reactionary decisions with which the Court had shredded the major legal props of the New Deal.

A month later, in a major radio address, Roosevelt spoke directly to the main points, but by then it was too late. Broad opposition was developing in Congress, and a letter from Chief Justice Hughes informed Senator Burton K. Wheeler, chairman of the Senate Judiciary Committee, which was considering Roosevelt's bill, that "the Supreme Court is fully abreast of its work" and that any additions to the Court would hinder, not promote, its efficiency: "There would be more judges to hear, more judges to confer, more judges to discuss, more judges to be convinced and to decide."

The plan failed, but the battle was soon won. For even as the Senate was deliberating, the Court did something startling. On March 29, 1937, White Monday, it upheld the constitutionality of a minimum wage law for women, overruling a precedent squarely to the contrary. The decision was five to four; the shifting vote was that of Justice Roberts. On that same day, it upheld the National Firearms Act, requiring dealers to pay a tax, against a challenge that Congress's taxing power could not be used to regulate the firearms traffic. It also upheld an amended Railway Labor Act, a scheme to promote collective bargaining between railroads and workers. Finally, it upheld a slightly modified version of the Frazier-Lemke Act, which provided relief for farm mortgagors. It was the famous "switch in time that saved nine."

Two weeks later, the Court upheld the Wagner Act, the centerpiece of the New Deal's restructuring of the labor relations process in the United States. The Jones & Laughlin Steel Company had discharged employees active in union organizing. The new National Labor Relations Board found the company guilty of an unfair labor practice, and it appealed, insisting that Congress could not reach local employee practices. Said the Court: "The fact remains that the stoppage of those operations by industrial strife would have a most serious effect upon interstate commerce. In view of [the company's] far-flung activities, it is idle to say that the effect would be indirect or remote. It is obvious that it would be immediate and might be catastrophic. . . . When industries organize themselves on a national scale, making their relation to interstate commerce the dominant factor in their activities, how can it be maintained that their industrial labor relations constitute a forbidden field into

THE INGENIOUS QUARTERBACK!

which Congress may not enter when it is necessary to protect interstate commerce from the paralyzing consequences of industrial war?"

Other decisions too saw the previous majority now in heated dissent. And by the end of the term, it had sustained the Social Security Act, construing the general welfare clause of Article I for the first time in its history, finding in it an expansive power for Congress to act.

By the end of the term, Justice Van Devanter retired, giving FDR his first nomination to the Court, the liberal Alabaman, Hugo L. Black. Justice Sutherland retired the following year, giving the administration, with the appointment of Stanley F. Reed,

a majority that grew stronger with the successive appointments of Justices Felix Frankfurter, William O. Douglas, Frank Murphy, Robert H. Jackson, and Wiley Rutledge.

The Commerce Power Ascendant

By the early 1940s, the Court had reverted to a doctrine contained in a long line of cases around which it had detoured in the early decades of the century. This doctrine holds that Congress may regulate any activity that "affects" interstate commerce. Thus in the *Shreveport Rate Case* in 1914, the Court upheld an order of the Interstate Commerce Commission to railroads to cease discriminating against out-of-state shipments. Railroads had been charging less for longer distances wholly within one state than for shorter distances across state lines. The railroads argued that the ICC had no authority to set rates for trips within the borders of the state. Not so, said Justice Hughes: "Whenever the interstate and intrastate transactions of carriers are so related that the government of the one involves the control of the other, it is Congress, and not the State, that is entitled to prescribe the final and dominant rule." In another case, Justice Holmes spoke of the "current of commerce" in which local activities would eventuate in commerce across state lines, and the Court used this metaphor in sustaining federal regulations of stockyard dealers, because their practices affected the livestock that would be moving across the country.

In 1941, the Court upheld the Fair Labor Standards Act, against the challenge of a Georgia lumber dealer that the minimum wage and maximum hours provisions of the act were outside the scope of the commerce power. The Court's rationale was simple: since the lumber was intended for interstate sales, Congress could prescribe conditions for its production and prohibit sales of goods that did not measure up—in order that "interstate commerce should not be made the instrument of competition in the distribution of goods produced under substandard labor conditions."

In 1942, the Court showed just how broad is the commerce power it was finally willing to concede to Congress. Filburn raised a small amount of wheat on his farm, in excess of the amount allowed under the second Agricultural Adjustment Act. He used the excess entirely for his own consumption on the farm, for feeding livestock, making flour, and for seeding. Filburn refused to pay a fine for growing too much wheat and appealed his conviction. The Court upheld the conviction and fine. Consumption of wheat on the farm has an effect on market prices, since it competes with wheat that is sold. If everyone were to do what Filburn had done, interstate commerce in wheat would be seriously affected. As Justice Jackson later characteristically summed up the rule: "If it is interstate commerce that feels the pinch, it does not matter how local the operation that applies the squeeze."

The Modern Commerce Power

So definitively did the Court break away from its consumptive reading of the commerce power that Congress has since those days continually expanded the types of legislation justified by resort to the commerce clause. It is no longer confined to purely economic concerns. Numerous federal criminal statutes aimed at racketeering, loan sharking, gambling, and like crimes have been sustained as proper exercises of the commerce power. The commerce power is also the primary constitutional support for major civil rights statutes of the 1960s. The public accommodations section of the 1964 Civil Rights Act, for instance, prohibits discrimination on the basis of race, color, religion, or national origin in any lodging, restaurant, theater, or like establishment in which interstate commerce is involved. In upholding these provisions in cases brought by motel and restaurant owners, the Court pointed to the proximity of these establishments to interstate highways, to the purchase of food from other states, and to the number of patrons who come from other states.

In 1985, the Court upheld a federal law making it a criminal offense to set fire to any building used in interstate commerce or in any activity affecting interstate commerce. The defendant had attempted to burn down a two-unit apartment building that he rented out in Chicago. Merely renting real estate is an activity that affects commerce, said Justice Stevens for a unanimous Court. "The local rental of an apartment unit is merely an element of a much broader commercial market in rental properties. The congressional power to regulate the class of activities that constitute the rental market for real estate includes the power to regulate individual activity within that class."

So far does the commerce power extend that Congress may even regulate the wages and hours of state employees under the Fair Labor Standards Act, positions that on occasion have been supposed to be a sovereign function of state public governments and outside the federal power.

"Great Silences" of the Constitution: State Power to Regulate

To this point, we have been considering the power of Congress to *act* under the commerce clause. Suppose, however, that Congress had not acted. To what degree may the states regulate economic activities within their borders that have, or might have, an impact on the national economy?

The Constitution does not answer the question. Here again the courts must repair to what Justice Jackson called the "vision of the Founders," who saw the Nation as Market:

[This Court] has advanced the solidarity and prosperity of this Nation by the meaning it has given to these great silences of the Constitution. . . . The principle that our economic unit is the Nation, which alone has the gamut of powers necessary to control the economy, including the vital power of erecting customs barriers against foreign competition, has as its corollary that the states are not separable economic units. . . . The material success that has come to inhabitants of the states which make up this federal free trade unit has been the most impressive in the history of commerce, but the established interdependence of the states only emphasizes the necessity of protecting interstate movement of goods against local burdens. . . . This Court consistently has rebuffed attempts of states to advance their own commercial interests by curtailing the movement of articles of commerce, either into or out of the state, while generally supporting their right to impose even burdensome regulations in the interest of local health and safety. . . . Our system, fostered by the Commerce Clause, is that every farmer and every craftsman shall be encouraged to produce by the certainty that he will have free access to every market in the Nation, that no home embargoes will withhold his exports, and no foreign state will by customs duties or regulations exclude them. Likewise, every consumer may look to the free competition from every producing area in the Nation to protect him from exploitation by any. Such was the vision of the Founders; such has been the doctrine of this Court which has given it reality.

If the Nation serves as common market to all commercial interests, are the states forbidden from any acts that might trench on any trade that passes between them?

From earliest days, the power to regulate commerce has never been regarded as exclusively federal.

But by its very presence in the Constitution, the commerce clause has been seen as a barrier to unfettered state regulation. In 1851, the Taney Court steered a middle course in sustaining a Pennsylvania law that required ships entering or leaving the Philadelphia harbor to hire a local pilot to guide them. The First Congress in 1789 had enacted a statute specifically holding pilots to local regulations until Congress legislated otherwise. That was enough to show, said Justice Curtis, that pilotage is a local concern, which does not require a uniform national rule, unless Congress speaks to the contrary. Congress may constitutionally leave these matters to local authorities. What is local is for the states; only what is national is forbidden to them.

The distinction between "local" and "national" is difficult to draw, like all the talismanic phrases that have been uttered to incant the spirit of the Constitution. For a time, the courts distinguished between

Distinguishing between local and national legislative concerns, the Taney Court upheld local regulations over pilotage of the Philadelphia harbor.

the "direct" impact of a regulation on interstate commerce and its "indirect" effect. They also looked to the purpose of the regulation. But two seemingly identical cases could come to different conclusions. A Washington licensing scheme that prevented a passenger and freight carrier from operating between Portland and Seattle was upset because the Court discerned a desire to limit trade rather than to promote safety. The state said that it was denying a "certificate of convenience and necessity" to operate as an interstate carrier because the route was "already being adequately served by other carriers." But when Ohio some years later denied a certificate to run between Cleveland and Flint (Michigan) because highway congestion was so severe that additional carriers would create road hazards, the Court upheld the state. Justice Brandeis reasoned that Ohio desired to promote safety and that the effect of the denial was only an incidental burden on interstate commerce.

Today the Court far more frankly strikes a balance, case by case. In 1970, Justice Stewart stated the general rule:

> Where the statute regulates evenhandedly to effectuate a legitimate local interest, and its effects on interstate commerce are only incidental, it will be upheld unless the burden imposed on such commerce is clearly excessive in relation to the putative local benefits. If a legitimate local purpose is found, then the question becomes one of degree. And the extent of the burden that will be tolerated will of course depend on the nature of the local interest involved, and on whether it could be promoted as well with a lesser impact on interstate activities.

Whenever Congress has kept quiet, the balancing, in all cases, is for the courts, not the states. When Arizona limited the length of railroad trains running through the state, the Supreme Court voided the law as an unconstitutional burden on commerce. The standard practice of railroads was to run long trains over their main tracks throughout the country; state by state regulation of their length would severely impair their efficiency. "If the length of trains is to be regulated at all, national uniformity in the regulation adopted, such as only Congress can prescribe, is practically indispensable to the operation of an efficient and economical national railway system." Because Congress had not limited train length, railroads must remain free to couple as many cars as they wish. Likewise, an Iowa law was unconstitutional that prohibited sixty-five-foot double axle trucks from using its highways, when surrounding states permitted their use. The Court noted that Iowa failed to back up its claim that the sixty-five-foot "doubles" were less safe than smaller trucks that Iowa permitted.

The commerce clause stands also as a barrier to local protectionism through discriminatory legislation that confers benefits on residents or burdens on non-residents. Here too, the Court stands guard and imposes stern judgment on states whose laws might seem, at first blush, the product of sweet reason.

Citing important health and environmental concerns, New Jersey banned anyone from importing "solid or liquid waste" from outside the state. It had, after all, enough of its own. But the Supreme Court opened New Jersey's gates, seeing less a concern for health than for blocking "the importation of waste in an obvious effort to saddle those outside the State with the entire burden of slowing the flow of refuse into New Jersey's remaining landfill sites." Similarly, the Court struck down a Madison, Wisconsin, ordinance that refused entry to the markets of the city any milk pasteurized at a plant more than five miles from the center of town, thus protecting local farmers and processors from competition with farmers and processors in Illinois. This ban clearly burdened interstate commerce, without any sound countervailing reason—any health concerns could have been met by inspecting the imported milk and charging the foreign companies for the cost of the inspection.

Local protectionism is not confined to keeping competitors out of the home market. The reverse is also frequently a motivation: attempts to keep prod-

Supreme Court rulings prevent states from enacting laws banning the importation of solid or liquid waste.

ucts, especially natural resources, within the state's borders. Here too, the courts are suspicious. For example, the Supreme Court struck down an Oklahoma statute barring fishermen from shipping out of state any minnows caught in Oklahoma waters, and it likewise condemned a New Hampshire attempt to prohibit electric utilities from selling locally generated power in nearby states.

An exception to the general rule that has emerged since 1976 is for states acting as "market participants." If the state itself is an economic competitor—in contracting to buy supplies or in construction projects—then it may be permitted to adopt what would otherwise seem protectionist rules. For instance, a state or municipality paying for the construction of an office building may require that a certain percentage of the work force live in the state. The market participant exception to the usual federal commerce clause restraint on local restrictions is still new enough to foreclose confident description of its contours or depth.

The cases that illustrate the general rule are representative, not exhaustive. The impulse of business to attempt to monopolize its field is well known; even Adam Smith reflected on the tendency. The court reports are full of opinions dealing with ordinances regulating just about anything that can be imported. One time-honored way to beat the general rule of interstate commerce is to claim that you are involved in a profession or other occupation that is inherently local and that the state must necessarily regulate for the welfare of its residents. Lawyers, doctors, engineers, beauticians, and dozens of other possessors of arcane skills operate in all states behind a cloak of regulation that has tended to make it difficult for outside practitioners to move in. In recent years, the Court has declared that the practice of a profession is also a business and hence subject, at least under certain circumstances, to the federal antitrust laws. Lawyers have learned, for instance, that their once universal minimum fee schedules, by which they fixed the price of their services, violated the Sherman Act—

a holding that required a finding that the services of a lawyer can be part of interstate commerce. Nevertheless, the states continue to exert a considerable drag on the development of truly national markets in the now dominant sector of the economy, the service sector.

It should not be surprising that commerce cases are a staple of the judicial diet, for commerce is the lifeblood of the nation. In wisely assigning the principal and preemptive power to regulate to the national government, the framers not only foreshadowed an economy free enough from the crippling effects of insular interests to make American productivity the envy of the world but they also created, in just a few words, a judiciary to protect that freedom until the day that Congress acts.

Should Congress act unwisely or corruptly, what then? We must, in the final analysis, rely on the entire system that the Constitution has given us to control our government. As Chief Justice Waite trenchantly observed more than a century ago, a power that exists may always be abused, "but that is no argument against its existence. For protection against abuses by legislatures the people must resort to the polls."

378

Part 6 A Third Century of Constitutionalism

Chapter 19 **Reform and the Future of the Constitution**

Constitutional Change through Amendment

The Constitution endures. For two hundred years, Americans have lived in a nation whose political institutions, culture, and public philosophy have been shaped and animated by this short legal document. The branches of government that fifty-five delegates in Philadelphia created in 1787 abide. The press remains robustly free. Religious diversity flourishes. The people generally continue to respect the desirability of governmental regularity and freedom from bureaucratic whim and arbitrary rule.

Still, as is manifest from these pages, we do not live under the *same* Constitution. A fourth branch of government—unthinkable to the framers—has a significant voice in creating law. The Fourteenth Amendment has worked a revolution as fundamental as the original Constitution itself, restricting states in their power to act and empowering federal courts to oversee all governmental acts. Throughout our history, the Constitution has been contoured, within boundaries that themselves shift, to our changing needs—although not always quickly enough and sometimes even retrogressively. At considerable cost, we have learned to weather constitutional storms, transforming not only the meaning of the words but ourselves as well.

As is less manifest from these pages, the formal Constitution, authoritatively construed by the Supreme Court, has rarely been identical in all respects with *constitutionalism* as actually practiced. Some examples loom large in American history: the abysmal failure of the states to honor formal legal equality, even as the Court meagerly interpreted the term during the first half of the century; the blatant attempt by federal and state governments to suppress political protest, especially during wartime; the nonchalance of many law enforcement officials toward even the rudiments of legal procedure insofar as they affected certain groups. Some examples are more subtle, reflecting the failure of the courts to persuade significant minorities of the judicial interpretation of the Constitution, as suggested by the continued vitality of the practice of prayer in some public schools.

Nor is it a fair inference that constitutional interpretation always precedes a spirit or consciousness of constitutionalism. To the contrary, it might be more fairly argued that minority ideals of constitutionalism are forerunners of judicial interpretation, for courts are rarely innovators—slavery and its badges were abolished despite, not because of, judicial intervention, at least until recently.

Not only has the Constitution changed during the past two centuries but it will continue to take on new meanings—to comport with new realities or changing philosophies of a substantial number of people. Nevertheless, we ought to resist the temptation to equate social and political problems with constitutional shortcomings—an assumption often made throughout our history. If we do suppose that so many of our current problems are constitutional ones, we are bound to be gloomy about the possibility of change, for history teaches that the prospects of fundamental constitutional reform are especially unlikely.

The framers made it difficult to amend the Constitution formally. Article V spells out two methods by which the Constitution may be modified—the first method has been used successfully seventeen times (the ten amendments of the Bill of Rights were proposed to the states simultaneously, and sixteen other amendments have been adopted). The second method has never been used.

Amending the Constitution is a two-step process. By the first method, an amendment must be introduced in both the Senate and House and each chamber must pass it by a two-thirds vote. The amendment is then transmitted either to the state legislatures or to state conventions (the option is for Congress), and it must be ratified by three-fourths of them, or thirty-eight states. (Only the Twenty-first Amendment, repealing Prohibition, was submitted to state conventions, and these acted with alacrity, the requisite number ratifying the amendment between February 20 and December 5, 1933.)

What constitutes proper ratification has so far not been considered a judicial question but rests with Congress. In 1939, the question arose whether the Child Labor Amendment could still be ratified after a lapse of fifteen years. (It had been pending since 1924 as an attempt to overrule the Court's decision in 1918 that Congress could not regulate child labor in the states.) Three justices in a plurality opinion declared that the question was political, hence not for the courts to determine. (The Child Labor Amendment became politically moot when the Supreme Court two years later reversed itself, overturning the 1918 case. In proposing to the states a few subsequent amendments, including the unsuccessful Equal Rights Amendment, Congress has explicitly required ratification within seven years.)

Although Congress appears to control the amending process, its power is not absolute. Article V permits a second method: Two-thirds of the state legislatures may demand that Congress call an independent "convention for proposing amendments."

This means that if thirty-four state legislatures agree, Congress would be bound to call a constitutional convention, presumably like that which met in Philadelphia (and which has never since been duplicated).

In recent years, this second route to amendment has received considerable attention, because a call for a convention has been making the rounds of the state legislatures since the early 1970s. As of late 1986, thirty-two states had endorsed this application to Congress, just two states short of the required two-thirds majority. The impetus is the so-called balanced budget amendment (which Congress, under the spur of the potential convention and at the urging of President Reagan, has been considering independently). This amendment, or the congressional version at any rate, would require Congress to enact a budget each year that was in balance—but subject, according to its critics, to so many loopholes (a three-fifths majority could legislate deficits) that it would amount to flim-flam.

Many fear that a convention called to consider a single proposed amendment would become a "runaway," constituting itself a body to overhaul the entire Constitution. Congress has become alarmed enough to consider a Constitutional Convention Procedures Act, which would regulate the topics that any convention could consider. This act itself would be of dubious constitutionality, since Article V seems to permit the states to demand a convention that would have plenary powers—just as the Philadelphia Convention did (though itself called to consider an extremely limited agenda relating to navigation). However, the danger of a radical overhaul of the Constitution through the balanced budget route seems unlikely: Twenty-three of the state legislatures limited their application for a convention to the sole purpose of a balanced budget; they do not want a convention at all if it cannot be limited. Eleven of these states were even more direct about the danger of a runaway convention: Their applications explicitly stated that they are not to be counted in the total if

Proposed Constitutional Amendments

Of the thousands of proposals introduced in the Senate or House as constitutional amendments, many have been repetitive: Proposals were received by the dozens or scores to outlaw slavery, provide for uniform marriage and divorce laws throughout the United States, change the date on which sessions of Congress begin, regulate labor, prohibit polygamy, change the method of electing the president and senators, provide for women's suffrage, prohibit traffic in liquor, and even change the method of amending the Constitution.

Some, however, have been unusual, and show the range of concerns that our representatives have thought necessary to address at the highest possible legal level. For instance, in 1810, a serious effort was undertaken to strip Americans of their citizenship if they claimed or accepted titles of nobility or kept any presents from a king, emperor, or other foreign power. In the 1820s and 1830s, several proposals would have constitutionally abolished the practice of dueling. From time to time, members of Congress have wanted to strip themselves of the power to enact private bills—easier to point to the Constitution, apparently, than simply to refuse to enact a bill. Someone once also wanted to bar, constitutionally, anyone who owed a debt to the United States from serving in Congress.

Others have wanted to limit the length of soldiers' enlistment terms, require accounts of public moneys to be published, abolish the presidential veto, restrict the proposing of constitutional amendments to every tenth year, guarantee the "literal construction of the Constitution," provide an export tax on cotton, let the people elect postmasters, prohibit the contracting of convict labor, acknowledge the Deity in the Constitution, and even change the name of the country to the "United States of the World."

the convention could propose amendments other than that sought by the state legislature. These instructions should be sufficient for Congress constitutionally to refuse to call a convention, should two more states sign on.

In any event, chances are exceedingly slim that any particular constitutional amendment will emerge from Congress (or from a convention) and be ratified by three-fourths of the state legislatures. In two hundred years, some ten thousand amendments have been introduced in Congress; twenty-six have been adopted.

Still, the idea of massive constitutional reform to achieve political or social change remains beguiling to some. In 1974, Rexford G. Tugwell, one of President Franklin Roosevelt's original brain trust, presented the draft of a "Constitutional Model for the Newstates of America." The argument for it takes up most of a six-hundred-page book. In brief,

> [we] must worry about the competence of the newly devised institutions [that is, those in 1776] to meet the needs of the present. It is generally recognized that emergency has become an ever present potentiality; that vast and increasingly vaster powers are being concentrated in a president who is not physically or mentally different from the first president nearly two centuries ago; that both legislative and judiciary are very much changed; that striking alterations have been made in the Constitution, not by consciously undertaken revision but by other processes and that certainly the economic and social systems have been transformed since the existing Constitution was devised.

Twice as long as the present Constitution and amendments, Tugwell's is a curious document. He was drawn to renaming things; thus department secretaries became chancellors, the chief justice became the principal justice, the states "newstates." He also wanted to redraw maps: State boundaries could be modified beyond recognition. He proposed new branches of government: an electoral branch to supervise elections, a planning branch to engage in national economic planning, a judicial council, a judicial assembly,

and a regulatory branch with power over all economic enterprises. He wanted a president with a single nine-year term (an issue debated in 1787 but never entirely put to rest) and two vice presidents, the president to be recallable by a 40-percent popular veto in the third year (what is that but a second election, against no particular opponent?). He suggested life terms for senators (not all of them popularly elected). The model constitution even says that the salaries of lower judges should be two-thirds that of the principal justice, as if Congress could not be entrusted to determine proportionality for itself. On and on go Tugwell's suggestions—all bearing more than a faintly aristocratic odor.

Despite the sweeping detail of much of his model constitution, Tugwell was vague when it came to delineating rights (and responsibilities, which he considered necessary to be spelled out). His religion clause, for instance, said that "the practice of religion shall be privileged; but no religion shall be imposed by some on others, and none shall have public support." That clause achieves no discernible advantage over the present First Amendment. He proclaimed freedom of speech and press, but then took it away again by permitting their abridgment (to an unstated degree) in times of "declared emergency," a term left undefined. The due process clause he preserved intact, with all the ambiguities that we have seen. Though published in 1974, a year after *Roe v. Wade*, Tugwell's book devoted not a single word to the subject of abortion.

Is this document evidence of the waning powers of an eminent statesman in his final years or of the naiveté of one who has not thought hard about constitutionalism and judicial review? An acute analyst, Tugwell was no neophyte at assessing the perplexities and incongruities of modern American government, nor did he discount the difficulty of fundamental constitutional revision. Nevertheless, Tugwell's constitutional utopianism seems just that: the work of a scholar who can reassure his readers that "further

Founding Father

Caleb Strong

(did not sign the Constitution)

Caleb Strong was born in Northampton, Massachusetts, on January 9, 1745, and died there of a heart attack on November 7, 1819. In his early years, he was educated privately. Later, he studied at Harvard College, receiving his degree with highest honors in 1764. Soon after, he was taken ill with smallpox, which left him permanently poor sighted. Despite this handicap, in 1772 he was admitted to the bar, and that same year was appointed a selectman of Northampton. From 1774 through the close of the Revolution, he was on Northampton's town committee of safety. He was on the General Court in 1776, and acted as county attorney for the next twenty-four years. In 1779, he was part of the drafting committee of the Massachusetts state constitutional convention. The following year, he was a member of the last executively empowered Massachusetts Council. Also in 1780, he was appointed to the Continen-

tal Congress, but declined. He also declined an offer for a seat on the supreme judicial court (1783), serving instead as a state senator from 1780 to 1789. As a Massachusetts delegate to the Constitutional Convention, Strong was moderately active until August, when a family illness obliged him to leave the debates. In 1789, he was elected a U.S. senator. As senator, he was instrumental in framing the Judiciary Act, was selected to report Hamilton's national bank proposal to the Senate, and supported Jay's Treaty. He resigned in 1796 to resume his private law practice. In 1800, he was the Federalist candidate in the Massachusetts election for governor, and won. He was eventually defeated in 1807, though he ran again in 1812 and won, despite Governor Gerry's "gerrymandering" efforts. As governor, Strong was outspoken against national preparations for war with England, proclaiming a public fast on June 26 to symbolize opposition to the impending war "against the nation from which we are descended." In 1816, he retired from politics, though nominated to continue as governor of Massachusetts.

Strong was known as a religious, thoughtful, and moderate individual.

study and discussion should result in improvement," not the compromise of those whose votes count in making a constitution that will govern us all.

Still, Tugwell's hope is not an isolated case. A few years later, two Washingtonians, Morton Mintz, a well-known journalist, and Jerry S. Cohen, a Washington lawyer and former chief counsel to the Senate Antitrust and Monopoly Subcommittee, proposed that the remedy for all the ailments affecting the American public lay in a constitutional "happiness" amendment. They suggested giving citizens standing in federal court to challenge "any act or conduct of a person which act or conduct threatens to cause or is causing substantial harm to the safety or happiness of a consequential number of people." To choose only one among many difficulties, this standardless amendment would permit challenges both to doctors who do and do not perform abortions. Abortion was not Mintz and Cohen's target: They were concerned in the main with such things as environmental degradation. In this case, the problem is only sidestepped, for rather than settle it, they would delegate power to courts to rule as judges saw fit. But the proposal and its difficulties reflect the mentality of those who see all pressing problems as derangements of the political order and who see salvation only in constitutional rearrangement.

Political restructuring has largely been unnecessary, Don K. Price has suggested, because the "written Constitution of 1789 has been flexible enough to permit, within its formal framework, . . . the evolution of a richly varied unwritten constitution that can be adapted by political bargaining to new needs and circumstances." As James L. Sundquist notes, this unwritten constitution—the political possibilities that lie in the vague phrases of the written one—"has permitted the Congress to delegate extraordinary power to the president, as in wartime and during the economic catastrophe of the Great Depression, but to curtail that power when circumstances change. The Congress may submit to presidential leadership, but

it does so voluntarily and for only as long as it may choose. The president may act unilaterally, particularly in foreign relations, but he does so at the peril of having his policy undermined, or repudiated, by the Congress later."

Despite this flexibility, Sundquist writes of the perils in stalemated government—like the dangers of an ever-spiraling budget deficit, seemingly untamable (a Republican conservative president, deploring deficits, doubled the national debt in six years) and a war-making initiative left largely in the hands of the president without efficient check. In a serious and sophisticated proposal for constitutional change to remedy these defects, Sundquist concentrates on the truism "that the power to prevent bad acts can also be employed to prevent good ones, however those two adjectives may be defined by any individual."

From an analysis of the problems that beset us through an often divided and deadlocked government or an impotent one (because terms of office are arguably too short or for some other reason the particular administration has failed or is hopelessly at odds with Congress), Sundquist has suggested, "without regard to the question of what may or may not be politically feasible, an ideal series of amendments": (1) a "team ticket," under which every party's candidates for national office would be voted for as a single unit; (2) four-year House terms and eight-year Senate terms; (3) a special election to reconstitute a failed government; (4) removal of the Article I prohibition against congressional members' holding executive office (thus allowing the possibility of, but not requiring, a British parliamentary system); (5) a limited item veto, permitting the president to veto particular expenditures without having to veto an entire appropriation, while giving Congress by majority vote the power to override; (6) restoration of the legislative veto, struck down in *Chadha*; (7) a war powers amendment that would state clearly the degree to which the president can commit troops without a congressional declaration of war; (8) giving the House

George Wythe

(did not sign the Constitution)

George Wythe was born on his father's plantation on Black River, Elizabeth City County, Virginia, in 1726, and died in Virginia on June 8, 1806. Educated informally in Latin and Greek by his mother, he later attended the College of William and Mary grammar school. Later he studied law at Prince George County, and was admitted to the bar in 1746. He then formed an association with John Lewis in Spotsylvania County, remaining in this practice for eight years. In 1754, he became attorney general for several months while Peyton Randolph was away and unable to fulfill this post. He was a representative for Williamsburg in the House of Burgesses from 1754 to 1755. Continuing his legal studies, he was later admitted to the bar of the General Court. From 1758 to 1761, he again was in the House of Burgesses as a representative from the College of William and Mary. From 1761 to 1768, he represented Elizabeth City County. In 1768, he became mayor of Williamsburg, and the next year acted on the board of visitors for William and Mary, as well as clerk of the House of Burgesses (1769–1775). Wythe opposed the Stamp Act, in fact, drafted the Virginia resolutions of remonstrance for the act. At the outbreak of the Revolution, he volunteered his service, although he was soon called to the Continental Congress and served from 1775 to 1776. He signed the Declaration of Independence, was on the committee that created Virginia's seal, and with Jefferson and Edmund Pendleton, helped revise the laws of Virginia. In 1777, he was speaker of the House of Delegates. The following year, he became one of the three judges of Virginia's High Court of Chancery, later becoming sole chancellor. In 1779, he was named to the first chair of law in an American college (William and Mary), titled "Professorship of Law and Police." There, for the next twenty years, he proved himself an American innovator of jurisprudence and published several works. In 1799, he left the seat to form his own modest law school. As a Virginia delegate to the Constitutional Convention in 1787, he was an esteemed though little active framer. Other obligations took him away from the Convention.

Polite and conscientious, Wythe was known for his legal ethics. He turned down cases he considered unjust and refused to represent those he felt corrupt. He was a vestryman in the Episcopal Church, and opposed slavery (he freed his own slaves, even leaving one a legacy). Poisoned with arsenic by his grandnephew, who meant to kill Wythe's servant to free up additional inheritance money, he died at his home.

a concurrent power to ratify treaties (and reducing the power of minority veto by removing the two-thirds majority rule); and (9) some form of national referendum to allow the people to break deadlocks between the branches.

This is a tall list. Sundquist himself agrees that "nothing is likely to happen short of crisis." We have had crisis aplenty, and nothing like any of the items on his list has come close to passage. Are these proposals worthy of discussion, as Sundquist suggests? Certainly. Are they likely to become enshrined in the Constitution? Certainly not. Our history teaches that the most enduring part of the Constitution is the formal political structure it created, just because, as Price has said, the formal structure is so pliable after all.

Constitutional Change and Judicial Review

It would be rhetorically convenient but inaccurate to say that it is as easy to amend the Constitution by judicial interpretation as it is difficult to amend it formally by Congress. Not every constitutional decision that according to some critic's lights extends (or abridges) a constitutional right or broadens (or curtails) a constitutional power is for that reason alone the functional equivalent of an amendment. As history has shown, and as not even the most rigid proponent of judicial restraint argues, the courts must necessarily interpret the delphic constitutional phrases. To say, for instance, that the legislative veto is unconstitutional is not to amend the Constitution, likewise to say that prayers in school unconstitutionally encroach on religious freedom.

Still, the line is thin, and over time a line of decisions may work up to a sizable change in prior constitutional understanding—for example, the line of cases beginning in the 1920s that the Fourteenth Amendment incorporates most of the Bill of Rights.

Usually, constitutional change comes slowly, case by case, as in the evolving doctrine of incorporation. As we have seen, this is the mechanism by which the Constitution has come to be made workable from one generation to the next, or at least over a series of generations.

Sometimes, though, the Court has made genuinely revolutionary decisions—in a sudden leap. *Dred Scott* was one. Either the decision to permit states to segregate by race (in 1896) or the decision that states may not segregate by race in schools (in 1954) was revolutionary; take your pick. The reapportionment and abortion decisions were so. Arguably, so too were *Miranda v. Arizona* (criminal confessions and right to counsel) and *Allgeyer v. Louisiana* (economic due process), though each of these was foreshadowed by considerable judicial rumblings.

These changes were products not merely of logic or of sentiment but also of political fortuity. Timing, specific issues that may generate heat for a few months and then disappear, and personalities place presidents in the White House. Presidents, with the consent of the Senate, place justices on the Supreme Court. How many they get to appoint depends on judicial longevity. On that depends also the kind of Court we get. Washington named ten justices who were confirmed; Franklin Roosevelt, nine; Jackson, six; Lincoln, Grant, Taft, and Eisenhower, five each; Nixon, four; Carter, none.

The Supreme Court is a continuing body. No single appointment can change its course all at once. Nevertheless, at certain historical moments, major changes have been sealed, either because a justice of one persuasion or another comes to a Court delicately balanced between opposing views or because, in short order, a series of judges was named. The Court changed when Chief Justice Taney replaced John Marshall; it changed when FDR within four years named seven justices.

For the past thirty-two years, since 1954, the Court

has taken an activist course, no less under Chief Justice Burger than under Chief Justice Warren. (During that time, eleven of the twenty-three justices who served on the Court were appointed by Democratic presidents, and of these eleven, six served for four years or less.) That the Court has, over the political memory of so many Americans, played so large a role so often is something of a surprise—or so, looking ahead from 1953, it would have seemed.

Presidents often profess to be astonished by opinions of the justices they have appointed: Theodore Roosevelt said, apropos of Oliver Wendell Holmes's antitrust decisions ("I could carve out of a banana a judge with more backbone than that!"); Dwight Eisenhower lamented his appointment of Earl Warren ("biggest damnfool decision I ever made"); and Woodrow Wilson probably blanched on more than one occasion at decisions of James McReynolds, likely the most reactionary justice ever to sit on the Court. Yet as Laurence Tribe points out, the examples of presidential surprise are exceptions, not the rule, and most of these are myth, for what the presidents got was almost wholly predictable.

On the eve of the Constitution's bicentennial, the Court and the country seem to be at a rare historical crossroads. With Chief Justice Burger's retirement announced in the summer of 1986, President Reagan's naming of William Rehnquist as chief justice and Antonin Scalia as associate justice will assuredly solidify the conservative bloc, as conservative a bloc as has existed in at least half a century. Though immediate decisions are unlikely to deviate widely from the course of decisions that have lately been handed down, fundamental change could come with the next two appointments. For if the oldest and most liberal justices—Brennan and Marshall—leave the Court while Reagan is still in office, two more conservative justices with fundamentally different views on the power of the Court to interpret the Constitution could substantially alter much that has gone before. At the other

Chief Justice Warren Burger

Antonin Scalia is sworn in as associate justice by Warren Burger in September 1986. William Rehnquist appears on the left; President Reagan on the right.

extreme, should other conservatives, like Powell and O'Connor, leave the Court with a Democrat in the White House, the historical watershed that so many have begun to predict will simply evaporate.

But even a "radically" conservative Court is likely to change more the direction of a still evolving doctrine than a doctrine that has been largely articulated. It is inconceivable that any nominee whom the Senate would confirm would vote, once on the Court, to rescind the principles of *Brown v. Board,* though the highly controversial affirmative action doctrine might well be rendered toothless. It is equally unlikely that the Court will roll back six decades of Fourteenth Amendment jurisprudence to declare that the states are henceforth free to act in major ways not permitted the federal government under the Bill of Rights. Despite the apparent hint in speeches in 1985 and 1986 by the attorney general that suggest he would like the Court to abandon incorporation, the Court will not, at this date, permit states to establish their own churches or to censor newspapers, though the most controversial of the Warren Court's criminal rights deci-

sions, like *Miranda* and *Mapp,* could conceivably be reversed outright or reduced to impotence. *Roe v. Wade* and its associated decisions could certainly be overturned as well, especially if *Roe* remains the litmus test for conservative judicial nominees. But the far more likely impact of any radical realignment of judicial values is on what has not yet come to be.

Some Unanswered Questions

In no particular order, here are some of the major issues that remain unresolved and whose resolution, case by case, will affect us as individuals and groups, to a greater or lesser extent, in the immediate years to come.

Privacy. The question of personal privacy (containing within its possible definition the issue of autonomy to act in personal matters) was one that the framers either overlooked, or meant to leave to the states. As we have seen, various bits and pieces of privacy concerns (in the Fourth Amendment, for example) suggest the necessity for constitutionally protecting such a right. But its extent is highly controversial. Two aspects of personal privacy will be keenly contested in the next several years: the use of drug and polygraph (lie detector) testing by employers and others. To what degree may federal, state, or local governments demand that a worker, an applicant for a license, or a citizen be tested for drug use? In 1986, sharply increased concern over drug abuses (including the use of "crack," a potent form of cocaine that is highly addictive and can be lethal) led to numerous demands that athletes, teachers, police officers, firefighters, and others be tested at random. The president volunteered a urine specimen to demonstrate his support for testing. In such random tests between 1983 and 1985, the Pentagon discharged fifty-one thousand members of the armed forces for misusing drugs. Athletes playing on teams belonging to major leagues may have contractually agreed to be bound by rulings of their commissioners, including the power to test randomly. But many others, especially municipal workers, have argued, with some success in the lower courts, that without reasonable suspicion, random testing of any individual violates Fourth Amendment rights. Likewise, polygraph testing of employees has been condemned—though the argument to some is less that it violates the Fourth Amendment than that it is inherently faulty, and Congress is moving to bar lie detectors in private employment in both preemployment screening and on-the-job investigations. Public attention was dramatically focused on the issue when Secretary of State George Schultz said he would resign before submitting to a lie detector test, as President Reagan had suggested for senior government officials to stem the tide of official leaks. A still larger issue—the power of government to spy on citizens, or at least to maintain surveillance and gather unevaluated information that goes into files where, years later, it may do serious damage—remains largely open.

Polygraph testing will be a controversial aspect of the right to personal privacy during the next several years.

Robert Yates

(did not sign the Constitution)

Robert Yates was born in Schenectady, New York, on January 27, 1738, and died in Albany, on September 9, 1801. He was classically educated in New York City, and later studied law with William Livingston. In 1760, he was admitted to the bar in Albany, his home for the rest of his life. From 1771 to 1775, he was on the town board of aldermen, also serving on the Committee of Safety and as a representative from Albany in New York's four provincial congresses and one convention from 1775 to 1777. Between 1776 and 1777, as congressman, he was on the secret committee to block the Hudson channel, the Committee on Arrangements for the Continental regiments, and the Committee of Thirteen which drafted the first New York constitution. In 1777, he was named a justice to the New York Supreme Court and in 1790 was appointed chief justice, at which post he served until 1798, gaining a reputation for high ethics. In 1786, he was named to the commission to settle land disputes between New York and Massachusetts. Four years later, he helped do the same between New York and Vermont, and in 1795, he was on the commission that distributed funds from Vermont to New York claimants. An adamant Anti-Federalist, he was a delegate to the Philadelphia Convention and a member of the Committee of Revision. Along with fellow New York delegate Lansing, Yates left the Convention the day the committee made its report, on the grounds that the actions of the framers had exceeded their authority. Yates was active in his dissent over the Constitution. He wrote several essays under the names "Brutus" and "Sydney" attacking the documents, and opposed the Constitution at the New York state ratifying convention. Between 1789 and 1795, he ran for governor twice (once with Federalist support and once as an Anti-Federalist), but was defeated both times. In 1800, he was on the commission to settle land disputes in Onondaga County, New York. This was his last public service. He died the following year, with little means. In 1821, his wife published posthumously his notes on the proceedings of the Convention.

Though Yates did not attend the entire Convention, his notes have been useful to historians.

Financial Support for Religious Schools. The question is far from settled. Major change in the degree to which states could provide grants-in-aid to schools that carry out secular teaching and other secular functions remains very much open—as does the definition of *secular*.

Restrictions on Campaign Funding. One of the most heated long-term debates in American politics is the impact of money on campaigning. Various bills to regulate contributions and expenditures have been proposed and passed. The Court has cut some to shreds, allowed others. To what extent campaign financing can be regulated remains an open constitutional question.

The Distinction between "Public" and "Private". One of the most vexing and least resolved constitutional issues, though it may seem technical, is the type of activity that, though seemingly private, is in fact public enough to be governed by constitutional restrictions. When a "company town," wholly owned by a corporation in Alabama, refused to permit private individuals to distribute literature on its streets, the Supreme Court declared the town to be performing public functions subject to the First Amendment. Likewise, when a state leased a building on a public highway to a restaurant that discriminated, the Court held that the state's lease constituted "state action" sufficient to bring the restaurant within the antidiscrimination provisions of the equal protection clause. But may private clubs and other organizations discriminate on racial or sexual grounds in the absence of local legislation prohibiting it? The question remains open—and vital.

Press Freedoms. A spate of revelations, leading to espionage convictions, that American servicemen and federal employees sold or gave major intelligence secrets to the Soviet Union and China has prompted the federal government to demand anew more rigid laws against disclosure of official secrets. The United States has never had an "official secrets law." The constitutionality of such an act (permitting punishment of the press as well as leakers), should it come to be, might very well depend on who sits on the High Court in the next few years, and the answer could have a material impact on the conduct of journalism (and of government).

An Unfolding Constitution

For all its familiarity, the Constitution remains a document that is never wholly knowable, because the keepers of its flame, taking indirect dictation from the public itself, are a changing lot and because, more importantly, the society that the Constitution helped spawn is the most rapidly changing society ever known. This proposition needs no documentation here, but a small example makes the point better than ample numbers of surveys.

Comedian George Carlin's "seven dirty words" monologue was the subject of a 1978 Court decision allowing the FCC to regulate broadcasts containing indecent language.

In 1978, the Supreme Court held that the Federal Communications Commission may constitutionally regulate language on the radio (and by extension, network television) that is indecent, though not obscene. The case grew out of Pacifica Radio's broadcast of comedian George Carlin's twelve-minute monologue entitled "Filthy Words." It was undisputed, said Justice Stevens, that "the content of Pacifica's broadcast was 'vulgar,' 'offensive,' and 'shocking.'" What seemed to concern the Court most was that Pacifica broadcast Carlin's words during the middle of a weekday afternoon, when children might have been listening. The broadcast, Justice Stevens said, "could have enlarged a child's vocabulary in an instant" before a parent could exercise control at the source.

Less than a decade later, George Carlin appeared in a new medium—cable television—in a one-man comedy special in which some of these same vexing words were repeated without fear of regulation by the FCC. Why? The simple though inexplicable answer is that cable television is constitutionally freer than broadcast radio and television because the signal is not beamed out through the airwaves (there being fewer airwaves than cable channels). Does the child who turns the television dial distinguish such subtleties? Do you? In every facet of life, technology creates new possibilities and raises new constitutional questions. That ought no longer be surprising.

Of course, in every age, on any day, the "official" declaration of our constitutionalism may not square with its practice. The courts may say we are free to talk or walk or run and yet petty officials, high or low, may interfere with these rights. That may be cause for alarm, but never for defeat. Again and again, we come back as a nation to a practiced constitutionalism, and again and again things right themselves over time. Is this a consequence of the Constitution or of our national character and an open society? No simple answer can be given; it is one of our intellectual peculiarities that we seek solitary explanations for complex phenomena. But who can doubt that the Constitution has been instrumental in keeping this society open enough for reform to occur far more quickly and with far less bloodshed than attends reforms worldwide—as one glance at the tragedy unfolding in South Africa surely shows? Constitutionalism is not only an ideal but it is also a practical belief, bred in the bone. As rational creatures, we employ reason often merely to rationalize, and rationalization has from time to time been elevated to the highest art in defense of the constitutionally indefensible. But somehow those rationalizations do not last. People are free in America, under the Constitution, to see things in new ways and talk about them and make the force of that new way felt.

To assess the Constitution, we must learn to step back from this Supreme Court and this president and this Congress here and now and ask what the con-

The Supreme Court of the United States on the eve of the Constitution's Bicentennial.

stitutional system has been and has become. When we do, we find that the marvelously intricate system, set in motion two centuries ago, is capable of producing progressive and heartening change, even as it is always in danger of proceeding toward heartless change. But it is the possibility of peaceful reform— toward more equal rights and more equal possibilities, toward more freedom from arbitrary, unknown law, for more people, rather than for fewer—that distinguishes the American system from all the others on the globe. Remember that it is a Constitution we *all* are expounding. Still.

Notes and References

The notes and references collected here are keyed to specific passages in the text. No other references are given, for any attempt to exhaust the literature would itself be exhausting. Because this is not a scholarly text, no specific page references are given to quotations from court cases; each case is cited in full form when first discussed in the text. Subsequent discussion can be located in the Index of Cases. References to works frequently cited are given only once in full and thereafter are cited only by the author's name. The full citation can be located in the Bibliography that follows this section.

Prologue: To Celebrate a Constitution

Page 2: *Index to Legal Periodicals:* The *Index* shows 146 articles devoted to constitutional studies for the period September 1984 through August 1985, the last full year of listings as this is written. Headings included in this figure are Constitutional Amendments, Constitutional Conventions, Constitutional History, Constitutional Law, and Constitutional Law-U.S. A multitude of specific constitutional topics, like free speech and self-incrimination, are listed separately. Between 1976 and 1979, 741 articles were listed under this same general heading.

Page 2: Glossators have rivaled the work of biblical scholars—depending, of course, on what you mean by scholar and gloss. Perhaps I have taken some liberties here. Michael Grant, in his *Jesus, An Historian's Review of the Gospels* (New York: Charles Scribner's Sons, 1977), p. 197, notes that during the nineteenth century alone, sixty thousand biographies of Jesus were written. That does rather eclipse the torrent of commentary on the Constitution.

Page 2: United States Constitution Sesquicentennial Commission, *History of the Formation of the Union Under the Constitution* (Washington, D.C.: Government Printing Office, 1943); reprinted by Greenwood Press, New York, 1968. The story of Sol Bloom and the Sesquicentennial Commission is engagingly told in Michael Kammen, *A Machine That Would Go of Itself* (New York: Alfred A. Knopf, 1986), Chap. 10.

Page 3: On pseudoevents, see Daniel J. Boorstin, *The Image* (New York: Harper Colophon Books, 1964).

Page 3: Story in the *New York Times*, "Know Your Constitution," April 16, 1986, p. B8.

Page 3: Dallas: Quoted in W. Hickey, *The Constitution of the United States of America*, 4th ed. (Philadelphia, 1851), p. iii.

Page 4: Constitution we are expounding: McCulloch v. Maryland, 4 Wheat. 316, 407 (1819).

Page 4: Last time for real: There has been much hugger-mugger over the Court's abortion decision of 1973 (see p. 267), but the level of debate is less constitutional than political; those who damn the Court want the Constitution amended. The debate is not over the interpretation—as it was over whether Nixon could be tried before being impeached, or whether he should have to turn over the tapes despite his claim of executive privilege—but over the policy. Moreover, the entire American public was exercised in 1974; the abortion debate centers in more discrete quarters. Other sharp constitutional debates, still ongoing, are those on school prayer and rights of criminal defendants, one of the primary issues of President Nixon's 1968 campaign, an issue that has become somewhat muted over the past few years.

Page 4: The Supreme Court follows the election returns: This is the well-known aphorism of Mr. Dooley's creator, Finley Peter Dunne.

Page 4: Other books do that: Two of the most important are Harold W. Chase and Craig R. Ducat, *Corwin's The Constitution and What It Means Today* (Princeton, N.J.: Princeton University Press, 1978 ed., with 1980 Supplement), and Laurence H. Tribe, *American Constitutional Law* (Mineola, N.Y.: Foundation Press, 1978, with 1981 Supplement). I have relied greatly on both these treatises. Unfortunately, the rush of constitutional decision has made these books already somewhat out of date. I have also relied on Gerald Gunther, *Cases and Materials on Individual Rights in Constitutional Law*, 3d ed. (Mineola, N.Y.: Foundation Press, 1981, and 1984 Supplement), and Stephen A. Saltzburg, *American Criminal Procedure*, 2d ed. (St. Paul: West, 1984, with 1985 Supplement).

Chapter 1: The Search for Constitutionalism

Page 9: Divinely inspired: As late as 1936, Justice George Sutherland, for one, affirmed his belief in the divine inspiration of our fundamental charter; noted in Alexander M. Bickel, *The Supreme Court and the Idea of Progress* (New Haven: Yale University Press, 1978), pp. 14–15. The after-dinner expositor of the Constitution (1913): Quoted in Bickel, p. 15.

Page 10: Liberty is the happiness: Richard Price, quoted in Gordon S. Wood, *The Creation of the American Republic 1776–1787* (New York: W. W. Norton, 1972), p. 24.

Page 11: Leading scholar: Charles Howard McIlwain, *Constitutionalism Ancient and Modern* (Ithaca, N.Y.: Cornell University Press, rev. ed. 1947), pp. 21–22.

Page 11: Cicero: Quoted in Edwin S. Corwin, *The "Higher Law" Background of American Constitutional Law* (Ithaca, N.Y.: Cornell University Press, 1955), p. 10; a different translation of this same famous passage is by George Holland Sabine and Stanley Barney Smith, *On the Commonwealth* (Indianapolis: Bobbs-Merrill, 1976), pp. 215–216.

Page 12: Dr. Bonham's case: Coke, quoted in Corwin, p. 44.

Page 13: Parliament can do anything: Quoted in Corwin, p. 87.

Page 15: Locke, *Second Treatise of Government*, § 222; in Peter Laslett, *John Locke's Two Treatises of Government*, rev. ed. (New York: New American Library, 1965), pp. 460–461 (italics in the original).

Page 16: Rousseau noted: Jean-Jacques Rousseau, *The Social Contract*, Book 3, Chapter 4.

Page 16: Burke: Quoted in Wood, p. 175.

Page 17: Henry and Winthrop: Quoted in Benjamin R. Barber, "The Compromised Republic: Public Purposelessness in America," in Robert H. Horwitz, ed., *The Moral Foundations of the American Republic*, 2d ed. (Charlottesville: University Press of Virginia, 1979), p. 22.

Page 19: Jacob Shallus: The story of the detective work to uncover Shallus's identity is in John C. Fitzpatrick, "The

Man Who Engrossed the Constitution," in *History of the Formation of the Union Under the Constitution*, United States Sesquicentennial Commission (Washington, D.C.: Government Printing Office, 1943; reprinted New York: Greenwood Press, 1968).

Chapter 2: Constitutionalism Before the Constitution

Page 21: Mayflower Compact: Quoted in Page Smith, *The Constitution, A Documentary and Narrative History* (New York: Morrow Quill Paperbacks, 1980), pp. 24–25.

Page 22: Massachusetts Bay charter: Quoted in Lawrence M. Friedman, *A History of American Law* (New York: Simon and Schuster, 1973), p. 33.

Page 23: Articles of Confederation of United Colonies: Taken from Albert Bushness Hart and Edward Channing, eds., *American Historical Leaflets* (New York: Parker B. Simmons, 1917), No. 7, "Articles of Confederation of the United Colonies of New England, 1643–1684," p. 9.

Page 24: Chauncey: Quoted in Lawrence H. Leder, *Liberty and Authority: Early American Political Ideology, 1689–1763* (New York: W. W. Norton, 1976), pp. 82–83.

Page 24: Parliaments are not the Constitution: Quoted in Leder, p. 92.

Page 24: Throne as well as cottage: *New York Gazette*, November 1, 1756, quoted in Leder, p. 94.

Page 24: One New York lawyer argued in 1734: Quoted in Leder, pp. 96–97.

Page 24: Otis: Quoted in Cecelia M. Kenyon, "Constitutionalism in Revolutionary America," in J. Roland Pennock and John W. Chapman, eds., *Constitutionalism* (New York: New York University Press, 1979), p. 86.

Page 27: Lawrence Friedman, on strength of idea of constitutionalism: p. 102.

Page 27: State constitutions: Much of the material in this section is taken from Cecelia M. Kenyon, "Constitutionalism in Revolutionary America," in J. Roland Pennock and John W. Chapman, eds., *Constitutionalism* (New York: New York University Press, 1979), pp. 84–121.

Pages 27–28: Tidewater aristocracy: Kenyon, p. 96.

Page 28: Every state . . . needed a degree of virtue: Wood, p. 68.

Page 30: The most aristocratic or oligarchic of any: Kenyon, p. 109.

Page 30: Sun and moon shall endure: Memorial of the people of Pittsfield, Mass., quoted in Oscar and Mary Handlin, eds., *The Popular Sources of Political Authority: Documents on the Massachusetts Constitution of 1780* (Cambridge, Mass.: Harvard University Press, 1966), p. 64.

Page 30: Democratic despotism: Referred to in Wood, p. 404.

Page 30: Madison on legislatures' wantonly multiplying the laws: From his "Vices of the Political System of the United States," quoted in Wood, p. 406.

Page 31: Visible declension of religion: Quoting the Charleston S.C. and American Gazette, Jan. 21, 1779, in Wood, p. 417.

Page 31: Lawsuits like rabbits: Wood, p. 417.

Page 31: Correspondents to Jefferson: Quoted in Wood, p. 424.

Page 31: Otis: Quoted in Wood, p. 476.

Page 32: Sharply different economic interest: I follow here Merrill Jensen, *The New Nation, A History of the United States During the Confederation 1781–1789* (Boston: Northeastern University Press, 1981), pp. 18–27.

Page 33: Creation of responsible staff, and Joseph Nourse: Jensen, p. 360.

Page 33: James Wilson: Quoted in Broadus & Louise Mitchell, *A Biography of the Constitution of the United States* (New York: Oxford University Press, 1964), p. 7.

Page 34: Interest on debt estimated at 50 percent of states' budgets: Jensen, p. 304.

Page 35: John Quincy Adams: Quoted in Wood, p. 393.

Chapter 3: The Framing of the Constitution

Page 37: James Madison on commerce: Quoted in Farrand, *The Framing of the Constitution* (New Haven: Yale University Press, 1913), p. 7.

Page 38: Jefferson wrote Adams: Farrand, p. 39. Farrand notes that Jefferson's view was not universally shared. Writing at the time the delegates were being chosen, P. L. Ford, an opponent of the convention, noted: "I do not wish to detract from their merits, but I will venture to affirm, that twenty assemblies of equal number might be collected, equally respectable both in point of ability, integrity, and patriotism. Some of the characters which compose it I revere; others I consider as of small consequence, and a number are suspected of being great public defaulters, and to have been guilty of notorious peculation and fraud, with regard to public property in the hour of our distress" (p. 40). Farrand himself concluded that "the convention as a whole was composed of men such as would be appointed to a similar gathering at the present time [1912]: professional men, business men, and gentlemen of leisure; patriotic statesmen and clever, scheming politicians; some trained by experience and study for the task before them, and others utterly unfit. It was essentially a representative body, taking possibly a somewhat higher tone from the social conditions of the time, the seriousness of the crisis, and the character of the leaders" (pp. 40–41).

Page 38: Lee on possibility of second convention: Smith, p. 89.

Page 40: Madison on historical moment: Quoted in Farrand, p. 61.

Page 40: Morris and Wilson on convention import: Farrand, p. 62.

Page 41: Madison quoted in Max Farrand, *The Framing of the Constitution of the United States* p. 60.

Page 44: "Most trying and tiresome . . ": Smith, p. 214.

Page 46: Madison on Morris's prose: Farrand, p. 181.

Page 48: Sherman's rejoinder: Quoted in Catherine Drinker Bowen, *Miracle at Philadelphia* (Boston: Little, Brown, 1966), pp. 245–246.

Page 49: General William Thompson: Quoted in Smith, p. 241.

Page 49: Amos Singletary: Quoted in Smith, p. 242.

Page 49: Thompson for amending Articles of Confederation: Quoted in Smith, p. 242.

Page 49: Patrick Henry opposing Constitution: Quoted in Smith, p. 248.

Page 49–50: Light Horse Harry Lee: Quoted in Smith, pp. 242–250.

Page 50: Some contend: "*The Federalist* worked only a small influence upon the course of events during the struggle over ratifications. . . . The chief usefulness of *The Federalist* in the events of 1788 was as a kind of debater's handbook in Virginia and New York." Clinton Rossiter, Introduction to *The Federalist Papers* (New York: Mentor Books, 1961), p. xi.

Page 51: Greatest act of prestidigitation: Smith, p. 527.

Page 52: Max Farrand echoes Madison: Farrand, p. 204.

Page 53: Forty-three hundred words: The first seven articles of the Constitution take about 4,300 words, and the twenty-six amendments another 3,000.

Page 55: On no feudalism: Louis Hartz, *The Liberal Tradition in America* (New York: Harcourt Brace and World, 1955).

Page 55: William Henry Drayton, in 1776: Quoted in Wood, p. 39.

Page 55: Blessed beyond all others by the bounty of nature: See David Potter, *People of Plenty: Economic Abundance and the American Character* (Chicago: University of Chicago Press, 1954).

Chapter 4: The Legislative Power

Page 59: Mark Twain, *Around the Equator* (1897).

Page 61: Permanent capital: Art. I, Sect. 8, Cl. 17. The present District of Columbia is actually smaller than that, Virginia having regained in 1846 her portion of the original cession.

Page 61: Fisher Ames: Quoted in Alvin M. Josephy, Jr., *On the Hill: A History of the American Congress* (New York: Simon and Schuster, 1979), p. 10.

Page 61: Each house may write its own rules: Art. I, Sect. 5, Cl. 2.

Page 66: When taking his seat, but not on the day when elected. This understanding goes back to the election of Henry Clay to the Senate, then under thirty. He was deemed properly elected as long as he would turn thirty before taking the oath of office. By extension, the rules applies to representatives as well. See Senate Report 904, 74th Cong., 1st Sess. (1935).

Page 66: Senate divided into classes: Art. I, Sect. 3, Cl. 2.

Page 66: Powell v. McCormack, 395 U.S. 486 (1969).

Page 67: Roudebush v. Hartke, 405 U.S. 15 (1972).

Page 67: The contest over the election in Indiana's Eighth District resulted in a House determination (236–190) that incumbent Democrat Frank McCloskey had won by four votes, leading to a walkout by Republicans amid threats of severe reprisals. *New York Times*, May 2, 1985, p. A1.

Page 67: Libel and slander provision: Art. I, Sect. 6, Cl. 1.

Page 67: Ray v. Proxmire, 581 F.2d 998 (D.C. Cir. 1978), *cert. denied*, 99 S.Ct. 326 (1978); Hutchinson v. Proxmire, 99 S.Ct. 2675 (1979).

Page 68: Powers herein granted: Art. I, Sect. 1, Cl. 1.

Page 68: Taxing and spending power: Art. I, Sect. 8, Cl. 1.

Page 68: Original Constitution on taxing authority: Art. I, Sect. 2, Cl. 3 and Sect. 9, Cl. 4.

Page 68: Borrow money: Art. I, Sect. 8, Cl. 2.

Page 68: Regulate commerce: Art. I, Sect. 8, Cl. 3.

Page 68: Naturalization: Art. I, Sect. 8, Cl. 4.

Page 68: Bankruptcy power: Art. I, Sect. 8, Cl. 4.

Page 69: Coin and regulate money: Art. I, Sect. 8, Cl. 5.

Page 69: Weights and measures: Art. I, Sect. 8, Cl. 5.

Page 69: Counterfeiting: Art. I, Sect. 8, Cl. 6. Congress would have had this power without its specific enumeration, as an adjunct to its power to regulate money.

Page 69: Post office power: Art. I, Sect. 8, Cl. 7.

Page 69: Patents and copyrights: Art. I, Sect. 8, Cl. 8.

Page 70: Lower federal courts: Art. I, Sect. 8, Cl. 9.

Page 70: International law: Art. I, Sect. 8, Cl. 10.

Page 70: War powers: Art. I, Sect. 8, Cls. 11–14.

Page 70: Militia powers: Art. I, Sect. 8, Cl. 15–16.

Page 70: Except in two respects, Congress has complete control of the militia, having the power to tell the states how to organize the militia and what kind of training is necessary. The states may appoint officers of the militia (subject to standards set by the president) and train members of the militia (subject to congressional standards).

Page 70: National capital: Art. I, Sect. 8, Cl. 17.

Page 70: Succession to the presidency: Art. II, Sect. 1, Cl. 6 and the Twelfth, Twentieth, and Twenty-fifth Amendments.

Page 70: Vest appointments: Art. II, Sect. 2, Cl. 2.

Page 70: Control court jurisdiction: Art. III, Sect. 2, Cl. 2.

Page 70: Admit states: Art. IV, Sect. 3, Cl. 1–2.

Page 70: Citizens of Puerto Rico, Guam, and the Virgin Islands are citizens of the United States. Puerto Ricans, by virtue of their commonwealth status, are self-governing to the extent that the states are, but may not vote in national elections. American Samoans are not citizens but nationals of the United States. Guam and American Samoa are under the jurisdiction of the U.S. Interior Department. Wake Island is under the jurisdiction of the Air Force; the Midway Islands are under Navy administration. The Mariannas are about to become a commonwealth of the United States.

Page 70: Disposition of federal property: In 1982, the Supreme Court ruled that even if it was unconstitutional for the Department of Health, Education, and Welfare to donate a surplus U.S. military hospital to a church-related college, no one would have standing to challenge the statute, and hence as a practical matter Congress may do as it likes in disposing of federal property. Valley Forge Christian College v. Americans United for Separation of Church and State, Inc., 454 U.S. 464 (1982).

Page 71: Necessary and proper clause: Art. I, Sect. 8, Cl. 18.

Pages 71–72: Marshall's words: McCulloch v. Maryland, 17 U.S. (4 Wheat.) 315 (1819).

Page 72: Madison quoted in Louis Fisher, *Constitutional Conflicts Between Congress and the President* (Princeton, N.J.: Princeton University Press, 1985), p. 19.

Page 72: McCulloch v. Maryland, 17 U.S. (4 Wheat.) 316 (1819).

Page 72: Power to shape maritime law: In re Garnett, 141 U.S. 1 (1891).

Page 73: Apportionment requirement: Art. I, Sect. 2, Cl. 3 and Sect. 9, Cl. 4. The ruling against the income tax was Pollock v. Farmers Loan and Trust Co., 157 U.S. 429 and 158 U.S. 601 (1895). The Court did not rule that *all* income taxes were direct; it would have permitted taxation of incomes based on professional and occupational pursuits, but invalidated the federal income tax statute because it intermixed taxes on incomes from business activities and property. From then until 1913, when the Sixteenth Amendment was ratified, the Court wavered and might have ultimately overruled *Pollock*. Thus in Flint v. Tracy Co., 220 U.S. 107 (1911), it held that Congress could legitimately subject corporate income to an indirect tax on the theory that the income was merely a measure of the privilege of doing business in corporate form.

Page 73: Civil War income tax law: Springer v. United States, 102 U.S. 586 (1881).

Page 73: With one exception: A tax on stock dividends distributed to corporate stockholders is considered direct if taxed to the stockholder and may not be imposed unless apportioned equally among the states, making the tax impossible to lay. Eisner v. Macomber, 252 U.S. 189 (1920).

Page 73: Taxes on embezzled money: James v. United States, 366 U.S. 213 (1961).

Page 73: Retroactive operation of income tax: Shanahan v. United States, 447 F.2d 1082 (10th Cir. 1971); Welch v. Henry, 305 U.S. 134 (1938).

Page 74: Severely regulate a company: United States v. Sanchez, 340 U.S. 42 (1950).

Page 74: General welfare clause: Art. I, Sect. 8, Cl. 1.

Page 74: Hamilton's view on the spending power: Quoted in Tribe, p. 249, from 3 *Works of Alexander Hamilton* 372 (Lodge ed. 1885).

Page 74: Upholding the Social Security Act: Helvering v. Davis, 301 U.S. 619 (1937).

Page 74: Howard Phillips, "Let's De-Fund the Left," *Conservative Digest*, April 1982, p. 50.

Page 76: President Jackson's postmaster general directed to pay: Kendall v. United States, 37 U.S. (12 Pet.) 524 (1838).

Page 76: President Nixon's belief that the Senate must consent to his nominees to federal office: "Text of the President's Letter to Senator Saxbe Defending His Nomination of Carswell to High Court," *New York Times*, April 2, 1970, p. 28.

Page 76: President may not withhold funds because he does not like the program: Train v. City of New York, 420 U.S. 35 (1975).

Page 77: Schechter Poultry Corp. v. United States, 295 U.S. 495 (1935).

Page 78: 1881 case: Kilbourn v. Thompson, 103 U.S. 168 (1881).

Page 78: Quoted in Edward Dumbauld, *The Bill of Rights and What It Means Today* 174–75, 183, 199 (Norman: University of Oklahoma Press, 1957).

Page 78: Supreme Court has recently recognized: Buckley v. Valeo, 424 U.S. 1 (1976).

Page 78: Helms-Hunt race in North Carolina: William E. Schmidt, "Caustic N.C. Senate Race Is Ending Up a Dead Heat," *New York Times*, Nov. 4, 1984, p. 34; according to this article, the race cost $22 million and featured more than eight thousand television commercials.

Page 78: American pluralism at work: For a trenchant criticism of pluralist theory, see Henry S. Kariel, *The Decline of American Pluralism* (Stanford, Calif.: Stanford University Press, 1961), and Theodore J. Lowi, *The End of Liberalism* (New York: W. W. Norton, 1969).

Page 79: Capture of Congressional power: See Lowi, *The End of Liberalism.*

Chapter 5: The Executive Power

Page 81: "The President is at liberty": Woodrow Wilson, *Constitutional Government* (New York: Columbia University Press, 1921), p. 70.

Page 81: Character fit for republicanism: Americans, said one essayist in 1777, "instead of being sunk into that general licentiousness, profligacy and dissoluteness of manners, of which there is so much complaint in the ancient countries; are, for the most part, industrious, frugal, and honest." Quoted in Wood, p. 100.

Page 81: James Wilson, "Lectures on Law," in J. Wilson, ed., *The Works of James Wilson* (Cambridge, Mass.: Harvard University Press, 1967), p. 290.

Page 82: Benjamin Franklin: Quoted from Madison's notes, in Marcus Cunliffe, *The American Heritage History of the Presidency* (New York: American Heritage, 1968), p. 35.

Page 83: Franklin: Quoted in Cunliffe, p. 39.

Page 83: Ellsworth: Quoted in Cunliffe, p. 40.

Page 84: Some delegates thought to make the president a monarch, Farrand, p. 174.

Page 84: Since the term is "natural born," rather than "native born," the issue is open whether a person born abroad to American citizens could serve as president. The Constitution qualified all those who were citizens at the time it was adopted (this provision applied to Washington, Adams, Jefferson, Madison, Monroe, John Quincy Adams, Jackson, and William Henry Harrison. Martin Van Buren and all presidents since Harrison were born after 1788.

Page 84: Constitution denies power to grant titles of nobility: See Art. I, Sect. 9, Cl. 8, and Sect. 10, Cl. 1.

Page 84: Member of Congress may not hold executive office: Art. I, Sect. 6, Cl. 2.

Page 84: Washington to Lafayette: Quoted in Cunliffe, p. 48.

Page 84: Washington on precedent: Quoted in Cunliffe, p. 71.

Page 85: Debate on titles for president: Quoted in *Sesquicentennial History*, pp. 375–376.

Page 85: Washington, on how the winds blew: *Sesquicentennial History*, p. 380.

Page 86: Nixon's uniformed guards: *New York Times*, Jan. 28, 1970, p. 1.

Page 86: Washington to Harrison, *Sesquicentennial History*, p. 264.

Page 87: Headlines have made clear: During 1986, President Reagan's former assistant, Michael Deaver, was much in the news for his highly visible representation of foreign governments and other interests he might have had official connection to while in the White House. The "revolving door"—government officials going from industry to an agency that oversees the agency and then back to the industry—is an ethical problem, not a constitutional one, and is controlled to some degree by civil and criminal statutes and, perhaps to a lesser degree, by the moral scruples and political sensitivities of the incumbent.

Page 87: Two terms: Actually, the longest any president can serve under the Twenty-second Amendment is ten years. The amendment allows for the possibility that a vice president may succeed a president who has died in office. If the deceased president had finished more than half his term, then the new president is eligible to run for reelection twice.

Page 88: The term *electoral college* was used informally during several early elections and was first referred to officially by Congress in an enactment in 1845: See Andrew C. McLaughlin and Albert Bushnell Hart, eds., 1 *Cyclopedia of American Government* (Gloucester, Mass.: Peter Smith, 1963), p. 657.

Page 88: Under Art. II, Sect. 1, Cl. 4, the Twentieth Amendment, and supporting legislation, the electors meet on the first Monday after the second Wednesday of December following the November elections. They cast their ballots in each state, and these ballots are transmitted to Washington to be counted in the House of Representatives on January 6 at 1 P.M.

Page 88: Electoral vote for Harry Byrd: That was only the eighth defection in some fourteen thousand votes since 1789. There was some fear during the campaign that defections might make a difference in the 1968 election, but they did not, and the courts have never considered the issue.

Page 90: Art. II: Sect. 1, Cl. 6, on presidential powers devolving on the vice president.

Page 90: Congressional terms had traditionally ended March 4, but new sessions of Congress began the first Monday in December, so defeated members, "lame ducks," were able to take part in a Congress to which they did not belong. The Twentieth Amendment declares that the terms of president and vice president begin on January 20 and of members of Congress on January 3 and that each new Congress would also begin on that date.

Pages 90–91: President Kennedy's disability: Other presidents were disabled or ill as well: President Wilson was disabled by a stroke for more than a year, President Roosevelt was apparently sicker than the public was told during his final few months, and President Eisenhower had two heart attacks and another ailment while in office.

Page 92: Max Farrand on impeachment: Farrand, p. 203.

Page 92: Ford's statement on impeachable offenses: 116 Congressional Record 11913 (1970).

Pages 92–93 Jefferson quoted in Hearings on Judicial Fitness, Senate Committee on the Judiciary, 89th Cong., 2d Sess., February 15, 1966, pp. 3–4.

Page 93: Patrick Henry: Quoted in R. Hirschfield, ed., *The Power of the Presidency*, 2d ed. (Chicago: Aldine, 1973), p. 22.

Page 93: Necessity of stopping at red lights: Dan Cordtz, "The Imperial Life Style of the U.S. President," *Fortune*, October 1973, p. 144.

Page 93: When president does it: Quoted in Conlon, television interview, May 20, 1977, p. 223.

Page 94: A president may refuse to testify before Congress: This view was specifically upheld by a federal appeals court, which held that President Nixon could refuse to turn papers over to the Senate Watergate Committee: Senate Select Committee v. Nixon, 498 F.2d 725 (D.C. Cir. 1974).

Page 94: House Judiciary Committee in 1879: Quoted in *Watergate: Chronology of a Crisis* (Washington: Congressional Quarterly, 1973), Vol. 1, p. 190.

Page 94: Muskie and Kleindienst: 1973 *Congressional Quarterly Weekly Report*, p. 862.

Page 95: Lawyers warned darkly: Quoted in Leon Friedman, ed., *United States v. Nixon, The President Before the Supreme Court* (New York: R. R. Bowker, 1974), p. 397.

Page 95: Charles Alan Wright: Quoted in Friedman, ed., p. 8.

Page 95: United States v. Nixon, 418 U.S. 683 (1974). The story of this case is told in some detail in my *Milestones! 200 Years of American Law* (St. Paul: West, 1976), Chapter 20.

Page 95: Unanimously: Justice Rehnquist, having served in the Nixon White House, did not participate in the decision, so the vote was 8–0.

Page 95: Washington offered to serve for free: Forrest McDonald, *The Presidency of George Washington* (Lawrence: University of Kansas Press, 1973), p. 26.

Page 95: White House budget: Figures for White House operations in the early 1970s are given in Dan Cordtz, "The Imperial Life Style of the U.S. President," *Fortune*, October 1973, p. 143.

Page 97: Immunize a federal marshal: In re Neagle, 135 U.S. 1 (1890). The attorney general had sent a federal marshal to guard U.S. Supreme Court Justice Stephen Field, whose life had been threatened. One morning Justice Field was assaulted, and the marshal, after identifying himself, shot and killed the assailant. No federal law permitted the attorney general to send the marshal to guard the justice. The state wanted to try Neagle for murder. But the Justice Department successfully argued that the attorney general, acting as the surrogate for the president, was entitled to send Neagle under the general principle that the president's duty to faithfully execute the laws is not limited to enforcement of congressional enactments but extends to "the rights, duties and obligations growing out of the Constitution itself." That being the case, Neagle was properly performing a federal function and could not be prosecuted by state authorities.

Page 97: Executive orders: See Louis Fisher, *Constitutional Conflicts Between President and Congress*, pp. 128–134.

Page 98: Lendlease: Attorney General Jackson's rationalization for the president's power is given in 39 Ops. Atty.Gen. 484 (1941).

Page 98: Carter upheld: Dames and Moore v. Regan, 453 U.S. 654 (1981). Of course, what choice did the Supreme Court have? Had it failed to approve President Carter's actions, the United States might have been plunged into another long nightmare should the Iranians have chosen in some fashion to retaliate.

Page 98: Steel seizure case: Youngstown Sheet & Tube Co. v. Sawyer, 343 U.S. 579 (1952).

Page 100: Era of the imperial presidency: See Arthur M. Schlesinger, Jr., *The Imperial Presidency* (Boston: Houghton Mifflin, 1973).

Page 100: Congress's power to vest appointment: Art. II, Sect. 2, Cl. 2.

Page 101: The postmaster story is told in Louis Fisher, *Constitutional Conflicts*, pp. 61–66.

Page 101: Postmaster removal case: Myers v. United States, 272 U.S. 52 (1926).

Page 103: Humphrey's Executor v. United States, 295 U.S. 602 (1935).

Page 103: President Eisenhower denied power to dismiss member of War Claims Commission: Weiner v. United States, 357 U.S. 349 (1958).

Page 104: For the most part: Congress sometimes delegates authority directly to an agency head. For example, occupational health regulations are to be issued directly by the secretary of labor. The Federal Aviation Administration, part of the Department of Transportation, is by statute exclusively empowered to grant or deny a license to fly, and the law says that the administrator "shall not submit his decisions for the approval of, nor be bound by, the decisions or recommendations of any committee, board, or other organization created by Executive Order" 49 U.S.C. § 1341(a) (1970). Although the president presumably could not overrule the administrator's decision, he could nevertheless discharge the administrator, since the FAA is no longer an independent federal agency, having been brought under the wing of the Transportation Department.

Page 104: Report of the President's Committee on Administrative Management 36 (1937).

Page 104: One-house veto case: Immigration and Naturalization Service v. Chadha, 462 U.S. 919 (1983).

Page 104: Decision severely criticized: See Fisher, pp. 178–183.

Page 105: Three-judge panel's opinion in Gramm-Rudman: Synar v. United States, 626 F.Supp. 1374 (D.D.C.1986).

Page 105: Supreme Court's Gramm-Rudman decision: Bowsher v. Synar, 106 S.Ct. 3187 (1986).

Page 106: The five wars declared by Congress were (1) the War of 1812, (2) Mexican War of 1846, (3) Spanish-American War, (4) World War I, and (5) World War II. Neither the Korean war nor the war in Vietnam was fought as the result of a congressional declaration of war.

Page 107: Presidents, of course, have done so: Among other adventures, President Wilson toppled the government of Mexico when he sent troops to occupy Veracruz, Mexico, in 1914; he also sent troops to Haiti, where they remained for twenty years. President Truman sent the army to Korea in 1950; President Eisenhower committed the marines to Lebanon in 1958; President Johnson, to the Dominican Republic in 1965 and then and thereafter, to Vietnam; President Nixon bombed Cambodia, as did President Ford in rescuing the *Mayaguez* in 1975; President Carter ordered a commando operation into Iran in 1980, and President Reagan directed the invasion of Grenada in 1983.

Page 107: Japanese-American detention: Korematsu v. United States, 323 U.S. 214 (1944). Forty years later, federal courts have overturned convictions in two of the key cases, as new information turned up under the Freedom of Information Act suggests clearly that the military acted under no justifiable claim of necessity. See "The Japanese American Coram Nobis Cases: Exposing the Myth of Disloyalty," 13 *New York University Review of Law and Social Change* 199 (1984–1985). For details, see the discussion in the section on habeas corpus in Chapter 14, p. 279.

Page 107: Beyond the scope of this book: For more on the war powers resolution, see Louis Fisher, Chapter 9, and Gerald Jenkins, "The War Powers Resolution: Statutory

Limitations on the Commander in Chief," 11 *Harvard Journal on Legislation* 181 (1974); Louis Fischer, *The Politics of Shared Power, The Congress and the Executive* (Washington: Congressional Quarterly Press, 1981).

Page 107: Said Senator Minority Leader Robert C. Byrd: "We were not consulted. We were notified of a decision that had already been made." Quoted by Steven V. Roberts, "From Capitol Hill, Words of Support Are Mixed with Some Reservations," *New York Times*, April 15, 1986, p. A10. Roberts, "Lawmakers Say U.S. Failed to Consult Them Properly," *New York Times*, April 16, 1986, p. A17.

Chapter 6: The Judicial Power

Page 109: Supreme Court as Super Bad guidance counselor: Alex Heard, "Heard v. U.S.," *The New Republic,* April 28, 1986, p. 12.

Page 110: Norris LaGuardia Act: The ban on labor injunctions was upheld in Lauf v. E. G. Shinner & Co., 303 U.S. 323 (1938).

Page 110: Jefferson to Chief Justice Jay: Quoted in Henry M. Hart Jr., and Herbert Wechsler, *The Federal Courts and the Federal System* (Brooklyn, N.Y.: Foundation Press, 1953), p. 75. Letter of the justices to President Washington: Quoted in Arthur E. Sutherland, *Constitutionalism in America* (New York: Blaisdell, 1965), p. 248.

Pages 111–112: Court of Claims case: Gordon v. United States, 117 U.S., appendix (1864).

Page 112: Frothingham v. Mellon, 262 U.S. 447 (1923).

Page 112: Standing to contest federal grants for instruction in religious schools: Flast v. Cohen, 392 U.S. 83 (1968). Taxpayer's standing is not as broad as it might seem. In another case, Congress donated a surplus military hospital to a church-related college. The Court refused to hear a challenge that the donation violated the establishment of religion clause in the First Amendment because Congress acted under its Article IV, § 3 power to dispose of government property, rather than its Article I, § 8 spending power. Valley Forge Christian College v. Americans United for Separation of Church and State Inc., 454 U.S. 464 (1982).

Page 112: Reserve commissions case: Schlesinger v. Reservists Committee to Stop the War, 418 U.S. 208 (1974). Theoretically, the issue might be justiciable, if the secretary of defense himself decided to revoke the commissions on the constitutional ground and members of Congress directly affected sued to recover them.

Page 113: Imperial judiciary: Nathan Glazer, "The Imperial Judiciary," 41 *Public Interest* 118 (1975).

Page 114: Small and undignified chamber: Charles Warren, *The Supreme Court in United States History* (Boston: Little-Brown, 1926), Vol. 1, p. 171. For discussion of the Court's peregrinations to present, see "When the Supreme Court Was in the Capitol," 61 *American Bar Association Journal* 949 (1975).

Page 117: On medieval notions of finding, not making, law: See Fritz Kern, *Kingship and Law in the Middle Ages,* trans. S. B. Chrimes (New York: Harper Torchbooks, 1970), Part II, Chapter 1, esp. p. 165.

Page 117: The jurisprudence of common law is given in Benjamin N. Cardozo, *The Nature of the Judicial Process* (New Haven: Yale University Press, 1921).

Page 117: Could not invent rules on their own: See, for example, Wheaton v. Peters, 8 Pet. 591 (1834).

Page 118: Bushrod Washington: Quoted in Robert H. Jackson, "The Rise and Fall of *Swift v. Tyson,*" 24 *American Bar Association Journal* 609 (1938).

Page 118: Iowa bond cases: Gelpcke v. Dubuque, 68 U.S. (1 Wall.) 175 (1864).

Page 118: Most compelling explanation that of Jackson: Robert H. Jackson, "Rise and Fall . . ."

Page 119: Supreme Court finally reversed Justice Story: Erie Railroad v. Tompkins, 304 U.S. 64 (1938). The story is told in my *Milestones! 200 Years of American Law* (St. Paul: West, 1976), Chapter 11.

Page 119: Presidential immunity: Nixon v. Fitzgerald, 457 U.S. 731 (1982). The decision was 5–4. But that broad immunity does not extend to presidential assistants: Harlow v. Fitzgerald, 457 U.S. 800 (1982). The doctrine of immunity is a tangled one, and in recent years has become overgrown with exceptions. Judges, legislators, and prosecutors are absolutely immune from private damage suits. Since the mid-1970s, the Court has let a variety of damage suits go forward against other federal and state officials. Some of these cases were based on Reconstruction statutes, especially the Civil Rights Act of 1871, now codified in 42 U.S.C. § 1983. One doctrinal innovation is the damage suit for violation of constitutional rights based not on federal statute but on the Constitution itself; in Bivens v. Six Unknown Federal Narcotics Agents, 403 U.S. 388 (1971), the Court approved lawsuits against federal narcotics officials for allegedly violating the Fourth Amendment rights of defendants whose homes had been searched without proper warrants, and in Carlson v. Green, 446 U.S. 14 (1980), for cruel and unusual prison conditions.

Page 120: Authorities on scope of federal jurisdiction: Henry J. Friendly, *Federal Jurisdiction: A General View* (New York: Columbia University Press, 1973); Paul M. Bator, Paul J. Mishkin, David L. Shapiro, and Herbert Wechsler, eds., *Hart & Wechsler's The Federal Court and the Federal System*, 2d ed. (Mineola, N.Y.: Foundation, 1973).

Page 121: Ex parte Milligan, 71 U.S. (4 Wall.) 2 (1866).

Page 121: Ex parte McCardle, 74 U.S. (7 Wall.) 506 (1868).

Page 121: Serious argument: See Laurence H. Tribe, *Constitutional Choices* (Cambridge, Mass.: Harvard University Press, 1985), Chapter 5, "Silencing the Oracle: Carving Disfavored Rights Out of the Jurisdiction of Federal Courts."

Page 121: Always subject to the limitation: Williams v. Rhodes, 393 U.S. 23 (1968).

Page 121: Federal damage actions could be made available: Tribe, *Constitutional Choices*, p. 54.

Page 122: Marbury v. Madison, 5 U.S. (1 Cr.) 137 (1803). The story is told in some detail in my *Milestones!*, Chapter 4.

Page 122: Cox on Marshall's Hobson's choice: *The Supreme Court and the System of Government* (New York: Oxford University Press, 1976), p. 10.

Page 123: Propriety of judiciary's passing on constitutionality of legislation: See Alexander M. Bickel, *The Least Dangerous Branch* (Indianapolis: Bobbs-Merrill, 1962), pp. 3 ff. Chapter 1 sets out the major arguments for and against the Marshallian assumption.

Page 124: Madison on Gerry: Quoted in Max Farrand, 1 *The Records of the Federal Convention*, (New Haven: Yale University Press, 1911), p. 109.

Page 124: Madison on Court's power of constitutional review: Farrand, 2 *Records of the Federal Convention* (New Haven: Yale University Press, 1937), p. 430.

Page 124: As Leonard Levy demonstrates: Levy, "Judicial Review, History, and Democracy," in *Judgments, Essays in American Constitutional History* (Chicago: Quadrangle Books, 1972), p. 27 ff.

Page 125: Descriptions of Supreme Court building: Quoted in *Congressional Quarterly's Guide to the Supreme Court* (Washington, D.C.: Congressional Quarterly, 1979), p. 772.

Page 126: Frequently raised: In fact, the Court in 1794 in United States v. Todd apparently had already struck down a congressional enactment as unconstitutional. Marshall referred to it in *Marbury* but the earlier case was not officially reported and came to light only when mentioned in a Supreme Court case fifty-seven years later; see United States v. Ferreira, 13 How. 40, 52 (1851). For a brief discussion, see Sutherland, *Constitutionalism in America* pp. 261, 327–328, 331.

Page 126. Supreme Court's power to review state law: The proposition was first enunciated in Martin v. Hunter's Lessee, 14 U.S. (1 Wheat). 304 (1816); and a potentially troubling difficulty posed by the Eleventh Amendment, forbidding commencement of a suit by a citizen against a state, was held to be no bar to the Court's *review* of a state criminal case, since review is not a suit "commenced" or "prosecuted." Cohens v. Virginia, 19 U.S. (6 Wheat.) 264 (1821).

Page 126: Justice Holmes on power to review state decisions: "The Law and the Court," delivered in 1913, reprinted in *Collected Legal Papers* (New York: Peter Smith, 1952), p. 295.

Page 126: Vesting of the law so that Congress may not repeal it: Lynch v. United States, 292 U.S. 571 (1934).

Page 126: Private bills: "A law intended to rectify a particular problem that public laws either created or ignored. Private bills date back to the first Congress." Jeffrey M. Elliot and Sheikh R. Ali, *The Presidential-*

Congressional Political Dictionary (Santa Barbara, Calif.: ABC-Clio Information Services, 1984), p. 19. The courts have upheld private bills against the claim that they amount to bills of attainder and violate the separation of powers. Most private bills are for monetary claims against the government or to upgrade the petitioner's immigration status or to avert deportation.

Page 127: Constitution is what judges say it is: So the Court said in Cooper v. Aaron, 358 U.S. 1 (1958), responding to Governor Faubus's defiance of court orders to desegregate the public schools on the grounds that the state was not bound by Supreme Court rulings. Laurence Tribe suggests that although this principle is sound in cases in which the court interprets the Constitution to prohibit governmental action, it does not necessarily apply in relatively rare cases, like Katzenbach v. Morgan, 384 U.S. 641 (1966), in which Congress may be empowered under specific constitutional enforcement clauses to declare a broader constitutional right for private parties than the courts have (that is, Congress may have the power to declare a more sweeping prohibition on a state's action in racial matters than the courts have decreed). See Tribe, *American Constitutional Law,* § 3–4. Attorney General Meese has become a modern detractor of the principle of *Cooper v. Aaron;* in a 1986 speech at Tulane University, he declared that Supreme Court interpretations of the Constitution were not "the supreme law of the land." The speech sparked intense controversy that was soon lost in the growing Iran arms sales scandal. See Stuart Taylor, Jr., "Meese Says Court Doesn't Make Law," *New York Times,* Oct. 23, 1986, p. 1; "Liberties Union Denounces Meese," *New York Times,* Oct. 24, 1986, p. A17; "Meese and the Storm over the Court," Oct. 27, 1986, p. A20.

Page 127: McCulloch v. Maryland, 17 U.S. (4 Wheat.) 316 (1819).

Page 128: Meese and the flap over CICA: The story is told in Murray Waas and Jeffrey Toobin, "Meese's Power Grab," *New Republic,* May 19, 1986, p. 15. Court of Appeals ruling: Ameron, Inc. v. U.S. Army Corps of Engineers, 787 F.2d 875 (3d Cir. 1986). See also *Constitutionality of GAO's Bid Protest Function: Hearings Before the Subcommittee on Legislation and National Security of the House Committee on Government Operations,* 99th Cong., 1st Sess. (1985).

Page 129: Luther v. Borden, 48 U.S. (7 How.) 1 (1849). The case is discussed at length in William M. Wiecek, *The Guarantee Clause of the U.S. Constitution* (Ithaca, N.Y.: Cornell University Press, 1972). See also Marvin E. Gettleman, *The Dorr Rebellion* (New York: Random House, 1973). Congress may delegate to the president the power to determine whether a particular state government is "republican," as Taney held Congress had done in Luther's case.

Page 129: Reluctance to intervene in legislative malapportionment cases finally overcome: Baker v. Carr, 269 U.S. 186 (1962).

Page 129: Amending the Constitution: Coleman v. Miller, 307 U.S. 433 (1939).

Page 129: Democratic Convention case: O'Brien v. Brown, 409 U.S. 1 (1972).

Page 130: Constitutionality of Vietnam war: Atlee v. Laird, 347 F.Supp. 689 (E.D.Pa.1972) (dismissing claim that war was unconstitutional), affirmed, 411 U.S. 911 (1973).

Page 130: Justice Owen Roberts on constitutional interpretation: United States v. Butler, 297 U.S. 1 (1936).

Page 130: Learned Hand: *The Bill of Rights* (Cambridge, Mass.: Harvard University Press, 1958), p. 11.

Page 131: Legislators tempted into enacting unconstitutional laws: Congressman F. Edward Hebert advised the Justice Department in 1967 to prosecute war protestors even though he knew that any convictions would be overturned in higher courts as violations of the First Amendment. His comments are noted in my *How the Government Breaks the Law* (New York: Penguin, 1973), p. 254.

Page 131: Thayer: *John Marshall* (Cambridge: Houghton Mifflin, 1901), p. 107.

Page 131: Countermajoritarian force: The phrase, and its explication, are in Alexander M. Bickel, *The Least Dangerous Branch* (Indianapolis: Bobbs-Merrill, 1962), pp. 16–23.

Page 133: Medieval theologians crossing their fingers: The crossed finger is the outward sign of the mental reservation that persuaded many Scholastics their lies could be justified: See Sissela Bok, *Lying* (New York: Vintage Books, 1979), pp. 34–38.

Page 133: One perpetrates no violence: Louis Lusky, *By What Right?* (Charlottesville, Va.: The Michie Company, 1975), p. 21. Lusky's view is sharply criticized in Raoul Berger, *Government by Judiciary* (Cambridge, Mass.: Harvard University Press, 1977), Chapter 21.

Page 133: Brief accounting of the Supreme Court's modern caseload: The numbers are drawn from Part IV of "Leading Cases," 1984 term, 99 *Harvard Law Review* 322 (1985).

Page 134: The term *"interpretivism"* was given currency by John Hart Ely in *Democracy and Distrust* (Cambridge, Mass.: Harvard University Press, 1980). The whole subject is reviewed and Ely's partial noninterpretivist theory is criticized in Michael J. Perry, *The Constitution, Courts, and Human Rights* (New Haven: Yale University Press, 1982).

Page 134: Defining *interpretivist:* Ely, p. 1.

Page 134: Bork: "Neutral Principles and Some First Amendment Problems," 47 *Indiana Law Journal*, 1, 8, 10 (1971).

Page 134: Right of privacy and penumbras: Griswold v. Connecticut, 381 U.S. 479 (1965); Justice Douglas wrote the majority opinion in this case striking down Connecticut's antiquated law prohibiting the use of birth control devices even by married couples; without any explicit constitutional justification for the result, Douglas pointed to "penumbras" emanating from various privacy related provisions of the Constitution. Black dissented, because he could find no text to support the result.

Page 134: What kind of fundamental presupposition is it: Quoting Bork, in Perry, p. 94.

Page 134: No right answers: Ronald Dworkin supposes that judges can find the "right" answers; see, for example, "Hard Cases," 88 *Harvard Law Review* 1057 (1975). But his method seems unsatisfactory, and the kinds of judges he presupposes for this task (his ideal judge he calls "Hercules") are not to be found either; see R. Kent Greenawalt, "Discretion and Judicial Decision: The Elusive Quest for the Fetters that Bind Judges," 76 *Columbia Law Review* 243 (1975), and Greenawalt, "Policy, Rights, and Judicial Decision," 11 *Georgia Law Review* 991 (1977).

Pages 134–135: Justice Holmes, on words of the Constitution: Missouri v. Holland, 252 U.S. 416 (1920).

Pages 135–136: Robert H. Jackson, on Court's attaining supremacy: *The Struggle for Judicial Supremacy* (New York: Vintage Books, 1941), pp. ix–x.

Page 136: Remedial decrees: The subject is discussed in my *The Litigious Society* (New York: Harper Colophon Books, 1983), Chapter 5. See also Archibald Cox, *The Role of the Supreme Court in American Government* (New York: Oxford University Press, 1976), Chapter 4.

Page 137: Jackson on the Court's judgment being wrong: *The Struggle for Judicial Supremacy*, p. x.

Page 137: Levy, in *Judgments*, p. 50.

Page 137: Commager: From "Judicial Review and Democracy," 19 *Virginia Quarterly Review* 417, 428 (1943), quoted in Berger, p. 332. Commager overstates his point. The Court did intervene on behalf of some of these interests during 150 years, but because it was so sparing in doing so, the political branches felt few constraints to obey.

Page 137: Berger, on wretched performance, *id.*, p. 332.

Page 137: Levy, *Judgments*, p. 54. This passage was written before *Roe v. Wade,* the Court's basic abortion decision, which many would take to disprove Levy's contention that there has never been "a single case" hurtful to the moral sense of the community. But even *Roe* does not necessarily defeat the point. Unlike the Court's fallacious race rulings, in which there never was a valid substantive argument to be made for discrimination, *Roe* involves two distinct moral notions—life for the fetus and the sanctity of a woman's body. Moreover, it is difficult to contend that *Roe* has hurt the community's moral sense. Those who oppose the decision are morally outraged, and have let the nation know; the decision did not permit a morally objectionable practice to commence, since abortion was practiced, though clandestinely (and often barbarously) before.

Page 139: No social transformation as complete: I am speaking of the transformation in thought and conventional wisdom, not in the final integration of American society nor in the eradication of bigotry. Perhaps the only comparison was the dramatic reforms of

Cleisthenes in remaking the representative basis of ancient Athens in 502 B.C.; his reordering rendered irrelevant old tribal loyalties. See M. Rostovtzeff, *Greece* (New York: Oxford University Press, 1963), pp. 93–97.

Page 139: Cherokee treaty case: Worcester v. Georgia, 31 U.S. (6 Pet.) 515 (1832).

Chapter 7: Federalism: The Nation and the States

Page 141: Adams: Quoted in Wood, p. 526.

Page 141: Correspondent to New Hampshire president: Quoted in David M. Matteson, "The Organization of the Government under the Constitution," in *History of the Formation of the Union under the Constitution* (Washington, D.C.: Government Printing Office, 1943; New York: Greenwood Press, 1968), pp. 445.

Page 142: Winthrop and Mason: Quoted in Wood, p. 528.

Page 142: "Parallel lines": Edmund Pendleton of Virginia: Quoted in Wood, p. 529.

Page 142: Madison on the national-federal nature of the Constitution: "In its foundation it is federal, not national; in the sources from which the ordinary powers of the government are drawn, it is partly federal and partly national; in the operation of these powers, it is national, not federal; in the extent of them, again, it is federal, not national; and, finally in the authoritative mode of introducing amendments, it is neither wholly federal nor wholly national. Federalist 39.

Page 142: Wilson on sovereignty: Quoted in Wood, pp. 530, 532.

Page 142: San Francisco Vigilantes: Quoted in Harold M. Hyman and William M. Wiecek, *Equal Justice Under Law, Constitutional Development 1835–1875* (New York: Harper and Row, 1982), pp. 5–6.

Page 142: The other way lies chaos: In 1950, a young law school graduate was denied admission to the Illinois bar because he had stated his belief, quoting almost verbatim from the Declaration of Independence, in the right of the people to alter or abolish the government—he did not say violently—when the government fails to secure basic rights. The bar committee thought he was a communist—apparently the only noncommunist patriots entitled to rebel were dead ones. The bar committee seemed to have overlooked the right, guaranteed by Article V, that the people may indeed change the government as it sees fit. Who admitted *them* to the practice of law? In any event, the Supreme Court bought the committee's argument that its refusal to admit him (when he declined to answer questions, which on principle he thought improper, about his political affiliations) did not deny him any First Amendment right. In re Anastaplo, 366 U.S. 82 (1961). But the Court eventually reversed itself on the principle; political beliefs and membership in political organizations cannot be the basis for refusing vocational licenses. Baird v. State Bar of Arizona, 401 U.S. 1 (1971); In re Stolar, 401 U.S. 23 (1971).

Page 144: Telling the states what to do: Aside from its enforcement powers under the Civil War Amendments and later amendments dealing with voting rights, Congress is given power in Article I to preempt state rules for elections to Congress (see Chapter 8) and in Article IV to condition the means by which the states will give full faith and credit to the public acts and judgments of sister states.

Page 146: On plural office holding, see David M. Matteson, "The Organization of the Government under the Constitution," in *History of the Formation of the Union under the Constitution* (Washington, D.C.: Government Printing Office, 1943; New York: Greenwood Press, 1968), pp. 435–446.

Page 146: Suit against Georgia by citizen of South Carolina: Chisholm v. Georgia, 2 U.S. (2 Dall.) 419 (1793).

Page 147: Suits brought by a state's own citizens: Hans v. Louisiana, 134 U.S. 1 (1890); suits brought by a foreign state: Monaco v. Mississippi, 292 U.S. 313 (1934).

Page 147: Supreme Court may hear an appeal when the individual is defending a case brought by the state: Cohens v. Virginia, 19 U.S. (6 Wheat.) 264 (1821); federal jurisdiction to enjoin a state official enforcing an allegedly unconstitutional law: Ex parte Young, 209 U.S. 123 (1908).

Page 147: Oklahoma state capital: Coyle v. Smith, 221 U.S. 559 (1911).

Page 148: Original court must have jurisdiction for judgment to be valid in another state: Williams v. North Carolina, 325 U.S. 226 (1945).

Page 148: McCulloch v. Maryland, 17 U.S. (4 Wheat.) 316 (1819).

Page 149: Fair Labor Standards Act case: National League of Cities v. Usery, 426 U.S. 833 (1976).

Page 149: Overruling National League of Cities: Garcia v. San Antonio Metropolitan Transit Authority, 469 U.S. 528 (1985). *National League of Cities* had itself overruled a cause eight years earlier holding that the commerce clause could constitutionally be applied to states in the performance of governmental functions; Maryland v. Wirtz, 392 U.S. 183 (1968). Perplexing cases: See Laurence H. Tribe, *Constitutional Choices*, Chapter 9. The issue is alive; the minority in *Garcia* has pledged to attempt to restore the *National League of Cities* rule.

Page 149: Chief Justice Taney on federalism: Ableman v. Booth, 62 U.S. (21 How.) 506 (1859).

Page 149: President Eisenhower on states' rights: *Public Papers of the Presidents* 1957, pp. 494, 496, quoted in James L. Sundquist, *Making Federalism Work* (Washington: Brookings Institution, 1969), pp. 8–9.

Page 149: Joint federal-state committee proposed: Sundquist, p. 9.

Page 150: "New federalism": Nelson Rockefeller, *The Future of Federalism* (Cambridge: Harvard University Press, 1962).

Page 150: "Seek Life-Prolonging Treatment": Andrew H. Malcolm, "Ruling on Baby Doe: Impact Limited," *New York Times*, June 11, 1986, p. A16.

Page 150: Without legal authority: A plurality opinion held that the Rehabilitation Act of 1973, the law on which the Baby Doe regulations were based, did not permit federal intervention "in treatment decisions traditionally entrusted to state governments." Bowen v. American Hospital Association, 106 S.Ct. 2101 (1986).

Page 150: President Reagan quoted on meaning of Constitution: Robert Pear, "Reagan Seems to Mix Supreme Court Cases," *New York Times*, June 12, 1986, p. A21.

Page 152: Madison's draft of the Virginia interposition resolution: Quoted in Arthur E. Sutherland, *Constitutionalism in America*, p. 257.

Page 152: Jackson's South Carolina proclamation: Quoted in Hyman and Wiecek, p. 10.

Page 153: Ableman v. Booth, 62 U.S. (21 How.) 506 (1859). The Wisconsin Supreme Court backed down: Ableman v. Booth, 11 Wis. 517 (1860); Booth v. Ableman, 18 Wis. 519 (1864); see Hyman and Wiecek, pp. 198–201.

Page 153: Senator Eastland: Quoted in *Look* Magazine, April 3, 1956, p. 24.

Page 153: Peregrinations: The story of the transfers is told in Elizabeth Hawthorn Buck, "The Declaration as a Document," *Manuscripts*, Vol. 10, no. 5 (Library of Congress, Summer 1958); David C. Mearns, *The Declaration of Independence: The Story of a Parchment* (Library of Congress, 1950); Milton O. Gustafson, "The Empty Shrine: The Transfer of the Declaration of Independence and the Constitution to the National Archives," *The American Archivist*, Vol. 39, no. 3 (July 1976).

Page 154: Senator Byrd: Quoted in Richard Kluger, *Simple Justice* (New York: Random House, 1975), p. 710.

Page 154: Warring against the Constitution: Cooper v. Aaron, 358 U.S. 1 (1958).

Page 154: Violates Art. I of the Constitution: Sect. 10, Cl. 1.

Page 155: James Wilson on the bill of rights: Quoted in Gordon Wood, p. 536.

Page 155: Jefferson to Madison on bill of rights: Quoted in Wood, p. 537.

Page 155: Madison on bill of rights: Quoted in Wood, pp. 542–543.

Page 155: Madison's most valuable amendment: *Annals of Congress* I, p. 755, quoted in *The Constitution of the United States of America, Analysis and Interpretation* (Washington, D.C.: Government Printing Office, 1953), p. 750.

Page 156: John Barron's wharf case: Barron v. Baltimore, 32 U.S. (7 Pet.) 243 (1833).

Chapter 8: Voting Rights: Citizen Control of the Government

Page 160: Constitutional eligibility for voting: Art. I, Sect. 2, Cl. 1.

Page 160: Of these seven amendments, two concerned election of the president, considered in Chapter 5. The amendments: Twelfth (concerning election of the President), Fifteenth (blacks), Seventeenth (direct election of senators), Nineteenth (women's suffrage), Twenty-third (extending the right to vote for president to residents of the District of Columbia), Twenty-fourth (abolition of the poll tax), and Twenty-sixth (age).

Page 160: Congress could not legislate voting age for states: Oregon v. Mitchell, 400 U.S. 112 (1970).

Page 161: Poll taxes are unconstitutional: Harper v. Virginia Board of Elections, 383 U.S. 663 (1966).

Page 161: Generally observed them without fuss: Some difficulty arose during the 1972 campaign when students went to register in the towns in which they attended college, as opposed to the home states where their parents lived. Legally, an eighteen-year-old is entitled to vote where he lives and may declare either his college residence or his parents' home as his voting home. But for the most part, local voting registrars acquiesced and the issue never took on national import. See Manard v. Miller, 405 U.S. 982 (1972).

Page 161: Louisiana black voter registration 1896–1904: The figures are given in C. Vann Woodward, *The Strange Career of Jim Crow* (New York: Oxford University Press, 1974), p. 85.

Page 161: Supreme Court struck down these ploys: Guinn v. United States, 238 U.S. 347 (1915) (invalidating Oklahoma's grandfather clause requiring a reading and writing ability for all voters except those "entitled" to vote or descended from those entitled to vote as of January 1, 1866); Lane v. Wilson, 307 U.S. 268 (1939) (overturning twelve-day registration period for those grandfathered out of registering).

Page 161: Tuskegee's gerrymandering: Gomillion v. Lightfoot, 364 U.S. 339 (1960).

Page 162: Texas white primary law case: Nixon v. Herndon, 273 U.S. 536 (1927).

Page 162: Executive committee of party as agent of the state: Nixon v. Condon, 286 U.S. 73 (1932).

Page 162: Court upheld the subterfuge: Grovey v. Townsend, 295 U.S. 45 (1935).

Page 162: Primary is an election: United States v. Classic, 313 U.S. 299 (1941). The Louisiana primary, out of which this case grew, was paid for by public funds and regulated by state laws.

Page 162: Struck down discrimination in primaries: Smith v. Allwright, 321 U.S. 649 (1944). The 1941 Louisiana case concerned a criminal prosecution of a state official who tore up ballots in the primary. The Court had to wait until a discrimination case came along finally to wipe out discrimination in primaries. Actually, Texas tried again. A private political club known as the Jaybird Democratic Association ran candidates in its own primary in May. The Jaybirds had no official connection with the Democratic party, did not organize under state election laws, nor use state voting machinery or state funds. For sixty years, with one exception, the winner of the Jaybird primary ran unopposed in the July Democratic primary and won the November election. Blacks were excluded from the Jaybird voting. The Supreme Court struck down this final vestige of discrimination under the Fifteenth Amendment in Terry v. Adams, 345 U.S. 461 (1953).

Page 163: Supreme Court struck down most of the vital sections: See, for example, United States v. Reese, 92 U.S. 214 (1876).

Page 163: President Johnson's call for action: *New York Times*, March 16, 1965, p. 1.

Page 163: According to Laurence Tribe: Tribe, *American Constitutional Law*, p. 263.

Page 164: Supreme Court quickly upheld the act: South Carolina v. Katzenbach, 383 U.S. 301 (1966).

Page 164: Precluding suits against the attorney general: Morris v. Gressette, 432 U.S. 491 (1977); Briscoe v. Bell, 432 U.S. 404 (1977).

Page 165: 1898 literacy case: Williams v. Mississippi, 170 U.S. 213 (1898).

Page 165: Situation was squarely put: Davis v. Schnell, 336 U.S. 933 (1949).

Page 165: Constitutionality of requiring all voters to be literate: Lassiter v. Northampton Election Board, 360 U.S. 45 (1959).

Page 165: Literacy in Spanish: Katzenbach v. Morgan, 384 U.S. 641 (1966).

Page 166: Tennessee's claim: Dunn v. Blumstein, 405 U.S. 330 (1972).

Page 166: Fifty-day residency requirement: Marston v. Lewis, 410 U.S. 679 (1973) (per curiam).

Page 166: Constitutional requirement to apportion seats: Art. I, Sect. 2, Cl. 3, as amended by Sect. 2 of the Fourteenth Amendment.

Page 167: "Political thicket": Colegrove v. Green, 328 U.S. 549, 556 (1946).

Page 167: Not until 1962: In Baker v. Carr, 369 U.S. 186 (1962), the Supreme Court held for the first time that voters had standing to challenge the apportionment of legislative districts.

Page 167: Art. I language requiring equal voting districts: Sect. 2, Cl. 1. Congressional "one man-one vote" case: Wesberry v. Sanders, 376 U.S. 1 (1964).

Page 168: Chief Justice Warren, striking down unequal state legislative districts: Reynolds v. Sims, 377 U.S. 533 (1964).

Page 168: Among its many decisions involving state legislative apportionment: Maryland Committee for Fair Representation v. Tawes, 377 U.S. 656 (1964); Lucas v. Colorado General Assembly, 377 U.S. 713 (1964).

Page 168: One political wag: I recollect that the wag was Senator Everett McKinley Dirksen, but diligent search has failed to turn up authority to support that recollection. The jest sounds like Dirksen, and he was a leading foe of the Court's reapportionment decisions, several times having introduced constitutional amendments to overturn them.

Page 168: Equal voting rule applicable to local bodies: Avery v. Midland County, 390 U.S. 474 (1968); Hadley v. Junior College District, 397 U.S. 50 (1970).

Page 168: As nearly of equal population as is practicable: Reynolds v. Sims, 377 U.S. 656 (1964). The Supreme Court distinguishes between equality among congressional districts and state legislative districts, holding to a far higher standard in the former than the latter. Mahan v. Howell, 410 U.S. 315 (1973).

Page 168: Water district voting: Salyer Land Co. v. Tulare Lake Basin Water Storage District, 410 U.S. 719 (1973). But a state may not restrict voting on issuance of public utility revenue bonds to property taxpayers. Cipriano v. City of Houma, 395 U.S. 701 (1968); Phoenix v. Kolodziejski, 399 U.S. 204 (1970).

Page 169: Ohio election case: Williams v. Rhodes, 393 U.S. 23 (1968).

Page 169: Georgia election law: Jenness v. Fortson, 403 U.S. 431 (1971).

Page 170: Roman candidates: George Thayer, *Who Shakes the Money Tree? American Campaign Financing Practices from 1789 to the Present* (New York: Simon and Schuster, 1973), p. 26.

Page 170: Washington's liquor giveaway: Thayer, p. 25.

Page 170: Court's ruling on campaign election law: Buckley v. Valeo, 424 U.S. 1 (1976) (per curiam).

Page 171: "A group like ours could lie": Quoted in *New York Times*, June 1, 1986, p. 24E.

Page 171: Ambrose Bierce, *The Devil's Dictionary* (New York: Dover, 1958), p. 35.

Chapter 9: Realizing Freedom: The Abolition of Slavery

Page 175: Locke, Second Treatise, § 23: "[H]aving, by his fault, forfeited his own Life, by some Act that deserves Death; he, to whom he was forfeited it, may (when he has him in his Power) delay to take it, and make use of him to his own Service, and he does him no injury by it." § 24: "This is the perfect condition of *Slavery*, which *is nothing else, but the state of War continued, between a lawful Conquerour, and a Captive.*" (italics in original) § 85: ". . . another sort of Servants, which by a peculiar Name we call *Slaves*, who being Captives taken in a just War, are by the Right of Nature subjected to the Absolute Dominion and Arbitrary power of their Masters. These men having, as I say, forfeited their

Lives, and with it their Liberties, and lost their Estates; and being in the *State of Slavery*, not capable of any Property, cannot in that state be considered as any part of *Civil Society. . . .*"

Page 175: Locke as administrator of the Carolinas: See Peter Laslett, ed., *John Locke, Two Treatises of Government*, rev. ed. (New York: Mentor Books, 1965), footnote to § 24, Second Treatise, pp. 325–326.

Page 176: States alone were competent: William M. Wiecek, *The Sources of Antislavery Constitutionalism in America 1760–1848* (Ithaca, N.Y.: Cornell University Press, 1977), p. 16.

Page 176: Lynch and Franklin: Quoted in Wiecek, *Sources*, p. 57.

Page 176: Madison on the difference between North and South: In Farrand, ed., 2 *The Records of the Federal Convention*, (rev. ed. 1937), Vol. 2, p. 10 (14 July).

Page 176: Morris, denouncing Connecticut Compromise on slavery issue: Quoted in Wiecek, *Sources*, p. 71.

Page 177: What Farrand has called: Farrand, p. 151.

Page 179: Luther Martin explained: Quoted in Wiecek, *Sources*, p. 76.

Page 180: Repeatedly held to be constitutional: See Prigg v. Pennsylvania, 16 Pet. (41 U.S.) 608 (1842).

Page 181: Thousands of slaves were imported: Wiecek, *Sources*, p. 97, note 45.

Page 182: Congressmen they would not otherwise have had: Wiecek, *Sources*, p. 106.

Page 182: Senator King on Art. IV: Sect. 3, Cl.s 1 and 2.

Page 182: Communist claim: Wiecek, *Sources*, p. 113, quoting John Scott of Missouri (Feb. 15, 1819).

Page 182: Morison, *Oxford History of the American People* (New York: Oxford University Press, 1965), p. 405.

Page 183: "Calculated to excite discontent . . .": Quoted in Wiecek, *Sources*, p. 179.

Page 183: Gibson's ruling: Hobbs v. Fogg, 6 Watts 553 (Pa.1834).

Page 185: Med Maria case: Commonwealth v. Aves, 35 Mass. (18 Pick.) 193 (1836).

Page 186: John Quincy Adams: Quoted in Harold M. Hyman and William M. Wiecek, p. 119.

Page 188: "Narrowed constitutional options drastically . . .": Hyman and Wiecek, p. 166. In his "House Divided" speech, Lincoln had said: "[T]his government cannot endure, permanently half slave and half free. I do not expect the Union to be dissolved . . . but I do expect it will cease to be divided. . . . Either the opponents of slavery will arrest the further spread of it, and place it where the public mind shall rest in the belief that it is in the course of ultimate extinction; or its advocates will push it forward, till it shall become alike lawful in all the States, old as well as new, North, as well as South."

Page 188: For a complete account of the case, see Vincent C. Hopkins, *Dred Scott's Case* (New York: Fordham University Press, 1971), and Stanley I. Kutler, *The Dred Scott Decision: Law or Politics?* (Boston: Houghton Mifflin, 1967), from which this discussion is largely drawn.

Page 190: Strader v. Graham, 10 How. 82 (1852).

Page 190: Dred Scott v. Sandford, 19 How. 393 (1857).

Page 193: Thirteenth Amendment protects everyone: Hodges v. United States, 203 U.S. 1 (1906).

Page 193: Alabama farm laborers statute: Clyatt v. United States, 197 U.S. 207 (1905).

Page 193: Baseball players: Flood v. Kuhn, 316 F.Supp. 271 (S.D.N.Y.1971), *affirmed* 443 F.2d 264 (2d Cir. 1971), *affirmed on other grounds*, 407 U.S. 258 (1972).

Page 193: Thirteenth Amendment and the draft: Butler v. Perry, 240 U.S. 328 (1916); material witness: Hurtado v. United States, 410 U.S. 578 (1973).

Page 193: Supreme Court took a narrow view: Civil Rights Cases, 109 U.S. 3 (1883).

Chapter 10: Latent Possibilities: The Promise of the Fourteenth Amendment

Page 195: Jean Giraudoux, *Tiger at the Gates*, trans. Christopher Fry (New York: Oxford University Press, 1955).

Page 196: Acknowledged the Negroes' free status: Hyman and Wiecek, p. 319.

Page 196: Black Codes "recreating the race-control features," and so on: Quoting Hyman and Wiecek, p. 319.

Page 197: Two historians: Hyman and Wiecek, pp. 395–399.

Page 197: James Wilson: Quoted in Hyman and Wiecek, p. 404.

Page 198: For judicial thinking on the Civil Rights Act of 1866 before the Fourteenth Amendment, see Hyman and Wiecek, pp. 428–431.

Page 198: Fourteenth as not narrowing the scope of the Thirteenth Amendment: This argument is controversial. It is advanced at length in Hyman and Wiecek, Chapter 11, and is the core of the argument in Jacobus tenBroek, *Equal Under Law* (New York: Collier Books, 1965), originally published in 1951 as *The Antislavery Origins of the Fourteenth Amendment* (Berkeley: University of California Press).

Page 199: Privileges and immunities in Art. IV: Sect. 2, Cl. 1.

Page 199: One of four ways: See Chase and Ducat, pp. 255–256.

Page 199: Supreme Court's 1948 decision: Toomer v. Witsell, 334 U.S. 385 (1948).

Page 199: Georgia abortion case: Doe v. Bolton, 410 U.S. 179 (1973).

Page 199: Corfield v. Coryell, 6 Fed.Cas. 546 (C.C.E.D.Pa.1823) (on circuit).

Page 200: Vehement historical debate: For summaries of the debate and bibliography, see Henry J. Abraham, *Freedom and the Court,* 3d ed. (New York: Oxford University Press, 1977), pp. 36–48. See also Leonard W. Levy, "The Fourteenth Amendment and the Bill of Rights," in *Judgments,* pp. 64–79; and Henry Steele Commager, "Historical Background of the Fourteenth Amendment," in Bernard Schwartz, ed., *The Fourteenth Amendment* (New York: New York University Press, 1970), pp. 14–27. In *Government by Judiciary* (Cambridge, Mass.: Harvard University Press, 1977), Raoul Berger marshals evidence that he says definitively disproves any intention by the Thirty-Ninth Congress to incorporate the Bill of Rights in the Fourteenth Amendment. John Hart Ely takes strong exception to

Berger's approach in *Democracy and Distrust* (Cambridge, Mass.: Harvard University Press, 1980), esp. n. 66, pp. 198–200.

Page 200: Howard: Quoted in Abraham, p. 46.

Page 201: Slaughterhouse Cases (The Butchers' Benevolent Assn. of New Orleans v. Crescent City Live Stock Landing and Slaughter-House Co.), 83 U.S. (16 Wall.) 36 (1873).

Page 202: Interview of Justice Brennan with Stuart Taylor, Jr.: "An Inside Look at Supreme Court and Its Cases," *New York Times,* June 24, 1986, p. A24. For other perspectives on how the Court decides cases, see Walter F. Murphy, *Elements of Judicial Strategy* (Chicago: University of Chicago Press, 1964): Bob Woodward and Scott Armstrong, *The Brethren* (New York: Simon and Schuster, 1980); Robert M. Kaus, "They Were Wrong about *The Brethren*," *Washington Monthly,* March, 1981, p. 32, defending this controversial account against several harsh reviews, and Bernard Schwartz, *Swann's Way* (New York: Oxford University Press, 1986).

Page 204: Earlier decision: Paul v. Virginia, 75 U.S. (8 Wall.) 168 (1869).

Pages 205–206: Grand jury indictment case: Hurtado v. California, 110 U.S. 516 (1884).

Page 206: Utah eight-man jury case: Maxwell v. Dow, 176 U.S. 581 (1900).

Page 206: Self-incrimination case: Twining v. New Jersey, 211 U.S. 78 (1908).

Page 206: Property-taking case: Chicago, Burlington & Quincy R.R. v. Chicago, 166 U.S. 226 (1897).

Page 206: Harlan quoted on selecting Bill of Rights: Chicago, Burlington & Quincy R.R., *supra.*

Page 206: Benjamin Gitlow case: Gitlow v. New York, 268 U.S. 652 (1925).

Page 207: Series of cases: Fiske v. Kansas, 274 U.S. 380 (1927); Stromberg v. California, 283 U.S. 359 (1931); Near v. Minnesota, 283 U.S. 697 (1931).

Page 207: Scottsboro case: Powell v. Alabama, 287 U.S. 45 (1932). Though innocent, the Scottsboro boys were subsequently retried, this time with a noted New York lawyer as assigned counsel, and convicted by a jury uninterested in the facts. They served many years in jail; in 1976, Clarence (Willy) Norris, the lone surviving defendant, was finally pardoned. Although the Scottsboro case was the first criminal case to be reversed on the grounds that a specific procedural provision of the Bill of Rights had been violated, this was not the first case in which the Supreme Court reversed a state conviction on the grounds that the state procedures ran afoul of the due process clause. In Moore v. Dempsey, 261 U.S. 86 (1923), the Supreme Court sent a capital conviction of five blacks in Arkansas back to a federal court to inquire into the circumstances surrounding the trial. The atmosphere was so oppressive and the procedures so obviously aimed at conviction that they would amount to a deprivation of due process, the Court ruled, if the defendants' allegations were shown to be true.

Page 207: Freedom of religion: Hamilton v. Regents of the University of California, 293 U.S. 245 (1934). Freedom of assembly: DeJonge v. Oregon, 299 U.S. 353 (1937).

Page 207: Palko v. Connecticut, 302 U.S. 319 (1937).

Page 208: Separation of church and state: Everson v. Board of Education, 330 U.S. 1 (1947). Public trials: In re Oliver, 333 U.S. 257 (1948).

Page 208: Justice Black's incorporation theory: Adamson v. California, 332 U.S. 46 (1948).

Page 209: Shocks the conscience: Rochin v. California, 342 U.S. 165 (1952).

Page 209: Birth control case: Griswold v. Connecticut, 381 U.S. 479 (1965).

Page 210: Charles Fairman, "Does the Fourteenth Amendment Incorporate the Bill of Rights? The Original Understanding," 2 *Stanford Law Review* 5 (1949).

Page 210: Leonard Levy: *Judgments*, pp. 69–70.

Page 210: Other historians: See Alfred H. Kelly and Winfred A. Harbison, *The American Constitution: Its Origin and Development*, 4th ed. (New York: W. W. Norton, 1970), p. 463; Louis Henkin, "Selective Incorporation in the Fourteenth Amendment," 73 *Yale Law Journal* 74 (1963); Frank H. Walker, Jr., "Constitutional Law—Was It Intended that the Fourteenth Amendment Incorporates the Bill of Rights?" 42 *North Carolina Law Review* 925 (1964).

Chapter 11: Freedom of Expression

Page 213: Beguiling concept of liberty: For general treatment, see Harold Laski, "Liberty," in 9 *Encyclopedia of the Social Sciences* (New York: Macmillan, 1937), pp. 442–446 (and references cited); Isaiah Berlin, *Four Essays on Liberty* (New York: Oxford University Press, 1969); Herbert J. Muller, *Freedom in the Modern World* (New York: Harper and Row, 1966); J. P. Corbett, *Europe and the Social Order* (Leyden, Netherlands: A. W. Sythoff, 1959), Chapter 7; Friedrich A. Hayek, *The Constitution of Liberty* (Chicago: University of Chicago Press, 1960).

Page 213: Charleston paper: Charleston S.-C. *Gazette*, Sept. 26, 1775: Quoted in Wood, p. 63.

Page 213: Adams: Quoted in Wood, p. 63.

Pages 213–214: Jefferson to Madison: Quoted in Wood, p. 537.

Page 214: Jefferson observed: Quoted in Robert Allen Rutland, *The Birth of the Bill of Rights 1776–1791* (New York: Collier Books, 1962), p. 206.

Page 216: King Henry quoted in Zechariah Chafee, Jr., *Free Speech in the United States* (New York: Atheneum, 1969; originally published in 1941), p. 498.

Page 217: Licensing of the press: See Frederick Seaton Siebert, *Freedom of the Press in England, 1476–1776* (Urbana: University of Illinois Press, 1952), Chapter 2.

Page 217: Right to search and seize: Stationers Company Charter of Incorporation (1557): Quoted in Siebert, p. 82.

Page 218: Definition of seditious libel: Chafee, p. 19.

Page 219: Andrew Hamilton: Quoted in James Alexander, *A Brief Narrative of the Case and Trial of John Peter Zenger*, ed. Stanley Nider Katz, 2d ed. (Cambridge, Mass.: Harvard University Press, 1972), pp. 98–99.

Page 220: On Blackstone, see Daniel J. Boorstin, *The Mysterious Science of the Law* (Boston: Beacon Press, 1958).

Page 220: Blackstone, *Commentaries on the Laws of England*, Book 4, Chapter 2.

Page 220: Holmes in 1907: Patterson v. Colorado, 205 U.S. 454 (1907).

Page 220: Holmes later changed his mind: "I wholly disagree with the argument of the Government that the First Amendment left the common law as to seditious libel in force. History seems to me against the notion." Abrams v. United States, 250 U.S. 616, 630 (1919) (Holmes, dissenting).

Page 220: Levy, on a choice between two propositions: Leonard W. Levy, *Emergence of a Free Press* (New York: Oxford University Press, 1985), p. 281.

Page 220: Zengerian principles: Levy, *Emergence*, p. 219.

Page 220: Chafee, on the framers' intentions: pp. 21, 18, 19.

Pages 220–221: Van Alstyne on reconciling Chafee and Levy: William W. Van Alstyne, "Congressional Power and Free Speech: Levy's *Legacy* Revisited" (review of *Emergence of a Free Press*), 99 *Harvard Law Review* 1089, 1098 (1986).

Page 223: Falsely shouting fire: Schenck v. United States, 249 U.S. 47 (1919). Note that Holmes said "falsely." This sentence is often misquoted by omitting that word.

Page 223: Polish joke: Quoted in *New York Times*, May 11, 1986, p. A10.

Page 223: Connecticut judge declared: State v. McKee, 73 Conn. 18 (1900).

Page 223: Conception central to the Soviet Constitution: Article 129, 1968 Constitution ("In conformity with the interests of the working people, citizens shall be guaranteed . . ." freedom of speech, and so on), trans. and ed. Harold J. Berman and John B. Quigley Jr., *Basic Laws on the Structure of the Soviet State* (Cambridge, Mass.: Harvard University Press, 1969).

Page 223: A monopoly on defining injury: This view is set out in my article "The Relativity of Injury," 7 *Philosophy and Public Affairs* 60 (1977).

Page 223: "To argue that the federal Constitution . . .": Chafee, p. 14.

Page 223: "There is no such thing as a false idea": Gertz v. Robert Welch, Inc., 418 U.S. 323 (1974).

Pages 223–224: Justice Brandeis: Whitney v. California, 274 U.S. 357 (1927) (concurring).

Page 224: A leading constitutional law casebook: Gerald Gunther, *Cases and Materials on Individual Rights in Constitutional Law*, 3d ed. (Mineola, N.Y.: Foundation Press, 1981), Chapters 6 and 7.

Page 225: Leading constitutional law treatise: Laurence H. Tribe, *American Constitutional Law*, Chapter 12.

Page 225: "The Saturday Press" restraint case: Near v. Minnesota, 283 U.S. 697 (1931).

Page 226: Pentagon Papers case: New York Times Co. v. United States, 403 U.S. 713 (1971). In 1979, a federal court for the first time squarely enjoined a publication on the grounds that the article, if published, would have clearly affected national security. *The Progressive*, a monthly magazine, was about to publish technical material telling sophisticated readers how to manufacture a hydrogen bomb. Even though the material had been drawn from declassified sources, the court declared that by putting the concepts together, the article "could possibly provide sufficient information to allow a medium size nation to move faster in developing a hydrogen weapon." The lower court injunction in *The Progressive* case marks the high tide of prior restraint. The Supreme Court never heard an appeal, for in the midst of the proceedings another magazine published much of the same material. With the material made public, the government dropped the case. United States v. Progressive, Inc., 467 F.Supp. 990 (W.D.Wis.1979).

Page 226: "Lady Chatterley's" film case: Kingsley International Pictures Corp. v. Regents, 360 U.S. 684 (1959). Motion pictures as protected by the First Amendment: Joseph Burstyn, Inc. v. Wilson, 343 U.S. 495 (1952). The Court subsequently has held that film licensing systems are invalid without the strictest procedural safeguards: Freedman v. Maryland, 380 U.S. 51 (1965).

Page 226: Gag order case: Nebraska Press Assn. v. Stuart, 427 U.S. 539 (1976). The Court did approve an order barring a newspaper from disclosing material that it had uncovered in a lawsuit in which it was a party during the course of pretrial "discovery." The Court said that the paper was free to publish if it obtained the material from other sources. Seattle Times Co. v. Rinehart, 467 U.S. 20 (1984).

Page 226: Rape victim's name case: Cox Broadcasting Corp. v. Cohn, 420 U.S. 469 (1975).

Page 226: 1986 intelligence trials problem: Philip Shenon, "Casey Said to Consider Prosecuting Publications," *New York Times,* May 7, 1986, p. D31; Stephen Engelberg, "Giving the Espionage Laws a New Look," *New York Times,* May 25, 1986, p. 4E.

Page 227: Epidemic of school censorship: William Zeisel, ed., *Censorship, 500 Years of Conflict* (New York: New York Public Library, 1984), p. 111.

Page 227: Denounced as unconstitutional: Leonard Levy sees Jefferson as an incomplete libertarian because the basis of his opposition to the act was that the power to curb speech was reserved to the states, not Congress. Once he became president, he pardoned those convicted under the act, though he advocated selective prosecution of newspaper printing vicious libels about the new administration. See Leonard W. Levy, *Jefferson and Civil Liberties, The Darker Side* (New York: Quadrangle, 1973), pp. 56–60.

Page 228: Holmes on clear and present danger test: Schenck v. United States, 249 U.S. 47 (1919).

Page 228: One of the most famous declarations: "The most eloquent and moving defense of free speech since Milton's *Areopagitica,*" say Alfred H. Kelly and Winfred A. Harbison, *The American Constitution: Its Origins and Development,* 4th ed. (New York: W. W. Norton, 1970), p. 678. His statement "will live as long as English prose has power to thrill," said Justice Frankfurter, ed., *Mr. Justice Holmes* (New York: Coward-McCann, 1931), p. 72.

Page 228: "The government was confronted": Paul L. Murphy, *The Constitution in Crisis Times 1918–1969* (New York: Harper and Row, 1972), p. 25.

Page 229: Holme's dissent: Abrams v. United States, 250 U.S. 616 (1919).

Page 229: "Left a restrictive legal residue": Paul L. Murphy, p. 27. Red scare: See Robert K. Murray, *Red Scare: A Study in National Hysteria* (Minneapolis: University of Minnesota Press, 1955).

Page 229: On the American Civil Liberties Union, see Alan Reitman, ed., *The Pulse of Freedom, American Liberties: 1920–1970s* (New York: W. W. Norton, 1975).

Page 229: Oregon criminal syndicalism case: DeJonge v. Oregon, 299 U.S. 353 (1937).

Page 229: Other decisions: For example, Fiske v. Kansas, 274 U.S. 380 (1927); Herndon v. Lowry, 301 U.S. 242 (1937).

Page 229: For a time, Smith Act convictions were upheld, notably in Dennis v. United States, 341 U.S. 494 (1951). For a brief history of the period, see Paul L. Murphy, Chapter 9.

Page 230: One critic acidly charged: John P. Frank, *Marble Palace: The Supreme Court in American Life* (New York, Alfred A. Knopf, 1961), p. 252.

Page 230: Mere advocacy not enough: Brandenburg v. Ohio, 395 U.S. 444 (1969). See also Yates v. United States, 354 U.S. 298 (1957); Scales v. United States, 367 U.S. 203 (1960); Noto v. United States, 367 U.S. 290 (1961); Bond v. Floyd, 385 U.S. 116 (1966).

Page 231: Holmes, "Every idea is an incitement": Gitlow v. New York, 268 U.S. 652 (1925).

Page 231: On the litigious society: See my *The Litigious Society* (New York: Harper Colophon Books, 1983); Marc Galanter, "Reading the Landscape of Disputes: What We Know and Don't Know (and Think We Know) About Our Allegedly Contentious and Litigious Society," 31 *UCLA Law Review* 4 (1983).

Page 232: New York Times v. Sullivan, 376 U.S. 264 (1964).

Page 232: Public figures: Curtis Publishing Co. v. Butts (football coach) and Associated Press v. Walker (retired general), decided at 388 U.S. 130 (1967); private individual: Gertz v. Robert Welch, Inc., 418 U.S. 323 (1974).

Page 232: Fighting words doctrine: Chaplinsky v. New Hampshire, 315 U.S. 568 (1942).

Page 233: Marchers' breach of peace: Gregory v. Chicago, 394 U.S. 111 (1969).

Page 233: The draft case: Cohen v. California, 403 U.S. 15 (1971).

Page 233: The Skokie Nazi Party march: See Collin v. Smith, 578 F.2d 1197 (7th Cir. 1978); cert denied, Smith v. Collin, 436 U.S. 953 (1978). The problem and cases continue: See, for example, Gooding v. Wilson, 405 U.S. 518 (1972); Rosenfeld v. New Jersey, 408 U.S. 901 (1972); Lewis v. New Orleans, 408 U.S. 913 (1972); Brown v. Oklahoma, 408 U.S. 914 (1972); FCC v. Pacifica Foundation, 438 U.S. 726 (1978).

Page 234: "A message may be delivered": Clark v. Community for Creative Non-Violence, 468 U.S. 228 (1984) (Justice White).

Page 234: Flag cases: Stromberg v. California, 283 U.S. 359 (1931) (red flag case); United States v. O'Brien, 391 U.S. 367 (1968) (draft card burning); Spence v. Washington, 418 U.S. 405 (1974) (peace symbol).

Page 234: Demonstrators sleeping on park grounds: Clark v. Community for Creative Non-Violence, 468 U.S. 228 (1984).

Page 234: Handbills: Schneider v. State, 308 U.S. 147 (1939) (flat bans on distribution of leaflets is unconstitutional); Martin v. Struthers, 319 U.S. 1 (1943) (unconstitutional to prohibit canvassers from ringing doorbells to pass out leaflets); see also Hynes v. Mayor of Oradell, 425 U.S. 610 (1976) and United States Postal Service v. Greenburgh Civic Associations, 453 U.S. 114 (1981) (constitutional to prohibit placing unstamped "mailable matter" in mailboxes).

Page 234: Regulating marches: Lovell v. Griffin, 303 U.S. 444 (1938) (streets); Hague v. CIO, 307 U.S. 496 (1939) (streets); Cox v. New Hampshire, 312 U.S. 569 (1941); Edwards v. South Carolina, 372 U.S. 229 (1963) (march around South Carolina State House grounds to protest segregation); Cox v. Louisiana, 379 U.S. 536 and 379 U.S. 559 (1965) (courthouse demonstration); Bachellar v. Maryland, 397 U.S. 564 (1970) (Army recruiting station); Brown v. Louisiana, 383 U.S. 131 (1966) (public library); Adderley v. Florida, 385 U.S. 39 (1966) (county jail); Grayned v. Rockford, 408 U.S. 104 (1972) (school grounds); Greer v. Spock, 424 U.S. 828 (1976) (military bases); Heffron v. International Society for Krishna Consciousness, 452 U.S. 640 (1981) (state fair grounds).

Page 234: Loudspeakers: Saia v. New York, 334 U.S. 558 (1948); Kovacs v. Cooper, 336 U.S. 77 (1949).

Page 234: Justice Blackmun on overbreadth: Bates v. State Bar of Arizona, 433 U.S. 350 (1977).

Page 234: Birmingham parade permit case: Shuttlesworth v. Birmingham, 394 U.S. 147 (1969).

Page 235: School picketing: Police Department of the City of Chicago v. Mosley, 408 U.S. 92 (1972).

Page 235: Did not reach the Court until 1948: The Court affirmed without opinion the conviction of Doubleday & Co. for publishing Edmund Wilson's *Memoirs of Hecate County:* Doubleday & Co. v. New York, 335 U.S. 848 (1948). In Roth v. United States, 352 U.S. 964 (1957), the Court held that obscenity is not protected by the First Amendment.

Page 235: The story of the vice societies and the rise and fall of literary censorship is told in Paul S. Boyer, *Purity in Print* (New York: Charles Scribner's Sons, 1968).

Page 236: *Lady Chatterley's Lover* banned in Boston: Commonwealth v. Delacey, 271 Mass. 327, 171 N.E. 455 (1930).

Page 236: Pus to ether: Boyer, p. 215.

Page 236: Vague nineteenth century test: Regina v. Hicklin, L.R. 3 Q.B. 360 (1968).

Page 236: Edmund Wilson: People v. Doubleday & Co., 272 App.Div. 799, 71 N.Y.S.2d 736 (1947), aff'd 297 N.Y. 687, 77 N.E.2d 6 (1947).

Page 236: *Ulysses* decision: United States v. One Book Called "Ulysses," 5 F.Supp. 182 (S.D.N.Y.1933), aff'd 72 F.2d 705 (2d Cir. 1934).

Page 236: Walt Disney movie and black and white schoolchildren movie: *New York Times*, June 27, 1969, p. 1; noted in Henry J. Abraham, *Freedom and the Court*, 4th ed. (New York: Oxford University Press, 1982), pp. 188–189.

Page 236: The Supreme Court's first obscenity case: Roth v. United States, Alberts v. California, 354 U.S. 476 (1957).

Page 236: Three-pronged test: Memoirs v. Massachusetts, 383 U.S. 413 (1966).

Pages 237–238: Burger Court test for obscenity: Miller v. California, 413 U.S. 15 (1973).

Page 238: Carnal knowledge case: Jenkins v. Georgia, 418 U.S. 153 (1974).

Page 238: Justice Stewart's famous answer: Jacobellis v. Ohio, 378 U.S. 184 (1964).

Page 238: New commission on pornography: See, for example, Philip Shenon, "Two on U.S. Commission Dissent on a Pornography Link to Violence," *New York Times,* May 19, 1986, p. A17.

Page 238: Feminist groups and pornography: The Minneapolis ordinance was enacted in December 1983; the Indianapolis ordinance was adopted in April 1984 and preliminarily enjoined in May in American Booksellers Association, Inc. v. Hudnut, 598 F.Supp. 1316 (S.D.Ind.1984). On appeal, it was declared unconstitutional in August 1985, 771 F.2d 323 (7th Cir. 1985), and the Supreme Court summarily affirmed in February 1986, sub nom. Hudnut v. American Booksellers Assn., Inc., 106 S.Ct. 1172 (1986).

Page 238: New manifestation of vice societies, retail outlets, and the Attorney General's Commission on Pornography: Matthew L. Wald, " 'Adult' Magazines Lose Sales as 8,000 Stores Forbid Them," *New York Times,* June 16, 1986, p. 1.

Page 238: Maine referendum: Matthew L. Wald, "Maine Anti-Obscenity Plan Soundly Defeated," *New York Times,* June 12, 1986, p. A27.

Page 238: Minors have no constitutional right to pornography: Ginsberg v. New York, 390 U.S. 629 (1968).

Page 238: No right to depict children engaged in sexual conduct: New York v. Ferber, 458 U.S. 747 (1982).

Page 238: Material permissible for adults that is unsuitable for children: Butler v. Michigan, 352 U.S. 380 (1957).

Page 238: Private possession of obscene material: Stanley v. Georgia, 394 U.S. 557 (1969). Somewhat contradictorily, the Court has held that this basic right does not invalidate statutes barring mailing of obscene material: United States v. Reidel, 402 U.S. 351 (1971).

Page 238: Injunction against obscene films shown in an adults-only theater: Paris Adult Theater I v. Slaton, 413 U.S. 49 (1973).

Page 239: "The real case against pornography": Letter from Patrick Riley, *New York Times,* June 7, 1986, p. A26.

Page 239: Zoning movie theaters into red-light districts: Young v. American Mini-Theatres, Inc. 427 U.S. 50 (1979).

Page 239: Drive-in movie theater case: Erznoznik v. City of Jacksonville, 422 U.S. 205 (1975).

Page 239: "A painted girl": Boyer, p. 16.

Page 240: Submarine tour leaflet case: Valentine v. Chrestensen, 316 U.S. 52 (1942).

Page 240: Abortion advertisement case: Bigelow v. Virginia, 421 U.S. 809 (1975); pharmacists' drug price advertising case: Virginia State Board of Pharmacy v. Virginia Citizens Consumer Council, Inc., 425 & .S. 748 (1976).

Page 240: False advertising: Federal Trade Commission v. Colgate-Palmolive Co., 380 U.S. 374 (1965). Electric utility case: Central Hudson Gas v. Public Service Commission, 447 U.S. 557 (1980). "For sale" case: Linmark Associates, Inc. v. Willingboro, 431 U.S. 85 (1977). Help wanted case: Pittsburgh Press Co. v. Human Relations Commission, 413 U.S. 376 (1973).

Page 240: Puerto Rico casino case: Posadas de Puerto Rico Associates v. Tourism Co. of Puerto Rico, 106 S.Ct. 2968 (1986).

Page 240: Purity of French language: Otto Friedrich, "A Language that Has *Ausgeflippt,*" *Time,* June 16, 1986, p. 55.

Page 240: Many private individuals own printing presses: See J. Ben Lieberman, *Printing as a Hobby* (New York: Sterling, 1963).

Page 241: Right-of-reply law case: Miami Herald Publishing Co. v. Tornillo, 418 U.S. 241 (1974).

Page 241: Fairness doctrine case: Red Lion Broadcasting Co. v. FCC, 395 U.S. 367 (1969).

Page 241: Prisoner cases: Saxbe v. Washington Post, 417 U.S. 843 (1974) and Pell v. Procunier, 417 U.S. 817 (1974).

Page 241: Demand to cover pretrial hearings closed to public: Gannett Co. v. DePasquale, 443 U.S. 368 (1979).

Page 241: Independent Sixth Amendment right: Waller v. Georgia, 467 U.S. 39 (1984).

Page 241: Right to attend criminal trials: Richmond Newspapers, Inc. v. Virginia, 448 U.S. 555 (1980).

Page 241: "To pursue goals independently protected": Tribe, *American Constitutional Law*, p. 702; I borrow the structure (all but the second and fourth types in the text that follows) from Tribe, p. 703.

Page 241: Mere membership is not unlawful: Noto v. United States, 367 U.S. 290 (1961).

Pages 241–242: Subversive organizations and respect for American institutions case: Baggett v. Bullitt, 377 U.S. 360 (1964). Other cases that signaled the effective end of loyalty oaths include Elfbrandt v. Russell, 384 U.S. 11 (1966) and Keyishian v. Board of Regents, 385 U.S. 589 (1967).

Page 242: Defrocking a priest: Serbian Eastern Orthodox Diocese v. Milivojevich, 426 U.S. 696 (1976). Delegate seating: Cousins v. Wigoda, 419 U.S. 477 (1975).

Page 242: Justice Douglas quoted: Adderley v. Florida, 385 U.S. 39 (1966). See also Cox v. Louisiana, 379 U.S. 536 (1965).

Page 243: "No constitutional right to be a policeman": McAuliffe v. City of New Bedford, 155 Mass. 216, 29 N.E. 517 (1892).

Page 243: Conditioning privilege on surrender of constitutional right: See "Unconstitutional Conditions," 73 *Harvard Law Review* 1595 (1960). Also: "Nor may the . . . construction of the statute be saved from constitutional infirmity on the ground that unemployment compensation benefits are not appellant's 'right' but merely a 'privilege.' It is too late in the day to doubt that the liberties of religion and expression may be infringed by the denial of or placing of conditions upon a benefit or privilege." Sherbert v. Verner, 374 U.S. 398 (1963).

Page 243: Passport case: Aptheker v. Secretary of State, 378 U.S. 500 (1964); law practice case: Schware v. Board of Bar Examiners, 353 U.S. 232 (1957).

Page 243: NAACP membership list case: NAACP v. Alabama ex rel. Patterson, 357 U.S. 449 (1958).

Page 243: Arkansas public school teacher statute: Shelton v. Tucker, 364 U.S. 479 (1960).

Page 243: Preferred freedoms: The phrase was first used by Justice Harlan F. Stone in Jones v. Opelika, 316 U.S. 584 (1942).

Page 243: Justice Cardozo on the matrix: Palko v. Connecticut, 302 U.S. 319 (1937).

Page 243: Footnote 4: United States v. Carolene Products Company, 304 U.S. 144 (1938).

Page 243: Justice Rutledge: Thomas v. Collins, 323 U.S. 516 (1945).

Page 243: Justice Frankfurter disavowed the term: "[The preferred position of freedom of speech] is a phrase that has uncritically crept into some recent opinions of this Court. I deem it a mischievous phrase, if it carries the thought, which it may subtly imply, that any law touching communication is infected with presumptive invalidity." Kovacs v. Cooper, 336 U.S. 7 (1949) (concurring).

Page 243: John Stuart Mill, *On Liberty*, Chapter 2, in *John Stuart Mill, Three Essays* (New York: Oxford University Press, 1975), pp. 23–24.

Chapter 12: Freedom of Conscience

Page 246: Brief history of church establishment in colonies: From Leonard W. Levy, "No Establishment of Religion: The Original Understanding," in *Judgments*, pp. 191–201.

Page 246: Speaking impiously: Quoting Leo Pfeffer, *Religious Freedom* (Skokie: National Textbook Co., 1977), p. 8.

Page 247: Madison's "Remonstrances" as having "staggering" effect: Levy, *Judgments*, p. 201.

Page 247: Jefferson quoted on neighbor's belief in twenty gods or none: Dumas Malone, *Jefferson the Virginian* (Boston: Little, Brown, 1948), p. 275.

Page 247: Virginia Statute of Religious Liberty, Sect. 2, Quoted in Dumas Malone, p. 278.

Page 247: Madison on making laws for the human mind: Quoted in Dumas Malone, p. 279.

Page 247: Changes that broadened the text of the religion clauses: Madison first proposed an amendment that read: "The civil rights of none shall be abridged on account of religious belief or worship, nor shall any national religion be established, nor shall the full and equal rights of conscience be in any manner, or on any pretext, infringed." This was transformed by a select House committee to "No religion shall be established by law, nor shall the equal rights of conscience be infringed." When the House passed a set of amendments and sent them to the Senate, the religion provision had been changed again: "Congress shall make no law establishing religion, or prohibiting the free exercise thereof, nor shall the rights of conscience be infringed."

The Senate killed three amendments that would have limited the ban against religious entanglement to establishing one religion in preference to another. But it rewrote the provision this way: "Congress shall make no law establishing articles of faith or a mode of worship, or prohibiting the free exercise of religion."

The House, however, would not assent to this version, and the House members (including Madison) of a joint conference committee formed to reconcile the different versions of all the amendments likewise refused to let the Senate's wording stand. Eventually, the committee rewrote the language to its present form.

Page 248: Supreme Court unanimously struck down Tennessee ban on clergy in public office: McDaniel v. Paty, 435 U.S. 618 (1978). There was no majority opinion. Chief Justice Burger's plurality opinion spoke in terms of the status of clergy in the Tennessee provision, defined by "conduct and activity rather [than] belief." The plurality opinion said that the provision was unconstitutional because the state could not show that any dangers would flow from the clergy's participation in politics. Justice Brennan's concurring opinion said that the ban was unconstitutional because it directly interfered with the exercise of religion, manifested by a person's joining the ministry.

Page 249: Justice Black on the meaning of establishment of religion clause: Everson v. Board of Education, 330 U.S. 1 (1947).

Page 249: William F. Buckley, quoted in Leonard W. Levy, "School Prayers and the Founding Fathers," in *Judgments*, p. 226.

Page 250: The narrow interpretation and the position of the framers on the meaning of establishment: Leonard Levy demonstrates this point quite convincingly in his review of the meaning and practice of church establishments, in *Judgments*, pp. 169–224.

Page 250: Three-prong test: Quoting Committee for Public Education & Religious Liberty v. Regan, 444 U.S. 646 (1980). The test was first announced in Lemon v. Kurtzman, 403 U.S. 602 (1971).

Page 250: Justice Holmes, general propositions: Lochner v. New York, 198 U.S. 45 (1905).

Page 250: Leonard F. Manning, summing up financial aid to school doctrine: *The Law of Church-State Relations* (St. Paul: West, 1981), pp. 114–115. The cases are as follows:
(1) Police teaching of secular teacher in sectarian school: Meek v. Pittinger, 421 U.S. 349 (1975).
(2) Surveillance unnecessary in public school: *Meek.*
(3) State may lend text books to parochial students: Board of Education v. Allen, 392 U.S. 236 (1968); *Meek.*
(4) State may not lend movie projectors, etc.: *Meek.*
(5) State may exempt church property from taxation: Walz v. Tax Commissioner, 397 U.S. 664 (1970).
(6) State may not provide income tax credits or deductions for parents paying tuition to sectarian schools: Committee for Public Education v. Nyquist, 413 U.S. 756 (1973).
(7) State may provide free bus transportation to and from parochial schools: Everson v. Board of Education, 330 U.S. 1 (1947).
(8) State may not bus same students to programs designed to enrich their secular studies: Wolman v. Walter, 433 U.S. 229 (1977).
(9) State may fund church-related colleges: Tilton v. Richardson, 403 U.S. 672 (1971).
(10) State may not provide indirect, restricted aid to church-affiliated secondary schools: Lemon v. Kurtzman, 403 U.S. 602 (1971).
(11) State may not provide remedial and other services on nonpublic school premises: *Meek.*
(12) State may provide speech and hearing diagnostic services in nonpublic schools: *Wolman.*
(13) State may provide therapeutic services for handicapped nonpublic schoolchildren in public schools or other public places: *Wolman.*

(14) State may not provide therapeutic services for handicapped nonpublic schoolchildren in nonpublic school premises: *Meek.*

Page 251: "Released-time" programs: McCollum v. Board of Education, 333 U.S. 203 (1948)(unconstitutional because on school grounds); Zorach v. Clauson, 343 U.S. 306 (1952) (constitutional because off school premises).

Page 251: Chaplains in armed forces and prisons: As Justice Stewart said, "Spending federal funds to employ chaplains for the armed forces might be said to violate the Establishment Clause. Yet a lonely soldier stationed at some faraway outpost could surely complain that a government which did *not* provide him the opportunity for pastoral guidance was affirmatively prohibiting the free exercise of religion." Abington School District v. Schempp, 374 U.S. 203 (1963)(dissenting). In Cruz v. Beto, 405 U.S. 319 (1972), the Court questioned the failure of the Texas prisons to provide equal religious facilities to a Buddhist inmate, given that it established facilities for Christian and Jewish inmates; the Court did not question the establishment of religious facilities in and of themselves. In Marsh v. Chambers, 463 U.S. 783 (1983), the Court upheld the practice of the Nebraska Legislature to open each legislative day with a prayer by a chaplain paid by the state. This case was something of an anomaly: the "inmates" of the legislature were not "captives," like soldiers and prisoners, and the Court abandoned, only for this case, the three-pronged test, relying on "a long history of acceptance of legislative and other official prayers." In effect, the Court held simply that legislative prayers are an exception to the establishment clause.

Page 252: New York Board of Regents nondenominational prayer case: Engel v. Vitale, 370 U.S. 421 (1962).

Page 252: Pennsylvania Lord's Prayer case: Abington School District v. Schempp, 374 U.S. 203 (1963).

Page 253: Dean Griswold on the desirability of minorities tolerating the majority: Erwin S. Griswold, "Absolute Is in the Dark—A Discussion of the Approach of the Supreme Court to Constitutional Questions," 8 *Utah Law Review* 167, 177 (1963).

Page 253: Monkey law case: Epperson v. Arkansas, 393 U.S. 97 (1968).

Page 254: In God We Trust, never been tested: The motto may have been implicitly approved in Wooley v. Maynard, 430 U.S. 705 (1977)(note 15).

Page 254: Crèche case: Lynch v. Donnelly, 465 U.S. 668 (1984).

Page 255: Departure from ecclesiastical doctrine: Presbyterian Church in the United States v. Mary Elizabeth Blue Hull Memorial Presbyterian Church, 393 U.S. 440 (1969). See also Kedroff v. St. Nicholas Cathedral, 344 U.S. 94 (1952) (a New York cathedral may not be removed from the control of its Russian parent body: "St. Nicholas Cathedral is not just a piece of real estate. . . . What is at stake here is the power to exert religious authority."

Page 255: Defrocking a bishop: Serbian Orthodox Diocese v. Milivojevich, 426 U.S. 696 (1976).

Page 256: Phonograph on public street case: Cantwell v. Connecticut, 310 U.S. 296 (1940).

Page 256: First flag salute case: Minersville School District v. Gobitis, 310 U.S. 586 (1940).

Page 256: Literal interpretation of the Bible: Jehovah's Witnesses consider the flag an "image," and the Bible says "Thou shalt not make unto thee any graven image. . . . thou shalt not bow down thyself to them, nor serve them." Exodus: 20.3,4.

Page 256: Violent reactions to the Witnesses' very presence: "The Court's decision was announced on June 3, 1940. Between June 12 and June 20, hundreds of physical attacks on the Jehovah's Witnesses were reported in the United States Department of Justice. At Kennebunk, Maine, their Kingdom Hall was burned. At Rockville, Maryland, the police assisted a mob in dispersing a Jehovah's Witnesses Bible meeting. At Litchfield, Illinois, practically the entire town mobbed a company of some sixty Witnesses who were canvassing it. At Connersville, Indiana, several Witnesses were charged with riotous conspiracy, their attorney beaten, and all driven out of town. At Jackson, Mississippi, members of a veteran's organization forcibly removed a number of Witnesses and their trailer homes from the town. In Nebraska, a Witness was lured from his house, abducted, and castrated. In Richwood, West Virginia, the chief of police and deputy sheriff forced a group of Witnesses to drink large doses of castor oil and paraded the victims through the streets, tied together with police department rope. In the two years following the *Gobitis* decision, there was an uninterrupted record of violence and persecution of the Witnesses. Almost without exception, the flag and flag salute were the causes." Leo Pfeffer, *God, Caesar, and the Constitution* (Boston: Beacon Press, 1975), pp. 143–144

Page 256: Zechariah Chafee's phrase: in Chafee, p. 399.

Page 256: J. Skelly Wright concluded: "The Role of the Courts: Conscience of a Sovereign People," 29 *The Reporter*, September 26, 1963, p. 28; quoted in Levy, "Judicial Review, History, and Democracy," in *Judgments*, p. 55.

Page 256: Second flag salute case: West Virginia State Board of Education v. Barnette, 319 U.S. 624 (1943).

Page 256: Maryland notary public case: Torasco v. Watkins, 367 U.S. 488 (1961). The Court grounded its rejection of the belief-in-God oath on the free exercise clause, not Art. VI of the Constitution, which refers only to federal office.

Page 256: "Live Free or Die": Wooley v. Maynard, 430 U.S. 705 (1977).

Page 257: South Carolina Seventh-Day Adventist case: Sherbert v. Verner, 374 U.S. 398 (1963) (quoting Justice Brennan's majority opinion).

Page 257: Sunday closing case: Braunfeld v. Brown, 366 U.S. 599 (1961).

Pages 257–258: Draft exemption cases: Selective Draft Law Cases, 245 U.S. 366 (1918)(exemption is a matter of legislative grace); United States v. Seeger, 380 U.S. 163 (1965) (unnecessary to believe in "Supreme Being"); Welsh v. United States, 398 U.S. 333 (1970) (unnecessary for belief to be strictly "religious"); Gillette v. United States, 401 U.S. 437 (1971) (selective conscientious objection not embraced by exemption).

Page 258: Mail fraud case: United States v. Ballard, 322 U.S. 78 (1944). In the case, the court "stressed that the defendants had composed form-letter testimonials from non-existent persons claiming to have been healed and noted that the defendants had failed even to call their system a 'religion' until they were placed on trial." Tribe, *American Constitutional Law*, pp. 861–862.

Page 258: Live and vexing problem; ministers and tax exemptions: see Richard Haitch, "Follow-up on the News; Tax Rebellion," *New York Times*, March 13, 1983, Sect. 1, p. 49; State Board of Equalization and Assessment v. Kerwick, 52 N.Y.2d 557, 421 N.E.2d 803, 439 N.Y.S.2d 311 (1981). How to define religion? Professor Greenawalt suggests we cannot settle on a single definition: "Any dictionary approach oversimplifies the concept of religion, and the very phrase 'definition of religion' is potentially misleading. No specification of essential conditions will capture all and only the beliefs that are regarded as religious in modern culture and should be treated as such under the Constitution." Kent Greenawalt, "Religion as a Concept in Constitutional Law," 72 *California Law Review*, 753, 763 (1984).

Page 258: Polygamy case: Reynolds v. United States, 98 U.S. 145 (1878).

Page 259: Blood-transfusion case: Jehovah's Witnesses v. King County Hospital, 390 U.S. 598 (1968)(per curiam).

Page 259: Peyote case: People v. Woody, 61 Cal.2d 716, 40 Cal.Rptr. 69, 394 P.2d 813 (1964). The Native American Church uses peyote under strictly supervised circumstances and only once a week as part of a regular religious ritual, not indiscriminately. The prosecutor had argued that peyote "shackles the Indian to primitive conditions" and that it was up to the state to free him. The court responded that it knew of "no doctrine that the state, in its asserted omniscience, should undertake to deny to defendants the observance of their religion in order to free them from the suppositious 'shackles' of their 'unenlightened' and 'primitive condition.'"

Page 259: Amish public school case: Wisconsin v. Yoder, 406 U.S. 205 (1972).

Chapter 13: The Farther Reaches of Liberty

Page 261: Life plan: See John Rawls, *A Theory of Justice* (Cambridge, Mass.: Harvard University Press, 1971), pp. 94ff.

Page 262: "Promote the cause of human progress": Norman H. Clark, *Deliver Us From Evil* (New York: W. W. Norton, 1976), p. 10.

Page 262: Accomplished just that: Norman Clark in *Deliver Us From Evil* debunks the conventional wisdom that Prohibition was simply a moralistic movement that had no effect on saloon drinking or rates of consumption, even after repeal.

Pages 262–263: The passage from John Stuart Mill is from *On Liberty*, Chapter 1, in *John Stuart Mill, Three Essays* (New York: Oxford University Press, 1975), p. 15.

Page 263: Justice Chase's comments are from his opinion in Calder v. Bull, 3 Dall. 385 (1798)(italics in the original).

Page 264: Allgeyer v. Louisiana, 165 U.S. 578 (1897).

Page 264: Justice McReynolds, quoted from Meyer v. Nebraska, 262 U.S. 390 (1923).

Page 264: Oregon public school case: Pierce v. Society of Sisters, 268 U.S. 510 (1925).

Page 264: Military case: Pierce v. Hill Military Academy, 268 U.S. 510 (1928).

Pages 265–266: Justice Douglas: Quoted from Griswold v. Connecticut, 381 U.S. 479 (1965).

Page 266: Says one commentator: Edward Dumbauld, *The Bill of Rights and What It Means Today* (Norman: University of Oklahoma Press, 1957), p. 63.

Page 266: Charles L. Black, *Decision According to Law* (New York: W. W. Norton, 1981), p. 43.

Page 266: Black's solution to its meaning: Black, p. 50.

Page 267: Overturned laws against contraception: Carey v. Population Services International, 431 U.S. 678 (1977).

Page 267: Roe v. Wade, 410 U.S. 113 (1973).

Page 268: Decision to which the chief justice assented: Chief Justice Burger may have been changing his mind on the underlying rationale of *Roe*. In Thornburgh v. American College of Obstetricians and Gynecologists, 106 S.Ct. 2841 (1986), involving Pennsylvania "informed consent" regulations, Burger dissented, suggesting that it was time to "re-examine *Roe*" in view of the decisions that followed it. *New York Times*, June 12, 1986, p. B10.

Page 268: Tax reform: Senator Gordon J. Humphrey of New Hampshire had planned to offer an amendment to the reform bill that would have denied tax-exempt status to any hospital involved with abortions. President Reagan was called on to talk Senator Humphrey out of his plan, because the abortion issue might well have tangled the Senate in knots for weeks or months. David E. Rosenbaum, "Tax Debate Omits Issue of Abortion," *New York Times*, June 13, 1986, p. D1.

Page 268: Attorney General's Orwellian statement: "Reagan Nominee Is Voted Down," *New York Times*, June 8, 1986, p. E4.

Page 268: Missouri law: Planned Parenthood of Missouri v. Danforth, 428 U.S. 52 (1976). On the question of parental consent, the Court has generally held to the view that parents have the right to veto the choice of a daughter who is not "mature or emancipated," but only if there exists an independent judicial procedure for the girl to demonstrate that she is mature enough to make the decision or that the decision is nevertheless in her best interests. See H.L. v. Mathewson, 450 U.S. 398 (1981); Akron v. Akron Center for Reproductive Health, Inc., 462 U.S. 416 (1983); Planned Parenthood Association of Kansas City v. Ashcroft, 462 U.S. 476 (1983).

Page 268: Pennsylvania fetal survivability statute: Colautti v. Franklin, 439 U.S. 379 (1979).

Page 268: Funding decisions: Beal v. Doe, 432 &.S. 438 (1977); Maher v. Roe, 432 U.S. 464 (1977); Poelker v. Doe, 432 U.S. 519 (1977); Harris v. McRae, 448 U.S. 297 (1980)(sustaining the so-called "Hyde Amendment" prohibiting payments from federal funds for abortions, except those medically necessary to save the life of the mother, or as the result of incest or rape).

Page 269: 1986 Pennsylvania case: Thornburgh v. American College of Obstetricians and Gynecologists, 106 S.Ct. 2841 (1986). Eighty-two briefs: William K. Stevens, "Margin of Vote Is Called Key to Abortion Decision," *New York Times*, June 12, 1986, p. B11. Vigorously pressed the Court to reverse: Leslie H. Gelb, "U.S. Will Ask Court to Reverse Abortion Ruling," *New York Times*, July 15, 1985, p. 1.

Page 269: According to a Harris poll in January, 1985, 70 percent of the respondents agreed with this statement: "Any woman who is three months pregnant or less should have the right to decide, with her doctor's advice, whether or not she wants to have an abortion," and only

28 percent disagreed. See "The Spectrum of Opinion," *Harper's,* July 1986, p. 42.

Page 270: East Cleveland case: Moore v. City of East Cleveland, 431 U.S. 494 (1977).

Page 270: Belle Terre case: Village of Belle Terre v. Boraas, 416 U.S. 1 (1974). Tribe in *American Constitutional Law,* p. 975.

Page 271: Jaycees case: Roberts v. United States Jaycees, 468 U.S. 609 (1984).

Page 271: Liquor license case: Moose Lodge #107 v. Irvis, 407 U.S. 163 (1972). Two months later, the state human relations commission ruled that because Lodge #107 freely allowed guests, it had become a "public accommodation" and thus must serve anyone invited as a guest, and the Court dismissed its appeal of that decision, Loyal Order of Moose v. Pennsylvania Human Relations Commission, 409 U.S. 1052 (1972). Moreover, a state may, if it chooses, condition receipt of a liquor license on adherence to an antidiscrimination policy. B.P.O.E. Lodge #2403 v. Ingraham, 412 U.S. 913 (1973).

Page 271: Georgia sodomy law case: Bowers v. Hardwick, 106 S.Ct. 2841 (1986), excerpts of opinion reported in *New York Times,* July 1, 1986, p. A1 8.

Page 272: Slow the advancement of homosexual rights: Larry Rohter, "Friend and Foe See Homosexual Defeat," *New York Times,* July 1, 1986, p. A1 9.

Page 272: Sodomy laws as virtually unenforceable: In 1976, the Supreme Court affirmed without comment a lower court's dismissal of a similar challenge to the sodomy law on the ground that the plaintiff had not been arrested and was in no danger of prosecution. Doe v. Commonwealth's Attorney, 425 U.S. 901 (1976). The *Bowers* case was a fluke. The police had gone to Michael Hardwick's home to serve a warrant because he had not paid a fine for public drunkenness; a visitor answered the door and let the police in. The officer discovered Hardwick committing sodomy and arrested him. The state dropped the charge, but Hardwick challenged the law on the ground that the state could always reinstate the charges (at least until the statute of limitations expired in August 1986); hence he satisfied the standing requirement. That set of circumstances is unlikely to be repeated; the police will almost never have grounds to enter a person's home to witness sexual acts.

Page 272: Strikes at heterosexual conduct as well: The New Jersey Supreme Court has gone part of the way, finding a zone of privacy for heterosexuals in voiding a state antifornication law. State v. Saunders, 75 N.J. 200, 381 A.2d 333 (1977).

Pages 272–273: Sumptuary laws: J. M. Vincent, "Sumptuary Legislation," in Edwin R. A. Seligman, ed., 13 *Encyclopedia of the Social Sciences* (New York: Macmillan, 1937), pp. 464–466; Gustavus Myers, "Blue Laws," in 1 *Encyclopedia of the Social Sciences,* pp. 600–602.

Page 273: Policeman's hair case: Kelley v. Johnson, 435 U.S. 238 (1976).

Page 273: Lower courts liberating students: Massie v. Henry, 455 F.2d 779 (4th Cir. 1972)(blackboards); Bishop v. Colaw, 450 F.2d 1069 (8th Cir. 1971)(rest rooms).

Page 274: Wearing ties in public places: A lawyer was once held in criminal contempt for failing to wear a tie to court: Sandstrom v. State, 309 So.2d 17 (Fla.Dist.Ct.App.), aff'd 311 So.2d 804 (Fla.Dist.Ct.App.1975), cert. discharged, 336 So.2d 572 (Fla.1976).

Page 274: Helmetless on motorcycles: The Illinois Supreme Court has struck down a helmet law: People v. Fries, 42 Ill.2d 446, 250 N.E.2d 149 (1969).

Page 274: Quinlan case: Matter of Quinlan, 70 N.J. 10, 355 A.2d 647 (1976).

Page 275: Elizabeth Bouvia's plight has been chronicled in a series of articles; e.g., *New York Times,* January 22, 1986, p. A12 (sues to stop hospital from force-feeding her); February 9, 1986, p. A.25; February 13, 1986, p. A15; February 22, 1986, p. A6; March 16, 1986, p. A26 (a California appellate court rules out force-feeding). See also "Right to Refuse Treatment," 4 *Behavioral Sciences & L.* 247–327 (1986).

Page 275: California law against bringing indigents into the state: Edwards v. California, 314 U.S. 160 (1941). Welfare payments: Shapiro v. Thompson, 394 U.S. 618 (1969).

Page 275: Passports for communists: Aptheker v. Secretary of State, 378 U.S. 500 (1964). The Court has recently ruled that the president may place off limits, in the name of national security, certain countries to which Americans might wish to travel; for example, Cuba: Regan v. Wald, 468 U.S. 222 (1984).

Page 275: Jacksonville vagrancy case: Papachristou v. City of Jacksonville, 405 U.S. 156 (1972) (emphasis added to the quotation of the ordinance).

Page 275: California ordinance: Kolender v. Lawson, 461 U.S. 352 (1983). Although the Court voided the ordinance on the grounds that it gave no useful guidance to the police and potentially interfered with First Amendment rights, the impact of the law, it seems clear, was to interfere with the simple act of walking around.

Chapter 14: The Procedural Guarantees of Criminal Justice

Page 277: Ordered liberty: Palko v. Connecticut, 302 U.S. 319 (1937).

Page 278: Frankfurter on procedural safeguards: McNabb v. United States, 318 U.S. 332 (1943).

Page 278: On the distinctions between inquisitorial and accusatorial systems, see, most usefully, Marvin E. Frankel, *Partisan Justice* (New York: Hill and Wang, 1980).

Page 279: "Not so much that": I quote myself in a review of Marvin Frankel's *Partisan Justice* in 27 *New York Law School Law Review* 695 (1981).

Page 279: On the Star Chamber, see J. H. Baker, *An Introduction to English Legal History* (London: Butterworths, 1971), p. 51.

Page 280: Civil War suspension of habeas corpus: Ex parte Milligan, 71 U.S. (4 Wall.) 2 (1866).

Page 280: Federal habeas corpus statute: Habeas corpus relief is codified at 28 U.S.C. §2241 et seq.

Page 280: Federal habeas review of state proceedings: Fay v. Noia, 372 U.S. 391 (1963); Townsend v. Sain, 372 U.S. 293 (1963) (plenary power to try the facts de novo); Presier v. Rodriguez, 411 U.S. 475 (1973) (habeas is sole method of review in federal court; Civil Rights Act proceedings unavailable). But not every question is entitled to de novo hearing; for instance, Fourth Amendment claims "should be solely to the question of whether the petitioner was provided a full and fair opportunity to raise and have adjudicated the question in courts." Schneckcloth v. Bustamonte, 412 U.S. 218 (1973) (dictum); Stone v. Powell, 428 U.S. 465 (1976).

Page 280: "Race prejudice, war hysteria and a failure of political leadership" and Commission's 1982 study: *Personal Justice Denied*, Report of the Commission on Wartime Relocation and Internment of Civilians (Washington, D.C.: Government Printing Office, 1982), p. 18.

Page 280: Japanese exclusion cases: Korematsu v. United States, 323 U.S. 214 (1944); Hirabayashi v. United States, 320 U.S. 81 (1943); Yasui v. United States, 320 U.S. 115 (1943). The definitive dissection of these cases is in Eugene D. Rostow, "The Japanese-American Cases: A Disaster," 54 *Yale Law Journal* 489 (1945).

Page 280: Endo's case: Ex parte Endo, 323 U.S. 283 (1944). As the Commission on Wartime Relocation notes, however, "even this ruling was on the narrow ground that no statute or even an explicit executive order supported this course of conduct. The Supreme Court does not reach constitutional issues unnecessarily, but the tone of Justice Douglas's writing in *Endo* was nonetheless crabbed and confined. Even this very substantial and important victory for the evacuees did not come with an air of generosity or largeness of spirit." *Report*, p. 239. I am indebted to Angus Macbeth, special counsel to the commission, for pointing out the reluctance of the Japanese to engage in case-by-case habeas proceedings.

Page 281: Civil War bill of attainder cases: Cummings v. Missouri, 71 U.S. (4 Wall.) 277 (1867) (priests); Ex parte Garland, 71 U.S. (4 Wall.) 333 (1867) (attorneys).

Page 281: Modern attainder cases: United States v. Lovett, 328 U.S. 303 (1946) (denial of compensation to government employees); United States v. Brown, 381 U.S. 437 (1965) (outlawing Communist party member from serving as officer in labor union).

Page 281: Presidential papers case: Nixon v. Administrator of General Services, 433 U.S. 425 (1977). The Court stressed that the law did not invade a property or liberty interest—Nixon was free to pursue any calling and the law specifically provided for compensation in the event that GSA invaded any economic interest it might ultimately be determined he had in the papers—and in any event, Nixon "constituted a legitimate class of one" (the only president to have resigned and be pardoned for criminal acts).

Page 281: Definition of ex post facto law: Chief Justice Marshall in Fletcher v. Peck, 10 U.S. (6 Cranch.) 87 (1810).

Page 282: Ex post facto laws are only those with penal effect: Calder v. Bull, 3 U.S. (3 Dall.) 386 (1798) (will construction). Retroactive taxes: Welch v. Henry, 305 U.S. 134 (1938).

Page 282: Medical practice law not ex post facto: Hawker v. New York, 170 U.S. 189 (1898).

Page 282: Resident alien deportation case: Harisiades v. Shaughnessy, 342 U.S. 580 (1952). In a later case, Trop v. Dulles, 356 U.S. 86 (1958), the Court held that loss of citizenship is not only a punishment but also a cruel and unusual one that violates the Eighth Amendment. How can it be that it is not a punishment to exile a person from the home in which he has lived for a quarter-century for doing something that was not illegal when he did it?

Pages 282–283: Evidentiary rules changes not ex post facto: For instance, Dixon v. United States, 287 A.2d 89 (D.C.Ct.App.1972).

Page 283: Death penalty revocation case: Dobbert v. Florida, 432 U.S. 282 (1977).

Page 283: Chapter 29 of Magna Carta of 1225 (Chapters 39 and 40 of Magna Carta of 1215), quoted in Sir Ivor Jennings, *Magna Carta and Its Influence in the World Today* (London: British Information Services, 1965), p. 46 (emphasis added).

Pages 283–284: Frankfurter on the due process clause: Rochin v. California, 342 U.S. 165 (1952).

Page 284: Justice Cardozo on due process: Palko v. Connecticut, 302 U.S. 319 (1937); previous courts: Hebert v. Louisiana, 272 U.S. 312 (1926); Snyder v. Massachusetts, 291 U.S. 97 (1934).

Page 284: Open hearing: In re Oliver, 333 U.S. 257 (1948). Neutral judge and one-man grand jury: In re Murchison, 349 U.S. 133 (1955).

Page 284: Ohio mayor's case: Tumey v. Ohio, 273 U.S. 510 (1927). Ohio mayors didn't seem to learn. In a case nearly a half-century later, the Court struck down the practice of a mayor of another Ohio town, who sat as a traffic court judge and collected fines that constituted a substantial proportion of village funds; Ward v. Village of Monroeville, 409 U.S. 57 (1972).

Page 285: "Gangster" case: Lanzetta v. New Jersey, 306 U.S. 451 (1939).

Page 285: Vagrant case: "Papachristou v. City of Jacksonville, 405 U.S. 156 (1972).

Page 285: Annoying: Coates v. Cincinnati, 402 U.S. 611 (1971) (city ordinance made it an offense to act "in a manner annoying to persons passing by").

Page 285: Court's rejection of common law of seditious libel: United States v. Hudson & Goodwin, 11 U.S. (7 Cranch.) 32 (1812). Technically, this was not a due process holding; the Court ruled that federal courts lacked common law jurisdiction under Article III.

Page 285: Mob violence: Moore v. Dempsey, 261 U.S. 86 (1923).

Page 286: Perjured testimony: Mooney v. Holohan, 294 U.S. 103 (1935); Miller v. Pate, 386 U.S. 1 (1967). The Miller case is discussed in detail in my *How the Government Breaks the Law* (New York: Penguin Books, 1973), pp. 35–48.

Page 286: Entrapment: United States v. Russell, 411 U.S. 423 (1973); Hampton v. United States, 425 U.S. 484 (1976).

Page 286: Burden of proof: In re Winship, 397 U.S. 358 (1970).

Page 286: The incorporation table lists the first holding of the Supreme Court of each constitutional clause in the Bill of Rights incorporated in the Fourteenth Amendment. Because occasionally the Court has announced in dictum a right incorporated before it has actually applied that right in a case, some of the notes that follow list the earlier dictum. There is a minor historical debate over whether certain of the cases, like the 1897 case dealing with the just compensation clause, actually represent an incorporation or a construction of the due process clause as guaranteeing a fundamental right exclusive of the Bill of Rights. For a general discussion, see Abraham, 4th ed., Chapter 3.

Page 286: Freedom of speech incorporated: Gitlow v. New York, 268 U.S. 652 (1925)(dictum); Fiske v. Kansas, 274 U.S. 380 (1927); Stromberg v. California, 283 U.S. 359 (1931).

Page 286: Freedom of press incorporated: Near v. Minnesota, 283 U.S. 697 (1931).

Page 286: Freedom of assembly incorporated: DeJonge v. Oregon, 299 U.S. 353 (1937).

Page 286: Freedom of religion incorporated: Hamilton v. Regents of the University of California, 293 U.S. 245 (1934)(dictum); Cantwell v. Connecticut, 310 U.S. 296 (1940).

Page 286: Ban on religious establishment incorporated: Everson v. Board of Education, 330 U.S. 1 (1947) (dictum); McCollum v. Board of Education, 333 U.S. 203 (1948). See also Murdock v. Pennsylvania, 319 U.S. 105 (1943).

Page 286: Unreasonable search and seizure incorporated: Wolf v. Colorado, 338 U.S. 25 (1949). But the Court did not incorporate the exclusionary rule as a sanction for the violation of this constitutional provision until 1961 in Mapp v. Ohio, 367 U.S. 643 (1961).

Page 286: Extension of exclusionary rule to states: Mapp v. Ohio, 367 U.S. 643 (1961).

Page 286: Just compensation clause incorporated: Chicago, Burlington & Quincy R.R. v. Chicago, 166 U.S. 266 (1897).

Page 286: Ban against self-incrimination incorporated: Malloy v. Hogan, 378 U.S. 1 (1964); Murphy v. Waterfront Commission of New York Harbor, 378 U.S. 52 (1964).

Page 286: Ban on double jeopardy incorporated: Benton v. Maryland, 395 U.S. 784 (1969).

Page 286: Assistance of counsel in capital case incorporated: Powell v. Alabama, 287 U.S. 45 (1932).

Page 286: Public trials incorporated: In re Oliver, 33 U.S. 257 (1948). In Gannett v. DePasquale, 443 U.S. 368

(1979), the Court indicated that this right, at least in connection with pretrial suppression hearings, is personal to the defendant, and if he agrees with the prosecution and judge to close the courtroom, the judge may do so. This view was expressly confirmed in Waller v. Georgia, 467 U.S. 39 (1984); if a defendant wishes to have open a pretrial hearing on the suppression of evidence the judge may not close the court to the public or press. In Richmond Newspapers, Inc. v. Virginia, 448 U.S. 555 (1980), the Court held that in the absence of an "overriding interest articulated in findings," a criminal trial must be open to the public, and in Press-Enterprise Co. v. Superior Court, 464 U.S. 501 (1984), this was held to include open voir dire examination of jurors in a criminal trial involving even a crime as brutal as the rape and murder of a teenage girl.

Page 286: Assistance of counsel in felony cases: Gideon v. Wainwright, 372 U.S. 335 (1963). The full story of this case is told in Anthony Lewis, *Gideon's Trumpet* (New York: Random House, 1964).

Page 286: Right to confront adverse witnesses incorporated: Pointer v. Texas, 380 U.S. 400 (1965).

Page 286: Right to impartial jury incorporated: Parker v. Gladden, 385 U.S. 363 (1966).

Page 286: Right to subpoena favorable witness incorporated: Washington v. Texas, 388 U.S. 14 (1967).

Page 286: Right to speedy trial incorporated: Klopfer v. North Carolina, 386 U.S. 213 (1967).

Page 286: Right to trial by jury incorporated: Duncan v. Louisiana, 391 U.S. 145 (1968).

Page 286: Assistance of counsel in imprisonable misdemeanor cases: Argersinger v. Hamlin, 407 U.S. 25 (1972).

Page 286: Right of unanimous verdict when the jury consists of as few as six jurors incorporated: Burch v. Louisiana, 441 U.S. 130 (1979). The federal requirement of a twelve-person unanimous verdict was upheld in Apodaca v. Oregon, 406 U.S. 404 (1972)(dictum). Though eight justices in the *Apodaca* case held that Duncan v. Louisiana, 391 U.S. 145 (1968) stands for the proposition that each element of the Sixth Amendment jury trial applies to the states, they split on just what those elements are. In Williams v. Florida, 399 U.S. 78

(1970), the Court held that a twelve-person jury requirement is not mandated by the Sixth Amendment, as applied to the states, though by virtue of a five-member majority in *Apodaca*, the unanimity requirement was held to apply to federal prosecutions. In Ballew v. Georgia, 435 U.S. 223 (1978), the Court held that a state criminal jury must consist of at least six members. And in *Burch*, the Court held that if the state jury is as few as six, it must be unanimous in reaching a guilty verdict.

Page 286: Ban on cruel and unusual punishments incorporated: Robinson v. California, 370 U.S. 660 (1962). See also Louisiana ex rel. Francis v. Resweber, 329 U.S. 459 (1947).

Page 287: John Adams on Otis and independence: *2 Legal Papers of John Adams*, ed. L. Kinvin Wroth and Hiller B. Zobel (Cambridge: Belknap Press, 1965), pp. 106–47.

Page 287: Search of student newspaper: Zurcher v. Stanford Daily, 436 U.S. 547 (1978).

Page 287: Searches are per se unreasonable without warrant, subject to exceptions: Katz v. United States, 389 U.S. 347 (1967); Mincey v. Arizona, 437 U.S. 385 (1978).

Page 287: Arrests in a public place: United States v. Watson, 423 U.S. 411 (1976).

Page 287: Hot pursuit: United States v. Santana, 427 U.S. 38 (1976).

Page 287: Stop and frisk searches: Terry v. Ohio, 392 U.S. 1 (1968).

Page 287: Voluntary consent: Schneckloth v. Bustamonte, 412 U.S. 218 (1973). But if the suspect himself has not given consent, the question then remains who may consent; the Court has held that neither a hotel night clerk nor a landlord can constitutionally consent to have a suspect's hotel room or living quarters searched: Stoner v. California, 376 U.S. 483 (1964); Chapman v. United States, 365 U.S. 610 (1961).

Page 287: Searches incident to a valid arrest: Chimel v. California, 395 U.S. 752 (1969).

Page 287: Motor vehicles: South Dakota v. Opperman, 428 U.S. 364 (1976) (automobiles offer a diminished "expectation of privacy").

Page 287: Stomach pumping case: Rochin v. California, 342 U.S. 165 (1952).

Page 287: Blood samples: Breithaupt v. Abram, 352 U.S. 435 (1957); Schmerber v. California, 384 U.S. 757 (1966). *Schmerber* upheld the taking of the blood sample against a claim that it violated the defendant's Fifth Amendment right against self-incrimination.

Page 287: Courts have given varying answers: The cases are collected in Chase and Ducat, pp. 352–353.

Page 288: Border searches: United States v. Ramsey, 431 U.S. 606 (1976); roving border searches; Almeida-Sanchez v. United States, 413 U.S. 266 (1973); permanent checkpoints: United States v. Martinez-Fuerte, 428 U.S. 543 (1976).

Page 288: Airport screening: See cases collected in Chase and Ducat, p. 358.

Page 288: Sobriety roadblocks and spot checks: In Delaware v. Prouse, 440 U.S. 648 (1979), the Court held that spot checks of drivers' credentials violate the Fourth Amendment, but a roadblock to check for license and registration would be permissible.

Page 288: Justice Brandeis's wiretapping dissent: Olmstead v. United States, 277 U.S. 438 (1928).

Page 288: Microphones placed against walls: Goldman v. United States, 316 U.S. 129 (1942)(not a violation).

Page 288: Undercover agents wired for sound: On Lee v. United States, 343 U.S. 747 (1952)(not a violation).

Page 288: Microphone spikes stuck into walls: Silverman v. United States, 365 U.S. 505 (1961)(violation).

Page 288: Listening device held into wall with thumbtack: Clinton v. Virginia, 377 U.S. 158 (1964)(violation).

Page 288: Listening in on extension phone: Rathbun v. United States, 355 U.S. 107 (1957) (not a violation if one party consents).

Page 288: Wiretaps subject to Fourth Amendment: Katz v. United States, 389 U.S. 347 (1967).

Page 289: Domestic subversion wiretap case: United States v. United States District Court, 407 U.S. 297 (1972).

Page 289: Exclusionary rule applied to the states: Mapp v. Ohio, 367 U.S. 643 (1961). The story of this case is told in my *Milestones!*, Chapter 14.

Page 289: Exclusionary rule first announced: Weeks v. United States, 232 U.S. 383 (1914).

Page 289: Fruits of involuntary confession: Brown v. Illinois, 422 U.S. 590 (1975); Taylor v. Alabama, 455 U.S. 1014 (1982). Such evidence may be used by grand jury: United States v. Calandra, 414 U.S. 338 (1974).

Page 289: Bitterly denounced: The usual rationale against the exclusionary rule is that expressed by Justice Cardozo when he was a judge on the New York Court of Appeals: "The criminal is to go free because the constable has blundered." People v. Defore, 232 N.Y. 14 (1926). But the tone, if not the substance, of Cardozo's epigram is inaccurate: The major problems are not blunders, and for the most part the problem stems not from absent-minded "constables" but urban law enforcement agencies. In any event, the remedy for the blunder is a "good-faith" exception to the rule, which the Court has announced in 1984; it is too soon to evaluate how such an exception will work.

Page 289: Good-faith exception to exclusionary rule: United States v. Leon, 468 U.S. 897 (1984).

Page 289: Damage suits against police for violations of Fourth Amendment: Bivens v. Six Unknown Federal Narcotics Agents, 403 U.S. 388 (1971); Pierson v. Ray, 386 U.S. 547 (1967)(magistrates issuing warrants are absolutely immune from suit); Malley v. Briggs, 106 S.Ct. 1092 (1986)(no absolute immunity for police in acting on defective warrants).

Page 290: Lilburne's story is told in brief in Dumbauld, pp. 77–82.

Page 290: Witnesses as well as defendants: Counselman v. Hitchcock, 142 U.S. 547 (1892).

Page 290: Not corporations: Wilson v. United States, 221 U.S. 361 (1911).

Page 290: Registering members of the Communist party: Albertson v. Subversive Activities Control Board, 382 U.S. 70 (1965).

Page 290: Public employee may not be fired: Slochowerv. Board of Higher Education of New York City, 350 U.S. 551 (1956); attorney may not be disbarred: Spevack v. Klein, 385 U.S. 511 (1967).

Page 290: Comment on defendant's silence not permitted: Griffin v. California, 380 U.S. 609 (1965).

Page 290: Defendant subject to cross-examination: United States v. Murdock, 284 U.S. 141 (1931).

Page 290: Compelled testimony when immunity is granted: Ullmann v. United States, 350 U.S. 422 (1956); Murphy v. New York Waterfront Commission, 378 U.S. 52 (1964).

Page 290: Confession beaten out of a suspect: In Brown v. Mississippi, 297 U.S. 278 (1936), the Court first declared a confession obtained as the result of a severe whipping was a violation of the due process clause and any conviction based on it must be reversed. Abusive means need not be physical: the literature is rife with examples of false confessions wrung from weary and confused suspects after hours of questioning in the stationhouse: Lloyd Eldon Miller in Illinois: Willard J. Lassers, *Scapegoat Justice: Lloyd Eldon Miller and the Failure of the American Legal System* (Bloomington: Indiana University Press, 1973); Peter O'Reilly in Connecticut: Joan Barthel, *A Death in Canaan* (New York: Dutton, 1976). George Whitmore in New York, Fred C. Shapiro, *Whitmore* (Indianapolis: Bobbs-Merrill, 1969); to name only three of the most prominent examples.

Page 290: Miranda v. Arizona, 384 U.S. 436 (1966).

Page 290: Harris v. New York, 401 U.S. 222 (1971).

Page 291: Silence may be used to impeach: Fletcher v. Weir, 455 U.S. 603 (1982); but silence may not be used if at the time of his arrest the suspect is given *Miranda* warnings, chooses to remain silent, and later tells an exculpatory story: Doyle v. Ohio, 426 U.S. 610 (1976).

Page 291: Custody: No *Miranda* warning necessary if not, as IRS agents sat around a taxpayer's dining room table to discuss his income tax return: Beckwith v. United States, 425 U.S. 341 (1976).

Page 291: Complete warning: Failure to advise that an indigent is entitled to appointed counsel does not make the confession involuntary: Michigan v. Tucker, 417 U.S. 433 (1974).

Page 291: Resumption of questioning: Michigan v. Mosley, 423 U.S. 96 (1975) (permissible to resume questioning about a different crime when *Miranda* warnings again given). Impermissible when suspect requests counsel and has not yet been provided with a lawyer: Edwards v. Arizona, 451 U.S. 477 (1981).

Page 291: Volunteered statement is admissible: Rhode Island v. Innis, 446 U.S. 291 (1980).

Page 291: Informer in a cell: Yes, they may, as long as the informer does not ask the questions or actively "elicit" any admissions, Kulhmann v. Wilson, 106 S.Ct. 1712 (1986).

Page 291: Jeopardy attaches when jury is sworn: Crist v. Bretz, 437 U.S. 28 (1978). Insufficiency of evidence barring further trial: Burks v. United States, 437 U.S. 1 (1978); but retrial is permitted if the appeal held that the conviction was against the weight of the evidence: Tibbs v. Florida, 457 U.S. 31 (1982).

Page 291: Double jeopardy bars prosecution of lesser included offenses: Brown v. Ohio, 432 U.S. 161 (1977). The basic test is whether the one statutory provision requires the prosecutor to prove an additional fact not required to be proved by the other statutory provision; Blockburger v. United States, 284 U.S. 299 (1932).

Page 292: Double jeopardy does not preclude separate federal and state prosecutions: Bartkus v. Illinois, 359 U.S. 121 (1959), Abbate v. United States, 359 U.S. 187 (1959). But a city is not a sovereign separate from the state of which it is a part, and so they may not both prosecute the same offense. Waller v. Florida, 397 U.S. 387 (1970).

Page 292: Four factors: Barker v. Wingo, 407 U.S. 514 (1972) (five years not unconstitutionally long delay).

Page 292: Only possible remedy is dismissal of the charges: Strunk v. United States, 412 U.S. 434 (1973).

Page 293: List of tortures permitted once in England: Quoting David Fellman, *The Defendant's Rights Today* (Madison: University of Wisconsin Press, 1976), p. 384.

Page 293: Arkansas Penitentiary case: Holt v. Sarver, 309 F.Supp. 362 (E.D.Ark. 1970), aff'd 442 F.2d 304 (8th Cir. 1971). Its "degrading and disgusting conditions" included inadequate medical facilities, a scarcity of food, overcrowding, unpoliced stabbings and sexual assaults, free circulation of drugs and alcohol, grueling manual labor, and lack of rehabilitation.

Page 293: Loss of citizenship: Trop v. Dulles, 356 U.S. 86 (1958).

Page 293: Cruel and unusual to punish an addict: Robinson v. California, 370 U.S. 660 (1962).

Page 293: No capital punishment for rape not ending in death: Coker v. Georgia, 433 U.S. 584 (1977).

Page 293: Life sentence case: Rummel v. Estelle, 445 U.S. 263 (1980). The Court said that because the defendant has the possibility of parole in twelve years, the sentence was not as severe as it appeared. In a later case, Hutto v. Davis, 454 U.S. 370 (1982), the Court approved a forty-year sentence for possession and distribution of nine ounces of marijuana with a street value of $200. But in Solem v. Helm, 463 U.S. 277 (1983), the Court voided a life sentence without parole of a man convicted of a seventh offense under a habitual offender statute; his previous offenses were nonviolent, all committed under the influence of alcohol, and the offense that triggered the life sentence was a $100 bad check. On the crazy-quilt pattern of sentences, see Marvin E. Frankel, *Criminal Sentencing: Law Without Order* (New York: Hill and Wang, 1972).

Page 293: Death penalty case vacating death sentences: Furman v. Georgia, 408 U.S. 238 (1972).

Page 293: Death penalty not unconstitutional: Gregg v. Georgia, 428 U.S. 153 (1976).

Page 293: No death penalty in nonhomicide cases: Coker v. Georgia, 433 U.S. 584 (1977).

Page 293: Mandatory death sentence: Woodson v. North Carolina, 428 U.S. 280 (1976); Roberts v. Louisiana, 428 U.S. 325 (1976).

Page 293: *Miranda* and the furnace of social controversy: See Liva Baker, *Miranda: Crime, Law, and Politics* (New York: Atheneum, 1983); Yale Kamisar, *"Miranda:* The Case, the Man, and the Players," 82 *Michigan Law Review* 1074 (1984).

Page 293: Numerous studies have shown: These are summarized in Charles E. Silberman, *Criminal Violence, Criminal Justice* (New York: Vintage Books, 1980), pp. 354–357. "A recent federally funded study in Illinois, Michigan, and Pennsylvania found that convictions were lost as a result of judges throwing out confessions in only five out of the 7,035 cases studied, or

0.07 percent." Patrick A. Malone, "You Have the Right to Remain Silent, *Miranda* after Twenty Years," *American Scholar* (Summer 1986), p. 368.

Page 293: Most law-enforcement officials admit: Yale Kamisar, "The Miranda Case, 20 Years Later," *New York Times*, June 11, 1986, p. A35.

Page 293: Olmstead v. United States, 277 U.S. 438 (1928).

Chapter 15: Ending America's Original Sin

Page 298: Orientals as citizens: The law barring Asian immigrants from becoming citizens dated from 1875. The first naturalization law (1790) permitted the naturalization of "free white persons." It was intended to exclude blacks from being naturalized. In 1875, Congress amended the law to permit naturalization of those of "African descent" but did not repeal the word "white," which thereafter was held to contrast with "yellow." The ban was finally repealed by the Immigration and Naturalization Act of 1952 (the McCarran-Walter Act). The story is told in my *Are Americans Extinct?* (New York: Walker, 1967).

Page 299: C. Vann Woodward reports: Woodward, p. 54.

Page 300: Virginia editorialist, quoted in Woodward, p. 38.

Page 300: Warner: Quoted in Woodward, p. 42.

Page 300: In sum: Woodward, p. 74; the political and economic causes of the "capitulation to racism" is given in Woodward, Chapter 3.

Page 301: Sumner: Quoted in Walter L. Fleming, 2 *Documentary History of Reconstruction*, rev. ed. (New York: McGraw-Hill, 1966), p. 292.

Page 302: Civil Rights Cases (United States v. Singleton), 109 U.S. 3 (1883). The story is told by Alan F. Westin, "The Case of the Prejudiced Doorkeeper," Chapter 9, in John A. Garraty, ed., *Quarrels That Have Shaped the Constitution* (New York: Harper and Row, 1964).

Page 302: State action doctrine as mystifying: See Tribe, *American Constitutional Law*, Chapter 18.

Page 302: Restaurant on public highway: Burton v. Wilmington Parking Authority, 365 U.S. 715 (1961).

Page 302: Liquor license case: Moose Lodge No. 107 v. Irvis, 407 U.S. 163 (1972).

Page 303: Supreme Court on principle of republicanism: United States v. Cruikshank, 92 U.S. 542 (1876).

Page 303: Inaction vs. action: Before the possibility was choked off, the federal courts seemed inclined to make this very distinction: See United States v. Hall, 26 Fed.Cas. 79 (C.C.S.D.Ala. 1871): "Denying includes inaction as well as action, and denying the equal protection of the laws includes the omission to protect, as well as the omission to pass laws for protection."

Page 303: As Tribe points out: Tribe, *American Constitutional Law*, p. 1153, n. 16.

Page 304: Westin, in Garraty, p. 141.

Pages 304–305: Westin on delicate balance, in Garraty, p. 143.

Page 305: For a description of Jim Crow legislation, see Woodward, pp. 97–102.

Page 306: The *Plessy* discussion is drawn from my discussion in *Milestones!* (St. Paul: West, 1976), pp. 260–262.

Page 306: Plessy v. Ferguson, 163 U.S. 537 (1896).

Page 308: Jury service: Strauder v. West Virginia, 100 U.S. 303 (1880).

Page 308: Peremptory challenge case: Batson v. Kentucky, 106 S.Ct. 1712 (1986).

Page 308: Dining car case: McCabe v. Atchison, Topeka & Santa Fe R.R. Co., 235 U.S. 151 (1914).

Page 308: Residential case: Buchanan v. Warley, 245 U.S. 60 (1917).

Page 308: Racial covenant case: Shelley v. Kraemer, 334 U.S. 1 (1948).

Page 308: 1927 school segregation case: Gong Lum v. Rice, 275 U.S. 78 (1927).

Page 308: Missouri law school case: Missouri ex rel. Gaines v. Canada, 305 U.S. 337 (1938).

Page 309: Texas law school case: Sweatt v. Painter, 339

U.S. 629 (1950); Oklahoma University case: McLaurin v. Oklahoma State Regents, 339 &.s. 637 (1950).

Page 309: So well told: The story is movingly told in Richard Kluger, *Simple Justice: The History of Brown v. Board of Education and Black America's Struggle for Equality* (New York: Random House, 1976) and is summarized in Chapter 13 of my *Milestones!*

Page 309: Brown v. Board of Education, 347 U.S. 483 (1954).

Page 311: More analytical minds: In a famous lecture, Herbert Wechsler criticized *Brown* for failing to rest on "neutral principles": "Toward Neutral Principles of Constitutional Law," 73 *Harvard Law Review* 1, 19, 31–34 (1959).

Page 311: On need for unanimity: J. Harvie Wilkinson, III, *From Brown to Baake, The Supreme Court and School Integration: 1954–1978* (New York: Oxford University Press, 1979), p. 30.

Page 311: Evidence as suspect: Wilkinson, pp. 32–33.

Page 311: "By what right?": Louis Lusky, *By What Right* (Charlottesville, Va.: Michie, 1975).

Page 312: Raoul Berger, Chapter 7.

Page 312: Justice Jackson: Quoted in Kluger, p. 609.

Page 312: They meant for the courts to continue to engage in that process: Hyman and Wiecek suggest that "the framers of the Thirteenth Amendment included the enforcement clause precisely in order to allow posterity to cope with an imprecise future," p. 334.

Page 313: Shaw decision: Roberts v. City of Boston, 59 Mass. (5 Cush.) 198 (1849).

Page 314: "Rights of personal security": James F. Wilson, quoting Chancellor Kent, during debates in the thirty-ninth Congress: Quoted in turn by Berger, p. 27.

Page 314: That whites were equally forbidden from contracting to ride in black cars is beside the point: This was the point that the Court missed in Pace v. Alabama, 106 U.S. 583 (1883), an important precursor to *Plessy,* which held that it was constitutionally permissible to prohibit persons of different races to marry or live with each other on pain of jail sentences. The Court approved this prohibition because the state *also* punished on the same basis illicit sexual relations between persons of the *same* race. But this won't wash, because the state did not punish *marriage* between persons of the same race, a rather crucial distinction; in effect, the law violated the equal protection clause because it said whites could marry whites but blacks could not.

Pages 314–315: Raoul Berger on impossibility of undoing the past: Berger, pp. 412–413.

Page 315: Davis's story is told with great sympathy by William H. Harbaugh, *Lawyer's Lawyer: The Life of John W. Davis* (New York: Oxford University Press, 1974).

Page 315: Thurgood Marshall's prediction: Quoted in "N.A.A.C.P. Sets Advanced Goals," *New York Times,* May 18, 1954, p. 16.

Page 315: Second Brown case: Brown v. Board of Education, 349 U.S. 294 (1955).

Page 315: This time the Supreme Court upheld the laws: Heart of Atlanta Motel, Inc. v. United States, 379 U.S. 241 (1964); Katzenbach v. McClung, 379 U.S. 294 (1964); Katzenbach v. Morgan, 384 U.S. 641 (1966).

Page 316: Area after area: For example, beaches: Mayor of Baltimore v. Dawson, 350 U.S. 877; buses; Gayle v. Browder, 352 U.S. 903 (1956); golf courses: Holmes v. City of Atlanta, 350 U.S. 879 (1955); parks: New Orleans City Park Imp. Ass'n. v. Detiege, 358 U.S. 54 (1958).

Page 316: Miscegenation decision: Loving v. Virginia, 388 U.S. 1 (1967).

Page 316: On southern bar, see Jack Oppenheim, "The Abdication of the Southern Bar," in Leon Friedman, *Southern Justice* (New York: Random House, 1965); Marvin E. Frankel, "The *Alabama Lawyer* 1954–1964: Has the Official Organ Atrophied?" 64 *Columbia Law Review* 1243 (1964). On the Fifth Circuit judges, see Jack Bass, *Unlikely Heroes* (New York: Simon and Schuster, 1981).

Page 316: Court's abandonment of all deliberate speed: Alexander v. Holmes County Board of Education, 396 U.S. 19 (1969).

Page 316: Busing decision: Swann v. Charlotte-Mecklenburg Board of Education, 402 U.S. 1 (1971).

Page 316: The busing story is told in Wilkinson, Chapters 6–9.

Page 316: Housing case: Jones v. Mayer Co., 392 U.S. 409, 443 (1968).

Page 317: Private school case: Runyon v. McCrary, 427 U.S. 160 (1976).

Page 317: Invisible man: See Ralph Ellison, *Invisible Man* (New York: Random House, 1952).

Page 317: Administration pulled back: The Internal Revenue Service denied tax exempt status to private schools that discriminated on the basis of race. The Reagan Treasury Department reversed this rule, asserting that IRS had acted beyond powers delegated by Congress. The Supreme Court held that Congress had indeed intended that discriminating schools be denied tax breaks. Bob Jones University v. United States, 461 U.S. 574 (1983).

Chapter 16: Beyond Race

Page 320: "Reasonable differentiation": The phrase is Justice Jackson's in Railway Express Agency v. New York, 336 U.S. 106 (1949).

Page 320: Two-tier approach: Justice Marshall's phrase in Massachusetts Board of Retirement v. Murgia, 427 U.S. 307 (1976).

Page 320: Sterilization case: Skinner v. Oklahoma, 316 U.S. 535 (1942).

Page 320: "Most celebrated": The words are Justice Powell's in "Carolene Products Revisited," 82 *Columbia Law Review* 1087 n. 4 (1982).

Page 320: Discrete and insular minorities: United States v. Carolene Products Co., 304 U.S. 144, n. 4 (1938).

Page 322: Japanese exclusion case identifying race as suspect category: Korematsu v. United States, 323 U.S. 214 (1944).

Page 322: Railway Express Agency v. New York, 336 U.S. 106 (1949).

Page 323: Antiques vs. reproductions, etc.: See Richard Cohen, *Sunday in the Sixties* (New York: Public Affairs Committee, 1962).

Page 323: Chief Justice Warren, from McGowan v. Maryland, 366 U.S. 582 (1961). The other cases were Two Guys from Harrison-Allentown, Inc. v. McGinley, 366 U.S. 582 (1961); Gallagher v. Crown Kosher Super Market of Massachusetts, 366 U.S. 617 (1961); and Braunfeld v. Brown, 366 U.S. 599 (1961).

Page 323: New Orleans pushcart law: New Orleans v. Dukes, 427 U.S. 297 (1976).

Page 323: Railroad retirement system case: U.S. Railroad Retirement Board v. Fritz, 449 U.S. 166 (1980).

Page 323: Justice Bradley, concurring in Bradwell v. State, 83 U.S. (16 Wall.) 130 (1873).

Page 323: Case limiting number of hours women could work: Muller v. Oregon, 208 U.S. 412 (1908).

Page 323 Bartender case: Goesaert v. Cleary, 335 U.S. 464 (1948).

Page 324: "Romantic paternalism": Frontiero v. Richardson, 411 U.S. 677 (1973).

Page 324: Idaho estates case: Reed v. Reed, 404 U.S. 71 (1971).

Page 324: Effects of ERA on American society: Quoting Gilbert Y. Steiner, *Constitutional Inequality, The Political Fortunes of the Equal Rights Amendment* (Washington, D.C.: Brookings Institution, 1985), pp. 22–23.

Page 324: ERA's effects in 1983 debate: Steiner, p. 87.

Page 325: Justice Powell, in Frontiero v. Richardson.

Page 325: 3.2 beer: Craig v. Boren, 429 U.S. 190 (1976).

Page 325: Illegitimate children case: Caban v. Mohammed, 441 U.S. 380 (1979).

Pages 325–326: Mississippi School of Nursing case: Mississippi University for Women v. Hogan, 458 U.S. 718 (1982).

Page 326: Louisiana joint property case: Kirchberg v. Feenstra, 450 U.S. 455 (1981).

Page 326: Draft case: Rostker v. Goldberg, 453 U.S. 57 (1981).

Page 326: Statutory rape case: Michael M. v. Superior Court, 450 U.S. 464 (1981).

Page 326: Justice Brennan's announcement of rule: Heckler v. Matthews, 465 U.S. 728 (1984).

Page 326: New York public works projects case: Crane v. New York, 239 U.S. 195 (1915).

Page 326: Commercial fishing license case: Takahashi v. Fish & Game Commissioner, 334 U.S. 410 (1948).

Page 326: Welfare benefits: Graham v. Richardson, 403 U.S. 365 (1971).

Page 326: Practice of law: In re Griffiths, 413 U.S. 717 (1973); notaries public: Bernal v. Fainter, 467 U.S. 216 (1984); competitive civil service: Sugarman v. Dougall, 413 U.S. 634 (1973).

Page 327: Illegal school-age children: Plyler v. Doe, 457 U.S. 202 (1982).

Page 327: State troopers case: Foley v. Connelie, 435 U.S. 291 (1978); public school teacher case: Ambach v. Norwick, 441 U.S. 68 (1979); deputy probation officers: Cabell v. Chavez-Salido, 454 U.S. 432 (1982).

Page 329: Chief Justice Marshall in Indian case: Worcester v. Georgia, 31 U.S. (6 Pet.) 515 (1832). Later case: Williams v. Lee, 358 U.S. 217 (1959).

Page 329: Indians as self-governing: Williams v. Lee; Moe v. Confed. Salish and Kootenai Tribes, 425 U.S. 463 (1976).

Page 329: Indians may not be treated worse: United States v. Antelope, 523 F.2d 400 (9th Cir. 1975), reversed on other grounds, 430 U.S. 641 (1977).

Page 329: Wrongful death of mother case: Levy v. Louisiana, 391 U.S. 68 (1968).

Page 329: Inheritance priority to other relatives: Labine V. Vincent, 401 U.S. 532 (1971).

Page 329: Paternity to be proved within lifetime of father: Lalli v. Lalli, 439 U.S. 259 (1978).

Page 329: Absolute ban on inheritance from fathers: Trimble v. Gordon, 430 U.S. 762 (1977).

Page 329: Child support suit: Mills v. Habluetzel, 456 U.S. 91 (1982).

Page 329: Trial transcripts: Griffin v. Illinois, 351 U.S. 12 (1956).

Page 329: Jail in lieu of fine: Williams v. Illinois, 399 U.S. 235 (1970).

Page 329: Residency requirements for welfare benefits: Shapiro v. Thompson, 394 U.S. 618 (1969); for hospital benefits: Memorial Hospital v. Maricopa County, 415 U.S. 250 (1974); Alaska's income distribution statute: Zobel v. Williams, 457 U.S. 55 (1982).

Pages 329–330: Aid to Families with Dependent Children case: Dandridge v. Williams, 397 U.S. 471 (1970).

Page 330: San Antonio Independent School District v. Rodriguez, 411 U.S. 1 (1973).

Page 330: Construing state constitutions to require equalizing school funding throughout a state: See for example, Serrano v. Priest, 96 Cal.Rptr. 601, 487 P.2d 1241, 5 Cal.3d 584 (1971).

Page 330: Chinese laundry case: Yick Wo v. Hopkins, 118 U.S. 356 (1886).

Page 331: General intelligence tests: Griggs v. Duke Power Co., 401 U.S. 424 (1971).

Page 331: Justice White in Washington v. Davis, 426 U.S. 229 (1976).

Page 331: Veterans preference case: Personnel Administrator of Massachusetts v. Feeney, 442 U.S. 256 (1979).

Pages 331–332: Mobile at-large voter case: Mobile v. Bolden, 446 U.S. 55 (1980).

Page 332: University of California Regents v. Baake, 438 U.S. 265 (1978).

Page 334: Collectively bargained affirmative action plan: United Steelworkers v. Weber, 443 U.S. 193 (1979).

Page 334: Minority business enterprise "set aside" case: Fullilove v. Klutznick, 448 U.S. 448 (1980).

Pages 334–335: Memphis firefighter case: Firefighters Local Union No. 1784 v. Stotts, 467 U.S. 561 (1984).

Page 335: Michigan school board layoff policy case: Wynant v. Jackson Board of Education, 106 S.Ct. 1842 (1986).

Page 335: Administration's central argument: Linda Greenhouse, "Justice Official Terms Court's Ruling a 'Disappointment' and 'Unfortunate,' " *New York Times*, July 3, 1986, p. B9.

Page 335: July 1986 racial preference cases: Local 93, International Association of Firefighters v. Cleveland, 106 S.Ct. 3063 (1986); Local 28, Sheet Metal Workers International Association v. Equal Employment Opportunity Commission, 106 S.Ct. 3019 (1986).

Page 335: Zoning ordinances governing work at home: John Herbers, "Rising Cottage Industry Stirring Concern in U.S.," *New York Times*, May 13, 1986, p. A18.

Chapter 17: Protecting Property and Economic Interests

Page 339: For a history of the debate over the meaning of property, see especially Richard Schlatter, *Private Property* (New York: Russell and Russell, 1973), and Paschal Larkin, *Property in the Eighteenth Century* (London: Longmans, Green, 1930).

Pages 339–340: Justice Stewart on false dichotomy: Lynch v. Household Finance Corp., 405 U.S. 538 (1972).

Page 340: A capitalist market system: Care should be taken to distinguish capitalist from noncapitalist markets. The Chinese in recent years and the Yugoslavians for a longer period have begun to rely on market transactions in economies that are not capitalist because basic decisions on investment are not in private hands. See Karl Polyanyi, *The Great Transformation* (Boston: Beacon Press, 1947); Frederic L. Pryor, *Property and Industrial Organization in Communist and Capitalist Nations* (Bloomington: Indiana University Press, 1973); Charles E. Lindblom, *Politics and Markets* (New York: Basic Books, 1977), esp. Chapter 24.

Page 340: Absolutist monarchies: "Such loans [for government or private bonds in Spain] were fraught with political risk, since the state, being omnipotent, could treat the individual with contempt. In effect, there was no real law of financial property in Habsburg Spain, since the state seized and confiscated goods at will, altered contracts unilaterally, and if necessary simply went bankrupt, as it did in 1557, 1575, 1576, 1607, 1627, and 1647. The only section of society which could defend itself against the robber-state was the regular army, which enforced payment of its arrears of pay by well-organized mutinies. . . . France was the model of absolutist monarchy, and the rights of private property were only marginally better protected than in Spain. Until the Revolution, a successful trade or manufacturer could always be disposed of, and his fortune seized for the crown, by a *lettre de cachet*." Paul Johnson, *Enemies of Society* (New York: Atheneum, 1977), pp. 57–58.

Page 340: According to Hayek: Friedrich A. Hayek, *The Constitution of Liberty* (Chicago: University of Chicago Press, 1960), p. 208.

Page 340: On the enclosure movement, "Enclosures," 3 *Encyclopedia of the Social Sciences* (1937), pp. 523–527; A. E. Bland, P. A. Brown, and R. H. Tawney, eds., *English Economic History, Select Documents* (London, G. Bell, 1914), pp. 525–545; R. H. Tawney, *The Agrarian Problem in the Sixteenth Century* (London, 1912); J. L. and Barbara Hammond, *The Town Labourer* (New York: Anchor, 1968); E. P. Thompson, *The Making of the English Working Class* (New York: Vintage, 1966), esp. pp. 216–219; Karl Polanyi, *The Great Transformation* (Boston: Beacon, 1957), pp. 35ff.

Page 340: Paul Johnson has written: Johnson, p. 62.

Page 340: Redistribution without compensation in America: See Morton J. Horwitz, *The Transformation of American Law, 1780–1860* (Cambridge, Mass.: Harvard University Press, 1977), pp. 62–66.

Page 340: Locke on government's end as protection of property: Second Treatise, Sect. 94; Laslett ed., p. 373.

Page 341: Restrictions on state economic powers in original Constitution: Art. I, Sect. X.

Page 341: Two works: Robert E. Brown, *Charles Beard and the Constitution* (Princeton, N.J.: Princeton University Press, 1956); Forrest McDonald, *We the People: The Economic Origins of the Constitution* (Chicago: University of Chicago Press, 1958). For a discussion of the whole controversy, with pertinent excerpts from Beard, Brown, McDonald, and others, see Leonard W. Levy, ed., *Essays on the Making of the Constitution* (New York: Oxford University Press, 1969).

Page 342: Marmontel: The passage is from Birrell, *Seven Lectures on the Law and History of Copyright in Books* (1899), pp. 10–12, quoted in Benjamin Kaplan and Ralph S. Brown, Jr., *Cases on Copyright* (Mineola, N.Y.: Foundation Press, 1960), pp. 41–42.

Page 342: Walton Hamilton on property: 11 *Encyclopedia of the Social Sciences* 528 (1937).

Page 342: Modern legal definition of property: *Restatement of the Law: Property* (Philadelphia: American Law Institute, 1936), Introductory note.

Page 342: View of law that land was not an instrumental good: Horwitz, p. 36.

Page 342: On use value and exchange value and the dimensions of the change, see John R. Commons, *Legal Foundations of Capitalism* (Madison: University of Wisconsin Press, 1957; originally published 1924), Chapter 2.

Page 343: Fletcher v. Peck, 10 U.S. (6 Cranch) 87 (1810).

Page 343: Magrath on Yazoo: C. Peter Magrath, *Yazoo, Law and Politics in the New Republic* (New York: W. W. Norton, 1967), p. vii.

Page 343: Dartmouth College v. Woodward, 17 U.S. (4 Wheat.) 518 (1819).

Page 344: For Webster's plea, and the story of the case, see my *Milestones!*, Chapter 5.

Page 344: New York insolvency case: Sturges v. Crowninshield, 17 U.S. (4 Wheat.) 122 (1819).

Page 344: Ogden v. Saunders, 25 U.S. (12 Wheat.) 213 (1827).

Pages 344–345: Charles River Bridge v. Warren Bridge, 36 U.S. (11 Pet.) 420 (1837).

Page 345: Promising not to exercise its power of eminent domain: West River Bridge Co. v. Dix, 47 U.S. (6 How.) 507 (1848).

Page 345: Refrain from prohibiting lotteries: Stone v. Mississippi, 101 U.S. 814 (1880).

Page 345: Minnesota mortgage moratorium case: Home Building & Loan Ass'n. v. Blaisdell, 290 U.S. 398 (1934).

Page 345: Texas landowner case: El Paso v. Simmons, 379 U.S. 497 (1965). Texas had limited to five years the period in which the landowners could tender the delinquent interest to reclaim their lands; the law under which they had purchased the land permitted them to reclaim the land *indefinitely* by paying the interest.

Page 345: New Jersey Port Authority covenant case: United States Trust Co. v. New Jersey, 431 U.S. 1 (1977).

Page 345: Minnesota pension plan law: Allied Structural Steel Co. v. Spannaus, 438 U.S. 234 (1978).

Page 345: Kansas natural gas case: Energy Reserves Group v. Kansas Power & Light Co., 459 U.S. 400 (1983).

Page 346: New York prohibition case: Wynehamer v. People, 13 N.Y. 378 (1856).

Page 346: On social Darwinism, Spencer, and Sumner (not to be confused with Senator Charles Sumner; William Graham Sumner was, alas, a Yale professor), see Richard Hofstadter, *Social Darwinism in American Thought*, rev. ed. (Boston: Beacon Press, 1955).

Pages 346–347: Coke on Magna Carta and monopolies: Quoted in Hayek, p. 168.

Page 347: Granger Cases: Munn v. Illinois, 94 U.S. 113 (1877).

Page 348: Justice Miller, on a "strange misconception": Davidson v. New Orleans, 96 U.S. 97 (1877).

Page 348: Power to regulate not a power to destroy: Stone v. Farmers Loan & Trust Co. (The Railroad Commission Cases), 116 U.S. 307 (1886). See also Mugler v. Kansas, 123 U.S. 623 (1887).

Page 348: Corporations as persons case: Santa Clara County v. Southern Pacific Railroad, 118 U.S. 394 (1886). According to Howard Jay Graham, in "The Conspiracy Theory of the Fourteenth Amendment," 47 *Yale Law Journal* 371 (1938), the sponsors of the Fourteenth Amendment in the Thirty-ninth Congress intended the due process clause to "take in the whole range of national economy."

Page 348: Allgeyer v. Louisiana, 165 U.S. 578 (1897).

Page 348: Railroad rate regulation case: Smyth v. Ames, 169 U.S. 466 (1898).

Page 348: Fair value fallacy: Robert L. Hale, *Freedom Through Law: Public Control of Private Governing Power* New York: Columbia Univ. Press, 1952), p. 462.

Page 348: Court rejected the doctrine: FPC v. Hope Natural Gas Co., 320 U.S. 591 (1940).

Page 348: Laws upset and upheld during 1899 to 1937: Upset: Benjamin Wright, *The Growth of American Constitutional Law* (Boston: Reynal and Hitchcock, 1942), p. 154; upheld: Charles Warren, 3 *The Supreme Court in United States History* (Boston: Little Brown, 1922), pp. 463–465. Between 1899 and 1918, the Court rejected 53 laws enacted under state police power, but between 1920 and 1930, it threw out 140; Warren, p. 463; Murphy, p. 63.

Page 348: Lochner v. New York, 198 U.S. 45 (1905).

Page 349: Eight-hour day for miners: Holden v. Hardy, 169 U.S. 366 (1898). Six-day week for barbers: Petit v. Minnesota, 177 U.S. 164 (1900).

Page 349: "Perhaps too great embarrassments are better forgotten": The passage is from my *Tyranny of the Experts* (New York: Walker, 1970), p. 184.

Page 350: Federal yellow dog contract case: Adair v. United States, 208 U.S. 161 (1908); state case: Coppage v. Kansas, 236 U.S. 1 (1915).

Page 350: Special hour limitations for women: Muller v. Oregon, 208 U.S. 412 (1908); wage limitations impermissible: Adkins v. Children's Hospital, 261 U.S. 525 (1923).

Page 351: Unconstitutionality of price regulation: Williams v. Standard Oil Co., 278 U.S. 235 (1929).

Page 351: Ice case: New State Ice Co. v. Liebmann, 285 U.S. 262 (1932).

Page 351: Pharmacies case: Liggett Co. v. Baldridge, 278 U.S. 105 (1928).

Page 351: Shoddy mattress case: Weaver v. Palmer Bros. Co., 270 U.S. 402 (1926).

Page 351: New York milk price case: Nebbia v. New York, 291 U.S. 502 (1934).

Page 352: Minimum wage law case overruling earlier decision: West Coast Hotel Co. v. Parrish, 300 U.S. 379 (1937).

Page 352: Debt adjuster case: Ferguson v. Skrupa, 372 U.S. 726 (1963).

Page 352: Pennsylvania land taking case: M'Clenachan v. Curwin, 3 Yeates 362, 6 Binn. 509 (Pa. 1802). The case is discussed in Horwitz, pp. 64–65

Page 353: Missouri Pac. Ry. v. Nebraska, 164 U.S. 403 (1896).

Page 353: Just compensation principle applied to the states: Chicago, B & Q. R.R. Co. v. Chicago, 166 U.S. 226 (1897).

Page 353: Hawaii land oligopoly case: Hawaii Housing Authority v. Midkiff, 467 U.S. 229 (1984).

Page 354: Holmes on petty larceny of the police power: At the urging of his judicial brethren, who found it tasteless, this phrase was deleted from his final opinion in Jackson v. Rosenbaum Co., 260 U.S. 22 (1922); quoted in Gunther, p. 165.

Page 354: Justice Holmes on the police power and property: Pennsylvania Coal Co. v. Mahon, 260 U.S. 393 (1922).

Page 354: Zoning: Euclid v. Ambler Realty Co., 272 U.S. 365 (1926).

Page 354: Suburban land rezoning: Agins v. Tiburon, 447 U.S. 255 (1980).

Page 354: Legislative Reference Service estimate: 80 *Congressional Record,* June 8, 1936, pp. 9251ff.

Page 354: Wright estimates: Benjamin F. Wright, *The Growth of American Constitutional Law* (Boston: Houghton Mifflin, 1942), p. 243.

Page 354: Sutherland estimate: Arthur E. Sutherland, p. 331.

Page 354: Congressional Research Service 1972 data: Lester S. Jayson, supervising ed., *The Constitution of the United States of America, Analysis and Interpretation* (Washington, D.C.: Government Printing Office, 1978 and 1980 Supplement), pp. 1613–1619 and S305–309.

Page 355: Grand Central Terminal case: Penn Central Transportation Co. v. New York City, 438 U.S. 104 (1978).

Page 355: Flight path case: United States v. Causby, 328 U.S. 256 (1946).

Page 355: Cable television case: Loretto v. TelePrompTer Manhattan CATV Corp., 458 U.S. 419 (1982).

Page 355: Trade secrets case: Ruckelshaus v. Monsanto Co., 467 U.S. (1984).

Page 355: Charles Reich, "The New Property," 73 *Yale Law Journal* 733 (1964).

Page 355: Goldberg v. Kelly, 397 U.S. 254 (1970).

Page 355: Driver's license case: Bell v. Burson, 402 U.S. 535 (1971).

Page 355: School suspensions: Goss v. Lopez, 419 U.S. 565 (1975).

Page 355: Untenured faculty case: Board of Regents v. Roth, 408 U.S. 564 (1972).

Pages 356–357 Legitimate claim of entitlement stemming from faculty handbook: Perry v. Sindermann, 408 U.S. 593 (1972).

Page 357: Policeman not entitled to permanent employment: Bishop v. Wood, 426 U.S. (1976).

Page 357: No liberty interest invaded when defamed by police department: Paul v. Davis, 424 U.S. 693 (1976).

Page 357: Prisoner transfer case: Meachum v. Fano, 427 U.S. 215 (1976).

Page 357: Balancing test: Mathews v. Eldridge, 424 U.S. 319 (1976).

Page 357: Corporal punishment in school case: Ingraham v. Wright, 430 U.S. 651 (1977).

Chapter 18: Regulating Commerce

Page 360: Gibbons v. Ogden, 22 U.S. (9 Wheat.) 1 (1824). The story of the case is told by George Dangerfield in "The Steamboat Case," in Garraty, ed., pp. 49–61.

Page 360: Gunfire and war threatened: Page Smith, p. 375.

Page 360: Assemblage of ladies, quoting a reporter on the scene: Smith, p. 378.

Page 360: Release of every creek: Smith quotes Judge Wayne "about twenty years afterward," in Smith, p. 377.

Page 360: "Never experienced more intellectual pleasure": Webster quoted in Smith, p. 377.

Page 364: Edward Everett Hale quoted in Harold M. Hyman, *A More Perfect Union, The Impact of the Civil War and Reconstruction on the Constitution* (Boston: Houghton Mifflin, 1975), p. 548.

Page 364: Indiana criminal code, New York silver regulation, Sunday closing laws are all discussed in Lawrence Friedman, pp. 508–512.

Page 364: On multiplication of economic crimes: Quoting Friedman, p. 510.

Page 365: Broad codes of civil wrongs: The antitrust laws, for the most part, are used civilly, but they do contain criminal sanctions as well. Price fixing, one type of restraint of trade outlawed by Section 1 of the Sherman Act, has occasionally been the basis for criminal prosecutions and jail terms—for instance, in the General Electric price-fixing scandal in 1962.

Page 365: Sugar Trust Case: United States v. E. C. Knight Co., 156 U.S. 1 (1895).

Page 366: Price-fixing case as affecting commerce: Addyston Pipe & Steel Co. v. United States, 175 U.S. 211 (1899).

Page 366: Lottery case: Champion v. Ames, 188 U.S. 321 (1903).

Page 367: Seizure of adulterated foods: Hipolite Egg Co. v. United States, 220 U.S. 45 (1911).

Page 367: Transportation of women: Hoke v. United States, 227 U.S. 308 (1913).

Page 367: Child labor case: Hammer v. Dagenhart, 247 U.S. 251 (1918).

Pages 367–368: Overruled the Child Labor Case: United States v. Darby, 312 U.S. 100 (1941).

Page 368: Gold clauses and gold payments: Norman v. Baltimore & Ohio Railroad Co., 294 U.S. 240 (1935); Perry v. United States, 294 U.S. 330 (1935).

Page 368: Strike down the New Deal: The story of the New Deal and the Supreme Court has often been told; see, for example, Robert H. Jackson, *The Struggle for Judicial Supremacy*, and Arthur M. Schlesinger, Jr., *The Politics of Upheaval* (Boston: Houghton Mifflin, 1960).

Page 368: Hot oil case: Panama Refining Co. v. Ryan, 293 U.S. 388 (1935).

Page 368: Voiding the Railway Retirement Act: Railroad Retirement Board v. Alton Railroad Co., 295 U.S. 330 (1935).

Page 368: Sick chicken case: Schechter Poultry Corp. v. United States, 295 U.S. 495 (1935).

Page 368: Farm mortgagors' case: Louisville Bank v. Radford, 295 U.S. 555 (1935). President's removal power: Humphrey's Executor v. United States, 295 U.S. 602 (1935).

Page 368: Roosevelt quoted on horse-and-buggy days and relegating control to the states: Schlesinger, pp. 285–286.

Page 368: Vermont tax case: Colgate v. Harvey, 296 U.S. 404 (1935). Powell's remarks quoted in Schlesinger, p. 469.

Page 368: Court would overrule Colgate v. Harvey: Madden v. Kentucky, 309 U.S. 83 (1940).

Page 368: Coal mining regulations: Carter v. Carter Coal Co., 298 U.S. 238 (1936).

Page 368: Agricultural Act: United States v. Butler, 297 U.S. 1 (1936).

Page 368: Municipal Bankruptcy Act struck down: Ashton v. Cameron County Dist., 298 U.S. 513 (1936).

Page 368: The dual campaign against the powers of Congress: Jackson, pp. xii–xiii.

Page 369: Stone on Court's 1936 term: Alpheus T. Mason, *Harlan Fiske Stone: Pillar of the Law* (New York: Viking, 1956), pp. 425–426.

Page 369: Roosevelt on stopping a constitutional amendment cold: Quoted in Schlesinger, p. 493.

Page 370: Largest congressional majorities: Schlesinger, p. 642.

Page 370: Charging the justices with inefficiency: Quoting Jackson, p. 190.

Page 370: Chief Justice Hughes's letter to Senator Wheeler: The letter and other documents on the Court-packing plan are reprinted in *Reorganization of the Federal Judiciary—Adverse Report of the Committee on the Judiciary,* Senate Report No. 711, 75th Cong., 1st Sess. (1937).

Page 370: Minimum wage law for women: West Coast Hotel Co. v. Parrish, 300 U.S. 379 (1937), overruling Adkins v. Children's Hospital, 261 U.S. 525 (1923).

Page 370: Firearms decision: Sonzinsky v. United States, 300 U.S. 506 (1937).

Page 370: Railway Act: Virginian Ry. v. Federation, 300 U.S. 515 (1937).

Page 370: Farm mortgagors upheld: Wright v. Vinton Branch, 300 U.S. 440 (1937).

Page 370: Wagner Act upheld: National Labor Relations Board v. Jones & Laughlin Steel Corp., 301 U.S. 1 (1937).

Page 371: Social security cases: Steward Machine Co. v. Davis, 301 U.S. 548 (1937); Helvering v. Davis, 301 U.S. 619 (1937).

Page 371: Shreveport Rate Case: Houston E. & W. Texas Railraod Co. v. United States, 234 U.S. 342 (1914).

Page 372: Current of commerce: Swift & Co. v. United States, 196 U.S. 375 (1905) (upholding injunction against price-fixing against meat dealers).

Page 372: Livestock dealers: Stafford v. Wallace, 258 U.S. 495 (1922).

Page 372: Fair Labor Standards case: United States v. Darby, 312 U.S. 100 (1941).

Page 372: Filburn's case: Wickard v. Filburn, 317 U.S. 111 (1942).

Page 373: Justice Jackson on interstate commerce feeling the pinch: United States v. Women's Sportswear Manufacturers' Assn., 336 U.S. 460 (1949).

Page 373: Federal criminal statutes sustained: See, for example, Perez v. United States, 402 U.S. 146 (1971).

Page 373: Public accommodations cases: Heart of Atlanta Motel v. United States, 379 U.S. 241 (1964); Katzenbach v. McClung, 379 U.S. 294 (1964).

Page 373: Real estate rental and arson case: Russell v. United States, 105 S.Ct. 2455 (1985).

Page 373: Regulating wages and hours of state employees: Garcia v. San Antonio Metropolitan Transit Authority, (469 U.S. 528) (1985).

Page 373: Justice Jackson on the nation as economic unit: H. P. Hood & Sons v. Du Mond, 336 U.S. 525 (1949).

Page 374: Philadelphia harbor pilots' case: Cooley v. Board of Wardens of the Port of Philadelphia, 53 U.S. (12 How.) 299 (1851).

Page 375: Washington certificate of convenience and necessity case: Buck v. Kuykendall, 267 U.S. 307 (1925).

Page 375: Ohio certificate of convenience and necessity case: Bradley v. Public Utilities Commission, 289 U.S. 92 (1933).

Page 375: Justice Stewart on the general rule: Pike v. Bruce Church, Inc., 397 U.S. 137 (1970).

Page 375: Arizona train length case: Southern Pacific Co. v. Arizona, 325 U.S. 761 (1945).

Page 375: Iowa trucking case: Kassel v. Consolidated Freightways Corp., 450 U.S. 662 (1981).

Page 375: New Jersey landfill case: Philadelphia v. New Jersey, 437 U.S. 617 (1978).

Page 375: Madison milk case: Dean Milk Co. v. Madison, 340 U.S. 349 (1951).

Page 376: Oklahoma minnow case: Hughes v. Oklahoma, 441 U.S. 322 (1979).

Page 376: New Hampshire electric power case: New England Power Co. v. New Hampshire, 455 U.S. 331 (1982).

Page 376: Requiring a percentage of the work force to live in state: White v. Massachusetts Council of Construction Employers, 460 U.S. 204 (1983).

Page 376: Adam Smith reflected on the tendency: "People of the same trade seldom meet together, even for merriment and diversion, but the conversation ends in a conspiracy against the public, or in some contrivance to raise prices," in *The Wealth of Nations* (New York: Modern Library, 1937), p. 128.

Pages 376–377: Lawyers' minimum fee schedule case: Goldfarb v. Virginia State Bar, 421 U.S. 773 (1975). The Supreme Court has held that states may constitutionally exempt industries from the federal antitrust laws by the simple expedient of directing that the industries do so. Parker v. Brown, 317 U.S. 341 (1943) (the industry at issue there was raisins). This subject is discussed in considerable detail in my *Tyranny of the Experts* (1970).

Page 377: Chief Justice Waite, on resorting to polls to protect against abuses by legislatures: Munn v. Illinois, 94 U.S. 113 (1877).

Chapter 19: Reform and the Future of the Constitution

Page 382: Continued vitality of prayers in some public schools: see Wallace v. Jaffree, 105 S.Ct. 2479 (1985); "Plaintiff in Prayer Suit Says the Case Hurt His Children," *New York Times*, June 5, 1985, p. 1. See also

William K. Muir, Jr., *Law and Attitude Change, Prayer in the Public Schools* (Chicago: University of Chicago Press, 1973).

Page 382: Child labor case: Hammer v. Dagenhart, 247 U.S. 251 (1918).

Page 382: Time to ratify as a political question: Coleman v. Miller, 307 U.S. 433 (1939).

Page 382: Supreme Court reversed itself: United States v. Darby, 312 U.S. 100 (1941).

Page 383: Debate over balanced budget amendment: The drive seems to have run out of steam: *New York Times*, March 4, 1984, p. A22; editorial controversy, *New York Times*, March 2, 1984, p. A26; Sen. Owen H. Johnson replies, March 27, 1984, p. A.30; Sen. Harry F. Byrd, Jr. responds, April 2, 1984, p. A18; N.J. Senator Lee B. Laskin writes, July 29, 1984, sect. XI, p. 20; but "surprising signs of life," August 27, 1984, sect. IV, p. 2; William Safire sees threat, Sept. 3, 1984, p. A25; Martin Anderson on, August 30, 1985, p. A25. The Senate rejected the proposed amendment on March 25, 1986, by one vote: Jonathan Fuerbringer, "Budget-Balancing Change for Constitution Loses," *New York Times*, March 26, 1986, p. A11. Said Senator Slade Gorton of Washington, "The Constitution is no place for Congressional grafitti."

Pages 383–384: For an argument that Congress may reject the application of many state resolutions, see Walter Dellinger, "Con Con Con," *New Republic*, April 7, 1986, p. 10.

Page 384: According to H. Ames, *The Proposed Amendments to the Constitution* (American Historical Association, 1896), Congress considered 1,736 amendments during its first century (1789–1889). From 1890 to 1926, according to *Proposed Amendments to the Constitution of the United States*, Senate Doc. No. 93, 69th Congress, 1st Session (1926), another 1,316 amendments were introduced between 1890 and 1926. From 1926 through 1963, 2,340 more proposals were submitted, "Proposed Amendments to the Constitution of the United States of America," Sen. Doc. No. 163, 87th Cong., 2d Sess., 1962; and Steiner, p. 29, estimates that in all 10,000 amendments have been proposed, meaning that 5,000 have been introduced during the past quarter of a century.

Page 384: Tugwell's Model Constitution: He presents it as the final chapter of a 642-page book describing the failures of the American political system. Rexford G. Tugwell, *The Emerging Constitution* (New York: Harper's Magazine Press, 1974).

Page 384: Quoting Tugwell: Tugwell, p. xxxvi.

Page 384: Never entirely put to rest: See, for example, Griffin B. Bell, Herbert Brownell, William E. Simon, Cyrus R. Vance, "For a One-Term, Six-Year Presidency," *The New York Times*, December 31, 1985, p. A15.

Page 386: Result in improvements: Tugwell, p. xi.

Page 386: The Mintz and Cohen proposal is contained in Morton Mintz and Jerry S. Cohen, *Power, Inc.* (New York: Viking, 1976), p. 585. I discuss the difficulties with this proposal in *The Litigious Society*, p. 185.

Page 386: Price on the unwritten Constitution: Don K. Price, *America's Unwritten Constitution, Science, Religion, and Political Responsibility* (Baton Rouge: Louisiana State University Press, 1983), pp. 149–150.

Page 386: Sundquist quoted: James L. Sundquist, *Constitutional Reform and Effective Government* (Washington, D.C.: Brookings Institution, 1986), p. 73.

Page 386: Sundquist on "truism": Sundquist, p. 206.

Page 387: Short of crisis: Sundquist, p. 251.

Page 389: On the activist role of the Burger Court, see Vincent Blasi, *The Burger Court, The Counter-Revolution That Wasn't*, rev. ed. (New Haven: Yale University Press, 1985).

Page 389: Tribe points out: Laurence H. Tribe, *God Save This Honorable Court* (New York: Random House, 1985), pp. 51ff.

Page 389: Historical crossroads: For example, Benno C. Schmidt, Jr., "The Rehnquist Court: A Watershed," *New York Times*, June 22, 1986, p. E27.

Page 390: On the attorney general's speeches: Attorney General Meese has labeled "infamous" such decisions as *Miranda* and *Mapp* and has condemned as "intellectually shaky" the incorporation doctrine. The speech that sparked a year-long controversy, given at the American Bar Association's 1985 annual meeting, held that year in London, and delivered on July 9, has been "reinterpreted" on more than one occasion by the Justice Department's top PR operative, Terry Eastland, director of the Office of Public Affairs. See Terry Eastland, "Proper Interpretation of the Constitution," *New York Times*, January 9, 1986, p. A23. In a masterpiece of confusion (letter to *The New York Times* dated Aug. 1, 1986, *New York Times*, Aug. 16, 1986, p. A22), Eastland declared that Meese has not called for repealing the doctrine of incorporation, even though he appears to believe that the courts "should not presume the power to make such important decisions [as those prompted by the incorporation doctrine] without explicit constitutional warrant." According to Eastland, in other words (Meese having stopped trying to explain himself), Meese has not stated that he wants the doctrine repealed even though he "questions its particulars" as "intellectually shaky." What Meese really means and whether it matters is anybody's guess. But even Meese seems to concede (though that is not clear) that state churches and state censorship are constitutionally indefensible. On the controversy Meese has sparked, see Anthony Lewis, "Mr. Meese's Freedom," *New York Times*, September 30, 1985, p. A15; Philip Shenon, "Meese and His New Vision of the Constitution," *New York Times*, October 17, 1985, p. B10; Stuart Taylor, Jr., "Administration Trolling for Constitutional Debate," *New York Times*, October 28, 1985, p. A12; Stuart Taylor, Jr., "Meese v. Brennan," *New Republic*, January 6, 13, 1986, p. 17.

Page 391: Members of armed forces discharged for misusing drugs: Joel Brinkley, "U.S. Project Said to Curb Bolivia Drugs," *The New York Times*, August 6, 1986, p. B4.

Page 391: With some success: Jesus Rangel, "Court Bars Drug Testing of Teachers," *The New York Times*, August 12, 1986, p. B1.

Page 391: Polygraph testing in Congress: Linda Greenhouse, "A Privacy Issue Cuts Across Ideological Lines," *The New York Times*, June 20, 1986, p. A16.

Page 391: On government surveillance, see Frank J. Donner, *The Age of Surveillance, The Aims and Methods of America's Political Intelligence System* (New York: Knopf, 1980); David Wise, *The American Police State* (New York: Random House, 1976).

Pages 392–393: Company town case: Marsh v. Alabama, 326 U.S. 501 (1946).

Page 393: Leased building case: Burton v. Wilmington Parking Authority, 365 U.S. 715 (1961).

Page 394: FCC power to regulate indecent but nonobscene language on radio: Federal Communications Commission v. Pacifica Foundation, 438 U.S. 726 (1978).

Bibliography

This is not a comprehensive bibliography. Included here are only those works referred to more than once in the preceding Notes and References. Full bibliographic information is given in the Notes for works cited only once.

Abraham, Henry J. *Freedom and the Court.* 3d and 4th eds. New York: Oxford University Press, 1977 and 1982.

Berger, Raoul. *Government by Judiciary.* Cambridge, Mass.: Harvard University Press, 1977.

Bickel, Alexander M. *The Least Dangerous Branch.* Indianapolis: Bobbs-Merrill, 1962.

Bickel, Alexander M. *The Supreme Court and the Idea of Progress.* New Haven, Conn.: Yale University Press, 1978.

Black, Charles L. *Decision According to Law.* New York: W. W. Norton, 1981.

Blasi, Vincent, ed. *The Burger Court, The Counter-Revolution That Wasn't.* New Haven, Conn.: Yale University Press, 1983.

Boyer, Paul S. *Purity in Print.* New York: Charles Scribner's Sons, 1968.

Chafee, Zechariah, Jr. *Free Speech in the United States.* New York: Atheneum, 1969.

Chase, Harold W., and Craig R. Ducat. *Corwin's The Constitution and What It Means Today.* Princeton, N.J.: Princeton University Press, 1978 ed., with 1980 Supplement.

Corwin, Edwin S. *The "Higher Law" Background of American Constitutional Law.* Ithaca, N.Y.: Cornell University Press, 1955.

Cox, Archibald. *The Role of the Supreme Court in American Government.* New York: Oxford University Press, 1976.

Cunliffe, Marcus. *The American Heritage History of the Presidency.* New York: American Heritage, 1968.

Dumbauld, Edward. *The Bill of Rights and What It Means Today.* Norman: University of Oklahoma Press, 1957.

Ely, John Hart. *Democracy and Distrust.* Cambridge, Mass.: Harvard University Press, 1980.

Farrand, Max. *The Framing of the Constitution*. New Haven: Yale University Press, 1913.

Farrand, Max, ed. *The Records of the Federal Convention*. New Haven, Conn.: Yale University Press, 1937.

The Federalist. New York: Mentor Books, 1961.

Fisher, Louis. *Constitutional Conflicts Between Congress and the President*. Princeton, N.J.: Princeton University Press, 1985.

Friedman, Lawrence H. *A History of American Law*. New York: Simon and Schuster, 1973.

Garraty, John A., ed. *Quarrels That Have Shaped the Constitution*. New York: Harper and Row, 1964.

Gunther, Gerald. *Cases and Materials on Individual Rights in Constitutional Law*, 3d ed. Mineola, N.Y.: Foundation Press, 1981, and 1984 Supplement.

Horwitz, Morton J. *The Transformation of American Law: 1780–1860*. Cambridge, Mass.: Harvard University Press, 1977.

Hyman, Harold M. *A More Perfect Union, The Impact of the Civil War and Reconstruction on the Constitution*. Boston: Houghton Mifflin, 1975.

Hyman, Harold M., and William M. Wiecek. *Equal Justice Under Law: Constitutional Development: 1835–1875*. New York: Harper and Row, 1982.

Jackson, Robert H. *The Struggle for Judicial Supremacy*. New York: Vintage Books, 1941.

Jensen, Merrill. *The New Nation, A History of the United States During the Confederation: 1781–1789*. Boston: Northeastern University Press, 1981.

John Stuart Mill, Three Essays. New York: Oxford University Press, 1975.

Johnson, Paul. *Enemies of Society*. New York: Atheneum, 1977.

Kenyon, Cecelia M. "Constitutionalism in Revolutionary America," in *Constitutionalism*, edited by J. Roland Pennock and John W. Chapman. New York: New York University Press, 1979.

Laslett, Peter. *John Locke's Two Treatises of Government*. Rev. ed. New York: New American Library, 1965.

Leder, Lawrence H. *Liberty and Authority: Early American Political Ideology*. New York: W. W. Norton, 1976.

Levy, Leonard M. *Emergence of a Free Press*. New York: Oxford University Press, 1985.

Levy, Leonard M., ed. *Essays on the Making of the Constitution*. New York: Oxford University Press, 1969.

Levy, Leonard M. *Jefferson and Civil Liberties: The Darker Side*. New York: Quadrangle Books, 1973.

Levy, Leonard M. *Judgments: Essays in American Constitutional History*. Chicago: Quadrangle Books, 1972.

Lieberman, Jethro K. *Are Americans Extinct?* New York: Walker, 1967.

Lieberman, Jethro K. *How the Government Breaks the Law*. New York: Penguin, 1973.

Lieberman, Jethro K. *The Litigious Society*. New York: Harper Colophon Books, 1983.

Lieberman, Jethro K. *Milestones! 200 Years of American Law*. St. Paul and New York: West/Oxford University Press, 1976.

Lieberman, Jethro K. *The Tyranny of the Experts*. New York: Walker, 1970.

Lusky, Louis. *By What Right?* Charlottesville, Va.: Michie, 1975.

Malone, Dumas. *Jefferson the Virginian*. Boston: Little, Brown, 1948.

Manning, Leonard F. *The Law of Church-State Relations*. St. Paul: West, 1981.

McIlwain, Charles Howard. *Constitutionalism Ancient and Modern*. Rev. ed. Ithaca, N.Y.: Cornell University Press, 1947.

Mitchell, Broadus, and Louise Mitchell. *A Biography of the Constitution of the United States*. New York: Oxford University Press, 1964.

Murphy, Paul L. *The Constitution in Crisis Times: 1918–1969*. New York: Harper and Row, 1972.

Perry, Michael J. *The Constitution, Courts, and Human Rights.* New Haven, Conn.: Yale University Press, 1982.

Price, Don K. *America's Unwritten Constitution: Science, Religion, and Political Responsibility.* Baton Rouge: Louisiana State University Press, 1983.

Schlesinger, Arthur M. *The Politics of Upheaval.* Boston: Houghton Mifflin, 1960.

Sesquicentennial History: United States Constitution Sesquicentennial Commission. *History of the Formation of the Union Under the Constitution.* Washington, D.C.: Government Printing Office, 1943; reprinted by Greenwood Press, New York, 1968.

Smith, Page. *The Constitution: A Documentary and Narrative History.* New York: Morrow Quill Paperbacks, 1980.

Steiner, Gilbert Y. *Constitutional Inequality: The Political Fortunes of the Equal Rights Amendment.* Washington, D.C.: Brookings Institution, 1985.

Sundquist, James L. *Constitutional Reform and Effective Government.* Washington, D.C.: Brookings Institution, 1986.

Sutherland, Arthur E. *Constitutionalism in America.* New York: Blaisdell, 1965.

Tribe, Laurence H. *American Constitutional Law.* Mineola, N.Y.: Foundation Press, 1978, with 1981 Supplement.

Tribe, Laurence H. *Constitutional Choices.* Cambridge, Mass.: Harvard University Press, 1985.

Tribe, Laurence H. *God Save This Honorable Court.* New York: Random House, 1985.

Tugwell, Rexford G. *The Emerging Constitution.* New York: Harper's Magazine Press, 1974.

Wiecek, William M. *The Sources of Antislavery Constitutionalism in America: 1760–1848.* Ithaca, N.Y.: Cornell University Press, 1977.

Wood, Gordon S. *The Creation of the American Republic: 1776–1787.* New York: W. W. Norton, 1972.

Woodward, C. Vann. *The Strange Career of Jim Crow.* 3d rev. ed. New York: Oxford University Press, 1974.

Constitution of the United States

Author's Note: The following text omits much of the original capitalization but retains the original spelling. Numbers and words in brackets are not part of the text but have been included to make it easier to identify particular parts and clauses. Clauses or entire sections in brackets indicate that the text has been superseded by amendment. The word *Section* has been added or spelled out in the text of several amendments for the sake of consistency. Boldface numbers in the margins are references to the pages on which the line or section is discussed.

[PREAMBLE]

4, 47, 142

We, the people of the United States, in Order to form a more perfect Union, establish Justice, insure domestic Tranquility, provide for the common defence, promote the general Welfare, and secure the Blessings of Liberty to ourselves and our Posterity, do ordain and establish this Constitution for the United States of America.

59–79 Article I

77 *Sect. 1.* All legislative powers herein granted shall be vested in a Congress of the United States, which shall consist of a Senate and House of Representatives.

Sect. 2. [1] The House of Representatives shall be composed of members chosen every second year by the people of the several States, and the Electors in each State shall have the qualifications requisite for Electors of the most numerous branch of the State legislature.

[2] No person shall be a Representative who shall not have attained to the age of twenty-five years, and been seven years a citizen of the United States, and who shall not, when elected, be an inhabitant of that State in which he shall be chosen.

[3] [Representatives and direct taxes shall be apportioned among the several States which may be included within this Union, according to their respective numbers, which shall be determined by adding to the whole number of free persons, including those bound to service for a term of years, and excluding Indians not taxed, three-fifths of all other persons.] The actual enumeration shall be made within three years after the first meeting of the Congress of the United States, and within every subsequent term of ten years, in such manner as they shall by law direct. The number of Representatives shall not exceed one for every thirty thousand, but each State shall have at least one Representative; [and until such enumeration shall be made, the State of New-Hampshire shall be entitled to chuse three, Massachusetts eight, Rhode-Island and Providence Plantations one, Connecticut five, New-York six, New-Jersey four, Pennsylvania eight, Delaware one, Maryland six, Virginia ten, North-Carolina five, South-Carolina five, and Georgia three].

[4] When vacancies happen in the representation from any State, the Executive authority thereof shall issue writs of election to fill such vacancies.

[5] The House of Representatives shall chuse their Speaker and other officers; and shall have the sole power of impeachment.

Sect. 3. [1] The Senate of the United States shall be composed of two Senators from each State, [chosen by the legislature thereof,] for six years; and each Senator shall have one vote.

[2] [Immediately after they shall be assembled in consequence of the first election, they shall be divided as equally as may be into three classes. The seats of the Senators of the first class shall be vacated at the expiration of the second year, of the second class at the expiration of the fourth year, and of the third class at the expiration of the sixth year, so that one-third may be chosen every second year; and if vacancies happen by resignations, or otherwise, during the recess of the Legislature of any State, the Executive thereof may make temporary appointments until the next meeting of the Legislature, which shall then fill such vacancies].

[3] No person shall be a Senator who shall not have attained to the age of thirty years, and been nine years a citizen of the United States, and who shall not, when elected, be an inhabitant of that State for which he shall be chosen.

[4] The Vice-President of the United States shall be President of the Senate, but shall have no vote, unless they be equally divided.

[5] The Senate shall chuse their other officers, and also a President pro tempore, in the absence of the Vice-President, or when he shall exercise the office of President of the United States.

[6] The Senate shall have the sole power to try all empeachments. When sitting for that

purpose, they shall be on oath or affirmation. When the President of the United States is tried, the Chief Justice shall preside: And no person shall be convicted without the concurrence of two-thirds of the members present.

[7] Judgment in cases of impeachment shall not extend further than to removal from office, and disqualification to hold and enjoy any office of honor, trust or profit under the United States; but the party convicted shall nevertheless be liable and subject to indictment, trial, judgment and punishment, according to law.

Sect. 4. [1] The times, places and manner of holding elections for Senators and Representatives, shall be prescribed in each State by the legislature thereof; but the Congress may at any time by law make or alter such regulations, except as to the places of chusing Senators.

[2] The Congress shall assemble at least once in every year, and such meeting shall be on [the first Monday in December,] unless they shall by law appoint a different day.

Sect. 5. [1] Each House shall be the judge of the elections, returns and qualifications of its own members, and a majority of each shall constitute a quorum to do business; but a smaller number may adjourn from day to day, and may be authorized to compel the attendance of absent members, in such manner, and under such penalties as each House may provide.

[2] Each House may determine the rules of its proceedings, punish its members for disorderly behaviour, and, with the concurrence of two-thirds, expel a member.

[3] Each House shall keep a journal of its proceedings, and from time to time publish the same, excepting such parts as may in their judgment require secrecy; and the yeas and nays of the members of either House on any question shall, at the desire of one-fifth of those present, be entered on the journal.

[4] Neither House, during the session of Congress, shall, without the consent of the other, adjourn for more than three days, nor to any other place than that in which the two Houses shall be sitting.

Sect. 6. [1] The Senators and Representatives shall receive a compensation for their services, to be ascertained by law, and paid out of the Treasury of the United States. They shall in all cases, except treason, felony and breach of the peace, be privileged from arrest during their attendance at the session of their respective Houses, and in going to and returning from the same; and for any speech or debate in either House, they shall not be questioned in any other place.

[2] No Senator or Representative shall, during the time for which he was elected, be appointed to any civil office under the authority of the United States, which shall have been created, or the emoluments whereof shall have been encreased during such time; and no person holding any office under the United States, shall be a member of either House during his continuance in office.

Sect. 7. [1] All Bills for raising revenue shall originate in the House of Representatives; but the Senate may propose or concur with amendments as on other bills.

[2] Every bill which shall have passed the House of Representatives and the Senate, shall,

before it become a law, be presented to the President of the United States; if he approve he shall sign it, but if not he shall return it, with his objections to that House in which it shall have originated, who shall enter the objections at large on their journal, and proceed to reconsider it. If after such reconsideration two-thirds of that House shall agree to pass the bill, it shall be sent, together with the objections, to the other House, by which it shall likewise be reconsidered, and if approved by two-thirds of that House, it shall become a law. But in all such cases the votes of both Houses shall be determined by yeas and nays, and the names of the persons voting for and against the bill shall be entered on the journal of each House respectively. If any bill shall not be returned by the President within ten days (Sundays excepted) after it shall have been presented to him, the same shall be a law, in like manner as if he had signed it, unless the Congress by their adjournment prevent its return, in which case it shall not be a law.

[3] Every order, resolution, or vote to which the concurrence of the Senate and House of Representatives may be necessary (except on a question of adjournment) shall be presented to the President of the United States; and before the same shall take effect, shall be approved by him, or, being disapproved by him, shall be repassed by two-thirds of the Senate and House of Representatives, according to the rules and limitations prescribed in the case of a bill.

68, 371 *Sect. 8.* [1] The Congress shall have power to lay and collect taxes, duties, imposts and excises, to pay the debts and provide for the common defence and general welfare of the United States; but all duties, imposts and excises shall be uniform throughout the United States;

68 [2] To borrow money on the credit of the United States;

68, 359–377 [3] To regulate commerce with foreign nations, and among the several States, and with the Indian tribes;

68, 344 [4] To establish an uniform rule of naturalization, and uniform laws on the subject of bankruptcies throughout the United States;

69 [5] To coin money, regulate the value thereof, and of foreign coin, and fix the standard of weights and measures;

69 [6] To provide for the punishment of counterfeiting the securities and current coin of the United States;

[7] To establish post offices and post roads;

69 [8] To promote the progress of science and useful arts, by securing for limited times to authors and inventors the exclusive right to their respective writings and discoveries;

70 [9] To constitute tribunals inferior to the Supreme Court;

70 [10] To define and punish piracies and felonies committed on the high seas, and offences against the law of nations;

70 [11] To declare war, grant letters of marque
106–107 and reprisal, and make rules concerning captures on land and water;

70 [12] To raise and support armies, but no appropriation of money to that use shall be for a longer term than two years;

70 [13] To provide and maintain a navy;

70 [14] To make rules for the government and regulation of the land and naval forces;

70 [15] To provide for calling forth the militia to execute the laws of the union, suppress insurrections and repel invasions;

70 [16] To provide for organizing, arming, and

disciplining, the militia, and for governing such part of them as may be employed in the service of the United States, reserving to the States respectively, the appointment of the officers, and the authority of training the militia according to the discipline prescribed by Congress;

70 [17] To exercise exclusive legislation in all cases whatsoever, over such district (not exceeding ten miles square) as may, by cession of particular States, and the acceptance of Congress, become the seat of the government of the United States, and to exercise like authority over all places purchased by the consent of the legislature of the State in which the same shall be, for the erection of forts, magazines, arsenals, dock-yards, and other needful buildings;—And

71–72 [18] To make all laws which shall be necessary and proper for carrying into execution the foregoing powers, and all other powers vested by this Constitution in the government of the United States, or in any department or officer thereof.

Sect. 9. [1] [The migration or importation of such persons as any of the States now existing shall think proper to admit, shall not be prohibited by the Congress prior to the year one thousand eight hundred and eight, but a tax or duty may be imposed on such importation, not exceeding ten dollars for each person.]

279–281 [2] The privilege of the writ of habeas corpus shall not be suspended, unless when in cases of rebellion or invasion the public safety may require it.

281–283 [3] No bill of attainder or ex post facto law shall be passed.

68, 72–76 [4] No capitation, or other direct, tax shall be laid, unless in proportion to the census or enumeration herein before directed to be taken.

[5] No tax or duty shall be laid on articles exported from any State.

[6] No preference shall be given by any regulation of commerce or revenue to the ports of one State over those of another; nor shall vessels bound to, or from, one State, be obliged to enter, clear, or pay duties in another.

[7] No money shall be drawn from the Treasury, but in consequence of appropriations made by law; and a regular Statement and account of the receipts and expenditures of all public money shall be published from time to time.

[8] No title of nobility shall be granted by the United States:—And no person holding any office of profit or trust under them, shall, without the consent of the Congress, accept of any present, emolument, office, or title, of any kind whatever, from any king, prince, or foreign State.

Sect. 10. [1] No State shall enter into any treaty, alliance, or confederation; grant letters of marque and reprisal; coin money; emit bills of credit; make any thing but gold and silver coin a tender in payment of debts; pass any bill of **154, 343–346** attainder, ex post facto law, or law impairing the obligation of contracts, or grant any title of nobility.

[2] No State shall, without the consent of the Congress, lay any imposts or duties on imports or exports, except what may be absolutely necessary for executing its inspection laws; and the net produce of all duties and imposts, laid by any State on imports or exports, shall be for the use of the Treasury of the United States; and all such laws shall be subject to the revision and controul of the Congress.

[3] No State shall, without the consent of

Congress, lay any duty of tonnage, keep troops, or ships of war in time of peace, enter into any agreement or compact with another State, or with a foreign power, or engage in war, unless actually invaded, or in such imminent danger as will not admit of delay.

Article II

95–100   *Sect. 1.* [1] The executive power shall be vested in a President of the United States of America. He shall hold his office during the term of four years, and, together with the Vice-President, chosen for the same term, be elected as follows.

88   [2] Each State shall appoint, in such manner as the legislature thereof may direct, a number of Electors, equal to the whole number of Senators and Representatives to which the State may be entitled in the Congress: but no Senator or Representative, or person holding an office of trust or profit under the United States, shall be appointed an Elector.

[3] [The Electors shall meet in their respective States, and vote by ballot for two persons, of whom one at least shall not be an inhabitant of the same State with themselves. And they shall make a list of all the persons voted for, and of the number of votes for each; which list they shall sign and certify, and transmit sealed to the seat of the government of the United States, directed to the President of the Senate. The President of the Senate shall, in the presence of the Senate and House of Representatives, open all the certificates, and the votes shall then be counted. The person having the greatest number of votes shall be the President, if such number be a majority of the whole number of Electors appointed; and if there be more than one who have such majority, and have an equal number of votes, then the House of Representatives shall immediately chuse by ballot one of them for President; and if no person have a majority, then from the five highest on the list the said House shall in like manner chuse the President. But in chusing the President, the votes shall be taken by States, the representation from each State having one vote; a quorum for this purpose shall consist of a member or members from two-thirds of the States, and a majority of all the States shall be necessary to a choice. In every case, after the choice of the President, the person having the greatest number of votes of the Electors shall be the Vice-President. But if there should remain two or more who have equal votes, the Senate shall chuse from them by ballot the Vice-President.]

[4] The Congress may determine the time of chusing the Electors, and the day on which they shall give their votes; which day shall be the same throughout the United States.

84   [5] No person except a natural born citizen, or a citizen of the United States, at the time of the adoption of this Constitution, shall be eligible to the office of President; neither shall any person be eligible to that office who shall not have attained to the age of thirty-five years, and been fourteen years a resident within the United States.

90   [6] In case of the removal of the President from office, or of his death, resignation, or inability to discharge the powers and duties of the said office, the same shall devolve on the Vice-President, and the Congress may by law provide for the case of removal, death, resignation or inability, both of the President and Vice-President, declaring what officer shall then

act as President, and such officer shall act accordingly, until the disability be removed, or a President shall be elected.

[7] The President shall, at stated times, receive for his services, a compensation, which shall neither be encreased nor diminished during the period for which he shall have been elected, and he shall not receive within that period any other emolument from the United States, or any of them.

[8] Before he enter on the execution of his office, he shall take the following oath or affirmation:

"I do solemnly swear (or affirm) that I will faithfully execute the office of President of the United States, and will to the best of my ability, preserve, protect and defend the Constitution of the United States."

96 *Sect. 2.* [1] The President shall be commander in chief of the army and navy of the United States, and of the militia of the several States, when called into the actual service of the United States; he may require the opinion, in writing, of the principal officer in each of the executive departments, upon any subject relating to the duties of their respective offices, and he shall have power to grant reprieves and pardons for offences against the United States, except in cases of impeachment.

[2] He shall have power, by and with the advice and consent of the Senate, to make treaties, provided two-thirds of the Senators present concur; and he shall nominate, and by and with the advice and consent of the Senate, shall appoint ambassadors, other public ministers and consuls, judges of the Supreme Court, and all other officers of the United States, whose appointments are not herein otherwise pro-

vided for, and which shall be established by law. But the Congress may by law vest the appointment of such inferior officers, as they think proper, in the President alone, in the courts of law, or in the heads of departments.

[3] The President shall have power to fill up all vacancies that may happen during the recess of the Senate, by granting commissions which shall expire at the end of their next session.

Sect. 3. He shall from time to time give to the Congress information of the State of the union, and recommend to their consideration such measures as he shall judge necessary and expedient; he may, on extraordinary occasions, convene both Houses, or either of them, and in case of disagreement between them, with respect to the time of adjournment, he may adjourn them to such time as he shall think proper; he shall receive ambassadors and other public ministers; he shall take care that the laws be faithfully executed, and shall commission all the officers of the United States.

92-95 *Sect. 4.* The President, Vice-President and all civil officers of the United States, shall be removed from office on impeachment for, and conviction of, treason, bribery, or other high crimes and .misdemeanors.

Article III

109-139 *Sect. 1.* The judicial power of the United States, shall be vested in one Supreme Court, and in such inferior courts as the Congress may from time to time ordain and establish. The judges, both of the supreme and inferior courts, shall hold their offices during good behaviour, and shall, at stated times, receive for their services, a compensation, which shall not be diminished during their continuance in office.

110, 116 *Sect. 2.* [1] The judicial power shall extend to all cases, in law and equity, arising under this Constitution, the laws of the United States, and treaties made, or which shall be made, under their authority; to all cases affecting ambassadors, other public ministers and consuls; to all cases of admiralty and maritime jurisdiction; to controversies to which the United States shall be a party; to controversies between two or more States, between a State and citizens of another State, between citizens of different states, between citizens of the same State claiming lands under grants of different States, and between a State, or the citizens thereof, and foreign States, citizens or subjects.

119–121 [2] In all cases affecting ambassadors, other public ministers and consuls, and those in which a State shall be party, the Supreme Court shall have original jurisdiction. In all the other cases before mentioned, the Supreme Court shall have appellate jurisdiction, both as to law and fact, with such exceptions, and under such regulations as the Congress shall make.

[3] The trial of all crimes, except in cases of impeachment, shall be by jury; and such trial shall be held in the State where the said crimes shall have been committed; but when not committed within any State, the trial shall be at such place or places as the Congress may by law have directed.

Sect. 3. [1] Treason against the United States, shall consist only in levying war against them, or in adhering to their enemies, giving them aid and comfort. No person shall be convicted of treason unless on the testimony of two witnesses to the same overt act, or on confession in open court.

[2] The Congress shall have power to declare the punishment of treason, but no attainder of treason shall work corruption of blood, or forfeiture except during the life of the person attainted.

Article IV

147–148 *Sect. 1.* Full faith and credit shall be given in each State to the public acts, records, and judicial proceedings of every other State. And the Congress may by general laws prescribe the manner in which such acts, records and proceedings shall be proved, and the effect thereof.

145, 184, 199, 204, 368 *Sect. 2.* [1] The citizens of each State shall be entitled to all privileges and immunities of citizens in the several States.

[2] A person charged in any State with treason, felony, or other crime, who shall flee from justice, and be found in another State, shall, on demand of the executive authority of the State from which he fled, be delivered up, to be removed to the State having jurisdiction of the crime.

178 [3] [No person held to service or labour in one State, under the laws thereof, escaping into another, shall, in consequence of any law or regulation therein, be discharged from such service or labour, but shall be delivered up on claim of the party to whom such service or labour may be due.]

Sect. 3. [1] New States may be admitted by the Congress into this union; but no new State shall be formed or erected within the jurisdiction of any other State; nor any State be formed by the junction of two or more States, or parts of States, without the consent of the legislatures of the States concerned as well as of the Congress.

[2] The Congress shall have power to dispose of and make all needful rules and regulations respecting the territory or other property belonging to the United States; and nothing in this Constitution shall be so construed as to prejudice any claims of the United States, or of any particular State.

129, 145 *Sect. 4.* The United States shall guarantee to every State in this union a Republican form of government, and shall protect each of them against invasion; and on application of the legislature, or of the executive (when the legislature cannot be convened) against domestic violence.

Article V

70, 142, 382–388 The Congress, whenever two-thirds of both Houses shall deem it necessary, shall propose amendments to this Constitution, or, on the application of the legislatures of two-thirds of the several States, shall call a convention for proposing amendments, which, in either case, shall be valid to all intents and purposes, as part of this Constitution, when ratified by the legislatures of three-fourths of the several States, or by conventions in three-fourths thereof, as the one or the other mode of ratification may be proposed by the Congress; Provided, [that no amendment which may be made prior to the year one thousand eight hundred and eight shall in any manner affect the first and fourth clauses in the Ninth Section of the First Article; and] that no State, without its consent, shall be deprived of its equal suffrage in the Senate.

Article VI

[1] All debts contracted and engagements entered into, before the adoption of this Constitution, shall be as valid against the United States under this Constitution as under the Confederation.

53, 123, 144 [2] This Constitution, and the laws of the United States which shall be made in pursuance thereof; and all treaties made, or which shall be made, under the authority of the United States, shall be the supreme law of the land; and the judges in every State shall be bound thereby, any thing in the constitution or laws of any State to the contrary notwithstanding.

154 [3] The Senators and Representatives before mentioned, and the members of the several State legislatures, and all executive and judicial officers, both of the United States and of the several States, shall be bound by oath or affirmation, to support this Constitution;

247, 256 but no religious test shall ever be required as a qualification to any office or public trust under the United States.

Article VII

The ratification of the conventions of nine States, shall be sufficient for the establishment of this Constitution between the States so ratifying the same.

Done in Convention, by the unanimous consent of the States present, the seventeenth day of September, in the year of our Lord one thousand seven hundred and eighty-seven, and of the Independence of the United States of America the twelfth. In witness whereof we have hereunto subscribed our Names.

Delaware
Geo: Read
Gunning Bedford jun
John Dickinson
Richard Bassett
Jaco: Broom
James McHenry

Maryland
Dan of St Thos. Jenifer
Danl Carroll

Virginia
John Blair —
James Madison Jr.

North Carolina
Wm Blount
Rich'd Dobbs Spaight.
Hu Williamson

South Carolina
J. Rutledge
Charles Cotesworth Pinckney
Charles Pinckney
Pierce Butler.

Georgia
William Few
Abr Baldwin

G° Washington—Presid'
and deputy from Virginia

New Hampshire
John Langdon
Nicholas Gilman

Massachusetts
Nathaniel Gorham
Rufus King

Connecticut
Wm Saml Johnson
Roger Sherman

New York
Alexander Hamilton

New Jersey
Wil: Livingston
David Brearley.
Wm Paterson.
Jona: Dayton

Pennsylvania
B Franklin
Thomas Mifflin
Rob Morris
Geo. Clymer
Tho FitzSimons
Jared Ingersoll
James Wilson
Gouv Morris

458   CONSTITUTION OF THE UNITED STATES

Amendments to the Constitution

(with years ratified)

First Amendment
(1791)

74, 75, 78, 112, 156, 170, 206, 207, 213–243, 245–259, 264, 265, 392–393 Congress shall make no law respecting an establishment of religion, or prohibiting the free exercise thereof; or abridging the freedom of speech, or of the press; or the right of the people peaceably to assemble, and to petition the Government for a redress of grievances.

Second Amendment
(1791)

A well regulated militia, being necessary to the security of a free State, the right of the people to keep and bear Arms, shall not be infringed.

Third Amendment
(1791)

132, 265 No Soldier shall, in time of peace be quartered in any house, without the consent of the Owner, nor in time of war, but in a manner to be prescribed by law.

265 Fourth Amendment
(1791)

287–290, 391 The right of the people to be secure in their persons, houses, papers, and effects, against unreasonable searches and seizures, shall not be violated, and no warrants shall issue, but upon probable cause, supported by oath or affirmation, and particularly describing the place to be searched, and the persons or things to be seized.

Fifth Amendment
(1791)

265

No person shall be held to answer for a capital, or otherwise infamous crime, unless on a presentment or indictment of a grand jury, except in cases arising in the land or naval forces, or in the militia, when in actual service in time of war or public danger; nor shall any person be subject for the same offence to be twice put in jeopardy of life or limb; nor shall be compelled in any criminal case to be a witness against himself, nor be deprived of life, liberty, or property, without due process of law; nor shall private property be taken for public use, without just compensation.

205

266, 291

289–290
263
156, 206,
329,
352–355

Sixth Amendment
(1791)

In all criminal prosecutions, the accused shall enjoy the right to a speedy and public trial, by an impartial jury of the State and district wherein the crime shall have been committed, which district shall have been previously ascertained by law, and to be informed of the nature and cause of the accusation; to be confronted with the witnesses against him; to have compulsory process for obtaining witnesses in his favor, and to have the assistance of counsel for his defence.

292

207, 290

Seventh Amendment
(1791)

209

In suits at common law, where the value in controversy shall exceed twenty dollars, the right of trial by jury shall be preserved, and no fact tried by a jury, shall be otherwise reexamined in any courts of the United States, than according to the rules of the common law.

Eighth Amendment
(1791)

Excessive bail shall not be required, nor excessive fines imposed, nor cruel and unusual punishments inflicted.

293

Ninth Amendment
(1791)

The enumeration in the Constitution, of certain rights, shall not be construed to deny or disparage others retained by the people.

146,
266–267

Tenth Amendment
(1791)

72, 146,
148–149

The powers not delegated to the United States by the Constitution, nor prohibited by it to the States, are reserved to the States respectively, or to the people.

Eleventh Amendment
(1798)

146, 407

The Judicial power of the United States shall not be construed to extend to any suit in law or equity, commenced or prosecuted against one of the United States by citizens of another State, or by citizens or subjects of any foreign state.

Twelfth Amendment
(1804)

[1] Electors shall meet in their respective states, and vote by ballot for President and Vice-President, one of whom, at least, shall not be an inhabitant of the same state with themselves; they shall name in their ballots the person voted for as President, and in distinct ballots the person voted for as Vice-President, and they shall make distinct lists of all persons voted for as President, and of all persons voted for as Vice-President, and of the number of votes for each, which lists they shall sign and certify, and transmit sealed to the seat of government of the United States, directed to the President of the Senate;—The President of the Senate shall, in the presence of the Senate and House of Representatives, open all the certificates and the votes shall then be counted;—The person having the greatest number of votes for President, shall be the President, if such number be a majority of the whole number of Electors appointed; and if no person have such majority, then from the persons having the highest numbers not exceeding three on the list of those voted for as President, the House of Representatives shall choose immediately, by ballot, the President. But in choosing the President, the votes shall be taken by states, the representation from each state having one vote; a quorum for this purpose shall consist of a member or members from two-thirds of the states, and a majority of all the states shall be necessary to a choice. [And if the House of Representatives shall not choose a President whenever the right choice shall devolve upon them, before the fourth day of March next following, then the Vice-President shall act as President, as in the case of the death or other constitutional disability of the President.]

[2] The person having the greatest number of votes as Vice-President, shall be the Vice-President, if such number be a majority of the whole number of Electors appointed, and if no person have a majority, then from the two highest numbers on the list, the Senate shall choose the Vice-President; a quorum for the purpose shall consist of two-thirds of the whole number of Senators, and a majority of the whole number shall be necessary to a choice. But no person constitutionally ineligible to the office of President shall be eligible to that of Vice-President of the United States.

Thirteenth Amendment
(1865)

193,
196–197,
302, 307,
316–317

Section 1. Neither slavery nor involuntary servitude, except as a punishment for crime whereof the party shall have been duly convicted, shall exist within the United States, or any place subject to their jurisdiction.

Section 2. Congress shall have power to enforce this article by appropriate legislation.

297–317
154–157,
195–211,
267, 297

Fourteenth Amendment
(1868)

Section 1. All persons born or naturalized in the United States, and subject to the jurisdiction thereof, are citizens of the United States and of the State wherein they reside. No State shall make or enforce any law which shall

199

abridge the privileges or immunities of citizens of the United States; nor shall any State deprive any person of life, liberty, or property, without due process of law; nor deny to any

263,
277–293,
346–352

person within its jurisdiction the equal protection of the laws.

Section 2. Representatives shall be apportioned among the several States according to their respective numbers, counting the whole number of persons in each State, excluding Indians not taxed. But when the right to vote at any election for the choice of electors for President and Vice President of the United States, Representatives in Congress, the Executive and Judicial officers of a State, or the members of the Legislature thereof, is denied to any of the male inhabitants of such State, being twenty-one years of age, and citizens of the United States, or in any way abridged, except for participation in rebellion, or other crime, the basis of representation therein shall be reduced in the proportion which the number of such male citizens shall bear to the whole number of male citizens twenty-one years of age in such State.

Section 3. No person shall be a Senator or Representative in Congress, or elector of President and Vice President, or hold any office, civil or military, under the United States, or under any State, who, having previously taken an oath, as a member of Congress, or as an officer of the United States, or as a member of any State legislature, or as an executive or judicial officer of any State, to support the Constitution of the United States, shall have engaged in insurrection or rebellion against the same, or given aid or comfort to the enemies thereof. But Congress may by a vote of two-thirds of each House, remove such disability.

Section 4. The validity of the public debt of the United States, authorized by law, including debts incurred for payment of pensions and bounties for service in suppressing insurrection or rebellion, shall not be questioned. But neither the United States nor any State shall assume or pay any debt or obligation incurred in aid of insurrection or rebellion against the United States, or any claim for the loss or emancipation of any slave; but all such debts, obligations, and claims shall be held illegal and void.

Section 5. The Congress shall have power to enforce, by appropriate legislation, the provisions of this article.

Fifteenth Amendment
(1870)

Section 1. The right of citizens of the United States to vote shall not be denied or abridged by the United States or by any State on account of race, color, or previous condition of servitude.

Section 2. The Congress shall have power to enforce this article by appropriate legislation.

Sixteenth Amendment
(1913)

The Congress shall have power to lay and collect taxes on incomes, from whatever source derived, without apportionment among the several States, and without regard to any census or enumeration.

Seventeenth Amendment
(1913)

Section 1. The Senate of the United States shall be composed of two Senators from each State, elected by the people thereof, for six years; and each Senator shall have one vote. The electors in each State shall have the qualification requisite for electors of the most numerous branch of the State legislature.

Section 2. When vacancies happen in the representation of any State in the Senate, the executive authority of such State shall issue writs of election to fill such vacancies: *Provided,* That the legislature of any State may empower the executive thereof to make temporary appointments until the people fill the vacancies by election as the legislature may direct.

Section 3. This amendment shall not be so construed as to affect the election or term of any Senator chosen before it becomes valid as part of the Constitution.

Eighteenth Amendment
(1919)

[*Section 1.* After one year from the ratification of this article the manufacture, sale, or transportation of intoxicating liquors within, the importation thereof into, or the exportation thereof from the United States and all territory subject to the jurisdiction thereof for beverage purposes is hereby prohibited.

[*Section 2.* The Congress and the several States shall have concurrent power to enforce this article by appropriate legislation.

[*Section 3.* This article shall be inoperative unless it shall have been ratified as an amendment to the Constitution by the legislatures of the several States, as provided in the Constitution, within seven years from the date of the submission hereof to the States by the Congress.]

Nineteenth Amendment
(1920)

Section 1. The right of citizens of the United States to vote shall not be denied or abridged by the United States or by any State on account of sex.

Section 2. Congress shall have power to enforce this article by appropriate legislation.

Twentieth Amendment
(1933)

Section 1. The terms of the President and Vice President shall end at noon on the 20th day of January, and the terms of Senators and Representatives at noon on the 3d day of January, of the years in which such terms would have ended if this article had not been ratified; and the terms of their successors shall then begin.

Section 2. The Congress shall assemble at least once in every year, and such meeting shall begin at noon on the 3d day of January, unless they shall by law appoint a different day.

Section 3. If, at the time fixed for the beginning of the term of the President, the President elect shall have died, the Vice President elect shall become President. If a President shall not have been chosen before the time fixed for the beginning of his term, or if the President elect shall have failed to qualify, then the Vice President elect shall act as President until a President shall have qualified; and the Congress may by law provide for the case wherein neither a President elect nor a Vice President elect shall have qualified, declaring who shall then act as President, or the manner in which one who is to act shall be selected, and such person shall act accordingly until a President or Vice President shall have qualified.

Section 4. The Congress may by law provide for the case of the death of any of the persons from whom the House of Representatives may choose a President whenever the right of choice shall have devolved upon them, and for the case of the death of any of the persons from whom the Senate may choose a Vice President whenever the right of choice shall have devolved upon them.

Section 5. Sections 1 and 2 shall take effect on the 15th day of October following the ratification of this article.

Section 6. This article shall be inoperative unless it shall have been ratified as an amendment to the Constitution by the legislatures of three-fourths of the several States within seven years from the date of its submission.

382 **Twenty-first Amendment**
(1933)

Section 1. The eighteenth article of amendment to the Constitution of the United States is hereby repealed.

Section 2. The transportation or importation into any State, Territory, or possession of the United States for delivery or use therein of intoxicating liquors, in violation of the laws thereof, is hereby prohibited.

Section 3. This article shall be inoperative unless it shall have been ratified as an amendment to the Constitution by conventions in the several States, as provided in the Constitution, within seven years from the date of the submission hereof to the States by the Congress.

87, 403 **Twenty-second Amendment**
(1951)

Section 1. No person shall be elected to the office of the President more than twice, and no person who has held the office of President, or acted as President, for more than two years of a term to which some other person was elected President shall be elected to the office of the President more than once. But this Article shall not apply to any person holding the office of President when this Article was proposed by the Congress, and shall not prevent any person who may be holding the office of President, or acting as President, during the term within which this Article becomes operative from holding the office of President or acting as President during the remainder of such term.

Section 2. This article shall be inoperative unless it shall have been ratified as an amendment to the Constitution by the legislatures of three-fourths of the several States within seven years from the date of its submission to the States by the Congress.

Twenty-third Amendment
(1961)

Section 1. The District constituting the seat of Government of the United States shall appoint in such manner as the Congress may direct:

A number of electors of President and Vice President equal to the whole number of Senators and Representatives in Congress to which the District would be entitled if it were a State, but in no event more than the least populous State; they shall be in addition to those appointed by the States, but they shall be considered, for the purposes of the election of President and Vice President, to be electors appointed by a State; and they shall meet in the District and perform such duties as provided by the twelfth article of amendment.

Section 2. The Congress shall have power to enforce this article by appropriate legislation.

Twenty-fourth Amendment
(1964)

Section 1. The right of citizens of the United States to vote in any primary or other election for President or Vice President, for electors for President or Vice President, or for Senator or Representative in Congress, shall not be denied or abridged by the United States or any State by reason of failure to pay any poll tax or other tax.

Section 2. The Congress shall have power to enforce this article by appropriate legislation.

Twenty-fifth Amendment
(1967)

Section 1. In case of removal of the President from office or of his death or resignation, the Vice President shall become President.

Section 2. Whenever there is a vacancy in the office of the Vice President, the President shall nominate a Vice President who shall take office upon confirmation by a majority vote of both Houses of Congress.

Section 3. Whenever the President transmits to the President pro tempore of the Senate and the Speaker of the House of Representatives his written declaration that he is unable to discharge the powers and duties of his office, and until he transmits to them a written declaration to the contrary, such powers and duties shall be discharged by the Vice President as Acting President.

Section 4. Whenever the Vice President and a majority of either the principal officers of the executive departments or of such other body as Congress may by law provide, transmit to the President pro tempore of the Senate and the Speaker of the House of Representatives their written declaration that the President is unable to discharge the powers and duties of his office, the Vice President shall immediately assume the powers and duties of the office as Acting President.

Thereafter, when the President transmits to the President pro tempore of the Senate and the Speaker of the House of Representatives his written declaration that no inability exists, he shall resume the powers and duties of his office unless the Vice President and a majority of either the principal officers of the executive department or of such other body as Congress may by law provide, transmit within four days to the President pro tempore of the Senate and the Speaker of the House of Representatives their written declaration that the President is unable to discharge the powers and duties of his office. Thereupon Congress shall decide the issue, assembling within forty-eight hours for that purpose if not in session. If the Congress, within twenty-one days after receipt of the latter written declaration, or, if Congress is not in session, within twenty-one days after Congress is required to assemble, determines by two-thirds vote of both Houses that the President is unable to discharge the powers and duties of his office, the Vice President shall continue to discharge the same as Acting President; otherwise, the President shall resume the powers and duties of his office.

Twenty-sixth Amendment
(1971)

160

Section 1. The right of citizens of the United States, who are eighteen years of age or older, to vote shall not be denied or abridged by the United States or by any State on account of age.

Section 2. The Congress shall have power to enforce this article by appropriate legislation.

Table of Cases

(Numbers refer to pages in the text where the case is referred to by name. Numbers in parenthesis refer to pages on which the case is discussed, though not named.)

Martin v. Struthers, (234), 419
Martinez-Fuerte, United States v., (288), 430
Maryland Committee for Fair Representation v. Tawes, (168), 413
Massachusetts Bd. of Retirement v. Murgia, (320), 435
Massie v. Henry, (273), 426
Mathews v. Eldridge, (357), 440
Maxwell v. Dow, (206), 415
Mayor of Baltimore v. Dawson, (316), 434
McAuliffe v. City of New Bedford, (243), 421
McCabe v. Atchison, Topkea & Santa Fe R.R. Co., (308), 433
McCardle, Ex parte, (121), 407
McCollum v. Board of Education, (251), (286), 423, 429
McCulloch v. Maryland, (4), (71), 72, 127, 148, 363, 398, 408
McDaniel v. Paty, (248), 422
McGowan v. Maryland, (323), 435
McLaurin v. Oklahoma State Regents, (309), 434
McNabb v. United States, (278), 427
Meachum v. Fano, (357), 440
Meek v. Pittinger, (250), 422
Memoirs v. Massachusetts, (236), 419
Memorial Hospital v. Maricopa County, (329), 436
Meyer v. Nebraska, (264), 425
Miami Herald Publishing Co. v. Tornillo, (241), 420
Michael M. v. Superior Court, (326), 435
Michigan v. Mosley, (291), 431
Michigan v. Tucker, (291), 431
Miller v. California, (234–238), 419
Miller v. Pate, (286), 428
Milligan, Ex parte, (121), (280), 407, 427
Mills v. Habluetzel, (329), 436
Minersville School District v. Gobitis, (256), 423
Miranda v. Arizona, 290–291, 293, 388, 390, 431
Mississippi University for Women v. Hogan, (325–326), 435
Missouri ex rel. Gaines v. Canada, (308), 433
Missouri Pacific Ry. Co. v. Nebraska (353), 439
Missouri v. Holland, (134–135), 409
Mobile v. Bolden, (331–332), 436
Moe v. Confed. Salish and Kootenai Tribes, (329), 436
Monaco v. Mississippi, (147), 410
Mooney v. Holohan, (286), 428
Moore v. City of East Cleveland, (270), 426
Moore v. Dempsey, (207), (285), 416, 428
Moose Lodge No. 107 v. Irvis, (302), 433
Morris v. Gressette, (164), 412
Mugler v. Kansas, (348), 438
Muller v. Oregon, (323), (350), 435, 439
Munn v. Illinois (347), (377), 438, 442
Murchison, In re, (284), 428
Murdock v. Pennsylvania, (286), 429

Murdock, United States v., (290), 431
Murphy v. Waterfront Comn. of New York Harbor, (286), (290), 429, 431
Myers v. United States, (101), 405

NAACP v. Alabama ex rel. Patterson, (243), 421
National Labor Relations Board v. Jones & Laughlin Steel Corp., (370), 441
National League of Cities v. Usery, (149), 411
Neagle, In re, (97), 404
Near v. Minnesota, (207), (225), (286), 415, 417, 429
Nebbia v. New York, (351), 439
Nebraska Press Assn. v. Stuart, (226), 417
New England Power Co. v. New Hampshire, (376), 442
New Jersey v. Saunders, (272), 426
New Orleans City Park Imp. Assn. v. Detiege, (316), 434
New Orleans v. Dukes, (323), 435
New State Ice Co. v. Liebmann, (351), 439
New York Times Co. v. United States, (226), 417
New York Times v. Sullivan, 232, 418
New York v. Ferber, (238), 420
Nixon v. Administrator of General Services, (281), 427
Nixon v. Condon, (162), 412
Nixon v. Fitzgerald, (119), 406
Nixon v. Herndon, (162), 412
Nixon, United States v., (94), 95, 404
Norman v. Baltimore & Ohio R.R. Co., (368), 440
Noto v. United States, (230), (241), 418, 421

O'Brien v. Brown, (129), 408
O'Brien, United States v., (234), 419
Ogden v. Saunders, 344, 438
Oliver, In re, (208), (284), (286), 416, 428, 429
Olmstead v. United States, (288), (293), 430, 433
On Lee v. United States, (288), 430
One Book Called "Ulysses," United States v., (236), 419
Oregon v. Mitchell, (160), 412

Pace v. Alabama, (314), 434
Palko v. Connecticut, 207, (243), (277), (284), 416, 421, 427, 428
Panama Refining Co. v. Ryan, (368), 440
Papachristou v. City of Jacksonville, (275), (285), 427, 428
Paris Adult Theater I v. Slaton, (238), 420
Parker v. Gladden, (286), 429
Patterson v. Colorado, (220), 417
Paul v. Davis, (357), 440
Paul v. Virginia, (204), 415

Index

créche as secular symbol, 253–254
Crescent City Stock Landing and
    Slaughterhouse Co., 201, 264
cruel and unusual punishments, 293

Dallas, George M., 3
Dana, Francis, 394
Dartmouth College, 343–344
Darwin, Charles, 253
Davie, William Richardson, **321**
Davis, John W., 315
Davis, William R., Jr., 302, 369
Day, William R., 367
Dayton, Jonathan, 44, **96**
De Tocqueville, Alexis, 136
death
    penalty, 246, 293
    right to dare, 274
debt cases, 35, 344, 352
Declaration of Independence, 25
defamation, 231–232, 357
deficit reduction, 105
DeLancey, James, 218
delegation of power, 76–77, 405
democratic despotism, 30, 213
demonstrations, regulation of, 234–235
deportation, 282
Depression, 351–352
Dickinson, John, 45, **111**
die, right to, 274–275
Dirksen, Everett McKinley, 413
disability of president, 90–92
discrimination, administrative, 330–331;
    see also specific type
Disney, Walt, 236
district courts, 114–115
District of Columbia, 61, 70, 400
diversity jurisdiction, 117–119, 189
divine right of kings, 12–13
Dole, Robert, 332
Dooley, Mr., 4
Dorr, Thomas Wilson, 129
Dorr's Rebellion, 128–129, 142
Dos Passos, John, 236
double jeopardy, 266, 291–292
Douglas, William O., 92, 209, 242, 265,
    275, 371

Douglass, Frederick, 301
Dreiser, Theodore, 236
drug testing, 391
due process, 204, 261–264, 277–293, 346–
    352
    as a curb on arbitrary procedures, 283–
    286
Dunlap & Claypoole, 221
Dunlap, John, 221

Eastland, James O., 153
Eastland, Terry, 443
ecclesiastical interpretations, 255
economic due process, 346–352
Edison Electric Illuminating Co., 74
Eisenhower, Dwight D., 76, 103, 132,
    139, 149, 315, 388, 389, 403, 405
Electoral college, 88
Elizabeth I, 217
Ellsworth, Oliver, 44, 62, **327**
eminent domain, 206
enclosure movement, 340
Endo, Mitsuye, 280
entitlements, 355–357
entrapment, 285
enumerated powers, 72
Environmental Defense Fund, 75
Environmental Protection Agency, 355
equal protection clause, 297–313, 319–335
Equal Rights Amendment, 324–325, 382
equality, racial, 297–317
    aliens and, 326–328
    commercial classifications, 322–323
    general classifications, 323–326
    suspect classifications, 319–322
Ervin, Sam J., Jr., 324
ex post facto laws, 30, 281–283
exclusionary rule, 289–290
executive agreements, 98
executive orders, 97
executive privilege, 94
expression, freedom of, 216–243; see also
    speech

faction, Madison on, 18–19
Fair Labor Standards Act, 149
Fairman, Charles, 210

family rights, 270–271
Fanny Hill, 237
Farrand, Max, 41, 52, 53, 95
Faubus, Orval, 154
Federal Corrupt Practices Act, 170
federal courts, see also courts
    power over states, 126, 144
    structure of, 113–116
Federal Election Campaign Act, 170
federal number, 176
Federal Trade Commission, 103
federal vs. national, 141–142
federalism, 141–157
Federalist Papers, 50
Federalists, 141
Ferguson, John H., 306
Few, William, **282**
fighting words, 232–234
filibuster, 66
First Amendment, 74, 75, 78, 112, 156,
    170, 206, 213–243, 245, 259
Fitzsimmons, Thomas, **147**
flag salute, 256
Ford, Gerald R., 92, 405
Ford, Henry, 15
Ford, P. L., 400
Founding Fathers, see particular names
Fourth Branch, 103–104
Framers, see particular names
    intentions of, 132
Frankfurter, Felix, 167, 208–209, 278,
    283, 287, 371
Franklin, Benjamin, 23, 25, 39, 44, 47, 82,
    83, **102,** 176
Franklin, Temple, 40
Freud, Sigmund, 236
Friedman, Lawrence, 27, 364
Frothingham, Harriett, 112
fruit of poisonous tree, 289
Fugitive Slave Act, 180, 187, 304
full faith and credit, 147–148
Fulton, Robert, 360–362

gag order, 226
Gallatin, Albert, 66
Garner, John Nance, 89
Garrison, William Lloyd, 182–183

Photo Credits (continued)

Historical Park; **145,** Russ Kinne, Photo Researchers, Inc.; **148,** Van Bucher, Photo Researchers, Inc.; **150,** Jim Dixon, Photo Researchers, Inc.; **151,** The Granger Collection; **152,** Library of Congress; **155,** The Granger Collection; **156,** From the Collection of Independence National Historical Park; **158,** Eddie Adams, Gamma-Liaison; **160,** The Bettmann Archive; **161,** Dennis Brack, Black Star; **162,** From the Collection of Independence National Historical Park; **163,** Vernon Merritt, Black Star; **164,** UPI/Bettmann Newsphotos; **165,** Library of Congress; **167,** From the Collection of Independence National Historical Park; **169,** Leif Skoogfors, Photo Researchers, Inc.; **172,** Ferry, Gamma-Liaison; **174,** The Granger Collection; **177,** The Bettmann Archive; **178,** The Bettmann Archive; **180,** Photo Researchers, Inc.; **181,** The Granger Collection; **183,** Library of Congress; From Photo Researchers, Inc.; **184,** The Granger Collection; **185,** From the Collection of Independence National Historical Park; **186,** Bradford County Historical Society; **187,** The Granger Collection; **188,** The Bettmann Archive; **189,** The Granger Collection; **190,** Library of Congress; **191,** Special Collections, Langston Hughes Memorial Library, Lincoln University [PA]; **192,** From the Collection of Independence National Historical Park; **194,** Steve Schapiro, Black Star; **198,** The Granger Collection; **200,** Harvard Law Art Collection; **201,** Dictionary of American Portraits; **205,** National Archive; **207,** The Bettmann Archive; **209,** Library of Congress; **212,** Fred Ward, Black Star; **215, (top)** Peter Turnley, Black Star; **(bottom)** UPI/Bettmann Newsphotos; **216,** The Bettmann Archive; **217,** The Granger Collection; **219,** The Granger Collection; **222,** The Granger Collection; **225** The Bettmann Archive; **227,** UPI/Bettmann Newsphotos; **228,** Jeff Foxx, Black Star; **230,** UPI/Bettmann Newsphotos; **233,** Ethan Hoffman Archive Pictures; **235,** James L. Shaffer; **237,** The Bettmann Archive; **239,** Art Seitz, Gamma-Liaison; **242,** Larry Mulvehill, Photo Researchers, Inc.; **244,** Thomas B. Hollyman, Photo Researchers, Inc.; **246** The Bettmann Archive; **248,** *Harpers Weekly* February 25, 1871; **249,** From the Collection of Independence National Historical Park; **251,** Jack Schneider, U.S. Department of Agriculture; **252,** Library of Congress; **253,** Library of Congress; **254,** The Bettmann Archive; **255,** Edward Lettau, Photo Researchers, Inc.; **257,** The Bettmann Archive; **258,** Boston Public Library; **259,** John Launois, Black Star; **260,** Agence Vandystadt, Photo Researchers, Inc.; **262,** The Bettmann Archive; **265,** The Bettmann Archive; **266,** National Archives; **267,** Bill Janscha, AP/Wide World; **269, (left)** Tom Kane, Black Star; **(right)** Martin Adler Levick, Black Star; **270,** The Granger Collection; **272,** Stephen, Ferry, Gamma-Liaison; **273,** UPI; **274,** The Bettmann Archive; **276,** Charles Steiner, Sygma; **278,** U.S. Supreme Court; **279,** The Bettmann Archive; **281,** National Archives; **282,** From the Collection of Independence National Historical Park; **283,** Library of Congress; **284,** Jim Shaffer; **285,** The Bettmann Archive; **288,** Don Carl Steffen, Photo Researchers, Inc.; **289,** Joe Traver, Gamma-Liaison; **291,** UPI/Bettmann Newsphotos; **292,** From the Collection of Independence National Historical Park; **294,** The Granger Collection; **296,** Taurus Photos; **298,** National Archives; **299,** The Granger Collection; **301,** From the Collection of Independence National Historical Park; **303,** The Bettmann Archive; **304,** Library of Congress; **305,** The Granger Collection; **306,** Library of Congress; **309,** Bruce Roberts, Photo Researchers, Inc., **310,** Carl Iwasaki, Life Magazine © 1954 TIME INC.; **312,** The Bettmann Archive; **317,** Suzanne Szasz, Photo Researchers, Inc.; **318,** Peter Miller, The Image Bank; **321,** From the Collection of Independence National Historical Park; **322,** The Granger Collection; **324,** The Granger Collection; **325,** Arnold Zann, Black Star; **326,** Alex Webb, Magnum Photos, Inc.; **327,** From the Collection of Independence National Historical Park; **328,** UPI/Bettmann Newsphotos; **333, (left)** UPI/Bettmann Newsphotos; **(right)** UPI/Bettmann Newsphotos; **334,** Martin A. Levick, Black Star; **336,** Sandra Baker, Photo Researchers, Inc.; **338,** Naythons, Gamma-Liaison; **343,** Library of Congress; **344,** Library of Congress; **347,** The Bettmann Archive; **349** Library of Congress; **350,** The Bettmann Archive; **356,** From the Collection of Independence National Historical Park; **358,** Van Bucher, Photo Researchers, Inc.; **361, (left)** Collection of William L. Hopkins, Jr., Savannah, Georgia; **(right)** Courtesy of The New York Historical Society, New York City; **362,** The Granger Collection; **363,** From the Collection of Independence National Historical Park; **365,** Library of Congress, From Photo Researchers, Inc.; **366,** The Bettmann Archive; **367,** National Archives; **369,** Supreme Court of the United States; **371,** Library of Congress; **374,** The Granger Collection; **376,** UPI/Bettmann Newsphotos; **378,** Bill Carter, The Image Bank; **380,** Sloane, Gamma-Liaison; **385,** The Bettmann Archive; **387,** From the Collection of Independence National Historical Park; **389,** Steve Northup, Black Star; **390,** Sloane, Gamma-Liaison; **391,** Bruce Roberts, Photo Researchers, Inc.; **393,** Courtesy/NBC; **395,** UPI/Bettmann Newsphotos.